THE PRACTICE AND PROCEDURE OF THE INTER-AMERICAN COURT OF HUMAN RIGHTS

Jo M. Pasqualucci provides a comprehensive critique of the Inter-American Court of Human Rights, which is at once scholarly yet practical. She analyzes all aspects of the Court's advisory jurisdiction, contentious jurisdiction and provisional measures orders. When relevant, she compares the practice and procedure of the Inter-American Court with that of the European Court of Human Rights, the International Court of Justice and the United Nations Human Rights Committee. She also evaluates the new Rules of Procedure of the Inter-American Court and the Inter-American Commission, which entered into force in May and June of 2001 and bring about important procedural changes in the interrelationship of those organs. In addition, she cites the effectiveness of the Convention and the Court's rulings in the domestic law of the States Parties to the Convention. This book will provide an important resource for scholars, practitioners and students of international human rights law and practice.

JO M. PASQUALUCCI is Professor of Law at the University of South Dakota. She earned an SJD in International and Comparative Law from the George Washington University Law School, and she was affiliated with the Inter-American Court of Human Rights as a Fulbright scholar in Costa Rica. She has lived for several years in Central America. Her articles on the Inter-American Court have been published in journals such as the *Stanford Journal of International Law*, the *Michigan Journal of International Law* and the *Virginia Journal of International Law*.

THE PRACTICE AND PROCEDURE OF THE INTER-AMERICAN COURT OF HUMAN RIGHTS

JO M. PASQUALUCCI

PUBLISHED BY THE PRESS SYNDICATE OF THE UNIVERSITY OF CAMBRIDGE
The Pitt Building, Trumpington Street, Cambridge CB2 1RP, United Kingdom

CAMBRIDGE UNIVERSITY PRESS
The Edinburgh Building, Cambridge, CB2 2RU, UK
40 West 20th Street, New York, NY 10011–4211, USA
477 Williamstown Road, Port Melbourne, VIC 3207, Australia
Ruiz de Alarcón 13, 28014 Madrid, Spain
Dock House, The Waterfront, Cape Town 8001, South Africa

http://www.cambridge.org

© Jo M. Pasqualucci 2003

This book is in copyright. Subject to statutory exception
and to the provisions of relevant collective licensing agreements,
no reproduction of any part may take place without
the written permission of Cambridge University Press.

First published 2003

Printed in the United Kingdom at the University Press, Cambridge

Typeface Adobe Minion 10.75/12.75 pt. *System* LaTeX 2_ε [TB]

A catalogue record for this book is available from the British Library

ISBN 0 521 82595 4 hardback
ISBN 0 521 53335 X paperback

To my father,
Lorenzo Pasqualucci,
who sparked and nurtured my love of learning.

CONTENTS

FOREWORD

In 1978, when the American Convention on Human Rights entered into force, much of Central America and South America was ruled by dictatorships either of the right or the left. Of the eleven States whose ratifications had brought the Convention into force, fewer than one-half had democratically elected governments at the time. The remainder ratified for a variety of political reasons. Important also was the pressure brought to bear by the Carter Administration and the fact that some of these States were convinced that ratification posed no serious risks to them since the system established by the Convention would never be implemented. Effective human rights institutions were not something many governments in the region believed in at the time, but they were not opposed to a little window dressing for propaganda purposes. The attitude of these regimes towards human rights was graphically demonstrated when, shortly after the Convention entered into force, the General Assembly of the Organization of American States failed to adopt a budget for the newly created Inter-American Court of Human Rights. Had it not been for funds provided by Costa Rica, the Court would have been paralyzed even before it began to perform its functions.

Over the years, though, the political climate in the Americas changed gradually, making it possible for the Inter-American system for the protection of human rights to play an increasingly more important role. The fact that today all Latin American governments in the region, with the exception of Cuba, have been democratically elected has produced significant improvements in the human rights situation in these countries. These states have now also ratified the Convention and accepted the jurisdiction of the Court. This leaves only a small number of OAS member states – some Commonwealth Caribbean countries as well as the United States and Canada – out of the system established by the Convention. That is also true of Cuba whose government remains excluded from the OAS.

The increase in the number of ratifications of the Convention and acceptances of the Court's jurisdiction has made it possible for more and more cases to be referred to the Court. Today the Court can point to a significant body of law that has evolved from its judgments in contentious cases, its advisory opinions as well as its provisional measures. In her book, Professor Jo Pasqualucci provides the first truly comprehensive and up-to-date analysis of this practice. Here we have a book that needed to be written. It puts all of us interested in the work and role of the Inter-American Court in her debt for writing it and for the fine scholarship it represents.

Scholars and practitioners will find in this book a valuable review of all relevant elements of the Court's practice, including issues relating to admissibility, fact-finding, provisional measures, oral and written proceedings, scope of judgments, etc. Also discussed are those aspects of the practice of the Inter-American Commission on Human Rights that bear on the work of the Court. The author discusses the new Rules of Procedure of the Court and the Commission and the legal consequences they have for the interrelationship between these two institutions. Besides providing the reader with a practical guide to the Court's procedure and *modus operandi* which practitioners should find particularly useful, Professor Pasqualucci also succeeds in carefully analyzing the Court's practice in a creative and sound critical manner.

There is a great deal of material in these pages that scholars will find of value in seeking to understand the Court's jurisprudence and how it has evolved over the years. The book contains important insights about the Court's methodology and its transformation of the American Convention into an effective tool for the protection of human rights in the Americas, as well as various examples of the Court's contribution to international human rights law in general. No one trying to understand the manner in which the Court functions can afford to be without this book.

Professor Pasqualucci had been working on this book, which started as a doctoral dissertation, on and off for more than a decade. This led me and my successors as her dissertation supervisors to become increasingly concerned that the book would never see the light of day. Now it is clear, however, that at the time when we encouraged her to get on with the job, the Court's practice had not reached the level of judicial maturity or ripeness that would have enabled her to produce the truly valuable work she has now published. An impatient former professor herewith admits his error and expresses his delight with his former student's wisdom and patient scholarship that has resulted in the publication of this outstanding work.

Thomas Buergenthal
Judge, International Court of Justice
The Hague

PREFACE

This work is the culmination of fifteen years of study of the Inter-American Court of Human Rights. I did not set out to study the Inter-American Court. In 1986, during my final year of law school, I was in the office of Professor Richard Bilder at the University of Wisconsin. I had decided to apply for a Fulbright, and he was helping me formulate my proposal. At that moment, Professor Bilder received a telephone call from his long-time friend Thomas Buergenthal, a judge on the Inter-American Court of Human Rights. In their conversation Professor Bilder mentioned that there was a student in his office who spoke Spanish and who was applying for a Fulbright to Central America. Judge Buergenthal immediately saw the possibility of having assistance with legal research. He offered to write a letter to the Fulbright Commission inviting me to be affiliated with the Court. That serendipitous telephone call led to my long-term relationship with the Inter-American Court and to the focus of my subsequent scholarship.

I began my tenure at the Court in 1986 when it was considering its first contentious cases, the *Honduran Disappearance Cases*. The experience opened my eyes to the realities of human rights abuse. I cried over letters in the file from the father of Francisco Fairén Garbi, a Costa Rican youth who disappeared on a trip through Central America. I vacillated between despair at the cruelty reflected in the facts of the cases, and excitement and awe at being present and involved in this historic stage of the Court's evolution. The Court was only beginning to set its jurisdictional parameters and to establish its rules on practice and procedure. It was like clerking for the US Supreme Court in the days of John Marshall.

I remember long talks with Judge Buergenthal in which he expressed his absolute faith that we were slowly step-by-step building a system that would some day function effectively to protect human rights in the western hemisphere. At that time there was little evidence that his faith would be fulfilled. Even the mention of human rights in many Latin American countries could result in the speaker being labelled a 'communist'. The

Inter-American system was not functioning optimally. The Commission, which had been in existence since 1960, did not refer contentious cases to the Court for several years after the Court's formation. Thus, in the Court's first seven years of existence, the Court had handed down only advisory opinions. Judge Buergenthal's quiet optimism and his belief in a positive future had a profound influence on my outlook. He explained the basis for his attitude in a speech that he delivered in 1986, when he, a Jewish survivor of Auschwitz and Sachsenhausen, accepted an honorary doctorate from the University of Heidelberg Faculty of Law in Germany. In it he asked:

> Who would have thought in 1939, for example, that I would be standing here today; who would have believed in 1940 that there would exist a European Community composed of democratic nations, a European Parliament and a European Commission and Court of Human Rights, and that a new Germany would be a very important part of it all? Who would have believed then that at least a part of the Europe of old, with its nationalistic animosities and military rivalries, would undergo this transformation? Certainly no realist, and probably not even your average idealist. For an international lawyer who works in the field of human rights, these developments and the many others I could cite are a strong medicine against the loss of faith and a strong incentive for believing that what may appear impossible today may well come true tomorrow or the day after.

In every State, even those that appear to be the most recalcitrant human rights offenders, there are those attempting to enforce the rule of law. Those persons and organizations take great risks promoting democracy and human rights. Most others, although not active out of fear or malaise, would prefer to live in a State where human rights are observed. When the domestic institutions do not have the will or are not capable of prosecuting human rights violations and bringing human rights violators to justice, resort to international enforcement organs, such as the Inter-American Commission and Court, may be the only avenue to strengthen and support those on the domestic plane who are fighting for justice.

It is my hope that this study of the practice and procedure of the Inter-American Court will contribute to making possible the effective protection of human rights in the Americas. Procedural transparency, effectiveness and efficiency are essential to the enforcement of substantive human rights. As such, the procedural evolution and the practice of the Inter-American Court have direct bearing on the fulfillment of individual human rights in the Americas.

This book includes, when relevant, an analysis of the cases and opinions rendered by the Court until 1 January 2003 and of the Rules of Procedure of the Court and Commission which came into effect in 2002. Portions of earlier versions of chapters of this book have been published as 'Advisory Practice of the Inter-American Court of Human Rights: Contributing to the Evolution of International Human Rights Law', 38 *Stanford Journal of International Law*, 241 (2002); 'Preliminary Objections Before the Inter-American Court of Human Rights', 40 *Virginia Journal of International Law*, 1 (1999); 'Victim Reparations in the Inter-American Human Rights System: A Critical Assessment of Current Practice and Procedure', 18 *Michigan Journal of International Law*, 1 (1996); 'The Inter-American Human Rights System: Establishing Precedents and Procedure in Human Rights Law', 26 *University of Miami Inter-American Law Review*, 297 (1994–1995); 'The Whole Truth and Nothing But the Truth: Truth Commissions, Impunity and the Inter-American Human Rights System', 12 *Boston University International Law Journal*, 321 (1994); and 'Provisional Measures in the Inter-American Human Rights System: An Innovative Development in International Law', 26 *Vanderbilt Journal of Transnational Law*, 803 (1993).

The publisher has used its best endeavours to ensure that the URLs for external websites referred to in this book are correct and active at the time of going to press. However, the publisher has no responsibility for the websites and can make no guarantee that a site will remain live or that the content is or will remain appropriate.

ACKNOWLEDGMENTS

It seems to me, and to most people who know me, that I have been writing this book for my entire professional life. No sooner did I finish a chapter, than the Inter-American Court would render a judgment that would necessitate rewriting and updating it. Throughout this ordeal, my friends and colleagues have remained supportive, always asking the obligatory question, 'How is your book coming along?' and then listening to the recital of my latest insight or frustration. I would like to thank them for their interest and understanding.

I am especially grateful to Thomas Buergenthal, who has been my inspiration since 1986. Without his suggestion and encouragement I never would have undertaken this study of the Inter-American Court of Human Rights. His comments on drafts of the initial chapters, before he was elected judge of the International Court of Justice, were invaluable. I also wish to thank Professor Louis B. Sohn, who unfailingly gave of his precious time to inspire me and encourage me, and Professor Ralph G. Steinhardt, who encouraged me to complete it. In South Dakota I am indebted to Dean Barry Vickrey, who unfailingly provided his support and encouragement.

I must also express my gratitude to Christina Cerna, David Padilla, Veronica Gomez, Manuel Ventura Robles and the other attorneys and staff members of the Secretariats of the Court and Commission who patiently answered my questions, located documents for me, and published their own articles that clarified the law in action. All opinions and analysis are my own.

TABLE OF CASES

Inter-American Court of Human Rights Advisory Opinions

Inter-American Court of Human Rights Judgments and Resolutions in contentious cases

Provisional measures

Inter-American Commission on Human Rights decisions

United Nations Committee on Human Rights decisions

European Court of Human Rights judgments

European Commission on Human Rights

International Court of Justice judgments and decisions

Permanent Court of International Justice judgments and decisions

Other decisions and judgments

Council of Europe

Argentina

United States

TABLE OF ARTICLES OF THE AMERICAN CONVENTION ON HUMAN RIGHTS

TABLE OF 2001 RULES OF PROCEDURE OF THE INTER-AMERICAN COURT OF HUMAN RIGHTS

TABLE OF 2001 RULES OF PROCEDURE OF THE INTER-AMERICAN COMMISSION ON HUMAN RIGHTS

TABLE OF OTHER LEGAL INSTRUMENTS AND DOCUMENTS

1

Introduction

> For better or for worse, the problems of our Hemisphere are more unique to the Americas than they are universal or European. They can only be solved within the framework of our own legal, cultural, political, and social traditions.[1]

Introduction

The status of individuals under international law is no longer in doubt: individuals are subjects of international law and as such are accorded rights. Yet rights are illusory without the procedural capability to enforce them. They are no more than high-minded principles if individuals whose rights have been violated have no avenue for complaint and relief. International courts and commissions are often empowered to enforce human rights and to attribute responsibility to States that violate their obligations. These enforcement bodies must employ equitable procedures that balance victims' rights and States' treaty obligations. The practice and procedures of these bodies can ensure or impede an individual victim's access to justice.

The Inter-American Court of Human Rights is the sole judicial organ in the Inter-American human rights system. As such, it is the final arbiter of human rights in those American States that have ratified the American Convention on Human Rights. In 2001, the Court substantially revised its Rules of Procedure to more effectively address issues of timeliness and victim representation before the Court. In addition, the increasing numbers of decisions issued by the Inter-American Court in recent years has presented the Court with diverse procedural issues, allowing it to establish consistent practices in applying its procedures. This book analyzes the practice and procedures of the Inter-American Court and critiques the effectiveness of the Court in developing procedures and practices that

[1] Thomas Buergenthal, 'The American and European Conventions on Human Rights: Similarities and Differences', 30 *American University Law Review*, 155, 156 (1980–1).

protect the rights of individual applicants. It covers the period from the Court's inception in 1979 up to decisions issued in December 2002.

The Inter-American human rights system

A brief background of the Inter-American human rights system is necessary for a thorough understanding of the practice and procedure of the Inter-American Court.[2] The system was created by the Organization of American States (OAS) to provide for human rights protection in the Americas. The OAS, which has thirty-five Member States,[3] is open to all American States, although Cuba is excluded from participating.[4] In the past fifty years, the OAS Member States have worked together to structure a regional system to promote and protect human rights in the Americas. The organization has promulgated a series of instruments governing human rights in the region. These instruments include the Charter of the OAS,[5] which is the constitutive treaty forming the alliance between the American States. The Charter established the Inter-American Commission on Human Rights as an organ of the OAS.[6] Over time the Charter has been amended to incorporate other provisions on human rights. OAS documents and treaties specifically dedicated to human rights include: the American Declaration of the Rights and Duties of Man;[7] the American Convention on Human Rights;[8] two

[2] See Thomas Buergenthal and Dinah Shelton, *Protecting Human Rights in the Americas: Cases and Materials* (4th edn, Engel, 1995).

[3] The Member States of the OAS include Antigua and Barbuda, Argentina, Bahamas, Barbados, Belize, Bolivia, Brazil, Canada, Chile, Colombia, Costa Rica, Cuba, Dominica, Dominican Republic, Ecuador, El Salvador, Grenada, Guatemala, Guyana, Haiti, Honduras, Jamaica, Mexico, Nicaragua, Panama, Paraguay, Peru, Saint Kitts and Nevis, Saint Lucia, Saint Vincent and the Grenadines, Suriname, Trinidad and Tobago, United States, Uruguay and Venezuela. Reprinted in 2001 Basic Documents Pertaining to Human Rights in the Inter-American System, 23, OEA/Ser.L/V/I.4 rev. 8 (22 May 2001) (English), at back cover. The Basic Documents can be located online at http://www.cidh.oas.org.

[4] Cuba was excluded from participation in the OAS in 1962 for adopting a Marxist-Leninist form of government.

[5] Charter of the Organization of American States (as amended), 30 April 1948, entered into force on 13 December 1951, 2 UST 2394, TIAS No. 2361; amended effective 1970, 21 UST 607, TIAS No. 6847.

[6] *Ibid.*, Art. 51. See Francisco Cox, 'Analyzing the Inter-American Commission on Human Rights Under Three Theories of Compliance', 28 *Revista Inter-American Institute of Human Rights* 11 (1998).

[7] Adopted in 1948 by the OAS General Assembly, reprinted in 2001 Basic Documents, at 4.

[8] American Convention on Human Rights, 22 November 1969, 9 ILM 673, OEA/Ser.K/XVI/I.1, doc. 65 rev. 1 corr. 1 (1970), reprinted in 2001 Basic Documents. The American

Protocols to the American Convention (the Protocol on Economic, Social and Cultural Rights, known as the 'Protocol of San Salvador',[9] and the Protocol to Abolish the Death Penalty);[10] the Inter-American Convention to Prevent and Punish Torture;[11] the Inter-American Convention on the Forced Disappearance of Persons;[12] the Inter-American Convention on the Prevention, Punishment and Eradication of Violence Against Women;[13] and the Inter-American Convention on the Elimination of All Forms of Discrimination Against Persons with Disabilities.[14]

The American Convention on Human Rights, also known as the 'Pact of San José', sets forth the human rights protected. The Convention empowers two bodies, the already-established Inter-American Commission on Human Rights and the Inter-American Court of Human Rights,[15] to ensure State compliance with the human rights set forth in the instrument.[16] The American Convention protects some two dozen rights, many more than the number protected initially by the European Convention on Human Rights and Fundamental Freedoms.[17] The rights protected by the

Convention and other Inter-American human rights documents can be viewed on the website of the OAS, http://www.oas.org, or on the website of the Inter-American Court of Human Rights, http://www.corteidh.or.cr.

9 Additional Protocol to the American Convention on Human Rights in the Area of Economic, Social and Cultural Rights ('Protocol of San Salvador'), signed at San Salvador, El Salvador, on 17 November 1988 at the eighteenth regular session of the General Assembly, and entered into force on 16 November 1999.

10 Protocol to the American Convention on Human Rights to Abolish the Death Penalty, Approved at Asunción, Paraguay, on 8 June 1990, at the twentieth regular session of the General Assembly of the OAS, entered into force on 28 August 1991, reprinted in 2001 Basic Documents, 79.

11 Signed at Cartegana de Indias, Colombia, on 9 December 1985 at the fifteenth regular session of the General Assembly of the OAS, entered into force on 28 February 1987, reprinted in 2001 Basic Documents, 83.

12 Resolution Adopted at Belem do Pará, Brazil, 9 June 1994 at the twenty-fourth regular session of the General Assembly of the OAS, entered into force on 28 March 1996, reprinted in 2001 Basic Documents, 93.

13 Adopted in Belem do Pará, Brazil, on 9 June 1994 during the twenty-fourth regular session of the General Assembly of the OAS, entered into force on 5 March 1995, reprinted in 2001 Basic Documents, 101.

14 Adopted at Guatemala City, Guatemala, at the twenty-ninth regular session of the General Assembly of the OAS, 7 June 1999, reprinted in 2001 Basic Documents, 111.

15 See Cecilia Medina Quiroga, 'The Inter-American Commission on Human Rights and the Inter-American Court of Human Rights: Reflections on a Joint Venture', 12 *Human Rights Quarterly*, 439, at 440–3 (1990).

16 American Convention, Art. 33.

17 European Convention for the Protection of Human Rights and Fundamental Freedoms, as amended by Protocol No. 11, Rome, 4 November 1950, Art. 47(2). The homepage for the European Court of Human Rights Rules is located at http://www.echr.coe.int.

American Convention include, *inter alia*, the rights to life, a name, nationality, property, privacy, humane treatment, personal liberty, a fair trial, assembly and compensation when there has been a miscarriage of justice. It also provides for rights of the family and the child, and for freedom of religion, thought, expression, movement and residence. The ambitious nature of the American Convention did not deter States from ratifying it, as many had feared it would.[18] The Convention received the necessary eleven ratifications and entered into force in 1978. As of 1 January 2003, twenty-four of the thirty-five Member States of the OAS are States Parties to the American Convention. These States are Argentina, Barbados, Bolivia, Brazil, Chile, Colombia, Costa Rica, Dominica, Dominican Republic, Ecuador, El Salvador, Grenada, Guatemala, Haiti, Honduras, Jamaica, Mexico, Nicaragua, Panama, Paraguay, Peru, Suriname, Uruguay and Venezuela.[19] Trinidad and Tobago, which had been a State Party, denounced the American Convention on 26 May 1998, effective 26 May 1999.

Although the American Convention is modelled on the UN human rights instruments and on the European Convention for the Protection of Human Rights and Fundamental Freedoms, the drafters of the American Convention refused to simply replicate those treaties. Rather, the delegates to the drafting conference argued that 'it was appropriate to introduce any modifications that were desirable in the light of circumstances prevailing in the American Republics'.[20] The circumstances and social reality of the developed States – of which the European human rights system was then composed – differed greatly from those of the many underdeveloped States in the Inter-American system. Extremes of poverty and wealth contributed to political instability in the Inter-American system. Misery, injustice and exploitation were endemic. Not surprisingly, social and economic oppression gave rise to political oppression and to human rights violations. The distinctions between the European and American systems were also manifest in the types of human rights violations initially confronted. Until the inclusion of Eastern European States, the European human rights system primarily dealt with isolated instances of human rights abuse, involving 'arrest and detention

[18] Thomas Buergenthal, 'The American Convention on Human Rights: Illusions and Hopes', 21 *Buffalo Law Review*, 121 (1971).

[19] The States Parties are listed in 2001 Basic Documents, 48. See Appendix 1, p. 381.

[20] Council of Europe, *Report on the Inter-American Specialized Conference on Human Rights* (Strasbourg, 22 December 1969), reprinted in *Human Rights: The Inter-American System*, Booklet 15 vol. 3, at 67, 71 (Thomas B. Buergenthal and Robert E. Norris eds., 1982).

guarantees and fair administration of justice'.[21] Conversely, for many years the principal cases in the Inter-American system involved forced disappearances and extra-judicial executions resulting from intentional governmental policies. The Inter-American system benefited immeasurably from the European experience; but as a result of differences it also was forced to forge its own practice and procedures. As Buergenthal stated, '[t]he political and economic realities of the Americas, where non-democratic regimes and large-scale poverty persist, make enforcement of human rights in this region much more difficult than in Western Europe'.[22]

The drafters of the American Convention had the foresight to give individuals the right to petition. In a reversal of traditional international law, the American Convention allows individuals to file complaints against a State upon the State's ratification of the Convention.[23] Conversely, it provides that a State Party must make an express declaration recognizing the competence of the Commission to deal with complaints from other States.[24] Farer observed that '[s]urely this was to swallow a camel and shrink from a fly. For while the former were certain to occur, the latter were improbable at any time, much less among members of a political and military alliance waging a Cold War.'[25] As Farer accurately predicted, to date no inter-State complaints have been filed in the Inter-American system. Traditionally only States had automatic standing to file petitions or complaints against other States in international law. Individuals did not have standing, even when their own rights were violated. This was also true in international human rights law, which had been created to protect individuals. When injured by the action of a State, an individual's only recourse was to convince his or her government to file a complaint.[26] If that government were the violator, the victim had no recourse under international law. When human rights abuses became endemic, only rarely

[21] E. V. O. Dankwa, 'Conference on Regional Systems of Human Rights Protection in Africa, the Americas and Europe', 13 *Human Rights Law Journal*, 314, at 316 (1992); see also Rolv Ryssdal, 'The Future of the European Court of Human Rights', ECOUR90296.AB, 4 (1990).

[22] Thomas Buergenthal, 'The American and European Conventions on Human Rights: Similarities and Differences', 30 *American University Law Review*, 155, at 156 (1980–1). See also Scott Davidson, *The Inter-American Court of Human Rights* 4 (Dartmouth, 1992).

[23] American Convention, Art. 44 [24] *Ibid.*, Art. 45.

[25] Tom Farer, 'The Rise of the Inter-American Human Rights Regime: No Longer a Unicorn, Not Yet an Ox', in *The Inter-American System of Human Rights* 31, 36 (Harris and Livingstone eds., 1998).

[26] See Ian Brownlie, *Principles of Public International Law* (5th edn, Oxford, 1998).

did one State complain or take action against another,[27] and these reactions were often politically motivated. Even when concerned about human rights violations, political reality often inhibits a State from making accusations about another for fear of jeopardizing its economic interests or of having its own practices evaluated.

Standing to file an individual petition with the Commission is not limited to the individual victim or family members of the victim. Any person, group of persons or nongovernmental entity that is legally recognized in a Member State of the OAS may file a petition alleging that an individual's rights have been violated.[28] This provision has proved to be especially important in the Inter-American system, where victims or their family members may be too intimidated or indigent to submit a petition. A nongovernmental organization (NGO) often has more resources than the individuals involved and is less susceptible to threats of retaliation.

The Convention delineates the procedures the Commission and the Court are to apply in processing individual complaints of human rights abuse. These procedures specify that an individual who alleges that a State party to the American Convention has violated his or her rights must first file a complaint directly with the Inter-American Commission, located in Washington DC.[29] The Commission receives hundreds of complaints each year.[30] The Inter-American Commission is composed of seven commissioners, who are chosen from the Member States of the OAS.[31] The Commission's Secretariat, composed of a full-time staff of lawyers, an Executive Secretary, and a Deputy Executive Secretary, performs the routine work of the Commission, including the initial review of petitions. The Commission solicits information from the parties, makes a decision as to the admissibility of the petition, engages in fact-finding procedures, and attempts to bring about a friendly settlement between the parties. If the Commission attributes the human rights violation to the State, the Commission may make recommendations to the State.[32] A State that decides to challenge the Commission's attribution of responsibility may submit the case to the Inter-American Court.[33] The Commission may submit a case

[27] But see *The Greek Case*, 1969 Eur. YB 501 (Council of Europe).

[28] American Convention, Art. 44. See David Padilla, 'The Inter-American Commission on Human Rights of the Organization of American States: A Case Study', 9 *American University Journal of International Law and Policy*, 95, at 97–115 (1993).

[29] American Convention, Art. 44.

[30] Christina Cerna, 'Commission Organization and Petitions', in *The Inter-American System of Human Rights*, 65, 96 (Harris and Livingstone, eds., 1998).

[31] American Convention, Art. 34. [32] *Ibid.*, Art. 50(3). [33] *Ibid.*, Art. 61.

to the Court only if the State has accepted the Court's jurisdiction.[34] The Court then conducts contentious proceedings to determine whether the State is responsible for the human rights violation. If the Court holds the State accountable, the Court may order the State to make reparations.[35] The State Party is legally bound to comply with the judgment of the Court.[36]

A concise history of the Inter-American Court

The Inter-American Court of Human Rights was established in 1979. During its early years, the Court's prospects for improving the human rights of the people of the Americas appeared uninspiring. Dictatorships in the Western Hemisphere perpetrated gross and systematic violations of human rights.[37] State-sponsored forced disappearances, extra-judicial killings, and torture were commonplace. Few observers expected the Court to have a significant impact, and, initially, the sceptics were right. The Commission did not forward contentious cases to the Court until 1986, seven years after its inception. Although Costa Rica attempted to bypass the Commission in one instance by referring a case directly, the Court determined that the Convention-mandated procedures could not be circumvented.[38] The Court, therefore, refused to consider the case and sent it to the Commission.[39] The Court's principal vehicle for contributing to international law during that period was its advisory opinions.

When the Commission began to refer contentious cases to the Court, the governments of newly emerging democracies were shocked to be charged with human rights violations. These States equated the need for human rights enforcement with dictatorships. As a result, it was initially feared that States would refuse to participate in proceedings before the Court, a recurring problem before the International Court of Justice at that time. This did not happen. States responded to applications filed

[34] *Ibid.*, Art. 62(3).

[35] *Ibid.*, Art. 63(1). See Jo M. Pasqualucci, 'Victim Reparations in the Inter-American Human Rights System: A Critical Assessment of Current Practice and Procedure', 18 *Michigan Journal of International Law*, 1 (1996).

[36] American Convention, Art. 68(1).

[37] Cecilia Medina Quiroga, *The Battle of Human Rights: Gross Systematic Violations and the Inter-American System*, 2 (Kluwer, 1988).

[38] *In the Matter of Viviana Gallardo et al.*, Inter-Am. Ct HR, Decision of 13 November 1981, Ser. A, No. G101/81, para. 28.

[39] *Ibid.*, Resolutions 3 and 4.

against them by designating agents, filing memoranda, and appearing and arguing at public hearings. To be sure, States often filed preliminary objections, many of which were frivolous; but, when those objections were rejected, the States presented a defence.

The reputation of the Inter-American Court increased as a result of the quality of its jurisprudence. The status of the Court is reflected in the calibre of State witnesses who have appeared before it to defend State actions. For example, in the *Baena Ricardo Case*, in which 270 former State employees alleged that they were illegally dismissed from their jobs as a result of an *ex post facto* law, Guillermo Endara, the former president of Panama, and his vice-president testified before the Court.[40] Eventually, some States accepted responsibility for the human rights violations before the Court reached a judgment, leaving only the issue of reparations to be decided.[41] The acceptance of international responsibility was an indirect acknowledgment on the part of the State that an Inter-American Court judgment attributing responsibility to a State for human rights violations would be taken seriously domestically and internationally.

State compliance with Court-ordered reparations has similarly evolved. As the Court has no effective mechanism to enforce its judgments, it was initially feared that States would simply ignore them and refuse to make Court-ordered reparation to the victims. Honduras, under the presidency of Carlos Roberto Reina, a former Inter-American Court judge, eventually paid the compensation ordered in the *Honduran Disappearance Cases*, the first contentious cases decided by the Court. Most other States have also paid the pecuniary compensation ordered by the Court, although many have balked and delayed payment for extensive periods. Compensation, however, is not the only form of reparation ordered. The Court may also order the State to take action or to desist from particular acts. When Peru complied with the Court's order to release from prison María Elena Loayza Tamayo, a college professor,[42] a new level of State compliance was reached.

[40] *Baena Ricardo et al.* (*270 Workers* v. *Panama*) (Merits), Inter-Am. Ct HR, 2 February 2001, Ser. C, No. 72. paras. 65(h) and (i).

[41] Cases in which States have accepted international responsibility include *Barrios Altos* (*Chumbipuma Aguirre et al.* v. *Peru*) (Merits), Inter-Am. Ct HR, 14 March 2001, Ser. C, No. 75, para. 31(1); *Aloeboetoe et al.* v. *Suriname* (Merits), Inter-Am. Ct HR, 4 December 1991, Ser. C, No. 11, para. 22; *El Amparo* v. *Venezuela* (Merits), Inter-Am. Ct HR, 18 January 1995, Ser. C, No. 19, para. 19; *Garrido and Baigorria* v. *Argentina* (Merits), Inter-Am. Ct HR, 2 February 1996, Ser. C, No. 26, para. 25; *Del Caracazo* v. *Venezuela* (Merits), Inter-Am. Ct HR, 11 November 1999, Ser. C, No. 58, para. 37. *Las Palmeras* v. *Colombia* (Merits), Inter-Am. Ct HR, 6 December 2001, Ser. C, No. 90, para. 19, accepting partial responsibility.

[42] See *Loayza Tamayo* v. *Peru* (Merits), Inter-Am. Ct HR, 17 September 1997, Ser. C, No. 33, para. 84 and operative para. 5.

Peru also later released Cesti Hurtado from prison.[43] Subsequently, in certain cases when the Court has declared a domestic law or judgment to be in violation of the American Convention, States have amended the laws,[44] or domestic courts have declared them to be unconstitutional[45] or domestic court judgments have been annulled.[46] These developments are unprecedented in human rights law.

There is, however, another level of State compliance with Court-ordered reparations that is not yet commonly observed in the Inter-American system. The Court, in almost every case, orders the State to investigate, prosecute and punish the individuals responsible for the human rights violations. These orders are seldom fulfilled. In most States impunity reigns, and the State power structure lacks the means or the will to bring the perpetrators of human rights violations to justice. When Court orders to prosecute and punish the violators are consistently fulfilled, the Court will have contributed substantially to the fall of impunity and to the specific and general deterrence of human rights violations.

The initial fear that States would withdraw their acceptance of the Court's jurisdiction or denounce the American Convention has not been warranted. Only one State, Trinidad and Tobago, has denounced the Convention and the Court's jurisdiction.[47] Peru, which had announced its intention to withdraw its recognition of the Court's jurisdiction, has since reaffirmed its acceptance of the Court's jurisdiction.[48] Moreover, additional States have ratified the Convention and accepted the Court's jurisdiction.

Composition of the Court

The Court is composed of seven judges, who must be 'jurists of the highest moral authority' recognized for their competence in human rights law.[49] The judges must also 'possess the qualifications required for the exercise of the highest judicial functions in conformity with the law of the state of

[43] *Cesti Hurtado* v. *Peru* (Request for Interpretation of the Judgment of 29 September 1999), Inter-Am. Ct HR, Order of 19 November 1999, Ser. C, No. 62.

[44] *Cantoral Benavides* v. *Peru* (Reparations), Inter-Am. Ct HR, 3 December 2001, Ser. C, No. 88, para. 76.

[45] *Suárez Rosero* v. *Ecuador* (Reparations) (Art. 63(1) American Convention of Human Rights), Inter-Am. Ct HR, 20 January 1999, Ser. C, No. 44, paras. 81–3.

[46] *Cesti Hurtado* v. *Peru* (Reparations), Inter-Am Ct HR, 31 May 2001, Ser. C, No. 78, para. 15.

[47] See 2001 Basic Documents, 59.

[48] See Peruvian Legislative Resolution No. 271532 in the Inter-American Court of Human Rights Press Release CP2/01 on the Court's website at http://corteidh.or.cr.

[49] American Convention, Art. 52(1).

which they are nationals or of the state that proposes them as candidates'.[50] Judges are independent; they do not represent States. Although judges must be nationals of OAS Member States,[51] they need not be nationals of States that have ratified the American Convention or accepted the jurisdiction of the Court. Judges are elected by a vote of the States Parties to the Convention.[52] A State Party may propose up to three candidates for judge, provided that at least one of the three is a national of another Member State.[53] The judges are elected for six years and may serve no more than two terms.[54] They serve on a part-time basis, although the number of cases and requests for provisional measures is increasing the pressure for a full-time Court.[55] The judge who serves as President of the Court serves on a permanent basis.[56]

In addition to the seven sitting judges, the bench may also include interim and *ad hoc* judges for particular cases. When a sitting judge is a national of a State Party to a contentious case, that judge need not recuse himself or herself from consideration of the case. If, however, the President of the Court is a national of the respondent State or any party to the case, the President shall relinquish the Presidency for that case.[57] A State Party in a contentious case has the right to name a judge *ad hoc* for that case, if a sitting judge is not a national of that State.[58] With inter-State complaints, if a judge on the Court is a national of one of the States Parties to the case, the other State Party may designate a judge *ad hoc*.[59]

The Court has a full-time secretariat that is based at the seat of the Court in San José, Costa Rica. The Secretariat is composed of the Secretary, Deputy Secretary, four additional attorneys and five assistants. The Court

[50] *Ibid.*

[51] American Convention, Art. 52. The judges must be nationals of different States. *Ibid.*, Art. 52(1). Five judges constitute a quorum for the consideration of a case or the transaction of other Court business. *Ibid.*, Art. 56.

[52] American Convention, Art. 53(1). [53] *Ibid.*, Art. 53(2). [54] *Ibid.*, Art. 54.

[55] Evaluation of the Workings of the Inter-American System for the Protection and Promotion of Human Rights with a View to its Improvement and Strengthening, Resolution 1(e), AG/RES. 1828 (XXXI-O/01), Resolution adopted at the third plenary session, held on 5 June 2001 in which the OAS General Assembly suggested that the possibility of a permanent Court and Commission be examined. Available on the OAS website at www.oas.org.

[56] Statute of the Inter-American Court of Human Rights, adopted by the General Assembly of the OAS at its ninth regular session, held in La Paz, Bolivia, October 1979 (Resolution No. 448), Art. 16(2), reprinted in 2001 Basic Documents, 155.

[57] 2001 Rules of Procedure of the Inter-American Court of Human Rights, Art. 4(3), entered into force on 1 June 2001, approved by the Court at its forty-ninth regular session held 25 November 2000.

[58] American Convention, Art. 55(2). [59] *Ibid.*

usually convenes at its seat.[60] It may, however, meet in any State of the OAS, with the prior consent of that State, so long as a majority of the judges on the Court deem the alternative meeting place desirable.[61]

Overview of jurisdiction

Under its contentious jurisdiction, the Inter-American Court rules on whether a State has violated an individual's human rights. The Court must assess the truth of the applicant's allegations and determine whether the facts as proved constitute a violation of the Convention imputable to the State. The Court can only exercise contentious jurisdiction over States that have accepted its jurisdiction as binding *ipso facto* or on an *ad hoc* basis by special agreement for a particular case.[62] A State Party to the American Convention accepts the Court's jurisdiction as binding *ipso facto* when it files a special declaration to that effect.[63] As of 1 January 2003, twenty-one States Parties to the American Convention had accepted the compulsory jurisdiction of the Inter-American Court. The States subject to the Court's jurisdiction are Argentina, Barbados, Bolivia, Brazil, Chile, Colombia, Costa Rica, Dominican Republic, Ecuador, El Salvador, Guatemala, Haiti, Honduras, Mexico, Nicaragua, Panama, Paraguay, Peru, Suriname, Uruguay and Venezuela.[64] In denouncing the American Convention, Trinidad and Tobago also denounced the Court's jurisdiction.

The majority of the Court's contentious cases have dealt with disappearances or extra-judicial executions – as represented by the *Honduran Disappearance Cases*, the *Aloeboetoe Case*, the *Caballero Delgado and Santana Case* and the *Gangaram Panday Case*. In later years, a broader range of alleged violations has been submitted for the Court's consideration. In *'The Last Temptation of Christ' Case*, the Court held that Chile's prior censorship of the movie was in violation of freedom of expression as guaranteed by the American Convention.[65] In the *Constitutional Court*

[60] American Convention, Art. 58(1). 'The seat of the Court may be changed by a vote of two-thirds of the States Parties to the Convention, in the OAS General Assembly.' *Ibid.*

[61] *Ibid.*

[62] *Ibid.*, Art. 62. See Restrictions to the Death Penalty (Arts. 4(2) and 4(4) of the American Convention on Human Rights), Inter-Am. Ct HR, Advisory Opinion OC-3/83 of 8 September 1983, Ser. A, No. 3, para. 21.

[63] American Convention, Art. 62.

[64] See 2001 Basic Documents, 48.

[65] *'The Last Temptation of Christ' (Olmedo Bustos et al.* v. *Chile)* (Merits), Inter-Am. Ct HR, 5 February 2001, Ser. C, No. 73, operative para. 1.

Case, the Court ruled on the dismissal of three Peruvian Constitutional Court justices, who argued that they were impeached because they refused to hold constitutional a law that would allow President Fujimori to run for an additional term in office.[66] In the *Baena Ricardo et al. Case*, the Court ruled that 270 Panamanian government workers had been fired in violation of the American Convention for exercising their right of association.[67] The increasing breadth of rights litigated is important for the evolution of the Inter-American human rights system in that the Court's caseload is coming to reflect the spectrum of rights protected by the Convention.

The Inter-American Court also has advisory jurisdiction that can be exercised without the express consent of the States. Even OAS Member States that have not ratified the American Convention may request an advisory opinion or find their actions subject to the Court's advisory jurisdiction.[68] There are no 'parties' to an advisory procedure, and there is no case to be settled by the Court.[69] The Court's advisory jurisdiction enables it 'to perform a service for all of the members of the inter-American system and is designed to assist them in fulfilling their international human rights obligations'.[70] Through its advisory opinions, the Court fosters uniform legal standards throughout the Americas. While an advisory opinion is not binding (unlike the Court's judgment in a contentious case), it does have undeniable legal and moral effects on both national and international law.[71]

The Court is also empowered to act quickly in 'cases of extreme gravity and urgency' by ordering a State to protect persons who are in danger.[72] Whether the case is before the Court or is still under consideration by the Commission and has not yet been submitted to the Court, the Court

66 *Constitutional Court* v. *Peru* (Competence), Inter-Am. Ct HR, 24 September 1999, Ser. C, No. 55, para. 2.

67 *Baena Ricardo et al.* (*270 Workers* v. *Panama*) (Merits, 2001), operative para. 4.

68 Advisory Opinion OC-3/83, para. 43.

69 Reports of the Inter-American Commission of Human Rights (Art. 51 of the American Convention on Human Rights), Inter-Am. Ct HR, Advisory Opinion OC-15/97 of 14 November 1997, Ser. A, No. 15, para. 25.

70 *'Other Treaties' Subject to the Consultative Jurisdiction of the Court* (Art. 64 of the American Convention on Human Rights), Inter-Am. Ct HR, Advisory Opinion OC-1/82 of 24 September 1982, Ser. A, No. 1, para. 39, quoted in *Proposed Amendments to the Naturalization Provisions of the Constitution of Costa Rica*, Inter-Am. Ct HR, Advisory Opinion OC-4/84 of 19 January 1984, Ser. A, No. 4, para. 19; *The Right to Information on Consular Assistance within the Framework of the Guarantees of Legal Due Process*, Inter-Am. Ct HR, Advisory Opinion OC-16/99 of 1 October 1999, Ser. A. No. 16, para. 64.

71 Advisory Opinion OC-15/97, para. 26. See also 'State and institutional implementation of the Inter-American Court's advisory opinions', pp. 332–7 below.

72 American Convention, Art. 63(2).

may order a State to take provisional measures to protect persons from irreparable harm.[73] The Court has declared that its provisional measures orders are binding.[74] Requests for provisional measures have proliferated, putting a burden on both the Commission and the Court to oversee their implementation. The danger of irreparable harm and the corresponding duty of oversight often continues for years. Nonetheless, provisional measures have proved effective in protecting victims who are in imminent danger.

An illustrative contentious case

The facts and procedures of an actual contentious case may help the reader to better understand the subject matter of this book.[75] The *Velásquez Rodríguez Case* was one of the first three contentious cases decided by the Inter-American Court of Human Rights. The case is representative in that it involved all procedural phases. It is imperfect in that the Court and Commission were at that time still developing their procedures, and the Court did not fully exercise its authority to order reparations. There have been some changes in procedures at both the Commission and Court levels since the Court rendered the judgment.

Facts

The Court found the following facts to be proved.[76] Angel Manfredo Velásquez Rodríguez,[77] a Honduran university student, was seized in broad daylight in downtown Tegucigalpa, the capital of Honduras, on

[73] Various terms are used to denote the same meaning in international documents: 'provisional measures', 'interim measures', 'interim measures of protection', 'precautionary measures', 'emergency measures', 'urgent measures' and 'conservatory measures'. The term 'provisional measures' will be used in this book except when the applicable source uses an alternative term.

[74] *Constitutional Court* (Peru), Provisional Measures, Inter-Am. Ct HR, Order of 14 August 2000, Ser. E, para. 14.

[75] See Claudio Grossman, 'Disappearances in Honduras: The Need for Direct Victim Representation in Human Rights Litigation', 15 *Hastings International and Comparative Law Review*, 363 (1992); Juan Méndez and José Vivanco, 'Disappearances and the Inter-American Court: Reflections on a Litigation Experience', 13 *Hamline Law Review*, 507 (1990); and National Commission for the Protection of Human Rights, *The Facts Speak for Themselves, Preliminary Report on the Disappeared in Honduras 1980–1993* (1994).

[76] *Velásquez Rodríguez* v. *Honduras* (Merits), Inter-Am. Ct HR, 29 July 1988, Ser. C, No. 4, para. 147.

[77] Hereinafter 'Manfredo Velásquez' or 'Velásquez'.

12 September 1981. Several heavily-armed men in civilian clothes, driving a vehicle without licence plates, kidnapped him from a parking lot in front of eyewitnesses. He was thirty-five years old, married, and the father of three minor children. Various witnesses reported that he was detained and subject to torture in two military locations. His family filed three writs of *habeas corpus* and two criminal complaints without avail. The security forces and police denied all knowledge of him. He remains disappeared.

Between the years 1981 and 1984, the Government of Honduras engaged in a practice of forced disappearances to eliminate people whom the authorities considered to be dangerous to State security. During that three-year period, between 100 and 150 persons were forcibly disappeared in Honduras. The *modus operandi* of the disappearances was similar. The victims, who were often students and labour leaders, were kept under prolonged surveillance. The abductions often took place during the day in public places. Those who detained the victims were generally armed men wearing civilian clothes. Occasionally the military or police openly detained the victims. The abductors often drove vehicles with false or no licence plates and tinted windows which required official authorization. They carried arms of a type that were only permitted for official use by the police and military. The kidnappers often blindfolded the victims, took them to secret unofficial detention centres and moved them from one centre to another. They interrogated the victims and subjected them to cruel and humiliating treatment and torture. Some were ultimately murdered and their bodies were buried in clandestine cemeteries.

Honduras ratified the American Convention on 8 September 1977 and accepted the jurisdiction of the Court on 9 September 1981.[78]

Procedures before the Commission

On 7 October 1981, a petition in the case was filed with the Inter-American Commission on Human Rights. The Commission communicated the relevant parts of the petition to the government for a response, and then tried on several occasions to obtain information, but the government did not reply. On 4 October 1983, two years after the petition was originally filed, having received no response from Honduras, the Commission applied its regulations and presumed as true the allegations contained in the

[78] 2001 Basic Documents, 48.

petition. Only at that point did Honduras reply, requesting reconsideration of the Commission's determination on various grounds. On 30 May 1984, the Commission agreed to reconsider its resolution and again requested information from Honduras. Honduras did not respond. On 29 January 1985, the Commission informed Honduras that it would render a final decision in March 1985. On 1 March 1985, Honduras again requested an extension on the ground that it had set up an investigatory commission. The Commission granted an additional thirty-day extension. On 17 October 1985, Honduras gave the Commission a report of its investigation, in which charges against all officials were dismissed except for the charge against a former general who was in exile and out of favour with the government.[79]

Procedures before the Court

On 24 April 1986, four-and-a-half years after the petition was filed, the Commission referred the case to the Court. The Commission alleged that the Government of Honduras was responsible for violations of the rights to life, personal liberty and humane treatment of Angel Manfredo Velásquez Rodríguez.[80] The Court joined the *Velásquez Rodríguez Case* with two other cases in which the State of Honduras was charged with forcibly disappearing the alleged victims, the *Godínez Cruz Case* and the *Fairén Garbi and Solís Corrales Case.*

Preliminary objections

The Honduran Government filed preliminary objections asserting that the Commission had not followed several Convention-mandated procedures. The objections asserted that the Commission had failed (1) to make a formal declaration of admissibility; (2) to attempt a friendly settlement between the parties; (3) to engage in an on-site investigation in Honduras; (4) to hold a hearing; and (5) to comply properly with the Convention's reporting procedures. Honduras also objected that the petitioners had not exhausted domestic remedies.[81] The Commission filed a responding brief. The Court held a public hearing to hear the Commission's and the State's oral arguments on the objections.[82] After considering the evidence

[79] *Velásquez Rodríguez* v. *Honduras* (Preliminary Objections), Inter-Am. Ct HR, 26 June 1987, Ser. C, No. 1, paras. 1 and 15–24.

[80] *Ibid.*, paras. 1 and 2. [81] *Ibid.*, paras. 25 and 31. [82] *Ibid.*, para. 9.

and arguments, the Court rejected the preliminary objections to the procedures taken by the Commission.[83] It joined the preliminary objection of non-exhaustion of domestic remedies to the merits of the case.[84]

Proceedings on the merits

Pursuant to the order of the Court, the parties filed briefs on the merits and supporting documentary evidence. The Court also accepted *amicus* briefs from nongovernmental organizations.[85] The Court then held public hearings on the merits of the case. Commission witnesses testified as to the specific facts and that during the years in question in Honduras numerous persons disappeared and domestic remedies were ineffective.[86] The Commission submitted evidence from Honduran attorneys, persons who had been disappeared, relatives of disappeared persons, national legislators, and newspaper clippings to show that legal remedies were ineffective to free persons 'disappeared' pursuant to a government policy during the period in question.[87] The witnesses included a woman who testified that she had been held incommunicado and tortured for three months,[88] a Honduran attorney who defended political prisoners, who testified that he was held for ten days and tortured,[89] and a former death squad operative who testified that he had participated in kidnappings.[90] At the public hearing, the government did not offer witnesses or evidence to refute the Commission's allegations.[91] The Court then ordered the submission of additional documentary evidence and witness testimony, including the testimony of certain named Honduran military officers. Honduras requested, for security reasons, that the Court hold a private hearing to hear the testimony of military officers as to the organizational structure of the military battalion alleged to have committed the human rights abuses. The Court held the closed hearing in the presence of both parties.[92]

Provisional measures

Subsequent to the first public hearing, two witnesses were murdered, a person who had been summoned to testify was murdered and other

[83] *Ibid.*, operative para. 1. [84] *Ibid.*, operative para. 2.
[85] *Velásquez Rodríguez* v. *Honduras* (Merits), para. 38. [86] *Ibid.*, para. 28.
[87] *Ibid.*, para. 76. [88] *Ibid.*, para. 84. [89] *Ibid.*, para. 91.
[90] *Ibid.*, para. 100. [91] *Ibid.*, para. 79. [92] *Ibid.*, paras. 31 and 34.

persons related to the case received death threats.[93] The Court ordered the Government of Honduras to take provisional measures to protect the basic rights of former or future witnesses in the cases before the Court and to use all means to investigate the crimes, and identify and punish the perpetrators.[94] The Court subsequently held a public hearing to consider the Commission's and the State's views on subsequent provisional measures requested by the Commission. The Court ordered, as additional provisional measures, that the government report to the Court and submit documentation on the measures being taken to protect witnesses and investigate the threats and assassinations.[95] No further witnesses were killed.

Decision on the merits

In its decision on the merits, the Court rejected the government's claim that domestic remedies had not been exhausted, and held that Honduras had violated Manfredo Velásquez' right to life, personal liberty and humane treatment.[96] The Court also decided that the Commission and the government had a six-month period to determine the fair compensation to be paid to the family of the victim. The Court retained jurisdiction to approve the agreement or to act, if the parties failed to agree.[97]

Reparations

In this early case, the Court labelled and limited this phase of the proceedings to 'compensatory damages'.[98] During the six-month period specified by the Court for the parties to agree on compensation, the parties agreed only that the beneficiaries of the damages award were to be Velásquez' wife and three minor children.[99] Therefore, the Court ordered a public hearing and requested that the government submit documentary evidence such as the victim's birth certificate, salary and employment at the time of death, title to property in his name, academic and professional credentials, and the names and status of his wife and children.[100] The Court accepted *amicus curiae* briefs.[101] At the hearing, the Court heard expert psychiatric testimony as to the effect of Manfredo Velásquez' disappearance on the mental health of his family.[102]

93 *Ibid.*, paras. 39–41. 94 *Ibid.*, para. 41. 95 *Ibid.*, para. 45.
96 *Ibid.*, operative paras. 1–4. 97 *Ibid.*, operative para. 5.
98 *Velásquez Rodríguez* v. *Honduras* (Compensatory Damages), Inter-Am. Ct HR, 21 July 1989, Ser. C, No. 7.
99 *Ibid.*, para. 22. 100 *Ibid.*, para. 13. 101 *Ibid.*, para. 19. 102 *Ibid.*, para. 51.

The Court ordered compensation for the loss of earnings of the victim and moral damages to the family.[103] The wife's share of the damages award was to be paid directly to her. The children's share was to be placed in trust.[104] The Court refused to order punitive damages or to order the State to take other measures such as making a public condemnation of the practice of disappearances or naming a public place after the victims of disappearances.[105] The State was provided the option of paying the Court-ordered compensation in Honduran currency either as a lump sum within ninety days or in instalments with interest.[106] The Court supervised the government's compliance with the judgment.[107] The Commission subsequently requested that the Court interpret or amplify the damages judgment, because the government had not met the deadlines established for payment, and Honduran currency had been devalued in the interim. These factors had contributed to a more than 30 per cent loss in the purchasing power of the award.[108] The Court held a public hearing on the request, at which the Commission and the State presented oral arguments. Although the Court refused to formally interpret or amplify its compensatory damages judgment, in the exercise of its power to supervise compliance with the judgment, it ordered the State to compensate the family for the delay in payment.[109] Honduras protested. After an extended delay, however, the State eventually fully paid the Court-ordered compensation.[110]

Procedural advances made by the Court and the Commission

Since the initial contentious cases, the Court and the Commission have refined their procedures to enhance the role of the individual and to expedite the processing of cases. The Convention authorizes the Court and the Commission to draw up their Rules of Procedure.[111] Most of the advances have resulted from amendments to their Rules. The Court has revised its

[103] *Ibid.*, paras. 49–50. [104] *Ibid.*, para. 58.
[105] *Ibid.*, paras. 9, 38 and operative paras.
[106] *Ibid.*, para. 57. [107] *Ibid.*, operative para. 5.
[108] *Velásquez Rodríguez* v. *Honduras* (Interpretation of the Compensatory Damages), Inter-Am. Ct HR, 17 August 1990, Ser. C, No. 9, para. 22.
[109] *Ibid.*, operative paras. 1, 2 and 4.
[110] *La Tribuna* (Tegucigalpa, Honduras), 8 February 1996, Nacionales Section, 13
[111] American Convention, Arts. 39 and 60. For an excellent analysis of the changes to the Commission's and Court's Rules of Procedure, see Verónica Gómez, 'Inter-American Commission on Human Rights and the Inter-American Court of Human Rights: New Rules and Recent Cases', 1 *Human Rights Law Review*, 111 (2001).

Rules of Procedure several times, with a substantial revision entering into force on 1 June 2001.[112] In 2001, the Commission also made major changes in its Regulations, which were retitled 'Rules of Procedure'.[113]

One of the most pervasive criticisms of the Inter-American system has concerned the inadequacy of the role of the victim. Although petitioners have always been able to bring and present cases before the Commission, they had no recourse if the Commission chose not to forward the case to the Court, and no role before the Court if the Commission did submit the case. The Convention makes no provision for the victim or petitioner to seise the Court. The right of an individual to bring a case before a human rights court is a logical step in the evolution of human rights law. As explained with respect to the European system, '[t]he situation whereby the individual is granted rights but not given the possibility to exploit fully the control machinery provided for enforcing them, could today be regarded as inconsistent with the spirit of the Convention, not to mention incompatible with domestic-law procedures in states parties'.[114]

To circumvent this limitation, when the State involved has accepted the Court's jurisdiction, the 2001 amendments to the Commission's Rules of Procedure provide for automatic referral of a case 'unless there is a reasoned decision by an absolute majority of the members of the Commission to the contrary'.[115] A primary criterion in the Commission's decision is the petitioner's position as to whether the case should be referred to the Court.[116] If the petitioner is in favour of carrying the case forward, there is now a much greater possibility that the Commission will do so. This may be possible even when the Commission has ruled that the State has not violated the victim's human rights.[117] The Commission's Rules of Procedure do not address all limitations upon the individual's right to submit a case to the Court. Most fundamentally, the Commission, not the individual, still makes the ultimate decision.

112 2001 Rules of Procedure of the Inter-Am. Ct HR, Art. 66.

113 2001 Rules of Procedure of the Inter-American Commission on Human Rights, entered into force 1 May 2001, reprinted in 2001 Basic Documents, 127, also available at the website of the Inter-American Commission on Human Rights, http://www.cidh.oas.org. The Commission's Rules of Procedure were previously entitled 'Regulations'.

114 Explanatory Report to Protocol No. 9 to the Convention for the Protection of Human Rights and Fundamental Freedoms, reprinted in 12 *Human Rights Law Journal*, 51, at 52 (1991).

115 2001 Rules of Procedure of the Inter-Am. Comm. HR, Art. 44.

116 *Ibid.*, Art. 44(2).

117 Pedro Nikken, 'Observaciones Sobre el Fortalecimiento del Sistema Interamericano de Derechos Humanos en Vísperas de la Asamblea General de la OEA', 13 *Revista Inter-Americana Instituto de Derechos Humanos*, 26–8 (2001) (special edition).

Once an application is submitted, the Court's 2001 Rules of Procedure allow the victim to present his or her case autonomously.[118] Neither the Convention nor the Court's Statute provides a role for the victim before the Court; both specify that the Commission must appear in all cases.[119] The Statute of the Court goes further to provide that the Commission shall appear as a *party* in all contentious cases.[120] This provision was originally interpreted to require that the Commission represent the victim, which had the unfortunate repercussion of politicizing the Commission's position. The Commission served multiple roles in the individual petition process, not all of them complementary. It acted as factual investigator, as mediator in efforts at friendly settlements, and, if the case were not favourably resolved, as prosecutor before the Court.[121] Serving as prosecutor in one case often undermines the Commission's capacity as mediator in another case involving the same State. Under the 2001 Rules of Procedure, the Commission may play a role akin to that of the former European Commission on Human Rights. As such, it would serve as an objective and impartial participant rather than as an advocate of the victim. The former European Commission's role before the European Court has been described 'as that of an *amicus curiae*, an independent and impartial advisory organ with respect to questions of fact and law'.[122]

The Court took the initial step in enhancing the role of victims in 1991, when it amended its Rules of Procedure to allow the Commission to name the personal attorneys of the alleged victim to serve as its assistants.[123] Subsequently, the Court allowed the victim the right to direct representation in the reparations stage of the proceedings.[124] In 2001, the Court defined the term 'parties to the case' to include the 'victim or the alleged victim, the State and, only procedurally, the Commission'.[125] This alteration permits the alleged victim to participate at all stages of the proceedings before the Court once the application has been filed by the

[118] 2001 Rules of Procedure of the Inter-Am. Ct HR, Art. 23.

[119] American Convention, Art. 57; Statute of the Inter-Am. Ct HR, Art. 28.

[120] Statute of the Inter-Am. Ct HR, Art. 28 (emphasis added).

[121] *In the Matter of Viviana Gallardo*, Inter-Am. Ct HR, Decision of 13 November 1981, No. G101/81, para. 22, reprinted in 20 ILM 1424, 1428 (1981); see also Dinah Shelton, 'The Participation of Nongovernmental Organizations in International Judicial Proceedings', 88 *American Journal of International Law*, 611, at 615 (1994).

[122] Van Dijk and van Hoof, *Theory and Practice of the European Convention*, 225.

[123] See 1991 Rules of Procedure of the Inter-American Court of Human Rights, approved by the Court at its twenty-third regular session held 9–18 January 1991, Art. 22.

[124] See 1996 Rules of Procedure of the Inter-Am. Ct HR, Art. 23.

[125] 2001 Rules of Procedure of the Inter-Am. Ct HR, Art. 2(23).

Commission or the State.[126] The separation of roles is important to the victim because his or her objective in bringing the case may differ from that of the Commission. The role of the victim is to protect his or her individual interests, while that of the Commission is to fulfil its mandate under the Convention.

The Court and Commission have also streamlined their procedures to shorten the gap between the filing of a petition and a final judgment. Lengthy proceedings do not serve the needs of a victim who may be facing torture or death. As explained by a former member of the Commission, '[l]ong before all of these procedures have been completed, however, the patience of the complainant, although not his injury, may have come to an end, and in many cases it may be the end of the endurance or the life of the person tortured'.[127] To minimize the length of proceedings, the Commission curtailed the time period for response to communications and eliminated the possibility of repeated extensions. It also revised its procedures for hearings by creating chambers that report to the plenary Commission.[128] In addition, the Commission introduced practices that would enhance the transparency of its procedures. It registers petitions, issues a formal report on the admissibility of new cases, offers to mediate a friendly settlement between the parties in every case, and ensures confidentiality.[129]

The Court's amendments to its Rules of Procedure provide that, first, evidence must be submitted to the Court with the application.[130] Secondly, the respondent must raise preliminary objections in its answer to the application,[131] and the answer must be filed within two months after the notification of the application.[132] Thirdly, the Court's 2001 Rules of Procedure provide that '[e]vidence tendered to the Commission shall form part of the file, provided that it has been received in a procedure with the presence of both parties', unless the Court determines that the evidence must be repeated.[133] Finally, the Court no longer requires hearings when facts are not disputed. These advances reduce delay and duplication while maintaining procedural equality between the parties. The extensive changes in the practice and procedures of the Commission and Court

[126] *Ibid.*, Art. 23.
[127] Fernando Volio, 'The Inter-American Commission on Human Rights', 30 *American University Law Review*, 65, at 76–7 (1980).
[128] Claudio Grossman, 'Strengthening the Inter-American Human Rights System: The Current Debate', 92 *American Society of International Law Proceedings*, 186, 190 (1998).
[129] *Ibid.* [130] 2001 Rules of Procedure of the Inter-Am. Ct HR, Art. 33(1).
[131] *Ibid.*, Art. 36(1). [132] *Ibid.*, Art. 37(1). [133] *Ibid.*, Art. 43(2).

have, at least temporarily, diminished the need for a complete reform of the Inter-American human rights system similar to that undertaken in the European system.

Proposals for change to the Inter-American system

Certain States have proposed a complete reform of the American Convention. The proposals have been interpreted by some as attempts to weaken the system under the guise of improving it. Nikken challenged the States' underlying reasons for the proposals.[134] He argues that it is no more necessary to reform the American Convention to improve the Inter-American human rights system than it would be to tear down a cathedral to kill a mouse that was living in it, unless the real desire was to tear down the cathedral and the mouse was only a pretext to do it.[135] Instead of a full-scale reform of the Convention, the Commission and the Court, with the advice of States and civil society, have undertaken radical changes in their functioning through amendments to their rules of procedure.

The question had been raised as to whether the Inter-American human rights system should follow the example of the European system and eliminate the two-tiered system involving both a Commission and a Court. The main reasons put forward for the elimination of the Commission's role in processing individual complaints has been the lack of the victim's control of his or her own case and undue delay. Judge Piza Escalante, in his dissent in *In the Matter of Viviana Gallardo*, criticized the two-tiered system, stating:

> [I] have come to the conclusion that unfortunately the system of the Convention appears to make [the best protection of human rights] impossible because the American States in drafting it did not wish to accept the establishment of a swift and effective jurisdictional system but rather they hobbled it by interposing the impediment of the Commission, by establishing a veritable obstacle course that is almost insurmountable, on the long and arduous road that the basic rights of the individual are forced to travel.[136]

The elimination of the role of the Commission in processing individual petitions would not abolish the Commission in the Inter-American

[134] Nikken, 'Observaciones Sobre el Fortalecimiento del Sistema Interamericano', 13.

[135] *Ibid.*

[136] *In the Matter of Viviana Gallardo et al.*, Inter-Am. Ct HR, Ser. A, No. G101/81, para. 11 (1981).

human rights system, as its role is multifaceted. It is not confined to the processing of individual complaints. The mandate of the Commission is broader than that of the former European Commission. The primary purpose of the Commission is 'to promote respect for and defense of human rights'.[137] In doing so, it is charged with increasing awareness of human rights among the American peoples,[138] making recommendations on the adoption and implementation of human rights to State governments,[139] conducting country studies and writing reports on the human rights situation within any OAS Member State,[140] drafting new human rights treaties and instruments, requesting information from States, and advising States on human rights issues.[141] These additional responsibilities are of great importance to the peoples of the Americas. It would not be appropriate for the Court, a judicial body, to undertake these duties. The Commission could not be dissolved without eliminating those facets of the Commission's contributions. The Commission already functions on a limited budget with a small secretariat of human rights experts. This legal staff could not be eliminated by a merger of the Commission and the Court. In turn, the duties of responding to all individual petitions would greatly increase the workload of the Court and would require additional funding. Judges would be required to sit full-time on the Court, necessitating the payment of their living expenses and a salary. Currently judges receive honoraria when they attend sessions of the Court and are not paid for the extensive work they undertake while studying cases in their home States. Moreover, the pool of applicants who could serve on a full-time Court would necessarily be diminished.

The Court and the Commission could make additional modifications to better coordinate and streamline the processing of individual petitions. These changes could be made without a complete revision of the American Convention. The Commission and the Court, which independently modified their Rules of Procedure, could work together to avoid conflicting provisions. The Court could also allow all parties – the victim, State and Commission – to stipulate to a waiver of Commission proceedings. Limited protocols to the American Convention could be implemented, as was done initially in the European system. For example, a protocol could give individuals a right to petition the Court after completion of the

[137] American Convention, Art. 41. [138] *Ibid.*, Art. 41(a). [139] *Ibid.*, Art. 41(b).

[140] *Ibid.*, Art. 41(c). See Cecilia Medina Quiroga, 'The Role of Country Reports in the Inter-American System of Human Rights', in *The Inter-American System of Human Rights*, 115 (Harris and Livingstone eds., 1998).

[141] American Convention, Art. 41(d) and (e).

proceedings before the Commission. Such a protocol would not undermine the current Convention. It would be applied much like the Optional Protocol to the UN Covenant on Civil and Political Rights.[142] Another protocol, similar to Protocol No. 1 to the European Convention, could allow legal persons, such as corporations, to resort directly to the Commission and the Court when their property has been illegally confiscated by the State. Under the Court's most recent jurisprudence, shareholders of a corporation can resort to the Inter-American system.[143] Although this modification will resolve the problem in many instances, procedural difficulties could still arise.

Cançado Trindade, after meeting with the judges on the Court, Commissioners and leading experts on the system, proposed a limited Protocol to the American Convention.[144] The Protocol would incorporate into the American Convention the changes made in the Commission and Court's Rules of Procedure.[145] These changes, which authorize a greater role for individuals before the Court and streamline the procedures of the organs to permit more timely justice, would not then be subject to easy alteration. A second change would make the compulsory jurisdiction of the Court obligatory for all States Parties to the American Convention, as is currently the case in the European system.[146] Thirdly, the Permanent Council of the OAS would be required to continuously monitor State compliance with Court decisions. Fourthly, reservations to the Convention would not be permitted. Fifthly, the Commission would send its Article 50 report to the petitioners as well as to the State concerned. Sixthly, the Court would independently appoint its functionaries and secretariat.[147] The Court appoints its own Secretary, which gives the Court some independence as befits an 'autonomous judicial institution'.[148] Currently, the Statute of the Court specifies that the Attorney-General of the OAS, 'in consultation with the Secretary of the Court', shall appoint the Secretariat.[149] A source of contention for the Court is that the staff of the Secretariat, which

[142] Optional Protocol to the International Covenant on Civil and Political Rights, GA Res. 2200A (XXI), 21 UN GAOR Supp. (No. 16) at 59, UN Doc. A/6316 (1966), 999 UNTS 302, entered into force 23 March 1976.

[143] *Cantos* v. *Argentina* (Preliminary Objections), Inter-Am. Ct HR, 7 September 2001, Ser. C, No. 85, para. 29.

[144] Judge Cançado Trindade, 'Report and Proposals of the President of the Inter-American Court of Human Rights Before the Commission on Juridical and Legal Affairs of the Permanent Commission of the OAS', 5 April 2001, para. 54.

[145] *Ibid.* [146] *Ibid.* [147] *Ibid.*, paras. 55–7.

[148] American Convention, Art. 58(2), Statute of the Inter-Am. Court, Art. 1.

[149] Statute of the Inter-Am. Court, Art. 4.

includes its staff attorneys, are not chosen by the Court.[150] The Convention mandates that staff are appointed by the OAS Secretary General, in consultation with the Court's Secretary.[151] This provision does not allow the Court to hire or dismiss staff lawyers. As an autonomous judicial institution the Court must have sole control over its personnel.

Conclusion

This book analyzes and critiques the practice and procedure of the Inter-American Court of Human Rights. It examines the Court's advisory jurisdiction, its contentious jurisdiction and its authority to order provisional measures. Where relevant, it compares the practice and procedure of the Inter-American Court with those of the European Court of Human Rights, the International Court of Justice, the Permanent Court of International Justice and the United Nations Human Rights Committee. It does not treat the substantive rights protected by the American Convention except when those rights are relevant to the evaluation and discussion of the Court's procedures. Throughout, the study details the Court's contribution to the emergence and conceptual evolution of international human rights law.

The Inter-American Court's practice and procedures are of theoretical and practical importance on the national and international level. Understanding the Court's practices and procedures will help to better inform other international human rights bodies in the United Nations system as well as the developing African and expanding European human rights systems. In the Western Hemisphere, it will help to educate attorneys on how to represent victims and States. On a theoretical level, it will serve as a resource for scholarship on the system.

[150] See Cançado Trindade, 'Report and Proposals', para. 54.
[151] American Convention, Art. 59.

PART I

The advisory jurisdiction of the Inter-American Court

2

Advisory practice and procedure: contributing to the evolution of international human rights law

> Some of the most important advisory opinions would not have been issued if the Court 'had started from an outmoded voluntarist conception of International Law, with an instinctive attachment to the consent of the individual State for the exercise of not only the contentious but also the advisory jurisdictions of international tribunals.'[1]

Advisory opinions in general

In the last decade, States and international organizations, sometimes led by non-governmental human rights organizations, have emphasized the advisory jurisdiction of international courts to address controversial or developing issues in international law. An advisory opinion is an authoritative but non-binding explanation of a question or issue.[2] Advisory proceedings are less confrontational than contentious proceedings in that States are not parties and do not have to defend themselves against formal charges.[3] A tribunal does not have the authority under advisory jurisdiction to order judicial sanctions or impose duties or obligations on any State.[4] Although an advisory opinion cannot create legal obligations, it

1 *Reports of the Inter-American Commission of Human Rights (Art. 51 of the American Convention on Human Rights)*, Inter-Am. Ct HR, Advisory Opinion OC-15/97 of 14 November 1997, Ser. A, No. 15, Concurring Opinion of Judge A. A. Cançado Trindade, para. 17.

2 *Interpretation of Peace Treaties with Bulgaria, Hungary and Romania*, Advisory Opinion, 1950 ICJ Reports 65, 71 (30 March 1950). See Jo M. Pasqualucci, 'Advisory Practice of the Inter-American Court of Human Rights: Contributing to the Evolution of International Human Rights Law', 38 *Stanford Journal of International Law*, 241 (2002).

3 *Restrictions to the Death Penalty (Arts. 4(2) and 4(4) of the American Convention on Human Rights)*, Inter-Am. Ct HR, Advisory Opinion OC-3/83 of 8 September 1983, Ser. A, No. 3, para. 22. See also Thomas Buergenthal, 'The Inter-American Court, Human Rights and the OAS', Address by Judge Thomas Buergenthal, President, Inter-American Court of Human Rights, before a special session of the OAS Permanent Council, Washington DC, 3 December 1986, 7 *Human Rights Law Journal*, 157 (1986).

4 See Manley O. Hudson, *The Permanent Court of International Justice, 1920–1942*, 512 (Macmillan, New York, 1943).

often exerts moral authority on States. As stated by Judge Bustamante, 'there is a second difference of capital importance between an advisory opinion and a judgment of the Court, namely that the former is in no way binding upon those concerned, the opinion given having only moral authority, while the second imposes upon the parties a legal obligation having the force of res judicata'.[5] Thus, an advisory opinion may be more influential and authoritative than a judgment in a contentious case, in that it affects the general interpretation of international law for all States rather than for just the parties to an individual case. An advisory opinion, therefore, must encourage rather than compel a course of action.[6]

The authority to render an advisory opinion must be conferred on an international tribunal by the treaty under which it is created. Treaties that grant advisory jurisdiction do not require that the State independently accept advisory jurisdiction as they often require in relation to contentious jurisdiction. The ICJ explained that, although States must consent to the Court's contentious jurisdiction, their consent is not required for the exercise of its advisory jurisdiction.[7] Consequently, States cannot impede the exercise of advisory jurisdiction.

Most treaties that provide for tribunal oversight endow those tribunals with advisory jurisdiction. For example, the Charter of the United Nations authorizes the International Court of Justice to render advisory opinions.[8] The American Convention grants the Inter-American Court advisory jurisdiction.[9] The European Convention now accords the European Court of Human Rights a restricted advisory jurisdiction.[10] The Protocol to the African Charter of Human and Peoples' Rights, establishing an African

[5] *Case Concerning the Northern Cameroons* (*Cameroon* v. *UK*), 1963 ICJ Reports 15, 171 (Preliminary Objections Judgment of December 2), Judge Bustamante concurrence.

[6] Liz Heffernan, 'The Nuclear Weapons Opinions: Reflections on the Advisory Procedure of the International Court of Justice', 28 *Stetson Law Review*, 133, 139 (1998).

[7] *Interpretation of Peace Treaties with Bulgaria, Hungary and Romania*, Advisory Opinion, 1950 ICJ Reports 65, 71 (30 March 1950).

[8] Charter of the United Nations, 26 June 1945, 59 Stat. 1031, TS 993 entered into force 24 October 1945, Art. 96. See Dharma Pratap, *The Advisory Jurisdiction of the International Court*, 1–47 (Clarendon Press, Oxford, 1972); Kenneth Keith, *The Extent of the Advisory Jurisdiction of the ICJ* (A. W. Sijthoff, Leyden, 1971); Shabtai Rosenne, *The Law and Practice of the International Court, 1920–1996* (3rd edn, Nijhoff, 1997), vol. III, pp. 279–99; Michla Pomerance, *The Advisory Function of the International Court in the League and UN Eras* (Johns Hopkins, Baltimore, 1973).

[9] American Convention on Human Rights, 22 November 1969, 9 ILM 673, OEA/Ser.K/XVI/I.1, doc. 65 rev. 1 corr. 1 (1970), reprinted in 2001 Basic Documents, Art. 64(1).

[10] European Convention for the Protection of Human Rights and Fundamental Freedoms, as amended by Protocol No. 11, Rome, 4 November 1950, Art. 47(1).

Court to enforce human rights in the region, endows the future Court with a broad advisory jurisdiction.[11] The Law of the Sea Convention provides the Sea-Bed Disputes Chamber of the International Tribunal for the Law of the Sea with advisory jurisdiction.[12] Historically on the international plane several international bodies, including the International Bureau of the Universal Postal Union, the International Commission for Air Navigation and the League of Nations Advisory and Technical Committee for Communications and Transit have had the statutory authority to issue advisory opinions.[13] National courts in many countries also possess advisory jurisdiction. Courts in Colombia, Ecuador, Honduras, Panama, El Salvador, Norway and Sweden, among others, have long had this authority.[14] Although the United States Supreme Court holds that it does not have authority under the US Constitution to issue advisory opinions,[15] many individual state constitutions within the United States do authorize state supreme courts to respond to requests for advisory opinions.[16]

The utility of advisory opinions in international law has become widely accepted. In effect, advisory opinions contribute to an international common law and to the resolution of doctrinal differences. They also provide an alternative non-confrontational means to settle certain international disputes.

Character and scope of the Inter-American Court's advisory jurisdiction

The Inter-American Court's advisory jurisdiction is governed by Article 64 of the American Convention, which provides that:

[11] Protocol to the African Charter of Human and Peoples' Rights on the Establishment of an African Court of Human and Peoples' Rights, Adopted on 9 June 1998, Art. 4, reprinted in 20 *Human Rights Law Journal*, 269, 269 (1999); Vincent O. Orlu Nmehielle, 'Towards an African Court of Human Rights: Structuring and the Court', 6 *Annual Survey of International and Comparative Law*, 27 (2000).

[12] 10 December 1982, UN A/CONF. 62/122, 21 ILM 1261 (1982), entered into force on 16 November 1994, Art. 191.

[13] See Hudson, *The Permanent Court*, at 484–5.

[14] *Ibid.*, at 486, nn. 20 and 21.

[15] *Muskrat* v. *US*, 219 US 346 (1911).

[16] These States include but are not limited to Colorado, Florida, Maine, Massachusetts, New Hampshire, Rhode Island and South Dakota. Hudson, *The Permanent Court of International Justice*, at 485, n. 15. In other States, including Alabama and Delaware, the authority to issue advisory opinions has been conferred by statute. *Ibid.*, at 485, n. 16.

> 1. The member states of the Organization may consult the Court regarding the interpretation of this Convention or of other treaties concerning the protection of human rights in the American states. Within their spheres of competence, the organs listed in Chapter X of the Charter of the Organization of American States, as amended by the Protocol of Buenos Aires, may in like manner consult the Court.
>
> 2. The Court, at the request of a member state of the Organization, may provide that state with opinions regarding the compatibility of any of its domestic laws with the aforesaid international instruments.[17]

The legislative history of the American Convention reveals that the drafters intended to define the advisory jurisdiction of the Inter-American Court 'in the broadest terms possible'.[18] The original draft of the Convention provided only that the Inter-American Commission and the General Assembly and Permanent Council of the OAS could consult the Court concerning the interpretation of the American Convention or other treaties, and that the States Parties could consult the Court regarding the compatibility of their domestic laws with those international instruments.[19] The text of the provision was later expanded to its present form to allow other organs and Member States of the OAS to request advisory opinions in particular circumstances.[20] The Court views its advisory jurisdiction to be as extensive as may be necessary to safeguard the human rights in the Convention, restricted only by the limitations imposed by the Convention.[21]

The purpose of the advisory jurisdiction of the Inter-American Court is 'to assist the American States in fulfilling their international human rights obligations and to assist the different organs of the inter-American system to carry out the functions assigned to them'.[22] In the exercise of

[17] American Convention, Art. 64. See also Statute of the Inter-American Court of Human Rights, Adopted by the General Assembly of the OAS at its ninth regular session, held in La Paz, Bolivia, October 1979 (Resolution No. 448), Art. 2(2).

[18] *'Other Treaties' Subject to the Consultative Jurisdiction of the Court (Art. 64 of the American Convention on Human Rights)*, Inter-Am. Ct HR, Advisory Opinion OC-1/82 of 24 September 1982, Ser. A, No. 1, para. 17.

[19] OAS/Ser.G/V/C-d-1631, reprinted in *Human Rights: The Inter-American System*, Booklet 15, vol. 2, part 2, chapter 2, 20, Art. 53 (Thomas B. Buergenthal and Robert E. Norris eds., 1982).

[20] American Convention, Art. 64.

[21] *Proposed Amendments to the Naturalization Provisions of the Constitution of Costa Rica*, Inter-Am. Ct HR, Advisory Opinion OC-4/84 of 19 January 1984, Ser. A, No. 4, para. 25.

[22] Advisory Opinion OC-1/82, para. 25. See Manuel E. Ventura and Daniel Zovatto, *La Función Consultiva de la Corte Interamericana de Derechos Humanos: Naturaleza y Principios 1982–1987* (Instituto Interamericano de Derechos Humanos, Costa Rica ed., 1989).

this jurisdiction the Court clarifies the object, purpose and meaning of international human rights norms, and provides the requesting party with judicial interpretations of the law or provision in question.[23] These interpretations strengthen the protections provided by the Inter-American human rights system.[24] Especially important, through its advisory opinions the Court contributes to the evolving law of international human rights.

Compétence de la compétence

The Inter-American Court, in the exercise of the principle of *compétence de la compétence*, determines whether it has jurisdiction to issue an advisory opinion or a decision in a contentious case. This principle provides that the court itself is competent to decide the question of jurisdiction. As stated by the Court:

> The jurisdiction of the Court cannot be contingent upon events extraneous to its own actions. The instruments consenting to the optional clause concerning recognition of the Court's binding jurisdiction (Article 62(1) of the Convention) presuppose that the States submitting them accept the Court's right to settle any controversy relative to its jurisdiction.[25]

The Inter-American Court has explained that '[a]n objection or any other action taken by the State for the purpose of somehow affecting the Court's jurisdiction has no consequence whatever, as the Court retains the *compétence de la compétence*, as it is master of its own jurisdiction'.[26]

The principle of *compétence de la compétence* is codified in many treaties. The Statute of the International Court of Justice specifically provides that 'in the event of a dispute as to whether the court has jurisdiction, the matter shall be settled by the decision of the court'.[27] The European

[23] Advisory Opinion OC-1/82, para. 40.

[24] *The Right to Information on Consular Assistance Within the Framework of the Guarantees of Legal Due Process*, Inter-Am. Ct HR, Advisory Opinion OC-16/99 of 1 October 1999, Ser. A, No. 16, paras. 47 and 40.

[25] *Hilaire, Constantine and Benjamin et al.* v. *Trinidad and Tobago* (Merits), Inter-Am. Ct HR, 21 June 2002, Ser. C, No. 94, para. 18, quoting *Constitutional Court* v. *Peru* (Competence), Inter-Am. Ct HR, 24 September 1999, Ser. C, No. 55, para. 33; *Ivcher Bronstein* v. *Peru* (Competence), Inter-Am. Ct HR, 24 September 1999, Ser. C, No. 54, para. 34.

[26] *Benjamin et al.* v. *Trinidad and Tobago* (Preliminary Objections), Inter-Am. Ct HR, 1 September 2001, Ser. C, No. 81, para. 72; *Constitutional Court* v. *Peru* (Competence, 1999), para. 33; *Ivcher Bronstein* v. *Peru* (Competence, 1999), para. 34.

[27] Statute of the International Court of Justice, 59 Stat. 1055 (entered into force 24 October 1945), Art. 36(6).

Convention for the Protection of Human Rights and Fundamental Freedoms includes essentially the same provision.[28] It is not necessary, however, that this principle be delineated in the treaty. In the *Nottebohm Case*, the International Court of Justice held that the principle that 'an international tribunal has the right to decide as to its own jurisdiction' is 'a rule consistently accepted by general international law'.[29] The ICJ further stated that, even if its Statute did not contain this provision, 'the judicial character of the Court and the rule of general international law referred to above are sufficient to establish that the Court is competent to adjudicate on its own jurisdiction'.[30]

The American Convention and the Statute of the Inter-American Court do not include specific provisions establishing the Inter-American Court's competence to decide questions of its jurisdiction. The initial draft of the American Convention did contain such a provision. It provided that 'in the event of a dispute as to whether the Court has jurisdiction in a particular case, the matter shall be settled by decision of the Court'.[31] There is no explanation in the *travaux préparatoires* of the Convention as to why the provision, which was contained in several drafts, was not included in the final document of the Convention.

In its jurisprudence, the Inter-American Court specifies that it has the inherent authority to decide the question of its jurisdiction.[32] The Court has declared that 'as with any court or tribunal, [it] has the inherent authority to determine the scope of its own competence (*compétence de la compétence/Kompetenz-Kompetenz*)'.[33] The Court also grounded its authority in Article 62(3) of the Convention which provides that the Court has jurisdiction to interpret and apply the Convention.[34] This provision does not, however, clarify whether the Court shall make the determination that it has jurisdiction when the State challenges the Court's jurisdiction by arguing that the case does not involve the interpretation or application of the American Convention. The issue of whether the Court had such

[28] European Convention, Art. 32.

[29] *Nottebohm* (*Liechtenstein* v. *Guatemala*), 1953 ICJ Reports 111, at 119 (Preliminary Objections of November 18).

[30] *Ibid.*, at 120.

[31] See Buergenthal and Norris (eds.), *Human Rights: The Inter-American System*, Proposed Art. 51, Part 2, 13, at 20.

[32] *Hilaire, Constantine and Benjamin et al.* v. *Trinidad and Tobago* (Merits), Inter-Am. Ct HR, 21 June 2002, Ser. C, No. 94, para. 19.

[33] *Ivcher Bronstein* v. *Peru* (Competence, 1999), para. 32; *Cantos* v. *Argentina* (Preliminary Objections), Inter-Am. Ct HR, 7 September 2001, Ser. C, No. 85, para. 21.

[34] *Cantos* v. *Argentina* (Preliminary Objections, 2001), para. 21.

authority was raised when the Commission asked the Court for a determination of the effect of reservations on the entry into force of the American Convention.[35] Traditionally, all issues regarding reservations to treaties in the Inter-American system had been determined through consultations between the Secretary General of the OAS and the Member States.[36] The Court distinguished the American Convention by noting that the Convention, unlike other OAS treaties, establishes a formal process for the adjudication of disputes arising in reference to the interpretation of the Convention.[37] Thus, the Court held that the Inter-American Court itself is the most appropriate body to exercise jurisdiction to 'render an authoritative interpretation of all provisions of the Convention', including provisions relating to the entry into force of the Convention.[38] Also, when Peru attempted to withdraw its recognition of the jurisdiction of the Court, the Court refused to recognize the withdrawal, stating that a State's objection to the Court's jurisdiction is without consequence, because 'the Court retains the *compétence de la compétence*, as it is master of its own jurisdiction'.[39] For clarity, the Court should incorporate the principle of *compétence de la compétence* into the next revision of its Rules of Procedure in order to avoid future groundless objections. Government attorneys, who are responding to cases filed against the State, cannot be expected to be completely familiar with the case law of the Court.

The Court has also assumed the related inherent authority to clarify, define or reformulate the questions submitted to it so as to consider only those issues that fall within the jurisdiction of the Court.[40] This authority may be called for when an advisory request contains both acceptable and extraneous issues. In *The Enforceability of the Right to Reply or Correction*, Costa Rica combined two issues in its advisory opinion request.[41] The first issue concerned the interpretation of the American Convention, whereas the second issue was purely a matter within the domestic jurisdiction of the State.[42] The Court separated the two issues and dealt only with the former, over which it had jurisdiction.[43] The Court's only other option would have been to reject the entire request until the State had modified it. That approach would be unnecessarily time-consuming.

[35] *The Effect of Reservations on the Entry into Force of the American Convention on Human Rights (Arts. 74 and 75)*, Inter-Am. Ct HR, Advisory Opinion OC-2/82 of 24 September 1982, Ser. A, No. 2, para. 11.

[36] *Ibid.* [37] *Ibid.*, para. 13. [38] *Ibid.* [39] *Ibid.*

[40] *Enforceability of the Right to Reply or Correction (Arts. 14(1), 1(1) and 2 of the American Convention on Human Rights)*, Inter-Am. Ct HR, Advisory Opinion OC-7/86 of 29 August 1986, Ser. A, No. 7, para. 12, quoted in Advisory Opinion OC-16/99, para. 42.

[41] Advisory Opinion OC-7/86, para. 14. [42] *Ibid.* [43] *Ibid.*

The determination of whether the Court has jurisdiction must be made by the plenary Court.[44] In *Restrictions to the Death Penalty*, the Court rejected Guatemala's argument that the Permanent Commission of the Court, composed of the President, Vice President and a third Judge named by the President, should have ruled on the issue of jurisdiction.[45] The Court held that the Permanent Commission does not have the authority to make a decision on jurisdiction even in advisory proceedings.[46]

When the Inter-American Court is presented with a request for an advisory opinion, it must first determine whether the request is within its jurisdiction *ratione materiae* and *ratione personae*. This requires that it determine the nature of the advisory opinion request and the standing of the body submitting the request.[47] It will then determine whether there is a valid reason for the Court to decline to exercise its jurisdiction.

Jurisdiction ratione personae *(standing)*

All Member States of the OAS and all organs listed in the applicable section of the OAS Charter[48] have standing under Article 64 of the American Convention to request an advisory opinion of the Inter-American Court.[49] This is a much broader range of bodies than is or has been authorized for the Permanent Court of International Justice, which had the authority to issue an advisory opinion about disputes or questions referred by the Council or Assembly of the League of Nations,[50] the International Court of Justice, which may grant requests submitted by the General Assembly, Security Council and other UN organs and specialized agencies that are authorized by the General Assembly,[51] or the European Court of Human Rights.[52] The European Convention on Human Rights restricts standing to request an advisory opinion to the Committee of Ministers.[53] The

[44] Advisory Opinion OC-3/83, paras. 16–17.

[45] *Ibid.*, paras. 13 and 16.

[46] *Ibid.*, para. 16.

[47] *International Responsibility for the Promulgation and Enforcement of Laws in Violation of the Convention (Arts. 1 and 2 of the American Convention on Human Rights)*, Inter-Am. Ct HR, Advisory Opinion OC-14/94 of 9 December 1994, Ser. A, No. 14, para. 20.

[48] Charter of the Organization of American States (as amended), 30 April 1948, entered into force on 13 December 1951, 2 UST 2394, TIAS No. 2361; amended effective 1970, 21 UST 607, TIAS No. 6847, Art. 51.

[49] American Convention, Art. 64.

[50] Covenant of the League of Nations, 28 June 1919, 225 Consol. TS 188, Art. 14 available at http://www.tufts.edu/departments/fletcher/multi/www/ league-covenant.html.

[51] UN Charter, Art. 96.

[52] European Convention for the Protection of Human Rights, Art. 47(1).

[53] *Ibid.*

future African Court of Human and Peoples' Rights will have a more extensive jurisdiction *ratione personae* in that the Organization of African Unity itself, OAU Member States, any OAU organ and 'any African organization recognized by the OAU' will be authorized to request advisory opinions.[54]

One limitation on the advisory jurisdiction of the Inter-American Court is that it cannot render an advisory opinion on its own motion. Thus, the Inter-American Court cannot identify a problem and initiate advisory proceedings *motu proprio*. Scholars of the system are in disagreement as to whether the Court should have such power. Judge Cançado Trindade observed that, if the Court itself could freely offer advisory opinions, it 'would be tantamount to transforming itself, *ultra vires*, into an international legislator'.[55] Montalvo argues that, at least for the purpose of determining whether State reservations are consistent with the American Convention, the Court should have the jurisdiction to render an opinion *ex officio*.[56] This would be in accord with the UN Human Rights Committee statement that it is the responsibility of the Committee to determine the compatibility of a specific reservation with the object and purpose of the International Covenant on Civil and Political Rights.[57] Court authority to render advisory opinions *motu proprio* would contribute to clarity and consistency in the Inter-American human rights system.

Standing of Member States to request advisory opinions

Article 64(1) of the American Convention authorizes OAS Member States to request advisory opinions concerning the interpretation of the American Convention and other treaties.[58] A Member State of the OAS is any State that has ratified the OAS Charter. Thus any OAS Member State has an absolute right to request an advisory opinion, even if the State is not a State Party to the American Convention.[59] Cerna points out that '[i]t

[54] Protocol to the African Charter to Establish an African Court, Art. 4(1). See Vincent O. Orlu Nmehielle, *The African Human Rights System: Its Laws, Practice, and Institutions* (Martinus Nijhoff, The Hague, 2001).

[55] Advisory Opinion OC-15/97 of 14 November 1997, Ser. A, No. 15, concurring opinion, para. 37.

[56] Andrés E. Montalvo, 'Reservations to the American Convention on Human Rights: A New Approach', 16 *American University International Law Review*, 269, 271 (2001).

[57] Human Rights Committee, General Comment 24 (52), para. 18, General comment on issues relating to reservations made upon ratification or accession to the Covenant or the Optional Protocols thereto, or in relation to declarations under Article 41 of the Covenant, UN Doc. CCPR/C/21/Rev.1/Add.6 (1994).

[58] American Convention, Art. 64(1). [59] *Ibid.*

is an unusual feature of this multilateral convention that it grants certain rights to States which are not parties to it, and reflects the expectation of its drafters that its complete implementation would take some time, during which non-States parties should be granted a limited access to the Court in order to facilitate their eventual entry into the system'.[60]

OAS Member States also have standing under Article 64(2) of the American Convention to request advisory opinions as to whether their domestic laws are compatible with the American Convention and other treaties.[61] A request under this provision must be made by an entity empowered to speak for the State on the international plane.[62] In general, the executive branch of the government has the authority to engage in international relations, and is thus the proper authority to request an advisory opinion. In *Proposed Amendments to the Naturalization Provisions of the Constitution of Costa Rica*, a Committee of the Costa Rican Legislative Assembly, that was empowered to study amendments to the national Constitution, initially submitted the request to the Court.[63] The Court, however, did not become seised of the matter until the Minister of Foreign Affairs, who was entitled to act for the government, filed a formal request for an advisory opinion.[64] In no instance may one State utilize the advisory jurisdiction of the Court under Article 64(2) to elicit an opinion on another State's domestic laws, even if those laws have an effect on the requesting State.

States have accused the Inter-American Commission of encroaching on the right of States to request an advisory opinion in regard to their domestic laws.[65] When Peru's draft constitution broadened the application of the death penalty, Peru did not request an advisory opinion as to whether the proposed constitutional provisions were in keeping with the American Convention. The Commission, however, in *International Responsibility for the Promulgation and Enforcement of Laws in Violation of the Convention* asked the Court for an advisory opinion on the question.[66] Peru then accused the Commission of seeking 'to obtain indirectly what it is prevented from achieving directly',[67] meaning that the Commission could not bring

[60] Christina Cerna, 'The Structure and Functioning of the Inter-American Court of Human Rights (1979–1992)', 63 *British Yearbook of International Law*, 135, 141 (1992).

[61] American Convention, Art. 64(2).

[62] Advisory Opinion OC-4/84, para. 11. [63] *Ibid.* [64] *Ibid.*

[65] Advisory Opinion OC-14/94, para. 12. See Note of Ambassador Beatriz M. Ramacciotti, Permanent Representative of Peru before the OAS, to OAS Secretary General Cesar Gaviria, 1 July 1999, in *Castillo Petruzzi et al.* v. *Peru* (Compliance with Judgment), Inter-Am. Ct HR, 17 November 1999, Ser. C, No. 59, para. 3.

[66] Advisory Opinion OC-14/94, para. 1. [67] *Ibid.*, para. 12.

a contentious case against Peru. The Court held that the Commission had standing to request the advisory opinion under Article 64(1), in light of its function to make recommendations to Member States as to the compliance of their domestic laws with the American Convention.[68] Consequently, if the Commission phrases its request correctly, the Court will not find that it has infringed on the State's right to request an opinion on the compatibility of a domestic law with its international obligations.

Standing of OAS organs to request advisory opinions

Article 64(1) also authorizes OAS organs to request advisory opinions.[69] The Convention provides that 'the organs listed in Chapter X of the Charter of the Organization of American States, as amended by the Protocol of Buenos Aires', may consult the Court for an advisory opinion.[70] These organs are now listed in Chapter VIII of the Charter of the OAS, as amended by the 1985 Protocol of Cartagena de Indias. OAS organs include the General Assembly, the Meeting of Consultation of Ministers of Foreign Affairs, the Councils, the Inter-American Juridical Committee, the Inter-American Commission on Human Rights, the General Secretariat, the Specialized Conferences, and the Specialized Organizations.[71] The American Convention allows an OAS organ to request the opinion directly of the Court, thus eliminating the need for a middleman and the time-consuming procedures involved.[72] The United Nations Charter similarly allows UN agencies, under certain circumstances, to request advisory opinions on legal questions arising within the scope of their activities.[73] Conversely, under the Covenant of the League of Nations an international organization had to lobby the League's Assembly or Council to request an advisory opinion.[74]

The American Convention limits the standing of OAS organs to questions within 'their spheres of competence'.[75] A question within the sphere

[68] *Ibid.*, para. 25. [69] American Convention, Art. 64(1). [70] *Ibid.*

[71] See 2001 Basic Documents Pertaining to Human Rights in the Inter-American System, 23, OEA/Ser.L/V/I.4 rev. 8 (22 May 2001) (English), at 2–3 for a description of the functions of the OAS organs.

[72] American Convention, Art. 64(1).

[73] Under the Charter of the United Nations, '[t]he General Assembly or the Security Council may request the International Court of Justice to give an advisory opinion on any legal question'. Furthermore, '[o]ther organs of the United Nations and specialized agencies, which may at any time be so authorized by the General Assembly, may also request advisory opinions of the Court on legal questions arising within the scope of their activities'. UN Charter, Art. 96.

[74] Covenant of the League of Nations, Art. 14. [75] American Convention, Art. 64(1).

of competence of an OAS organ is one in which that entity has a 'legitimate institutional interest'.[76] It is initially for each organ to decide whether its request falls within its sphere of competence.[77] Ultimately, however, it is within the province of the Court, based on the Charter of the OAS, the constitutive instrument of the organ, and the legal practice of that particular organ, to determine whether the subject matter of a request is within a particular organ's sphere of competence.[78] The Court has specified that the Inter-American Commission on Human Rights has an absolute right to request advisory opinions on the American Convention.[79] When the Commission requests an opinion concerning other treaties, however, it is required to explain its competence to make the request.[80] The ICJ, when confronted with the question of the scope of an agency's responsibilities, has taken a restricted view. For example, when the World Health Organization (WHO) requested an ICJ advisory opinion as to whether the dangerous health and environmental effects that would result from a State's deployment of nuclear weapons would breach the State's international obligations, including those set forth in the WHO Constitution, the ICJ rejected the request.[81] The Court found that the question was outside the scope of the WHO's responsibilities.[82]

Advisory opinions could be instrumental in allowing organs that regularly deal with human rights matters to effectively carry out their activities. These opinions could facilitate the efficient functioning of the OAS organs by clarifying difficult legal questions that impede their action. For example, the Inter-American Commission of Women would be eligible to submit an advisory request to the Court concerning its efforts to promote human rights relating to women in the United Nations, the International Labor Organization and under OAS treaties.[83] Also, the OAS General Assembly could request an advisory opinion to resolve questions on any draft resolution calling upon an OAS Member State to comply with its human rights obligations under the American Convention or other treaty.[84] Buergenthal opined that the General Assembly of the OAS should

[76] Advisory Opinion OC-2/82, para. 14. [77] *Ibid.* [78] *Ibid.* [79] *Ibid.*, para. 16.

[80] 2001 Rules of Procedure of the Inter-Am. Ct HR, Art. 60(2).

[81] *Legality of the Use by a State of Nuclear Weapons in Armed Conflict*, 1996 ICJ Reports 66 (8 July), available at http://www.icj-cij.org. The ICJ did issue an advisory opinion requested by the UN General Assembly on the *Legality of the Threat or Use of Nuclear Weapons*, 1996 ICJ Reports 226 (8 July).

[82] *Legality of the Use by a State of Nuclear Weapons in Armed Conflict*, 1996 ICJ Reports 66 (8 July).

[83] See Thomas Buergenthal, 'The Advisory Practice of the Inter-American Human Rights Court', 79 *American Journal of International Law*, 1, 5 (1985).

[84] *Ibid.*, at 4. See also Scott Davidson, *The Inter-American Court of Human Rights* (Dartmouth, 1992), at 102.

also have an absolute right to request advisory opinions of the Court, due to the broad nature of its sphere of competence.[85] Notwithstanding the advantages that would accrue to organs that request advisory opinions, the Inter-American Commission is the only organ that has availed itself of the Court's advisory jurisdiction to date.

Additional entities within the OAS could benefit from standing to request an advisory opinion. For example, in view of the political powers of the Secretary General, the position would be aided by the authority to ask the Inter-American Court for advice on legal questions concerning human rights.[86] The Legal Counsel to the OAS, who may be presented with questions concerning human rights, could also benefit from standing to request an advisory opinion. The Legal Counsel should not be obliged to make a preliminary determination of human rights issues before a State or authorized organ can raise the issue with the Court. This was the case in the Court's advisory opinion on the *Effect of Reservations*, in which the Inter-American Commission requested an advisory opinion after the OAS Legal Counsel determined that a State, upon deposit of its instrument of ratification, was not necessarily a party to the American Convention.[87] The Court disagreed with the decision of the Legal Counsel and determined that the Convention did enter into force for a State as of the moment of deposit of the State's instrument of ratification or adherence.[88] It would be more efficient if the Legal Counsel had standing to request an advisory opinion in relevant cases.

The advisory jurisdiction of the Inter-American Court could also be expanded to allow domestic courts in OAS member States to directly request advisory opinions on questions of compliance of domestic law with the American Convention or other treaties ratified by the State. This procedure is successful in the European Union, where any court in a Member State has standing to request a ruling from the European Court of Justice on questions of European Union law that arise before a national tribunal.[89] The American Bar Association recommended that the United

[85] See Buergenthal, 'The Advisory Practice of the Inter-American Human Rights Court', at 4.

[86] See Cerna, 'The Structure and Functioning of the Inter-American Court', at 139. See generally Stephen M. Schwebel, 'Authorizing the Secretary-General of the United Nations to Request Advisory Opinions of the International Court of Justice', 78 *American Journal of International Law*, 869 (1984).

[87] See Buergenthal, 'The Advisory Practice of the Inter-American Human Rights Court', at 21.

[88] Advisory Opinion OC-2/82, para. 37.

[89] Treaty Establishing the European Economic Community (or Treaty of Rome), Art. 234 (ex Art. 177), 25 March 1957, 298 UNTS 3 at http://www.hri.org/docs/Rome57.

States approve the expansion of the advisory jurisdiction of the ICJ to allow it to consider international law questions referred to it by national courts.[90] Such a procedure would also be beneficial in the Inter-American system.

Alternatively, domestic courts could be authorized to request an advisory opinion through an already-established OAS organ or through the executive branch of the domestic government. The primary benefit of this change would be that the procedure would not necessitate an amendment to the American Convention. The primary limitation would be the time factor, in that the domestic court must petition the OAS organ, and that organ must then resolve to make the request of the Court. The OAS organ that would be appropriate to carry out this function would be the Inter-American Juridical Committee, which serves as an advisory body to the OAS on legal matters, and promotes the codification and progressive development of international law.[91] The possibility of creating a new organ to promote advisory opinion requests would not be possible under the American Convention, which provides that only those organs listed in the OAS Charter are authorized to request advisory opinions.[92] A new organ should not be necessary, however, in light of the functions and purpose of the Juridical Committee.

Non-governmental organizations that are legally recognized in any OAS Member State could also be authorized to request advisory opinions, although this change would require a protocol to the American Convention. Human rights organizations could be expected to make requests for opinions in areas of broad public interest that States or OAS organs, which are composed of States, would not be likely to raise before the Court. Even the organ most involved in human rights questions, the Inter-American Commission, is not likely to submit many advisory opinion requests due to limited financing.[93] Moreover, the conflicting roles of the Commission may deter it from making a request that would be adverse to the interest

[90] American Bar Association, Summary of Action of the House of Delegates, 1982 Midyear Meeting 12 (Chicago, 1982), as cited in Louis B. Sohn, 'Broadening the Advisory Jurisdiction of the International Court of Justice', 77 *American Journal of International Law*, 124, 126 (1983). See also Stephen M. Schwebel, 'Widening the Advisory Jurisdiction of the International Court of Justice Without Amending its Statute', 33 *Catholic University Law Review*, 355, 359 (1984).

[91] See 2001 Basic Documents, at 2.

[92] American Convention, Art. 64(1).

[93] Report prepared by the Office of the Secretary General of the Organization of American States for the Ad Hoc Working Group on Human Rights, created by the Foreign Ministers meeting of 22 November 1999, *Financing the Inter-American Human Rights System*, 11 (28 April 2000).

of a State that is complying with Commission recommendations in other areas. Precedent already suggests an expanded role for NGOs in the Inter-American system in that NGOs are authorized to file petitions with the Commission.[94] Moreover, limited persuasive authority exists internationally in that the proposed African Court will have jurisdiction to respond to advisory opinion requests from 'any African organization recognized by the OAU'.[95]

At present, the only avenue available to NGOs in the Inter-American system is to attempt to convince States or authorized organs to request an advisory opinion.[96] In *Compulsory Membership in an Association Prescribed by Law for the Practice of Journalism*, the Inter-American Press Association successfully petitioned the Costa Rican Government to request an advisory opinion concerning the compatibility of a Costa Rican law with the American Convention. The law, which was similar to laws in other Latin American countries, mandated the compulsory membership of journalists in associations that often required a specific type of university degree.[97] Costa Rica's compliance in submitting the request, although it disagreed with the position of the Inter-American Press Association,[98] was an anomaly. Cerna posited that a possible reason for Costa Rica's submission of the request to the Court was 'its support for the continued survival of the Court, sometimes to the point of appearing adversely to affect its own self-interest'.[99] Seldom have NGOs been successful in finding a champion to espouse their requests. For instance, a consortium of thirty NGOs could not convince the Inter-American Commission to request an advisory opinion as to whether a candidate for the position of judge on the Inter-American Court had the Convention-mandated credentials.[100] Although the possibility exists that States or authorized organs may be

94 American Convention, Art. 44.

95 Protocol to the African Charter to Establish an African Court, Art. 4.

96 See Edda Kristjansdottir, 'The Legality of the Threat or Use of Nuclear Weapons Under Current International Law: The Arguments Behind the World Court's Advisory Opinion', 30 *New York University Journal of International Law and Policy*, 291 (1997–8) (stating that the requests for an ICJ advisory opinion on the legality of nuclear weapons was 'the result of intensive lobbying by a network of anti-nuclear activists and non-governmental organizations, known as the World Court project (WCP)').

97 *Compulsory Membership in an Association Prescribed by Law for the Practice of Journalism (Arts. 13 and 29 of the American Convention on Human Rights)*, Inter-Am. Ct HR, Advisory Opinion OC-5/85 of 13 November 1985, Ser. A, No. 5, paras. 14 and 61.

98 *Ibid.*, para. 15.

99 Cerna, 'The Structure and Functioning of the Inter-American Court', at 176.

100 Douglass Cassel Jr, 'Somoza's Revenge: A New Judge for the Inter-American Court of Human Rights', 13 *Human Rights Law Journal*, 137, 139 (1992).

persuaded to request advisory opinions on issues of general interest, most individuals and organizations will not have this level of influence, and few States are likely to be amenable to this avenue. Given standing, human rights organizations could be expected to make requests for opinions in areas of broad public interest that States or OAS organs, controlled by Member States, would not be likely to raise before the Court.

It would be impractical, however, to open the floodgates of the Court by permitting unlimited access to request advisory opinions to all legally recognized NGOs in the Americas. Consequently, the Court would need to exercise discretion, in accordance with a transparent and impartial decision-making procedure, in considering such requests. A possible model would require NGOs to ask leave of the Court to file a request, setting forth the reasoning underlying the importance of the issue which would be raised. A panel of judges could then be authorized to accept only those requests that raise important or novel questions that would contribute to the development of international human rights law. When the Court rejected a request, it could be required to write a short statement outlining the reasons for its refusal to consider the issue raised.

Jurisdiction ratione materiae *(subject matter jurisdiction)*

The subject matter, or *ratione materiae*, of the Court's advisory jurisdiction encompasses three areas: (1) questions concerning interpretation of the American Convention under Article 64(1), which extends to the interpretation of its two protocols (the Protocol to Abolish the Death Penalty[101] and the Additional Protocol in the Area of Economic, Social and Cultural Rights, known as the 'Protocol of San Salvador'[102]); (2) questions relating to the interpretation of 'other treaties concerning the protection of human rights in the American States' under Article 64(1); and (3) requests pertaining to whether a State's domestic laws are compatible with the American Convention or 'other treaties' under Article 64(2). Although this subject matter is relatively broad, it is limited to the interpretation of legal questions.

[101] Protocol to the American Convention on Human Rights to Abolish the Death Penalty, approved at Asunción, Paraguay, on 8 June 1990, at the twentieth regular session of the General Assembly of the OAS, entered into force on 28 August 1991.

[102] Additional Protocol to the American Convention on Human Rights in the Area of Economic, Social and Cultural Rights ('Protocol of San Salvador'), signed at San Salvador, El Salvador, on 17 November 1988, at the eighteenth regular session of the General Assembly, and entered into force on 16 November 1999.

The Court does not have jurisdiction to issue an advisory opinion on other issues in dispute which could affect the human rights of the peoples of the Americas. Precedent exists for an international court to issue advisory opinions on matters in dispute between States. The Permanent Court of International Justice had the authority to issue an advisory opinion on 'any dispute or question'.[103] Although the States involved in a dispute could not request an advisory opinion directly from the Court, the League of Nations Assembly or Council could do so, perhaps at the suggestion of a State or the States involved in a dispute or a neighbouring State that was suffering repercussions from the hostilities.[104] Judge Hudson stated that '[i]n the broad sense of the term, it may be said that each of the requests for an advisory opinion which have been made by the Council has related to a *dispute*'.[105] The States involved in the dispute could, of course, have turned to the Court's contentious jurisdiction but chose not to do so.

The expansiveness of the subject matter of the advisory jurisdiction of the Permanent Court of International Justice to cover disputes has not been extended to other international tribunals. The Charter of the United Nations authorizes the International Court of Justice to issue advisory opinions solely on 'legal questions'.[106] The subject matter of the advisory jurisdiction of the future African Court encompasses only 'legal matters' that are not related to a matter before the African Commission.[107] The European Court of Human Rights is even more limited in that it may issue advisory opinions dealing only with legal questions interpreting the European Convention and its protocols, excluding questions related to the scope or content of protected rights or with any other question which the European Court or the Committee of Ministers might consider in relation to Convention proceedings.[108] Scholars of the European system have commented that '[i]t is obvious that a high degree of inventiveness is required for the formulation of a question of any importance which could stand the test'.[109] As a result of the limitations to the advisory jurisdiction of the European Court, to date it has not received any requests for advisory opinions.

[103] Covenant of the League of Nations, Art. 14.
[104] Hudson, *The Permanent Court*, at 486–7.
[105] *Ibid.*, at 495. [106] Charter of the United Nations, Art. 96.
[107] Protocol to the African Charter, Art. 4(1).
[108] European Convention, Art. 47. See also Advisory Opinion OC-1/82, para. 16.
[109] P. van Dijk and G. J. H. van Hoof, *Theory and Practice of the European Convention on Human Rights*, 265 (3rd edn, Kluwer, The Hague, 1998).

Jurisdiction to issue advisory opinions interpreting the American Convention

The Court's advisory jurisdiction to interpret the American Convention provides a means to resolve uncertainties and contradictions in the text of the Convention. Despite precautions, it is inevitable that there will be varying interpretations of provisions in a complex treaty. An additional problem with the American Convention is that there are irreconcilable differences between the English, Spanish, Portuguese and French versions of certain provisions.

When called upon to interpret the American Convention, the Court applies the Vienna Convention on the Law of Treaties, which specifies that 'a treaty shall be interpreted in good faith, in accordance with the ordinary meaning to be given to the terms of the treaty in their context and in the light of its object and purpose'.[110] The object and purpose of the American Convention 'is the protection of the basic rights of individual human beings irrespective of their nationality, both against the State of their nationality and all other contracting States'.[111] In accordance with that objective, the Court has stated that it must interpret the Convention so 'as to give full effect to the system of human rights protection'.[112] The Court also applies the principles of legal certainty, procedural equality and proportionality in its interpretations.[113] The Court reasons that it must interpret the Convention and State declarations 'in accordance with the canons and practice of International Law in general, and with International Human Rights Law specifically, and [in a manner] which awards the greatest degree of protection to the human beings under its guardianship'.[114] In doing so, the Court must preserve the integrity of the Convention and of the Court's jurisdiction.

The Court does not take a strict constructionist position in its interpretation of the Convention. In light of changing societal conditions, interpretation of the rights protected by the Convention and the procedures employed by the Commission and Court may evolve over time. In this regard, the Court has stated that it may not ignore the important developments in the last fifty years that have enriched human rights law.[115] Therefore, it interprets the Convention 'within the framework of the entire legal system prevailing at the time of the interpretation'.[116] In

[110] 1969 Vienna Convention on the Law of Treaties, Art. 31.

[111] Advisory Opinion OC-2/82, para. 29.

[112] Advisory Opinion OC-15/97, para. 29. [113] *Ibid.*, paras. 39 and 48.

[114] *Benjamin et al.* v. *Trinidad and Tobago* (Preliminary Objections, 2001), para. 70.

[115] Advisory Opinion OC-16/99, para. 113. [116] *Ibid.*

doing so, the Court may exercise its advisory jurisdiction to answer both procedural and substantive questions.

Interpretation of the substantive provisions of the American Convention An advisory opinion interpreting the substantive provisions of the American Convention accords the States Parties to the Convention a uniform understanding of the meaning and scope of the human rights they have committed themselves to respect. It also provides the people of the Americas with more explicit knowledge of the rights ensured to them by the Convention. On a larger scale, the Inter-American Court's interpretation of the substantive provisions of the American Convention contributes to the general field of international human rights law by providing consistency in the interpretation of the rights protected and fostering uniformity in the development of international substantive rights.

There is no formal rule of *stare decisis* in the Inter-American system, although the Inter-American Court regularly cites to and quotes its *jurisprudencia constante*, or well-established case law. While admitting that its 'case law may establish precedents', the Court maintains that 'it cannot be invoked as a criterion to be universally applied; instead, each case needs to be examined individually'.[117] The Court also reinforces internationally recognized rights and principles by relying on and citing the jurisprudence of the Permanent Court of International Justice, the International Court of Justice, the European Court of Human Rights, international arbitral decisions, and scholarly writings. The Inter-American Court, however, does not merely follow external authority. As Davidson observed, 'it is apparent that the Court's own jurisprudence is distinctive in certain areas, most particularly in its identification of the philosophical bases of human rights obligations and ideological issues concerning the relationship of human rights to the concept of the rule of law and to democratic ideals'.[118]

For example, the Court has emphasized the fundamental principle that a democratic form of government is essential to the protection and enforcement of human rights. In its advisory opinion, *The Word 'Laws'*, the Court determined that laws which permit the restriction of certain rights include only 'formal law'.[119] According to the Court, a formal law in

[117] *El Amparo* v. *Venezuela* (Reparations), Inter-Am. Ct HR, 14 September 1996, Ser. C, No. 28, para. 34; see also *Paniagua Morales et al.* v. *Guatemala* (Reparations), Inter-Am. Ct HR, 25 May 2001, Ser. C, No. 76, para. 104.

[118] Davidson, *The Inter-American Court*, at 130.

[119] *The Word 'Laws' in Article 30 of the American Convention on Human Rights*, Inter-Am. Ct HR, Advisory Opinion OC-6/86 of 9 May 1986, Ser. A, No. 6, para. 27.

this context is a legal norm passed by a democratically elected legislature and promulgated by a democratically elected executive branch, pursuant to procedures set forth in the domestic law of that State.[120] The Court reasoned that it is the 'effective exercise of representative democracy' that underlies the enjoyment of human rights.[121] In contrast, the Court held that laws promulgated by governments that are not democratically elected, as has occurred in the past in several Latin American States, would not be recognized under the American Convention as legally restricting the enjoyment or exercise of human rights.[122] The Court stated that '[t]o affirm otherwise would be to recognize in those who govern, virtually absolute power over their subjects'.[123] The Court also emphasized the democratic form of government as the basis for the effective protection of human rights in *Compulsory Membership in an Association Prescribed by Law for the Practice of Journalism*.[124] The Court therein rejected the view that the form of government does not affect State compliance with human rights standards.[125]

The Court addressed the issue of the non-derogability of certain human rights in its advisory opinion on the meaning of 'judicial guarantees' from which no State derogation is permitted.[126] Judicial guarantees are of primary importance in regions that suffer gross and systematic violations of human rights. In *Habeas Corpus in Emergency Situations*, the Court responded to a Commission request for clarification as to which judicial rights are guaranteed even during a state of emergency.[127] In times of emergency, such as war or public danger that threaten the security or independence of a State Party, international law in general, and the American Convention in particular, permit a State to suspend certain protected rights on a temporary basis.[128] Some rights, however, such as the rights to life and to humane treatment, are so crucial that even during a state of emergency the American Convention does not allow State derogation.[129]

[120] *Ibid.*, paras. 27 and 38. [121] *Ibid.*, para. 32. [122] *Ibid.*, para. 27.

[123] *Ibid.* [124] Advisory Opinion OC-5/85, para. 42.

[125] *Ibid.*; Thomas Buergenthal, 'The Normative and Institutional Evolution of International Human Rights', 19 *Human Rights Quarterly*, 703, 714 (1997).

[126] *Habeas Corpus in Emergency Situations (Arts. 27(2) and 7(6) of the American Convention on Human Rights)*, Inter-Am. Ct HR, Advisory Opinion OC-8/87 of 30 January 1987, Ser. A, No. 8, para. 11.

[127] *Ibid.*, para. 11.

[128] American Convention, Art. 27(1). For a more comprehensive discussion in Spanish of states of emergency and human rights in Latin America, see Daniel Zovatto, *Los Estados de Excepción y los Derechos Humanos en América Latina* (Editorial Juridica Venezolana, Caracas, 1990).

[129] American Convention, Art. 27(2).

Included in the Convention's prohibitions of those rights that cannot be suspended are essential judicial guarantees.[130]

The Convention does not specify which judicial guarantees are deemed 'essential', however, and therefore that issue remained for the Court to clarify. The Commission particularly questioned whether the right of a prisoner to *habeas corpus* was included in the judicial guarantees that cannot be suspended.[131] The purpose of a writ of *habeas corpus* is to bring a detained person before a judge, who can then verify that the prisoner is alive, and that he or she has not been tortured.[132] The Commission argued in its request that certain States had laws or a practice under which detainees could be held incommunicado for as long as fifteen days.[133] In its advisory opinion on *Habeas Corpus in Emergency Situations*, the Court verified that the peoples of the Americas have a right to the judicial guarantee of *habeas corpus* even during a state of emergency.[134] In so finding, it reasoned that 'the realities that have been the experience of some of the peoples of this hemisphere in recent decades, particularly disappearances, torture and murder committed or tolerated by some governments' has repeatedly demonstrated that the rights to life and to humane treatment are threatened whenever the right to *habeas corpus* is partially or wholly suspended.[135] The Court stated that '[h]abeas corpus performs a vital role in ensuring that a person's life and physical integrity are respected, in preventing his disappearance or the keeping of his whereabouts secret and in protecting him against torture or cruel, inhumane, or degrading punishment or treatment'.[136] The Court's determination in this area has effects not only in the Inter-American human rights system, but throughout international human rights law and domestic law.

The Inter-American Court linked the concept of the non-derogability of select fundamental human rights to the incompatibility of certain State reservations. In *Restrictions to the Death Penalty*, the Commission's request for an advisory opinion questioned the effect and scope of

[130] *Ibid.*, Art. 27. [131] Advisory Opinion OC-8/87, para. 11.
[132] *Ibid.*, paras. 33 and 35. [133] *Ibid.*, para. 12. [134] *Ibid.*, para. 42.
[135] *Ibid.*, para. 36; see generally Informe de la Comisión Nacional de Verdad y Reconciliación, Chile (National Commission on Truth and Reconciliation Report, Chile), March 1991; UN Truth Commission Report for El Salvador, *From Madness to Hope: The Twelve-Year War in El Salvador* (United Nations, New York and San Salvador, 1993); *Honduras: The Facts Speak for Themselves: The Preliminary Report of the Commissioner for the Protection of Human Rights in Honduras* (Human Rights Watch, New York, 1994).
[136] *Judicial Guarantees in States of Emergency (Arts. 27(2), 25 and 8 of the American Convention on Human Rights)*, Inter-Am. Ct HR, Advisory Opinion OC-9/87 of 6 October 1987, Ser. A, No. 9, para. 35. See generally Elizabeth Faulkner, 'The Right to Habeas Corpus: Only in the Americas', 9 *American University Journal of International Law and Policy*, 653 (1994).

Guatemala's reservation to the death penalty provision of the Convention.[137] Guatemala's reservation stated that it 'only exclude[d] the application of the death penalty to political crimes, but not common crimes related to political crimes'.[138] The Court found that the Guatemalan reservation did not contravene the object and purpose of the Convention.[139] The Court, however, made the important statement that 'a reservation which was designed to enable a State to suspend any of the non-derogable fundamental rights must be deemed to be incompatible with the object and purpose of the Convention, and, consequently, not permitted by it'.[140] The UN Human Rights Committee has also commented on the relationship between reservations and non-derogable rights. Its statement, although similar to that of the Inter-American Court, was not as absolute. The Human Rights Committee declared that '[w]hile there is no automatic correlation between reservations to non-derogable provisions, and reservations which offend against the object and purpose of the Covenant [which are not permitted], a State has a heavy onus to justify such a reservation'.[141]

Another basis of international human rights law which was addressed by the Court in its advisory opinion on *Proposed Amendments to the Naturalization Provisions of the Constitution of Costa Rica* is the underlying philosophy of the essential principle of non-discrimination.[142] International law, and human rights law in particular, has long provided that the rights of all individuals must be respected without discrimination of any type.[143] The American Convention provides that there can be no discrimination on the basis of 'race, color, sex, language, religion, political or other opinion, national or social origin, economic status, birth, or any other social condition'.[144] In *Proposed Amendments*, the Court relied on natural law in theorizing that equality arises directly from the unity of the human family and is inextricably linked to the dignity of the individual.[145] The Court went on to state that:

137 Advisory Opinion OC-3/83, para. 13.

138 Guatemalan Reservation to the American Convention on Human Rights, reprinted in 2001 Basic Documents, at 84.

139 Advisory Opinion OC-3/83, para. 61.

140 *Ibid.*

141 Human Rights Committee, General Comment 24 (52), para. 10.

142 Advisory Opinion OC-4/84, para. 55.

143 See the International Covenant on Civil and Political Rights, Art. 2(1), opened for signature 16 December 1966, 999 UNTS 171, entered into force on 23 March 1976.

144 American Convention, Art. 1(1). In addition, Art. 24 provides that '[a]ll persons are equal before the law. Consequently, they are entitled, without discrimination, to equal protection of the law.' *Ibid.*

145 Advisory Opinion OC-4/84, para. 55.

> [t]hat principle cannot be reconciled with the notion that a given group has the right to privileged treatment because of its perceived superiority. It is equally irreconcilable with that notion to characterize a group as inferior and treat it with hostility or otherwise subject it to discrimination in the enjoyment of rights which are accorded to others not so classified. It is impermissible to subject human beings to differences in treatment that are inconsistent with their unique and congenerous character.[146]

The Court did not find all discrepancies in legal treatment to be *per se* discriminatory but rather only those that have 'no objective and reasonable justification'.[147] According to the Court, certain inequalities may be instrumental in attaining justice for those who are in a 'weak legal position'.[148] Thus, although States have the right to confer and regulate nationality, State regulations and procedures in this area cannot conflict with superior norms such as the right to non-discrimination. The Court held in its advisory opinion on the *Legal Status and Human Rights of the Child* that States can and must adopt specific legal measures to protect children.[149] These measures would not violate the Convention's mandate that all persons 'are entitled without discrimination, to equal protection of the law' because of the more vulnerable nature of children.[150]

The Inter-American Court has affirmed that States have a margin of appreciation, meaning a certain degree of flexibility, in implementing the Convention's substantive provisions. In its advisory opinion on *Proposed Amendments to the Naturalization Provisions of the Constitution of Costa Rica*, the Court cited with approval the general principle of 'margin of appreciation', which is frequently raised by the European Commission and Court.[151] A margin of appreciation allows a State some latitude in judgment or discretion in implementing international rules in the domestic sphere. In *Proposed Amendments*, the Court recognized that a margin of appreciation was reserved to States in establishing requirements for the acquisition of nationality.[152] Therefore, although a State must comply with the substantive provisions of the American Convention, it has discretion in determining the means to fulfil its international obligations.

The interpretation or scope of other substantive provisions of the American Convention could also be addressed through advisory opinions.

[146] *Ibid.* [147] *Ibid.*, para. 56. [148] *Ibid.*

[149] *The Legal Status and Human Rights of the Child*, Inter-Am. Ct HR, Advisory Opinion OC-17/2002 of 28 August 2002, Ser. A, No. 17, operative para. 3.

[150] *Ibid.*; American Convention, Art. 24.

[151] Advisory Opinion OC-4/84, paras. 58 and 62–3; see van Dijk and van Hoof, *Theory and Practice*, at 282–95.

[152] *Ibid.*, para. 62.

For example, questions have been raised concerning the meaning and justiciability of the provision of the American Convention on the 'progressive development' of economic, social and cultural rights[153] and the Additional Protocol to the American Convention on Human Rights in the Area of Economic, Social and Cultural Rights.[154] Also, an advisory opinion on the question of whether widespread corruption, which robs the public treasury of the monies needed to provide for these rights, is a violation of the Convention could give a judicial imprimatur to the movements that are attempting to eliminate official corruption. Another question which is being debated in international human rights law is whether individuals can violate human rights treaties. A request for an advisory opinion on Article 32 of the American Convention, which affirms the principle of individual responsibility while limiting individual freedom by reference to general welfare and security, could result in a much anticipated judicial pronouncement on the issue.

Interpretation of the procedural provisions of the American Convention The American Convention specifies the procedures that shall be followed by the organs that oversee State compliance.[155] The Court's resolution of procedural issues in the application of the Convention also provides for legal certainty and procedural equality between the parties, which contributes to the credibility of the Commission and the Court. Just as the States Parties to the Convention must comply with their substantive obligations, the Court and Commission must comply with their procedural obligations. When a procedural question arises in a contentious case that is before the Court, the State Party involved may raise it as a preliminary objection claiming that the case should be dismissed due to an irregularity in the processing of the case.[156] Alternatively, if a case is not before the Court, the State could request an advisory opinion as to whether the procedures used by the Commission comply with the mandate of the Convention.

A far-reaching procedural issue resolved by the Court in its advisory opinion, *Exceptions to the Exhaustion of Domestic Remedies*, involved the question of when a petitioner must exhaust internal state remedies before

[153] American Convention, Art. 26. [154] Protocol of San Salvador.

[155] American Convention, Arts. 48–51.

[156] See generally Jo M. Pasqualucci, 'Preliminary Objections Before the Inter-American Court of Human Rights', 40 *Virginia Journal of International Law*, 1, 6 (1999).

filing a complaint with the Inter-American Commission.[157] Under the American Convention, unless there is a relevant exception, legal remedies in the State where the violation occurred must normally be 'pursued and exhausted' before a petitioner can turn to the Inter-American system for relief.[158] This generally recognized rule allows a state to attempt a resolution of the case under its internal law before being confronted with an international proceeding.[159] The requirement of exhaustion of remedies is not, however, absolute. It is based on the availability of effective domestic remedies in the State in question. The American Convention, therefore, enumerates specific exceptions to the rule of exhaustion that are applicable in limited situations.[160] In *Exceptions to the Exhaustion of Domestic Remedies*, the Commission asked the Court to determine whether an exception to the doctrine of exhaustion was applicable to an individual petitioner who could not secure legal representation due to either indigence or an atmosphere of fear.[161] The Court advised that, under the American Convention, if indigence or general fear prevented a petitioner from securing an attorney to represent him or her before domestic authorities, the petitioner need not exhaust domestic remedies before filing a complaint with the Commission.[162] This opinion paved the way for many victims in the Americas to find recourse before the Inter-American human rights system. It may also serve as persuasive authority in cases before the European Court of Human Rights arising in countries of Eastern Europe that suffer from poverty and authoritarian traditions, or in cases before the future African Court on Human and Peoples' Rights.

The Court has also clarified certain procedural requirements that the Commission must apply when processing a complaint.[163] The Commission had difficulty adequately addressing these complaints due to the number of individual petitions filed with the Commission and its limited staff and resources. As a result of two advisory opinions issued by the Court, *Reports of the Inter-American Commission of Human Rights* and *Certain Attributes of the Inter-American Commission on Human Rights*,[164]

[157] *Exceptions to the Exhaustion of Domestic Remedies (Arts. 46(1), 46(2)(a), and 46(2)(b) of the American Convention on Human Rights)*, Inter-Am. Ct HR, Advisory Opinion OC-11/90 of 10 August 1990, Ser. A, No. 11.

[158] American Convention, Art. 46(1)(a).

[159] *Velásquez Rodríguez* v. *Honduras* (Merits), Inter-Am. Ct HR, 29 July 1988, Ser. C, No. 4, paras. 35–7.

[160] American Convention, Art. 46(2).

[161] Advisory Opinion OC-11/90, para. 2.

[162] *Ibid.*, operative para. 1.

[163] Advisory Opinion OC-15/97; Advisory Opinion OC-13/93.

[164] Advisory Opinion OC-15/97; Advisory Opinion OC-13/93.

and preliminary objections in contentious cases that were resolved against the Commission, the Commission eventually restructured the manner in which it processes individual cases.[165]

Although the resulting transparency of the Commission's procedures contributes to confidence in the Inter-American human rights system, the Court's interpretations of the Convention's procedural requirements have not been universally applauded. In *Certain Attributes of the Inter-American Commission on Human Rights*, the Court advised that the American Convention does not permit the Commission to send its preliminary report to both the State and the petitioner.[166] The Convention provision states that '[t]he report shall be transmitted to the States concerned, which shall not be at liberty to publish it'.[167] The Court interpreted the provision to provide that *only* States have a right to the report.[168] Thus, the petitioner does not receive timely notice of the Commission's ruling when the Commission finds that the State has violated the victim's rights. The petitioner is notified only that the Commission has adopted a report and has transmitted it to the State concerned, but is not informed of the contents of the report.[169] Critics argue that this results in procedural inequality of the parties and violates a basic tenet of human rights law, that laws should be interpreted in favour of the individual.[170]

States continue to question whether the Commission strictly adheres to Convention-mandated procedures in all instances. Some of these procedural questions could be submitted to the Inter-American Court for advisory opinions. For example, the Inter-American Commission currently publishes its admissibility decisions in its annual report[171] despite the opposition of certain States and the recommendation of the OAS General Assembly.[172] States argue that the Convention does not authorize the publication of interim decisions.[173] The Chair of the Commission

[165] Claudio Grossman, 'Strengthening the Inter-American Human Rights System: The Current Debate', 92 *American Society of International Law Proceedings*, 186, 190 (1998).

[166] Advisory Opinion OC-13/93, paras. 48–9. [167] American Convention, Art. 50(2).

[168] Advisory Opinion OC-13/93, paras. 48–9.

[169] 2001 Rules of Procedure of the Inter-American Commission on Human Rights, entered into force 1 May 2001, Art. 43(2).

[170] See Pedro Nikken, 'Observaciones Sobre el Fortalecimiento del Sistema Interamericano de Derechos Humanos en Visperas de la Asamblea General de la OEA', 13 *Revista Inter-Americano Instituto de Derechos Humanos*, 13 (2001), at 33 (special edition).

[171] 2001 Rules of Procedure of the Inter-Am. Comm. HR, Art. 37(1).

[172] Resolution AG/RES. 1701 (XXX-O/00), para. 6(b).

[173] Dialogue on the Inter-American System for the Promotion and Protection of Human Rights, Permanent Council of the OEA/Ser.G/OAS CP/CAJP-1610/00 rev. 2, 24 April 2000, Committee on Juridical and Political Affairs, at 9 of 20.

suggested in response that the State raise the issue in an advisory opinion request.[174] States have also questioned the legitimacy of some changes in the Court's and Commission's Rules of Procedure.[175] For instance, a new Commission rule specifies that the Commission may follow up on State compliance with Commission recommendations and friendly settlements by holding hearings or by requesting information from the parties[176] – practices that the States challenge.[177] One State delegation to the OAS suggested that the reforms to the Rules of Procedure of the Commission and the Court be submitted to the Sub-Secretariat of the OAS Juridical Committee to determine if the new Rules comply with the American Convention.[178] The OAS General Assembly instructed the Permanent Council of the OAS to study 'the relationship between the rules of procedure of [the Commission and the Court] and the provisions of their statutes and the American Convention on Human Rights'.[179] These are not the proper bodies to determine the compatibility of human rights instruments with the American Convention. The American Convention specifies that questions concerning the interpretation of the Convention are to be submitted to the Inter-American Court.[180] The questions should therefore be submitted to the Court in the form of a request for an advisory opinion.

Jurisdiction to issue advisory opinions interpreting other treaties

The States of the Americas have ratified various regional and international treaties that impose human rights obligations on the ratifying States. For the benefit of the American States that must comply with these obligations and the OAS organs that may be called upon to apply these treaty provisions, the Court has jurisdiction *ratione materiae* under Article 64(1) of the American Convention to interpret 'other treaties concerning the protection of human rights in the American states' and to clarify the scope of the human rights obligations created by all such treaties.[181]

The scope of the Court's jurisdiction in regard to 'other treaties' is not clearly delineated in the American Convention. Consequently, the

174 *Ibid.*, at 6.

175 See Nikken, 'Observaciones Sobre el Fortalecimiento del Sistema', at 33.

176 2001 Rules of Procedure of the Inter-Am. Comm. HR, Art. 46.

177 *Ibid.*

178 See Nikken, 'Observaciones Sobre el Fortalecimiento del Sistema', at 30.

179 Evaluation of the Workings of the Inter-American System for the Protection and Promotion of Human Rights with a View to its Improvement and Strengthening, AG/RES. 1828 (XXXI-O/01), available at http://www.oas.org. Resolution adopted at the third plenary session, held on 5 June 2001.

180 American Convention, Art. 64(1).

181 *Ibid.*

Government of Peru presented the Court with its first opportunity to render an advisory opinion by requesting an interpretation of the phrase 'other treaties concerning the protection of human rights in the American states'.[182] In its opinion *'Other Treaties'*, the Court interpreted the phrase 'other treaties' to include:

> any provision dealing with the protection of human rights set forth in any international treaty applicable in the American States, regardless of whether it be bilateral or multilateral, whatever be the principal purpose of such a treaty, and whether or not non-Member States of the inter-American system are or have the right to become parties thereto.[183]

The Court defined the word 'treaty' to be 'an international instrument' in accordance with the definitions in the 1969 Vienna Convention on the Law of Treaties[184] and the 1986 Vienna Convention on the Law of Treaties Among States and International Organizations or Among International Organizations.[185] It understood the term 'American State' to mean all States that may ratify the American Convention, which is any Member State of the OAS.[186] The Court further determined that a treaty concerns the protection of human rights if it 'has bearing upon, affects or is of interest' in the area of human rights.[187] The principal purpose of the treaty need not be the protection of human rights; it is necessary only that the pertinent provision concerns human rights.[188] Thus, the Court determined that 'a treaty can concern the protection of human rights, regardless of what the principal purpose of that treaty might be'.[189] As such, the source of the obligation, the main purpose of the treaty, and the bilateral or multilateral nature of the treaty are not determining factors.[190] This interpretation gives the Court the broadest possible jurisdiction to interpret human rights provisions.

Mexico's request in *The Right to Information on Consular Assistance* seeking an advisory opinion on the Vienna Convention on Consular Relations raised the question of whether a specific treaty provision falls within the Court's advisory jurisdiction.[191] The United States objected to the Court's consideration of the request for an interpretation of the

[182] Advisory Opinion OC-1/82, paras. 20 and 8. [183] *Ibid.*, operative para. 1.

[184] 1969 Vienna Convention on the Law of Treaties, Art. 2(1)(a).

[185] *Interpretation of the American Declaration of the Rights and Duties of Man Within the Framework of Article 64 of the American Convention on Human Rights*, Inter-Am. Ct HR, Advisory Opinion OC-10/89 of 14 July 1989, Ser. A, No. 10, para. 32.

[186] Advisory Opinion OC-1/82, para. 35. [187] Advisory Opinion OC-16/99, para. 72.

[188] *Ibid.*, para. 76. [189] *Ibid.*, para. 76.

[190] Advisory Opinion OC-1/82, para. 34. [191] Advisory Opinion OC-16/99, para. 3.

Vienna Convention, on the grounds that it was neither a human rights treaty nor a treaty concerning the protection of human rights, and that it was not intended by the ratifying States to confer rights on individuals.[192] The United States claimed that it was a multilateral treaty 'of the traditional type concluded to accomplish reciprocal exchange of rights for the mutual benefit of the contracting States',[193] which the Court had earlier contrasted to human rights treaties.[194] The Court rejected this argument. While refusing to involve itself in the underlying controversy between the States, the Court interpreted the relevant provisions of the Vienna Convention to confer rights on the individual and clarified that those rights qualified as human rights.[195]

Other Inter-American treaties The Court's jurisdiction to interpret 'other treaties' may encompass specialized OAS human rights treaties including the Inter-American Convention to Prevent and Punish Torture,[196] the Inter-American Convention on the Forced Disappearance of Persons,[197] the Inter-American Convention on the Prevention, Punishment and Eradication of Violence Against Women,[198] as well as the human rights provisions of the Charter of the OAS.[199] Although the Court held that the American Declaration of the Rights and Duties of Man[200] is not a treaty *per se*, the Court issued an advisory opinion concluding that the Declaration is an authoritative interpretation of the Charter of the OAS and the American Convention.[201] Consequently, the Court is authorized to interpret the American Declaration when necessary to interpret the OAS Charter or the American Convention.[202]

Non-regional treaties In determining that its advisory jurisdiction extends beyond the Inter-American system to the interpretation of human rights provisions in any treaty ratified by an American State, the

192 *Ibid.*, para. 26. 193 *Ibid.*, quoting Advisory Opinion OC-1/82, para. 24.
194 Advisory Opinion OC-2/82, para. 29.
195 Advisory Opinion OC-16/99, paras. 82, 84, 86, 87 and operative paras. 1 and 2.
196 Reprinted in 2001 Basic Documents, at 83.
197 Resolution Adopted at Belem do Pará, Brazil, 9 June 1994, at the twenty-fourth regular session of the General Assembly of the Organization of American States, entered into force on 29 March 1996.
198 Adopted in Belem do Pará, Brazil, on 9 June 1994, during the twenty-fourth regular session of the General Assembly of the OAS, entered into force on 5 March 1995.
199 Charter of the Organization of American States.
200 Adopted at the Ninth International Conference of American States, Bogotá, Colombia, 1948, reprinted in 2001 Basic Documents, at 15.
201 Advisory Opinion OC-10/89, paras. 33 and 44. 202 *Ibid.*, para. 44.

Inter-American Court took a position on another long-standing debate among human rights commentators: whether human rights are universal or culturally relative in character.[203] The Court reasoned that distinctions based on a regional character of obligations would 'deny the existence of the common core of basic human rights standards'.[204] Thus, the Court gave its judicial imprimatur to the universality of human rights.[205] The principle that rights are culturally relative would allow for distinctions and exceptions on the basis of religious or cultural differences, distinctions which sometimes support human rights violations. Subsequent to the Court's opinion, universalism also found support at the World Conference on Human Rights in Vienna.[206]

To date, the Inter-American Court has interpreted provisions of two non-regional treaties. In response to Mexico's request in *The Right to Information on Consular Assistance*, the Court held that an individual's right to information conferred by the Vienna Convention gives practical effect in concrete cases to the right to due process recognized by the International Covenant on Civil and Political Rights.[207] The Court further advised that the Articles in question of the International Covenant of Civil and Political Rights do 'concern the protection of human rights in the American States'.[208]

Jurisdiction to issue advisory opinions on the compatibility of domestic laws of a Member State

Any Member State of the OAS can request an advisory opinion under Article 64(2) as to whether its domestic laws are compatible with the American Convention or with any treaty that concerns human rights protection in the American States.[209] The American Convention's use of the unqualified term 'domestic laws' in this context has been interpreted by the Court to mean that it has jurisdiction to determine the compatibility of 'all national legislation and legal norms' of any character.[210] In

[203] Advisory Opinion OC-1/82, para. 40. [204] *Ibid.* [205] *Ibid.*

[206] 1993 Vienna Declaration on Human Rights, UN Secretary-General, Report of the World Conference on Human Rights, UN Doc. A/Conf. 157/24 (1993).

[207] Advisory Opinion OC-16/99, paras. 6 and 141(7); see also International Covenant on Civil and Political Rights, GA Res. 2200A, UN GAOR, 21st Sess., UN Doc. A/6316, 999 UNTS 171 (1966).

[208] Advisory Opinion OC-16/99, operative para. 5 (referring to Articles 2, 6, 14 and 50).

[209] American Convention, Art. 64(2). See *Compatibility of Draft Legislation with Article 8(2)(h) of the American Convention on Human Rights*, Inter-Am. Ct HR, Advisory Opinion OC-12/91 of 6 December 1991, Ser. A, No. 12, para. 14.

[210] Advisory Opinion OC-4/84, para. 14.

Proposed Amendments to the Naturalization Provisions of the Constitution of Costa Rica, the State asked for an advisory opinion on whether proposed constitutional amendments, which had not yet been adopted by the legislative assembly, were compatible with the American Convention.[211] The Convention does not specify whether domestic laws must be in force to be the subject of an advisory opinion request. Therefore, the initial issue to be decided was whether the Court's advisory jurisdiction extended to draft laws, such as proposed constitutional amendments, or only to those laws already enacted.[212] The Court determined that it did have jurisdiction to interpret draft legislation, given that a restrictive reading of the Convention would 'unduly limit the advisory function of the Court'.[213] The Court reasoned that, by refusing to issue an advisory opinion on draft laws, a State might adopt and perhaps apply a law that would be in violation of its human rights obligations.[214] The authority of the Inter-American Court to provide opinions on draft legislation could become increasingly important as the emphasis of regional systems shifts to implementing rights in the domestic arena. In this regard, the European human rights system is considering the option of systematically screening all draft legislation of Contracting States to the European Convention to ensure its compatibility with the States' human rights obligations under the European Convention.[215]

The Court cannot use its advisory jurisdiction to order a State to reform its laws. This power is reserved for the Court's contentious jurisdiction. An advisory opinion, however, may clarify the legal issue of whether the law is in violation of the State's international legal obligations, and thereby inform the national political debate on the law in question.[216] Whether a State has a monist or dualist system, a State is in violation of its international obligations if its domestic laws are in conflict with the international treaties it has ratified. One way for a State to avoid inadvertently violating its international human rights obligations is to request an advisory opinion as to the compatibility of its laws with its treaty obligations. This aspect of the Court's jurisdiction enables the Court 'to perform a service for all of the members of the Inter-American system and is designed to assist them in fulfilling their international human rights obligations'.[217]

[211] *Ibid.*, para. 1. [212] *Ibid.*, para. 13. [213] *Ibid.*, para. 28.

[214] *Ibid.*, para. 26, quoted in Advisory Opinion OC-12/91, para. 20.

[215] See Statement of Mr Pierre-Henri Imbert, Director General of Human Rights at the Council of Europe, delivered at the 57th Session of the United Nations Commission on Human Rights, Geneva, 29 March 2001.

[216] Buergenthal, 'The Inter-American Court, Human Rights and the OAS', at 160.

[217] Advisory Opinion OC-1/82, para. 39, quoted in Advisory Opinion OC-4/84, para. 19.

In some cases, the Court may choose not to issue an advisory opinion on the compatibility of domestic laws if there is a danger that by granting the request the Court will be embroiled in national partisan politics.[218] In this regard, the Court has stated that it will 'exercise great care to ensure that its advisory jurisdiction in such instances is not resorted to in order to affect the outcome of the domestic legislative process for narrow partisan political ends'.[219] The Court should not be overly cautious in this area, because there is political opposition to almost any position taken by a government. The Court has admitted that 'an advisory opinion might either weaken or strengthen a State's legal position in a current or future controversy'.[220] Although this may be true, the Court's purpose is to help State governments comply with their international human rights obligations. Thus, when the government of a State makes a request, the Court should generally render an advisory opinion.

Jurisdiction ratione temporis *following the attempted withdrawal of a request for an advisory opinion*

The Inter-American Court continues to have jurisdiction *ratione temporis* even after the party requesting the opinion has attempted to withdraw the request.[221] For example, in *Reports of the Inter-American Commission of Human Rights*, Chile submitted a request for an advisory opinion and later attempted to withdraw it.[222] The Court determined that the State's attempted withdrawal 'raised a substantive question concerning the scope and nature of the Court's advisory jurisdiction'.[223] It reasoned that other OAS Member States might also have an interest in the issue raised in the request.[224] The Court emphasized that an advisory opinion request is communicated to all Member States of the OAS, and those States may then submit their observations to the Court in writing or participate in the oral hearing.[225] At the time that Chile attempted to withdraw its request, two States had already submitted their briefs on the issue to the Court.[226] The Court maintained that 'the State requesting an advisory opinion is not the only interested party and that even if it withdraws the request, that withdrawal is not binding on the Court'.[227] Consequently, the

[218] Advisory Opinion OC-4/84, para. 30. [219] *Ibid.*
[220] Advisory Opinion OC-3/83, para. 24. [221] Advisory Opinion OC-15/97, para. 28.
[222] *Ibid.*, para. 24. [223] *Ibid.* [224] *Ibid.*, para. 28.
[225] *Ibid.*, para. 26. [226] *Ibid.*, paras. 10 and 12.
[227] *Ibid.*, para. 28, quoting Order of Inter-Am. Ct HR, 14 April 1997, 'Considering' section, para. 5, reprinted in the 1997 Annual Report of the Inter-American Court of Human

Court determined that the scope of its advisory jurisdiction allowed it to process the request.[228] The Court also analogized its advisory jurisdiction to its jurisdiction in contentious cases, in which an applicant's attempted withdrawal also does not obligate the Court to close the case.[229]

In contrast, when confronted with the same issue, the Permanent Court of International Justice did permit the withdrawal of a request for an advisory opinion.[230] That, however, may have been a result of the circumstances of the specific case in which the underlying problem had already been resolved. The Council of the League of Nations had requested a decision on its competence to deal with a dispute between Greece and Turkey.[231] The dispute was resolved by the States before the Court issued an opinion. Moreover, the question did not affect other entities and was not influential in international law in general, so there was no need for the Court to issue an opinion.[232]

Advisory jurisdiction subject to the Court's discretion

The Inter-American Court retains discretion to decline to exercise its advisory jurisdiction, even when the request meets the requirements set forth in the Convention and in the Court's Rules of Procedure.[233] When the Court's jurisdiction to issue an advisory opinion is challenged, the Court will first determine whether it has the requisite jurisdiction. If it finds that it has, the Court will then determine whether it will exercise that jurisdiction.[234] The Court explained that 'its advisory jurisdiction is permissive in character in the sense that it empowers the Court to

Rights, OAS/Ser.L/V/III.39 doc. 5, 21 January 1998. The Court's denial of the requested withdrawal in no way prejudges the admissibility or merits of the advisory request. Advisory Opinion OC-15/97, para. 28.

228 Advisory Opinion OC-15/97, para. 28.

229 Request for Advisory Opinion OC-15, Inter-Am. Ct HR, Order of 14 April 1997, 'Considering' section, para. 5, reprinted in 1997 Annual Report of the Inter-Am. Ct HR, at 111.

230 Judge Hudson opined that:

> The Council or Assembly may withdraw a request for an advisory opinion: the withdrawal may certainly be made at any time prior to the opening of oral proceedings, and it would seem that it might be made at any time prior to the actual delivery of the opinion in open court.

Hudson, *The Permanent Court*, at 509.

231 See *League of Nations Official Journal*, 1925, pp. 579, 637, cited in Hudson, *The Permanent Court*, at 510, n. 67.

232 *Ibid.*, at 509–10.

233 Advisory Opinion OC-16/99, para. 31.

234 See *ibid.*, para. 42.

decide whether the circumstances of a request for an advisory opinion justify a decision rejecting the request'.[235] The wording of the American Convention, which provides that the Court 'may' provide a Member State with an opinion on the compatibility of its domestic laws, supports the Court's discretion.[236] The Convention is not equally clear as to whether the Court has the authority to refuse to consider requests for interpretations of the American Convention or other treaties, but that would follow from the nature of the Court's jurisdiction in this area.[237] The Statute of the International Court of Justice similarly provides that the Court 'may' render an advisory opinion.[238] The Inter-American Court's decision is also consistent with the jurisprudence of the ICJ in this regard.[239] In reference to the PCIJ Rosenne explained that 'the permissive character of the advisory competence . . . included not only discretion whether the Court would give the requested opinion at all, but also broad discretion regarding the procedure to be followed in any specific advisory cases'.[240]

The Inter-American Court bases its decision to accept or reject an advisory opinion request 'on considerations that transcend merely formal aspects'.[241] Principally, the Court will refuse to consider 'any request for an advisory opinion which is likely to undermine the Court's contentious jurisdiction or, in general, to weaken or alter the system established by the Convention, in a manner that would impair the rights of potential victims of human rights violations'.[242] However, the Court would possibly consider an advisory opinion request on a subject when the Commission's failure to refer a case to the Count impairs 'the delicate balance of the protective system established by the Convention'.[243] The Court could also exercise its discretion to abstain from issuing an advisory opinion when the issue raised by a request is a juridical question that does not refer to a specific fact situation.[244] The Court reasoned that its advisory jurisdiction 'should not, in principle, be used for purely academic speculation, without a foreseeable application to concrete situations justifying the need for an advisory opinion'.[245]

235 Advisory Opinion OC-1/82, para. 27. 236 American Convention, Art. 64(2).
237 *Ibid.*, Art. 64(1). 238 Statute of the International Court of Justice, Art. 65.
239 *Interpretation of Peace Treaties*, 150 ICJ Reports 65.
240 Rosenne, *The Law and Practice of the International Court*, at 282.
241 *The Right to Information on Consular Assistance Within the Framework of the Guarantees of Legal Due Process*, Inter-Am. Ct HR, Advisory Opinion OC-16/99 of 1 October 1999, Ser. A. No. 16, para. 31.
242 Advisory Opinion OC-1/82, para. 31, quoted in Advisory Opinion OC-5/85, para. 21; Advisory Opinion OC-16/99, para. 44.
243 Advisory Opinion OC-5/85, para. 26. 244 Advisory Opinion OC-9/87, para. 16.
245 *Ibid.*

On only one occasion to date, in *Compatibility of Draft Legislation*, has the Inter-American Court refused to exercise its jurisdiction to render an advisory opinion.[246] In that matter, Costa Rica requested the Court's opinion on whether its draft legislation, establishing a court of criminal appeals and providing for the right to appeal, complied with the requirements of the American Convention.[247] Although the Court held that it has jurisdiction to issue an advisory opinion on draft laws, it refused to render the requested opinion. The Court reasoned that the questions presented 'could produce under the guise of an advisory opinion, a determination of contentious matters not yet referred to the Court, without providing the victims with the opportunity to participate in the proceedings'.[248]

The Court's discretion to deny a request for an advisory opinion is not unfettered.[249] The Court 'must have compelling reasons found in the conviction that the request exceeds the limits of its advisory jurisdiction under the Convention before it may refrain from complying with a request for an opinion'.[250] Similarly, the International Court of Justice has stated that '[a] reply to a request for an Opinion should not, in principle, be refused'.[251] If, however, after considering the circumstances of a request, the Inter-American Court decides that there are compelling reasons to decline to consider an advisory request, it must still issue a statement that includes an explanation of its reasons for the refusal.[252]

Discretion to exercise advisory jurisdiction over a case in dispute between two States or between a State and an international organization

Historically there has been controversy as to whether international courts can or should consider advisory opinion requests that concern issues in dispute between States or between a State and an international organization. States object that an international tribunal's exercise of advisory jurisdiction in those instances can serve to evade the principle of State consent to the adjudication of a legal dispute.[253] The State concerned may argue that the 'advisory opinion is a disguised contentious case and that it should be heard only if all the parties have accepted the tribunal's contentious jurisdiction'.[254]

246 Advisory Opinion OC-12/91, para. 30. 247 *Ibid.*

248 *Ibid.*, para. 28. 249 Advisory Opinion OC-1/82, para. 30. 250 *Ibid.*

251 *Reservations to the Convention on the Prevention and Punishment of the Crime of Genocide*, 1951 ICJ Reports 15, at 19 (28 May).

252 Advisory Opinion OC-1/82, paras. 30 and 31. 253 *Ibid.*, para. 23.

254 Buergenthal, 'The Advisory Practice of the Inter-American Human Rights Court', at 8.

The Inter-American Court has categorically rejected the argument that it should decline to render an advisory opinion simply because the request is based on an underlying case that is in dispute between States.[255] In *The Right to Information on Consular Assistance*, the United States alleged that Mexico had submitted a 'contentious case in the guise of a request for an advisory opinion'.[256] The United States argued that the request was 'an attempt to subject the United States to the contentious jurisdiction of the Court' even though the US had not ratified the American Convention nor accepted the Court's contentious jurisdiction.[257] The basis of the underlying dispute was an acrimonious controversy between the United States and several other States, including Mexico, concerning the failure of US authorities to advise foreign detainees that they had the right to contact their consulates in accordance with the Vienna Convention on Consular Relations.[258] Some of the foreign citizens arrested had been tried without the assistance of their consulate and had been sentenced to death. In its request for the advisory opinion, Mexico described six specific cases involving its nationals who had received the death penalty in the United States without being advised of their right to communicate with Mexican consular authorities.[259] Other States had brought cases in US courts alleging that their nationals were not informed of their right to contact their national consulate as provided for in the Vienna Convention.[260] The Inter-American Court rejected the arguments of the United States, and held that it could examine the subject matter of the request without ruling on the underlying contentious cases.[261]

The Court will also entertain a request for an advisory opinion when the dispute is between a State and an international organization, such as the Inter-American Commission.[262] States have argued that the Court should not consider a request for an advisory opinion from the Commission concerning a disputed case.[263] Many of the Commission's activities, including its authority to conduct country studies of human rights violations in any

[255] Advisory Opinion OC-15/97, para. 40; Advisory Opinion OC-16/99, para. 50; and Advisory Opinion OC-3/83, para. 13.
[256] Advisory Opinion OC-16/99, para. 26. [257] *Ibid.* [258] *Ibid.*, para. 46.
[259] *Ibid.*, para. 46. See generally Jordan J. Paust, 'Breard and Treaty-Based Rights Under the Consular Convention', 92 *American Journal of International Law*, 691 (1998); Erik G. Luna and Douglas J. Sylvester, 'Beyond Breard', 17 *Berkeley Journal of International Law*, 147 (1999).
[260] See generally *Federal Republic of Germany* v. *United States*, 526 US 111 (1999); *Republic of Paraguay* v. *Allen*, 134 F 3d 622 (4th Cir.).
[261] Advisory Opinion OC-16/99, para. 50.
[262] Advisory Opinion OC-3/83, para. 13. [263] *Ibid.*, para. 30.

Member State of the OAS or to process individual petitions alleging State human rights abuses, may result in disputes with States over the proper interpretation of a treaty provision concerning human rights. In *Restrictions to the Death Penalty*, the Court ruled that the Inter-American Commission is not barred from seeking an advisory opinion from the Court 'merely because one or more governments are involved in a controversy with the Commission'.[264] The Commission's request in that instance dealt with the effect and scope of reservations to the American Convention's right to life.[265] Guatemala challenged the Court's jurisdiction by essentially alleging that the Commission's request was a veiled contentious case which the Court could not consider because Guatemala had not accepted the Court's jurisdiction.[266] The Court clarified that 'the mere fact that there exists a dispute' between the Commission and the State Party regarding the meaning of a provision of the Convention would not justify the Court in declining to exercise its advisory jurisdiction.[267] The Court reasoned that the Commission, as an organ of the OAS, had the right to ask the Court to resolve disputed legal issues that arise within the performance of its Convention-mandated activities.[268] The Court also pointed out that, if it would not consider advisory opinion requests when one or more States were involved in a controversy with an international organization, it would not be able to consider advisory opinion requests from the OAS General Assembly regarding draft resolutions calling upon Member States to fulfil their international human rights obligations.[269]

The Court also refused to dismiss an advisory opinion request in the opposite situation, when the Commission complained that the State was submitting a disguised contentious case.[270] The Court explained that its decision to render an advisory opinion was 'in full conformity with the international jurisprudence on the subject, which has repeatedly rejected any request that it refrain from exercising its advisory jurisdiction in situations in which it is claimed that, because the matter is in dispute, the Court is being asked to rule on a disguised contentious case'.[271] The Court

264 *Ibid.*, para. 13. 265 *Ibid.*, para. 8. 266 *Ibid.*, para. 11. 267 *Ibid.*
268 *Ibid.*, para. 39. 269 *Ibid.*, para. 38 270 Advisory Opinion OC-15/97, para. 22(c).
271 *Ibid.*, para. 40. The Court cited *Interpretation of Peace Treaties with Bulgaria, Hungary and Romania*, Advisory Opinion, 1950 ICJ Reports 65; *Reservations to the Convention on the Prevention and Punishment of the Crime of Genocide*, 1951 ICJ Reports 15, at 65 (28 May); *Legal Consequences for States of the Continued Presence of South Africa in Namibia (South West Africa) Notwithstanding Security Council Resolution 276 (1970)*, 1971 ICJ Reports 16 (21 June); *Western Sahara*, 1975 ICJ Reports 12 (16 October); *Applicability of Article VI, Section 22, of the Convention on Privileges and Immunities of the United Nations*, Advisory Opinion, 1989 ICJ Reports 177.

relied on the ICJ's advisory opinion in *Interpretation of Peace Treaties* in which the ICJ rendered an advisory opinion despite States' objections that the ICJ could not render the requested opinion 'without violating the well-established principle of international law according to which no judicial proceedings relating to a legal question pending between States can take place without their consent'.[272] The ICJ responded that the consent of States to the Court's jurisdiction is a requirement only in contentious cases but not in advisory proceedings.[273]

In actuality, international authority, although favouring the acceptance of a request over matters in dispute, is not unanimous. The Permanent Court of International Justice, the forerunner to the ICJ, refused to exercise its advisory jurisdiction when a related argument was made in the *Eastern Caralia Opinion*.[274] The European Court of Human Rights, which has an extremely limited advisory jurisdiction, does not have authority to consider a case in dispute.[275] Even leading commentators who advocate broadening the scope of the European Court's jurisdiction do so with the caveat that 'the request must not directly relate to a dispute which is pending before the Commission or the Court'.[276]

In accepting requests based on underlying disputes, the Court has analyzed and rejected the arguments supporting the objections. One argument put forward is that advisory proceedings are summary in nature and, therefore, are not suitable to decide complex factual issues in dispute.[277] States contend that, because there is no provision for the introduction or examination of evidence, the Court cannot resolve the factual contentions necessary to the analysis of the advisory opinion request.[278] The Inter-American Court agreed, in principle, that the Court may not rule on charges against a State or on the alleged supporting evidence, because to do so would deny the State the opportunities provided in a contentious proceeding to establish its defence.[279] The Court observed, however, that in the exercise of its advisory jurisdiction, there is no need for it to settle questions of fact; rather, the Court is only called upon to interpret the meaning, object and purpose of international human rights norms.[280] Although the Court can interpret a provision of the Convention that is at issue in a disputed case, it is not authorized to examine the case itself.[281]

272 *Interpretation of Peace Treaties with Bulgaria, Hungary and Romania*, Advisory Opinion, 1950 ICJ Reports 65, 71 (30 March 1950).

273 *Ibid.* 274 *Eastern Caralia Opinion*, 1923 PCIJ, Ser. B. No. 5.

275 European Convention for the Protection of Human Rights, Art. 47.

276 Van Dijk and van Hoof, *Theory and Practice*, at 265.

277 Advisory Opinion OC-16/99, para. 27. 278 *Ibid.* 279 *Ibid.*, para. 47.

280 *Ibid.*, para. 52. 281 Advisory Opinion OC-15/97, para. 33.

Therefore, to avoid reaching a conclusion that could distort the Convention system by eliminating the victims' opportunity to participate in contentious proceedings, the Court is 'particularly careful' when exercising its advisory jurisdiction on matters based on an underlying specific case.[282]

Another argument put forward by States is that, when the underlying facts are based on a case in dispute, the international tribunal cannot or should not render an advisory opinion, because the request may be politically motivated. In such instances, the ICJ has held that any alleged political motivation for an advisory opinion request and any eventual 'political implications' of the advisory opinion are irrelevant to the Court's determination of its competence to render the advisory opinion.[283] The Inter-American Court, if confronted by a similar argument, should adopt the ICJ's well-founded position.

Discretion to exercise advisory jurisdiction over a dispute that is before another international body

The Inter-American Court is likely to exercise its discretion to render an advisory opinion even though the core issue of the request is under consideration by another international tribunal such as the ICJ.[284] States argue against the Court's acceptance of jurisdiction in such cases contending that there is a risk that there will be inconsistency between the findings of the tribunals.[285] This situation could occur, for example, if the Inter-American Court exercises its advisory jurisdiction to interpret a treaty concerning human rights that was not propagated in the Inter-American system. The Inter-American Court dismissed this argument, stating that:

> the possibility of conflicting interpretations is a phenomenon common to all those legal systems that have certain courts which are not hierarchically integrated. Such courts have jurisdiction to apply and, consequently, interpret the same body of law. Here it is, therefore, not unusual to find that on certain occasions courts reach conflicting or at the very least different conclusions in interpreting the same rule of law.[286]

[282] *Ibid.*, para. 37, citing and quoting Advisory Opinion OC-12/91, para. 28.
[283] *Legality of the Use by a State of Nuclear Weapons in Armed Conflict*, 1996 ICJ Reports 66, at 73–4 (8 July).
[284] Advisory Opinion OC-16/99, para. 57.
[285] *Ibid.*, paras. 26 and 27. [286] *Ibid.*, para. 61.

States further contend that for reasons of comity the Inter-American Court should refrain from exercising its advisory jurisdiction when the case is before another international tribunal. In *The Right to Information on Consular Assistance*, the United States argued that prudence and comity were compelling reasons to decline jurisdiction in view of the contentious cases brought by Paraguay and Germany against the United States before the ICJ.[287] The issues and subject matter of those cases were similar to many of the central issues raised in the request for an advisory opinion before the Inter-American Court. The Court dismissed that argument and chose to exercise its advisory jurisdiction.[288]

Also, certain globally ratified treaties specify the international mechanism that shall be employed to settle disputes between States Parties to the treaty. States may object to the consideration of a request by a tribunal, such as the Inter-American Court, when resort to that tribunal is not included as an option for dispute settlement under the treaty. In *The Right to Information on Consular Assistance*, the Inter-American Court rejected the United States' argument that disputes concerning the Vienna Convention on Consular Relations could be settled only by the Convention's specified means of conciliation, arbitration or referral to the ICJ.[289] The ICJ also rejected this argument in its advisory opinion on *Reservations to the Convention on the Prevention and Punishment of the Crime of Genocide*.[290] Buergenthal subsequently argued that the Inter-American Court should have limited its holding to an interpretation of the provision within the context of the Inter-American system.[291] He argued that the legitimacy of international judicial pronouncements could be jeopardized unless regional courts adopt a policy of judicial deference.[292] If, however, tribunals 'stay within their respective spheres of competence, apply traditional international legal reasoning, show judicial restraint by seeking to avoid unnecessary conflicts, and remain open to reconsider their prior legal pronouncements', there should be less risk of major conflict.[293]

Court procedures applicable to an advisory opinion request

The Inter-American Court's liberalization of the procedures applicable to an advisory opinion proceeding has also contributed to the evolution

287 *Ibid.*, para. 27. 288 *Ibid.* 289 *Ibid.*, para. 26.

290 1951 ICJ Reports 15, at 20 (28 May).

291 Thomas Buergenthal, 'Proliferation of International Courts and Tribunals: Is it Good or Bad?', 14 *Leiden Journal of International Law*, 267, 273 (2001).

292 *Ibid.*, at 272. 293 *Ibid.*, at 273.

of international human rights law. Through a broad interpretation of its Rules of Procedure and subsequent amendments to those Rules, the Court has enhanced the role of individuals and *amici* without sacrificing the Convention's structure or procedural equality between the alleged victims and the States Parties.[294]

The procedures followed by the Inter-American Court in the consideration of an advisory request generally track the procedures it follows in contentious proceedings. The Rules of Procedure of the Court specify that the procedural rules for contentious cases shall be applied by analogy in advisory proceedings to the extent that the Court finds them compatible.[295] Thus, the Court has broad discretion to determine to what extent the specific circumstances of an advisory request lead to the analogous application of contentious procedures.[296] Advisory opinions are considered by the full Court. Unlike contentious proceedings, however, neither the American Convention nor the Rules of Procedure of the Court provide for an *ad hoc* judge during advisory proceedings. As in contentious cases, advisory proceedings are generally divided into a written phase and an oral phase, although the Court may decide to dispense with the oral phase.[297]

The Inter-American Court should provide an expedited procedure for time-sensitive advisory opinion requests. At present the Court's Rules lack a provision, akin to that in the ICJ Rules, to provide for expedited procedures when a request for an advisory opinion necessitates an urgent answer.[298] Under the Rules of the ICJ, when the requesting party 'informs the Court that its request necessitates an urgent answer, or the Court finds that an early answer would be desirable, the Court shall take all necessary steps to accelerate the procedure, and it shall convene as early as possible for the purpose of proceeding to a hearing and deliberation on the request'.[299] To date, the Inter-American Court has considered at least two advisory opinion requests that were time-sensitive and would have benefited from expedited proceedings. In *Restrictions to the Death Penalty*, the underlying fact situation involved the execution of prisoners who had been

[294] Statute of the Inter-Am. Court, Art. 25(1).

[295] 2001 Rules of Procedure of the Inter-Am. Ct HR, Art. 63. See also Statute of the ICJ, Art. 68, for a similar provision.

[296] Advisory Opinion OC-4/84, para. 17.

[297] 2001 Rules of Procedure of the Inter-Am. Ct HR, Art. 62(4). 'Prior consultation with the Agent is required in cases governed by Article 64(2) of the Convention.' *Ibid.*

[298] See International Court of Justice, Rules of Court, Adopted on 14 April 1978, amended on 5 December 2000, Art. 103.

[299] *Ibid.*

tried by 'faceless courts' in accordance with a law that reinstituted the death penalty in Guatemala in violation of the American Convention.[300] Also, in *The Right to Information on Consular Assistance*, the Court's opinion applied to the legitimacy of the application of the death penalty to certain foreign prisoners on death row in the United States.[301] When lives are at stake, a rapid response is necessary. Although the Inter-American Court attempts to deliver advisory opinions in a timely fashion, the process is still lengthy. The average duration of an advisory proceeding before the Court has been approximately ten months.[302] The proceedings may take longer. For example, the request for an advisory opinion in *The Right to Information on Consular Assistance* was filed on 9 December 1997 and the Court's advisory opinion was not issued until almost two years later on 1 October 1999.[303]

The Court could incorporate a provision in its Rules of Procedure to expedite consideration of advisory requests when the circumstances so require. The amended Rules could provide that the State or organ requesting the expedited review inform the Court of the need to accelerate the opinion and the reasons therefor. If the Court is not in session, the President of the Court could have the discretion to determine if an expedited opinion is necessary under the specified circumstances. If such a finding is made, the President could be authorized to determine the extent of the accelerated proceedings, including whether written briefs would be necessary. In all likelihood, written briefs would be necessary as the Court cannot make an informed decision without the availability of adequate information. Rosenne, in reference to the ICJ, opines that the issuance of an advisory opinion without written briefs would be a 'questionable development' in that it would accentuate the summary character of the advisory decision and severely reduce the Court's authority.[304] Time periods for the submission of written observations in such cases should be kept to a minimum. If adequate information is made available to the Court through written briefs and documents, the Rules could allow the Court the discretion to dispense with the oral proceedings. To protect

[300] See Charles Moyer and David Padilla, 'Executions in Guatemala as Decreed by the Courts of Special Jurisdiction in 1982–83: A Case Study', 6 *Human Rights Quarterly*, 507 (1984).

[301] Advisory Opinion OC-16/99, para. 2.

[302] Report prepared by the Office of the Secretary General of the Organization of American States for the Ad Hoc Working Group on Human Rights, created by the Foreign Ministers meeting of 22 November 1999, *Financing the Inter-American Human Rights System*, 11 (28 April 2000).

[303] Advisory Opinion OC-16/99, para. 1 and opinion title.

[304] Rosenne, *The Law and Practice of the International Court*, vol. III at 1719.

the legitimacy of the Court, this step should be taken with caution, as the transparency of the Court's proceedings are of as much importance as their expeditiousness. Moreover, dispensing with oral proceedings may not necessarily accelerate the process, since the Court still must convene for deliberations on the request. Oral proceedings could be held during the same special session of the Court.

Requirements of the request

A formal request for an advisory opinion is necessary to initiate advisory proceedings. The Convention-mandated contents of a request depend to some extent on the type of question raised and whether it falls under Article 64(1) or (2) of the American Convention. The Court Rules provide that a request for interpretation of the Convention under Article 64(1) must state the questions on which the Court's opinion is being sought, the provisions of the American Convention to be interpreted, the considerations that gave rise to the request and the names and addresses of the State's Agent as the Commission's Delegates.[305] Moreover, if the advisory opinion request is made by an OAS organ, the request must also explain how the request relates to the sphere of competence of the requesting organ.[306] If the request is for the interpretation of a treaty other than the American Convention, it must also specify: (1) the title of the treaty; (2) the parties to the treaty; (3) the specific questions being put to the Court; and (4) the considerations which gave rise to the request.[307] A State's request for an advisory opinion on the compatibility of its domestic laws under Article 64(2) must specify the applicable domestic law provisions and list the pertinent provisions of the American Convention or other treaties to which the request relates.[308] It must also be accompanied by a copy of the law in question[309] and must set out the specific questions to be answered by the Court.[310]

Admissibility

A request for an advisory opinion is admissible if it is submitted by an entity authorized by the Convention (jurisdiction *ratione personae*), falls within the subject matter jurisdiction of the Court (jurisdiction *ratione materiae*), and contains the information required by the Convention. The

[305] 2001 Rules of Procedure of the Inter-Am. Ct HR, Art. 59(1) and (2).
[306] *Ibid.*, Art. 59(3). [307] *Ibid.*, Art. 60. [308] *Ibid.*, Art. 61(1)(a).
[309] *Ibid.*, Art. 61(2). [310] *Ibid.*, Art. 61(1)(b).

Court specified that, when a request seeks an interpretation of the American Convention, it fulfils the requisites of admissibility.[311] In *Interpretation of the American Declaration of the Rights and Duties of Man*, the admissibility of the request was at issue, because the American Declaration is not a treaty within the meaning of Article 64(1).[312] The Court determined, however, that the question of the legal status of the American Declaration went to the merits of the request rather than to its admissibility, because, even if the Court concluded that the Declaration was not a treaty within the context of Article 64(1) of the American Convention, the decision would be based on an interpretation of the American Convention rather than the Declaration.[313] The Court clarified that:

> [t]he mere fact, however, that the interpretation of the Convention or other treaties concerning human rights might require the Court to analyze international instruments which may or may not be treaties *strictu sensu* does not mean that the request for an advisory opinion is inadmissible, provided that the context is the interpretation of the instruments mentioned in Article 64(1) of the Convention.[314]

The Court's holding respected the voluntary nature of the State's treaty obligations but did not extend them.

Notification of the submission

When the Court receives a request for an advisory opinion, the Court's Rules require that the Secretary transmit the request to all OAS Member States, the OAS Secretary General and Permanent Council, the Inter-American Commission, and the OAS organs whose spheres of competence include the subject matter of the request.[315] In practice, the Court also transmits the request to all the Chapter VIII organs of the OAS Charter through the Secretary General of the OAS. By having the request transmitted to all OAS organs, the Court avoids making a determination as to which organs are entitled to a copy of the request in a particular case.

Initially, the Rules of the Court did not require that the Court notify OAS Member States and organs when a State requested an advisory opinion on the compatibility of its domestic laws with international human rights treaties.[316] This difference was apparently based on the assumption that only the requesting State could be interested in the issues raised.

311 Advisory Opinion OC-10/89, para. 24. 312 *Ibid.*, para. 12. 313 *Ibid.*, para. 26.
314 *Ibid.*, para. 25. 315 2001 Rules of Procedure of the Inter-Am. Ct HR, Art. 62(1).
316 See Advisory Opinion OC-4/84, para. 17.

Buergenthal pointed out, however, that the function of the Court in Article 64(2) proceedings was not to interpret the domestic law of the State but rather to interpret the Convention or other human rights treaties, which could be of interest to other States and organs.[317] Consequently, the Court's Rules now require full notification of all requests for advisory opinions.[318] Non-governmental organizations and individuals generally learn of requests for advisory opinions through Court-issued press releases, which are also transmitted by fax and e-mail to interested persons.

Written proceedings

The written proceedings commence when the President of the Court sets a deadline for the submission of briefs and supporting documents.[319] With one exception, the President is authorized to invite any interested party to submit a written brief on the relevant issues.[320] The Court has explained that '[t]he legitimate interests that any Member State has in the outcome of an advisory proceeding are protected by the opportunity it is given to participate fully in those proceedings and to make known to the Court its views on the legal norms to be interpreted'.[321] The exception arises when a State asks the Court for an advisory opinion on the compatibility of its laws under Article 64(2).[322] In that case, the President must first consult the agent of the State before inviting or authorizing interested parties to file a brief.[323] The Court may find it useful to invite comments from the State's governmental bodies or entities that are or will potentially be affected by the law in question. In *Proposed Amendments to the Naturalization Provisions of the Constitution of Costa Rica*, the Court invited Costa Rican juridical institutions to submit briefs, information or relevant documents on the issue.[324]

The written aspect of the proceedings continues following the public hearing. At that point, the Court forwards the transcript of the hearing

317 Buergenthal, 'The Advisory Practice of the Inter-American Human Rights Court', at 16, n. 65.

318 2001 Rules of Procedure of the Inter-Am. Ct HR, Art. 62(1).

319 *Ibid.*, Art. 62(2).

320 *Ibid.*, Art. 62(3).

321 Advisory Opinion OC-16/99, para. 63; see also Advisory Opinion OC-3/83, para. 24; see Statute of the ICJ, Art. 66.

322 American Convention, Art. 64(2).

323 *Ibid.* See Adalberto José Urbina Briceño, 'La Competencia Consultiva de la Corte Interamericana de Derechos Humanos', 90 *Revista de la Facultad de Ciencias Jurídicas y Políticas, Universidad Central de Venezuela* 355, 404 (1993).

324 Advisory Opinion OC-4/84, para. 4.

to all participants in the hearing and receives final briefs from those who had appeared before the Court.[325]

Amicus *briefs*

Although the Convention and the Statute of the Court do not authorize *amicus* briefs, the Court has amended its Rules to permit parties other than States and OAS organs to submit briefs at the invitation of the President.[326] The practice of the Court is to accept *amicus* briefs from NGOs and even from individuals.[327] An *amicus curiae* is a person or organization that has a strong interest in the subject matter before a court, who, as a 'friend of the court', submits a brief which suggests a rationale for deciding the case that is consistent with its views.[328] '*Amici*, with permission, suggest to a court matters of fact and law within their knowledge.'[329] *Amicus* briefs are often filed by human rights organizations, and as such can be expected to advocate a liberal interpretation of the American Convention.[330] In *The Right to Information on Consular Assistance*, which raised the issue of the right of foreign nationals to contact their consulate when they are charged with capital crimes, *amicus* briefs were filed by twenty-two NGOs and individuals.[331] One such brief was filed on behalf of José Trinidad Loza, a Mexican national, on death row in Ohio, who allegedly had not been given the right to contact the Mexican consulate when he was arrested.[332] Ten major news organizations, including *Newsweek*, the *Wall Street Journal*, the American Newspaper Publishers Association, the Fédération Internationale des Editeurs de Journaux, and the Inter-American Press Association, filed *amicus* briefs in another advisory proceeding, *The Enforceability of the Right to Reply or Correction*, which concerned the State's duty to ensure that newspapers and radio and television stations provide individuals injured by an inaccurate statement with a right to reply.[333] The Court also

[325] Advisory Opinion OC-16/99, paras. 19, 21 and 22.

[326] 2001 Rules of Procedure of the Inter-Am. Ct HR, Art. 62(3). See Charles Moyer, 'The Role of Amicus Curiae in the Inter-American Court of Human Rights', in *La Corte Interamericana de Derechos Humanos: Estudios y Documentos*, 103, 104 (1986).

[327] See generally Dinah Shelton, 'The Participation of Nongovernmental Organizations in International Judicial Proceedings', 88 *American Journal of International Law*, 611, 615 (1994).

[328] See *Black's Law Dictionary*.

[329] Shelton, 'The Participation of Nongovernmental Organizations', at 611.

[330] Moyer, 'The Role of Amicus Curiae in the Inter-American Court', at 105.

[331] Advisory Opinion OC-16/99, para. 62.

[332] *Ibid.*

[333] Advisory Opinion OC-7/86, para. 5.

received several *amicus* briefs from international NGOs in *Restrictions to the Death Penalty*.[334]

The Court's acceptance of *amicus* briefs in advisory proceedings provides NGOs and individuals with a forum to present an alternative viewpoint and thereby influence the development of international law. These organizations are more likely to support the position of the individual, a position that may not receive adequate support in the briefs submitted by States. As such, *amicus* briefs offer valuable assistance to the Court and Commission, which operate with small legal staffs.[335] Shelton reports that, although the Inter-American Court has rarely quoted from or cited *amicus* briefs, there is evidence in the opinions that the Court has relied on the research and analysis provided by them.[336] Although individuals and NGOs are not allowed to request advisory opinions in any international forum, they can influence States or OAS organs to request advisory opinions, and then submit their legal arguments in the form of *amicus* briefs.[337] The Court is not required to accept or consider every *amicus* brief submitted, although there is no formal procedure for the rejection of briefs. The potential for abuse exists in that organizations with a primarily political agenda could attempt to convert the *amicus* process into a forum for their political viewpoints. The Court should use its authority to reject such briefs, insofar as they do not contribute to the Court's understanding of the legitimate legal issues that are before it.

Preliminary objections to an advisory request

States may file preliminary objections to the Court's consideration of an advisory opinion request. Although most preliminary objections arise in the context of contentious proceedings, there have also been objections in advisory proceedings.[338] The State may object that the request is inadmissible, that the Court does not have jurisdiction, or that the Court is not following all the procedural requirements of the treaty. A State could also raise an objection to the composition of the Court to hear an advisory

[334] Advisory Opinion OC-3/83, para. 5.

[335] Moyer, 'The Role of Amicus Curiae in the Inter-American Court of Human Rights', at 113.

[336] Shelton, 'The Participation of Nongovernmental Organizations', at 639.

[337] See Sohn, 'Broadening the Advisory Jurisdiction', at 125, citing the 1971 Report of the Secretary-General summarizing the views of various governments concerning the role of the International Court of Justice, UN Doc. A/8382, paras. 263–305, at 90–101 (1971).

[338] See Advisory Opinion OC-3/83, para. 21.

opinion. The Statute of the Court provides that '[j]udges may not take part in matters in which, in the opinion of the Court, they or members of their family have a direct interest or in which they have previously taken part as agents, counsel or advocates, or as members of a national or international court or an investigatory committee, or in any other capacity'.[339] The use of the term 'matters' rather than 'cases' in the Statute would seem to imply that this provision is applicable not only to contentious but also to advisory proceedings. To date, no objection to the composition of the Court has been raised in the Inter-American system. This objection has been raised in advisory proceedings before the ICJ, which has taken a narrow view of the objections. In the *Namibia Case*, the ICJ rejected South Africa's objection to three judges for reasons of their past participation as governmental representatives to the UN.[340] Moreover, the ICJ rejected objections to judges sitting in cases interpreting texts which they had participated in drafting.[341] The limitations in the Inter-American Court's statute would most likely require that judges recuse themselves in similar circumstances.

During advisory proceedings the Court will consider a preliminary objection to an advisory request in the same phase in which it considers the substance of the request.[342] Guatemala objected to the Court's exercise of jurisdiction in *Restrictions to the Death Penalty* and requested that the Court consider its objection in a separate preliminary proceeding.[343] The Court held that it was unnecessary to hold a separate phase of the proceedings to consider the objection, because the only purpose of advisory proceedings is to provide a judicial interpretation of the relevant treaty.[344] The Court also reasoned that the resulting delay from the separation of the proceedings 'would seriously impair the purpose and utility of the advisory power' of the Court.[345] The practice of the ICJ is in accordance with that of the Inter-American Court in that it has not made a preliminary determination as to the composition or competence of the Court in advisory proceedings.[346]

[339] Statute of the Inter-Am. Court, Art. 19(1).

[340] *Legal Consequences for States of the Continued Presence of South Africa in Namibia (South West Africa) Notwithstanding Security Council Resolution 276 (1970)*, 1971 ICJ Reports 16, para. 9 (21 June).

[341] *Ibid.* [342] Advisory Opinion OC-3/83, para. 22.

[343] *Ibid.* [344] *Ibid.*, para. 22. [345] *Ibid.*, para. 25.

[346] *Legal Consequences for States of the Continued Presence of South Africa in Namibia (South West Africa) Notwithstanding Security Council Resolution 276 (1970)*, 1971 ICJ Reports 16, para. 38 (21 June).

Oral proceedings

At the conclusion of the initial written stage of the proceedings, the Court shall determine whether it will hold oral proceedings.[347] If the Court exercises its discretion to hold oral proceedings, those proceedings must be public, unless exceptional circumstances warrant private hearings.[348] Previous practice indicates the unlikelihood that such exceptional circumstances would be present in advisory proceedings, which are limited to legal questions of interpretation. To date, oral hearings have been held for all seventeen of the advisory requests submitted to the Court. Consequently, the criteria that may be applied by the Court in determining the necessity of oral hearings have not been formalized. From a practical perspective, oral hearings are not necessary in all advisory proceedings, as the proceedings are intended to be non-factual in nature. Absent an underlying dispute which would require greater transparency, the Court should be able to issue advisory opinions, such as those requesting an interpretation of a provision of the American Convention, on the basis of written briefs alone.

The Court has made the statement that under its advisory jurisdiction it 'does not exercise any fact-finding functions; instead, it is called upon to render opinions interpreting legal norms'.[349] This statement may be too broad. There are often factual questions underlying the legal question presented to the Court that could, on occasion, necessitate a limited fact-finding function. Reisman and Levit state that 'the Inter-American Court's advisory mode seems to allow for the submission of cases that have factual components which themselves may be in contention'.[350] The Court at times hears oral testimony and receives documentary evidence during the hearing,[351] and the judges may pose questions to those testifying.[352] The ICJ finds that it 'must also be acquainted with, take into account and, if necessary, make findings as to the relevant factual

347 2001 Rules of Procedure of the Inter-Am. Ct HR, Art. 62(4). 'Prior consultation with the Agent is required in cases governed by Article 64(2) of the Convention.' *Ibid.* If the Court determines that there will be a hearing, it must set a date. *Ibid.*

348 2001 Rules of Procedure of the Inter-Am. Ct HR, Art. 14(1).

349 Advisory Opinion OC-3/83, para. 32, quoting Advisory Opinion OC-1/82, para. 51.

350 Michael Reisman and Janet Koven Levit, 'Fact-Finding Initiatives for the Inter-American Court of Human Rights', in *La Corte y el Sistema Interamericano de Derechos Humanos* 443, 453 (Rafael Nieto Navia ed., 1994).

351 Advisory Opinion OC-16/99, para. 18.

352 See Advisory Opinion OC-10/89, para. 10.

issues'[353] in order to decide on legal questions posed in advisory requests. Although there are no evidentiary rules or burden of proof standards in advisory proceedings before the Inter-American Court, should it be necessary the Court could apply the rules of contentious proceedings by analogy.[354]

Initially, only member States and organs of the OAS were permitted to present oral arguments to the Court.[355] Then, in *Proposed Amendments to the Naturalization Provisions of the Constitution of Costa Rica*, which involved domestic State laws, the Court invited Costa Rican Government officials with a knowledge of the laws in question to testify.[356] Subsequently, in a proceeding also concerning a State's domestic law, *Compulsory Membership in an Association Prescribed by Law for the Practice of Journalism*, the Court invited the Inter-American Press Association and the Colegio de Periodistas of Costa Rica to testify.[357] Although there is no provision in the Rules of the Court authorizing the Court to hear such oral arguments, the Court applies by analogy the rule applicable to contentious proceedings. That rule states that the Court 'may hear as a witness, expert witness, or in any other capacity, any person whose evidence, statement or opinion it deems to be relevant'.[358] Since 1994, the Court has invited all parties that submitted written comments, including NGOs and individuals, to present arguments during the oral proceedings.[359]

The opportunity for NGOs and even individuals to provide input before an international human rights tribunal is significant. Although the participation of these bodies through *amicus* briefs has been permitted in certain international tribunals, the occasion to present oral arguments is a breakthrough. This step increases opportunities for nongovernmental actors to influence the development of international law, and it further erodes the exclusive role of States. It is neither possible nor desirable, however, for every organization or individual that submits a brief to also present an oral argument before the Court. These briefs have

[353] *Legal Consequences for States of the Continued Presence of South Africa in Namibia (South West Africa) Notwithstanding Security Council Resolution 276 (1970)*, 1971 ICJ Reports 16, para. 40 (21 June).

[354] Advisory Opinion OC-15/97, para. 19, citing *Western Sahara*, 1975 ICJ Reports 12, at 18–42 and 26–9 (16 October).

[355] See Advisory Opinion OC-3/83, para. 6.

[356] Advisory Opinion OC-4/84, para. 5.

[357] Advisory Opinion OC-5/85, para. 7. The Court invited the organizations to make presentations at the public hearing only after consultation with the Government of Costa Rica. *Ibid.*

[358] 2001 Rules of Procedure of the Inter-Am. Ct HR, Art. 44(1).

[359] See Advisory Opinion OC-16/99, para. 8; Advisory Opinion OC-14/94, para. 10.

increased in number, and accommodating the corresponding oral arguments has the potential to overwhelm the resources of the Court. While States Parties and OAS organs have automatic access to address the Court, other participants should only have that opportunity when invited by the Court to address a particular argument raised in the brief. Moreover, time limits should be placed on the presentations in order to expedite the proceeding.

Content, delivery and publication of advisory opinions

An advisory opinion must contain: (a) the names of the President, the judges who rendered the opinion, the Secretary, and Deputy Secretary; (b) the issues presented to the Court; (c) a description of the various steps in the proceedings; (d) the legal arguments; (e) the opinion of the Court; and (f) a statement indicating which text is authentic.[360] Any judge who was involved in the delivery of the advisory opinion is authorized to attach an individual dissenting or concurring opinion to the Court's opinion.[361] The Court's Rules of Procedure require that in matters to be voted upon '[e]ach judge shall vote either in the affirmative or the negative'.[362] The Rules further mandate that no judge can abstain from a vote on an advisory opinion.[363] In its advisory opinion on the *Enforceability of the Right to Reply or Correction*, those judges who dissented from the majority holding that the request was admissible opined that they should then have been allowed to abstain from addressing the merits of the question.[364] However, in light of that provision, they voted affirmatively on the merits.[365]

In the interest of 'economic and procedural efficiency', the Court reformed its Rules of Procedure to eliminate the practice of reading its advisory decisions and judgments in open court.[366] Initially, advisory opinions were delivered at a separate public hearing at the seat of the Court. Advisory opinions are now delivered to the requesting party, the operative points are disseminated in a press release, the entire opinion is posted on the Court's web page, and the opinions are subsequently published in the Court's annual report and in Series A of the Court's opinions.

[360] 2001 Rules of Procedure of the Inter-Am. Ct HR, Art. 64(2).
[361] *Ibid.*, Art. 64(3). [362] *Ibid.*, Art. 15(1). [363] *Ibid.*
[364] Advisory Opinion OC-7/86, para. 17(A) and para. 2.
[365] *Ibid.*, para. 17(B) and para. 3.
[366] 1998 Annual Report of the Inter-American Court, OAS/Ser.L/V/III.43 doc. 11, 18 January 1999 at 14.

Conclusion

In summary, the Inter-American Court of Human Rights currently has the broadest advisory jurisdiction of any international tribunal. The Court has exercised this jurisdiction to make important conceptual contributions to international human rights law. Its advisory opinions have contributed to the emergence of international human rights law from the traditional principles of public international law that govern relations between States. An advisory opinion, a vehicle much less confrontational than a contentious case and not limited to the specific facts placed in evidence, serves to give judicial expression to the underlying principles of the law.

The Court also contributes to the evolution of human rights law through the procedures it applies in advisory proceedings. The Court accepts *amicus* briefs submitted by NGOs and individuals. Although *amicus* briefs increase the Court's workload, they provide a public interest perspective that otherwise might be under-represented in the proceedings. In later proceedings, the Court has also allowed the *amici* to make oral presentations to the Court during the public hearings. Thus, through the broad interpretation of its Rules of Procedure and subsequent amendments thereto, the Inter-American Court has enhanced the role of individuals and *amici* in advisory proceedings without sacrificing the Convention structure and procedural equality essential to States Parties.

Through its advisory jurisdiction the Court has contributed to the uniformity and consistency of the interpretation of the substantive and procedural provisions of the American Convention and other human rights treaties. It has also given its judicial imprimatur to foundational yet disputed concepts of human rights law, including the non-reciprocal character of human rights treaties, non-discrimination, the incompatibility of reservations to non-derogable rights, democracy as the basis for human rights, and the universal nature of human rights. Thus, the Inter-American Court's advisory opinions provide a forum from which the Court influences important fundamental doctrinal principles and questions in the evolving law governing international human rights

PART II

The contentious jurisdiction of the Inter-American Court of Human Rights

3

Preliminary objections: legitimate issues and illegitimate tactics

> [A State] has the right to resort to every legitimate judicial remedy and procedure to defend itself against charges that it has violated the treaty. What it may not do is interpose manifestly ill-founded and trivial motions whose sole purpose can only be to disrupt and delay the orderly and timely completion of the proceedings.[1]

Preliminary objections: an overview

A preliminary objection is an objection to a tribunal's consideration of a case. When a party submits a case to a tribunal, the respondent may make legal objections to the Court's authority to act. The respondent may object that the case was initially inadmissible, that the enforcement organs did not have jurisdiction, or that the enforcement organs did not follow all the procedural or technical requirements of the treaty. As articulated by the International Court of Justice, 'the object of a preliminary objection is to avoid not merely a decision on, but even any discussion of the merits'.[2] Before an international tribunal can consider whether the State has violated substantive provisions it must first rule on any preliminary objections. If certain of these objections are admitted by the Court, it may result in the dismissal of an otherwise factually verifiable case. Rosenne lamented the English use of the term 'preliminary objection' rather than 'preliminary question' because he believed that it resulted in unnecessary difficulties:

[1] *Neira Alegría et al.* v. *Peru* (Requests for Revision and Interpretation of Judgment of 11 December 1991 on Preliminary Objections), Inter-Am. Ct HR, Order of 3 July 1992, Declaration by Judge Thomas Buergenthal, 1992 Annual Report of the Inter-Am. Ct HR 75, 85, OAS/Ser.L/V/III.27.

[2] *Barcelona Traction, Light and Power Company, Limited (New Application: 1962) (Belgium* v. *Spain)*, 1964 ICJ Reports 6, 44 (Preliminary Objections Judgment of 24 July).

> It is to be regretted that the English language has to use the word 'objection' and not 'question'; it incorporates misleading overtones absent from the corresponding French term *exception*, redolent of the exceptiones of Roman law. It is possible that much of the political difficulty recently experienced over preliminary objections can trace its origin to this.[3]

Preliminary objections exist not only in international law but also in domestic common law and civil law systems. In Latin American civil law codes, preliminary objections are called *excepciónes preliminares* and may be designated as *excepciónes de previo* and *excepciónes de especial pronunciamiento.*[4] In the United States, a preliminary objection is a 'motion to dismiss'.[5] Preliminary objections have often played an important role in international adjudications. In *Military and Paramilitary Activities in and Against Nicaragua* before the ICJ, in which Nicaragua charged the US with mining its harbours in contravention of international law, the US raised preliminary objections.[6] When the Court dismissed those objections, the United States withdrew from the case[7] and then withdrew its acceptance of the compulsory jurisdiction of the Court.[8]

States Parties to human rights treaties consider the option to interpose preliminary objections essential to their sovereignty. Under international law, States are obligated to submit to rulings of international tribunals only if they have consented to do so.[9] When a State ratifies an international treaty, it relinquishes its traditional sovereignty over the subject matter of the treaty, but only to the extent provided by the treaty.[10] If the treaty has an enforcement organ such as an international court, the State submits

[3] Shabtai Rosenne, *Procedure in the International Court: A Commentary on the 1978 Rules of the International Court of Justice*, 159 (Nijhoff, Kluwer, The Hague, 1983).

[4] See Juan Carlos Hitters, *Derecho Internacional de Los Derechos Humanos*, Vol. II, at 490 (Ediar Sociedad Anonima Editora, Buenos Aires, 1991–3).

[5] See US Federal Rules of Civil Procedure, Rule 12.

[6] Preliminary Objections, 1984 ICJ Reports 392 (26 November), reprinted in 24 ILM 59 (1985).

[7] Statement by Department of State on US Withdrawal from Nicaragua Proceedings, 18 January 1985, in 'Contemporary Practice of the United States', 79 *American Journal of International Law*, reprinted in 24 ILM 1743 (1985).

[8] United States: Department of State, Letter and Statement Concerning Termination of Acceptance of ICJ Compulsory Jurisdiction, 7 October 1985, reprinted in 24 ILM 1742 (1985).

[9] See Edward McWhinney, *Judicial Settlement of International Disputes: Jurisdiction, Justiciability and Judicial Law-Making on the Contemporary International Court*, 58 (Nijhoff, 1991)

[10] See generally Paul Sieghart, *The International Law of Human Rights*, 11 (Oxford, 1983); Ian Brownlie, *Principles of Public International Law*, 289–99 (5th edn, Oxford, 1998).

to that court's jurisdiction only if it explicitly agrees to do so, either by ratifying the treaty or by taking any additional measure required by the treaty. Thus, States may refuse to allow their conduct to be scrutinized by an international tribunal unless they have conferred jurisdiction on the tribunal.

The treaty also specifies the procedures that shall be followed by the court or any other enforcement organ in the exercise of its jurisdiction. The enforcement organ must comply strictly with all treaty-mandated procedures or the State may file preliminary objections. Therefore, before the Inter-American Court can consider whether the State has violated substantive issues it must first rule on any preliminary objections.

A State has a legal right to interpose preliminary objections provided that it does not abuse the 'due course of justice'.[11] Preliminary objections have an important role in the operation of a legal system in that: (1) they enable a court to dismiss an untenable application early in the proceeding; (2) they contribute to the clarification of individual cases and to the adequate functioning of the legal system; (3) they positively influence the care exercised by complainants and enforcement organs in following statutorily mandated procedures; and (4) they encourage States to accept the jurisdiction of enforcement organs. An applicant before the ICJ once asked the Court 'to adjudge and declare that [the respondent] had abused its right to raise preliminary objections'.[12] The Court refused, explaining that 'such objections as are raised by the Respondent may be useful to clarify the legal situation'.[13]

Preliminary objections may be misused, however. By ratifying a treaty, a State submits itself to the 'legal order' established by the treaty and is expected to uphold the object and purpose of the treaty.[14] In the case of human rights treaties, that object and purpose is 'the protection of the basic rights of individual human beings'.[15] Although there is a valid basis for many objections, others seem to be filed primarily as a delaying tactic. An example of such tactics occurred in the *Neira Alegría Case*, in which Peru not only raised several groundless preliminary objections which the

[11] Shabtai Rosenne, *The Law and Practice of the International Court, 1920–1996*, 446 (3rd edn, Nijhoff, The Hague and Boston, 1997).

[12] *Application of the Convention on the Prevention and Punishment of the Crime of Genocide (Bosnia and Herzegovina* v. *Yugoslavia)*, 1996 ICJ Reports 803, at 609 (11 July).

[13] *Ibid.*, at 622.

[14] *The Effect of Reservations on the Entry into Force of the American Convention on Human Rights (Arts. 74 and 75)*, Inter-Am. Ct HR, Advisory Opinion OC-2/82 of 24 September 1982, Ser. A, No. 2, para. 29.

[15] *Ibid.*

Court dismissed, but then also requested a revision and interpretation of the Court's rejection of those objections.[16] Judge Buergenthal, in his final opinion after twelve years on the Court, wrote a scathing reproach of the use of trivial tactics meant to delay or disrupt a timely decision on the merits.[17] He counselled that:

> Such tactics violate the object and purpose of the human rights machinery established by the Convention. They can also not be reconciled with the intention of the States Parties to the Convention, reaffirmed in paragraph one of its Preamble, 'to consolidate in this hemisphere, within the framework of democratic institutions, a system of personal liberty and social justice based on respect for the essential rights of man'.[18]

In the *Loayza Tamayo Case*, Peru filed a motion requesting the nullification of the Court's decision rejecting its preliminary objection. The Court rejected the motion, admonishing that the filing of motions that 'are flagrantly out of order slows down the speed with which justice should be imparted in the field of human rights'. The Court went on to state that 'it is the opinion of this Court that parties to human rights cases have a duty to refrain from making applications of this nature'.[19] States have also filed conflicting preliminary objections. In the *Cantoral Benavides Case*, in which the victim was first tried and acquitted in the military courts and then tried and convicted in the civilian courts, Peru argued that the domestic proceedings in Peru had never been exhausted by the complainants, and conversely that the complainants filed their petition with the Commission more than six months after the final judgment, which exhausted domestic remedies, was rendered in the domestic proceedings.[20]

An international tribunal is unlikely to go further than an occasional admonishment of a State for the misuse of preliminary objections. Unlike municipal law, wherein the respondent is a private party and the likely culprit is an overzealous lawyer, in the case of international tribunals, the party most likely to raise objections is a sovereign State.

The Inter-American Court can and has, however, through its jurisprudence and the amendment of its Rules of Procedure, eliminated the bases for several objections that do not contribute to procedural fairness or

[16] *Neira Alegría et al.* v. *Peru* (Request for Revision and Interpretation), 1992 Annual Report of the Inter-Am. Ct HR, at 75, OAS/Ser.L/V/III.27.

[17] *Ibid.*, Declaration by Judge Thomas Buergenthal. [18] *Ibid.*

[19] Inter-Am. Ct HR, Order of 27 June 1996, OAS/Ser.L/V/III.35, doc. 4, para. 9.

[20] *Cantoral Benavides* v. *Peru* (Preliminary Objections), Inter-Am. Ct HR, 3 September 1998, Ser. C, No. 40, para. 15.

clarification of the legal situation. Beyond that, when ruling on preliminary objections the Court has stated that it 'must preserve a fair balance between the protection of human rights, which is the ultimate purpose of the system, and the legal certainty and procedural equity that will ensure the stability and reliability of the international protection mechanism'.[21]

Preliminary objections to jurisdiction

Parties often interpose preliminary objections challenging some aspect of the jurisdiction of an international court. Jurisdiction is the legal authority of a court to consider matters brought before it. Essentially the jurisdiction of the court is a condition precedent to the court's decision on the substantive legal issues in the case. Successful objections to the jurisdiction of the tribunal may terminate 'all proceedings in the case, since they strike at the competence of the tribunal to give rulings as to the merits or admissibility of the claim'.[22]

The scope of the court's jurisdiction is determined by the treaty under which the court is established. A treaty establishing a permanent court to oversee compliance with its provisions may make jurisdiction of the court over all ratifying parties obligatory *strictu senso*. In such a case, a ratifying State subjects itself *ipso facto* to the court's jurisdiction simply by ratifying the treaty. Alternatively, the treaty may make acceptance of the jurisdiction of the court optional. Then an additional act of recognition of the jurisdiction of the court, as specified in the governing instrument, is required of the State. In such a case, the State may make a conditional or unconditional declaration recognizing the court's jurisdiction. State conditions usually go to jurisdiction *ratione materiae*, *personae*, *temporis* or *loci*. A State that is not willing to grant the court jurisdiction in general may still consent to be bound by the court on an *ad hoc* basis for special cases.

A court has an inherent power to raise preliminary questions with respect to its jurisdiction in the case under consideration. The ICJ stated in this regard that the Court must always 'be satisfied that it has jurisdiction, and must if necessary go into that matter *proprio motu*'.[23] When there

[21] *Cayara* v. *Peru* (Preliminary Objections), Inter-Am. Ct HR, 3 February 1993, Ser. C, No. 14, para. 63.

[22] See Ian Brownlie, *Principles of Public International Law*, 479.

[23] *Appeal Relating to the Jurisdiction of the ICAO Council (India* v. *Pakistan)*, 1972 ICJ Reports 46, 52 (Jurisdiction of the Court Judgment of 18 August). See Rosenne, *Procedure in the International Court*, at 158–68.

is a preliminary objection as to whether an international tribunal has jurisdiction in a particular case, under the general principle of *compétence de la compétence* the court itself is competent to determine whether it has jurisdiction.[24] Moreover, although the court may have jurisdiction in a given case, it is not obligated to exercise it. In exceptional instances, the court may decline to exercise its jurisdiction on the ground of judicial propriety.

Manner in which a State may accept the jurisdiction of the Inter-American Court

The American Convention provides that:

> [a] State Party may, upon depositing its instrument of ratification or adherence to this Convention, or at any subsequent time, declare that it recognizes as binding, *ipso facto*, and not requiring special agreement, the jurisdiction of the Court on all matters relating to the interpretation or application of this Convention. Such declaration may be made unconditionally, on the condition of reciprocity, for a specified period, or for specific cases.[25]

It is a matter for the Court to determine whether a State's reservation, condition or limitation to its acceptance of the Court's compulsory jurisdiction deprives the Court of jurisdiction in a given case.[26] The only limitations permissible to the jurisdiction of the Court are those expressly provided for in the Convention. The Court holds that a State Party cannot limit its jurisdiction by subsequently adding terms to its recognition of the Court's jurisdiction.[27] The Court rejected Trinidad and Tobago's preliminary objection that the ambiguously worded limitation in its acceptance of the Court's compulsory jurisdiction barred the Court from considering the subject matter in the *Benjamin*,[28] *Hilaire*[29] and *Constantine et al.*

[24] *Nottebohm (Liechtenstein* v. *Guatemala)*, 1953 ICJ Reports 111, at 119 (Preliminary Objections of 18 November).

[25] American Convention, Art. 62(2). See generally Sergio García Ramírez, *Los Derechos Humanos y la Jurisdicción Interamericana* (Universidad Nacional Autónoma de México, 2002).

[26] *Hilaire* v. *Trinidad and Tobago* (Preliminary Objections), Inter-Am. Ct HR, 1 September 2001, Ser. C, No. 80, 78.

[27] *Constitutional Court Case* (Competence), Inter-Am. Ct HR, 24 September 1999, Ser. C, No. 55, para. 34.

[28] *Benjamin et al.* v. *Trinidad and Tobago* (Preliminary Objections), Inter-Am. Ct HR, 1 September 2001, Ser. C, No. 81, operative para. 1.

[29] *Hilaire* v. *Trinidad and Tobago* (Preliminary Objections, 2001), operative para. 1.

Cases.[30] The acceptance stated that '[t]he Government of the Republic of Trinidad and Tobago recognizes the compulsory jurisdiction of the Inter-American Court of Human Rights as stated in the said article only to such extent that recognition is consistent with the relevant sections of the Constitution of the Republic of Trinidad and Tobago; and provided that any judgment of the Court does not infringe, create or abolish any existing rights or duties of any private citizen'.[31]

The State objected *inter alia* that the Court's consideration of its domestic law, which mandates the death penalty in convictions for murder, did not fall within the subject matter of its acceptance of the jurisdiction of the Court.[32] The Court rejected the preliminary objection, finding that the limitation's general scope 'completely subordinates the application of the American Convention to the internal legislation of Trinidad and Tobago as decided by its courts'.[33] The Court reasoned that the clause setting forth the allowable procedure for the acceptance of the Court's jurisdiction was 'essential to the efficacy of the mechanism of international protection', and therefore 'must be interpreted and applied in such a way that the guarantee that it establishes is truly practical and effective, given the special nature of human rights treaties and their collective enforcement'.[34] The Court reasoned that it is obligated to interpret the Convention's mechanism for State acceptance of the compulsory jurisdiction of the Court in a manner that preserves its integrity.[35] The Court further explained that it was unacceptable to subordinate the acceptance of the Court's jurisdiction to restrictions that would render the protection of human rights and the Court's jurisdiction inoperative.[36]

30 *Constantine et al.* v. *Trinidad and Tobago* (Preliminary Objections), Inter-Am. Ct HR, 1 September 2001, Ser. C, No. 82, operative para. 1.

31 Reprinted in 2001 Basic Documents Pertaining to Human Rights in the Inter-American System, 23, OEA/Ser.L/V/I.4 rev. 8 (22 May 2001) (English), at 59.

32 *Benjamin et al.* v. *Trinidad and Tobago* (Preliminary Objections, 2001), para. 43; *Hilaire* v. *Trinidad and Tobago* (Preliminary Objections, 2001), para. 44.

33 *Benjamin et al.* v. *Trinidad and Tobago* (Preliminary Objections, 2001), para. 79; *Hilaire* v. *Trinidad and Tobago* (Preliminary Objections, 2001), para. 88.

34 *Benjamin et al.* v. *Trinidad and Tobago* (Preliminary Objections, 2001), para. 74; *Hilaire* v. *Trinidad and Tobago* (Preliminary Objections, 2001), para. 83, quoting *Constitutional Court* v. *Peru* (Competence), Inter-Am. Ct HR, 24 September 1999, Ser. C, No. 55, para. 36; *Ivcher Bronstein* v. *Peru* (Competence), Inter-Am. Ct HR, 24 September 1999, Ser. C, No. 54, para. 37.

35 *Benjamin et al.* v. *Trinidad and Tobago* (Preliminary Objections, 2001), para. 73; *Hilaire* v. *Trinidad and Tobago* (Preliminary Objections, 2001), para. 82.

36 *Benjamin et al.* v. *Trinidad and Tobago* (Preliminary Objections, 2001), para. 73; *Hilaire* v. *Trinidad and Tobago* (Preliminary Objections, 2001), para. 82.

Objections to jurisdiction ratione materiae

An objection to jurisdiction *ratione materiae* is an objection that the subject matter of the application is not within the jurisdiction of the enforcement organs. Under the American Convention, the jurisdiction *ratione materiae* of the Inter-American Court extends to 'all matters relating to the interpretation or application of [the American] Convention'.[37] Moreover, as certain provisions of the Convention make reference to other treaties, in limited relevant circumstances those treaties may come within the jurisdiction *ratione materiae* of the Inter-American Court. In addition, the Court has jurisdiction *ratione materiae* to determine if there has been a violation of other treaties that confer jurisdiction on the Inter-American Court, which have been ratified by the respondent State.[38] The only other Inter-American treaty that expressly confers jurisdiction on the Inter-American Court is the Inter-American Convention on Forced Disappearance of Persons.[39] The relevant provision provides that:

> [f]or the purposes of this Convention, the processing of petitions or communications presented to the Inter-American Commission on Human Rights alleging the forced disappearance of persons shall be subject to the procedures established in the American Convention on Human Rights and to the Statute and Regulations of the Inter-American Commission on Human Rights and to the Statute and Rules of Procedure of the Inter-American Court of Human Rights, including the provisions on precautionary measures.[40]

The Inter-American Convention to Prevent and Punish Torture provides that, after the exhaustion of domestic remedies, 'the case may be submitted to the international fora whose competence has been recognized by that State'.[41] Those 'international fora' include the Inter-American Court when the State has accepted the Court's jurisdiction. The Court has held in several cases, including the *Paniagua Morales* v. *Guatemala Case*,[42] the

[37] American Convention, Art. 62(1).

[38] *Las Palmeras* (Preliminary Objections), Inter-Am. Ct HR, 4 February 2000, Ser. C, No. 67, para. 34.

[39] Inter-American Convention on Forced Disappearance of Persons, Resolution Adopted at Belem do Pará, Brazil, 9 June 1994, at the twenty-fourth regular session of the General Assembly of the Organization of American States, entered into force on 28 March 1996, Art. XIII.

[40] *Ibid.* [41] Inter-American Convention to Prevent and Punish Torture, Art. 8.

[42] *Paniagua Morales et al.* v. *Guatemala* (*The White Van Case*) (Merits), Inter-Am. Ct HR, 8 March 1998, Ser. C, No. 37, para. 136 and Resolution 3.

Bámaca Velásquez v. *Guatemala Case*,[43] the *Cantoral Benavides* v. *Peru Case*[44] and the *Villagrán Morales et al.* v. *Guatemala Case*[45] that the State did not comply with its obligation to prevent and punish torture under the Inter-American Convention to Prevent and Punish Torture.[46]

The Additional Protocol to the American Convention on Human Rights in the Area of Economic, Social and Cultural Rights, more commonly known as the 'Protocol of San Salvador', grants the Inter-American Court limited jurisdiction *ratione materiae* for violations of the rights of trade unions and the right to education.[47] In the *Baena Ricardo Case* in which 270 trade union members were dismissed from their jobs for a walk-out, the Commission alleged that Panama had violated the Protocol of San Salvador.[48] The State objected to the application of the Protocol.[49] The Court dismissed the claim, holding that it did not have jurisdiction, because Panama had not ratified the Protocol at the time of the violations.[50]

The Inter-American Court does not have jurisdiction to render judgments on violations of other treaties, which do not confer jurisdiction on the Inter-American Court, even if the respondent State has ratified the treaty.[51] The American Convention provides only that the Court may interpret other treaties in the exercise of its advisory jurisdiction.[52] For example, the Inter-American Convention on the Prevention, Punishment and Eradication of Violence Against Women provides only that the Commission has competence to consider complaints of violations of the Convention, and that the States Parties to the Convention or the Inter-American Commission can resort to the Inter-American Court's advisory jurisdiction.[53] Therefore, the Inter-American Court does not have

43 *Bámaca Velásquez* (Merits), Inter-Am. Ct HR, 25 November 2000, Ser. C, No. 70, para. 223.

44 *Cantoral Benavides* v. *Peru* (Merits), Inter-Am. Ct HR, 18 August 2000, Ser. C, No. 69, para. 191.

45 *Villagrán Morales et al.* v. *Guatemala* (*The Street Children Case*) (Merits), Inter-Am. Ct HR, 19 November 1999, Ser. C, No. 63, para. 252.

46 *Paniagua Morales et al.* v. *Guatemala* (Merits, 1998), para. 126.

47 Additional Protocol to the American Convention on Human Rights in the Area of Economic, Social and Cultural Rights ('Protocol of San Salvador'), signed at San Salvador, El Salvador, on 17 November 1988, at the eighteenth regular session of the General Assembly, and entered into force on 16 November 1999, Art. 19(6), referring to Arts. 8 and 13.

48 *Baena Ricardo et al. (270 Workers* v. *Panama)* (Merits), Inter-Am. Ct HR, 2 February 2001, Ser. C, No. 72, para. 95.

49 *Ibid.*, para. 96.

50 *Ibid.*, para. 99.

51 *Las Palmeras* (Preliminary Objections, 2000), para. 33 and operative para. 2.

52 American Convention, Art. 64(1).

53 2001 Basic Documents, Arts. 11 and 12.

contentious jurisdiction to deal with complaints under that treaty. In the *Castillo Petruzzi Case*, the Commission charged Peru with a violation of the Vienna Convention on Consular Relations, because Peru allegedly refused to allow a Chilean delegation to visit the Chilean victims who were imprisoned in Peru. Although the Court upheld Peru's preliminary objection to the claim, and therefore did not consider the issue, it did so on the grounds that the Commission had not raised the complaint in its final report to the State.[54] The Court could also have found that the Vienna Convention on Consular Relations does not confer jurisdiction on the Inter-American Court. In the *Las Palmeras Case*, the Court held that it did not have jurisdiction to rule on the State's liability for the violation of common Article 3 of the 1949 Geneva Conventions.[55]

Although the Court lacks jurisdiction to hold a State internationally responsible for the violation of international treaties that do not confer jurisdiction on the Court, it may take the relevant provisions of those treaties into consideration in its interpretation of the American Convention, particularly if those provisions are *jus cogens*, as are many of the norms of humanitarian law.[56] The Court has also declared that it 'is competent to determine whether any norm of domestic or international law applied by a State, in times of peace or armed conflict, is compatible or not with the American Convention'.[57] This authority of the Inter-American Court results in a more consistent and uniform interpretation of human rights in the Inter-American system.

The American Convention allows a State to place specific limitations on the Inter-American Court's jurisdiction. The only specific limitation set out in the Convention that could affect the Court's jurisdiction *ratione materiae* is that which allows States to recognize the Court's jurisdiction only 'for specific cases'.[58]

The 'fourth instance formula'

It is not within the jurisdiction *ratione materiae* of either the Inter-American Court or Commission to assume the role of the national authorities and become an appeals court of fourth instance. It is within the jurisdiction *ratione materiae* of the Inter-American supervisory organs

[54] *Castillo Petruzzi et al.* v. *Peru* (Preliminary Objections), Inter-Am. Ct HR, 4 September 1998, Ser. C, No. 41, paras. 65–6 and 68–9.

[55] *Las Palmeras* (Preliminary Objections, 2000), para. 16, Resolutions 2 and 3.

[56] *Ibid.*, para. 32; *Bámaca Velásquez* (Merits, 2000), Inter-Am. Ct HR, 25 November 2000, Ser. C, No. 70, paras. 208–9, and Separate Concurring Opinion of Judge Sergio García Ramírez, paras. 24–5.

[57] *Las Palmeras* (Preliminary Objections, 2000), para. 32.

[58] American Convention, Art. 62(2).

to determine whether a State Party has violated the international human rights obligations that it contracted to observe when it ratified the American Convention.[59] It is not within their jurisdiction to act as appellate bodies with the authority to examine alleged errors of domestic law or fact that national courts may have committed while acting within their jurisdiction.[60] The 'fourth instance formula' specifies that international and regional human rights organs, such as the Commission and the Court, are subsidiary to the States' domestic judicial bodies.[61] Under this doctrine, when domestic law has already held that there is a violation of an individual's human rights, and the question is definitively settled, there is no need for the matter to be brought before the Inter-American Court for its 'confirmation' or 'approval'.[62] International supervisory organs may not overturn domestic court decisions that applied national law, unless the procedures followed by the national court were in violation of the international treaty.[63] If the petition contains nothing more than the allegation that the domestic court's decision was wrong or unjust, the Commission must apply the fourth instance formula and declare the petition inadmissible *ratione materiae*.[64] If, however, the organs of the Inter-American system do not have the benefit of fact-finding and decision-making by domestic courts, they must take on more than a subsidiary role.

International human rights law provides individuals with a means of protecting internationally recognized human rights against the State. The Commission and Court have jurisdiction *ratione materiae* to decide whether the national court's decision or procedures violated the right to a fair trial or other guarantees set forth in the Convention.[65] In the *Villagrán Morales Case*, Guatemala objected that the Inter-American Court did not

[59] *Cesti Hurtado* v. *Peru* (Preliminary Objections), Inter-Am. Ct HR, 26 January 1999, Ser. C, No. 49, para. 47.

[60] Case 11.673, *Santiago Marzioni (Argentina)*, Inter-Am. Comm. HR 86, para. 51, OEA/Ser.L/V/II.95, doc. 7 rev. (1996). Inter-American Commission reports are on the Internet at http://www.cidh.org.

[61] Case 11.597, *Emiliano Castro Tortrino (Argentina)*, Inter-Am. Comm. HR 54, para. 17, OEA/Ser.L/V/II.98, doc. 7 rev. (2 March 1998).

[62] *Las Palmeras* (Merits), Inter-Am. Ct HR, 6 December 2001, Ser. C, No. 90, para. 33.

[63] *Villagrán Morales et al.* v. *Guatemala (The Street Children Case)* (Preliminary Objections), Inter-Am. Ct HR, 11 September 1997, Ser. C, No. 32, paras. 17–18.

[64] Case 11.137, *Juan Carlos Abella (Argentina)*, Inter-Am. Comm. HR, 18 November 1997, 271, 302, para. 142, OEA/Ser.L/V/II.98, doc. 7 rev. (1997).

[65] See José Miguel Vivanco and Lisa L. Bhansali, 'Procedural Shortcomings in the Defense of Human Rights: An Inequality of Arms', in *The Inter-American System of Human Rights*, 430 (Harris and Livingstone eds., Clarendon Press, Oxford, and Oxford University Press, New York, 1998).

have jurisdiction to review a decision of the Guatemalan Supreme Court.[66] The government argued that, under its Constitution, final judgments by its domestic courts could only be reviewed by domestic courts, and that no other authority could intervene in the State's administration of justice.[67] The Inter-American Court dismissed the preliminary objection on the ground that it was not reviewing the judgment of the Guatemalan courts but rather determining whether the State was responsible for the violation of the American Convention.[68] Likewise, in the *Castillo Petruzzi* and *Cesti Hurtado* cases, Peru objected that the Inter-American Court did not have authority to question a decision of the Peruvian courts.[69] In both cases, the Inter-American Court reminded the State that:

> [o]n becoming a State Party to the Convention, Peru accepted the competence of the organs of the Inter-American system for the protection of human rights, and therefore obligated itself, also in the exercise of its sovereignty, to participate in proceedings before the Commission and the Court and to assume the obligations that derive from them.[70]

States Parties to the American Convention often allege that the Inter-American Commission and Court are infringing their sovereignty. The Court's statement should serve to remind States of the nature of the commitments they undertook on ratifying the American Convention and the functions of the Inter-American Commission and Court.

The fourth instance doctrine is also consistently applied by the European Court of Human Rights. The European Court has explained that the protection provided by the European Convention is meant to be subsidiary to the national systems safeguarding human rights.[71] Likewise, it has explained that the purpose of the jurisdiction of an international court is not to replace the competent domestic courts, but rather to review the

66 *Villagrán Morales et al.* v. *Guatemala (The Street Children Case)* (Preliminary Objections, 1997), para. 17.

67 *Ibid.*, para. 15.

68 *Ibid.*, para. 18.

69 *Castillo Petruzzi et al.* v. *Peru* (Preliminary Objections, 1998), para. 100; *Cesti Hurtado* v. *Peru* (Preliminary Objections, 1999), para. 35. In the *Cesti Hurtado Case*, the State alleged that, if the Court ruled in favour of the Commission, it would 'destabilize current [Peruvian] constitutional institutions'. *Ibid.*

70 *Castillo Petruzzi et al.* v. *Peru* (Preliminary Objections, 1998), para. 102; *Cesti Hurtado* v. *Peru* (Preliminary Objections, 1999), para. 45.

71 See '*Relating to Certain Aspects of the Laws on the Use of Languages in Education in Belgium*' v. *Belgium*, 6 ECHR (Ser. A) (1968), para. B10; see also *National Union of Belgian Police* v. *Belgium*, 19 ECHR (Ser. A), para. 47 (1975) ('review by the Court concerns only the conformity of these measures with the requirements of the Convention').

judgments they render.[72] Like the Inter-American Court, the European Court evaluates the domestic court proceedings as a whole and then determines if the domestic procedures were applied fairly.[73] The United Nations Human Rights Committee also refuses to re-evaluate the facts and evidence of a domestic court case and to interpret domestic law. The Committee noted that 'it is in general for the courts of States Parties, and not for the Committee, to evaluate the facts in a particular case and to interpret domestic legislation'.[74] It is only when the domestic court's evaluation of the facts and interpretation of the applicable law are 'manifestly arbitrary or amount to a denial of justice' that the claim is admissible.

Manifestly groundless petitions

Most individual petitions to which the State could make an objection *ratione materiae* are declared inadmissible by the Commission because they are manifestly groundless or do not cite a violation of a right protected by the Convention. A petition must 'state facts that tend to establish a violation of the rights guaranteed by [the] Convention' to be admissible and to fall within the jurisdiction *ratione materiae* of the enforcement organs.[75] Therefore, when the petition is manifestly groundless, in that the complaints of the petitioners do not fall within the provisions of the Convention, the Commission must declare the petition inadmissible.[76] If the Commission should fail to do so and refer the case to the Court, the Court would be required to find that it did not have jurisdiction *ratione materiae*.[77] The standard applied by the Court to determine whether a case is manifestly groundless under the Convention 'exclude[s] any conclusion based on appearance and demands a "clear, manifest certainty so perceptible that nobody may rationally place it in doubt" '.[78] The provisions of the American Convention specify in great detail the rights protected. For this reason, objections *ratione materiae*, except for those challenging the

[72] *Handyside* v. *United Kingdom*, 24 ECHR (Ser. A), paras. 48–50 (1976).

[73] *Edwards* v. *United Kingdom*, Judgment of 16 December 1992, Series A, No. 247-B, para. 34; and *Vidal* v. *Belgium*, 235-B ECHR (Ser. A) (1992), para. 33.

[74] See *Ms G. (Name Deleted)* v. *Canada*, Communication No. 934/2000, para. 4(3), UN GAOR, Hum. Rts. Comm., 69th Sess., UN Doc. CCPR/C/69/D/934/2000 (2000).

[75] American Convention, Art. 47(b).

[76] *Ibid.* See Donna Gomien, D. J. Harris and Leo Zwaak, *Law and Practice of the European Convention on Human Rights and the European Social Charter*, 66 (Council of Europe Publishing, Strasbourg, 1996), for a discussion of the treatment of applications that are 'manifestly ill-founded' in the European system.

[77] American Convention, Art. 61(2).

[78] *Genie Lacayo* (Preliminary Objections), Inter-Am. Ct HR, 27 January 1995, Ser. C, No. 21, para. 36.

Court's jurisdiction to review the decisions of national courts for violations of the Convention, have not been frequent or problematic for the Court.

State reservations modifying the *ratione materiae* of the Convention

Even though a right is protected by the Convention, if that right is subject to a valid reservation by the State charged with its violation, the Court must find that it does not have jurisdiction *ratione materiae*. A State on ratifying a treaty may do so with reservations that exclude or modify the legal effect of provisions of the treaty.[79] Such reservations modify the subject matter jurisdiction of any enforcing institution as to that State.[80] Therefore, if a State makes a valid reservation to the treaty, it cannot be brought before the Commission or the Court for certain violations of rights subject to that reservation, because the organs would not have jurisdiction *ratione materiae* over the complaint. Several States in the Inter-American system have made reservations to the subject matter of the Convention. For instance, although the American Convention directs that capital punishment shall not be imposed on those who were under the age of eighteen at the time they committed the crime,[81] Barbados ratified the Convention with the reservation that 'persons of 16 years and over, or over 70 years of age, may be executed under Barbadian law'.[82] Mexico made a reservation to the Convention's general right to participate in government, specifying that religious ministers do not have 'an active or passive vote, nor the right to associate for political purposes'.[83]

There are limitations on the reservations that States Parties are permitted to make to the American Convention. The Convention specifically provides that it is subject only to those reservations that conform to the Vienna Convention on the Law of Treaties.[84] The Vienna Convention specifies that a ratifying State may not make a reservation that is expressly prohibited by the treaty or that is 'incompatible with the object and purpose of the treaty'.[85] There is no consensus on what reservations

[79] See 1969 Vienna Convention on the Law of Treaties, UN Doc. A/CONF.39/27, 23 May 1969, entered into force 27 January 1988, Arts. 19 and 21; Ian Brownlie, *Principles of Public International Law*, at 612–15.

[80] Vienna Convention on the Law of Treaties, Art. 19.

[81] American Convention, Art. 4(5).

[82] Barbados, reservation made at the time of its ratification of the American Convention on 5 November 1981, reprinted in 2001 Basic Documents, at 51.

[83] Reservation to Mexico's ratification of the American Convention, received 24 March 1981, reprinted in 2001 Basic Documents, at 55.

[84] American Convention, Art. 75.

[85] Vienna Convention on the Law of Treaties, Art. 19.

would not be compatible with the object and purpose of the Convention. The United Nations Human Rights Committee has commented in this regard that peremptory norms and non-derogable rights and judicial guarantees should not be the subject of reservations.[86] Although the Inter-American Court has dealt with the subject of reservations in two advisory opinions, it has not yet considered the question of what rights cannot be modified through State reservations.[87]

There is a question as to whether a human rights treaty should permit reservations. The object and purpose of a human rights treaty is to protect delineated rights of individuals. Article 1 of the American Convention specifies that the States Parties undertake to respect and ensure the rights recognized in the Convention.[88] As such, there is a convincing argument that the State is not warranted in declaring that certain rights will not be observed in that State. Cançado Trindade proposes that any future protocol to the American Convention specify that '[t]his Convention does not permit reservations'.[89]

Objections to jurisdiction ratione personae

A State may object to the Court's consideration of a case because the Court lacks jurisdiction *ratione personae* over the State. Jurisdiction *ratione personae* is the general equivalent of two principles: personal jurisdiction and standing. In the passive sense, it means that the State can be brought into the Court as a respondent. In its active sense, jurisdiction *ratione personae* means a party has *locus standi* to bring a case before the Court.

Jurisdiction *ratione personae*: passive legitimation

Jurisdiction *ratione personae* in its passive sense provides that a case can be brought before the tribunal only if 'the respondent State is subject to the compulsory jurisdiction of the Court or consents *ad hoc*' to the Court's consideration of a particular case.[90] The treaty generally specifies

[86] Human Rights Committee, General Comment 24(52), General comment on issues relating to reservations made upon ratification or accession to the Covenant or the Optional Protocols thereto, or in relation to declarations under Article 41 of the Covenant, para. 8, UN Doc. CCPR/C/21/Rev.1/Add.6 (1994).

[87] See Advisory Opinion OC-2/82; and Advisory Opinion OC-3/83.

[88] American Convention, Art. 1(1).

[89] Judge Cançado Trindade, *Report and Proposals of the President of the Inter-American Court of Human Rights before the Commission on Juridical and Legal Affairs of the Permanent Commission of the OAS*, 5 April 2001, para. 63.

[90] P. van Dijk and G. J. H. van Hoof, *Theory and Practice of the European Convention on Human Rights*, 200 (3rd edn, Kluwer, The Hague, 1998).

the manner in which the States Parties may accept the Court's jurisdiction. A State Party to the American Convention may make a declaration accepting the jurisdiction of the Court as binding *ipso facto* or by special agreement.[91] Twenty-one States are subject to the compulsory jurisdiction of the Inter-American Court, and can therefore be named as respondents before the Court.[92] The American Convention also provides that a State may accept the jurisdiction of the Court on an *ad hoc* basis by special agreement for a particular case.[93] To date, Nicaragua in the *Genie Lacayo Case* is the only State to have done so.[94] The Inter-American Court has explained that:

> in contentious cases the exercise of the Court's jurisdiction ordinarily depends upon a preliminary and basic question, involving the State's acceptance of or consent to such jurisdiction. If the consent has been given, the States which participate in the proceedings become, technically speaking, parties to the proceedings and are bound to comply with the resulting decision of the Court [American Convention, Art. 68(1)]. By the same token, the Court cannot exercise its jurisdiction where such consent has not been given.[95]

Many treaties, including the American Convention, authorize States to accept jurisdiction on the condition of reciprocity, which allows a State to bring a case against another State only if both States have accepted the tribunal's jurisdiction.[96] This condition, however, has proved to be of little relevance to date in the Inter-American system, because States have not initiated cases. Most cases are brought before the Commission by individual petitioners and before the Court by the Commission.[97]

Jurisdiction *ratione personae*: active legitimation

Under the American Convention, only the Commission and States Parties can seise the Inter-American Court.[98] Individuals do not have standing to bring a case before the Court. Despite the limitations in the Convention,

[91] American Convention, Art. 62(1).

[92] See chapter 1, text at note 64 for a listing of States that have accepted the jurisdiction of the Inter-American Court.

[93] See American Convention, Art. 62(3).

[94] *Genie Lacayo* (Preliminary Objections, 1995), paras. 21 and 23–4.

[95] *Restrictions to the Death Penalty (Arts. 4(2) and 4(4) of the American Convention on Human Rights)*, Inter-Am. Ct HR, Advisory Opinion OC-3/83 of 8 September 1983, Ser. A, No. 3, para. 21.

[96] See, e.g., American Convention, Art. 45(2); Statute of the ICJ, Art. 36(3).

[97] American Convention, Arts. 44 and 51.

[98] *Ibid.*, Art. 61(1).

both the Commission and the Court are moving in the direction of giving the petitioner greater autonomy. Changes in the 2001 Commission Rules provide that the Commission 'shall' refer a case to the Court when the State involved has recognized the Court's jurisdiction and has not followed the Commission's recommendations 'unless there is a reasoned decision by an absolute majority of the members of the Commission to the contrary'.[99] Before submitting the case, the Commission asks the petitioner's position on whether to submit the case to the Court.[100] The Commission's decision is then based on 'the position of the petitioner; the nature and seriousness of the violation; the need to develop or clarify the case-law of the system; the future effect of the decision within the legal systems of the Member States; and the quality of the evidence available'.[101]

Jurisdiction *ratione personae*: standing to file a complaint with the Commission

The American Commission must have competence *ratione personae* to consider a petition in order for the Inter-American Court to later have jurisdiction *ratione personae* to consider an application arising from that petition. The petitioner must, therefore, have standing to file a petition before the Commission. The Rules of Procedure of the Commission also provide that the Commission may, *motu proprio*, initiate the processing of a petition that *prima facie* meets the necessary requirements.[102] The Court cited this provision in the *Blake Case*, in which the Court expressly stated that it was 'surprised that the Commission did not use its authority' to include another alleged victim in the application.[103] It would only have been appropriate for the second victim to be added to the application to the Court if the proceedings before the Commission had also included the second victim.

Jurisdiction *ratione personae* to consider petitions filed by any person or group of persons Any State Party that ratifies the American Convention automatically empowers individuals to petition the Commission.[104] Individuals claiming that their rights have been violated by a State need not be a citizen of that State or citizens of Member States of the OAS.

[99] 2001 Rules of Procedure of the Inter-American Commission on Human Rights, entered into force on 1 May 2001, approved by the Commission at its one hundred and ninth regular session held 4–8 December 2000, Art. 44(1).

[100] *Ibid.*, Art. 43(3). [101] *Ibid.*, Art. 44(2). [102] *Ibid.*, Art. 24.

[103] *Blake* v. *Guatemala* (Merits), Inter-Am. Ct HR, 24 January 1998, Ser. C, No. 36, para. 85.

[104] American Convention, Art. 44.

The claimant need only have been subject to the jurisdiction of the State charged with the violation, when the violation occurred.[105]

The right of petition before the Inter-American Commission is not limited to alleged victims and their relatives. Any 'person or group of persons, or any nongovernmental entity legally recognized in one or more member states' of the OAS has the right to petition in the Inter-American system.[106] Consequently, nongovernmental organizations, such as Amnesty International and Americas Watch, have standing to file complaints on behalf of victims in any State that has ratified the American Convention.[107] Under this provision, national human rights committees and human rights ombudsmen are able to file petitions on behalf of victims. For instance, in the *Baena Ricardo et al. Case*, in which 270 public employees were dismissed from their jobs for participating in a public demonstration, the petition was filed by the Panamanian Human Rights Committee.[108] In the *Barrios Altos Case*, the Peruvian National Human Rights Coordinator submitted a petition against the State for granting amnesty to State agents who were being tried for the assassinations of several persons.[109]

The American Convention basically allows anyone to file a human rights petition with the Inter-American Commission, even without the authorization of the actual victim. In the *Constitutional Court Case*, in which three Peruvian Constitutional Court justices were dismissed from the Court, the complaint was signed by twenty-seven Peruvian Congressional Representatives.[110] In the *Castillo Petruzzi Case*, Peru objected that the Chilean organization, Fundacion de Ayuda Social de las Iglesias Cristianas (Foundation of Christian Churches for Social Assistance), the entity that had filed a petition on behalf of four Chilean prisoners who were sentenced to life imprisonment in Peru, did not have standing to do so.[111] Peru's objection was based on the argument that the organization was not officially recognized as a nongovernmental

[105] *Ibid.*, Art. 1(1). [106] *Ibid.*, Art. 44.

[107] See generally David Padilla, 'The Inter-American Commission on Human Rights of the Organization of American States: A Case Study', 9 *American University Journal of International Law and Policy*, 95, 97–115 (1993).

[108] *Baena Ricardo et al. (270 Workers* v. *Panama)* (Merits), Inter-Am. Court HR, Judgment of 2 February 2001, Ser. C, No. 72, para. 6.

[109] *Barrios Altos (Chumbipuma Aguirre et al.* v. *Peru)* (Merits), Inter-Am. Ct HR, 14 March 2001, Ser. C, No. 75, para. 4.

[110] *Constitutional Court Case (Aguirre Roca, Rey Terry and Revoredo Marsano* v. *Peru)* (Competence), Inter-Am. Ct HR, 24 September 1999, Ser. C, No. 55, para. 3.

[111] *Castillo Petruzzi et al.* v. *Peru* (Preliminary Objections, 1998), paras. 75–7.

organization in Chile.[112] The Court dismissed the objection without examining the legal status of the organization,[113] reasoning that the Convention authorizes 'any group of persons to lodge petitions' with the Commission, and that, therefore, it was irrelevant whether the petitioner was a legally recognized nongovernmental organization.[114] From the viewpoint of strict statutory construction, this interpretation basically makes superfluous the inclusion of the clause that authorizes 'any nongovernmental entity legally recognized in one or more member states' to file a petition.

A more likely interpretation of the provision would require that when an organization is not legally recognized the leaders of that organization must file the complaint as a 'group of persons'. Although this interpretation would appear to be more in keeping with the letter of the Convention, it adds an unnecessary element of form over substance. The Court's holding is more consistent with the spirit of the American Convention in that it maintains the broad basis for standing in the Inter-American system. The Court emphasized in this regard that 'certain formalities may be excused, provided that there is a suitable balance between justice and legal certainty'.[115] It is important that any person or organization that is willing and able to support human rights victims in the Inter-American system be permitted to do so. The broad wording of the American Convention and the subsequent holding of the Court on the subject should eliminate groundless preliminary objections that would require an examination of the credentials of those organizations that file petitions.

The innovative provision allowing unrelated parties to complain of human rights violations has proven particularly effective in the Inter-American system where poverty, lack of education and lack of legal assistance might otherwise hinder access to the enforcement organs of the regional system.[116] Many victims of human rights violations are rural villagers with a limited education who are also too poor to hire a lawyer.[117] Moreover, in some countries human rights lawyers are exposed to the same intimidation and retaliation as the victims and their families. The victim's

[112] See *ibid.*, para. 76. [113] See *ibid.*, paras. 77–9. [114] *Ibid.*, para. 77.

[115] *Ibid.*, para. 78 (citing *Cayara* v. *Peru* (Preliminary Objections, 1993), para. 42).

[116] See Burns H. Weston, 'Regional Human Rights Regimes: A Comparison and Appraisal', 20 *Vanderbilt Journal of Transnational Law*, 585, at 617–18 (1987).

[117] *Exceptions to the Exhaustion of Domestic Remedies (Arts. 46(1), 46(2)(a) and 46(2)(b) of the American Convention on Human Rights)*, Inter-Am. Ct HR, Advisory Opinion OC-11/90 of 10 August 1990, Ser. A, No. 11, para. 3.

lawyer sometimes becomes the next victim. Consequently, even those family members of victims who are willing to suffer the consequences of filing a complaint may encounter difficulty finding a lawyer willing to take their case.[118] For this reason, many of the petitions received by the Inter-American Commission have been filed by international organizations, which are less susceptible to intimidation. Moreover, the publicity that an organization can generate may provide some protection to the domestic witnesses.

Although any party may petition the Inter-American Commission on behalf of the alleged victim, an unrelated party must have the alleged victim's permission to represent him or her before the Inter-American Court. The Rules of the Court provide that, once the application has been submitted by the Commission or the State, only 'the alleged victims, their next of kin or their duly accredited representatives' may communicate with the Court.[119] Those representing the victims must submit a power of attorney signed by the victim or the family of the victim.

The United Nations Human Rights Committee's requirements for communications under Optional Protocol 1 compare to those of the Inter-American Court. Under the Rules of the UNHRC, the communication must be filed by the victim, the victim's family members or duly authorized counsel.[120] Counsel before the UNHRC must demonstrate actual authorization from the alleged victims or their family to act on their behalf or show a close past relationship between the alleged victim and counsel so as to give rise to an assumption that the alleged victim authorized the communication.[121] In one case before the UNHCR, the alleged victim was a Vietnamese refugee who had settled in China and then arrived in Australia without authorization. Purported counsel presented only the transcript of a telephone call to the alleged victim, in which 'counsel told Mr Y that he wished to address a question of principle to the Human Rights Committee (whether the State party has an obligation to inform unlawful entrants into Australia of their right to consult a lawyer) and asked whether Mr Y would agree to counsel submitting a communication

[118] See *ibid.*

[119] 2001 Rules of Procedure of the Inter-American Court of Human Rights, entered into force on 1 June 2001, approved by the Court at its forty-ninth regular session held 25 November 2000, Art. 23(1).

[120] Rules of Procedure of the United Nations Human Rights Committee, Rule 90(b), UN Doc. CCPR/C/3/Rev.6 (24 April 2001).

[121] Mr Colin McDonald and Mr Nicholas Poynder on behalf of *Mr Y (Name Deleted)* v. *Australia*, Communication No. 772/1997, para. 6.3, UN GAOR, Hum. Rts. Comm., 69th Sess., UN Doc. CCPR/C/69/D/772/1997 (2000).

in Mr Y's name in order to test this question'.[122] Counsel had no signed authorization from the alleged victim and no information as to the whereabouts of the victim, who later could not be located. The Human Rights Committee ruled that the communication was inadmissible *ratione personae*, because counsel could not show authorization to act for the alleged victim.[123]

Under similar circumstances, the Inter-American Court would not rule that the application was inadmissible *ratione personae*, because it would have been submitted by the Commission. However, the counsel would not be authorized to directly represent the victim. The Commission could name the counsel as an advisor to the Commission before the Court.

Jurisdiction *ratione personae* to consider State-filed complaints The American Convention also allows States Parties to recognize the competence of the Commission to consider complaints 'in which a State Party alleges that another State Party has committed a violation of a human right set forth in this Convention'.[124] State-filed complaints are limited by the principle of reciprocity. Only States that have recognized the Commission's competence to receive State-filed communications against it can file such communications against other States.[125] Nine States have accepted the Commission's competence to receive inter-State filings as of 1 January 2003: Argentina, Chile, Colombia, Costa Rica, Ecuador, Jamaica, Peru, Uruguay and Venezuela.[126] To date there have been no inter-State filings in the Inter-American system.

Jurisdiction *ratione personae* to consider concrete cases The Commission and the Court do not have jurisdiction *ratione personae* to consider a case filed *in abstracto*.[127] The Court has stated that '[t]he contentious jurisdiction of the Court is intended to protect the rights and freedoms of specific individuals, not to resolve abstract questions'.[128] Therefore, the Commission must receive a petition that alleges a concrete violation of a specific person's human rights.[129] A person who was in no way affected by

[122] *Ibid.*, para. 6.2. [123] *Ibid.*, para. 6.3 and 7.a. [124] American Convention, Art. 45(1).

[125] *Ibid.*, Art. 45(2). [126] See 2001 Basic Documents, at 48.

[127] Case 11.553, Inter-Am. Comm. HR 125, paras. 28 and 31, OEA/Ser.L/V/II.95, doc. 7 rev. (1996).

[128] *International Responsibility for the Promulgation and Enforcement of Laws in Violation of the Convention (Arts. 1 and 2 of the American Convention on Human Rights)*, Inter-Am. Ct HR, Advisory Opinion OC-14/94 of 9 December 1994, Ser. A, No. 14, para. 49.

[129] *Ibid.*, para. 45.

a domestic law cannot bring the matter before the Commission and the Court. Convention provisions mandate that the Court cannot consider a case until all proceedings before the Commission are completed.[130] Those proceedings cannot be initiated by the Commission unless the applicant alleges that all domestic remedies have been exhausted and the complaint is brought within six months of a final domestic judgment.[131] If the Commission is presented with an abstract petition it must declare itself incompetent *ratione personae* to consider it.[132] The United Nations Human Rights Committee, in considering applications under the Optional Protocol to the International Covenant on Civil and Political Rights,[133] also requires that the alleged victim be 'actually and personally affected' by the law in question.[134]

However, when a law is passed that would result in the violation of the rights of the petitioner, the Court may find the law to be *per se* a violation of the American Convention, and therefore a potential victim may have the right to file a complaint. In the *Hilaire, Constantine and Benjamin et al. Case*, in which thirty-two persons had been sentenced to death by hanging, pursuant to a law that the Court held to be in violation of the Convention, the Court found that all those sentenced were victims of the law even though only one of them had been executed.[135] Likewise, in the *Suárez Rosero Case*, the Court observed that, because Ecuador's Law on Narcotic Drugs and Psychotropic Substances left persons charged under the law without certain legal protections, the law was *per se* a violation of the American Convention 'whether or not it was enforced in the instant case'.[136]

Similarly, the European human rights system has adopted the concept of 'potential victim'. In the *Klass Case*, the European Court held that 'a law may by itself violate the rights of an individual if the individual is directly affected by the law in the absence of any specific measure of

[130] American Convention, Art. 61(2). [131] *Ibid.*, Art. 46(1)(a) and (b).

[132] Case 11.553, Inter-Am. Comm. HR 125, para. 28, OEA/Ser.L/V/II.95, doc. 7 rev. (1996).

[133] Optional Protocol to the International Covenant on Civil and Political Rights, GA Res. 2200A (XXI), 21 UN GAOR Supp. (No. 16) at 59, UN Doc. A/6316 (1966), 999 UNTS 302, entered into force 23 March 1976.

[134] *Disabled and Handicapped Persons in Italy – Not Specified* v. *Italy*, Communication No. 163/1984 (9 January 1984), UN Doc. Supp. No. 40, Sess. 39 (A/39/40) at 197, para. 6.2 (1984). CCPR/C/69/D/936/2000 (2000).

[135] *Hilaire, Constantine and Benjamin et al.* v. *Trinidad and Tobago* (Merits), Inter-Am. Ct HR, 21 June 2002, Ser. C, No. 94, paras. 116–17.

[136] *Suárez Rosero* v. *Ecuador* (Merits), Inter-Am. Ct HR, 12 November 1997, Ser. C, No. 35, para. 98.

implementation'.[137] The Inter-American Court cited the European *Klass Case* with approval in its advisory opinion on *International Responsibility for the Promulgation and Enforcement of Laws in Violation of the Convention.*[138] In that advisory opinion, the Inter-American Court differentiated between laws of immediate application, in which persons subject to the legal norm are affected solely by the adoption of the law, and a law that is not of immediate application which merely empowers State authorities to take measures under the law.[139] The Court stated that a law that deprives a portion of the population of some of its rights – for example, because of race – automatically injures all the members of that race.[140] Those people are potential victims of the law and may bring a case in the Inter-American system. It is difficult in many instances, however, to differentiate between those who may be considered potential victims and those who do not meet the requirements.

Jurisdiction *ratione personae* to consider cases in which the victim is an individual or shareholder in a business entity The Court has determined that it has jurisdiction *ratione personae* when the victim is a natural person or the shareholder of a business entity.[141] The American Convention does not expressly recognize the rights of legal persons, such as corporations. The Convention requires that States ensure human rights to 'all persons subject to their jurisdiction'.[142] The term 'person' is defined in the Convention as 'every human being'.[143] In earlier cases, the Inter-American Commission refused to consider a complaint alleging the violation of a corporation's right to property under the American Convention.[144] The Commission declared that the complaint was inadmissible *ratione personae* 'given the lack of jurisdiction of the Commission over the rights of legal entities and over operations or legal acts of a commercial nature'.[145]

137 *Klass and Others* v. *Germany*, 28 ECHR 17–18, para. 33. (Ser. A) (1978). See Antonio Augusto Cançado Trindade, *Co-existence and Co-ordination of Mechanisms of International Protection of Human Rights (at Global and Regional Levels)*, 271–82 (Nijhoff, The Hague, 1990); van Dijk and van Hoof, *Theory and Practice*, at 52–4.

138 Advisory Opinion OC-14/94, para. 45. 139 *Ibid.*, para. 41. 140 *Ibid.*, para. 43.

141 *Cantos* v. *Argentina* (Preliminary Objections), Inter-Am. Ct HR, 7 September 2001, Ser. C, No. 85, para. 29.

142 American Convention, Art. 1(1). 143 *Ibid.*, Art. 1(2).

144 Report No. 47/97, Inter-Am. Comm. HR 231, para. 35, OEA/Ser.L/V/II.98, doc. 7 rev. (1997). Conversely, the Commission did entertain claims filed by corporations or juridical persons under the American Declaration on the Rights and Duties of Man, Case No. 9250, *ABC Color* v. *Paraguay*, Inter-Am. Comm. HR, 72, OAS/Ser.L/V/II.63 doc. 10 rev. 1.

145 Report No. 47/97, Inter-Am. Comm. HR 231, para. 35, OEA/Ser.L/V/II.98, doc. 7 rev. (1997).

The Inter-American Court overruled this limited interpretation of the Convention in the *Cantos* v. *Argentina Case*, when the complaint was brought by a person involved in the business.[146] In the *Cantos Case*, the petitioner, who was the owner of a business group composed of various corporations, alleged that his right to property was violated when an agency of the provincial government confiscated all the documentation from the businesses, thereby impeding their further operation.[147] Argentina objected that the American Convention is not applicable to legal persons, and that, therefore, the petitioner's businesses were not protected by the Convention.[148] The Court rejected Argentina's preliminary objection.[149] The Court reasoned that, under Argentina's interpretation, if one farmer bought a piece of farm equipment, which was confiscated by the authorities, the farmer could resort to the Inter-American system. If two poor farmers bought the same piece of equipment together in joint ownership, and that equipment was confiscated, they could also resort to the Inter-American system. Conversely, if the two poor farmers formed a corporation and their corporation bought the equipment that was confiscated, they could not file a complaint in the Inter-American system.[150] The Court noted that, in general, the obligations and rights attributed to legal persons are also the obligations and rights of the human beings who have invested in or represent the legal entity.[151] Business entities are composed of a voluntary association of persons who invest therein for their personal benefit.[152] Consequently, the Court determined that it will entertain cases in which allegations of violations of the rights of legal persons are brought by the shareholders.[153]

The question of whether a business entity has the right to bring a case before an international body has not been uniformly decided under international law. The UN Human Rights Committee refused to entertain a complaint by a newspaper company incorporated under the laws of Trinidad and Tobago.[154] The Court held that the complaint was inadmissible, because the Optional Protocol only authorized individuals to submit communications to the Committee.[155] Although the managing director had made the complaint on behalf of the company, he had not alleged

[146] *Cantos* v. *Argentina* (Preliminary Objections, 2001), para. 29. [147] *Ibid.*, para. 2.
[148] *Ibid.*, para. 22. [149] *Ibid.*, para. 42(1). [150] *Ibid.*, para. 25.
[151] *Ibid.*, para. 27. [152] *Ibid.*, para. 26. [153] *Ibid.*, para. 29.
[154] Communication No. 360/1989, Trinidad and Tobago, 7 August 1989, CCPR/C/36/D/360/1989.
[155] *Ibid.*, para. 3.2. Optional Protocol to the International Covenant on Civil and Political Rights, Art. 1.

that his individual rights were violated, and therefore the complaint was barred.[156] The European States adopted Protocol 1 to the European Convention specifically providing that '[e]very natural and legal person is entitled to the peaceful enjoyment of his possessions'.[157]

Although the Inter-American Court's jurisprudence has now established that an individual shareholder can bring a case in the Inter-American system, one difficulty that may arise is the failure of the shareholder to exhaust domestic remedies. In some States, shareholders in legal entities do not have standing to assert the company's claims against third parties, meaning that they would be prohibited from exhausting remedies in their own names.[158] A limited protocol to the American Convention, although not strictly necessary, would eliminate any such problems. The protocol could approximate the first Protocol to the European Convention.

Objections to jurisdiction ratione temporis

An international human rights court has jurisdiction *ratione temporis* if the alleged violation takes place during a time when the court has jurisdiction over the State. A State can object that the court does not have jurisdiction either because the violation occurred before the entry into force of the treaty for that State, after the State's denunciation of the treaty became effective, or because the State placed conditional time limits on its recognition of the court's jurisdiction.

Lack of jurisdiction *ratione temporis* if the violation took place before the State ratified the treaty

It is a generally recognized principle of international law that treaties are not retrospective in effect.[159] The Vienna Convention on the Law of Treaties codifies this principle by providing that, in general, treaty provisions do not bind a party 'in relation to any act or fact which took place or any situation which ceased to exist before the date of the entry

[156] Communication No. 360/1989, Trinidad and Tobago, 7 August 1989, CCPR/C/36/D/360/1989, paras. 3.2 and 4(a).

[157] Protocol 1 to the European Convention for the Protection of Human Rights and Fundamental Freedoms, Art. 1.

[158] See Diego Rodríguez Pinzon, 'The Victim Requirement, the Fourth Instance Formula and the Notion of "Person" in the Individual Complaint Procedure of the Inter-American Human Rights System', 7 *International Law Students Association Journal of International and Comparative Law*, 82 (2001).

[159] Vienna Convention on the Law of Treaties, Art. 28.

into force of the treaty with respect to that party'.[160] In the case of the American Convention, it became binding on the initial eleven ratifying States when it entered into force in 1978.[161] As to States that ratified or adhered to the Convention subsequent to that date, the Convention entered into force for each State on the date the State's instrument of ratification or adherence was deposited with the OAS.[162] Thus, in general, a State Party can only be held responsible for violations of the Convention that took place subsequent to the date of entry into force of the American Convention with respect to that State.

In the European human rights system as it was formerly constituted, a State, arguably, could be held responsible for a violation that took place after the State ratified the Convention but before it recognized the competence of the Commission to examine individual petitions.[163] Under this view, the State's acceptance of competence could be found to have retrospective effect to the moment of that State's ratification of the Convention.[164] Thus, a State could be brought before the Court for an alleged violation of the Convention that took place after the Convention came into force for that State but before the date it filed its declaration.[165] This question has not been raised before the Inter-American system. It could be reasoned, however, that once the State has ratified a treaty, such as the American Convention, it has committed itself to be bound by its provisions. The State should, therefore, be accountable for any violation of the rights protected by the treaty subsequent to its ratification.

State acceptance of jurisdiction with temporal conditions

A State may exclude the retrospective effect of jurisdiction if the treaty so permits. The State does so by placing a condition *ratione temporis* on its acceptance of jurisdiction.[166] When the treaty provides that declarations recognizing jurisdiction may be made 'for a certain time', such provisions

[160] *Ibid.* See also *Restatement of the Law (Third) of the Foreign Relations Law of the United States*, § 322.

[161] American Convention, Art. 74(2). [162] See *ibid.*

[163] See van Dijk and van Hoof, *Theory and Practice*, at 13; Tom Zwart, *The Admissibility of Human Rights Petitions: The Case Law of the European Commission of Human Rights and the Human Rights Committee*, 134 (Kluwer, Boston, 1994).

[164] See van Dijk and van Hoof, *Theory and Practice*, at 13; Tom Zwart, *The Admissibility of Human Rights Petitions*, at 134.

[165] See van Dijk and van Hoof, *Theory and Practice*, at 13; Tom Zwart, *The Admissibility of Human Rights Petitions*, at 134.

[166] See Shabtai Rosenne, *The Time Factor in the Jurisdiction of the International Court of Justice*, at 12 (Sijthoff, Leyden, 1960).

inter alia authorize the State to exclude the retrospective effect of jurisdiction by expressly conditioning its acceptance of jurisdiction. Such conditions 'make it possible for States to insert into the specific attribution of jurisdiction such temporal limitations as they think fit'.[167] For instance, a State may specify that its acceptance of the court's jurisdiction applies to the future only.

The American Convention specifically authorizes States Parties to place a condition *ratione temporis* on their acceptance of the jurisdiction of the Inter-American Court. A State's declaration of acceptance 'may be made unconditionally, on the condition of reciprocity, *for a specified period*, or for specific cases'.[168] Certain States Parties to the American Convention have accepted the Court's jurisdiction with a condition limiting it to events that occurred after the date on which they filed their declarations of acceptance. For example, Colombia recognized the jurisdiction of the Inter-American Court on the condition of 'nonretroactivity',[169] and Chile recognized jurisdiction only as to 'situations occurring subsequent to the date of deposit of this instrument of ratification, or, in any event, to circumstances which arose after 11 March 1990'.[170] Likewise, Nicaragua, Paraguay and El Salvador incorporated conditions of non-retroactivity in their instruments of acceptance.[171]

Nicaragua objected to the Court jurisdiction *ratione temporis* in the *Genie Lacayo Case*, in which a sixteen-year-old boy who attempted to pass a military convoy was allegedly shot several times by machine gun and left to die in his car. Nicaragua objected that the Court did not have jurisdiction *ratione temporis*, because the alleged victim died more than three months before Nicaragua accepted the Court's jurisdiction.[172] Nicaragua's general declaration of acceptance included a condition *ratione temporis* in which it stated that 'this recognition of competence applies only to cases arising solely out of events subsequent to, and out of acts which began to be committed after, the date of deposit of this declaration'.[173] Nicaragua therefore argued that the Court did not have jurisdiction to rule on events that occurred before its acceptance of the Court's jurisdiction, events which the Commission alleged amounted to an obstruction of justice. These events included the murder of the police officer in charge of the investigation, the disappearance of evidence, the refusal of military

167 *Ibid.*, at 12. 168 American Convention, Art. 62(2) (emphasis added).
169 Reprinted in 2001 Basic Documents, at 62–3.
170 *Ibid.*, at 58. 171 *Ibid.*, at 59, 60 and 62.
172 *Genie Lacayo* (Preliminary Objections, 1995), paras. 11 and 21–6.
173 2001 Basic Documents, at 59.

witnesses to appear and testify, and the unreasonable delay of the domestic courts in processing the case.[174] The Inter-American Court did not rule on the validity of Nicaragua's condition, because Nicaragua had also provided a second basis for jurisdiction which did not include a condition *ratione temporis*.[175]

Jurisdiction *ratione temporis* over continuing violations

International law, however, imposes a basic limitation on the State's ability to condition its acceptance of jurisdiction *ratione temporis*. A State cannot effectively limit jurisdiction over events occurring after its acceptance of jurisdiction. In this way, the Court may have jurisdiction over the effects of events that took place before the State accepted the Court's jurisdiction but continued or had effects, which themselves constituted violations, after the date of the State's acceptance of jurisdiction.[176] When a violation that originated before the State's ratification of the treaty or acceptance of jurisdiction continues thereafter, the State can be held responsible for a continuing violation. The concept of continuing violations 'extends jurisdiction to cases that originated before the entry into force of the declaration of acceptance (the "critical date"), but that produced legal effects after that date'.[177]

States Parties, relying on a condition limiting jurisdiction to events occurring after their acceptance of jurisdiction, have objected to the Court's consideration of cases because the events in question began or took place at an earlier date.[178] In the *Blake Case*, the Inter-American Court held that the forced disappearance of a person is a continuing violation of the Convention until the whereabouts or fate of the person is known, and that, therefore, the Court had jurisdiction despite the State's condition *ratione temporis* in its acceptance.[179] The State objected to the Court's jurisdiction to hear the case, because the undisputed evidence identified

[174] *Genie Lacayo* (Preliminary Objections, 1995), paras. 12 and 13.

[175] *Ibid.*, paras. 21 and 23–4.

[176] See *J. L.* v. *Australia*, Communication No. 491/1992, para. 4.2; UN GAOR, Hum. Rts. Comm., 45th Sess., UN Doc. CCPR/C/45/D/491/1992 (1994); Zwart, *The Admissibility of Human Rights Petitions*, at 130.

[177] Beate Rudolf, 'International Decision: Loizidou v. Turkey', 91 *American Journal of International Law*, 532, 534–5 (1997).

[178] See *Blake* v. *Guatemala* (Preliminary Objections), Inter-Am. Ct HR, 2 July 1996, Ser. C, No. 27, paras. 23–4 and 29; *Genie Lacayo* (Preliminary Objections, 1995), para. 21; see also *Ibrahima Gueye et al.* v. *France*, Communication No. 196/1985, pp. 191–2, UN GAOR, Hum. Rts. Comm., 44th Sess., Supp. No. 40, UN Doc. A/44/40 (1989).

[179] *Blake* v. *Guatemala* (Preliminary Objections, 1996), paras. 29–40.

the date of death of the victim to have occurred almost two years before Guatemala accepted the jurisdiction of the Court.[180] The facts of the case as proved were that Ned Blake, an American journalist, and his companion disappeared in the highlands of Guatemala in March 1985. Blake's death occurred on 29 March 1985, and Guatemala did not file its declaration of acceptance of the jurisdiction of the Court until 9 March 1987.[181] Guatemala, in its declaration of acceptance of the Court's jurisdiction, had included the limitation that 'cases in which the competence of the court is recognized are exclusively those that shall have taken place after the date that this declaration is presented to the Secretary General of the Organization of American States'.[182] The Commission, however, alleged that, although the government knew of the murder, it had concealed that knowledge and evidence from his relatives, and had subsequently attempted to dispose of his remains.[183]

In *Blake*, the Court held that lack of jurisdiction *ratione temporis* 'does not apply to continuous crimes'.[184] The Court agreed with the State that the violations of deprivation of liberty and murder were completed before the date of the State's acceptance of the Court's jurisdiction and could not, therefore, 'be considered per se to be continuous'.[185] It found, however, that the effects of those crimes are 'prolonged continuously or permanently until such time as the victim's fate or whereabouts is established'.[186] In the *Blake Case*, the victim's fate was determined in June 1992, five years after Guatemala had accepted the Court's jurisdiction. The Court relied on several international documents, including its own jurisprudence, which held that forced disappearance is a 'continuous crime' or 'continuing offense'.[187] It also pointed out that Guatemalan domestic legislation stipulates that the crime of forced disappearance 'shall be deemed to be continuing until such time as the victim is freed'.[188] The Court commented:

[180] See *ibid.*, paras. 29 and 23. [181] *Ibid.*, para. 29.

[182] Reservation of Guatemala to the American Convention, 9 March 1987, reprinted in 2001 Basic Documents, at 53–4. Guatemala withdrew its reservation in 1986. *Ibid.*, at 54.

[183] *Blake* v. *Guatemala* (Preliminary Objections, 1996), para. 34.

[184] *Ibid.*, para. 24. [185] *Ibid.*, para. 33. [186] *Ibid.*, para. 39.

[187] The Inter-American Convention on Forced Disappearance of Persons, Art. III, reprinted in 2001 Basic Documents, at 93 and 94; the United Nations Declaration on the Protection of All Persons from Enforced Disappearance, Art. 17(1); *Velásquez Rodríguez* v. *Honduras* (Merits), Inter-Am. Ct HR, 29 July 1988, Ser. C, No. 4, para. 155; *Godínez Cruz* (Merits), Inter-Am. Ct HR, 20 January 1989, Ser. C, No. 5, para. 163.

[188] *Blake* v. *Guatemala* (Preliminary Objections, 1996), para. 38.

> In accordance with the aforementioned principles of international law which are also embodied in Guatemalan legislation, forced disappearance implies the violation of various human rights recognized in international human rights treaties, including the American Convention, and that the effects of such infringements – even though some may have been completed, as in the instant case – may be prolonged continuously or permanently until such time as the victim's fate or whereabouts are established.[189]

Other than in the case of disappearances, it is not clear in what circumstances the Inter-American Court will deem there to be continuing violations. In the *Cantos* v. *Argentina Case*, in which the petitioner's property had allegedly been confiscated by Argentine authorities before Argentina ratified the American Convention and had never been returned to him, the State objected to the Court's consideration of aspects of the case that took place before its ratification.[190] Argentina had limited its acceptance of the jurisdiction of the Court to events that took place after it ratified the Convention.[191] The Commission alleged that the effects of the deprivation of the petitioner's property continued to the present and, therefore, constituted a continuing violation of the Convention.[192] The Court, in application of the Vienna Convention's provision against non-retroactivity of treaty obligations and the State's limitation in its acceptance of jurisdiction, stated that it did not consider it necessary to examine the theory of continuing violations, and that, if any of the acts imputed to the State took place before the State's ratification, the Court would not consider them.[193] The Court gave no further explanation of its reasoning, nor did it expressly overrule its holding in *Blake*. Thus, the future jurisprudence of continuing violations in the Inter-American system is unclear. It may be that the Court will not find continuing violations solely when property rights are at issue, that the Court will find continuing violations solely when disappearances are at issue, or that the Court will no longer consider allegations of continuing violations in any context.

The UN Human Rights Committee[194] and the European human rights system hold that they have jurisdiction over continuing violations, although whether a violation will be considered to be continuing by either

[189] *Ibid.*, para. 38. [190] *Cantos* v. *Argentina* (Preliminary Objections, 2001), para. 32.
[191] *Ibid.* [192] *Ibid.*, para. 39.
[193] See Vienna Convention on the Law of Treaties, Art. 28.
[194] *Lovelace* v. *Canada*, Communication No. 24/1977, at 83, UN GAOR, Hum. Rts. Comm., 36th Sess., Supp. No. 40, UN Doc. CCPR/C/OP/1 (1984). See also Zwart, *The Admissibility of Human Rights Petitions*, at 130 and n. 24.

body may be difficult to ascertain in advance of a ruling.[195] The UN HRC maintains that it has competence over events occurring before the Optional Protocol entered into force for a State 'when the effects of the event continued to have an effect on the rights of a victim subsequent to that date', even when the State has filed a reservation attempting to limit the jurisdiction *ratione temporis* of the Committee.[196] The European Court of Human Rights has found a violation of the right to property, when the property has not been returned to the victims, to be a continuing violation.[197] Moreover, the European Court has held that restrictions in a State's declaration of acceptance of jurisdiction may be declared invalid without invalidating the declarations itself.[198] This controversial interpretation has not been tested yet in the Inter-American system.

Jurisdiction *ratione temporis* over States that denounce the Convention

The Vienna Convention on the Law of Treaties specifies that, when a treaty has no provision governing denunciation or withdrawal from the treaty, a party must give at least twelve months' notice of its intention to withdraw from or denounce the treaty.[199] An international tribunal continues to have jurisdiction over proceedings that are pending against a State Party when that State denounces the treaty.[200] Generally, if the treaty does not provide otherwise, the lapse of jurisdiction takes effect only for the future and removes the foundation for the court's jurisdiction 'in respect to proceedings not instituted prior to the effective lapse'.[201] The date on which the proceedings are introduced is the 'critical date' for the determination of questions of both jurisdiction and admissibility.[202]

The American Convention provides that States Parties may denounce the American Convention 'at the expiration of a five-year period from the date of its entry into force and by means of notice given one year

[195] *Yagci and Sargin* v. *Turkey*, 319-A ECHR (Ser. A), paras. 37 and 40 (1995). See also *Mansur* v. *Turkey*, 319-B ECHR (Ser. A) (1995), para. 44.

[196] Human Rights Committee, General Comment 24 (52), para. 14.

[197] *Loizidou* v. *Turkey* (Merits), 1996-VI ECHR 2216, para. 41 (18 December); *Papamichalopoulos and Others* v. *Greece*, 260-B ECHR (Ser. A) paras. 40 and 45–6 (1993).

[198] *Loizidou* v. *Turkey* (Preliminary Objections), 310 Eur. Ct HR (Ser. A), paras. 89 and 95 (1995) (holding that a declaration of jurisdiction stands although an original condition or restriction of that acceptance fails).

[199] Vienna Convention on the Law of Treaties, Art. 56(2).

[200] See Rosenne, *The Time Factor*, at 26.

[201] *Ibid.*, at 28.

[202] *Ibid.*, at 28–9 and n. 1.

in advance'.[203] The effective date of the denunciation will then be one year from the date of the notice of denunciation. The Convention specifies that '[s]uch a denunciation shall not have the effect of releasing the State Party concerned from the obligations contained in this Convention with respect to any act that may constitute a violation of those obligations and that has been taken by that state prior to the effective date of denunciation'.[204] Trinidad and Tobago denounced the American Convention on 26 May 1998 in response to a Commission order that the State suspend the execution of prisoners on death row while the cases were being reviewed.[205] Under the Convention, because the denunciation did not enter into effect for one year from that date, the Commission and the Court had jurisdiction over any violation of human rights committed by the State until 26 May 1999.[206] Thus, in the *Hilaire, Constantine and Benjamin et al. Case*, the Court asserted jurisdiction to rule on alleged violations that had occurred while the Convention was in effect for Trinidad and Tobago.[207] In the *James et al. Case*, the Court asserted its jurisdiction in August 2000 to continue the orders of provisional measures that it had made in 1998 and 1999 for acts that took place prior to the effective date of its denunciation.[208] The State complied with the Court's order by submitting bi-monthly reports on the status of those death row prisoners who were the subject of provisional measures.[209]

The Inter-American Court's jurisprudence in this area conforms to generally accepted international principles. States have also attempted to denounce the jurisdiction of the ICJ and the organs of the European human rights system as a means of expressing dissatisfaction with litigation pending before them. Both the ICJ and the European Commission held that they continue to have jurisdiction *ratione temporis* over the

[203] American Convention, Art. 78(1). The State must give notice of its denunciation to the Secretary General of the OAS, who shall then inform the other States Parties to the Convention. *Ibid.*

[204] American Convention, Art. 78(2).

[205] Reprinted in 2001 Basic Documents, at 59.

[206] *Benjamin et al.* v. *Trinidad and Tobago* (Preliminary Objections, 2001), para. 22; *James et al.* (Trinidad and Tobago), Provisional Measures, Inter-Am. Ct HR, Order of 16 August 2000, Ser. E, Considering paras. 2–7. See generally Natasha Parassram Concepción, 'The Legal Implications of Trinidad and Tobago's Withdrawal from the American Convention on Human Rights', 16 *American University International Law Review*, 847 (2001).

[207] *Hilaire, Constantine and Benjamin et al. Case* (Merits), Inter-Am. Ct HR, 21 June 2002, Ser. C, No. 94, para. 13.

[208] *Ibid.*, para. 6.

[209] *James et al.* (Trinidad and Tobago), Provisional Measures, Inter-Am. Ct HR, Order of 24 November 2000, Ser. E, para. 4.

cases.[210] In 1969, Greece denounced the European Convention. The Commission held that Greece remained bound by the Convention for six months following its denunciation, and any violation of the Convention by Greek authorities during those six months remained subject to the jurisdiction *ratione temporis* of the Commission.[211]

If States are to be permitted to withdraw from human rights treaties, it is especially important that the withdrawal or denunciation not be effective for an extended period. The immediate effectiveness of a denunciation would allow a government that is about to undertake an action which will violate human rights to denounce the treaty, and thereby immediately free itself of its international human rights obligations. This would encourage rather than discourage denunciations of human rights treaties.

Jurisdiction *ratione temporis* over States that attempt to withdraw acceptance of the jurisdiction of the Court

The Inter-American Court has held that a State cannot withdraw its acceptance of the jurisdiction of the Inter-American Court unless the State denounces the American Convention.[212] The Court specified that, if a treaty provision that provides for the State to recognize the jurisdiction of an international tribunal does not also provide for denunciation of that recognition, the State must denounce the treaty to free itself from the jurisdiction of the Court.[213] The American Convention does not have a provision that expressly permits a State Party to withdraw its acceptance of the binding jurisdiction of the Inter-American Court. On 9 July 1999, Peru attempted to withdraw its recognition of the jurisdiction of the Inter-American Court without denouncing the American Convention.[214] The

210 See *Military and Paramilitary Activities (Nicaragua* v. *US)*, Preliminary Objections, 1984 ICJ Reports 392 (26 November); see also Rosenne, *The Time Factor*, at 28 (discussing the *Anglo-Iranian Oil Co.* case, in which the Iranian Government denounced its declaration 'to express its dissatisfaction because of litigation pending against it').

211 See Gomien, Harris, and Zwaak, *Law and Practice of the European Convention*, at 65 (citing the *Second Greek* case, Application to the Commission No. 4448/70, Decision of 26 May 1970, Yearbook 13, at 108 and 116–20).

212 *Ivcher Bronstein* v. *Peru* (Competence, 1999), paras. 40 and 46; *Constitutional Court* v. *Peru* (Competence, 1999), paras. 39 and 45.

213 *Ibid.*

214 See Letter from Fernando de Trazegnies Granda, Minister for Foreign Affairs of the Republic of Peru, reprinted in the 1999 Annual Report of the Inter-American Court of Human Rights, OEA/Ser.L/V/III.47 Doc. 6 (24 January 2000); *Ivcher Bronstein* v. *Peru* (Competence, 1999), para. 23; *Constitutional Court* v. *Peru* (Competence, 1999), para. 23.

Court held that Peru's attempted withdrawal was ineffective.[215] Peru had accepted the compulsory jurisdiction of the Court without limitation in 1981.[216] A hypothesis put forward for Peru's attempted withdrawal was that the State wished to avoid a Court ruling in the *Constitutional Court Case*.[217] In that case, which was pending before the Court, the victims were three Peruvian Constitutional Court Justices who had been removed from the Constitutional Court allegedly for a ruling which would have had the effect of limiting President Fujimori's run for another consecutive term.[218] After ruling that Peru's withdrawal was ineffective, the Court continued to consider the cases before it. Peru has since announced that, by means of a 18 January 2001 Legislative Resolution, the government considers itself subject to the contentious jurisdiction of the Court in accordance with the Court's decisions.[219]

Even a State's explicit reservation of the right to withdraw its acceptance of jurisdiction probably would not be considered valid in the Inter-American system.[220] In the *Ivcher Bronstein* and *Constitutional Court Cases*, the Court stated '[e]ven supposing, for the sake of argument, that "release" was possible – a hypothetical that this Court rejects . . . .'[221] Peru's declaration of acceptance of the Court's jurisdiction made no provision for the withdrawal of its acceptance.[222] Three States, however, that accepted the contentious jurisdiction of the Inter-American Court, therein reserved the right to withdraw their acceptances.[223] For example, the declaration of acceptance of Ecuador provides in relevant part that '[t]he Ecuadorian State reserves the right to withdraw its recognition of this competence and this jurisdiction whenever it may deem it advisable to

215 *Ivcher Bronstein* v. *Peru* (Competence, 1999), operative para. 1; *Constitutional Court* v. *Peru* (Competence, 1999), operative para. 1.

216 Reprinted in 2001 Basic Documents, at 56.

217 Douglass Cassel, 'Peru Withdraws from the Court: Will the Inter-American Human Rights System Meet the Challenge?', 20 *Human Rights Law Journal*, 167, 173 (1999).

218 *Constitutional Court* v. *Peru* (Competence, 1999), Inter-Am. Ct HR, 24 September 1999, Ser. C, No. 55, para. 2.

219 See letters from the Peruvian Minister of Justice to the Court dated 1 February 2001 and 16 February 2001, reprinted in the 2001 Annual Report of the Inter-American Court of Human Rights, at 1169–72.

220 *Ivcher Bronstein* v. *Peru* (Competence, 1999), paras. 51–2; *Constitutional Court* v. *Peru* (Competence, 1999), paras. 50–1.

221 *Ibid.*

222 See *Ivcher Bronstein* v. *Peru* (Competence, 1999), para. 30; *Constitutional Court* v. *Peru* (Competence, 1999), para. 29.

223 The States are Ecuador, Colombia and El Salvador. Their respective Declarations of Competence are reprinted in 2001 Basic Documents, at 52, 57 and 62.

do so'.[224] Colombia and El Salvador also attempted to reserve the right to withdraw their recognition of competence of the Inter-American Court at will.[225] A State might, however, achieve that result by accepting the Court's jurisdiction for a specific but limited period of time.

Objections to jurisdiction ratione loci

An objection to jurisdiction *ratione loci* is an objection that the act in question is not within the jurisdiction of the enforcement organs because it did not take place within the jurisdiction of the State. The Vienna Convention on the Law of Treaties provides that a treaty is binding upon a party with respect to its entire territory, unless the treaty or other circumstances establish a different intention.[226] Human rights treaties establish a different and broader intention in that they generally provide for a more encompassing scope. Under human rights treaties, a State is generally responsible for violations of the rights of persons within the State's 'jurisdiction'. For instance, the American Convention specifies that the States Parties undertake to respect the rights and freedoms recognized in the Convention and 'to ensure to all persons *subject to their jurisdiction* the free and full exercise of those rights'.[227] Likewise, the European Convention states that 'the High Contracting Parties shall secure to everyone *within their jurisdiction* the rights and freedoms' set forth in the Convention.[228]

Jurisdiction *ratione loci* not limited to a State's physical territory

The reference to the State's 'jurisdiction' in human rights treaties is not restricted to a State's national territory.[229] It is a general principle of international law that a State has jurisdiction as to acts of its nationals outside its territory.[230] When a State violates a right protected by the treaty anywhere

[224] Declaration of Recognition of Competence made by the State of Ecuador, reprinted in 2001 Basic Documents, at 52.

[225] Declaration of Recognition of Competence made by the State of Colombia, reprinted in 2001 Basic Documents, at 57–8.

[226] See 1969 Vienna Convention on the Law of Treaties, Art. 29; *Restatement (Third) of the Foreign Relations Law of the United States*, Note 3 to § 322(2).

[227] American Convention, Art. 1(1) (emphasis added).

[228] European Convention for the Protection of Human Rights and Fundamental Freedoms, as amended by Protocol No. 11, Rome, 4 November 1950, Art. 1 (emphasis added).

[229] *Loizidou* v. *Turkey* (Preliminary Objections), 310 Eur. Ct HR (Ser. A), para. 62 (1995).

[230] See Oscar Schachter, *International Law in Theory and Practice*, 254 (Martinus Nijhoff, The Hague, 1991).

in which that State exercises authority, the treaty may be applicable and the enforcement organs may have jurisdiction over the violation. For instance, when a State engages in lawful or unlawful military control outside its national territory, it may be responsible for any human rights violations caused.[231] In accordance with that principle, the European Court held that Turkey had jurisdiction over the area on Cyprus, because it exercised effective control through military occupation.[232] The Court further clarified that the State's human rights obligations derive 'from the fact of such control whether it be exercised directly, through its armed forces, or through a subordinate local administration'.[233] It reasoned that States are responsible for the 'acts of their authorities, whether performed within or outside national boundaries, which produce effects outside their own territory'.[234]

Although no objection to jurisdiction *ratione loci* has been raised to date before the Inter-American Court, the question has come before the Inter-American Commission with reference to the legal status of persons detained by the United States at Guantanamo Bay, Cuba. In its order of precautionary measures, the Commission implicitly held that the Guantanamo detainees, although outside the physical territory of the United States, were subject to its jurisdiction, because they were 'wholly within the authority and control of the United States Government'.[235] The Commission observed that the Guantanamo detainees were held at the 'unfettered discretion' of the US.[236] A US federal district court had dismissed a writ of *habeas corpus* filed on behalf of the Guantanamo detainees, holding that the right to any federal court review of their detention was foreclosed because the detainees were outside the sovereign territory of the United States.[237] The question of whether the United States has jurisdiction over the detainees in Guantanamo Bay, and therefore has international human rights obligations towards them, can only be raised before the Inter-American Court, if the United States accepts the Court's jurisdiction on an *ad hoc* basis or a more general request is made under the Court's advisory

[231] *Loizidou* v. *Turkey* (Preliminary Objections), 310 Eur. Ct HR (Ser. A), para. 62 (1995); *Cyprus* v. *Turkey*, App. No. 25781/94, 23 EHRR 244, para. 14 (1997) (Commission report).

[232] *Loizidou* v. *Turkey* (Preliminary Objections), 310 Eur. Ct HR (Ser. A), paras. 63–4 (1995).

[233] *Ibid.*, para. 62. [234] *Ibid.*

[235] Precautionary Measures issued by the Commission on 12 March 2002 in *Detainees at Guantanamo Bay, Cuba.*

[236] *Ibid.*

[237] See Request for Precautionary Measures, in *Coalition of Clergy et al., Petitioners* v. *George Walker Bush et al., Respondents*, Case No. CV 02-570 AHM, 21 February 2002.

jurisdiction. Should the Court be confronted with this question, it should follow international jurisprudence and hold that, if the State is exercising effective control over the area or the persons in question, it has jurisdiction for the purpose of its human rights obligations. A State should not be permitted to act with impunity on foreign territory which it effectively controls.

Limitation of jurisdiction *ratione loci* must be expressly permitted by treaty

A State may not limit the jurisdictional scope of the application of a treaty or the competence of the enforcement organs unless the treaty so permits. There is no provision in the American Convention permitting limitation of its scope, although a State Party can make reservations to the Convention. The American Convention provides that a State's acceptance of the jurisdiction of the Inter-American Court may be unconditional, reciprocal, for specific cases, or for a specified period.[238] The question of what is meant by a permissible limitation 'for specific cases' has not been raised before the Inter-American Court, but it should not be interpreted to permit a State to declare that no cases arising in a specific area of its jurisdiction be permitted. Consequently, it does not appear that a State Party could condition its acceptance to exclude human rights violations in particular areas over which it has jurisdiction.

States Parties to the American Convention that have accepted the jurisdiction of the Inter-American Court have not attempted to include territorial restrictions in their declarations of acceptance.[239] The issue, however, could arise in future State declarations of acceptance. This question came before the European human rights system. In the *Loizidou* v. *Turkey* case before the European Court, the applicant, a Cypriot national,

[238] American Convention, Art. 62(2).

[239] The Inter-American Court has not yet confronted an objection that it does not have jurisdiction *ratione loci* because the victim filed the petition from a third country. The violation may fall within the jurisdiction *ratione loci* of the enforcement organ even if the victim has left the State that allegedly violated his rights before submitting the complaint. The United Nations Human Rights Committee has set forth the relevant international law principles. See Dominic McGoldrick, *The Human Rights Committee: Its Role in the Development of the International Covenant on Civil and Political Rights*, 177 (Oxford, 1991). In several cases, Uruguay objected that the Human Rights Committee did not have jurisdiction *ratione loci* to examine a communication submitted under the Optional Protocol when the victim filed the communication from outside the jurisdiction of the State that allegedly violated the victim's rights. *Ibid.*

claimed that Turkey was violating her right to the peaceful enjoyment of her property in northern Cyprus, which has been occupied by Turkey since 1974.[240] Turkey objected that the European Court and Commission did not have jurisdiction *ratione loci* with respect to acts of Turkey in Cyprus, due to conditions Turkey made in its acceptance of the competence of those organs.[241] At that time, the European Convention only permitted State acceptance of jurisdiction to be conditioned on the bases of reciprocity or 'for a specified period'.[242] It did not authorize the limitation of jurisdiction on the basis of location. Consequently, the European Court held that Turkey's territorial restriction or limitation set forth in its declaration accepting the jurisdiction of the Court was null and void and had no legal effect.[243]

Protection of human rights is particularly necessary in territories that are ruled by another State, as was demonstrated when Namibia was governed by South Africa.[244] An interpretation that allows States to condition jurisdiction on the basis of location would effectively neutralize the effect of human rights treaties in disputed territories where the enforcement of human rights protections is most necessary. Consequently, it would diminish the effectiveness of the American Convention and weaken the role of the Inter-American Commission and Court. It is therefore necessary, to the extent possible, to specify in advance that such a condition would not be acceptable in the Inter-American system.

Additional jurisdictional issues

The Inter-American Court continues to have jurisdiction over a case even when one or both parties notify the Court that they wish to discontinue the proceedings.[245] This may occur when the parties reach a friendly

240 *Loizidou* v. *Turkey* (Preliminary Objections), 310 Eur. Ct HR (Ser. A), paras. 10–11 (1995).

241 Renewed Declaration of Turkey, 28 January 1990 (quoted in *Loizidou* v. *Turkey* (Preliminary Objections)), 310 Eur. Ct HR (Ser. A), paras. 25–7 (1995).

242 *Loizidou* v. *Turkey* (Preliminary Objections), 310 Eur. Ct HR (Ser. A), paras. 65–6 (1995); American Convention, Arts. 25 and 46.

243 *Ibid.*

244 See *Legal Consequences for States of the Continued Presence of South Africa in Namibia (South West Africa) Notwithstanding Security Council Resolution 276* (1970), 1971 ICJ Reports 16, 57, 79–80 (21 June).

245 2001 Rules of Procedure of the Inter-Am. Ct HR, Arts. 52 and 53. See generally Manuel Ventura Robles, 'The Discontinuance and Acceptance of Claims in the Jurisprudence of the Inter-American Court of Human Rights', 5 *International Law Students Association Journal of International and Comparative Law*, 603 (1999).

settlement,[246] the applicant decides to discontinue the case,[247] or the State pardons the victim[248] or accepts responsibility for the violation.[249] The Court, after considering the opinion of the other parties involved, including the representatives of the victim or the victim's next of kin, may continue to hear the case, close the case and strike it from its docket, oversee compliance with the parties' agreement, or, in the event the State accepts responsibility, proceed to a determination of reparations and costs.[250]

The State and the victim reached a friendly settlement after the Court was seised of the case in *Maqueda* v. *Argentina*, in which the Commission had found that Argentina had violated due process protections in the victim's trial.[251] Under the settlement, Argentina agreed to commute Maqueda's sentence to time served, and Maqueda's representatives agreed to petition the Commission to discontinue the case and to petition the Court to approve the agreement.[252] The Court, in accordance with the Rules of Procedure then in effect, consulted the parties to the case and the representatives of the victim, to determine whether all those affected acquiesced in the discontinuance.[253] As all the Court's findings were positive, and Maqueda had already been conditionally released from prison, the Court granted the discontinuance and reserved the right to reopen the case should there be a change in relevant circumstances.[254] The provision in the Court's Rules providing for the Court's consideration of the opinions of the victims in the case of a friendly settlement or request for a discontinuance was a positive step in the necessary recognition that the individual should be accorded a stronger voice in human rights proceedings.[255] Although this provision has been technically removed

[246] 2001 Rules of Procedure of the Inter-American Ct HR, Art. 53. *Benavides Cevallos* v. *Ecuador* (Merits), Inter-Am. Court HR, 19 June 1998, Ser. C, No. 38, Resolutions 3 and 5.

[247] 2001 Rules of Procedure of the Inter-Am. Ct HR, Art. 52(1).

[248] *Cantoral Benavides* v. *Peru* (Merits), Inter-Am. Ct HR, 18 August 2000, Ser. C, No. 69, para. 17.

[249] 2001 Rules of Procedure of the Inter-American Ct HR, Art. 52(2).

[250] *Ibid.*, Art. 52. The European Court of Human Rights also makes an independent decision as to whether to continue the consideration of the case when the parties agree not to proceed. See van Dijk and van Hoof, *Theory and Practice*, at 221–2.

[251] *Maqueda* v. *Argentina*, Inter-Am. Ct HR, 17 January 1995, Ser. C, No. 18, para. 18.

[252] *Ibid.* [253] *Ibid.*, paras. 26–7.

[254] *Maqueda* v. *Argentina*, 1995 Resolution, Decisions 1 and 3 of the Court.

[255] 1996 Rules of Procedure of the Inter-American Court of Human Rights, approved by the Court at its twenty-fourth regular session held on 9–20 September 1996, Arts. 52 and 53.

from the 2001 Rules, the status of the victim in this regard has not changed: the victim is now a party to the case,[256] and the parties to the case are to be consulted.[257]

The Court may also maintain jurisdiction over a case when the victim has been pardoned. In the *Cantoral Benavides Case*, in which Peru commuted the sentence of the victim and released him from prison after the Court was seised of the case, the State requested that the Court forego the preliminary proceedings and the merits and instead consider only the issue of compensation.[258] The Court refused the request, because the State refused to withdraw its preliminary objections which went to issues of admissibility and jurisdiction.[259] Although this decision increased the workload of the Court, general principles of law obligated the Court to consider the State's objections, because, if the application had been inadmissible or the Court had lacked jurisdiction, it would have had no authority to rule on the issue of reparations.

When the State accepts international responsibility in a case, the Court will normally proceed to the reparations stage of the proceedings. The possibility also exists that the government may acquiesce to only some of the facts raised in the petition. The Court could then continue to consider the remaining claims.[260] The Court is not bound by the parties' classification of which Articles of the Convention were violated by the facts acquiesced to by the State. The determination of the human rights law violated is reserved to the judicial powers of the Court.

In general, international courts also have jurisdiction, in accordance with national and international law, to consider additional facts which occur during the proceedings before the court and which consist of mere extensions of the facts complained of in the case.[261] The court can also consider facts that occurred subsequent to the filing of the application but which were directly related to those facts specified in the application.[262]

[256] 2001 Rules of Procedure of the Inter-Am. Ct HR, Art. 2(23).

[257] *Ibid.*, Arts. 52 and 53.

[258] *Cantoral Benavides*, Order of 18 June 1998, Inter-Am. Ct HR, reprinted in 1998 Annual Report of the Inter-Am. Ct HR, at 223–5.

[259] *Ibid.*

[260] *Villagrán Morales et al.* v. *Guatemala (The Street Children Case)* (Merits, 1999), paras. 24–7.

[261] *Stögmüller* v. *Austria*, 9 Eur. Ct HR (Ser. A), para. 7 (1969).

[262] *Neumeister* v. *Austria*, 8 Eur. Ct HR (Ser. A), Section as to the Law, para. 7 (1968).

Preliminary objections to admissibility

Once a tribunal has determined that it has jurisdiction, it may address preliminary objections directed to the admissibility of the case. Treaties, particularly human rights treaties, which permit States or individuals to petition the enforcing bodies for redress of violations, generally specify requisites that a petition must meet to be admissible. Treaties also set forth procedures that the enforcing bodies must follow in their consideration of a petition.[263] These requirements are meant to protect both the victim and State sovereignty, and, as such, any perceived deviation from them must be considered carefully.

States Parties to the American Convention often file preliminary objections alleging that the case is not admissible before the Court on the ground that either the petitioner or the Commission failed to comply with the Convention-mandated requirements or procedures.[264] In ruling on these preliminary objections, the Court has refused to take a strictly formalistic view. The Court interprets the Convention in favour of the individual.[265] The Court has made it clear that 'the procedural system is a means of attaining justice and that [justice] cannot be sacrificed for the sake of mere formalities'.[266] Furthermore, the Court has held that 'failure to observe certain formalities is not necessarily relevant when dealing on the international plane. What is essential is that the conditions necessary for the preservation of the procedural rights of the parties not be diminished or unbalanced and that the objectives of the different procedures be met.'[267] The Court's position promotes substance over form and provides greater protection of human rights. The Court, however, will uphold objections to serious procedural defects in the Commission's processing of a case, even if, as in the *Cayara Case*, it results in dismissal of the case.[268]

[263] The American Convention, like the European Convention, sets forth admissibility requirements and procedural rules. American Convention, Arts. 46–51.

[264] See *Velásquez Rodríguez* v. *Honduras* (Preliminary Objections), Inter-Am. Ct HR, 26 June 1987, Ser. C, No. 1. See Bertha Santoscoy, *La Commission interaméricaine des droits de l'homme et le développement de sa compétence par le système des petitions individuelles* (Presses Universitaires de France, Paris, 1995); Monica Pinto, *La Denuncia ante la Comisión Interamericana de Derechos Humanos*, 49 (Editores del Puerto, Buenos Aires, 1993).

[265] *In the Matter of Viviana Gallardo et al.*, Inter-Am. Ct HR, Decision of 13 November 1981, Ser. A, No. G101/81, para. 16.

[266] *Cayara* v. *Peru* (Preliminary Objections, 1993), para. 42.

[267] *Velásquez Rodríguez* v. *Honduras* (Preliminary Objections, 1987), para. 33.

[268] *Cayara* v. *Peru* (Preliminary Objections, 1993), para. 63.

Objections that the petition to the Commission was inadmissible because the petitioner did not comply with the formal requirements of the Convention

The Executive Secretariat of the Commission is responsible during the initial processing of a complaint for determining whether the complaint meets the requirements for consideration by the Commission.[269] If the petition is initially lacking in some respect, the Secretariat may request additional information from the petitioner.[270] Since many of the petitions in the Inter-American system are lodged by uneducated and desperate people, the Commission's flexibility in this area is essential.

Technical informational requirements

A petition or complaint to the Commission alleging human rights abuses under the American Convention must be in writing and must contain specific information.[271] It must set forth the facts, including the location and date of the alleged violation and the State allegedly responsible. These facts must make a *prima facie* showing of a violation of the Convention or other treaty over which the Commission and Court have jurisdiction.[272] If possible, the petition should provide the name of the victim and of any public authority who is aware of the facts.[273] The petition must contain the name, nationality and signature of the person lodging it.[274] As the Convention and the Rules of the Commission and Court do not provide a definition of signature, petitioners could conceivably use electronic signatures. The requirements that the petitioner list an occupation and postal address or legal domicile have been eliminated.[275] In place of the former address requirements, the Commission now requests an address to which the Commission can send correspondence and, when available,

[269] 2001 Rules of Procedure of the Inter-Am. Comm. HR, Art. 24. The requirements for consideration of petitions are listed in Art. 28 *ibid.*

[270] *Ibid.*, Art. 26(2). See Christina Cerna, 'Commission Organization and Petitions', in *The Inter-American System of Human Rights*, 79 (Harris and Livingstone, eds., Clarendon Press, Oxford, and Oxford University Press, New York, 1998).

[271] 2001 Rules of Procedure of the Inter-Am. Comm. HR, Art. 28. For those OAS Member States that are not parties to the American Convention, the Commission considers individual complaints that the State violated the rights set forth in the American Declaration of the Rights and Duties of Man. These complaints cannot be submitted to the Court, however, and, therefore, the technical requirements and Commission procedures are beyond the subject matter of this book.

[272] American Convention, Art. 47(b).

[273] 2001 Rules of Procedure of the Inter-Am. Comm. HR, Art. 28(e).

[274] American Convention, Art. 46(1)(d).

[275] See Former Regulations of the Inter-Am. Comm., Art. 32(a).

a telephone and fax number and email address.[276] The change in this requirement, and the express authorization that the petitioner may request that his or her identity not be revealed to the State,[277] protects the petitioner from possible retribution. The petition must also indicate whether actions have been taken to exhaust domestic remedies, whether the facts of the complaint have been submitted to another international settlement body and whether the petition has been lodged within six months of the final domestic judgment.[278]

It is not necessary for the petitioner to specifically list the Article of the Convention that was allegedly violated.[279] It is enough that the petition allege all the facts relevant to deduce a violation of the Convention.[280] In the *Hilaire* v. *Trinidad and Tobago Case*, the State objected that the Court did not have jurisdiction to hold that the State had violated a particular Article of the Convention, because the petitioners had not alleged its violation within the six-month time limit.[281] The petitioners had filed their complaint in a timely manner, stating all the relevant facts. It was not, however, until their third supplement to the petition that they expressly argued that the State had violated the Article of the Convention in question. That supplement had been filed outside the required time limit. The Court dismissed the preliminary objection, reasoning that, as long as the essential facts are pleaded in a timely manner, it is immaterial that an additional legal argument is not raised until a later date.[282] The lack of the technical requirement and the Court's holding are important, because some petitioners file a complaint on their own and only subsequently acquire legal counsel who can cite the specific violations of the Convention.

Six-month rule

A petition is admissible only if it was lodged with the Commission within six months from the date that the party alleging the violation was notified of the final domestic judgment in the State where the violation allegedly occurred.[283] The six-month rule serves much like a statute of

276 2001 Rules of Procedure of the Inter-Am. Comm. HR, Art. 28(c).

277 *Ibid.*, Art. 28(b). 278 *Ibid.*, Art. 28(g)–(i).

279 *Ibid.*, Art. 28(f).

280 *Hilaire* v. *Trinidad and Tobago* (Preliminary Objections, 2001), Inter-Am. Ct HR, 1 September 2001, Ser. C, No. 80.

281 *Ibid.*, paras. 29–33. 282 *Ibid.*, para. 42.

283 See American Convention, Art. 46(1)(b); and 2001 Rules of Procedure of the Inter-Am. Comm. HR, Art. 32.

limitations that eliminates stale claims and provides a date of closure for the State. The Commission explained that the 'rule exists to allow for juridical certainty while still providing sufficient time for a potential petitioner to consider her position'.[284] In cases in which the petitioner alleges a denial of domestic justice, however, the petitioner never receives a final judgment. In those cases, the Commission will consider a petition that is presented within a reasonable time after the date of the alleged violation.[285]

Neither the six-month rule nor the reasonable time test is a bar to admissibility when the violation is found to be ongoing at the time of the filing of the petition.[286] It is justifiable to have no time limit for the filing of complaints when the State could take action to correct an ongoing violation. For example, the State could return property to a victim who has been deprived of its peaceful enjoyment or free a victim who continues to be incarcerated. In the case of forced disappearances, however, which have been held to be ongoing violations, there may be no way for the State to inform the victim's relatives of the whereabouts or fate of the victim. If the victim disappeared in the distant past, evidence may no longer be available to put an end to the case. International treaties, however, have declared disappearances to be an ongoing violation which puts them within the jurisdiction *ratione temporis* of the Inter-American Commission and Court.[287] In such cases it would be preferable for the Commission to apply the 'reasonable time' test to avoid consideration of unreasonably old cases when no additional facts appear to be available and the State has accepted international responsibility for the disappearances. The situation differed in the *Trujillo Oroza Case*, however, in which the petitioner filed a petition in 1992 alleging that her son had been disappeared by Bolivian authorities in 1971, because the State had not yet accepted responsibility for the disappearance when the petition was filed.[288]

[284] Case 11.625, Inter-Am. Comm. HR 144, 151, para. 29, OEA/Ser.L/V/II.98, doc. 7 rev. (1998). See Alexander H. E. Morawa, 'The Individual as a Party to International Human Rights Litigation, with Particular Reference to the Issue of "Abuse of the Right to Petition" ', 4 *Journal of International Relations*, 11 (1997).

[285] See 2001 Rules of Procedure of the Inter-Am. Comm. HR, Art. 32(2). The Commission will consider the 'circumstances of each case' in determining what constitutes 'a reasonable period of time'. *Ibid.*

[286] See Christina Cerna, 'Commission Organization and Petitions', at 93.

[287] See pp. 110–12 above.

[288] *Trujillo Oroza* v. *Bolivia* (Merits), Inter-Am. Ct HR, 26 January 2000, Ser. C, No. 64, para. 2.

Lis pendens: petition not substantially the same as one previously studied or pending before another international body

A petition is not admissible if it is substantially the same as a communication or petition currently pending before or previously studied by the Inter-American Commission or another international organization.[289] A petition is considered to be 'substantially the same' as another if it involves the same parties, is based on the same facts, and asserts identical legal grounds.[290] The Court held in the *Durand and Ugarte Case*, which was based on the same Peruvian prison massacre as the *Neira Alegría Case* which had already been considered by the Commission, that, as long as different persons are named as the alleged victims, the case does not involve the same parties and can therefore be heard by the Commission and the Court.[291] Moreover, if the alleged victims were not individualized in the other proceeding, there is not sufficient identity of the parties so as to bar consideration of the petition.[292] The complaints are based on the same facts if 'the behavior or the event that is a violation of some human rights' is identical.[293] It is questionable if the Court will find that the legal grounds are identical if the alleged violation is of provisions of different treaties but involves the same right, such as freedom of association.[294] If the same right is involved, it should be considered the same legal ground regardless of which treaty is cited. The Inter-American Court will also base its determination on whether there is a duplication of procedures on the nature of the outcome of proceedings before the conflicting body. If the other international organization merely issues recommendations to the State, as compared to the binding judgments awarding reparations which are rendered by the Inter-American Court, the Court will allow the case to go forward in the Inter-American system.[295]

In the *Baena Ricardo et al. Case*, Panama unsuccessfully objected that the petition was barred due to duplication of procedures.[296] The International Labor Organization had previously considered a complaint and issued a resolution condemning the State for the mass dismissal of the

289 See American Convention, Arts. 46(1)(c) and 47(d). See also 2001 Rules of Procedure of the Inter-Am. Comm. HR, Art. 33.

290 *Baena Ricardo et al.* v. *Panama* (Preliminary Objections, 1999), Inter-Am. Ct HR, Judgment of 18 November 1999, Ser. C, No. 61, para. 53.

291 *Durand and Ugarte* (Preliminary Objections), Inter-Am. Ct HR, Judgment of 28 May 1999, Ser. C, No. 50, para. 43.

292 *Baena Ricardo et al.* v. *Panama* (Preliminary Objections, 1999), para. 54.

293 *Ibid.*, para. 55, quoting *Durand and Ugarte* (Preliminary Objections), para. 43.

294 See *Baena Ricardo et al.* v. *Panama* (Preliminary Objections, 1999), para. 56.

295 *Ibid.*, para. 57.

296 *Ibid.*, para. 58.

workers. The ILO resolution was based on the same laws and incidents as those alleged in the complaint to the Commission.[297] The Inter-American Court rejected the State's preliminary objection because the 270 workers had been individually named in the petition to the Commission, whereas the ILO petitioners were the trade unions. Furthermore, the Court did not find that the facts were entirely overlapping, because the State had taken additional actions violating the workers' human rights after the ILO case. The Inter-American Court held that the legal grounds were much more extensive before the Inter-American Court, in that the complaint alleged the violation of *inter alia* the American Convention's right to a free trial, freedom from *ex post facto* laws, the right to compensation, rights of assembly and association, and the right to judicial protection, whereas before the ILO the complainants predominantly raised the violation of workers' rights and freedom of association.[298] Moreover, the ILO merely issued a resolution and recommendation to the State; the workers did not receive a remedy.[299]

The most likely conflict would be between the Inter-American enforcement organs and the UN Human Rights Committee, which examines individual complaints pursuant to the First Optional Protocol to the UN Covenant on Civil and Political Rights.[300] The Human Rights Committee also has a rule of procedure which provides that to be admissible the Committee must ascertain that the matter is not 'being examined under another procedure of international investigation or settlement'.[301] These provisions are meant to eliminate duplication of procedures rather than to limit the victims' opportunity to have their cases heard individually.

The Inter-American Commission interprets the requirement of non-duplication in a broad sense. Its Rules of Procedure permit the Commission to examine petitions that are or have been before another international organization in two circumstances.[302] First, the Inter-American Commission may consider a petition when the other international organization has only examined the general human rights situation in the State in question and has not made a decision on the specific facts contained in the petition.[303] Thus, the Inter-American Commission would not be barred from considering cases that are before the UN Human

[297] *Ibid.*, paras. 48 and 58. [298] *Ibid.*, paras. 54–6 and 58. [299] *Ibid.*, para. 57.

[300] Optional Protocol to the UN Covenant on Civil and Political Rights, reprinted in (1967) 6 ILM 383, Arts. 1–2.

[301] Rules of Procedure of the United Nations Human Rights Committee, Rule 90(e).

[302] 2001 Rules of Procedure of the Inter-Am. Comm. HR, Art. 33(2).

[303] *Ibid.*, Art. 33(2)(a).

Rights Commission and the Economic and Social Council, whose mandates are to study and report publicly on the human rights situations in specific countries and on major types of human rights violations throughout the world. Although in studying the more global human rights situation, these organs may take into consideration information about individual cases, they do not make a ruling on individual cases or order the State to make reparations to the victims. The victims are afforded no relief, except insofar as the negative publicity encourages the State to refrain from future violations. Thus, this exception is in the best interests of the petitioner and poses no additional burden for the State. The UN Human Rights Committee also determined that it would not be barred from considering communications that have been before these bodies.[304]

Secondly, the Inter-American Commission will consider the petition when the petitioner before the Commission is the alleged victim of the violation or a family member of the victim, and the petitioner before the other organization is a non-governmental entity or other third party who was not authorized by the victim or his family to file the complaint.[305] This exception is justifiable because the victim and his or her family should always be given precedence in their choice of forum. If those who suffered the human rights violations choose to litigate a case within the Inter-American system, the Commission should not dismiss the complaint because a third party has filed a similar petition with another international body. The Commission's interpretation of this Convention requirement allows for a procedural balance between the parties. The individual victim has the right to have his or her claim processed and reparations awarded in an international forum, and the State is not required to defend itself on the same facts in two fora.

Exhaustion of domestic remedies

Perhaps the most common preliminary objection is that the petitioner did not exhaust domestic remedies in the State of the alleged violation before lodging the petition with the Commission. It is a generally recognized principle of international law that a victim of human rights abuse must

[304] Decision of 25 March 1996, Views of the Human Rights Committee under Article 5, para. 4, of the Optional Protocol to the International Covenant on Civil and Political Rights. *Ms G. (Name Deleted)* v. *Canada*, Communication No. 934/2000, UN GAOR, Hum. Rts. Comm., 69th Sess., UN Doc. CCPR/C/69/D/934/2000 (2000). UN Human Rights Committee decisions are available on the Internet at www.umn.edu/humanrts/undocs/.

[305] See 2001 Rules of Procedure of the Inter-Am. Comm. HR, Art. 33(2)(b).

pursue and exhaust all available remedies in the local legal system before resorting to an international forum.[306] Brownlie reasoned that 'this is a rule which is justified by practical and political considerations and not by any logical necessity deriving from international law as a whole'.[307] It gives the State an opportunity to attempt to resolve the case under its internal law before being confronted in an international proceeding.[308]

The American Convention, in accordance with international law, provides that the petitioner must, when possible, first exhaust domestic remedies before filing a petition with the Commission.[309] In this regard, the petitioner must provide information on which domestic remedies he or she has attempted to use and the outcome of those attempts. When the case has been heard in a domestic court, the petition must include information about the judgment, any appeal, and the date of the final judgment.[310] In the *Cantoral Benavides Case*, for example, the petitioner specified that the victim had been subjected to a trial and four judgments in military courts and then to a trial in a civilian court.[311] Nonetheless, the State objected that domestic remedies had not been exhausted when the petitioners lodged the complaint with the Commission.[312] The Court rejected the preliminary objection.[313]

If the Commission receives a petition before domestic remedies have been exhausted, it may not begin its consideration of the matter. It may, however, hold the petition until the final judgment in the State and then process it. In the *Castillo Petruzzi Case*, the petitioners filed their complaint with the Commission while their cases were still pending before a military tribunal in Peru.[314] For that reason, the State later objected that the petitioners had not met the admissibility requirement that domestic remedies had been exhausted.[315] The Court rejected the preliminary objection, because the Commission had not acted on the case until after the final judgment in Peru.[316] The Commission did not transmit the

[306] See American Convention, Art. 46(1)(a); European Convention, Art. 35(1); Optional Protocol to the UN Covenant on Civil and Political Rights, Arts. 2 and 5(2)(b).

[307] Ian Brownlie, *Principles of Public International Law*, at 497. See A. A. Cançado Trindade, *The Application of the Rule of Exhaustion of Local Remedies in International Law* (Cambridge, 1983).

[308] *Velásquez Rodríguez* v. *Honduras* (Merits, 1988), para. 61.

[309] American Convention, Art. 46(1)(a); 2001 Rules of Procedure of the Inter-Am. Comm. HR, Arts. 28(h) and 31.

[310] See Cerna, 'Commission Organization and Petitions', at 79.

[311] *Cantoral Benavides* v. *Peru* (Preliminary Objections, 1998), paras. 28 and 32.

[312] *Ibid.* [313] *Ibid.*, para. 47 and operative para. 1.

[314] *Castillo Petruzzi et al.* v. *Peru* (Preliminary Objections, 1998), para. 52.

[315] See *ibid.* [316] See *ibid.*, paras. 54–5.

notification of the petition to Peru until the Peruvian military tribunal convicted the petitioners, which was the final judgment in the State.[317] The Court reasoned that the Commission's receipt of a petition must not be confused with the admission of and consideration of a case.[318] This holding takes into account practical considerations in the Inter-American system and is not so overly formalistic that it discourages petitioners from resorting to the Commission. It would be inefficient for the Commission to send back the petition and force the petitioners to resubmit it later. Petitioners often do not understand the requisites of admissibility and need to be advised that they must await a final ruling before the Commission can act on the petition. It would only prove confusing and frustrating to victims and their families if the Commission returned the petition until such time as a final ruling in the domestic courts was provided, especially as justice in the national systems is often delayed.

Domestic remedies must be adequate and effective When a State objects that domestic remedies have not been exhausted, it then has the burden of proving which domestic remedies remain.[319] It is not sufficient that domestic remedies formally exist.[320] The State must show that those remedies are both 'adequate' and 'effective' for the type of violation alleged.[321] A domestic remedy is adequate only if it is suitable to address the infringement of the specific legal right allegedly violated.[322] For instance, although *habeas corpus* is the normal remedy used to locate a person detained by the authorities, it is not adequate to locate a person who has disappeared, if the domestic law requires that the person filing

[317] *Ibid.* [318] See *ibid.*

[319] *Cantoral Benavides* v. *Peru* (Preliminary Objections, 1998), para. 31; *Loayza Tamayo* v. *Peru* (Preliminary Objections), Inter-Am. Ct HR, 31 January 1996, Ser. C, No. 25, para. 40; *Castillo Páez* v. *Peru* (Preliminary Objections), Inter-Am. Ct HR, 30 January 1996, Ser. C, No. 24, para. 40; *Neira Alegría et al.* v. *Peru* (Preliminary Objections), Inter-Am. Ct HR, 11 December 1991, Ser. C, No. 13, para. 30; *Gangaram Panday* v. *Suriname* (Preliminary Objections), Inter-Am. Ct HR, 4 December 1991, Ser. C, No. 12, para. 38; *Fairén Garbi and Solís Corrales* (Preliminary Objections), Inter-Am. Ct HR, 26 June 1987, Ser. C, No. 2, para. 87; *Godínez Cruz* (Preliminary Objections), Inter-Am. Ct HR, 26 June 1987, Ser. D, No. 3, para. 90; *Velásquez Rodríguez* v. *Honduras* (Preliminary Objections, 1987), para. 88.

[320] *Las Palmeras* v. *Colombia* (Merits, 2001), para. 58.

[321] *Velásquez Rodríguez* v. *Honduras* (Merits), Inter-Am. Ct HR, 29 July 1988, Ser. C, No. 4, paras. 63–4.

[322] *Ibid.*, para. 64; *Godínez Cruz* (Merits), Inter-Am. Ct HR, 20 January 1989, Ser. C, No. 5, para. 67; *Fairén Garbi and Solís Corrales* (Merits), Inter-Am. Ct HR, 15 March 1989, Ser. C, No. 6, para. 88.

the writ identify the detention area.[323] The Court first explained this reasoning in the *Velásquez Rodríguez Case* against Honduras, in which the victim had been picked up on a busy street of the nation's capital in broad daylight by government agents.[324] The victim's family did not know where he was being held. After unsuccessfully filing three writs of *habeas corpus* and two criminal complaints, the family filed a petition with the Inter-American Commission.[325] Honduras objected that domestic remedies had not been exhausted, because the petitioner had not identified both the place of detention and the detaining authority in the writ of *habeas corpus*, as required under Honduran law.[326] The Court did not accept this objection, reasoning that a norm should not be interpreted so as to 'lead to a result that is manifestly absurd or unreasonable'.[327]

Furthermore, the remedy must also be effective, meaning that it is capable of producing the anticipated result.[328] In the *Fairén Garbi and Solís Corrales Case*, the Court rejected the State's argument that the exhumation of a body found in a mass clandestine grave in Honduras would have been an effective remedy to guarantee the rights of a person who was presumed to have disappeared.[329] The Court has also held that *habeas corpus* cannot be considered an effective remedy if it is not applied impartially by the government, or if the party invoking it is thereby placed in danger.[330] Moreover, domestic remedies that prove illusory due to the circumstances of the case or the general situation in the State cannot be considered effective.[331] In the *Constitutional Court Case*, in which the victims had filed applications for the remedy of *amparo*, and the domestic courts had waited for six months to reject them, the Inter-American Court held that the remedy was illusory and ineffective because of the unjustified delay of the State authorities in reaching a decision.[332]

The Court reasoned that resorting to domestic remedies becomes a 'senseless formality' if they 'are denied for trivial reasons or without an

[323] *Velásquez Rodríguez* v. *Honduras* (Merits, 1988), paras. 64–5. The Court reasoned that 'in such cases there is only hearsay evidence of the detention, and the whereabouts of the victim is unknown'. *Ibid.*, para. 65.

[324] *Velásquez Rodríguez* v. *Honduras* (Preliminary Objections, 1987), para. 15.

[325] *Velásquez Rodríguez* v. *Honduras* (Merits, 1988), para. 74.

[326] *Ibid.*, para. 75. [327] *Ibid.*, para. 64. [328] *Ibid.*, para. 66.

[329] *Fairén Garbi and Solís Corrales* (Merits, 1989), para. 89.

[330] *Velásquez Rodríguez* v. *Honduras* (Merits, 1988), para. 66.

[331] *Las Palmeras* v. *Colombia* (Merits, 2001), para. 58; *Constitutional Court* v. *Peru* (Merits, 2001), para. 93.

[332] *Constitutional Court* v. *Peru* (Merits, 2001), para. 93; see also *Mayagna (SUMO) Awas Tingni Community* v. *Nicaragua* (Merits), Inter-Am. Ct HR, 31 August 2001, Ser. C, No. 79, para. 134.

examination of the merits, or if there is proof of the existence of a practice or policy ordered or tolerated by the government'.[333] The rule of exhaustion is not meant to be a procedural obstacle course that requires victims and their families to jump every possible hurdle before resorting to an international forum. It is intended to give the State a reasonable opportunity to provide relief. If that relief is not available in the domestic system, the victim should be allowed immediate recourse to international channels. In short, the domestic remedies available must be adequate and effective; if they are not, the victim may be exempted from pursuing them.

Although domestic remedies differ somewhat in different legal systems, the Court has been able to set forth a few general principles that allow for more certainty as to the remedies that need or need not be exhausted in the case of particular human rights violations. The Court has categorically stated that *habeas corpus* is 'the normal means of finding a person presumably detained by the authorities, of ascertaining whether he is legally detained and, given the case, of obtaining his liberty'.[334] Therefore, if the petitioners unsuccessfully file a writ of *habeas corpus* in such cases, they would normally have exhausted domestic remedies, and can turn to the Inter-American system. The Court has also held that the civil law procedural remedy of *amparo* has the characteristics necessary for the protection of certain fundamental rights.[335] Conversely, the Court specified that a civil proceeding which permits a presumptive finding of death so as to allow the heirs to divide the estate or the spouse to remarry is not an adequate remedy to find a person who has been disappeared.[336] Additional statements by the Inter-American Court detailing concrete limitations and adequate remedies would further reduce preliminary objections.

Exceptions to the exhaustion of domestic remedies Victims of human rights abuse and their family members frequently encounter difficulties in pursuing legal remedies in the State of the alleged violation. Under certain circumstances international law does not require that the petitioner exhaust domestic remedies. The Inter-American Court has stated that 'the

[333] *Velásquez Rodríguez* v. *Honduras* (Merits, 1988), para. 68.

[334] *Caballero Delgado and Santana* v. *Colombia* (Preliminary Objections), Inter-Am. Ct HR, 21 January 1994, Ser. C, No. 17, para. 64 (citing *Velásquez Rodríguez* v. *Honduras* (Merits, 1988), para. 65; *Godínez Cruz* (Merits, 1989), para. 68; and *Fairén Garbi and Solís Corrales* (Merits, 1989), para. 90).

[335] *Mayagna (SUMO) Awas Tingni Community* v. *Nicaragua* (Merits, 2001), para. 131, citing *Judicial Guarantees in States of Emergency (Articles 27(2), 25 and 8 American Convention on Human Rights)*, Advisory Opinion OC-9/87 of 6 October 1987, Ser. A, No. 9, para. 23.

[336] *Fairén Garbi and Solís Corrales* (Merits, 1989), para. 88.

rule of prior exhaustion must never lead to a halt or delay that would render international action in support of the defenseless victim ineffective'.[337] For this reason, the American Convention sets forth specific exceptions to the doctrine of the exhaustion of domestic remedies.[338] These statutory exceptions are applicable when: (1) due process of law does not exist for protection of the right allegedly violated; (2) local authorities deny access to or prevent a party from exhausting such remedies; or (3) there is unwarranted delay in the rendering of a final domestic judgment.[339] The Inter-American Court has repeatedly held that there has been an unwarranted delay in issuing a final judgment when a period of five years has transpired from the initiation of proceedings to the time when the case is brought before the Commission.[340] The State must provide a convincing explanation to justify a longer delay.[341]

In its jurisprudence, the Court has interpreted the statutorily recognized exceptions to hold that the victim need not comply with the exhaustion doctrine if he or she is indigent or unable to find a lawyer due to the fear of governmental reprisals.[342] Indigence may trigger an exception to the duty of exhaustion if a person does not have the financial resources to pay mandatory filing fees or secure legal representation.[343] Moreover, when a claimant is unable to secure legal representation because domestic lawyers are afraid to accept the case, the claimant need not exhaust domestic remedies.[344] The Inter-American Court's interpretation of the exceptions are particularly important for those victims who live under a regime that has engaged in a policy of using gross and systematic violations of human rights to intimidate the population.

A question arises when the petitioner makes no attempt to exhaust domestic remedies even though the situation that interfered with doing so has arguably passed. In the *Trujillo Oroza Case*, a twenty-one-year old university student was arrested by Bolivian authorities and subsequently disappeared. The violation occurred in 1971.[345] In 1992, the victim's mother filed a complaint with the Inter-American Commission. Although she had complained and taken action before executive and legislative authorities, she had never filed a writ of *habeas corpus* or any complaint with the

[337] *Velásquez Rodríguez* v. *Honduras* (Preliminary Objections, 1987), para. 93.
[338] See American Convention, Art. 46(2). [339] See *ibid.*
[340] *Genie Lacayo* (Merits, 1997), para. 81; *Las Palmeras* v. *Colombia* (Preliminary Objections, 2000), para. 38.
[341] *Las Palmeras* v. *Colombia* (Preliminary Objections, 2000), para. 38.
[342] See Advisory Opinion OC-11/90, paras. 30 and 35. [343] See *ibid.*, para. 30.
[344] See *ibid.*, paras. 34–5. [345] *Trujillo Oroza* v. *Bolivia* (Merits, 2000), para. 2(a).

Bolivian courts.[346] She explained this failure by citing the political instability of the country, the fear of reprisal and the dependence of the courts on the executive.[347] Bolivia objected that it had returned to democracy ten years before she filed the complaint with the Commission, and that she should have pursued domestic remedies subsequent to that time.[348] This argument was not pursued before the Court, because the State withdrew its preliminary objections and accepted international responsibility for the disappearance.[349] Filing a writ of *habeas corpus* or pursuing other domestic remedies years after a person has disappeared would be a needless formality, the only purpose of which would be to satisfy a statutory requirement. It could not be expected that the remedy would be effective, and therefore it should be excused.

Objections that the Commission failed to follow the procedures mandated by the Convention

An understanding of the Convention-mandated Commission procedures is necessary to an analysis of whether the Commission met its procedural obligations in a specific case and, thus, whether a given preliminary objection was well-founded. Prior to the entry into force of the American Convention, procedures before the Commission were relatively informal.[350] With the advent of the Convention, States Parties, petitioners and the Court came to expect and demand technical competence, formal procedures and explicit deadlines.[351] For a time, however, due to its commitments in other areas, the Commission continued its casual handling of cases.[352] As a result, before the Commission restructured its procedures, the Court made several rulings in response to States' objections to the procedures applied by the Commission.

The Convention and the Rules of Procedure of the Commission set forth the steps that the Commission must employ when dealing with a complaint.[353] A procedural oversight, however, will not necessarily result in dismissal of a case unless it diminishes the State's procedural rights or hampers its ability to present a defence.[354] The Court holds in this regard

346 *Ibid.*, para. 2(f). 347 *Ibid.* 348 *Ibid.*, paras. 8 and 17. 349 *Ibid.*, para. 33.

350 See Tom Farer, 'The Rise of the Inter-American Human Rights Regime: No Longer a Unicorn, Not Yet an Ox', in *The Inter-American System of Human Rights*, 61–2.

351 See *ibid.*, at 62. 352 See *ibid.*

353 American Convention, Arts. 48–51; 2001 Rules of Procedure of the Inter-Am. Comm. HR, Arts. 26–47.

354 *Velásquez Rodríguez* v. *Honduras* (Preliminary Objections, 1987), para. 74.

that '[i]t would be contrary to the object and purpose of the Convention, and would fail to take into account its context, to apply the regulatory norms without the criterion of reasonableness, resulting in an imbalance between the parties and compromising the realization of justice'.[355] To date, the only case dismissed by the Court due to faulty procedures employed by the Commission was the *Cayara Case*.[356]

Decision on admissibility

The Commission's 2001 Rules of Procedure set forth a detailed schema of steps that must be taken by the Commission upon its receipt of a complaint. When an individual complaint is lodged with the Commission, the Executive Secretariat processes the petition and makes a *prima facie* determination of admissibility based on the Convention's requirements.[357] The Secretariat will register a petition that is *prima facie* admissible, record the date of receipt, and notify the petitioner.[358] If the petition does not meet the basic requirements of admissibility, the Secretariat, on behalf of the Commission, may request that the petitioner or the petitioner's representative complete it.[359] The Secretariat transmits the pertinent parts of a petition that is *prima facie* admissible to the government concerned and requests information.[360] The request for information is not a prejudgment as to the admissibility of the petition.[361] The Commission will withhold the identity of the petitioner from the State, unless the petitioner expressly authorizes the disclosure.[362]

The State must respond to the Commission by providing relevant information within two months of the date the communication is transmitted.[363] The State may, with just cause, request an extension to

[355] *Paniagua Morales et al.* v. *Guatemala* (Preliminary Objections, 1996), para. 40, cited in *Case of the Nineteen Merchants* v. *Colombia* (Preliminary Objections), Inter-Am. Ct HR, 12 June 2002, Ser. C. No. 93, para. 28.

[356] *Cayara* v. *Peru* (Preliminary Objections, 1993), Resolutions 1 and 3.

[357] 2001 Rules of Procedure of the Inter-Am. Comm. HR, Art. 29(1). See also Cerna, 'Commission Organization and Petitions', at 80.

[358] 2001 Rules of Procedure of the Inter-Am. Comm. HR, Art. 29(1)(a).

[359] *Ibid.*, Arts. 26(2) and 29(1)(b).

[360] See American Convention, Art. 48(1)(a); 2001 Rules of Procedure of the Inter-Am. Comm. HR, Art. 30(2) and (3).

[361] 2001 Rules of Procedure of the Inter-Am. Comm. HR, Art. 30(2).

[362] *Ibid.*, Art. 30(2).

[363] *Ibid.*, Art. 30(3). American Convention, Art. 48(1)(a). The 2001 Rules of Procedure of the Commission also provide that '[i]n serious or urgent cases, or when it is believed that the life or personal integrity of a person is in real or imminent danger, the Commission shall request the promptest reply from the State, using for this purpose the means it considers most expeditious'. 2001 Rules of Procedure of the Inter-Am. Comm. HR, Art. 30(4).

respond, but the Executive Secretariat may not acquiesce in an extension of more than three months from the date the original communication was sent to the State.[364] Cerna noted that, in part due to the heavy workload of the Secretariat, when a government 'promises' to reply, the Secretariat generally grants an extension request.[365] The Commission may ask the parties to submit additional information in writing or at a hearing before it makes a decision on admissibility.[366] When the Commission receives the requested information, or the time periods expire, the Commission will determine if there are grounds for the petition.[367] If there are not, it will archive the case.[368] It is possible that the petitioner may notify the Commission in writing that it wishes to desist from pursuing the petition or case.[369] The Commission, however, is not bound by the petitioner's decision to desist. After an analysis of the petitioner's statement, the Commission may deem it appropriate to continue to process the petition.[370] It is important that the Commission have the option to continue a case despite a petitioner's request so as to minimize State pressure on individuals to withdraw the case. Also, a particular petition may provide the Commission with an opportunity to make conclusions on aspects of specific rights that will further develop human rights protections in that area.

Prior to the Commission's regular session, a working group of Commissioners meet to study the petitions and prepare recommendations on admissibility for the plenary Commission.[371] The plenary Commission then considers the positions of the petitioner and the State, and makes a formal decision on admissibility.[372] Subsequently, the Commission issues a public report on admissibility which is published in its Annual Report.[373] Some States have contested the legality of the publication of the admissibility report, claiming that the Convention only authorizes the publication of one report.[374] In its admissibility report, the Commission sets forth the facts of the case, the proceedings before the Commission, the positions of the parties, and its determination as to whether the complaint meets each of the requirements for admissibility, providing its reasoning and stating its conclusions. The Commission instituted the practice of issuing a separate ruling on admissibility for 'the purpose not only of producing

[364] 2001 Rules of Procedure of the Inter-Am. Comm. HR, Art. 30(3).

[365] Cerna, 'Commission Organization and Petitions', at 96.

[366] 2001 Rules of Procedure of the Inter-Am. Comm. HR, Art. 30(5).

[367] *Ibid.*, Art. 30(6). [368] *Ibid.* [369] *Ibid.*, Art. 35. [370] *Ibid.*

[371] *Ibid.*, Art. 36. [372] *Ibid.*, Art. 37(1). [373] *Ibid.*, Art. 37(1).

[374] Dialogue on the Inter-American System for the Promotion and Protection of Human Rights (Report by the Chair), Permanent Council of the OEA/Ser.G OAS CP/CAJP rev. 2 (24 April 2000).

greater clarity and legal certainty in its decisions but also focusing the parties on the central issues of the case'.[375] The Commission has specified that this practice is not absolute, as the Commission must analyze the specific circumstances of each case and determine 'the advantages that might derive from that decision'.[376] In exceptional circumstances, the Commission may open the case but defer its decision on admissibility until it makes a decision on the merits.[377]

Although the Convention does not mandate that the Commission make an express decision on admissibility, the Commission's earlier failure to do so resulted in preliminary objections and scholarly criticism.[378] In response to a preliminary objection interposed by Honduras, the Court held that, while the Commission must always make an express declaration if it determines that the petition is inadmissible, the Commission need not make an express and formal determination that a petition is admissible unless the government raises the issue.[379] If further facts emerge showing that the statutory requisites have not been met, the Commission must adopt a final decision of inadmissibility and close the case.[380] The Commission then informs the petitioner of its decision and its reasons for the finding of inadmissibility.[381]

The Commission's decision to make an express decision on admissibility and to write a detailed report on admissibility contributes to the transparency of the procedures of the Commission. In doing so, it should also eliminate the basis for certain preliminary objections and allow the Court to place more reliance on the Commission's decisions, thus obviating the need for the Court's reconsideration of factual issues already decided by the Commission. It does, however, have the negative effect of delaying the proceedings. The UN Human Rights Committee has moved to combine decisions on admissibility and merits whenever possible to

[375] Case 11.597, Inter-Am. Comm. HR 54, Report No. 7/98 (2 March 1998), OEA/Ser.L/V/II.98, doc. 7 rev., para. 15 (citing Case 11.520, Inter-Am. Comm. HR 669–70, Report No. 49/97 (18 February 1998), OEA/Ser.L/V/II.98, doc. 7 rev. (1998), para. 50).

[376] Case 11.520, Inter-Am. Comm. HR 669–70, Report No. 49/97 (18 February 1998), OEA/Ser.L/V/II.98, doc. 7 rev., para. 50.

[377] 2001 Rules of Procedure of the Inter-Am. Comm., Art. 37(3).

[378] See Vivanco and Bhansali, 'Procedural Shortcomings', at 428.

[379] *Velásquez Rodríguez* v. *Honduras* (Preliminary Objections, 1987), para. 40; *Godínez Cruz* (Preliminary Objections, 1987), para. 43; *Fairén Garbi and Solís Corrales* (Preliminary Objections, 1987), para. 45.

[380] See Cerna, 'Commission Organization and Petitions', at 79–80; American Convention, Art. 48(1)(c).

[381] See Cerna, 'Commission Organization and Petitions', at 80.

reduce the time expended on initial proceedings. In light of former preliminary objections, however, the Inter-American Commission's institution of a separate admissibility decision was warranted.

The Court's review of the Commission's admissibility decision

The Inter-American Court has determined that it may review all issues involved in the Commission's decision to go forward with a case,[382] and holds that it is authorized by the Convention to verify the Commission's compliance with the procedural norms set forth in the Convention.[383] In this regard the Court stated that:

> [i]n exercising these powers, the Court is not bound by what the Commission may have previously decided, rather, its authority to render judgment is in no way restricted. The Court does not act as a court of review, of appeal or other similar court in its dealings with the Commission. Its power to examine and review all actions and decisions of the Commission derives from its character as sole judicial organ in matters concerning the Convention. This not only affords greater protection to the human rights guaranteed by the Convention, but it also assures the States Parties that have accepted the jurisdiction of the Court that the provisions of the Convention will be strictly observed.[384]

The Inter-American Commission objected to this role of the Court in the *Velásquez Rodríguez Case* in which it argued that the Court is 'not an appellate tribunal in relation to the Commission'.[385] In the view of the Commission, the Court possessed only a limited jurisdiction which prevented it from reviewing 'all aspects relating to compliance with the prerequisites for the admissibility of a petition or with the procedural norms required in a case filed with the Commission'.[386] The Court rejected that argument, holding that the terms of the Convention authorize the Court to exercise 'full jurisdiction over all issues relevant to a case'.[387]

This broad authority is similar to the power that the European Court of Human Rights had to reexamine the European Commission's decisions on admissibility when the European system was two-tiered.[388] In response to a similar objection made by the European Commission, the European

382 *Velásquez Rodríguez* v. *Honduras* (Preliminary Objections, 1987), para. 29 (citing American Convention, Art. 62(1)).

383 See *ibid.* 384 *Ibid.* 385 *Ibid.*, para. 28. 386 *Ibid.* 387 *Ibid.*, para. 29.

388 Gomien, Harris and Zwaak, *Law and Practice of the European Convention*, at 75–6. See *De Wilde, Ooms and Versyp ('Vagrancy' Cases)*, 12 Eur. Ct HR (Ser. A) (1971), paras. 49–52.

Court held that, when it considered such questions, it was not acting in the capacity of an appeals court. The European Court explained that it was merely ascertaining whether the preliminary conditions necessary to allow the Court to consider the merits of the case had been satisfied.[389] Leading scholars on the European system criticized this practice, fearing that judicial review of Commission decisions would have a negative effect on the overall procedure.[390]

Similarly, Judge Cançado Trindade has objected to the Inter-American Court's reconsideration of Commission decisions on admissibility.[391] In his concurring opinion in the *Loayza Tamayo Case*, Judge Cançado Trindade stated that a Commission decision regarding admissibility 'should be considered definitive, impeding the Government to reopen it, and the Court to review it'.[392] Cançado Trindade objected that 'reopening or review by the Court of a decision on admissibility by the Commission creates an imbalance between the parties, in favor of the respondent governments'.[393]

The Court's reconsideration of the admissibility of the petition can have particularly harsh effects on petitioners in the Inter-American system. Witnesses who come forward and are willing to testify before the Inter-American Commission about governmental human rights abuses, and the national lawyers who assist them, often risk torture or death because of it. In the *Honduran Disappearance Cases*, three persons who had testified before the Inter-American Court or who were scheduled to testify were murdered.[394] These risks are difficult to bear when the Court may later dismiss the case because the petition was initially deficient in some respect.

Furthermore, unlike the European human rights system, the Inter-American system does not provide legal aid for petitioners. If the Commission's decision on admissibility is not definitive, petitioners could spend several years and a considerable amount of money arguing before the Commission only to have the Inter-American Court dismiss the case because the petitioner unknowingly had not met an initial admissibility requirement. Moreover, by the time the case reaches the Court, it is too late for the petitioner to correct any deficiency. A dismissal of a case after

389 *Airey* v. *Ireland*, 32 Eur. Ct HR (Ser. A), para. 17 (1979).

390 See Gomien, Harris and Zwaak, *Law and Practice of the European Convention*, at 75; van Dijk and van Hoof, *Theory and Practice*, at 146–7.

391 *Loayza Tamayo* v. *Peru* (Preliminary Objections, 1996), Separate Concurring Opinion of Judge Cançado Trindade, para. 8.

392 *Ibid.*, para. 13. 393 *Ibid.*, para. 8.

394 *Velásquez Rodríguez* v. *Honduras* (Merits, 1988), paras. 40–1; *Godínez Cruz* (Merits, 1989), paras. 42–3; *Fairén Garbi and Solís Corrales* (Merits), paras. 63–4.

many years of processing undermines public confidence in the human rights system.

A final consideration is that, when the Court reconsiders the Commission's admissibility decision, the State is given two opportunities to challenge the petition: first before the Commission, and later before the Court. The victim, however, is not treated equally. Should the Commission determine that the application is inadmissible, the victim or party petitioning has no further recourse. The case is closed and there is no appeal. Thus, there is no equality of arms.

The Court may be stepping back from its decision to reconsider the Commission's decisions on admissibility. In the *Cesti Hurtado Case*, the State objected that the petitioner had not exhausted domestic remedies when the Commission commenced its consideration of the case.[395] The Court summarized the arguments of both parties and then, without stating its reasoning, rejected the preliminary objection, simply stating that the Commission had determined and stated in its report that domestic remedies had been exhausted with the decision on *habeas corpus*.[396]

Fact-finding before the Commission

Preliminary objections may also go to certain aspects of the Commission's fact-finding procedures. The Commission engages in the initial fact-finding procedures when a complaint is filed.[397] The Convention, the Statute of the Commission and the Rules of Procedure of the Commission set forth the evidence-gathering procedures that the Commission can employ.[398] Due to the limited staff and resources of the Commission, however, the petitioner should supplement the complaint with all available evidence. A well-tried domestic case may assist the Commission to establish the facts, but often the petitioner alleges that the domestic trial was riddled with due process violations which make the findings of the domestic court less useful to the Commission.

In general, the Commission relies on the written information supplied by the parties in gathering evidence.[399] It may, however, hold hearings and consider witnesses, eye witnesses, documents and admissions by the

[395] *Cesti Hurtado* v. *Peru* (Preliminary Objections, 1999), para. 30.

[396] See *ibid.*, para. 33. [397] *In the Matter of Viviana Gallardo* (1981), para. 25.

[398] American Convention, Art. 48; Statute of the Inter-American Commission on Human Rights, Art. 1(1), approved by General Assembly Resolution 447 at its ninth regular session, held in La Paz, Bolivia, Art. 18, October 1979; 2001 Rules of Procedure of the Inter-Am. Comm. HR, Arts. 59–68.

[399] See Cerna, 'Commission Organization and Petitions', at 97.

State.[400] When appropriate, it may also take judicial notice of facts or conduct or make an on-site visit to the State where the violation allegedly occurred.[401] States have filed various preliminary objections before the Court alleging irregularities in the Commission's fact-finding procedures, which have given the Court the opportunity to clarify which procedures are optional and which are required by the Convention.

Hearings before the Commission are not required When necessary, the Commission may decide to hold hearings in a matter, either at a party's request or on its own initiative.[402] The Commission need not hold a hearing in every case. In the *Honduran Disappearance Cases*, the State objected that the cases were not admissible before the Court, because the Commission had not held a preliminary hearing to clarify the petitioners' allegations.[403] The Court dismissed the objection, stating that a 'preliminary hearing is a procedural requirement only when the Commission considers it necessary to complete the information or when the parties expressly request a hearing'.[404] Honduras had not requested a hearing before the Commission, and the Commission had not considered a hearing to be necessary, so it was not required.[405] Hearings are only necessary when there are questions of fact that may be resolved by the presence of the parties and an interrogation of live witnesses. Moreover, the Commission does not have the resources to hold a public hearing in every case. Finally, if the State refuses to participate in the proceedings before the Commission, as Honduras did in the *Disappearance Cases*, a hearing would be ineffective.

Hearings before the Commission have not resembled adversarial trials, although counsel for both parties are present. Generally, the petitioner and perhaps a few witnesses briefly address the Commission and are questioned by Commissioners rather than by opposing counsel.[406] Subsequent to the entry into force of the 2001 Rules of Procedure of the Court, which

400 See *ibid.*; 2001 Rules of Procedure of the Inter-Am. Comm. HR, Arts. 43 and 44.

401 See Cerna, 'Commission Organization and Petitions', at 97.

402 2001 Rules of Procedure of the Inter-Am. Comm. HR, Art. 59.

403 *Velásquez Rodríguez* v. *Honduras* (Preliminary Objections, 1987), para. 51; *Godínez Cruz* (Preliminary Objections, 1987), para. 54.

404 *Velásquez Rodríguez* v. *Honduras* (Preliminary Objections, 1987), para. 53; *Godínez Cruz* (Preliminary Objections, 1987), para. 56.

405 *Velásquez Rodríguez* v. *Honduras* (Preliminary Objections, 1987), para. 54; *Godínez Cruz* (Preliminary Objections, 1987), para. 57.

406 Douglass Cassel, 'Fact-Finding in the Inter-American System', 105, 106, in *The UN Human Rights Treaty System in the 21st Century* (Bayefsky ed., Kluwer, The Hague, 2000).

give greater weight to evidence established by the Commission, States may demand a more active role in Commission hearings. The purpose of the hearing may be to elicit new facts and information or to supplement that which the parties have already produced.[407] The additional facts or information may be necessary to determine whether a petition is admissible or whether there is a possibility that the parties could reach a friendly settlement.[408] Alternately, the Commission could call for a hearing to verify facts already presented to the Commission, to consider the merits of the petition, to follow up on its recommendations, or for any other reason relevant to the processing of the petition.[409] If a duly notified party does not appear when it is summoned by the Commission, the Commission shall nonetheless hold the hearing.[410] Attendance at the hearings is generally limited to the Commissioners, the staff of the Executive Secretariat, the representatives of the parties, and the recording secretaries, although the Commission, in its sole discretion, may permit other persons to be present at a hearing.[411] When the Commission makes the decision to allow the presence of other persons, it must inform the parties either orally or in writing prior to the commencement of the hearing.[412] The Commission's President forms working groups of Commissioners to participate in the hearings.[413]

Parties may submit any item of evidence at the hearing, including documents, expert reports and the testimony of witnesses and experts.[414] The party that proposes the evidence must bear the expense of its production.[415] When a party produces documentary evidence at a hearing, the opposing party shall be granted a reasonable time to respond.[416] The documents submitted by either party are eventually annexed to the minutes of the hearing.[417] The minutes are internal to the Commission, but copies may be furnished to the parties on their request, unless the contents of the minutes entail a risk to anyone.[418]

The testimony of a witness or expert may be requested by the Commission or by any of the parties. When a party proposes that the Commission hear testimony during a hearing, that party must identify the witnesses and set forth the purpose of the testimony in its request for a hearing.[419] The Commission shall decide whether to hear the proposed testimony when it decides whether to grant the request for the hearing.[420] In most instances, the Commission will notify all parties of testimony proposed by

[407] 2001 Rules of Procedure of the Inter-Am. Comm. HR, Art. 62(1). [408] *Ibid.*
[409] *Ibid.* [410] *Ibid.*, Art. 62(3). [411] *Ibid.*, Art. 66. [412] *Ibid.* [413] *Ibid.*, Art. 65.
[414] *Ibid.*, Art. 63(1). [415] *Ibid.*, Art. 67. [416] *Ibid.*, Art. 63(2). [417] *Ibid.*, Art. 68(1).
[418] *Ibid.*, Art. 68(2). [419] *Ibid.*, Art. 63(3). [420] *Ibid.*, Art. 63(4).

an opposing party.[421] In extraordinary circumstances, however, when it is necessary to safeguard the evidence or protect the proposed witness, the Commission may exercise its discretion to forego prior notification.[422] In such instances, the Commission will take all necessary measures to protect the procedural interests of the parties.[423] Also, if the State does not attend a hearing despite receiving notification thereof, and the Commission determines that the witnesses or experts require protection, the Commission may withhold the identity of witnesses.[424] The Commission hears the testimony of each witness separately, while the other witnesses are sequestered.[425] The Commission's Rules of Procedure further specify that witnesses who take the stand may not read their presentations.[426]

Witnesses who testify against a State before the Commission or the Court are often in danger. The Commission's Rules of Procedure, therefore, specifically mandate that the State shall accord the necessary guarantees to all persons who provide oral or written testimony or who attend the hearing in any capacity.[427] The Commission's Rules explicitly specify that in no instance may the State prosecute those who provide testimony before the Commission, nor may the State carry out reprisals against witnesses or their families.[428] Every witness or expert witness must first identify himself or herself and make a solemn promise to testify truthfully.[429] When necessary to protect the witness, the Commission will maintain his or her identity in confidence.[430]

On-site investigations in the State are not required The American Convention provides that 'if necessary and advisable' the Commission shall carry out an on-site investigation.[431] When the Commission carries out an on-site investigation, members of the Commission and its staff go to the State charged with the human rights violation and gather first-hand information about the facts.[432] Fact-finding missions are not unprecedented. The former European Commission also engaged in fact-finding missions. In the *Dhoest Case*, for instance, a delegation from the European Commission visited a mental institution in Belgium to assist in its determination of whether the conditions complained of by the petitioner violated the Convention.[433] The Inter-American Commission's authority, however, is dependent upon the State's cooperation.[434] Even in

[421] *Ibid.*, Art. 63(5). [422] *Ibid.*, Art. 63(6). [423] *Ibid.* [424] *Ibid.*, Art. 62(3).
[425] *Ibid.*, Art. 63(7). [426] *Ibid.* [427] *Ibid.*, Art. 61. [428] *Ibid.* [429] *Ibid.*, Art. 63(8).
[430] *Ibid.* [431] American Convention, Art. 48(1)(d). [432] *Ibid.*
[433] *Dhoest* v. *Belgium*, Report, 14 May 1987, DR 55, 5 at 66 *et seq.*, para. 61.
[434] American Convention, Art. 48(1)(d).

serious and urgent cases, the Commission must have the prior consent of the State to conduct an on-site investigation within a State's territory.[435] The Convention requires that the State furnish the Commission with all necessary facilities and provide it with any pertinent information when the Commission visits a State concerned in a matter.[436] In the *Honduran Disappearance Cases*, Honduras objected that the Commission had not carried out an on-site investigation in Honduras to verify the facts of the petitions.[437] The Court dismissed the objection, ruling that such an investigation was not mandatory under the Convention.[438] The Court held that the Commission has discretion as to whether to conduct such a factual investigation.[439]

In practice, the Commission does not have the financing or staff to enable it to undertake an on-site investigation for every petition.[440] Farer observed that:

> [o]nce the case load metastasized, practical obstacles to effective investigation made the formal ones largely irrelevant. In 1976, the Commission's professional staff hardly existed, and during the succeeding decade, when it reached the acme of its prominence and efficacy, the effective staff was less than a dozen. But without the active cooperation of governments, even three or four dozen could have investigated only a tiny fraction of the thousands of cases appearing on the Commission's agenda.[441]

An on-site visit is not necessary when there are no facts that are available only in the State of the alleged violation. Some cases can be resolved by reference to the briefs of the parties. In other cases, when the facts are in dispute, the Commission may hold hearings at its seat in Washington DC

[435] *Ibid.*, Art. 48(2). 'The State controls the means to verify acts occurring within its territory.' *Velásquez Rodríguez* v. *Honduras* (Merits, 1988), para. 136; *Godínez Cruz* (Merits, 1988), para. 142.

[436] American Convention, Art. 48(1)(d) and (e).

[437] *Velásquez Rodríguez* v. *Honduras* (Preliminary Objections, 1987), para. 47; *Godínez Cruz* (Preliminary Objections, 1987), para. 50; *Fairén Garbi and Solís Corrales* (Preliminary Objections, 1987), para. 52.

[438] *Velásquez Rodríguez* v. *Honduras* (Preliminary Objections, 1987), paras. 49–50; *Godínez Cruz* (Preliminary Objections, 1987), paras. 52–3; *Fairén Garbi and Solís Corrales* (Preliminary Objections, 1987), paras. 54–5.

[439] *Velásquez Rodríguez* v. *Honduras* (Preliminary Objections, 1987), para. 49; *Godínez Cruz* (Preliminary Objections, 1987), para. 52; *Fairén Garbi and Solís Corrales* (Preliminary Objections, 1987), para. 54.

[440] See Cerna, 'Commission Organization and Petitions', at 96 (explaining that 'over 12,000 individual petitions have been registered by a Secretariat which consists of thirteen staff lawyers, and for many years comprised less than half that number').

[441] Farer, 'No Longer a Unicorn, Not Yet an Ox', at 47–8.

to consider the oral testimony of relevant witnesses and to hear the arguments of the parties. Witnesses may feel less intimidated giving testimony against the State when they are in another country. On-site visits must be reserved for those cases in which the relevant facts can be unearthed only by the presence of members of the Commission in the State concerned.

Presumption of the truth of the allegations in the complaint If the State does not cooperate with the Commission's requests for pertinent information during the fact-finding stage, the Commission can presume the truth of the facts in the petition, provided that 'other evidence does not lead to a different conclusion'.[442] The presumption effectively serves as a default judgment. Thus, the State cannot avoid responsibility for a human rights violation simply by refusing to respond to the Commission's requests for information. In the *Gangaram Panday Case*, Suriname objected that the Commission had inappropriately employed the presumption of truth of the allegations although the State had produced evidence that could lead to a different conclusion.[443] The Court rejected the objection, finding no evidence that the Commission had even resorted to the presumption.[444]

The Commission decides the facts of the case based on the information before it. In most cases this information is limited to that provided by the parties. The petitioners must initially set forth enough information to establish an alleged violation of the Convention. The burden is then on the State to refute the allegations. If the State chooses not to investigate the facts or not to provide the Commission with evidence, the presumption of the truth of the petitioners' allegations takes effect and the case can go forward. The presumption was essential in the 1970s and 1980s, when many States used human rights violations as a tool of intimidation and refused to cooperate with the Commission.[445] It continues to be important to the proper functioning of the Inter-American system as it provides a strong incentive to the State to provide the requested information. Thus, it permits the Commission to resolve the cases before it rather than resorting to a referral of the case to the Court to coerce the State into taking the petitioners' claims seriously. The UN Human Rights Committee will also find in favour of the author of a petition, when the author

[442] 2001 Rules of Procedure of the Inter-Am. Comm. HR, Art. 39.

[443] *Gangaram Panday* v. *Suriname* (Preliminary Objections, 1991), para. 34.

[444] *Ibid.*, para. 35.

[445] See Cecilia Medina Quiroga, *The Battle of Human Rights: Gross Systematic Violations and the Inter-American System*, at 149 (Kluwer, The Hague, 1988).

substantiates the allegations and the State fails to provide the requested information.[446]

Friendly settlement

States have also objected that the Commission did not attempt to promote a friendly settlement between the petitioner and the State in compliance with procedures mandated by the Convention.[447] Friendly settlements are designed to facilitate negotiations without judicial intervention. Thus, the task of promoting such settlements is assigned to the Commission, 'precisely because it is not a judicial body'.[448] The American Convention provides that '[t]he Commission shall place itself at the disposal of the parties concerned with a view to reaching a friendly settlement of the matter on the basis of respect for the human rights recognized in this Convention'.[449] A friendly settlement is beneficial to the petitioner in that it provides an expedited opportunity to obtain a remedy.[450] It is advantageous to the State in that it allows the State to resolve the dispute without a finding by the Inter-American Commission or a binding judgment by the Court that the State has violated human rights.[451] Friendly settlements must be approved by the Commission, because the stipulations of the settlement may have ramifications that go beyond the interests of the victim and the State.[452]

The Court's jurisprudence on preliminary objections has evolved from its initial holding that the promotion of a friendly settlement was essentially within the discretion of the Commission, to the position that the Commission can withhold its good offices only in exceptional situations. In the *Honduran Disappearance Cases*, the Court initially held that the

446 See *Andre Alphonse Mpaka-Nsusu* v. *Zaire*, Communication No. 157/1983 (26 March 1986), UN Doc. Supp. No. 40 (A/41/40) at 142, para. 56 (1986). P. R. Ghandhi, *The Human Rights Committee and the Right of Individual Communication: Law and Practice* (Ashgate, Dartmouth, 1998).

447 *Velásquez Rodríguez* v. *Honduras* (Preliminary Objections, 1987), para. 25(5); *Caballero Delgado and Santana* v. *Colombia* (Preliminary Objections, 1994), para. 19.

448 *In the Matter of Viviana Gallardo*, 1985, para. 24.

449 American Convention, Art. 48(1)(f); see Pedro Nikken, *La Protección Internacional de los Derechos Humanos: su Desarrollo Progresivo*, 158 (Instituto Interamericano de Derechos Humanos, Costa Rica, 1987).

450 *Velásquez Rodríguez* v. *Honduras* (Preliminary Objections, 1987), para. 60.

451 See Charles Moyer, 'Friendly Settlement in the Inter-American System: The Verbitsky Case – When Push Needn't Come to Shove', in *La Corte y el Sistema Interamericano de Derechos Humanos*, 347, 352 (Rafael Nieto Navia ed., Costa Rica, Corte Interamericana de Derechos Humanos, San José, 1994).

452 *Ibid.*

Commission was only required to attempt a friendly settlement if, in its discretion, it determined that such a settlement was suitable or necessary under the circumstances.[453] The Court subsequently tempered this holding in the *Caballero Delgado and Santana Case* by clarifying that the Commission could only exercise its discretion not to initiate a friendly settlement in 'exceptional cases' and for good reason.[454] The Court refused to dismiss the case, however, because the State had not exercised its prerogative to request a friendly settlement.[455] The Court aptly stated that 'one cannot demand of another an action that one could have taken under the very same conditions but chose not to'.[456] In the *Genie Lacayo Case*, the Court further clarified that 'the Commission does not have arbitrary powers in this respect, but that it may, exceptionally and on the basis of essential arguments, circumvent the reconciliation procedure'.[457]

The Commission's Rules of Procedure provide that '[o]n its own initiative or at the request of any of the parties, the Commission *shall* place itself at the disposal of the parties concerned' for the purpose of reaching a friendly settlement.[458] The Commission's practice is to ask both parties in cases before it if they would consider a friendly settlement.[459] If either party declines, the Commission documents the offer and response and makes no further attempt at a friendly settlement.[460] The offer on the part of the Commission fulfils the conciliatory role assigned it by the Convention.[461] If the parties enter into friendly settlement negotiations that are not fruitful, the Commission may terminate its intervention.[462]

Although the Court's holding does not require that the Commission attempt a friendly settlement in every case, the Commission has wisely undertaken the more certain and transparent path of always offering its

453 *Velásquez Rodríguez* v. *Honduras* (Preliminary Objections, 1987), para. 44; *Godínez Cruz* v. *Honduras* (Preliminary Objections, 1987), para. 47; *Fairén Garbi and Solís Corrales* (Preliminary Objections, 1987), para. 49. The Court stated, however, that the Commission's power could not be exercised arbitrarily. *Velásquez Rodríguez* v. *Honduras* (Preliminary Objections, 1987), para. 45; *Godínez Cruz* v. *Honduras* (Preliminary Objections, 1987), para. 48. See also American Convention, Art. 48(1)(f) (provision on friendly settlements).

454 *Caballero Delgado and Santana* v. *Colombia* (Preliminary Objections, 1994), para. 27.

455 *Ibid.*, paras. 29–30. See 2001 Rules of Procedure of the Inter-Am. Comm. HR, Art. 45(1).

456 *Caballero Delgado and Santana* v. *Colombia* (Preliminary Objections, 1994), para. 30.

457 *Genie Lacayo* v. *Nicaragua* (Preliminary Objections, 1995), para. 39.

458 2001 Rules of Procedure of the Inter-Am. Comm. HR, Art. 41(1) (emphasis added).

459 See Cerna, 'Commission Organization and Petitions', at 102.

460 See *ibid.*

461 American Convention, Art. 48(1)(f); see *Caballero Delgado and Santana* v. *Colombia* (Preliminary Objections, 1994), para. 27.

462 Rules of Procedure of the Inter-Am. Comm., Art. 41(4).

good offices and documenting that offer. The Commission thereby forces the State either to avail itself of the friendly settlement procedure set forth in the Convention for its advantage, or to forego a future preliminary objection before the Court which could result in the delay or dismissal of the case.[463] The Commission's 2001 Rules of Procedure and practice in this area have effectively eliminated this particular preliminary objection, thereby expediting the resolution of cases before the Court.

Even when the case is before the Court, it is in the interest of judicial economy for the Commission to continue its role of conciliator if the parties so desire. From the perspective of both the victim and the State, an immediate settlement may be preferable to a future uncertain Court judgment. If the petitioners and the State reach a friendly settlement when the case is before the Court, the Court must approve the settlement before striking the case from its docket.[464] Conversely, the Court may refuse to approve the settlement and continue to consider the case and rule thereon even if it receives notice of a friendly settlement or a discontinuance.[465]

Friendly settlement procedures are available in most international human rights systems. There are also provisions for friendly settlement in the International Covenant on Civil and Political Rights for inter-State complaints.[466] The future African Court will have the authority to 'try to reach an amicable settlement in a case pending before it'.[467] The European Convention provides for a friendly settlement procedure, and retains jurisdiction following a friendly settlement.[468] In *Ireland* v. *United Kingdom*, the Court decided to rule on the merits of the case, 'notwithstanding the [friendly] initiatives taken by the respondent state'.[469] Human rights courts must not only police the settlement to be certain that it complies with the principles of human rights law, but must also look beyond the case before the Court and judge its effects on other victims in the system.

463 Lillian J. Lopez Miranda, 'Analysis of the Use of Preliminary Objections in the Inter-American Court of Human Rights: 1979–1996', at 50–1 (unpublished Master's Thesis, University of South Dakota, 1999, on file with the University of South Dakota).

464 *Velásquez Rodríguez* v. *Honduras* (Preliminary Objections, 1987), para. 75.

465 See Manuel E. Ventura Robles, 'Los Articulos 50 y 51 de la Convención Americana sobre Derechos Humanos', in *La Corte y el Sistema Interamericano de Derechos Humanos*, 553 (1994).

466 United Nations Covenant on Civil and Political Rights, Art. 41(1)(e).

467 Protocol to the African Charter of Human and Peoples' Rights on the Establishment of an African Court of Human and Peoples' Rights, adopted on 9 June 1998, Art. 9, reprinted in 20 *Human Rights Law Journal*, 269 (1999).

468 European Convention, Art. 38; Rules of the European Court, entered into force 1 November 1998, Art. 62.

469 25 Eur. Ct HR (Ser. A) (No. 25), paras. 153–5 (1978).

Reporting requirements

If the parties do not come to a friendly settlement while the matter is before the Commission, the Convention requires that the Commission draw up a report setting forth the facts of the case and stating its conclusions.[470] This report is the last step in the Commission's proceedings before the case can be submitted to the Court.[471] The State is provided with one final opportunity to resolve the case before the Commission can submit the matter for a judicial decision.[472] The Commission sends the report with its proposals and recommendations to the State concerned.[473]

The Convention does not require the Commission to send the report to the petitioners. Nevertheless, the Commission's practice originally had been to send a copy of the report to the petitioners so as to keep them informed of the status of their complaint.[474] The Governments of Argentina and Uruguay questioned this practice, not in a preliminary objection, but rather by requesting an advisory opinion from the Inter-American Court.[475] In its advisory opinion, the Court determined that the Commission's regulation permitting transmittal of the report to the petitioners was not in conformity with the Convention, which only specifies that the report be sent confidentially to the State.[476] Thereafter, the Commission altered its practice, and ceased to send the petitioners the preliminary report.[477] The petitioners are notified only that a report has been adopted and transmitted to the State.[478] Commentators have criticized this change, alleging that the failure to keep the petitioners informed constitutes a lack of respect for due process and results in an inequality of arms between the parties.[479] The purpose of the confidentiality requirement is to offer the State an incentive to comply with the Commission's recommendations, before the Commission's findings and recommendations are made public.[480] Although it is important for the Commission and Court to offer incentives for State compliance, those incentives should not be offered at

[470] American Convention, Art. 50(1). See *Certain Attributes of the Inter-American Commission on Human Rights (Arts. 41, 42, 44, 46, 47, 50 and 51 of the American Convention on Human Rights)*, Inter-Am. Ct HR, Advisory Opinion OC-13/93 of 16 July 1993, Ser. A, No. 13, para. 48.

[471] *Velásquez Rodríguez* v. *Honduras* (Preliminary Objections, 1987), para. 61.

[472] *Ibid.*, para. 62. [473] American Convention, Art. 50(2) and (3).

[474] Former Regulations of the Inter-American Commission, Art. 47(6) (cited in Advisory Opinion OC-13/93, para. 49).

[475] Advisory Opinion OC-13/93. [476] See *ibid.*, para. 49.

[477] See Vivanco and Bhansali, 'Procedural Shortcomings', at 437–8.

[478] 2001 Rules of Procedure of the Inter-Am. Comm. HR, Art. 43(3).

[479] See Vivanco and Bhansali, 'Procedural Shortcomings', at 437–8. [480] See *ibid.*

the expense of the individual. The Court should reinterpret this provision of the Convention, or any future changes to the Convention should provide that the preliminary report be sent to both the State and the petitioners.[481]

If neither the Commission nor the State submits the case to the Court, the Convention specifies that the Commission may then draft another report setting forth 'its opinion and conclusions' about the case.[482] The Commission may also make 'pertinent recommendations' in this second report and set a period within which the State must remedy the situation.[483] This report is sent to both the petitioners and the State.[484] Both parties must then submit information regarding the State's compliance with the Commission's recommendations.[485] If the State does not take the required measures, the Commission may publish the report.[486]

States have filed various objections related to the Commission's procedures concerning its reports. In the *Velásquez Rodríguez Case*, Honduras objected that the Commission had applied the procedures for both reports simultaneously.[487] Although the Court found that the Commission's procedures in its consideration of the case had been somewhat irregular due to the various extensions which it had granted at the State's request, the Court rejected the State's objection, holding that the irregularities did not amount to a 'procedural flaw that diminished the Government's procedural rights or ability to present its defense'.[488] In the *Gangaram Panday Case*, Suriname objected that the Commission had abused its powers by 'appropriating for itself the right to find a State responsible for violations of human rights'.[489] The Court rejected the preliminary objection, because the Convention specifically authorizes the Commission to draw up a report 'stating its conclusions'.[490] Suriname also objected that the Commission had broken 'the confidentiality rule' by publicizing certain facts about the case.[491] The Court also rejected this objection, finding that the Commission only made reference to the case in its annual report and had not published the case report itself.[492] Colombia argued that the Commission

[481] See Cançado Trindade, *Report and Proposals*, para. 57.
[482] American Convention, Art. 51(1). [483] *Ibid.*, Art. 51(2).
[484] 2001 Rules of Procedure of the Inter-Am. Comm. HR, Art. 45(2).
[485] *Ibid.* [486] American Convention, Art. 51(3).
[487] *Velásquez Rodríguez* v. *Honduras* (Preliminary Objections, 1987), para. 64.
[488] *Ibid.*, para. 74.
[489] *Gangaram Panday* v. *Suriname* (Preliminary Objections, 1991), para. 29.
[490] *Ibid.*, para. 31 (citing the American Convention, Art. 50).
[491] *Ibid.*, paras. 29 and 32. [492] See *ibid.*, para. 33.

had not adequately considered its response to the State's preliminary report before it submitted the case to the Court.[493] The Court rejected the objection, holding that the Commission is required only to wait until the State provides a response or until the deadline passes before it submits a case to the Court.[494] If the State responds, the Commission must evaluate its statement.[495] In doing so, the Commission has discretion, which it may not exercise in an arbitrary manner, to decide if the State has adopted positive measures to comply with the Commission's recommendations.[496] The Commission must determine whether submitting the case to the Court is the most favourable alternative for the protection of human rights.[497]

Extension of time for reconsideration of the report or an attempt to reach a friendly settlement The Commission may reconsider a report at the State's request, even though the Convention does not provide for such a possibility.[498] An implicit consequence of such a reconsideration is an extension of the applicable deadlines. Although the Court recognized that reconsideration could 'have negative effects on the petitioner's right to obtain the international protection offered by the Convention within the legally established time frames', the Court determined that the grant of such a request could be justified in certain situations.[499] Specifically, the Court stated that 'a request for reconsideration that is based on the will to resolve a case through the domestic channels available to the State' may achieve a 'satisfactory solution of the alleged violation through the State's cooperation, and therefore would satisfy the aims of the Commission's procedures'.[500] Such extensions should not be granted, however, unless the State can show evidence that it is making a concerted effort to comply with the Commission's recommendations.

The Commission's report may also result in further attempts between the State and the petitioners to reach a friendly settlement. In that event, the State may request additional time for negotiations.[501] The Commission, with the concurrence of the petitioners, may suspend the applicable deadlines.[502]

[493] *Case of the Nineteen Merchants* v. *Colombia* (Preliminary Objections, 2002), para. 24.
[494] *Ibid.*, para. 35. [495] *Ibid.* [496] *Ibid.*
[497] *Ibid.*, para. 33, citing *Baena Ricardo et al.* v. *Panama* (Preliminary Objections, 1999), para. 37.
[498] See *Velásquez Rodríguez* v. *Honduras* (Preliminary Objections, 1987), para. 69.
[499] *Ibid.* [500] *Ibid.*
[501] See *Las Palmeras* (Preliminary Objections, 2000), para. 9. [502] *Ibid.*

Treatment of claims not asserted by the Commission The Commission may implicitly waive certain claims before the Court, if it does not raise them in its report to the State.[503] The State should not be required to defend itself against novel allegations based on facts that were not brought forward before the case was referred to the Court. In its application in the *Castillo Petruzzi et al. Case*, the Commission claimed that Peru had violated international law by refusing to allow a Chilean delegation to visit Chilean prisoners in the Peruvian jails.[504] The Court admitted Peru's preliminary objection, holding that the Commission could not raise such claims against the State for the first time before the Court when it did not raise them in its earlier report to the State.[505] Although the Court agreed with the Commission that the application need not be a 'simple reiteration' of the Commission's report, the Court held that the application may not raise for the first time violations of which the State was not apprised during the proceedings before the Commission.[506] The Court reasoned that, in such cases, the State does not have the opportunity to admit the claim, reject it, or request a friendly settlement.[507] This holding of the Court satisfies the principle of 'equality of arms' providing a balance between the rights of the parties, in that it is analogous to the Court's holding that the State waives a claim that it did not first raise before the Commission.[508]

Conversely, the Court does not hold that all claims which the Commission fails to raise are waived.[509] The Court asserts the inherent authority to find a violation of a general obligation of the Convention even though the Commission did not find a violation or did not express an opinion as to whether there was a violation.[510] For example, the Court held that it can examine whether the State complied with its duty to investigate and punish those responsible for violations of the human rights, and that, therefore, it was not necessary for the Commission to have included that recommendation in its report to the State.[511] In the *Cantoral Benavides Case*, Peru objected that the Commission's allegation that the Peruvian anti-subversion law was not compatible with the American Convention

[503] *Castillo Petruzzi et al.* v. *Peru* (Preliminary Objections, 1998), paras. 68–9.
[504] *Ibid.*, paras. 65–6. [505] *Ibid.*, paras. 68–9.
[506] See *ibid.*, para. 68. [507] See *ibid.*
[508] See pp. 169–71 below for a discussion of State waiver for failing to raise claims before the Commission.
[509] *Cantoral Benavides* v. *Peru* (Preliminary Objections, 1998), para. 45.
[510] See *ibid.*, para. 46.
[511] *Cesti Hurtado* v. *Peru* (Preliminary Objections, 1999), para. 52.

had not been raised by the petitioners before the Commission or by the Commission in its report to the Court.[512] The Court held that this objection was inadmissible inasmuch as the Court, in the context of a concrete case, can examine the legal effect of a State's domestic law to determine its compatibility with the American Convention and international law.[513] The Court held that it has an official duty to examine the States Parties' fulfillment of the general obligations set forth in Article 1(1) and Article 2 of the Convention in conjunction with the specific obligations of each protected right.[514]

The Inter-American Court can also examine specific violations of the American Convention that are not raised by the Commission in its final report to the State or are not raised in its application to the Court, provided that the application includes the facts necessary to establish the violation. In the *Hilaire, Constantine and Benjamin et al. Case*, the Commission did not allege the violation of particular provisions of the right to life, even though it raised the issue in its final argument.[515] The Court held that, pursuant to the general legal principle of *iura novit curia*, the Court has both the authority and the obligation to find a violation of the applicable provision of the American Convention even when the violation is not expressly invoked by a party to the case.[516] Moreover, the Inter-American Court will hold that Convention provisions were violated to the detriment of particular petitioners, even if the Commission did not identify those petitioners as having suffered the violation. In the *Hilaire, Constantine and Benjamin et al. Case*, the Commission alleged that Trinidad and Tobago violated the Convention's prohibition against cruel, inhuman or degrading punishment by subjecting twenty-one of the thirty-one surviving prisoners to appalling prison conditions.[517] The Court, on the basis of the evidence presented and the general principle of *iura novit curia*, held that the prison conditions violated the rights of all the victims in the case.[518]

The European Court of Human Rights also has held that it is for the Court to determine, even *ex officio*, whether the facts as alleged in the application reveal violations of rights protected by the Convention even though

512 *Cantoral Benavides* v. *Peru* (Preliminary Objections, 1998), para. 44.

513 *Ibid.*, para. 45. 514 *Ibid.*, para. 46.

515 *Hilaire, Constantine and Benjamin et al.* v. *Trinidad and Tobago* (Merits), Inter-Am. Ct HR, 21 June 2002, Ser. C, No. 94, 107, 187.

516 *Ibid.*

517 *Hilaire, Constantine and Benjamin et al.* v. *Trinidad and Tobago* (Merits, 2002), para. 153.

518 *Ibid.*, para. 170.

the application has not alleged such violations.[519] Under the European system, as it was previously structured with a Commission and a Court, the European Court could find a violation of the Convention even though the Commission's report did not cite a violation or express an opinion as to whether there was a violation.[520] In human rights cases, the State argues that the events in question did not happen, or if they happened they are not attributable to the government. Therefore, the State is not placed at a major procedural disadvantage if the stated events are found to violate an additional provision of the Convention.

Partial referral of only some of the claims cited in the Commission's report The Commission may make a partial referral to the Court of only some of the violations cited in its report. This issue arose in the *Genie Lacayo Case*, in which the Commission declared that the State was responsible for the violation of the right to life of Genie Lacayo in its report to the State, but did not make that claim in its application to the Court.[521] The Court pointed out that, under the OAS Charter, the Commission has an obligation to 'promote the observance and protection of human rights' in all Member States of the OAS, whereas the Commission can only refer claims to the Inter-American Court that fall within the jurisdiction of the Court.[522] Since Nicaragua had not yet ratified the American Convention at the time of Genie Lacayo's death, the Court did not have jurisdiction *ratione temporis* to consider the claim.[523] Therefore, the Commission could not raise the claim before the Court.

The question remains, however, as to whether the applicant can choose to bring only certain claims before the Court, when the Court would have jurisdiction over the excluded claims. This issue was raised by the European Court of Human Rights, but it was not resolved because the respondent State did not object to the limited scope of the case.[524] There is no specific barrier in the American Convention or in the Court's Rules of Procedure that would prohibit a partial referral. If neither party objects, it is in the interest of judicial economy for the Court to consider only the disputed questions. The Court's Rules of Procedure should be amended,

519 See *Lawless* v. *Ireland*, 3 Eur. Ct HR (Ser. A), 'The Law' section, para. 40 (1961); *Neumeister* v. *Austria*, 8 Eur. Ct HR (Ser. A), 'As to the Law' section, para. 16 (1968).

520 See *Airey* v. *Ireland*, 32 Eur. Ct HR (Ser. A), paras. 14 and 33 (1979).

521 *Genie Lacayo* (Preliminary Objections, 1987), para. 46.

522 See *ibid.*

523 See pp. 107–9 above for an explanation of jurisdiction *ratione temporis*.

524 *Loizidou* v. *Turkey* (Preliminary Objections), 310 Eur. Ct HR (Ser. A), paras. 53–4 (1995).

however, to explicitly permit the applicant to make only a partial referral of some of the claims resolved by the Commission and to allow the respondent to counterclaim as to any or all remaining issues. The Rules of Procedure should also establish time limits for such counterclaims. It should also be noted that, as the original petitioner does not have standing before the Court, the petitioner is in the somewhat inequitable position of having no basis on which to object to the State's referral of only certain claims. The petitioner must depend on the Commission to raise other issues in such a case. A further stage in the evolution of the Inter-American system would be to allow the petitioner to litigate additional counterclaims or to require that the Commission do so. Normally, however, a partial referral should not prejudice the petitioner to any greater extent than he or she is already prejudiced by lack of standing to bring the case before the Court. At least, in the case of partial referral, some of the claims would be decided by the Court.

The Commission's decision to submit the case to the Court

The Convention does not specify procedures that the Commission must follow in reaching a decision to submit a case to the Court. In the *Baena Ricardo Case*, Panama objected that the Commission had employed an informal and irregular procedure based on an erroneous and bad faith interpretation of the Convention when it made the formal decision to submit the case to the Court in a telephone conference call between the commissioners.[525] The minutes of the conference call had been recorded as are the minutes of other Commission meetings. The Court rejected the preliminary objection, explaining that '[i]t is important that a non-permanent body such as the Commission may keep abreast of the times and make use of technological advances and modern electronic means to facilitate its communications, so that it may operate smoothly and promptly, without endangering legal certainty and procedural rights'.[526] The Commission risks having an application rejected as untimely if it is not filed with the Court within three months of notification to the State of the preliminary report. It should not have to call a special meeting before the end of that three-month period, with all the expense and inconvenience that entails, if the State does not comply with its recommendations.

525 *Baena Ricardo et al.* v. *Panama* (Preliminary Objections, 1999), paras. 32 and 40.

526 *Ibid.*, para. 43, citing *Paniagua Morales et al.* v. *Guatemala* (Preliminary Objections, 1996), para. 35.

Objections that the Commission did not comply with Convention requirements in submitting the case to the Court

The Court's Rules of Procedure set forth a detailed blueprint of the appropriate steps to follow in submitting a case to the Court.[527] The submission of a case commences with the filing of an application with the Court's Secretariat.[528] The Court's Rules provide that the application must be submitted to the Court in each of its working languages.[529] Those languages may be any of the official languages of the OAS: Spanish, English, French and Portuguese. Each year the Court agrees on its working languages.[530] 'The working languages for each case shall be determined at the start of the proceedings, unless they are the same as those already being employed by the Court.'[531] To date the working languages of the Court have generally been Spanish and English, the languages of the judges on the Court. In a specific case, the language of one of the parties may also be adopted as a working language, if it is one of the official languages of the OAS.[532] To allow the applicant time for translation, the filing of the case in only one working language will not suspend the proceedings, provided that translations into the other languages are provided to the Court within thirty days.[533]

Deadline for submission of a case to the Court

The Convention specifies that there is a three-month deadline for either the Commission or the State to submit the case to the Court if the matter has not been settled.[534] The three-month period runs from the date the Commission transmits the report to the States concerned.[535] In the *Cayara Case*, the Court upheld Peru's preliminary objection that the Commission had not met this statutory deadline, and therefore it dismissed the case.[536] The Commission had initially filed the case with the Court within the time limit specified by the Convention but had then withdrawn the case and resubmitted it six months later.[537] Although the Court reasoned that some delays and omissions in complying with Convention procedures might be excused, it determined that the case had to be dismissed to 'preserve a fair balance between the protection of human rights, which is the ultimate purpose of the system, and the legal certainty and procedural equity that

527 The American Convention authorizes the Court to adopt its own Rules of Procedure. See American Convention, Art. 60.

528 See 2001 Rules of Procedure of the Inter-Am. Ct HR, Art. 32. 529 *Ibid.*

530 *Ibid.*, Art. 20(2). 531 *Ibid.*, Art. 20(3). 532 *Ibid.* 533 *Ibid.*, Art. 32.

534 See American Convention, Art. 51(1). 535 *Ibid.*

536 *Cayara* v. *Peru* (Preliminary Objections, 1993), paras. 60–3. 537 *Ibid.*, para. 60.

will ensure the stability and reliability of the international protection mechanism'.[538]

If, however, the State requests an extension that results in the expiration of a Convention-mandated deadline, the Court has held that the principles of good faith which govern international relations prohibit the State from invoking the expiration of the deadline as a preliminary objection to the consideration of the case on the merits.[539] The Court has explained that 'without falling into a rigid formalism which distorts the purpose and object of the Convention, the States and the organs of the Convention must comply with the provisions which regulate the procedure, for the juridical security of the parties depends upon it'.[540] The European Court of Human Rights also subscribes to strict deadlines unless the file demonstrates special circumstances that justify the suspension of the time limits or the establishment of new time limits.[541]

Any blatant irregularities in the Inter-American Commission's or Court's processing of cases could raise State doubts as to whether its procedural rights were being respected, which could provide an excuse for State withdrawal from the system. During the processing of the *Cayara Case*, Peru sent a note to the Commission with a veiled threat of such action. In the note, Peru suggested that the Commission's irregularities in the handling of the case 'nullify any other proceeding to which [they] could give rise and allow Peru to disqualify itself in the future from validating such acts with its participation'.[542] In the interest of strengthening the Inter-American system, even at the loss of bringing justice in one case, the Court must dismiss applications that do not comply with the Convention-mandated procedures.

Method of computing time periods Neither the American Convention nor the Statute of the Court specify the manner in which time limits, such as the three-month deadline, shall be computed. The Court's Rules of Procedure provide that a 'day' is a 'natural day' and a 'month' is a 'calendar month'.[543] The Court's case law clarifies additional questions of how to measure the time periods specified in the Convention and Rules. In

538 *Ibid.*, para. 63.

539 *Neira Alegría et al.* v. *Peru* (Preliminary Objections, 1991), paras. 34–5.

540 Advisory Opinion OC-13/93, para. 41 (citing *Cayara* v. *Peru* (Preliminary Objections, 1993), paras. 42 and 63).

541 See *Istituto di Vigilanza* v. *Italy*, 265-C Eur. Ct HR para. 14 (Ser. A) (1993) (dismissing a case because it was filed one day after the deadline established by the European Convention).

542 *Cayara* v. *Peru* (Preliminary Objections, 1993), para. 57.

543 2001 Rules of Procedure of the Inter-Am. Ct HR, Arts. 2(11) and (21).

the *Paniagua Morales Case*, Guatemala objected that the Commission had submitted the case to the Court after the expiration of the deadline.[544] The State maintained that three months is the equivalent of ninety days, and that the Commission's application was therefore untimely.[545] The Court rejected that preliminary objection and held that, when the Convention specifies a time limit as a period of months, it is based on the Gregorian calendar month, which means that it is measured from date to date.[546] The Court disavowed an earlier opinion in which it had inadvertently stated that the three-month deadline in Article 51(1) was equivalent to ninety days.[547] Thus, a three-month period commencing on 17 September would expire on 17 December. The Court reiterated this principle when Trinidad and Tobago erroneously objected that the Commission had submitted the case to the Court one day after the three-month period for submission had expired in the *Benjamin et al. Case*.[548] Trinidad and Tobago also erroneously argued that Article 51 of the American Convention, which requires the case to be submitted by the Commission or the State concerned to the Court and 'its jurisdiction accepted' within a three-month period, was not satisfied, because the Court had not accepted jurisdiction of the case within the three-month time period.[549] The Court explained that the Convention's requirement referred to the State's acceptance of the Court's jurisdiction and not to the Court's acceptance of jurisdiction in the case.[550] It would be useful for the Court to include a provision in its Rules of Procedure on the measurement of time periods. Government attorneys who must prepare the answer to an application and preliminary objections cannot be expected to be familiar with the entire body of the Court's jurisprudence.

Extension of the time period for submission of application The three-month deadline for submission of a case to the Court may be extended. The Court held in response to a preliminary objection in the *Velásquez Rodríguez Case* that 'the extension of the time limit for submission of an application to the Court does not impair the procedural position of the State when the State itself requests an extension'.[551] In such a case, the

[544] *Paniagua Morales et al.* v. *Guatemala* (Preliminary Objections), Inter-Am. Ct HR, 25 January 1996, Ser. C, No. 23, para. 24.

[545] See *ibid.* [546] *Ibid.*, para. 26.

[547] *Ibid.*, para. 29, referring to *Caballero Delgado and Santana* v. *Colombia* (Preliminary Objections, 1994), para. 43.

[548] *Benjamin et al.* v. *Trinidad and Tobago* (Preliminary Objections, 2001), para. 38.

[549] *Ibid.*, para. 27. [550] *Ibid.*, para. 40.

[551] *Velásquez Rodríguez* v. *Honduras* (Preliminary Objections, 1987), para. 70.

Court reasoned that 'neither the State's procedural rights nor its opportunity to provide a remedy were in any way diminished'.[552] The Court expanded on that ruling in the *Cayara Case*, explaining that various circumstances could toll the time period for submission of an application or require a new report with the resumption of the three-month period from the beginning.[553] The Court added that each case will require a determination and analysis of the circumstances.[554]

The principal application of this rule in the Inter-American system has been in response to requests by States for a delay for the reconsideration of a report.[555] In later cases, the Commission has avoided a possible preliminary objection by expressly informing the State that it will grant the request for an extension but that the delay will prolong the deadline for the Commission to submit the case to the Court.[556]

Methods of filing the application

The application and all other documents submitted in the case may be delivered to the Court by any method in general use.[557] If the applicant uses an electronic means of transmission, the original documents must be submitted to the Court within fifteen days thereafter.[558] Prior to the Court's amendment of its Rules to explicitly authorize alternative methods of delivery, that issue was raised by a State as a preliminary objection.[559] In the *Paniagua Morales Case*, Guatemala objected to the admission of the Commission's faxed application to the Court.[560] Although the original documents were forwarded to the Court a few days after the faxed transmission, they arrived after the expiration of the deadline for the Commission's submission of the case to the Court. The State objected that the application was inadmissible because it was untimely.[561] The Rules of Procedure then in effect simply stated that the application was to be filed with the Secretariat of the Court, without specifying a required means of transmission.[562] The Court dismissed the objection, holding

552 *Ibid.*

553 *Cayara* v. *Peru* (Preliminary Objections, 1993), para. 39 (quoted in *Caballero Delgado and Santana* v. *Colombia* (Preliminary Objections, 1994), para. 42).

554 *Ibid.*

555 *Neira Alegría et al.* v. *Peru* (Preliminary Objections, 1991), paras. 34–5; *Caballero Delgado and Santana* v. *Colombia* (Preliminary Objections, 1994), para. 38.

556 *Ivcher Bronstein* v. *Peru* (Merits), Inter-Am. Ct HR, 6 February 2001, Ser. C, No. 74, para. 16.

557 2001 Rules of Procedure of the Inter-Am. Ct HR, Art. 26(1).

558 *Ibid.*

559 *Paniagua Morales* (Preliminary Objections, 1996), para. 31.

560 *Ibid.*

561 *Ibid.*

562 Former 1991 Rules of Procedure of the Inter-American Court of Human Rights, adopted by the Inter-American Court at its twenty-third regular session, held 9–18 January 1991, Art. 26, reprinted in 2001 Basic Documents, at 145.

that filing the application by fax was valid and that, therefore, the submission had been timely.[563] The Court noted that it is important that an international human rights tribunal use modern electronic means to facilitate rapid communications with the parties.[564] Expeditious means of communication are particularly important in the Inter-American human rights system, because the Commission is seated in Washington DC, the Court is located in San José, Costa Rica, and the victims may be anywhere in the western hemisphere.

Contents of the application

The application provides detailed information about the case. That information must include the identity of the parties to the case, the names of the delegates or agents, and a statement of the facts on which the application is based.[565] The application must also cite the supporting evidence, specify the facts on which each item of evidence will bear, identify the witnesses and expert witnesses and the purpose of their statements, and give the legal arguments and conclusions in the case.[566] It must also set forth the applicant's prayer for reparations and costs.[567] The Commission resolutions that initiated the proceeding and determined admissibility must accompany the application.[568] Also, if the application is filed by the Commission, it must be accompanied by the report referred to in Article 50 of the American Convention.[569]

This information is sufficient to allow the President of the Court to conduct a preliminary review of the application to be certain that all the basic requirements have been met.[570] If the President identifies any deficiencies, the Secretariat of the Court notifies the applicant and allows the party twenty days to correct the defect.[571] Although this provision was primarily adopted to fill in informational deficiencies, the Court now makes use of it to allow the parties to correct any formal procedural defects that do not constitute a procedural injury to the other party.[572] For instance, the Court relied on this provision when the State objected that the Commission failed to file copies of the application, a former requirement that is no longer in the Court's Rules of Procedure.[573] The Court pointed out that 'what is essential is that the conditions necessary for the preservation of the procedural rights of the parties not

[563] *Paniagua Morales* (Preliminary Objections, 1996), para. 36. [564] *Ibid.*, para. 35.

[565] 2001 Rules of Procedure of the Inter-Am. Ct HR, Art. 33(1). [566] *Ibid.*, Art. 33(1).

[567] *Ibid.* [568] *Ibid.* [569] *Ibid.*, Art. 33(2). [570] *Ibid.*, Art. 34. [571] *Ibid.*

[572] *Paniagua Morales* (Preliminary Objections, 1996), paras. 37 and 42.

[573] *Cayara* v. *Peru* (Preliminary Objections, 1996), para. 42; *Paniagua Morales* (Preliminary Objections, 1996), para. 37.

be diminished or unbalanced, and that the objectives of the different procedures be met'.[574] This use of the provision eliminates preliminary objections based on matters of pure form that do not prejudice the other party.[575] The President retains the right, however, to reject any communication from the parties that he considers unacceptable,[576] although no criteria to aid such a determination are listed in the Rules of Procedure.

The Court has made another concession to modern technology by eliminating the requirement of a signature on the application. The Court's earlier Rules of Procedure required that the Commission's application be signed.[577] In the *Gangaram Panday Case*, the Commission signed its application to the Court but failed to sign the supporting brief. The brief had been faxed to the Court under a cover sheet that verified the authenticity of the document.[578] Suriname objected that all documents initiating international human rights proceedings must be signed by the party that filed the application.[579] The Court disagreed, holding that the application had been signed, and that the Convention does not require that the Commission also sign its supporting brief.[580] Despite its holding, the Court reprimanded the Commission for the lapse, stating that 'it goes without saying that all documents presented to the Court should bear a signature and that the Commission should have made sure that this was so in the instant case'.[581] Following that case, the Court eliminated the signature requirement altogether, a change which is being made worldwide in statutes and rules of procedure.

[574] *Velásquez Rodríguez* v. *Honduras* (Preliminary Objections, 1987), para. 33; *Godínez Cruz* (Preliminary Objections, 1987), para. 3; *Fairén Garbi and Solís Corrales* (Preliminary Objections, 1987), para. 38 (quoted in *Paniagua Morales* (Preliminary Objections, 1996), para. 42).

[575] See *Paniagua Morales* v. *Guatemala* (Preliminary Objections, 1996), paras. 37 and 42. The Court has also stated that procedural rules 'must not be applied in a way that distorts the object and purpose of the Convention'. *Cayara* v. *Peru* (Preliminary Objections, 1993), para. 42.

[576] The President may take such action only in consultation with the Permanent Commission of the Court, which is composed of the President, Vice-President and any judge appointed by the President. See 2001 Rules of Procedure of the Inter-Am. Ct HR, Art. 26(2). If the President rejects the application or other filing, he orders that it be returned to the party, and the Court takes no further action on it. *Ibid.*

[577] See *Gangaram Panday* v. *Suriname* (Preliminary Objections, 1991), para. 21 (citing Art. 25(2) of the former Rules of the Court).

[578] *Ibid.*, para. 20.

[579] *Ibid.*, para. 19. Suriname did not characterize its comment as an objection but rather as an initial 'question of form'. *Ibid.*, para. 17.

[580] *Ibid.*, para. 23.

[581] *Ibid.*, para. 24.

Amendment of the application

The Court may permit the Commission to amend or modify the application subsequent to its submission.[582] In response to the State's objection, the Court has stated that 'in proceedings before an international court a party may modify its application, provided that the other party has the procedural opportunity to state its views on the subject'.[583] When the opposing party has been provided that opportunity, the Court will incorporate the amendment into the pleadings. This objection arose and was rejected by the Court in the *Aloeboetoe et al.* v. *Suriname Case*, wherein the Commission first requested moral damages at the reparations stage of the proceedings.[584] Likewise, pursuant to the principle of equality of arms, the respondent must be allowed to amend the answer to the application.

Proceedings before the Court

The submission of the case to the Court concludes the proceedings before the Commission.[585] Upon the filing of the application, the Secretary of the Court notifies all entities that have an interest in the case.[586] These entities include the State that allegedly violated the victim's rights, the Commission, the President and judges of the Court, the original claimant, if identified, and the alleged victim, family of a deceased or disappeared alleged victim, or their duly accredited representatives.[587] The Secretary also informs the other States Parties to the American Convention and the Permanent Council and Secretary General of the OAS.[588] The alleged victim, family members or representatives are informed that they have thirty days to independently submit their motions, arguments and evidence.[589] In conjunction with the notification of the application, the Secretary of the Court advises the parties that they have one month in which to designate the persons who will represent them before the Court.[590]

The Commission must appoint its delegates.[591] Until the delegates are appointed, the Commission is deemed to be represented by its President

582 This practice is similar to a US court's authority to grant the plaintiff leave to amend a complaint. Jack H. Friedenthal *et al.*, *Civil Procedure* 5.22, at 296 (2nd edn, West, St Paul, MN, 1993).

583 *Las Palmeras* (Merits, 2001), para. 31, quoting *Aloeboetoe et al.* v. *Suriname* (Reparations), Inter-Am. Ct HR, 10 September 1993, Ser. C, No. 15, para. 81; see also *The Factory at Chorzów* (Merits), 1928 PCIJ (Ser. A) No. 17, 7 (13 September).

584 *Aloeboetoe et al.* v. *Suriname* (Reparations, 1993), para. 81.

585 *Velásquez Rodríguez* v. *Honduras* (Preliminary Objections, 1987), para. 75.

586 2001 Rules of Procedure of the Inter-Am. Ct HR, Art. 35(1).

587 *Ibid.*

588 *Ibid.*, Art. 35(2).

589 *Ibid.*, Art. 35(4).

590 *Ibid.*, Art. 35(3).

591 *Ibid.*

for the purposes of the case.[592] Ordinarily, the delegates of the Commission include a Commissioner and members of its staff. In the *Gangaram Panday Case*, Suriname alleged that the Commission had not complied with the applicable rules when it designated its Executive Secretary and Assistant Executive Secretary as delegates, because they were members of the staff of the Commission and not Commissioners.[593] The Court dismissed the issue, quoting its Rules of Procedure which stated that 'the Commission shall be represented by the delegates whom it designates'.[594] The Court also held that the appointment of the victim's attorney to the Commission's delegation was also within the Rules.[595] Formerly, the Commission often chose to be assisted by the representative of the original claimant or of the victims or the families of deceased or disappeared victims. Under the 2001 Court Rules, the alleged victim, family members of the alleged victim, or their duly appointed representatives have the right to directly participate before the Court, and thus no longer need to participate as assistants to the Commission.[596]

It is important but not strictly required that at least one Commissioner represent the Commission before the Court, as it is only the Commissioners who have the authority to vote to bring the case before the Court, and the State deserves the respect that is evidenced by the presence of a Commissioner trying the case. As the Commissioners do not serve on a full-time basis, however, it is often the legal staff of the Commission who has detailed information on the facts of each case and who can best clarify contested issues during Court hearings. Therefore, it is important that the Commission also be allowed to name members of its Secretariat as delegates before the Court. The Court's Rules provide for an equality of arms as the State's Agent and Deputy Agent may also appoint other persons to assist in the presentation of the case.[597]

The respondent State must designate an agent.[598] The Court places no limitations on the persons who may serve as State agents or advocates before the Court. To date, this has not presented a problem. As the case

592 *Ibid.* 593 *Gangaram Panday* v. *Suriname* (Preliminary Objections, 1991), para. 25.

594 *Ibid.*, para. 27. Rule 22 of the 2001 Rules provides that 'the Commission shall be represented by the Delegates it has designated for the purpose. The Delegates may be assisted by any persons of their choice.' 2001 Rules of Procedure of the Inter-Am. Ct HR.

595 *Gangaram Panday* v. *Suriname* (Preliminary Objections, 1991), para. 27.

596 2001 Rules of Procedure of the Inter-Am. Ct HR, Art. 23.

597 *Ibid.*, Art. 21(1). The State's Deputy Agent has the same authority as the State's Agent. *Ibid.*, Art. 21(3).

598 *Ibid.*

load of the Court increases, however, it could be possible for the State to name the same person as a judge *ad hoc* in one case and State agent in another. Similarly, under the current Rules, the State could designate as agent or advocate a person who has recently served as a judge on the Court or a former staff attorney or employee. Such persons could carry greater weight with the judges or at least appear to do so. Even the appearance of impropriety should be avoided. As stated by the ICJ in its recent Practice Directions which discourage such conflicting appointments, they are 'not in the interest of the sound administration of justice'.[599] The Inter-American Court should also incorporate a procedural rule discouraging conflicting appointments, or the appointments of persons who have been closely connected to the Court, to any position except judge *ad hoc*, for a set period of time after their relationship with the Court terminates.

Deadline for filing preliminary objections

The respondent must raise preliminary objections in its answer to the application, which must be filed within two months after the notification of the application.[600] Under the 1996 Rules of Procedure, the respondent had two months from the Court's issuance of the notification of the application to file preliminary objections, although those objections were not included in the answer.[601] Thus, in effect, there is no change in the two-month period allowed for the interposition of objections. Other parties to the case have thirty days to submit written briefs in response to the objections.[602] The Court will not necessarily refuse to consider motions that are filed late, although it has begun enforcing deadlines more strictly. In the *Castillo Páez Case*, the State filed its preliminary objections a few days after the deadline prescribed in the Court's Rules of Procedure.[603] The Court accepted the filing, stating that 'this delay cannot

599 ICJ Practice Directions VII and VIII.

600 2001 Rules of Procedure of the Inter-Am. Ct HR, Art. 37(1). In the interest of judicial economy, the ICJ also amended its Rules of Procedure to limit the time for raising preliminary objections. International Court of Justice, Rules of Court, adopted on 14 April 1978, amended on 5 December 2000, Art. 79(1).

601 Former 1996 Rules of Procedure of the Inter-Am. Ct, Art. 36(1). See Ana María Reina, 'Las Excepciones Preliminares en el Sistema Interamericano de Derechos Humanos', in *La Corte y el Sistema Interamericano de Derechos Humanos*, 421, 425 (1994).

602 2001 Rules of Procedure of the Inter-Am. Ct HR, Art. 36(4).

603 *Castillo Páez* v. *Peru* (Preliminary Objections, 1996), para. 35.

be considered excessive within the limits of timeliness and reasonableness considered by this Tribunal as necessary for excusing a delay in meeting a deadline'.[604]

The Court may grant extensions of deadlines when the party making the request shows 'reasonable cause'.[605] The Court will not, however, grant extensions *de rigueur*. In the *Benavides Cevallos Case*, the Court denied Ecuador's request for an extension to submit preliminary objections although granting the State an additional period in which to file its answer.[606] As a consequence of the denial, Ecuador did not file preliminary objections in that case.[607] The Court has also refused to accept supplementary briefs on preliminary objections that are submitted after the deadline. In the *Cayara Case*, the Court did not allow the State to submit an additional brief that expanded the scope of the preliminary objections.[608] The Court explained that 'the proceeding would be reopened, the steps already taken at the appropriate time would be infringed and, furthermore, the procedural balance and equality of the parties would be seriously affected'.[609] It follows that, if a State fails to file a preliminary objection and then raises it later at the public hearing, the objection is rejected as out of time.[610] In the interests of judicial economy it is important that the objections be raised and dealt with at the outset of the proceedings.

Specificity of and support for preliminary objections

States have, at times, filed preliminary objections that are broad and unsupported.[611] The Court will refuse to consider arguments that are not pertinent to an objection in question. The Court, therefore, requires that the State making the objection specify the Article of the Convention upon which the objection is based or support its objections in some other way.[612] The Rules of the Court also specify that the brief in support of preliminary objections must set forth the facts, legal arguments, conclusions and supporting documents, and an offer of evidence.[613] The Court's interposition of these requirements may encourage States to consider future objections with care.

[604] *Ibid.* [605] *Ibid.* [606] *Benavides Cevallos* v. *Ecuador* (Merits, 1998), para. 14.
[607] *Ibid.* [608] *Cayara* v. *Peru* (Preliminary Objections, 1993), para. 13.
[609] *Ibid.* [610] See Gomien, Harris and Zwaak, *Law and Practice*, at 75–6.
[611] See *Genie Lacayo* (Preliminary Objections, 1995), paras. 33–5. [612] *Ibid.*, para. 35.
[613] 2001 Rules of Procedure of the Inter-Am. Ct HR, Art. 36(2).

Deadlines and consideration of the merits are not suspended during consideration of preliminary objections

There is no mandatory preliminary objection phase of proceedings before the Inter-American Court. In its 2001 Rules, the Court established that, in the interest of procedural economy, it may resolve any preliminary objections and the merits of the case in the same judgment.[614] In past contentious cases, the Court has generally ruled on the State's objections in interlocutory proceedings and has then issued a separate judgment on preliminary objections. Although there are limited issues, such as certain challenges to the Court's jurisdiction, that would be better resolved at a preliminary stage, it is generally more efficient for the Court to issue only one judgment.

The presentation of preliminary objections, in the Inter-American system, does not suspend the proceedings on the merits of the case.[615] In the *Loayza Tamayo Case*, Peru requested that the Court suspend the proceedings on the merits until its preliminary objections were resolved.[616] The Court rejected the request, as there was no evidence of an 'exceptional situation' and the request could not be justified on any other grounds.[617] The International Court of Justice suspends the proceedings on the merits when preliminary objections are filed. The suspension before the ICJ continues in effect until it has ruled on the objections.[618] The difference between the practice of the ICJ and that of the Inter-American Court can be attributed to the type of objections filed in the two systems. Most preliminary objections interposed before the ICJ challenge the Court's jurisdiction to hear the overall case. If such an objection is upheld, the case must be dismissed. It is in the interests of judicial economy that such preliminary objections be decided at an initial stage of the proceedings, thereby avoiding the time and expense to the parties. In the *Barcelona Traction Case* before the ICJ, the Court upheld a preliminary objection to its jurisdiction after the case had been before the Court for six years.[619] Thereafter, the ICJ changed the rules to suspend the proceedings on the merits until it reaches a decision on preliminary objections.

In the regional human rights systems, however, there are fewer objections to the jurisdiction of the court to hear a case, because jurisdiction

[614] *Ibid.*, Art. 36(6). [615] *Ibid.*, Art. 36(3).
[616] *Loayza Tamayo* v. *Peru* (Preliminary Objections, 1996), para. 8.
[617] *Ibid.* [618] Rules of the ICJ, Art. 79(5).
[619] *Barcelona Traction, Light and Power Company, Limited (New Application, 1962) (Belgium* v. *Spain)*, 1964 ICJ Reports 6 (Preliminary Objections Judgment of 24 July).

is based on an express acceptance of the compulsory jurisdiction of the tribunal by each State.[620] The non-suspension of the proceedings is more efficient for the Inter-American system, because States have often appeared to use preliminary objections to delay the proceedings. This may be for the purpose of avoiding justice or it may simply be a means of gaining time to research the alleged facts.

Public hearings on preliminary objections

Public hearings on preliminary objections are not mandated by the American Convention or the Statute or Rules of the Court. The Court, in its 2001 Rules, has determined that it will hold a special public hearing on preliminary objections only when it considers the hearing to be 'indispensable'.[621] Formerly, the Court's Rules provided that the Court could hold a public hearing on preliminary objections when it found it to be appropriate.[622] To date, the Court has convened public hearings in all but one case in which a State interposed preliminary objections.[623] A public hearing on preliminary objections was not necessary in many of these cases, because the issues involved only questions of law. Most preliminary objections can be decided on the briefs without the time and expense involved in holding hearings before the Court. Any objection that involves issues of fact rather than of pure law could be dealt with at the public hearing on the merits, as the Court has repeatedly done with the preliminary objection of non-exhaustion of domestic remedies.

Hearings on preliminary objections delay the processing of cases in the Inter-American system because the Inter-American Court does not sit on a full-time basis. The seven judges must be summoned from their respective States throughout the Americas to the seat of the Court in San José, Costa Rica, for public hearings and deliberations. Only in relatively rare cases should a hearing be necessary to decide on preliminary objections. The Court need not even meet in session to discuss preliminary objections when there are no issues of fact. The Court could instead employ electronic means used by boards of directors, such as secure e-mail, fax and telephone and video conferences, to allow the judges to discuss non-sensitive preliminary objections without going to the seat of the Court.

620 See American Convention, Arts. 62(1) and (2).

621 Former 1996 Rules of Procedure of the Inter-Am. Ct HR, Art. 36(5).

622 *Ibid.*, Art. 36(6).

623 The Court did not hold a public hearing in *Villagrán Morales et al.* v. *Guatemala (The Street Children Case)* (Preliminary Objections, 1997).

They could also arrange for voting on the objections without convening in person. Human rights cases should not be delayed unnecessarily. A public hearing on preliminary objections in most cases is an unnecessary expenditure of time and resources.

Application of the doctrines of waiver, estoppel and good faith to preliminary objections

The Court applies general principles of law in its consideration of contentious cases and advisory opinion requests. Waiver, estoppel and good faith are general principles of law applicable in most domestic and international legal systems. They are applied consistently in the jurisprudence of the Inter-American Court.

Waiver

It is a generally recognized principle of international law that the State may waive certain admissibility requirements.[624] The State's waiver may be express or implied.[625] In *In the Matter of Viviana Gallardo et al.*, Costa Rica expressly waived the exhaustion requirement when it attempted to bring the case before the Court.[626] The European Court of Human Rights also permits a State to expressly waive domestic remedies.[627] In the '*Vagrancy*' cases, the European Court stated that 'there is nothing to prevent States from waiving the benefit of the rule of exhaustion of domestic remedies, the essential aim of which is to protect their national legal order'.[628] The admissibility requirements are of a purely procedural nature which have been established for the benefit of the States. Therefore, these requirements may be waived by the States, and it is in the interest of judicial economy to allow them to do so.

A State may also implicitly waive an objection to the admissibility of a petition by failing to raise it in a timely manner. The State must raise such objections at the early stages of the Commission's consideration of the case or be estopped from raising them later before the Commission

624 *Castillo Petruzzi et al.* v. *Peru* (Preliminary Objections, 1998), para. 56; *Velásquez Rodríguez* v. *Honduras* (Preliminary Objections, 1987), para. 88.

625 See *Castillo Páez* v. *Peru* (Preliminary Objections, 1996), para. 40; *Loayza Tamayo* v. *Peru* (Preliminary Objections, 1996), para. 40.

626 *In the Matter of Viviana Gallardo*, 1981, at 13.

627 *De Wilde, Ooms and Versyp ('Vagrancy')* v. *Belgium* (Merits), 12 Eur. Ct HR (Ser. A) para. 55 (1971).

628 *Ibid.*

or before the Court.[629] State waiver most often occurs with respect to the State's objection of non-exhaustion of domestic remedies. The Court treats the failure to raise the objection initially before the Commission as a 'tacit admission' of the lack of domestic remedies.[630] The European Court of Human Rights also holds that objections of inadmissibility must be specifically invoked by the State in a timely fashion or the time-limit for presentation by the State will expire, and the Court will not examine them.[631] As in the Inter-American system, the appropriate time to raise the objection in the European system prior to Protocol 11 was at the beginning of the proceedings before the European Commission, when the Commission was determining the admissibility of the petition. For example, in the *Loizidou* case, the European Court rejected Turkey's preliminary objection that the aim of the application against it was 'political propaganda', because Turkey had not raised the objection in the proceedings before the Commission. The Court held that the State was estopped from raising the objection before the Court.[632] Neither the Inter-American Court nor the European Court will hold that the State waived an objection, however, if it was initially impossible for the State to interpose the defence for reasons that cannot be attributed to the State.[633]

In earlier cases, such as the *Honduran Disappearance Cases*, the Inter-American Court commented that the State had not raised the objection before the Commission and therefore had waived it. However, the Court then joined the objection of non-exhaustion to the merits.[634] This decision could perhaps be justified at that time because States were not familiar with the requirements and functioning of the Court, and the Commission's procedures were at times unclear and inconsistent. In later cases, however, when the Court has ruled that the State failed to raise the objection in a timely manner, the Court has held that the objection was waived and has therefore dismissed it.[635] When a party has waived a procedure established

[629] *Castillo Petruzzi et al.* v. *Peru* (Preliminary Objections, 1998), para. 56.

[630] *Ibid.*, para. 56.

[631] See *Artico* v. *Italy*, 37 Eur. Ct HR (Ser. A), paras. 23 *et seq.* (1980) (cited in *Caballero Delgado and Santana* v. *Colombia* (Preliminary Objections, 1994), para. 60). See Gomien, Harris and Zwaak, *Law and Practice of the European Convention*, at 75–6.

[632] *Loizidou* v. *Turkey* (Preliminary Objections), 310 Eur. Ct HR (Ser. A), paras. 42–5 (1995).

[633] *Castillo Petruzzi et al.* v. *Peru* (Preliminary Objections, 1998), para. 56; *Artico* v. *Italy*, 37 Eur. Ct HR (Ser. A), paras. 23 *et seq.* (1980).

[634] *Velásquez Rodríguez* v. *Honduras* (Preliminary Objections, 1987), para. 90 and Resolution 1.

[635] *Castillo Petruzzi et al.* v. *Peru* (Preliminary Objections, 1998), paras. 56–7; *Loayza Tamayo* v. *Peru* (Preliminary Objections, 1996), paras. 41–3; *Castillo Páez* v. *Peru* (Preliminary Objections, 1996), paras. 41–3.

for its benefit, in the interest of judicial economy and equality of arms between the parties, that party should be estopped from later raising it before the Court.

If a case is to be dismissed due to the petitioner's failure to fulfil a Convention-mandated requirement of admissibility, the dismissal must occur at the initial stage before the Commission to avoid the petitioner's expenditure of time and money and the exposure of witnesses to possible reprisals. For these reasons, if the State does not raise the failure of the petitioner to meet an admissibility requirement in a timely manner, the Court must find that the State waived its right to raise the issue. The Court must then refuse to reopen the issue. An advantage of the Court's consistent application of waiver is that it will ensure that States participate in and understand the importance of the proceedings before the Commission, and it will, thus, contribute to the efficient functioning of the system.

Estoppel

In accordance with international law, a State is estopped from taking conflicting positions on an issue. The Inter-American Court holds that, 'when a party in a case adopts a position that is either beneficial to it or detrimental to the other party the principle of estoppel prevents it from subsequently assuming the contrary position'.[636] As a result, a State is estopped from interposing conflicting preliminary objections in a case. In the *Neira Alegría Case*, the Court held that Peru was estopped from filing the contradictory objections that the petitioner had failed to exhaust domestic remedies and that the petition was inadmissible because it was not lodged with the Commission within the required six-month period after the exhaustion of domestic remedies.[637] The Court also applied the doctrine of estoppel in the *Mayagna (SUMO) Awas Tingni Community Case*, in which the State informed the Commission that it would comply with the Commission's recommendations, but later before the Court attempted to raise the objection that domestic remedies had not been exhausted.[638] Venezuela was estopped from retracting its acceptance of State responsibility in the *Del Caracazo Case* and also from contesting

[636] *Neira Alegría et al.* v. *Peru* (Preliminary Objections, 1991), paras. 29–30.

[637] *Ibid.*, paras. 28–30; American Convention, Art. 46(1)(b). See pp. 125–6 above for a discussion of the six-month requirement.

[638] *Mayagna (SUMO) Awas Tingni Community* v. *Nicaragua* (Preliminary Objections), Inter-Am. Ct HR, 1 February 2000, Ser. C, No. 67, para. 57.

certain reparations issues after withdrawing its responding reparations brief.[639]

Not only will the Court apply estoppel when a State raises conflicting arguments before the Inter-American Court, it will also apply estoppel when a State has taken a contrary position before another international court. In its advisory opinion on *The Right to Information on Consular Assistance*, the Court held that the United States was estopped from arguing that the Vienna Convention on Consular Relations did not confer rights on individuals, because it had argued the opposite position in the *Case Concerning United States Diplomatic and Consular Staff in Tehran* before the ICJ.[640] The Court's application of estoppel is important to judicial economy, the efficiency of the system, and the equitable treatment of the petitioners. It is also a step forward in ensuring the overall coordination of an international human rights system. Moreover, States must not be allowed to reach into a grab bag of preliminary objections and raise any or all of them without regard to their nature or applicability to the case.

Good faith

The Court also requires that the parties exercise good faith in accordance with general principles of law and the Vienna Convention on the Law of Treaties.[641] The basic international law principle of *pacta sunt servanda* provides that 'every international agreement in force is binding upon the parties to it and must be performed by them in good faith'.[642] In the *Neira Alegría Case*, the State ingenuously objected that the Commission had not submitted the case to the Court within the Convention's three-month deadline, a delay which resulted from Peru's request that the Commission grant it a thirty-day extension to consider the Commission's recommendations.[643] The Court rejected the objection, reasoning that 'in accordance with elementary principles of good faith that govern all international relations, Peru cannot invoke the expiration of a time-limit that was extended at its own behest'.[644] In the *Cantoral Benavides Case*, Peru raised the same conflicting objections again, and the Court

[639] *Del Caracazo* v. *Venezuela* (Reparations), Inter-Am. Ct HR, 29 August 2002, Ser. C, No. 95, paras. 52 and 53.

[640] Advisory Opinion OC-16/99, para. 75.

[641] Advisory Opinion OC-15/97, para. 29. See also *Restatement (Third) of Foreign Relations Law of the United States*, § 321 (1986).

[642] Vienna Convention on the Law of Treaties, Art. 26. See also *Restatement (Third) of the Foreign Relations Law of the United States*, § 321 (1987).

[643] *Neira Alegría et al.* v. *Peru* (Preliminary Objections, 1991), paras. 32–3.

[644] *Ibid.*, para. 34.

reminded the State that good faith must be exercised in an international proceeding.[645] Similarly, the Court applied the basic principle of good faith in the *Caballero Delgado and Santana Case*, when it refused to allow Colombia to request an extension for the reconsideration of the report and also to claim that the Commission had waived a deadline by granting that request.[646]

Especially in the field of human rights, all parties should be held to a high standard of good faith and fair dealing. States are familiar with the principles of waiver, estoppel and good faith, which are applicable in most domestic and international legal systems. Therefore, the Court's reliance on these principles should be expected and respected by the States Parties to the Inter-American system.

Character of the Court's decision on preliminary objections

Traditionally, the Court has three options in ruling on preliminary objections; it may admit the objection; it may reject the objection; or it may join the objection to the merits of the case. This is also true for the International Court of Justice. The ICJ Rules of the Court provide in relevant part that the Court 'shall either uphold the objection, reject it, or declare that the objection does not possess, in the circumstances of the case, an exclusively preliminary character'.[647]

Admit the objection

When the Court admits a preliminary objection that goes to the overall admissibility of the case or the jurisdiction of the Court, the Court does not go on to analyze other objections.[648] The case is dismissed with prejudice, and the Court never reaches the merits of the case, no matter how egregious the human rights violation alleged.[649]

A preliminary objection may, however, go to only one of several claims of human rights violations made in the application. In that case, if the objection is admitted, the particular claim will be dismissed, but the Court will continue to hear the other claims. For instance, in the *Genie Lacayo Case*, Nicaragua objected to the Commission's claim that certain domestic laws of Nicaragua were incompatible with the American Convention.[650]

645 *Cantoral Benavides* v. *Peru* (Preliminary Objections, 1998), para. 30.

646 *Caballero Delgado and Santana* v. *Colombia* (Preliminary Objections, 1994), para. 38, citing *Neira Alegría et al.* v. *Peru* (Preliminary Objections, 1991), para. 35.

647 Art. 79(9).

648 See *Cayara* v. *Peru* (Preliminary Objections, 1993), paras. 61–2.

649 *Ibid.*

650 *Genie Lacayo* (Preliminary Objections, 1995), paras. 2 and 47.

The Court upheld that objection, but did not dismiss the case. The Court explained that 'as far as the other aspects of the application are concerned, the jurisdiction of the Court remains unalterable due to the fact that this matter is independent of the Commission's remaining requests'.[651] In the *Las Palmeras Case*, the Court upheld Colombia's objection that the Court did not have jurisdiction to determine whether the State had violated common Article 3 of the 1949 Geneva Conventions.[652] The Court did have jurisdiction, however, to consider claims relating to the American Convention.[653] When only one claim is dismissed, the results for the petitioners is not so drastic, as the Court will go on to rule on the other alleged violations.

Join the objection to the merits

Certain objections may qualify as preliminary objections but not be of an exclusively preliminary character. In such a case, the Court cannot decide on an objection without going into the merits. In these cases, it may join the preliminary objection to the merits of the case.[654] There may be various reasons for joining an objection to the merits. First, the questions of law and fact raised by the objection may be so intimately linked to the merits that a ruling on the objection could prejudice the merits of the case.[655] Secondly, it may not be possible for the Court to determine if the objection is actually a defence to the merits of the case at an early stage in the proceedings. Thirdly, it may also be necessary to hear evidence of the alleged facts for the Court to make a ruling on the objection.

The preliminary objection most commonly joined to the merits of the case in the Inter-American system has been the non-exhaustion of domestic remedies. Petitioners' responses to the State's non-exhaustion objection generally are that the remedies available are not effective or adequate or that the victim has been denied access to domestic remedies.

651 *Ibid.*, para. 51.

652 *Las Palmeras* (Preliminary Objections, 2000), para. 33 and operative para. 2.

653 *Ibid.*, operative para. 1.

654 The Permanent Court of International Justice stated in the *Panevezys-Saldutiskis Railway Case* that 'the Court may order the joinder of preliminary objections to the merits, whenever the interests of the good administration of justice require it'. 1938 PCIJ (Ser. A/B) No. 75, at 55–6, quoted in *Barcelona Traction, Light and Power Company, Limited (New Application, 1962) (Belgium* v. *Spain)*, 1964 ICJ Reports 6, 42 (Preliminary Objections Judgment of 24 July).

655 See Reina, 'Las Excepciones Preliminares en el Sistema Interamericano de Derechos Humanos', 430 n. 24 (citing Judge Cançado Trindade).

These responses may raise questions of fact that require a hearing. The applicant may present witnesses or written proof which will likely be disputed by the State. In the *Honduran Disappearance Cases*, in which the State raised the objection of non-exhaustion, the Court joined the objection to the merits, reasoning that 'given the interplay between the problem of domestic remedies and the very violation of human rights, the question of their prior exhaustion must be taken up together with the merits of the case'.[656] Because decisions on whether domestic remedies have been exhausted or whether an exception to exhaustion is applicable in the particular case may often necessitate witness testimony, a preliminary hearing on the matter could result in the duplication of testimony as well as an undue delay in the proceedings. In this regard, the Inter-American Court has remarked that:

> [o]f course, when the State interposes this objection in timely fashion it should be heard and resolved; however, the relationship between the decision regarding applicability of the rule [of exhaustion of domestic remedies] and the need for timely international action in the absence of effective domestic remedies may frequently recommend the hearing of questions relating to that rule together with the merits, in order to prevent unnecessary delays due to preliminary objections.[657]

Earlier Rules of Procedure of the Inter-American Court specifically provided that the Court 'shall rule on the objections or order that they be joined to the merits'.[658] The Court's 1996 Rules of Procedure did not address the issue of whether a preliminary objection could be joined to the merits, although the Court regularly did so. Under the Court's 2001 Rules, the question is of minimal importance, because the Court need not hold a separate hearing or issue a separate report on preliminary objections.

Indications in later cases are that the Inter-American Court is more likely to decide the non-exhaustion objection at the preliminary objections phase of the proceedings rather than joining it to the merits. In the *Cantoral Benavides Case*, the Court considered and rejected the State's objection of failure to exhaust domestic remedies in its preliminary decision,

656 *Velásquez Rodríguez* v. *Honduras* (Preliminary Objections), para. 94; *Godínez Cruz* (Preliminary Objections), para. 96; *Fairén Garbi and Solís Corrales* (Preliminary Objections), para. 93.

657 *Velásquez Rodríguez* v. *Honduras* (Preliminary Objections), para. 93; *Godínez Cruz* (Preliminary Objections), para. 95; *Fairén Garbi and Solís Corrales* (Preliminary Objections), para. 92.

658 1991 Rules of Procedure of the Inter-American Court of Human Rights, approved by the Court at its twenty-third regular session held 9–18 January 1991, Art. 31(6).

and, therefore, did not join the objection to the merits.[659] In the *Castillo Petruzzi Case*, the Court held that the State had waived the objection by not raising it in a timely manner and then rejected the objection.[660] Moreover, in the *Cesti Hurtado Case*, the Court simply accepted the Commission's decision that domestic remedies had been exhausted without even engaging in an independent analysis of the facts.[661] In the interest of judicial economy and fairness to the petitioner, the Court should establish a rebuttable presumption in favour of the exhaustion of domestic remedies if the Commission has so decided, and render its decision on exhaustion in the preliminary objections phase of the proceedings. If the State has failed to raise the objection before the Commission, it should be estopped from doing so before the Court.

The Rules of the International Court of Justice explicitly provide for joinder of a preliminary objection to the merits.[662] The European Court has also joined the objection of non-exhaustion of domestic remedies to the merits.[663] Moreover, it has joined the objection to the Commission's and the Court's jurisdiction *ratione temporis* to the merits of the case, because of the legal and factual issues involved.[664]

Reject some or all objections

The Court may reject preliminary objections that are unsubstantiated by the party interposing the objection.[665] In the *Gangaram Panday Case*, Suriname did not provide evidence to support its objections that the Commission had abused its right of petition by filing an application before the Court and by not fully complying with the provisions of the Convention.[666] The Court rejected the objections and proceeded to consider the merits of the case.[667]

The Court will also reject a preliminary objection as being completely without grounds. In the preliminary objections stage of the *Cesti Hurtado Case*, the State raised the issue of the political affiliation of the defenders of the victim who, the State claimed, were radically opposed to the

659 *Cantoral Benavides* v. *Peru* (Preliminary Objections, 1998), para. 34.
660 *Castillo Petruzzi et al.* v. *Peru* (Preliminary Objections, 1998), para. 56.
661 See *Cesti Hurtado* v. *Peru* (Preliminary Objections, 1999), para. 33.
662 International Court of Justice, Rules of Court, adopted on 14 April 1978, amended on 5 December 2000, Arts. 79(9) and (10).
663 *Yasa* v. *Turkey* (1998-VI) Eur. Ct HR (1998), para. IIB.
664 *Loizidou* v. *Turkey* (Preliminary Objections), 310 Eur. Ct HR (Ser. A), paras. 103–5 (1995).
665 *Gangaram Panday* v. *Suriname* (Preliminary Objections, 1991), paras. 36 and 41.
666 See *ibid.* 667 *Ibid.*, paras. 41–2.

government of Peru.[668] The Court refused even to consider that issue, stating that it was irrelevant to the Court.[669] The Court may also reject an objection that it finds is possibly well-founded but not of a preliminary character. In such an instance, the Court can allow the party to take it up again in support of the case on the merits.[670] If the Court rejects all the preliminary objections interposed, it goes on to consider the merits of the case.

The Court's decision to reject preliminary objections cannot be contested by the State.[671] The American Convention provides that '[t]he judgment of the Court shall be final and not subject to appeal'.[672] The Court has held that all its decisions 'which are not purely procedural, that is, those traditionally called "interlocutory decisions or judgments", may not be challenged in any way'.[673] The Court reasoned that 'a contentious proceeding before this Court must be concentrated inasmuch as protection of the human rights enshrined in the American Convention requires that such a proceeding be as brief as possible; it cannot, therefore, be subject to the excessive formalities of an ordinary domestic trial'.[674]

Withdrawal of preliminary objections

A party may withdraw a preliminary objection that is no longer relevant. The withdrawal of a preliminary objection, which the respondent has decided not to interpose, is of obvious utility in that it saves the Court the time and resources it would expend determining the validity of issues to which the respondent no longer objects. Although there is no provision in the Rules of the Inter-American Court that explicitly allows a party to withdraw a preliminary objection, the jurisprudence of the Court has permitted such withdrawals. In the *Bámaca Velásquez Case*, Guatemala partially accepted international responsibility for a violation

668 *Cesti Hurtado* v. *Peru* (Preliminary Objections, 1999), para. 35.
669 See *ibid.*, para. 38.
670 See *Electricity Company of Sofia and Bulgaria (Bulgaria* v. *Belgium)*, Preliminary Objections, 1939 PCIJ (Ser. A/B) No. 77.
671 *Loayza Tamayo* v. *Peru*, Order of the Inter-American Court of Human Rights, 27 June 1996, paras. 6–7, reprinted in 1996 Annual Reports of the Inter-Am. Ct HR 112.
672 American Convention, Art. 67.
673 *Loayza Tamayo* v. *Peru*, Order of the Inter-American Court of Human Rights, 27 June 1996, para. 6, reprinted in 1996 Annual Report of the Inter-Am. Ct HR 112.
674 *Ibid.*, para. 7.

of the Convention, and in its brief specified that its acceptance implied the withdrawal of its preliminary objection.[675] The Court deemed the preliminary objection to be withdrawn and proceeded to consider the merits of the case.[676] Also, in the *Trujillo Oroza Case*, Bolivia withdrew its preliminary objections and accepted international responsibility for the human rights violations alleged in the application.[677] If the State accepts international responsibility for a violation or for other reasons requests that the Court eliminate the merits of the case and go directly to the reparations stage, the Court will only comply with that request if the State withdraws its preliminary objections.[678]

There is also precedent in the ICJ for the withdrawal of preliminary objections although there is no rule specifically providing for such withdrawal. In the *Genocide Convention Case (Bosnia* v. *Yugoslavia)*, the ICJ allowed Yugoslavia to withdraw a preliminary objection which it had interposed.[679]

The Court has also permitted a State to withdraw its brief raising preliminary objections and to file another within the time limits originally set by the Court.[680] In the *Villagrán Morales Case*, in which the Commission alleged that the Guatemalan Government was responsible for the murder of five street children, the State initially filed a brief interposing four preliminary objections, but, with the permission of the Court, it substituted another in its place within the prescribed time period.[681] When the time period has not passed for the submission of preliminary objections, the Court should permit the respondent to withdraw its brief and file another in its place. This action may have the unfortunate consequence of resulting in additional work for the applicant who may have already begun research to respond to the objections, but it is in the interest of procedural economy for the Court.

[675] *Bámaca Velásquez*, Withdrawal of Preliminary Objection, Order of the Inter-Am. Court HR, 16 April 1997, para. 9, reprinted in 1997 Annual Report of the Inter-Am. Ct HR, OAS/Ser.L/V/III.39 doc. 5, 21 January 1998, at 120.

[676] *Ibid.*, Resolutions 1 and 2.

[677] *Trujillo Oroza* v. *Bolivia* (Merits, 2002), para. 33.

[678] See *Cantoral Benavides*, Order of the Inter-Am. Ct HR, 18 June 1998, reprinted in 1998 Annual Report of the Inter-Am. Court HR, OAS/Ser.L/V/III.43 doc. 11, 18 January 1999, at 223–5.

[679] *Application of the Convention on the Prevention and Punishment of the Crime of Genocide (Bosnia and Herzegovina* v. *Yugoslavia)*, Preliminary Objections, 1996 ICJ Reports 803, para. 16 (11 July).

[680] *Villagrán Morales et al.* v. *Guatemala (The Street Children Case)* (Preliminary Objections, 1997), paras. 8–10.

[681] *Ibid.*

Conclusion

While States may properly raise preliminary objections to legitimate issues before the Inter-American Court, it is impermissible to use preliminary objections as a means to delay or subvert justice in human rights cases. The enforcement organs of the Inter-American human rights system have taken several important measures to guarantee that States use preliminary objections legitimately and efficiently. The Inter-American Court, while establishing new precedents in the defence of victims of human rights abuse, is also applying accepted principles of international law and the general principles of law observed by civilized nations in its decisions on preliminary objections. The Commission has eliminated certain State objections altogether by implementing changes in the processing of petitions. Although the Commission was initially somewhat informal in its handling of individual petitions, it is now instituting and documenting practices which explicitly comply with or go beyond Convention-mandated procedures. For instance, although the Court has ruled that the Commission does not have to issue a formal decision on admissibility, the Commission has chosen, in the interests of transparency and legal certainty, to issue a separate detailed admissibility report in most instances. Also, although the Court ruled that the Commission has some discretion in deciding when to make available its good offices for the purpose of facilitating a friendly settlement between the victim and the State, the Commission has instituted a consistent practice of asking both the State and the petitioner if they would consider a friendly settlement. The Commission then documents the response of each party. As a result, this basis for a preliminary objection has been effectively eliminated.

The Court has made changes to its Rules of Procedure and the processing of cases to eliminate the basis for those objections that do not contribute to a clarification of the legal situation. The Court now allows the applicant to amend a timely application and grants the applicant a limited additional time to remedy certain deficiencies.[682] Thus, purely formal procedural deficiencies in the application are no longer cause for preliminary objections and the consequent dismissal of the case. The Court has made changes in its Rules of Procedure to avoid delays in processing a case. The Court now requires that preliminary objections be specified in the answer to the petition, that a public hearing be held on preliminary objections only when the Court considers it indispensable, and that the

[682] *Paniagua Morales* (Preliminary Objections, 1996), para. 37.

Court can issue one judgment incorporating its response to preliminary objections and its decision on the merits.

Despite these advancements by the Commission and the Court, the frequency and quantity of preliminary objections do not appear to be substantially decreasing. These objections serve to delay the resolution of cases and infringe upon a petitioner's right to prompt justice. Additional steps should be taken to improve the use of preliminary objections and eliminate delays in the proceedings. First, the Court should refuse to reopen the Commission's decision on admissibility. Such a change would prevent the Court from dismissing a case on the grounds that the initial petition to the Commission did not fulfil the requisites of admissibility after the petitioners and witnesses to the alleged violation, at great personal risk and expense, have spent years processing a case before the Commission. It would also provide for an equality of arms between the petitioner and the State. Secondly, the Court should avail itself of its new Rule and not convene public hearings on preliminary objections unless there is an issue of fact or other reason necessitating oral argument. The briefs submitted by the parties contain extensive information, which would allow the Court to decide on most objections without the presence of the parties. Moreover, when appropriate, the Court should use modern technology to eliminate the need for the judges, who sit on a part-time basis, to travel to the seat of the Court to discuss and vote on the objections.

Finally, the Court and other international institutions should attempt to educate States' attorneys in the proper manner of responding to a petition lodged with the Inter-American Commission or an application submitted to the Court. Yearly seminars for high-level government functionaries who have authority to settle cases on behalf of the State could contribute to the prompt resolution of cases in the Inter-American system. In addition, a complete manual on procedure and practice before the Inter-American human rights organs would educate attorneys who are assigned to cases in a system about which they may know very little. This education would supplement the successful efforts of the Inter-American Institute of Human Rights and other international organizations to rehabilitate the concept of 'human rights', which in the 1970s and 1980s was considered a leftist catchphrase in Latin America, but which is now proudly embraced by many governments.

4

Proceedings on the merits: fact-finding and attribution of State responsibility

> The importance and transcendence of the evidence in a jurisdictional proceeding is obvious. It has even been said that the proceeding constitutes, in essence, a broad probative opportunity directed at verifying the *de facto* conditions that support the legal claims. The juridical consequences are constructed on the basis of the facts. Consequently, the judge must give special attention to the issue of the evidence before beginning the juridical consideration, and, particularly, do so in a firm and reasonably certain way, so that justice may be done in the specific case.[1]

Introduction

If the case is not dismissed in the preliminary objections stage of the proceedings, the Court will consider the merits of the case. During the merits phase, the Court engages in fact-finding and determines whether the State is responsible for the alleged violation. The function of fact-finding in the judicial process is 'to enable the tribunal to discover the truth concerning the conflicting claims of the parties before it'.[2] In doing so, the judges must evaluate the evidence presented to the tribunal.

Cases before international tribunals are generally heard by judges who were trained in different legal traditions. The two primary legal systems are civil and common law. The integration of these systems is most obvious in the area of fact-finding, where the evidentiary practices between the civil and common law systems differ in significant respects. Under common law, the parties are adversaries who bear the initiative in presenting evidence. The function of the judge is to serve as a disinterested umpire. It has been argued that the objective of common law proceedings is not to reveal the absolute truth but rather to 'see that evidence is brought before the court in accordance with the established rules and to render a verdict

[1] Separate Concurring Opinion of Judge Sergio García Ramírez in *Bámaca Velásquez* (Merits), Inter-Am. Ct HR, 25 November 2000, Ser. C, No. 70, para. 3.

[2] Durward Sandifer, *Evidence Before International Tribunals*, 1 (revised edn, 1975).

in favor of the party who succeeded in presenting the most convincing evidence through the rules'.[3] Under civil law, the functions of the judge are more comprehensive than under common law. Judges take a much more active part in the direction of the proceedings and in the examination of the witnesses.[4] Therefore, the rules of evidence, especially with respect to admission and exclusion, are not as technical as they are under common law.

Evidentiary practice in international law more closely parallels that of civil law in that it is encumbered by fewer technical and restrictive rules, and the judges determine the weight to be given to the evidence submitted.[5] Consequently, international tribunals have not adopted as detailed and complex a body of rules of evidence as has been adopted in common law systems.[6] Although 'fair and efficient regulation of the various issues related to proof is critical for a harmonious and peaceful development of social relations', there is no absolute law of evidence in international practice.[7] Sandifer, in his well-known treatise, *Evidence Before International Tribunals*, stated that '[n]o rule of evidence thus finds more frequent statement in the cases than the one that international tribunals are "not bound to adhere to strict judicial rules of evidence" '.[8]

The Inter-American Court, like the International Court of Justice and the European Court of Human Rights, is composed of judges from both common and civil law traditions. Many of the judges are scholars and have extensive knowledge of comparative law. Although the Inter-American Court initially had few rules of evidence, with each succeeding adoption of its Rules of Procedure, it has expanded and clarified those rules. Nonetheless, the judges will consider almost all evidence which is timely presented and will accord the evidence a relative weight.

Joinder of cases and proceedings before the Court

The Rules of Procedure of the Inter-American Court,[9] like those of the European Court of Human Rights,[10] the United Nations Human Rights

[3] *Ibid.*, at 2. [4] *Ibid.* [5] *Ibid.*, at 11–12.

[6] Mojtaba Kazazi, *Burden of Proof and Related Issues: A Study of Evidence Before International Tribunals*, 3 (Kluwer, The Hague, 1996).

[7] Joe Verhoeven, 'Foreword', in Kazazi, *Burden of Proof*, at vii.

[8] Sandifer, *Evidence Before International Tribunals*, at 9.

[9] 2001 Rules of Procedure of the Inter-American Court of Human Rights, entered into force on 1 June 2001, approved by the Court at its forty-ninth regular session held 25 November 2000, Art. 28.

[10] European Court of Human Rights, Rules of Court, entered into force on 1 November 1998, Rule 43.

Committee[11] and the Inter-American Commission[12] permit the joinder or simultaneous consideration of interrelated cases. In the interests of judicial economy, when more than one case involving similar alleged violations against the same State is submitted concurrently, the court may join the cases. Alternatively, the court may decide not to formally join the cases but rather to order that certain aspects of the written or oral proceedings be carried out jointly, including the introduction of witnesses.[13] The court may also conduct two or more cases simultaneously.[14]

The Inter-American Court may join cases at any stage of the proceedings when there is a commonality of 'identity of parties, subject matter, and ruling law'.[15] On this basis, the Court joined the *Hilaire, Constantine et al. and Benjamin et al. Cases* against Trinidad and Tobago.[16] First, the parties to the cases, the Inter-American Commission and the State of Trinidad and Tobago, were the same. Secondly, the subject matter of the three cases, which dealt with due process guarantees when the imposition of the death penalty was mandatory in the State, was essentially identical.[17] Thirdly, the application alleged that the State had violated many of the same provisions of the American Convention.[18] The only differences involved the circumstances of each individual's case. The joinder of cases eliminates duplication of procedures before the Court and the expense of bringing the same witnesses before the Court on different occasions.

A foreseeable difficulty in this area may result from the requirement that all alleged victims in a case before the Court must designate only one representative to present evidence, submit requests and present arguments before the Court.[19] The alleged victims may not be in agreement on these issues. The Court's Rules provide that the decision shall fall to the Court if the parties do not agree on a representative.[20] The Court might, in such an instance, request that the Commission make a recommendation to the Court in this regard. The Commission will have dealt with the parties in earlier proceedings and will, thus, have more knowledge of the

[11] The Rules of Procedure of the United Nations Human Rights Committee, UN Doc. CCPR/C/3/Rev. 6 (24 April 2001), Rule 88(2).

[12] 2001 Rules of Procedure of the Inter-Am. Comm. on Human Rights, entered into force on 1 May 2001, approved by the Commission at its 109th special session, held 4–8 December 2000, Art. 29(1)(d).

[13] 2001 Rules of Procedure of the Inter-Am. Ct HR, Art. 28(2).

[14] *Ibid.*, Art. 28(3). [15] *Ibid.*, Art. 28(1).

[16] *Hilaire, Constantine et al. and Benjamin et al.* v. *Trinidad and Tobago* (Joinder of Cases), Inter-Am. Ct HR, Resolution of 30 November 2001, reprinted in 2002 Annual Report of the Inter-Am. Ct HR.

[17] *Ibid.*, para. 6. [18] *Ibid.*, para. 7.

[19] 2001 Rules of Procedure of the Inter-Am. Ct HR, Art. 23(2). [20] *Ibid.*, Art. 23(3).

interrelationships to be considered. The Commission may also designate other victims' representatives as Commission assistants.[21]

Failure of a party to appear or to continue proceedings

The American Convention does not address the possibility that a party will default and fail to participate in proceedings before the Court. The Court's Rules, however, provide that, when a party fails to appear before the Court or withdraws from the proceedings, the Court may, on its own motion, take whatever measures it considers necessary to complete its consideration of the case.[22] The Inter-American Court holds that a State has a 'procedural responsibility' to present evidence.[23] When the State does not contest claims set forth in the application, 'the facts on which [the State] remains silent are presumed to be true, provided that the existing evidence leads to conclusions consistent with those facts'.[24] The Court will then consider all the evidence in reaching a conclusion.[25] Likewise, the Statute of the ICJ provides that, when a party fails to appear or to defend its case before the Court, the Court may find in favour of the applicant provided that 'the claim is well founded in fact and law'.[26] These provisions are essential to discourage States from boycotting international proceedings and encourage them to become seriously involved in the representation of their cases.

The Inter-American Court clarified that:

> procedural inactivity does not give rise to a specific sanction against the parties, nor does it affect the development of the proceeding; but it may eventually prejudice them, if they take the decision not to exercise fully their right to defense or to execute the appropriate procedural actions that are in their interests, in accordance with the *audi alteram partem* principle.[27]

Trinidad and Tobago failed to participate in the *Hilaire, Constantine and Benjamin et al. Cases*, except to file a preliminary objection.[28] Peru failed

[21] *Ibid.*, Art. 22. [22] *Ibid.*, Art. 27(1).

[23] *Hilaire, Constantine and Benjamin et al.* v. *Trinidad and Tobago* (Merits), Inter-Am. Ct HR, 21 June 2002, Ser. C, No. 94, para. 67.

[24] *Ibid.* [25] *Ibid.*, para. 68.

[26] Statute of the International Court of Justice, 59 Stat. 1055, entered into force 24 October 1945, Art. 53.

[27] *Constitutional Court* v. *Peru (Aguirre Roca, Rey Terry and Revoredo Marsano* v. *Peru)* (Merits), Inter-Am. Ct HR, 31 January 2001, Ser. C, No. 71, para. 60; see also *Ivcher Bronstein* v. *Peru* (Merits), Inter-Am. Ct HR, 6 February 2001, Ser. C, No. 74, para. 80.

[28] *Hilaire, Constantine and Benjamin et al.* v. *Trinidad and Tobago* (Merits, 2002), paras. 16 and 17.

to appear in the proceedings on the merits in the *Ivcher Bronstein Case* and the *Constitutional Court Case*.[29] The Inter-American Court, citing several ICJ cases, including the *Case Concerning Military and Paramilitary Activities In and Against Nicaragua*, affirmed that 'the absence of one of the parties at any stage of the case, does not affect the validity of the judgment', and thus the defaulting party is still bound to comply with the Court's decision.[30]

The scope of the Court's fact-finding powers

The American Convention does not specify whether the Inter-American Court, the only judicial organ in the Inter-American system, is a court of first instance or an appellate court. As stated, all individual petitions alleging human rights violations must first be brought before the Inter-American Commission. The Commission makes a determination of the facts of the case, and then, if it finds that the State has violated the American Convention, makes recommendations to the State. If the State does not comply with the Commission's recommendations or if the State is not in agreement with the Commission's findings, either the Commission or the State may bring the case before the Court. The Court's judgment in a case is not subject to appeal.[31] The Court has asserted that the Court and the Commission perform different but complementary functions when they consider matters concerning the States Parties' compliance with the Convention, and that the Court has jurisdiction over all issues relevant in a case.[32] It maintains that it:

> is not bound by what the Commission may have previously decided; rather, its authority to render judgment is in no way restricted. The Court does not act as a Court of review, of appeal or other similar court in its dealings with the Commission. Its power to examine and review all actions and decisions of the Commission derives from its character as sole juridical organ in matters concerning the Convention.[33]

[29] *Constitutional Court Case* (Peru) (Merits, 2001), para. 48; *Ivcher Bronstein* v. *Peru* (Merits, 2001), para. 68.

[30] *Constitutional Court Case* (Peru) (Merits, 2001), para. 62; *Ivcher Bronstein* v. *Peru* (Merits, 2001), para. 82.

[31] American Convention, Art. 67.

[32] *Gangaram Panday* v. *Suriname* (Merits), Inter-Am. Ct HR, 21 January 1994, Ser. C, No. 16, para. 41, citing *Velásquez Rodriguez* (Preliminary Objections), Inter-Am. Ct HR, 26 June 1987, Ser. C, No. 1, para. 29; *Nineteen Merchants* v. *Colombia* (Preliminary Objections), Inter-Am. Ct HR, 12 June 2002, Ser. C. No. 93, para. 27.

[33] *Velásquez Rodríguez* v. *Honduras* (Preliminary Objections, 1987), para. 29; *Godínez Cruz* (Preliminary Objections), Inter-Am. Ct HR, 26 June 1987, Ser. C, No. 3, para. 32; *Fairén*

This position has been criticized by many scholars of the Court who argue that the duplication of procedures is time-consuming and expensive.[34]

The Court's 2001 Rules of Procedure promise to eliminate at least some of the duplication of procedures between the Commission and the Court. The Rules now provide that '[e]vidence tendered to the Commission shall form part of the file, provided that it has been received in a procedure with the presence of both parties', unless the Court determines that the evidence must be repeated.[35] This change is meant to avoid repetition, speed up the proceedings, and save on the costs of evidence production.[36] The Commission creates a complete factual record that has been developed through proceedings which provide due process guarantees to both parties. Although many States originally failed to participate in proceedings before the Commission, by the late 1990s State participation was nearly 100 per cent.[37] Therefore, most evidence will be admitted before the Court, unless the Court determines that it must be repeated. Key witnesses may be called again to testify, as the judges may have questions for them or the Court may wish to evaluate the demeanour of the witness. Danger to witnesses who testified before the Commission will be minimized, however, because that testimony will be part of the Court record, thereby diminishing any benefit to the State of preventing them from testifying before the Court.

The requirement that evidence tendered only in an adversarial proceeding before the Commission form a part of the Court's files does not serve to discourage States from refusing to provide information in response to the Commission's requests for information. The State's non-participation in Commission proceedings forces the Commission to rely on a presumption

Garbi and Solís Corrales (Preliminary Objections), Inter-Am. Ct HR, 26 June 1987, Ser. C, No. 2, para. 34.

[34] Thomas Buergenthal, 'Judicial Fact-Finding: The Inter-American Human Rights Court', in *Fact-Finding Before International Tribunals: Eleventh Sokol Colloquium*, 263, at 264 (Richard Lillich ed., Transnational Publishers, Ardsley-on-Hudson, NY, 1992); Michael Reisman and Janet Koven Levit, 'Fact-Finding Initiatives for the Inter-American Court of Human Rights', in *La Corte y el Sistema Interamericano de Derechos Humanos*, 443, at 445 (Rafael Nieto Navia ed., 1994).

[35] 2001 Rules of Procedure of the Inter-Am. Ct HR, Art. 43(2).

[36] Informe y Propuestas del Presidente y Relator de la Corte Interamericana de Derechos Humanos, Juez Antonio A. Cançado Trindade, Ante la Comisión de Asuntos Jurídicos y Políticos del Consejo Permanente de la Organización de los Estados Americanos, en el Marco del Diálogo Sobre el Sistema Interamericano de Protección de los Derechos Humanos Bases para un Proyecto de Protocolo a la Convención Americana Sobre Derechos Humanos, para Fortalecer su Mecanismo de Protección, 5 April 2001, para. 35.

[37] Cassel, 'Fact-Finding in the Inter-American System', in *The UN Human Rights Treaty System in the 21st Century*, 106 at 107 (Bayefsky ed., Kluwer, The Hague, 2000), at 107.

that the facts reported in the complainant's petition were true.[38] The State had the opportunity to present its evidence. If it chose to waive the opportunity, it has received due process. Re-establishing the facts of such a case before the Court would not have a deterrent effect on States and would not provide the necessary encouragement to the State to present all facts to the Commission.

The Court's Rules do not specify that the Commission's findings of fact with respect to the evidence will be incorporated into the Court's file. Such a rule would be more useful in that it would effectively shift the burden to the State to persuade the Court that the evidence should not be accorded the status of *res judicata*. OAS Secretary General Gaviria suggested that the duplication of fact-finding efforts could be reduced if the Court were to afford greater deference to the Commission's findings either by regarding the Commission's factual findings as dispositive or by permitting the development of a rebuttable presumption in favour of the Commission's factual findings.[39]

State obligations to comply with Court orders

Respondent States are also obligated to cooperate with the Court by ensuring that 'all notices, communications or summonses addressed to persons subject to their jurisdiction are duly executed'.[40] The Court has the authority to summon witnesses to testify before the Court.[41] The summons shall state the witness' or expert witness' name. In the case of a testimonial witness, the summons must also state the facts that will be the subject of the examination. In respect to an expert witness, the summons will specify the object of the expert opinion.[42] In most cases, States have made an effort to comply with Court orders to produce the witnesses summoned. In the *Cantoral Benavides Case*, however, Peru objected to the Court summons of a naval investigating judge identified only by a code number.[43] The State justified its failure to produce the witness on the ground that domestic legislation mandated that the names of those judges participating in trials for treason or terrorism be kept secret.[44] The Court, while noting

[38] 2001 Rules of Procedure of the Inter-Am. Comm. HR, Art. 39.

[39] Cesar Gaviria, 'Toward a New Vision of the Inter-American Human Rights System', 4 *Journal of Latin American Affairs*, 4, at 11 (1996).

[40] 2001 Rules of Procedure of the Inter-Am. Ct HR, Art. 24(1).

[41] *Ibid.*, Art. 46. [42] *Ibid.*, Art. 46(2).

[43] *Cantoral Benavides* v. *Peru* (Merits), Inter-Am. Ct HR, 18 August 2000, Ser. C, No. 69, para. 53.

[44] *Ibid.*

the objection, maintained that States have an obligation to comply with the Court's summons and could not use domestic laws or considerations as an excuse for a failure to comply.[45]

The Court may also request that States that are not parties to a case assist the Court in ensuring that summonses in their territory are duly executed and that witnesses in their territory comply with those summonses.[46] In the *Ivcher Bronstein Case*, the Secretariat of the Court addressed Panama's diplomatic authorities in an attempt to summon the witness, Vladimiro Montesinos, former director of the Peruvian National Intelligence Service.[47] The proposed witness did not appear to testify.

The Inter-American Court asserts its power to compel testimony through the domestic courts where the witness resides. If a witness who has been summoned by the Court to testify fails to appear without good reason, refuses to provide evidence, or violates the oath, the Court will inform the State of residence 'so that the appropriate action may be taken under the relevant domestic legislation'.[48]

Unquestionably, the State is obligated to refrain from harming witnesses who appear before the Court and, in certain instances, to provide them with protection. There have been several instances in which witnesses who testified before the Court have been threatened or murdered.[49] The Court demands that the State refrain from taking actions against witnesses. The Court's Rules of Procedure provide that 'States may neither institute proceedings against witnesses or expert witnesses nor bring illicit pressure to bear on them or on their families on account of declarations or opinions they have delivered before the Court.'[50] This rule has not, however, been the most effective mechanism for providing witness protection. The Court has been more successful by ordering a State to take provisional measures to provide protection for persons who are in danger of irreparable harm.[51]

Admission of evidence

Except to the limited extent that procedural rules have been established by the American Convention and the Statute of the Court, the

[45] *Ibid.*, para. 54. [46] 2001 Rules of Procedure of the Inter-Am. Ct HR, Art. 24(3).

[47] *Ivcher Bronstein* v. *Peru* (Merits), para. 39.

[48] 2001 Rules of Procedure of the Inter-Am. Ct HR, Art. 51.

[49] See *Velásquez Rodríguez, Fairén Garbi and Solís Corrales, and Godínez Cruz*, Provisional Measures, Inter-Am. Ct HR, Order of 15 January 1988, Ser. E, para. 1.

[50] 2001 Rules of Procedure of the Inter-Am. Ct HR, Art. 50.

[51] See American Convention, Art. 63(2).

Inter-American Court is empowered to elaborate its rules on fact-finding and evidentiary matters.[52] Like most international courts, the Inter-American Court, therefore, enjoys considerable freedom to develop, interpret and apply rules of evidence. In general, the rules heretofore adopted by the Court are based on general principles of evidence from both the civil and common law traditions.

The Court's procedures in assessing the evidence 'are less formal and more flexible' than fact-finding procedures under domestic law, without disregarding legal protection and the procedural equality of the parties.[53] The Court affirms that:

> the international protection of human rights should not be confused with criminal justice. When States appear before the Court, they do so not as defendants in a criminal proceeding, since the Court does not impose punishment on those responsible for violating human rights. Its function is to protect the victims and to determine the reparation of the damages caused by the States responsible for such actions.[54]

The Court maintains that its proceedings involve unique procedures and characteristics, 'that distinguish them from domestic legal proceedings'.[55] The proceedings 'are not bound by the same formalities that bind domestic courts in their proceedings'.[56]

In its evaluation of the evidence, the Court uses logic and experience.[57] The criteria used by a human rights tribunal to evaluate evidence embody special characteristics, arising from its authority to determine a State's international responsibility for the violation of a person's rights.[58] This authority bestows on the Court greater latitude in its admission and evaluation of evidence.[59] The Court has stated in this regard that it has discretion to evaluate the written and testimonial evidence submitted to it.[60]

52 *Ibid.*, Art. 60.

53 *Cantoral Benavides* v. *Peru* (Merits, 2000), para. 45; see also *Castillo Páez* v. *Peru* (Reparations), Inter-Am. Ct HR, 27 November 1998, para. 38.

54 *Constitutional Court Case* v. *Peru* (Merits, 1999), para. 47; see also *Cantoral Benavides* v. *Peru* (Merits, 2000), para. 46.

55 *Castillo Páez* v. *Peru* (Reparations, 1998), para. 38; see also *Cantoral Benavides* v. *Peru* (Merits, 2000), para. 45.

56 *Loayza Tamayo* v. *Peru* (Reparations), Inter-Am. Ct HR, 27 November 1998, Ser. C, No. 42, para. 38.

57 *Loayza Tamayo* v. *Peru* (Merits), Inter-Am. Ct HR, 17 September 1997, Ser. C, No. 33, para. 42.

58 *Ibid.* 59 *Ibid.*

60 *Castillo Páez* v. *Peru* (Reparations, 1998), para. 40, citing *Paniagua Morales et al.* v. *Guatemala (The White Van Case)* (Merits), Inter-Am. Ct HR, 8 March 1998, Ser. C, No. 37, para. 76; and *Loayza Tamayo* v. *Peru* (Reparations, 1998), para. 57.

In doing so, the Court applies the rule of *sana critica*, which has been variously translated in the Court's opinions as 'reasoned judgment',[61] 'sound criticism',[62] 'competent analysis'[63] and 'sound judicial discretion',[64] balancing the circumstances of the case under consideration and 'respect for legal certainty and the equality of the parties'.[65]

Order and time of submission of evidence

Except under special circumstances, the parties must introduce evidence in the initial documents filed with the Court.[66] The Court's Rules provide that evidence must be listed in the application, the reply to the application, the brief raising preliminary objections, or in the answer to the preliminary objections brief.[67] In its brief containing the application, the applicant must provide, *inter alia*, a statement of the facts and specify the evidence supporting each fact.[68] The brief must also identify and provide information about the witnesses and expert witnesses and set forth the substance of their anticipated statements to the Court.[69] Evidence submitted by the Commission with its application may include reports, photographs, sketches, documents, copies of witness statements, and video recordings of interviews.

The respondent's answer must also include the evidentiary information which will be part of the respondent's case, including a statement of the facts, supporting evidence, a list of witnesses and the substance of the witnesses' statements.[70] Moreover, the respondent, in its answer, must also stipulate to those facts and claims set forth in the application that it accepts as true.[71] If the respondent does not file an answer to the

61 *Cantoral Benavides* v. *Peru* (Merits, 2000), para. 52.

62 *Loayza Tamayo* v. *Peru* (Reparations, 1998), para. 57.

63 *Mayagna (SUMO) Awas Tingni Community* v. *Nicaragua* (Merits), Inter-Am. Ct HR, 31 August 2001, Ser. C, No. 79, para. 88.

64 *Paniagua Morales et al.* v. *Guatemala* (Reparations), Inter-Am. Ct HR, 25 May 2001, Ser. C, No. 76, para. 51.

65 *Ibid.*; *Ivcher Bronstein* v. *Peru* (Merits), Inter-Am. Ct HR, 6 February 2001, Ser. C. No. 74, paras. 65–6; *Castillo Páez* v. *Peru* (Reparations), para. 40.

66 2001 Rules of Procedure of the Inter-Am. Ct HR, Art. 43(1) and (3).

67 *Ibid.*, Art. 43(1). The ICJ applies similar rules on the timing of the presentation of evidence. The Statute of the ICJ provides that '[a]fter the Court has received the proofs and evidence within the time specified for the purpose, it may refuse to accept any further oral or written evidence that one party may desire to present unless the other side consents'. Statute of the ICJ, Art. 52.

68 2001 Rules of Procedure of the Inter-Am. Ct HR, Art. 33(1).

69 *Ibid.*

70 *Ibid.*, Art. 37(1), stating that the answer must meet the content requirements for the application.

71 *Ibid.*, Art. 37(2).

application or does not address relevant facts, the Court 'presume[s] that the facts about which it remains silent are true, provided that consistent conclusions about them can be inferred from the evidence presented'.[72] The Court, however, will examine and evaluate all the evidence in the case, employing its sound judicial discretion to reach a decision on the truth of the allegations.[73] The respondent that files an answer may set forth additional evidence in a brief on preliminary objections, which must be filed with the answer.[74] The brief on preliminary objections must provide the facts underlying the objection and set forth evidence which the respondent intends to produce in support of the objection.[75]

The Court specifies that, in the interest of 'the principles of expeditiousness and diligence' that govern human rights proceedings, it is the procedural responsibility of the parties to set forth in their initial communications with the Court the evidence they intend to introduce 'indicating and identifying the witnesses and experts; the place and circumstances of any inspections; the purpose of the expert evidence and any other information necessary for the gathering of evidence'.[76] Under the 2001 Court Rules, in which the victim plays a more active role in the proceedings, the alleged victim, family, or duly accredited representatives may independently submit evidence to the Court.[77] This evidence must be submitted within thirty days of when the party is notified of the application.[78]

The Court interprets its rules on the admission of evidence in such a way that the parties may tender evidence 'in the original brief each party submits for each stage of the proceeding'.[79] Thus, at the reparations stage, the parties and the petitioner present briefs and specify any additional evidence they will present on reparations. For example, in the reparations decision in the *Blake Case*, when the family of the victim wished to introduce into evidence statements made at the oral hearing on the merits, the Court stated, '[t]he body of evidence of a case is unique and indivisible and is made up of the evidence submitted during all stages of the proceedings'.[80] The Court considers the entire body of evidence in a

72 *Constitutional Court Case (Aguirre Roca, Rey Terry, and Revoredo Marsano* v. *Peru)* (Merits, 2001), para. 48; *Bámaca Velásquez* (Merits, 2000), para. 100.

73 *Constitutional Court Case* (Merits, 2001), para. 49; *Bámaca Velásquez* (Merits, 2000), para. 100.

74 2001 Rules of Procedure of the Inter-Am. Ct HR, Art. 36(2).

75 *Ibid.*

76 Order of the Inter-Am. Ct HR, 2 February 1996, reprinted in the 1996 Annual Report of the Inter-Am. Ct HR, at 94.

77 2001 Rules of Procedure of the Inter-Am. Ct HR, Art. 35(4).

78 *Ibid.*

79 *Loayza Tamayo* v. *Peru* (Reparations, 1998), para. 15(b).

80 *Blake* v. *Guatemala* (Reparations), Inter-Am Ct HR, 22 January 1999, Ser. C, No. 48, para. 28.

case. Therefore, at any stage of the proceedings, the Court may choose to consider evidence elicited at a prior stage.

Exceptions to timely submission of evidence

The parties may present additional evidence at a later date if they allege and prove an authorized excuse. The Court's Rules provide that 'should any of the parties allege *force majeure*, serious impediment or the emergence of supervening events as grounds for producing an item of evidence, the Court may, in that particular instance, admit such evidence at a time other than those indicated above, provided that the opposing parties are guaranteed the right of defense'.[81] The Commission alleged supervening events when, during the public hearing in the *Constitutional Court Case*, it submitted documentation showing that, subsequent to its application, the Peruvian Congress had annulled the dismissals and reinstated the justices.[82] The Court incorporated the evidence into the file. In the *Bámaca Velásquez Case*, the Commission attempted to introduce at a late stage of the proceedings documents collected by the US Government concerning information about the victim.[83] The Court, after examining the documents, refused to take formal consideration of them, ruling that their submission was time-barred.[84] The Court held that the Commission had not satisfied the evidentiary requirement to justify an exception to the rule of timeliness.[85] In the *Paniagua Morales Case*, the Court refused to consider the extemporaneous presentation of evidence, reasoning that such evidence is admissible only in 'extremely aggravated circumstances which the State has in no way justified'.[86]

The Court's discretion to admit extemporaneous evidence

The Court may, in its discretion, admit extemporaneous evidence which does not result from an authorized excuse. The Court's Rules permit the Court to '[o]btain, on its own motion, any evidence it considers helpful'.[87]

[81] 2001 Rules of Procedure of the Inter-Am. Ct HR, Art. 43(3).

[82] *Constitutional Court Case (Aguirre Roca, Rey Terry, and Revoredo Marsano* v. *Peru)* (Merits, 2001), para. 51.

[83] *Bámaca Velásquez*, Order of the Inter-Am. Ct HR, 19 June 1998, reprinted in the 1998 Annual Report of the Inter-Am. Ct HR, OAS/Ser.L/V/III.43 doc. 11, 18 January 1999, at 245–7.

[84] *Ibid.* [85] *Ibid.*, Concurring Opinion of Judge Sergio García-Ramírez, para. 1.

[86] *Paniagua Morales et al.* v. *Guatemala (The White Van Case)* (Merits, 1998), para. 46.

[87] 2001 Rules of Procedure of the Inter-Am. Ct HR, Art. 44(1). This rule goes on to specify that: '[i]n particular, it may hear as a witness, expert witness, or in any other capacity, any person whose evidence, statement or opinion it deems to be relevant'. *Ibid.*

The Court exercised this option in the *Paniagua Morales Case* when the Commission objected to the State's offer to present the testimony of a Guatemalan judge whom the State alleged had been in ill health at the time of the public hearing. Guatemala had never named the judge as a witness, and therefore his illness was not considered *force majeure*.[88] The Court, however, chose, in accordance with its broad discretionary powers, to call for the testimony of the judge at a special public hearing.[89] The exception permits some latitude in receiving evidence while maintaining due regard for the preservation of 'the principle of legal certainty and the balanced procedural rights of the parties'.[90] Likewise, the ICJ has attempted to eliminate procedural delays by instituting Practice Directions, which require parties attempting to produce additional documents after the close of the Court's written proceedings to explain the need for the document and the reason for the delay. Then, if the opposing party does not consent to the introduction of the document, the ICJ will authorize the production only in 'exceptional circumstances if it considers it necessary and if the production of the document at this stage of the proceedings appears justified to the Court'.[91]

The Inter-American Court can request additional evidence at any stage of the proceedings. The Rules provide that at any stage of the proceedings the Court may '[r]equest any entity, office, organ or authority of its choice to obtain information, express an opinion, or deliver a report or pronouncement on any given point'.[92] For example, at the reparations stage of the *Loayza Tamayo Case*, the Court requested independent physical and psychiatric examinations of the victim and psychiatric examinations of her children.[93]

Oral proceedings

Oral proceedings are not mandated in the Inter-American system. The Court's Rules of Procedure provide that the President of the Court 'shall call such hearings as may be necessary'.[94] The Court's Rules seem

88 *Paniagua Morales et al.* v. *Guatemala* (Order of the President), Inter-Am. Ct HR, 16 October 1997, para. 2, reprinted in 1997 Annual Report of the Inter-Am. Ct HR, OAS/Ser.L/V/III.39 doc. 5, 21 January 1998, at 240.

89 *Ibid.*, paras. 3–7, at 240.

90 *Loayza Tamayo* v. *Peru* (Reparations, 1998), para. 38.

91 Practice Direction IX, http://www.icj-cij.org.

92 2001 Rules of Procedure of the Inter-Am. Ct HR, Art. 44(3).

93 *Loayza Tamayo* v. *Peru*, Order of the Inter-Am. Ct of 29 August 1998, reprinted in the 1998 Annual Report of the Inter-Am. Ct HR, OAS/Ser.L/V/III.43 doc. 11, 18 January 1999, at 331–3.

94 2001 Rules of Procedure of the Inter-Am. Ct HR, Art. 39. The President also announces the date for the opening of oral proceedings. *Ibid.*

to assume, without mandating it, that there will be a stage of oral proceedings.[95] To date, the Court generally has held more than one oral hearing in each case. Often there are oral hearings at the preliminary objections, merits and reparations stages of the proceedings. In principle, oral hearings should be necessary only when there is a question of fact that can be clarified by witnesses or experts. Questions of fact usually arise at the merits and reparations stages of the proceedings.

In general, proceedings before international tribunals include oral hearings. These hearings, however, historically did not necessarily involve the oral testimony of witnesses. Oral proceedings before the Permanent Court of International Justice generally consisted of oral arguments made by counsel, agents and advocates of the parties.[96] Testimonial evidence was generally submitted in written form.[97] Sandifer pointed out that, although testimonial evidence in the form of depositions was often considered in international judicial procedure, the direct testimony of witnesses was rarely taken. He attributed the 'sparing use of direct testimonial evidence' to 'practical considerations, rather than to any technical rules limiting the intrinsic merit or the admission of testimonial evidence per se'.[98] Conversely, the Statute of the International Court of Justice specifies that the procedure before the Court shall be both oral and written, and that the oral proceedings shall include a hearing before the Court with 'witnesses, experts, agents, counsel, and advocates'.[99] Rosenne explained that the mandatory character of the Statute 'has been emphasized by the Court which has insisted that even with the consent of the parties the Court is not authorized to waive the oral proceedings in the merits phase of the case'.[100] The Rules of the European Court of Human Rights allow the Court to dispense with oral hearings in exceptional cases.[101]

The Inter-American Court determines the working language for each case at the beginning of the proceedings. Generally, the working languages of the Court are English or Spanish. In a specific case, however, the Court may adopt the language of one of the parties as the Court's working

95 *Ibid.*, Art. 38.

96 Manley O. Hudson, *The Permanent Court of International Justice, 1920–1942*, at 563 (Macmillan, New York, 1943).

97 Sandifer, *Evidence Before International Tribunals*, at 289.

98 *Ibid.* 99 Statute of the ICJ, Art. 43(1) and (5).

100 Shabtai Rosenne, *The Law and Practice of the International Court, 1920–1996*, at 1318–19 and 1324 (3rd edn, Nijhoff, 1997).

101 European Court of Human Rights, Rules of Court, Rule 59(2); see *Obasa* v. *United Kingdom*, ECHR (Ser. A), para. 7 (16 January 2003).

language, provided that it is an OAS official language – Spanish, English, Portuguese or French.[102]

Public hearings barring exceptional circumstances

Hearings before the Inter-American Court are public unless the Court determines that exceptional circumstances warrant a private hearing.[103] Public hearings generate international publicity, and are therefore more likely to put pressure on offending States and their supporters. Governments that engage in a policy of disappearances, extra-judicial executions and torture are often surrounded by an atmosphere of conspiracy and intimidation. When victims and witnesses not only speak out publicly, but do so in an international court, the acts of States and their agents are no longer shrouded in secrecy. Thus, the public airing of the facts underlying human rights violations may have a deterrent effect on agents of the State in question. Moreover, more powerful States that have been backing the objectionable regimes or international companies with enterprises in the offending State, that may be willing to look the other way when the human rights violations are not a subject of world press, may exert pressure for reform when the violations are publicized. Farer argues that the 'shaming effect' of international publicity is actually aimed at the liberal democratic States that are funding and supporting the States that violate human rights.[104] Presently, there is no live television coverage of the trials. News photographers are given a few minutes before the beginning of a public hearing to take pictures of the judges. Additional media coverage might in fact do much to put pressure on States to comply with the Convention. Conversely, the negative implication of news coverage is that it could result in additional danger to witnesses who reside in the State concerned in the case.

Not all human rights bodies hold oral hearings. The United Nations Human Rights Committee decides cases based solely on the written testimony of the parties.[105] Hearings before an international body are

[102] 2001 Rules of Procedure of the Inter-Am. Ct HR, Art. 20(1) and (2).

[103] Statute of the Inter-American Court of Human Rights, adopted by the General Assembly of the OAS at its ninth regular session, held in La Paz, Bolivia, October 1979 (Resolution No. 448), Art. 24(1); see also 2001 Rules of Procedure of the Inter-Am. Ct HR, Art. 14(1).

[104] Tom J. Farer, 'The Rise of the Inter-American Human Rights Regime: No Longer a Unicorn, Not Yet an Ox', in *The Inter-American System of Human Rights*, 26, at 37 (Harris and Livingstone eds., 1998).

[105] Rules of Procedure of the UN Human Rights Committee, Rule 94(1).

time-consuming and expensive. Also, witnesses must travel great distances and often at prohibitive expense to testify.

The Inter-American Court has held a private hearing on only one occasion, in the *Honduran Disappearance Cases* at the request of the Government of Honduras.[106] As the subject of the closed hearing was the organizational structure of a top secret division of the Honduran military, the government requested the private hearing for reasons of State security.[107] Although the hearing was not public, it was otherwise conducted like other Court hearings in that the Commission's delegates had the opportunity to cross-examine the witnesses.[108] The Court heard the testimony of three officers then on active duty in the Honduran military. The Court's decision in the case stated that the Court 'received the testimony of persons *who identified themselves as* Lt Col. Alexander Hernandez and Lt Marco Tulio Regalado Hernandez'.[109] In reality, the Court could not determine if the witnesses were who they claimed to be, because no member of the Court or Commission could identify them by sight.[110] In future private hearings, the Court is likely to require that both parties stipulate to the identity of the witnesses.

Location of hearings

The Court's Rules of Procedure also provide that hearings will take place at the seat of the Court in San José, Costa Rica, unless there are exceptional circumstances.[111] In exceptional circumstances, however, the hearings may be held in another location.[112] For example, a special public hearing on the merits of the *Bámaca Velásquez Case* was held in Washington DC before a delegation of three judges of the Court to hear the oral testimony of a witness who, for immigration reasons, had been unable to attend the public hearing held earlier at the seat of the Court.[113] In the *Honduran Disappearance Cases*, the Court held a private hearing to

[106] *Velásquez Rodríguez* v. *Honduras* (Merits, 1988), para. 31; *Godínez Cruz* (Merits, 1989), para. 33; *Fairén Garbi and Solís Corrales* (Merits), para. 32.

[107] *Velásquez Rodríguez* v. *Honduras* (Merits, 1988), para. 31; *Godínez Cruz* (Merits, 1989), para. 33; *Fairén Garbi and Solís Corrales* (Merits), para. 32.

[108] Juan Méndez and José Vivanco, 'Disappearances and the Inter-American Court: Reflections on a Litigation Experience', 13 *Hamline Law Review* 507, 560 (1990).

[109] *Velásquez Rodríguez* v. *Honduras* (Merits, 1988), para. 34 (emphasis added). See also *Fairén Garbi and Solís Corrales* (Merits, 1989), para. 36.

[110] Méndez and Vivanco, 'Disappearances and the Inter-American Court', at 560.

[111] 2001 Rules of Procedure of the Inter-Am. Ct HR, Art. 14(1). [112] *Ibid.*

[113] 1998 Annual Report of the Inter-Am. Ct HR, OAS/Ser.L/V/III.43 doc. 11, 18 January 1999, at 23–4.

interview Honduran military officers at a police facility at the airport in San José, Costa Rica.[114]

Structure of hearings

Hearings are held before the plenary Court. The President of the Court directs the hearings by establishing the order of testimony and by instituting any measures necessary for the smooth administration of the hearing.[115] The State's designated Agent generally represents the State before the Court.[116] The Agent may be assisted by a Deputy Agent and by any additional persons that he or she chooses.[117] The Inter-American Commission also 'appear[s] in all cases before the Court', pursuant to the mandate of the American Convention.[118] The Statute of the Court goes further in providing that the Commission shall be a party in all contentious cases considered by the Court.[119] The 2001 Court Rules specify that the Commission is now only a procedural party to the case.[120] It is unclear at present what role the Commission will play. Initially, the role of the Commission was to represent the victim in contentious cases.

The 2001 Court Rules allow the individual victim to represent him- or herself before the Court at all stages of the proceedings.[121] The Rules provide that '[w]hen the application has been admitted, the alleged victims, their next of kin or their duly accredited representatives may submit their requests, arguments and evidence, autonomously, throughout the proceeding'.[122] A representative of the victim is duly accredited when the victim or the victim's next of kin has thereby certified that fact to the Court. When there is more than one alleged victim, they must 'designate a common intervenor'.[123] Only the common intervenor shall have the authority to represent the victim at the public hearing and to present evidence, arguments and requests.[124]

The questioning of the witnesses is subject to the control of the Court's President.[125] The State's Agent, Commission's delegates, assistants to the Commission's delegates and representative of the victims question the

[114] Méndez and Vivanco, 'Disappearances and the Inter-American Court', at 560. The Commission objected to the government's request to hold private hearings. *Velásquez Rodríguez v. Honduras* (Merits, 1988), para. 32; *Godínez Cruz* (Merits, 1989), para. 34; *Fairén Garbi and Solís Corrales* (Merits, 1989), para. 33.

[115] 2001 Rules of Procedure of the Inter-Am. Ct HR, Art. 40. [116] *Ibid.*, Art. 21(1).

[117] *Ibid.*, Art. 21(3) and (1). [118] American Convention, Art. 57.

[119] Statute of the Inter-Am. Ct HR, Art. 28.

[120] 2001 Rules of Procedure of the Inter-Am. Ct HR, Art. 2(23).

[121] *Ibid.*, Art. 23(1). [122] *Ibid.*

[123] *Ibid.*, Art. 23(2). [124] *Ibid.* [125] *Ibid.*, Art. 41(2).

witnesses.[126] The President rules on the relevance of questions and may excuse a witness from replying unless the Court decides to hear the reply.[127] The judges may also cross-examine witnesses and ask them 'any questions they deem proper' from the bench.[128] The Rules of the Court prohibit a party from asking the witness leading questions.[129] The Court may permit any witness to testify in his or her own language, if the witness cannot communicate adequately in the Court's working languages.[130] In such a case, an interpreter shall be present to translate the testimony.[131] Oral proceedings before the Court are simultaneously translated into Spanish and English. Speakers provide the translators with written texts when possible. Of course, there can be no written text for the examination of witnesses.

Testimonial evidence

Testimonial evidence is the transmission of information by a person who acquired it directly through the use of his or her senses.[132] The identity of a witness who is to testify must first be established to the satisfaction of the Court.[133] Every witness is then required to recite an oath or solemn declaration before testifying.[134] The oath or solemn declaration made by the witness states that the witness 'will speak the truth, the whole truth and nothing but the truth'.[135] It must be made before the Court, the President of the Court, or any of the judges whom the Court has delegated to hear the oath or declaration.[136] The Court will admit testimonial and expert evidence that goes to the purpose of the testimony that was stated by the party proposing the witness.

[126] *Ibid.* In the trial of Jean-Paul Akayesu before the ICTR, the accused himself was also permitted to cross-examine the Prosecution witnesses. *Prosecutor* v. *Jean-Paul Akayesu*, ICTR-96-4-T, UN General Assembly Security Council, A/52/582, S/1997/868, at 9, para. 16. There does not, however, appear to be an express statutory provision permitting such a practice in the ICTR Rules of Procedure and Evidence.

[127] 2001 Rules of Procedure of the Inter-Am. Ct HR, Art. 41(3).

[128] *Ibid.*, Art. 41(1). The ICTR's Rules of Procedure and Evidence contain a similar provision permitting judges to question witnesses at any point in the proceedings. ICTR Rules of Procedure and Evidence, Rule 85(B).

[129] 2001 Rules of Procedure of the Inter-Am. Ct HR, Art. 41(3).

[130] *Ibid.*, Art. 20(4). [131] *Ibid.*

[132] Separate Concurring Opinion of Judge Sergio García Ramírez, para. 2 in *Bámaca Velásquez*, Order of the Inter-Am. Ct HR, 19 June 1998, reprinted in 1998 Annual Report of the Inter-Am. Court HR, at 251.

[133] 2001 Rules of Procedure of the Inter-Am. Ct HR, Art. 47(1).

[134] *Ibid.* [135] *Ibid.* [136] *Ibid.*, Art. 47(3).

At the merits stage of the proceedings, a strong argument can be made that the Court should hear the testimony of the victims or their family members if they request to be heard. Even if the Court incorporates into its file the evidence tendered in adversarial proceedings before the Commission, victims and their families may need an opportunity to tell their stories in public in the Court proceeding. This in itself may be considered to be a remedy for human rights violations.[137]

Prior to the introduction of the Court's 2001 Rules of Procedure, which provide for the incorporation into the Court's file of evidence received by the Commission in the presence of both parties,[138] the Court refused to admit videotape of the testimony of a witness before the Commission. In future cases, provided that the testimony was taken before the adverse party, it should be admissible.

The Court should treat as evidence only statements of facts as to matters over which the witness has direct knowledge. The Inter-American Court has permitted witnesses to testify as to hearsay. In the *Blake Case*, a Guatemalan school teacher testified as to what local villagers had told him about how Blake had been murdered and by whom.[139] This type of testimony cannot serve as proof, although, in conjunction with other information, it could assist the Court in establishing the facts of the case.[140] In this regard, the Court must not give evidentiary weight to the suppositions or opinions of witnesses. Such evidence is subjective and does not allow for effective cross-examination.

In the interest of procedural speed and economy, the Court has requested, at least at the reparations stage of the proceedings, that sworn affidavits be submitted whenever possible in place of live testimonial and expert evidence.[141] The Court justified its request for the submission of sworn affidavits on the basis that it would expedite the oral proceedings while still protecting the rights of the victim, the Commission and the State to offer any oral testimony that should be heard by the Court.[142] Another advantage of allowing the victims and their family to participate in this manner is the savings on the cost of bringing additional witnesses to the Court. The party that requests the production of evidence must

[137] See Jo M. Pasqualucci, 'The Whole Truth and Nothing But the Truth: Truth Commissions, Impunity and the Inter-American Human Rights System', 12 *Boston University International Law Journal*, 321, 332–3 (1994).

[138] 2001 Rules of Procedure of the Inter-Am. Ct HR, Art. 43(2).

[139] *Blake* v. *Guatemala* (Merits), Inter-Am. Ct HR, 24 January 1998, Ser. C, No. 36, para. 31.

[140] See *Military and Paramilitary Activities In and Against Nicaragua (Nicaragua* v. *US)*, Merits, 1986 ICJ Reports 40 (27 June), para. 68.

[141] *Loayza Tamayo* (Reparations, 1998), para. 13. [142] *Ibid.*

defray its costs.[143] In the interest of procedural equality, the opposing party is then given the opportunity to refute or comment on the contents of the affidavits.[144] If the testimony in the affidavit is controversial, however, the Court should insist on the presence of the witness, as the State must be allowed to cross-examine the witness.

Objections to testimonial evidence

Any party may object to a witness before the witness testifies.[145] States have objected to the testimony of witnesses for reasons that would bar the testimony in their domestic courts. For example, in the *Loayza Tamayo Case*, Peru objected to the testimony of several witnesses, because they had been convicted of crimes.[146] In each case, the Inter-American Court overruled the objections. The Court quoted its ruling in the *Honduran Disappearance Cases*, in which it stated that 'under the American Convention on Human Rights, it is contradictory to deny a witness *a priori* – on the ground that he has been prosecuted or even convicted in the domestic courts – the opportunity to testify on facts in a case submitted to the Court, even if that case refers to matters that affect him'.[147]

States have also repeatedly objected to the testimony of 'interested persons'.[148] Interested persons often include the victim, and persons who have a direct relationship with the victim, such as family members. The Court will hear their testimony. The Court clarified that it is the well-established case law of the Court that a person's interest in the outcome of a case is not sufficient, *per se*, to disqualify him or her as a witness.[149] In human rights cases, often the only witnesses who are willing to put themselves at risk to testify are those who have a personal interest in the case. The Court particularly stated that the testimony of the victim has a 'unique import', as the victim may be the only person who can provide necessary information.[150] Such testimony is particularly useful in the reparations stage to provide information on the consequences of the

[143] 2001 Rules of Procedure of the Inter-Am. Ct HR, Art. 45.
[144] *Castillo Páez* v. *Peru* (Reparations, 1998), para. 41.
[145] 2001 Rules of Procedure of the Inter-Am. Ct HR, Art. 48(1).
[146] *Loayza Tamayo* v. *Peru* (Merits, 1997), para. 13.
[147] *Velásquez Rodríguez* v. *Honduras* (Merits, 1988), para. 145, quoted in *Loayza Tamayo* v. *Peru* (Merits, 1997), para. 42.
[148] *Castillo Páez* v. *Peru* (Reparations, 1998), para. 40.
[149] *Suárez Rosero* v. *Ecuador* (Merits), Inter-Am. Ct HR, 12 November 1997, Ser. C, No. 35, para. 32.
[150] *Loayza Tamayo* v. *Peru* (Reparations, 1998), para. 73.

violations.[151] In the *Loayza Tamayo Case*, the Court stated that '[b]ecause Ms. Loayza Tamayo is the victim in the instant case and has an immediate interest in it, her testimony cannot be weighed separately; instead, it must be weighed with the full body of evidence in this case'.[152] The Court admits the testimony when it is consistent with a relevant line of questioning.[153] The Court generally adds the testimony of interested parties to the body of evidence in the case and weighs it in conjunction with the other evidence.[154]

The Court will also evaluate the testimony of witnesses who were not present at the actual events to provide it with information on the general context of the case.[155] The Court has broad discretion to hear the testimony of any person for informational purposes, when the Court considers it necessary.[156] This is true even when a person does not qualify as a witness.[157] The Court has stated that:

> the criteria for evaluating evidence in an international human rights tribunal are endowed with special characteristics. This Court is not a criminal court; the grounds for objecting to witnesses do not operate in the same way, so that the investigation into a State's international liability for human rights violations bestows on the Court greater latitude to use logic and experience in its evaluation of oral testimony.[158]

In determining whether to hear a witness, the Court will weigh the value of the proposed testimony against the objections of the party.[159]

It is important that the Court consider all relevant evidence in its effort to ascertain the truth of the allegations. Judges, in contrast to juries, are not likely to be swayed by emotional or inflammatory testimony. Moreover, judges have more experience in evaluating the demeanour of witnesses and in balancing the witnesses' personal interest in the outcome with the value of their testimony.

[151] *Paniagua Morales et al.* v. *Guatemala* (Reparations, 2001), para. 70.
[152] *Loayza Tamayo* v. *Peru* (Reparations, 1998), para. 72.
[153] *Paniagua Morales et al.* v. *Guatemala* (Reparations, 2001), para. 70.
[154] *Ibid.*; *Suárez Rosero* v. *Ecuador* (Merits, 1997), para. 33.
[155] *Villagrán Morales et al.* v. *Guatemala (The Street Children Case)* (Merits), Inter-Am. Ct HR, 19 November 1999, Ser. C, No. 63, para. 73.
[156] 2001 Rules of Procedure of the Inter-Am. Ct HR, Art. 48(2).
[157] *Ibid.*
[158] *Loayza Tamayo* v. *Peru* (Merits, 1997), para. 42; *Blake* v. *Guatemala* (Merits, 1998), para. 50.
[159] 2001 Rules of Procedure of the Inter-Am. Ct HR, Art. 48(3).

Expert witnesses

An expert witness is 'a witness qualified by knowledge, skill, expertise, training, or education to provide a scientific, technical, or other specialized opinion about the evidence or a fact issue'.[160] The Court will admit testimony from a qualified expert when it is consistent with the purpose for which it is proposed.[161] Experts may testify regarding a wide range of topics. They are often called to testify as to the domestic law in the respondent State. For example, in *'The Last Temptation of Christ' Case*, experts testified on censorship laws in Chile.[162] In the *Hilaire, Constantine and Benjamin et al. Cases*, experts testified as to the prison conditions in Trinidad and Tobago.[163] In the *Mayagna Awas Tingni Community* v. *Nicaragua Case*, experts testified as to the life style of the indigenous petitioners.[164] The Inter-American Court requires that expert reports must be 'prepared by professionals who are competent in their field and include, in proper form, the information that the Court requires'.[165] The Court does not require that the experts' reports conform to international guidelines as a prerequisite to their admissibility.[166] If there is no objection and the expert testimony is not contested nor its authenticity questioned, the Court will consider the testimony to be valid.[167]

Any party can name expert witnesses. A party that proposes an expert witness must provide the identity of the expert and the subject of the expert's statement in the application or in the answer.[168] The Court will summon the witness.[169] The summons states the name of the expert and the object of the expert's opinion or the facts on which the examination of the expert will bear.[170]

The Court also may appoint expert witnesses. The Rules of the Inter-American Court authorize it to call for any evidence that it considers will

160 *Black's Law Dictionary*, citing the US Fed. R. Evid. 702–6.

161 *Paniagua Morales* v. *Guatemala* (Reparations, 2001), para. 71.

162 *'The Last Temptation of Christ' (Olmedo Bustos et al.* v. *Chile)* (Merits), Inter-Am. Ct HR, 5 February 2001, Ser. C, No. 73, para. 45(c)–(g).

163 *Hilaire, Constantine and Benjamin et al.* v. *Trinidad and Tobago* (Merits, 2002), para. 76(b) and (c).

164 *Mayagna (SUMO) Awas Tingni Community* v. *Nicaragua* (Merits, 2001), para. 83(d), (e) and (f).

165 *Loayza Tamayo* v. *Peru* (Reparations, 1998), para. 81. See generally Auxiliadora Solano Monge, 'La Prueba Pericial Ante La Corte Interamericana De Derechos Humanos', in *Liber Amicorum Héctor Fix-Zamudio*, Vol II, 1451 (1998).

166 *Loayza Tamayo* v. *Peru* (Reparations, 1998), para. 81.

167 *Bámaca Velásquez* (Merits, 2000), para. 113.

168 2001 Rules of Procedure of the Inter-Am. Ct HR, Arts. 33 and 37.

169 *Ibid.*, Art. 46(1).

170 *Ibid.*, Art. 46(2).

be of use.[171] 'In particular, it may hear as a witness, expert witness, or in any other capacity, any person whose evidence, statement or opinion it deems to be relevant.'[172] International tribunals are 'intolerant of any restrictive rules of evidence that might tend to confine the scope of a search after those facts. With certain exceptions, they do not hesitate to supplement, upon their own initiative, the evidence supplied by the parties if they regard it as inadequate.'[173] The Court appointed a handwriting expert in the *Fairén Garbi and Solís Corrales Case* to testify as to whether the victim's signature on a tourist visa was genuine.[174] In the *Palmeras Case*, in which the manner of death of two alleged victims was at issue, the Court appointed as experts two members of the Argentine Forensic Anthropology Team to exhume and examine the bodies.[175] The Court has also appointed experts at the reparations stage of proceedings to evaluate the injured party. In the *Loayza Tamayo Case*, the Court requested independent medical and psychiatric evaluations of the victim and her children.[176] The expert's psychiatric diagnosis of the victim provided that she suffered from 'post-traumatic stress syndrome as a consequence of systematic torture and rape'.[177]

An expert may be designated by the Court to visit a place and interview witnesses, when the trip itself would be difficult or expensive for the entire Court. In the *Loayza Tamayo Case*, the Commission named several witnesses who were imprisoned in Peru.[178] These witnesses could not appear at the seat of the Court, so the Commission requested that the Court proceedings be held at various Peruvian penitentiaries.[179] Instead, after informing the State, the Court appointed an expert to interrogate the witnesses where they were incarcerated.[180] Thus the Court was saved the time and expense of travelling to various locations in the State.

A party may object to the qualifications of a proposed expert witness. The objection must be made within fifteen days of when the party is notified of the expert witness' appointment.[181] In addition to the allegation that the proposed expert does not have the professional or experiential qualifications to give an expert opinion on a given subject, a proposed expert may be disqualified for personal reasons. For instance, a person

[171] *Ibid.*, Art. 44(1). [172] *Ibid.*

[173] Sandifer, *Evidence Before International Tribunals*, at 3–4.

[174] *Fairén Garbi and Solís Corrales* v. *Honduras* (Merits, 1987), para. 117.

[175] *Las Palmeras* v. *Colombia*, Inter-Am. Ct HR, Order of 30 May 2001, 'Considering' section, para. 3.

[176] *Loayza Tamayo* v. *Peru* (Reparations, 1998), para. 74.

[177] *Ibid.*, para. 76. [178] *Loayza Tamayo* v. *Peru* (Merits, 1997), para. 13.

[179] *Ibid.* [180] *Ibid.*, para. 15.

[181] 2001 Rules of the Procedure of the Inter-Am. Ct HR, Art. 49(2).

may not serve as an expert witness on a matter in which that person or his or her family members have a 'direct interest'.[182] Also, a person may not serve as an expert witness in a case in which he or she has been involved as an agent, advocate, counsel, member of a court or investigatory committee, or in any capacity whatsoever.[183] The Court shall rule on the grounds put forth for contesting the expert, if the expert challenges the objection.[184] If the Court is not in session when the objection is made to the proposed expert testimony, the President with the advice of the Permanent Commission of the Court shall make the decision as to whether the expert shall be heard.[185]

Documentary evidence

Documentary evidence consists of evidence in the form of a written or other document. Examples of documentary evidence submitted to the Inter-American Court include the victim's birth certificates, school and job credentials, tax records, certificate of nationality, medical records, State laws and resolutions, domestic court judgments, governmental reports and property deeds. Documents must normally be authenticated before they can be admitted as evidence. Authentication proves that the document is true or genuine. In domestic proceedings, certain types of evidence are considered to be self-authenticating. For instance, certified copies of public records and notarized documents may be admitted into evidence without extrinsic evidence of the document's genuineness or truth.

Although the Inter-American Court has not set forth in detail its requirements for documentary authentication, it has made clear that, at a minimum, it must be possible to establish precisely the source of the document and the procedure by which it was obtained.[186] The Court found domestic court decisions to be authentic when they held no inconsistencies and originated from 'reliable sources'.[187] Only complete, original and legible documents should be admitted as authentic to avoid the possible

[182] See *Ibid.*, Art. 49(1) (providing that the grounds that apply under the Statute of the Court to disqualify judges also apply to expert witnesses); Statute of the Inter-Am. Ct HR, Art. 19(1).

[183] See 2001 Rules of Procedure of the Inter-Am. Ct HR, Art. 49(1); and Statute of the Inter-Am. Court HR, Art. 19(1).

[184] 2001 Rules of Procedure of the Inter-Am. Ct HR, Art. 49(3).

[185] *Ibid.* [186] *Bámaca Velásquez* (Merits, 2000), para. 105.

[187] *Hilaire, Constantine and Benjamin et al.* v. *Trinidad and Tobago* (Merits, 2002), para. 79(a).

adulteration of photocopies, unless the copy has been certified by reliable authorities. It should not, however, be necessary for the official who certified the document to be present in Court. Nor should the chain of custody of evidence be proved though the live testimony of the people who handled it. These procedures, which often require the presence of bureaucrats who have no actual memory of the certification, would be much too expensive to be feasible in an international court to which witnesses must travel.

The opposing party can object to the inclusion in the file of documentary evidence that is not authenticated. In the *Bámaca Velásquez Case*, Guatemala objected to the inclusion of documents attributed to the US Central Intelligence Agency, arguing that they were not signed, were from another State, and were produced unilaterally by the Commission.[188] The documents in question contained deletions, which blocked out parts of the information and the names of those who wrote them.[189] The documents also included statements from unknown witnesses. As such, the government could not cross-examine the persons who wrote the documents and the judges could not question them to make a critical assessment of the veracity of the information contained therein. The Court refused to admit them, confirming that the documents in question did not meet the 'minimum formal requirements for admissibility'.[190]

Copies of documents submitted by a party are forwarded to the other party for their approval before they are included in the case file.[191] If the documents presented are not challenged, or their authenticity questioned, the Court accepts them as valid and orders their incorporation into the body of evidence in the case.[192] For example, the government did not object in the *Bámaca Velásquez Case* to the incorporation of the Report of the Inter-Diocesan Recovery of the Historical Memory Project prepared by the Archbishop of Guatemala's Human Rights Office, which documented human rights abuse in Guatemala.[193]

Documents may be requested independently by the Court. The Court's Rules provide that the Court may '[r]equest any entity, office, organ or authority of its choice to obtain information, express an opinion, or deliver

[188] *Bámaca Velásquez* (Merits, 2000), para. 104.

[189] *Bámaca Velásquez* (Merits, 2000), Separate Concurring Opinion of Judge Sergio García Ramírez, para. 27.

[190] *Ibid.* [191] *Bámaca Velásquez* (Merits, 2000), para. 58.

[192] *Paniagua Morales et al.* v. *Guatemala* (Reparations, 2001), para. 69; *Blake* v. *Guatemala* (Reparations, 1999), para. 27; *Loayza Tamayo* v. *Peru* (Reparations, 1998), para. 53; *Ivcher Bronstein* v. *Peru* (Merits, 2001), para. 70.

[193] *Bámaca Velásquez* (Merits, 2000), para. 31.

a report or pronouncement on any given point'.[194] The documents produced through Court requests may only be published with the Court's authorization.[195] Furthermore, when cases are sufficiently similar, the Court may, on its own motion or at the request of a party, incorporate documents into the file that had been submitted to the Court in a previous case.[196] This practice serves the interest of judicial economy as it avoids the expense of producing and copying identical documents, and minimizes the need for Court storage space.

Official records of national or international organizations may provide documentary evidence. Statements made by State officials reported in records which acknowledge facts in dispute or are unfavourable to the party making the statement may qualify as admissions against interest. For example, police records that a person, who then disappeared, was taken into custody would serve as an admission. The Court has considered the written declarations of witnesses sworn before a notary to qualify as documentary evidence, even though they did not meet the criteria of testimonial evidence.[197]

The Inter-American Court holds that newspaper clippings are not documentary evidence *per se*.[198] Newspaper articles may be important, however, if they corroborate other evidence or confirm the public nature and general knowledge of pertinent facts.[199] In such cases, the Court will add the articles to the body of evidence to aid in verifying the facts of the case.[200] The Inter-American Court specified in the *Honduran Disappearance Cases* that some newspaper articles have evidentiary value when they reproduce the text of public statements made by high-ranking public officials or when they corroborate testimony.[201] Likewise, the ICJ held in *Military and Paramilitary Activities In and Against Nicaragua* that press reports and excerpts from books do not qualify as 'evidence capable of proving facts'.[202] The ICJ reasoned, however, that this type of material could serve to corroborate a fact when introduced with other evidence.[203]

[194] 2001 Rules of Procedure of the Inter-Am. Ct HR, Art. 44(3). [195] *Ibid.*

[196] *Cantoral Benavides* v. *Peru* (Merits, 2000), paras. 16 and 32.

[197] *Bámaca Velásquez* (Merits, 2000), para. 108.

[198] *Velásquez Rodríguez* v. *Honduras* (Merits, 1998), para. 146; *Ivcher Bronstein* v. *Peru* (Merits, 2001), para. 70.

[199] *Ivcher Bronstein* v. *Peru* (Merits, 2001), para. 70; *Mayagna (SUMO) Awas Tingni Community* v. *Nicaragua* (Merits, 2001), para. 94.

[200] *Ibid.* [201] *Velásquez Rodríguez* v. *Honduras* (Merits, 1998), para. 146.

[202] *Military and Paramilitary Activities In and Against Nicaragua (Nicaragua* v. *US)*, Merits, 1986 ICJ Reports 40 (27 June), paras. 62–4.

[203] *Ibid.*

The number of documents submitted for the Court's consideration is increasing dramatically in some of the more complex cases. In the *Ivcher Bronstein Case*, in which the majority shareholder of a Peruvian television station was stripped of his nationality because the station reported on political malfeasance and scandals, the Commission submitted 433 documents, eight videos and several newspaper articles.[204] In the *Baena Ricardo et al Case (270 Workers* v. *Panama)*, the State attached 272 documents to its answer and the Commission submitted 195.[205] In the *Constitutional Court Case*, the Commission initially submitted 190 documents and then added a further eighty-one documents.[206] Although the information may be useful in deciding a case, it may soon overwhelm the human resources of the Court, which sits on a part-time basis and has a limited number of staff attorneys. Other international courts have a similar problem. The ICJ recently issued a practice instruction noting the proliferation of annexes to the pleadings and strongly urging the parties to strictly select the documents to be submitted to the Court.[207]

Demonstrative evidence

The parties may tender demonstrative evidence, for the purpose of making other evidence more understandable to the judges. Demonstrative evidence may include maps, models, drawings, charts and other tangible items.[208] These items may be crucial in assisting a witness to explain testimony to the Court. The admission or exclusion of demonstrative evidence lies within the Court's discretion. At the reparations stage in the *Loayza Tamayo Case*, the victim presented a chart of expenses incurred.[209] The Court held that the chart illustrated the victim's claims and supplemented the brief, but that it did not constitute evidence.[210] Therefore, the Court did not include the chart in the body of evidence in the case.[211]

[204] *Ivcher Bronstein* v. *Peru* (Merits, 2001), para. 58.

[205] *Baena Ricardo et al. (270 Workers* v. *Panama)* (Merits), Inter-Am. Ct HR, 2 February 2001, Ser. C, No. 72, paras. 57–9.

[206] *Constitutional Court Case (Aguirre Roca, Rey Terry, and Revoredo Marsano* v. *Peru)* (Merits), Inter-Am. Ct HR, 24 September 1999, Ser. C, No. 55, paras. 37 and 41.

[207] ICJ Practice Direction III.

[208] See Kenneth S. Broun, George E. Dix, Michael H. Graham, D. H. Kaye, Robert P. Mosteller and E. F. Roberts, *McCormick on Evidence*, 341 (John W. Strong *et al.* ed., 5th edn, West, St Paul, MN, 1992).

[209] *Loayza Tamayo* v. *Peru* (Reparations), para. 48. [210] *Ibid.*, para. 49. [211] *Ibid.*

Presumptions and circumstantial evidence

The practice of international and domestic courts shows that direct evidence, whether testimonial or documentary, can be supplemented by circumstantial evidence and presumptions. The Inter-American Court has consistently applied the principles of international law in considering and weighing all types of evidence. The Court stated in this regard that '[i]n the exercise of its judicial functions and when ascertaining and weighing the evidence necessary to decide the cases before it, the Court may, in certain circumstances, make use of both circumstantial evidence and indications or presumptions on which to base its pronouncements when they lead to consistent conclusions as regards the facts of the case'.[212]

Circumstantial evidence is indirect evidence that is not based on the personal knowledge or observations of a witness. The Court has held that circumstantial evidence 'is especially important in allegations of disappearances, because this type of repression is characterized by an attempt to suppress all information about the kidnapping or the whereabouts and fate of the victim'.[213] In this regard, the Court stated that it:

> deems it possible for the disappearance of a specific individual to be demonstrated by means of indirect and circumstantial testimonial evidence, when taken together with their logical inferences, and in the context of the widespread practice of disappearances. In a case such as this, the Court has always maintained that a judgment can be based on evidence other than direct documentary and testimonial evidence. Circumstantial evidence, indications, and presumptions may also be admitted when they lead to consistent conclusions with regard to the facts.[214]

For example, the Court has accorded the status of circumstantial evidence to police reports.[215] The police reports may contain ballistic reports, descriptions of the autopsy, statements, interrogations, descriptions of places, reports on the removal of the victim's corpse, and reports attributing responsibility.

[212] *Blake* v. *Guatemala* (Merits, 1998), para. 47, quoting *Gangaram Panday* v. *Suriname* (Merits, 1994), para. 49; *Villagrán Morales et al.* v. *Guatemala (The Street Children Case)* (Merits, 1999), para. 69, citing *Castillo Petruzzi et al.* v. *Peru* (Merits), Inter-Am. Ct HR, 30 May 1999, Ser. C, No. 52, para. 62.

[213] *Velásquez Rodríguez* v. *Honduras* (Merits, 1988), para. 131; *Godínez Cruz* (Merits, 1989), para. 137, quoted in *Blake* v. *Guatemala* (Merits, 1998), para. 49.

[214] *Blake* v. *Guatemala* (Merits, 1998), para. 49.

[215] *Villagrán Morales et al.* v. *Guatemala (The Street Children Case)* (Merits, 1999), paras. 70 and 71.

A presumption is '[a] legal inference or assumption that a fact exists, based on the known or proven existence of some other fact or group of facts'.[216] The Court generally presumes to be true facts stated in the application unless the State specifically contests those facts, provided that the evidence presented is consistent with those facts.[217] If the State fails to present evidence to refute the applicant's claims, the Court may 'presume that the facts set out in the application about which the State has kept silent are true, provided that conclusions consistent with such facts may be inferred from them'.[218] In such cases, the State deprives itself of an opportunity to present evidence and to challenge the evidence presented by the applicant. In both the *Ivcher Bronstein Case* and the *Constitutional Court Case*, the Court applied this presumption.[219]

The Court should also employ a presumption when the State or other parties do not comply with their obligation to provide any evidence requested by the Court or to supply any statement or explanation that the Court regards as useful to the resolution of the case.[220] It is often necessary for the State to furnish additional evidence as it is often the State that exercises sole control over necessary evidence, making it difficult for the alleged victim to clarify certain events without the State's cooperation.[221] Although States usually comply with Court requests, State compliance has not been consistent. For example, in the *Cantoral Benavides Case*, Peru failed to produce requested documents such as the records of the military trial of the petitioner, and a certified copy of a motion to review a Supreme Council of Military Justice judgment.[222] In the *Fairén Garbi and Solis Corrales Case*, the Court rebuked Honduras for its 'lack of diligence, sometimes approaching obstructionism, shown by the Government in not responding to repeated requests'.[223]

The Inter-American Court has employed several presumptions including the presumption that persons who disappeared in violent situations and who remain disappeared after many years are dead; that

[216] *Black's Law Dictionary.*

[217] *Villagrán Morales et al.* v. *Guatemala (The Street Children Case)* (Merits, 1999), para. 68.

[218] *Constitutional Court* v. *Peru* (Merits, 2001), para. 48; *Ivcher Bronstein* v. *Peru* (Merits, 2001), para. 68; see also *Gangaram Panday* v. *Suriname* (Merits, 1994), para. 51.

[219] *Constitutional Court* v. *Peru* (Merits, 2001), para. 48; *Ivcher Bronstein* v. *Peru* (Merits, 2001), para. 68.

[220] 2001 Rules of Procedure of the Inter-Am. Ct HR, Art. 44.

[221] *Cantoral Benavides* v. *Peru* (Merits, 2000), para. 55 (citing *Neira Alegría et al.* v. *Peru* (Merits), Inter-Am. Ct HR, 19 January 1995, Ser. C, No. 20, para. 65).

[222] *Cantoral Benavides* v. *Peru* (Merits, 2000), para. 56.

[223] *Fairén Garbi and Solís Corrales* (Merits, 1989), para. 160.

adults spend most of their income on family necessities; that relatives of a victim pay for the funeral; that all adults engage in productive activities and receive at least the minimum wage, even if the victim was unemployed at the time of the violation; and that the violation and the resulting impunity causes anguish, pain and sadness to the victims as well as their families.[224] In the *Street Children Case*, in which the Court found that the children had been abducted by members of the Guatemalan National Police Force, the Court adopted the presumption established by the European Court of Human Rights, that the State is responsible for the ill-treatment of persons in the custody of State agents, unless the authorities can demonstrate that the agents did not engage in such behaviour.[225] The Court, therefore, presumed that the torture that had been inflicted on the children between their seizure and their murders was carried out by State agents.[226] The Court also holds that there is a presumption in favour of a victim's testimony regarding the conditions of imprisonment, when the victim has been held incommunicado.[227] Moreover, the presumptive value of the victim's statements increases when the State is unable or unwilling to furnish information on the treatment accorded the prisoner during the incommunicado detention.[228] Also, when a State accepts international responsibility for a violation of the Convention, the Court will presume the truth of the facts relating to that violation.[229] In the *Blake Case*, Guatemala accepted responsibility for the delay in justice until 1995.[230] The Court, therefore, held that all the facts relating to that violation until that date were presumed to be true.[231]

Burden of proof

Generally, the Inter-American Court complies with basic principles of law which assign the burden of proof to the party making the allegations of a fact on which the claim is based.[232] There are instances, however, when the burden of proof is reversed, and assigned to the party who denies the fact if that party is in a better position to prove it. In human rights

[224] *Del Caracazo* v. *Venezuela* (Reparations), Inter-Am. Ct HR, 29 August 2002, Ser. C, No. 95, para. 50.

[225] *Villagrán Morales et al.* v. *Guatemala (The Street Children Case)* (Merits, 1999), paras. 169, 128 and 142 (citing *Aksoy* v. *Turkey*, 1996-VI, ECHR, para. 61 (1996)).

[226] *Ibid.*, para. 169.

[227] *Suárez Rosero* v. *Ecuador* (Merits, 1997), para. 33.

[228] *Ibid.*

[229] *Blake* v. *Guatemala* (Merits, 1998), para. 89.

[230] *Ibid.*

[231] *Ibid.*

[232] *Velásquez Rodríguez* v. *Honduras* (Merits, 1988), para. 123.

proceedings, the State's defence cannot rest on the applicant's inability to submit evidence, when that evidence cannot be produced without the State's cooperation.[233] For example, the victim's family can seldom provide direct evidence when the State perpetrators of disappearances attempt to avoid accountability by eliminating all evidence of the kidnapping or of the victim's fate.[234] The State is in control of the means to clarify the facts of the disappearance and as such may bear the burden of proof.[235] The Inter-American Court quoted with approval the United Nations Human Rights Committee, which held that:

> the burden of proof cannot fall solely on the author of the communication, considering, in particular, that the author and the State Party do not always have equal access to the evidence and that, frequently, it is only the State Party that has access to the pertinent information . . . In cases when the authors have presented charges supported by attesting evidence to the Committee . . . and in which subsequent clarification of the case depends on information that is exclusively in the hands of the State Party, the Committee may consider that those charges are justified unless the State Party presents satisfactory evidence and explanations to the contrary.[236]

In cases of forced disappearances for example, the State cannot rest its defence on the applicant's inability to present direct evidence, because the State controls the means of establishing the facts of the case.[237]

The Inter-American Court created a two-pronged test to determine the burden of proof in disappearance cases. Under the first prong, the applicant alleging the disappearance of a particular individual is required to show that the State engaged in an official practice of disappearances or at least tolerated such a practice.[238] Under the second prong, the applicant must establish a link between the particular disappearance and the State practice.[239] The Court explained that:

> [d]ue to the nature of the phenomenon and its probative difficulties, the Court has established that if it has been proved that the State promotes or tolerates the practice of forced disappearance of persons, and the case

[233] *Cantoral Benavides* v. *Peru* (Merits, 2000), para. 189; *Gangaram Panday* v. *Suriname* (Merits, 1994), para. 49; *Velásquez Rodríguez* v. *Honduras* (Merits, 1988), para. 135.

[234] *Velásquez Rodríguez* v. *Honduras* (Merits, 1988), para. 131.

[235] *Bámaca Velásquez* (Merits, 2000), para. 152.

[236] *Hiber Conteris* v. *Uruguay*, Communication No. 139/1983, paras. 182–6, quoted in *Bámaca Velásquez* (Merits, 2000), para. 153.

[237] *Bámaca Velásquez* (Merits, 2000), para. 152, citing *Neira Alegría et al.* v. *Peru* (Merits, 1995), para. 65.

[238] *Velásquez Rodríguez* v. *Honduras* (Merits, 1988), para. 125.

[239] *Ibid.*

> of a specific person can be linked to this practice, either by circumstantial or indirect evidence, or both, or by pertinent logical inference, then this specific disappearance may be considered to have been proven.[240]

In the *Velásquez Rodríguez Case*, the Commission established that a State practice of disappearances existed, by proving that between one hundred and one hundred and fifty persons were disappeared in Honduras from 1981 to 1984.[241] It further proved that '[i]t was public and notorious knowledge in Honduras that the kidnappings were carried out by military personnel or the police, or persons acting under their orders'.[242] The victims, many of whom had been under surveillance before their disappearances, were often labour leaders, student leaders or persons that the government deemed a threat to State security.[243] The kidnappers drove vehicles with tinted glass, which required official authorization, and carried arms reserved for use by the police and military.[244] At times, state security agents cleared the areas just prior to the kidnappings.[245] The Commission then established a link between the governmental policy and the disappearance of the particular victims. In *Velásquez Rodríguez*, the Commission demonstrated the requisite link by showing that the victim was a student leader who had been under governmental surveillance, and who was kidnapped in broad daylight under circumstances similar to those shown, under the first prong of the test, to be common in Honduras at that time.[246] When the applicant met its burden of proof, a rebuttable presumption was established that the government was responsible for the disappearance.[247] The burden then shifted to the government to refute the presumption.[248] The government could do so by showing that the alleged victim was not the type of person who was traditionally disappeared, or that there were other likely reasons for the disappearance. Honduras, however, did not present evidence to rebut the presumption in the *Velásquez Rodríguez Case*.

The Court also relied on the two-pronged test in the *Bámaca Velásquez Case* in which a guerrilla leader disappeared after being captured by the

240 *Bámaca Velásquez* (Merits, 2000), para. 130.

241 *Velásquez Rodríguez* v. *Honduras*, para. 147(a).

242 *Ibid.*, para. 147(b) and (c).

243 *Ibid.* (Merits, 1988), para. 147(i). See National Commission for the Protection of Human Rights, 'The Facts Speak for Themselves, Preliminary Report on the Disappeared in Honduras 1980–1993', at 385 (1994).

244 *Velásquez Rodríguez* v. *Honduras* (Merits, 1988), para. 147(ii).

245 *Ibid.*

246 *Ibid.*, para. 147.

247 Thomas Buergenthal, 'Judicial Fact-Finding', at 269. Buergenthal was President of the Inter-American Court during consideration of the Honduran cases.

248 *Ibid.*

military in Guatemala. In that case, the Commission proved that the Guatemalan army engaged in a practice of detaining captured guerrillas clandestinely without notifying the proper authorities, torturing the guerrillas to obtain information, and then executing them extrajudicially.[249] It also proved that the disappearance of Efraín Bámaca Velásquez was related to the State practice, and, thus, that his disappearance was attributable to the State.[250]

Standard of proof

No statutory authority in the Inter-American system establishes the standard of proof required in cases before the Court. International jurisprudence generally avoids rigid rules establishing the measure of proof required to support the judgment.[251] Rather, it 'has recognized the power of the courts to weigh the evidence freely'.[252] The Inter-American Court explained that the standard of proof is 'less formal in an international legal proceeding than in a domestic one'.[253] The Court maintains its authority to avoid 'making a rigid determination of the amount of evidence required to support a judgment' and 'to evaluate the evidence within the limits of sound judicial discretion'.[254] Thus, the Inter-American Court is flexible with respect to the standard of proof required depending on the violation to be proved.

Judicial notice

Judicial notice of a fact may substitute for formal proof, relieving a party of the duty to introduce evidence as to that fact.[255] 'Judicial notice allows a

249 *Bámaca Velásquez* (Merits, 2000), para. 132.
250 *Ibid.*, paras. 132–3.
251 *Velásquez Rodríguez* v. *Honduras* (Merits, 1988), para. 127 (citing *Corfu Channel Case* (*UK* v. *Albania*), 1949 ICJ Reports 4 (Merits Judgment of 9 April); *Military and Paramilitary Activities In and Against Nicaragua* (*Nicaragua* v. *US*), Merits, Judgment, 1986 ICJ Reports, paras. 29–30 and 59–60; *Godínez Cruz* (Merits), para. 133; *Fairén Garbi and Solís Corrales* (Merits, 1989), para. 130.
252 *Castillo Páez* v. *Peru* (Reparations, 1998), para. 38, citing the *Corfu Channel Case* (*UK* v. *Albania*), 1949 ICJ Reports 4 (Merits Judgment of 9 April); *Military and Paramilitary Activities In and Against Nicaragua* (*Nicaragua* v. *US*), Merits, Judgment, ICJ Reports 1986, paras. 29–30 and 59–60.
253 *Velásquez Rodríguez* v. *Honduras* (Merits, 1988), para. 128; *Godínez Cruz* (Merits, 1989), para. 134; *Fairén Garbi and Solís Corrales* (Merits, 1989), para. 131.
254 *Cesti Hurtado* v. *Peru* (Reparations), Inter-Am Ct HR, 31 May 2001, Ser. C, No. 78, para. 21.
255 Graham C. Lilly, *An Introduction to the Law of Evidence*, 13 (3rd edn, West, St Paul, MN, 1996).

court to accept as true, without formal evidentiary proof, non-contested facts.'[256] Sandifer noted that judicial notice derives from common law rather than from civil law.[257] Under the US Federal Rules of Evidence, '[a] judicially noticed fact must be one not subject to reasonable dispute in that it is either (1) generally known within the territorial jurisdiction of the trial court or (2) capable of accurate and ready determination by resort to sources whose accuracy cannot reasonably be questioned'.[258] The Rules of Procedure for the International Criminal Tribunal for Rwanda provide that '[a] Trial Chamber shall not require proof of facts of common knowledge but shall take judicial notice thereof'.[259]

The Inter-American Court employed judicial notice in the *Honduran Disappearance Cases*, in which the Commission demonstrated a State practice of disappearances in Honduras between 1981 and 1984, partially through newspaper reports.[260] Although the Court found that many of the newspaper accounts could not be considered to be documentary evidence, it stated that 'many of them contain public and well-known facts which, as such, do not require proof'.[261] More frequent use of this judicial tool when facts are not in dispute will serve to lighten the Court's increasing fact-finding burdens.[262]

Amicus curiae *briefs*

The Court regularly accepts *amicus curiae* briefs, although they are not evidence. *Amicus* briefs are not formally included in the file or case record.[263] *Amicus* briefs can be particularly helpful to the Court in that they often represent the public interest. In the *Mayagna (SUMO) Awas Tingni Community Case*, which raised questions of indigenous communal land rights, the Court received *amicus* briefs from *inter alia* the Assembly of First Nations of Canada, the Organization of Indigenous Syndics

256 Reisman and Levit, 'Fact-Finding Initiatives for the Inter-American Court of Human Rights', at 456.

257 Sandifer, *Evidence Before International Tribunals*, at 382. Sandifer also explained that 'under Italian and Mexican law notorious facts or those personally known to the Court do not need to be proved'. *Ibid.*, citing Chevallier, 'Remarques sur l'utilization par le juge de ses informations personnelles', 60 *Revue Trimestrielle de Droit Civil* 5 (1962).

258 US Fed. R. Evid. 201(a).

259 International Criminal Tribunal for Rwanda Rules of Procedure and Evidence, Rule 94.

260 *Velásquez Rodríguez* v. *Honduras* (Merits, 1988), para. 106.

261 *Ibid.*, para. 146.

262 Reisman and Levit, 'Fact-Finding Initiatives for the Inter-American Court of Human Rights', at 456.

263 *Benavides Cevallos* v. *Ecuador* (Merits, 1998), nn. 2 and 3; *Loayza Tamayo* v. *Peru* (Merits, 1997), para. 22.

of the Nicaraguan Caribbean, the Mohawks Indigenous Community of Akewsasne, and the National Congress of American Indians.[264]

Amici curiae have also requested to participate 'in all the oral and written instances that the rules of procedures allow',[265] which is essentially a request to intervene in the case. In '*The Last Temptation of Christ' Case*, the *amici* who made the request were the persons who had moved to have the movie censored in Chile 'in the name of Jesus Christ, the Catholic Church and themselves'.[266] The Court denied the request, explaining that (under the prior rules) only the Commission and the State could be heard until the reparations stage of the proceedings.[267] Even under the current rules of the Court, there is no provision for intervention in the case. If *amici* or other States have evidence to contribute to the proceedings, they could be named by either party as a witness or they could request that the Court call them as witnesses.

Written closing arguments

It is the uniform practice of the Court to invite the parties to submit written closing arguments.[268] A closing argument is a summary of the evidence and arguments presented by the party at the public hearing and in earlier briefs. Additional contradictory comments may not be inserted into the final briefs.[269] The parties have access to the transcripts of the public hearings to prepare their arguments.[270]

Deliberations and notification of judgment

At the conclusion of the hearings in which the parties presented their cases and after the parties have made their final arguments, the Court conducts private deliberations which remain confidential.[271] Normally, the deliberations are held during the Court's next session, and the judgment is handed down at the conclusion of that session. Only the judges take part in the actual deliberations, although other members of the staff of

[264] *Mayagna (SUMO) Awas Tingni Community* v. *Nicaragua* (Merits, 2001), paras. 38, 41, 52 and 61.

[265] *'The Last Temptation of Christ' Case (Olmedo Bustos et al.* v. *Chile)* (Merits, 2001), para. 21.

[266] *Ibid.*, para. 21 and n. 8.

[267] *Ibid.*, para. 21.

[268] *Paniagua Morales et al.* v. *Guatemala (The White Van Case)* (Merits, 1998), para. 43.

[269] *Mayagna (SUMO) Awas Tingni Community* v. *Nicaragua* (Merits, 2001), para. 70.

[270] 2001 Rules of Procedure of the Inter-Am. Ct HR, Art. 42(2).

[271] *Ibid.*, Art. 14(2). The Statute of the Court provides that '[t]he Court shall deliberate in private. Its deliberations shall remain secret, unless the Court decides otherwise.' Statute of the Inter-Am Ct HR, Art. 24(2).

the Secretariat, such as the Secretary and Deputy Secretary, may be in attendance.[272] All staff of the Secretariat take an oath of secrecy. The minutes of the deliberations are limited to 'a statement of the subject of the discussion and the decisions taken. Separate opinions, dissenting and concurring, and declarations made for the record shall also be noted.'[273] The Convention requires that the Court notify the parties to the case and the States Parties to the Convention of the Court's judgment.[274]

Request for interpretation of judgment

When the parties disagree about the meaning or scope of a judgment on the merits or on reparations, the Convention authorizes a party to ask the Court for an interpretation of the judgment in question.[275] Previously, only the Commission or the State concerned were authorized to make the request, because they were the sole parties to a case. Under the Court's 2001 Rules, however, the victim is also a party and can therefore request an interpretation without the intervention of the Commission. In the *Cesti Hurtado Case*, it was the victim who requested an interpretation of the Court's reparations judgment.[276] The Court had ordered the victim to return to the national courts for a determination of the pecuniary damages owed to him.[277] In turn, the victim requested an interpretation of the Court's reparations judgment to determine the parameters of the damages that were to be awarded by the Peruvian court.[278]

The request for interpretation must be made within ninety days from the date the party is notified of the judgment,[279] and it must precisely identify the issues relating to the scope or meaning of the judgment that the party considers to be unclear or imprecise.[280] The Court then notifies the other parties, including the Commission, and invites them to submit relevant written comments.[281] In the interest of judicial economy, whenever possible the request is considered by the same judges that issued the judgment being interpreted.[282]

[272] 2001 Rules of Procedure of the Inter-Am. Ct HR, Art. 14(2).
[273] *Ibid.*, Art. 14(4). [274] American Convention, Art. 69.
[275] *Ibid.*, Art. 67; 2001 Rules of Procedure of the Inter-Am. Ct HR, Art. 58(1).
[276] *Cesti Hurtado* v. *Peru* (Interpretation of Judgment on Reparations), Inter-Am Ct HR, 27 November 2001, Ser. C, No. 86, para. 9.
[277] *Cesti Hurtado* v. *Peru* (Reparations, 2001), para. 46 and Resolution 1.
[278] *Cesti Hurtado* v. *Peru* (Interpretation of Judgment on Reparations, 2001), para. 10.
[279] American Convention, Art. 67.
[280] 2001 Rules of Procedure of the Inter-Am. Ct HR, Art. 58(1).
[281] *Ibid.*, Art. 58(2). [282] *Ibid.*, Art. 58(3).

While the request is under consideration, the Court's Rules of Procedure specify that the effects of the judgment are not suspended.[283] In its request for interpretation in the *Cesti Hurtado Case*, Peru declared that the rule of non-suspension was not applicable, because its request specifically dealt with the issue of the judgment's execution.[284] The Court disagreed, maintaining that 'the nature of the proceedings before a human rights court does not permit the parties to withdraw from the application of set procedural rules, since they are by nature of a public procedural order'.[285] It would not be in the best interest of the victim if the State could delay the execution of the Court's judgment by simply interposing a request for an interpretation of the judgment.

An interpretation of a judgment may enhance the transparency of the Court's proceedings in appropriate cases by dissipating any doubts about the content and scope of a judgment.[286] The Court has reiterated a rule established by the case law of other international courts that '[t]he interpretation of a judgment involves not only precisely defining the text of the operative parts of the judgment, but also specifying its scope, meaning and purpose, based on the considerations of the judgment'.[287] For example, in the *Suárez Rosero Case*, Ecuador asked for an interpretation as to whether the interest earned from the compensatory damages and the use made of those damages was to be free of taxation.[288] In the *Blake Case*, Guatemala requested an interpretation of certain aspects of the judgment on reparations as related to the judgment on the merits of the case.[289] In the *Velásquez* and *Godínez Cruz Cases*, the Commission requested an interpretation of the Court's judgment on compensatory damages. The Court had ordered that the judgment be paid in Honduran national currency, which was decreasing rapidly in value, and be placed in trust for the

283 *Ibid.*, Art. 58(4).

284 *Cesti Hurtado* v. *Peru* (Interpretation of the Judgment on the Merits), Inter-Am. Ct HR, 29 January 2000, Ser. C, No. 65, para. 2.

285 *Cesti Hurtado* v. *Peru* (Request for Interpretation of Judgment of 29 September 1999), Inter-Am. Ct HR, 19 November 1999, Ser. C, No. 62, 'Considering' section, para. 3.

286 *Suárez Rosero* v. *Ecuador* (Interpretation of the Judgment on Reparations), Inter-Am. Ct HR, 29 May 1999, Ser. C, No. 51, para. 17, citing *El Amparo* v. *Venezuela* (Request for Interpretation of the Judgment of September 14, 1996), Inter-Am. Ct HR, 16 April 1997, Ser. C, No. 46, para. 1.

287 *Velásquez Rodríguez* v. *Honduras* (Interpretation of the Compensatory Damages), Inter-Am. Ct HR, 17 August 1990, Ser. C, No. 9, para. 26; *Godínez Cruz* (Interpretation of the Compensatory Damages), Inter-Am. Ct HR, 17 August 1990, Ser. C, No. 10, para. 26, citing *Ringeisen* v. *Austria* (Interpretation), 16 ECHR (Ser. A) (1973), para. 13.

288 *Suárez Rosero* v. *Ecuador* (Interpretation of Judgment on Reparations, 1999), para. 10.

289 *Blake* v. *Guatemala* (Interpretation of Judgment on Reparations), Inter-Am. Ct HR, 1 October 1999, Ser. C, No. 57, para. 8.

minor children of the victims 'under the most favorable conditions permitted by Honduran banking practice'.[290] Although the Court refused to interpret the judgment, under its authority to supervise the State's compliance, it held that the amount of damages should be in hard currencies which would preserve the purchasing power of the trust in the case of inflation and the devaluation of the national currency.[291]

A request for interpretation may not be used by a party to seek an amendment or nullification of the judgment in question, nor can it be used as a means of challenging the Court's judgment.[292] In its request for an interpretation of the reparations judgment in the *Suárez Rosero Case*, Ecuador argued that payment made to the victim's attorney pursuant to the Court's reparations judgment was equivalent to the earnings of any practising attorney and, therefore, could not be exempted from taxation.[293] The Court, although not obliged to do so because its order was clear, proffered an explanation as to why it had ordered that costs and expenses be tax-exempt.[294] In its request for an interpretation in the *Loayza Tamayo Case*, Peru argued *inter alia* that certain of the witnesses in the case had not been impartial, and that, therefore, the Court should rule that their statements were invalid.[295] The Court rejected the State's request, finding that it was 'an improper attempt' to amend the judgment on the merits.[296]

Revision of judgment on the basis of newly discovered facts or fraudulent evidence

There is no provision for a revision of an Inter-American Court judgment in the Convention, Statute or Rules of the Court. The Court's jurisprudence, however, permits a remedy of revision in exceptional circumstances. The Court admitted the Commission's request for revision

[290] *Velásquez Rodríguez* v. *Honduras* (Compensatory Damages), para. 58; *Godínez Cruz* (Compensatory Damages, 1989), para. 53.

[291] *Velásquez Rodríguez* v. *Honduras* (Interpretation of the Compensatory Damages, 1990), para. 31 and Resolution 3; *Godínez Cruz* (Interpretation of the Compensatory Damages, 1990), para. 31 and Resolution 3.

[292] *Loayza Tamayo* v. *Peru*, Order of the Inter-Am. Ct HR of 8 March 1998, para. 16, reprinted in 1998 Annual Report of the Inter-Am Ct HR, OAS/Ser.L/V/III.43 doc. 11, 18 January 1999, at 209.

[293] *Suárez Rosero* v. *Ecuador* (Interpretation of Judgment on Reparations, 1999), para. 18.

[294] *Ibid.* paras. 21 and 33–44.

[295] *Loayza Tamayo* v. *Peru*, Order of the Inter-Am. Ct HR of 8 March 1998, reprinted in 1998 Annual Report of the Inter-Am Court HR, OAS/Ser.L/V/III.43 doc. 11, 18 January 1999, at 206–8.

[296] *Ibid.* para. 17 and Resolution.

in the *Genie Lacayo Case*, but held that there were no exceptional reasons which could justify the amendment of its decision on the merits of the case.[297]

Other international Courts do make provision for a revision of a judgment. According to the Statute of the International Court of Justice:

> an application for revision of judgment may be made only when it is based upon the discovery of some fact of such a nature as to be a decisive factor, which fact was, when the judgment was given, unknown to the Court and also to the party claiming revision, always provided that such ignorance was not due to negligence.[298]

The European Convention on Human Rights also does not make provision for the remedy of revision. Such a recourse has, however, been included in the Rules of the European Court.[299]

The unappealable nature of a judgment of the Inter-American Court is not incompatible with the remedy of revision. The recourse of revision is essential to a court. Some would call it a power inherent to the judicial function of the Court.[300] If, for example, a State were found to be internationally responsible for the disappearance of a victim, and subsequently the person in question were discovered to be alive and not within the control of the State, it would be necessary for the Court to revise its judgment.

Attribution of State responsibility

Once the Court has determined the relevant facts proved, it will decide whether those facts establish a violation of the Convention that is attributable to the State. Many of the principles of attribution of State responsibility for violations of international law are well established and have been codified by the United Nations International Law Commission (ILC).[301] The American Convention, as interpreted by the

[297] *Genie Lacayo* v. *Nicaragua* (Request for Revision of the Judgment of January 29, 1997), Order of the Inter-Am. Ct HR, Order of 13 September 1997, Ser. C, No. 43, para. 13.

[298] Statute of the ICJ, Art. 61.

[299] Rules of Court, European Court of Human Rights, Rule 80, as in force at 1 November 1998. See http://www.echr.coe.int.

[300] *Genie Lacayo* v. *Nicaragua* (Request for Revision of the Judgment of January 29, 1997), Inter-Am. Ct HR, Order of 13 September 1997, Ser. C, No. 43, Dissenting Opinion of Judge Cançado Trindade, para. 7, at 184.

[301] The International Law Commission's Articles on State Responsibility, annexed to GA Res. 56/83, 12 December 2001, at 382 and *passim*. See James Crawford, *The International Law Commission's Articles on State Responsibility: Introduction, Text and Commentaries*

Inter-American Court, establishes broad bases of State responsibility which are in keeping with those codified principles of international law. States in the Inter-American human rights system are increasingly acknowledging these principles and accepting responsibility for actions which are in violation of international law.[302] The failure of States to recognize consistently their international responsibility, even when the facts are not in question, has, however, resulted in the needless prolongation of cases before the Commission or the Court. States have often denied responsibility before the Commission, only later to acknowledge international legal responsibility before the Court. Several cases before the Inter-American system test most, if not all, of the codified principles. These cases exhibit some of the more complex and difficult issues in the attribution of State responsibility for human rights violations.

Article 1(1) of the American Convention provides the basis for State responsibility in the Inter-American system.[303] Article 1(1) reads:

> [t]he States Parties to this Convention undertake to respect the rights and freedoms recognized herein and to ensure to all persons subject to their jurisdiction the free and full exercise of those rights and freedoms, without any discrimination for reasons of race, color, sex, language, religion, political or other opinion, national or social origin, economic status, birth, or any other social condition.[304]

In general, Article 1 requires that the States Parties to the Convention both respect and ensure the exercise of the rights and freedoms recognized by the Convention to all persons subject to their jurisdiction.[305]

The Court specifically recognizes the role of international law in stating that any impairment of the rights recognized by the Convention 'which can be attributed under the rules of international law to the action or omission of any public authority constitutes an act imputable to the State, which assumes responsibility in the terms provided by the Convention'.[306]

(Cambridge University Press, Cambridge, 2002); James Crawford, Pierre Bodeau and Jacqueline Peel, 'The ILC's Draft Articles on State Responsibility: Toward Completion of a Second Reading', 94 *American Journal of International Law*, 660 (2000).

302 *El Amparo* v. *Venezuela* (Merits), Inter-Am. Ct HR, 18 January 1995, Ser. C, No. 19, para. 19; *Aloeboetoe et al.* v. *Suriname* (Merits), Inter-Am. Ct HR, 4 December 1991, Ser. C, No. 11, para. 22; *Garrido and Baigorria* v. *Argentina* (Merits), Inter-Am. Ct HR, 2 February 1996, Ser. C, No. 26, para. 25.

303 See *Velásquez Rodríguez* v. *Honduras* (Merits, 1988), para. 164.

304 American Convention, Art. 1(1).

305 *Ibid.*

306 *Velásquez Rodríguez* v. *Honduras* (Merits, 1988), para. 164. See also Louis Sohn and R. Baxter, 'Responsibility of States for Injuries to the Economic Interests of Aliens', 55 *American Journal of International Law*, 545, 546 (1961).

In *'The Last Temptation of Christ' Case*, in which the Chilean Government argued that an act of the judiciary that contravened international law was not attributable to the State unless the executive power of the State acquiesced in it, the Court again clarified that:

> the international responsibility of the State may be engaged by acts or omissions of any power or organ of the State, whatsoever its rank, that violate the American Convention. That is, any act or omission that may be attributed to the State, in violation of the norms of international human rights law, engages the international responsibility of the State.[307]

Therefore, whether the violation of the American Convention is committed by the executive, legislative or judicial branch of the government, the violation is attributable to the State.

Violations committed by agents of the State including agents of territorial governments

When a State official or public entity, in its official capacity, violates a right protected under international law, that violation is attributable to the State.[308] The governmental position or status of the offending party does not affect the issue of imputability. The official who commits the violation may belong to any branch of government and may hold a high-level or subordinate position.[309] The Court specified that 'any exercise of public power that violates the rights recognized by the Convention is illegal'.[310]

The official actions of State agents have resulted in State responsibility in several cases before the Inter-American Court. For example, in the *Aloeboetoe et al. Case*, Surinamese soldiers murdered seven men of a rural tribe.[311] Fifty eye witnesses saw the soldiers beating the victims and taking them away, and one of the victims lived long enough to describe the murders.[312] Initially Suriname denied responsibility before the Inter-American Commission. Subsequently, however, confronted by overwhelming evidence before the Inter-American Court, the State accepted international responsibility for the violations committed by its agents.[313]

307 *'The Last Temptation of Christ' Case (Olmedo Bustos et al.* v. *Chile)* (Merits, 2001), para. 72.
308 *Velásquez Rodríguez* v. *Honduras* (Merits, 1988), para. 169.
309 ILC's Articles on State Responsibility, Art. 4 and comments 6 and 7.
310 *Velásquez Rodríguez* v. *Honduras* (Merits, 1988), para. 169.
311 *Aloeboetoe et al.* v. *Suriname* (Merits, 1991), paras. 11–14.
312 *Ibid.*, paras. 11 and 15.
313 *Ibid.*, para. 22.

Likewise, in the *El Amparo Case*, members of a special military unit in Venezuela murdered fourteen Venezuelan fishermen.[314] Two fishermen escaped and described the massacre.[315] Although Venezuela initially disputed liability before the Commission, when the case was referred to the Court the State accepted responsibility for the violation of the right to life of the victims.[316] In the *Gangaram Panday Case*, in which the Surinamese military police were found to have illegally incarcerated the victim, the Court held that the State incurred international responsibility for the violation of the victim's right to personal liberty.[317]

A violation of international law resulting from the conduct of an organ or official of a territorial government is also attributable to the State.[318] Thus, in a federal system, such as the United States, Argentina and Canada, the federal government is also responsible on the international plane for violations committed by officials of an individual state or territory. For instance, in the *Garrido and Baigorria Case*, four uniformed police officers of the Argentine province of Mendoza detained Garrido Calderón and Baigorria Balmaceda in front of eye witnesses near the city's central park.[319] The police were driving official vehicles, and the victims' automobile was found later at a police facility.[320] Garrido and Baigorria never reappeared. The Government of Argentina, which initially questioned its responsibility for the acts of provincial government agents, ultimately accepted international responsibility for the human rights violations.[321]

Violations committed by non-governmental groups or individuals acting under the direction or control of the State

A State cannot avoid international responsibility by exercising control over groups or individual non-governmental agents and directing them to commit human rights violations.[322] In certain States Parties to the Inter-American Convention, death squads reportedly operated under the auspices of the government.[323] The names of the members of the death squads were concealed. Although those comprising the death squads may in some

314 *El Amparo* v. *Venezuela* (Merits, 1995), para. 10. 315 *Ibid.*

316 *Ibid.*, para. 19. 317 *Gangaram Panday* v. *Suriname* (Merits, 1994), paras. 5 and 68.

318 ILC's Articles on State Responsibility, Art. 4 and comments 8–10.

319 *Garrido and Baigorria* v. *Argentina* (Merits, 1996), paras. 10 and 27.

320 *Ibid.*, paras. 10 and 12. 321 *Ibid.*, para. 24.

322 ILC's Articles on State Responsibility, Art. 8. See generally Stephanie Farrior, 'State Responsibility for Human Rights Abuses by Non-State Actors', 92 *American Society of International Law Proceedings*, 299 (1998).

323 See *Velásquez Rodriguez* v. *Honduras* (Merits, 1988), para. 147.

instances be private individuals, if they are directed or controlled by the government, the State is internationally responsible for their actions.

The Guatemalan Government acted through other groups by establishing civil defence patrols made up of the civilian males from Guatemala villages.[324] These patrols, whose stated purpose was the protection of highland villages from guerrillas, were accused of various human rights violations. In 1990, members of civil patrols in the highlands of Guatemala allegedly murdered several members of a local human rights monitoring group. Even the two judges who issued arrest warrants received death threats and were forced into hiding.[325] In another case, it was established that members of a highland civil patrol violated the rights of Nicholas Blake, an American citizen, who disappeared in Guatemala.[326] Whether the conduct of private individuals or groups can be attributed to the State depends on the degree of control exercised over them by the State.[327]

Ultra vires *acts of State agents or those empowered by the State*

Even when the human rights violations of government agents or those empowered to exercise governmental authority are *ultra vires*, the violation may be attributable to the State. The Inter-American Court clarified that 'a State is responsible for the acts of its agents, undertaken in their official capacity, and for their omissions, even when those agents act outside the sphere of their authority or violate internal law'.[328] Although the government officials may have exceeded their competence under internal law or contravened the instructions they were given, the State is still liable internationally for their actions if they had apparent authority.[329] The Inter-American Court, in accordance with this principle, stated: '[i]f acts of public power that exceed the State's authority or are illegal under its own laws were not considered to compromise that State's obligations under the treaty, the system of protection provided for in the Convention would be illusory'.[330] In the *Caballero Delgado and Santana Case*, involving the

324 Annual Report of the Inter-American Commission on Human Rights, 446, OEA/Ser.L/V/II.79, doc. 12 rev. 1 (1990–1).

325 *Chunimá*, Case 10.674, Request for Provisional Measures, Inter-Am. Comm. HR, June 1991, para. 3.

326 *Blake* (Guatemala), Provisional Measures, Inter-Am. Ct HR, Order of the President, Order of 16 August 1995, Ser. E, para. 3.

327 ILC's Articles on State Responsibility, Art. 8 and comments 3–5.

328 *Velásquez Rodríguez* v. *Honduras* (Merits, 1988), para. 170.

329 ILC's Articles on State Responsibility, Art. 7 and comments 7 and 8.

330 See *Velásquez Rodríguez* v. *Honduras* (Merits, 1988), para. 171.

disappearance of a man and a woman, Colombian army officers directing a group of soldiers and civilian paramilitaries were found to have illegally detained and disappeared the victims.[331] The Court, in attributing responsibility to Colombia, did not make a finding as to whether the soldiers' actions were *ultra vires* or taken under orders from their superiors, because the State is responsible in either case.[332]

If, however, government officials act in a purely personal capacity, that act is treated as the act of a private individual and is not attributable to the State. The line between the *ultra vires* acts of a state official taken within his or her official capacity and his or her acts as a private individual is not always obvious. The dissenting judge in the *Caballero Delgado and Santana Case* argued that the actions of the army officers should not be attributed to the State because the commanding officer had mental problems and had been treated for paranoia, and some of the soldiers had been charged with other crimes such as common robbery.[333] He opined that such acts should be attributed solely to the individuals and not to the State Party.[334] The Court had discredited this argument earlier in the *Velásquez Rodríguez Case*, stating that '[v]iolations of the Convention cannot be founded upon rules that take psychological factors into account in establishing individual culpability'.[335] The motivation of the State agent who violates the rights recognized by the American Convention is irrelevant to a determination of State responsibility.[336] The Court summarized the position thus: '[i]n principle, any violation of rights recognized by the Convention carried out by an act of public authority or by persons who use their position of authority is imputable to the State'.[337]

Failure to investigate and punish violations by persons not acting on behalf of the State

As a general principle, violations committed by individuals are not considered attributable to the State under international law, provided that they were not undertaken either *de jure* or *de facto* on behalf of the State.[338] The State can, however, incur international responsibility on other grounds for the acts of natural persons. As explained by the Inter-American Court:

[331] *Caballero Delgado and Santana* v. *Colombia* (Merits), Inter-Am. Ct HR, 8 December 1995, Ser. C, No. 22, para. 53.
[332] *Ibid.*, para. 53.
[333] *Ibid.*, dissent of Judge Nieto Navia.
[334] *Ibid.* [335] *Velásquez Rodríguez* v. *Honduras* (Merits, 1988), para. 173. [336] *Ibid.*
[337] *Ibid.*, para. 172. [338] ILC's Articles on State Responsibility, comment 1 to Art. 8.

> [a]n illegal act which violated human rights and which is initially not directly imputable to a State (for example, because it is the act of a private person or because the person responsible has not been identified) can lead to international responsibility of the State, not because of the act itself, but because of the lack of due diligence to prevent the violation or to respond to it as required by the Convention.[339]

For example, a State may be charged with non-compliance of its duties under international law by its failure to prevent injuries or to provide remedies.[340] In its Order for Provisional Measures in the *Urso Branco Prison Case*, in which several prison inmates had been murdered by other inmates, the Inter-American Court stated that there is a presumption of State responsibility when the victims are persons incarcerated in a State prison, and the State has not adopted security measures that protect them.[341]

In criminal cases, a State's failure to investigate the crime promptly or to capture, prosecute and adequately punish the guilty parties may result in international responsibility.[342] Also, the State may be liable if it had or should have had knowledge that a crime could take place but failed to take proper precautions to prevent it or subsequently to investigate the crime or to punish the person who committed it.[343] In such a case, the State has failed in its duty and may be held responsible under the American Convention and international law in general for the initial violation and also for the subsequent denial of justice.[344] In accordance with this principle, the Inter-American Court explained that '[t]he State has a legal duty to take reasonable steps to prevent human rights violations and to use the means at its disposal to carry out a serious investigation of violations committed within its jurisdiction, to identify those responsible, to impose the appropriate punishment and to ensure the victim adequate compensation'.[345] 'This duty to prevent includes all those means of a legal,

339 *Velásquez Rodríguez* v. *Honduras* (Merits), para. 172.

340 Marjorie M. Whiteman, *Damages in International Law*, 24 (Government Printing Office, Washington DC, 1937).

341 *Urso Branco Prison Case* (Brazil), Provisional Measures, Inter-Am. Ct HR, Order of 18 June 2002, Ser. E, 'Considering' section, para. 8.

342 Whiteman, *Damages in International Law*, at 24.

343 See Janet M. Baldwin (*United States* v. *Mexico*), (1888) *Foreign Relations*, Pt II, at 1087. See Whiteman, *Damages in International Law*, at 24–7, for a discussion of several relevant cases.

344 Whiteman, *Damages in International Law*, at 13.

345 *Velásquez Rodríguez* v. *Honduras* (Merits, 1988), para. 174; see generally Naomi Roht-Arriaza, Comment, 'State Responsibility to Investigate and Prosecute Grave Human Rights Violations in International Law', 78 *California Law Review*, 449 (1990).

political, administrative, and cultural nature that promote the protection of human rights and ensure that any violations are considered and treated as illegal acts, which, as such, may lead to the punishment of those responsible and the obligation to indemnify the victims for damages.'[346] The Court maintains that:

> [u]nlike domestic criminal law, it is not necessary to determine the perpetrators' culpability or intentionality in order to establish that the rights enshrined in the Convention have been violated, nor is it essential to identify individually the agents to whom the acts of violation are attributed. The sole requirement is to demonstrate that the State authorities supported or tolerated infringement of the rights recognized in the Convention. Moreover, the State's international responsibility is also at issue when it does not take the necessary steps under its domestic law to identify and, where appropriate, punish the author of such violations.[347]

If, however, the State provides the injured party with an adequate means of redressing the wrong which was committed by a private individual, there is no violation of international law.[348]

The decisive issue 'is whether a violation of the rights recognized by the Convention has occurred with the support or the acquiescence of the government, or whether the State has allowed the act to take place without taking measures to prevent it or to punish those responsible'.[349] An example of the latter situation occurred in Nicaragua when Arnoldo Aléman Lacayo, a candidate for the presidency, was injured during an attack by armed men while he was on a campaign tour.[350] The events took place in an area of the country where 'groups of heavily armed delinquents', who had ties with ex-members of the Sandinista army and the US-backed Contras, operated.[351] The Government of Nicaragua did not apparently have control over those who attacked the presidential candidate. The Government did, however, have a duty to attempt to prevent such attacks, to investigate the crime and to punish those responsible; if it failed to do so, it would bear international responsibility.[352]

[346] *Velásquez Rodríguez* v. *Honduras* (Merits, 1988), para. 175.

[347] *Villagrán Morales et al.* v. *Guatemala (The Street Children Case)* (Merits, 1999), para. 75, citing *Paniagua Morales et al.* v. *Guatemala (The White Van Case)* (Merits, 1998), para. 91.

[348] Whiteman, *Damages in International Law*, at 14.

[349] *Velásquez Rodríguez* v. *Honduras* (Merits, 1988), para. 173.

[350] *Aléman Lacayo* (Nicaragua), Provisional Measures, Inter-Am. Ct HR, Order of 2 February 1996, Ser. E.

[351] *Ibid.*, para. 3.

[352] *Ibid.*, operative para. 6.

Furthermore, a government must not interfere in the investigation of human rights violations or obstruct justice in any way. In the *Genie Lacayo Case*, the Commission claimed that the State was responsible for the denial of justice.[353] Nicaragua had not yet accepted the contentious jurisdiction of the Inter-American Court at the time that government soldiers allegedly shot a sixteen-year-old boy who attempted to pass their caravan of vehicles on the highway.[354] Therefore, the Court did not have jurisdiction to adjudicate the issue of State responsibility for the violation of the boy's right to life. Shortly thereafter, however, Nicaragua did accept the jurisdiction of the Court. Subsequently, government agents allegedly murdered the prosecutor who was investigating the crime and destroyed the evidence.[355] The Court held that Nicaragua had engaged in the obstruction of justice and was therefore responsible for violating the American Convention.[356]

No basis of reparations for violations committed by groups rebelling against the government unless the group is successful

In general, the State is not responsible for human rights violations committed by an unsuccessful insurrectional movement.[357] If lawlessness exists in a state and the state takes all measures it can reasonably be expected to take under the circumstances, the State is not internationally responsible for violations.[358] If, however, the insurrectional movement triumphs and becomes the government of the State or forms a new State, it is responsible for its earlier actions.[359] All successor governments are internationally responsible for violations committed by their predecessor governments which have not been repaired.[360]

353 *Genie Lacayo* (Preliminary Objections), Inter-Am. Ct HR, 27 January 1995, Ser. C, No. 21, para. 13.

354 *Ibid.* 355 *Ibid.*, paras. 12 and 13.

356 *Genie Lacayo* (Merits), Inter-Am. Ct HR, 29 January 1997, Ser. C, No. 30, Resolution 2.

357 ILC's Articles on State Responsibility, Art. 10 and comment 2.

358 Whiteman, *Damages in International Law*, at 34. For example, in the early 1900s, the Spanish Treaty Claims Commission determined that for claimants to recover for damages caused by insurgents they needed to allege and prove 'that at the time and place when and where the injury was done the Spanish authorities could, by due diligence, and should have prevented such injury'. Fuller's Report (1907) 25, in Whiteman, *Damages in International Law*, at 35.

359 ILC's Articles on State Responsibility, Art. 10 and comment 4.

360 See Theo Van Boven, *Study Concerning the Right to Restitution, Compensation and Rehabilitation for Victims of Gross Violations of Human Rights and Fundamental Freedoms*, 16, UN Human Rights Commission E/CN.4/Sub.2/1993/8 (2 July 1993); ILC's Articles on State Responsibility, comment 5 to Art. 10.

If the rebels continue to operate as rebels and never come to power, there is no established principle to place international liability on them. States Parties to international human rights treaties sometimes complain that, while States are held responsible for human rights violations, the international enforcement organs ignore the violations of rebel groups operating within their territories.[361] Generally under international human rights law, only the States Parties to the treaties incur a duty to respect human rights. The International Criminal Court, however, will have jurisdiction to try individuals charged with crimes against humanity. The United Nations Truth Commission for El Salvador also established some limited precedent for holding rebel groups liable, by stating that:

> [i]t is true that, in theory, international human rights law is applicable only to Governments, while in some armed conflicts international humanitarian law is binding on both sides: in other words, binding on both insurgents and Government forces. However, it must be recognized that when insurgents assume government powers in territories under their control, they too can be required to observe certain human rights obligations that are binding on the State under international law.[362]

This principle is justifiable and will perhaps find more support in the future. However, presently individuals or rebel groups that violate international human rights cannot be brought before the Inter-American Court.

Conclusion

The Inter-American Court implements fact-finding procedures that are more flexible and less formal than domestic fact-finding procedures.[363] This allows the Court to exercise logic and experience in evaluating the evidence submitted while ensuring legal certainty and maintaining procedural balance between the parties.

The Inter-American Court's application of the well-established principles of attribution of responsibility in holding States responsible for

[361] The Representative of the Peruvian Government made this complaint at the public hearing on Advisory Opinion OC-14, before the Inter-American Court of Human Rights on 31 January 1994.

[362] Report of the Commission on Truth for El Salvador, 'From Madness to Hope: The 12-Year War in El Salvador', 20 (United Nations 1993).

[363] *Cantoral Benavides* v. *Peru* (Merits, 2000), para. 45.

human rights violations has been in accordance with those principles as codified by the ILC. This consistency has perhaps resulted in States voluntarily accepting international responsibility, and thereby eliminating the need for a Court judgment on the merits. It bodes well for the future of international human rights law in general and the Inter-American human rights system in particular that more States are voluntarily acknowledging international responsibility for violations of human rights.

5

Victim reparations

> When a wrongful act occurs that is imputable to a State, the latter incurs international responsibility for violation of an international rule, and thus incurs a duty to make reparation.[1]

Introduction

It is a basic principle of international law that a State must make adequate reparation for the harm caused by the breach of its international obligations.[2] 'Reparation is a generic term that covers the various ways a State can redress the international responsibility it has incurred.'[3] All aspects of a State's obligation to make the reparations ordered by an international court are governed by international law.[4] The State may not invoke its domestic law to alter any aspect of the decision, including its scope, nature, means and the determination of beneficiaries.[5] The purpose of reparations is twofold: first, to require States to observe certain standards of law and order; and, secondly, to repair, to the extent

[1] *Castillo Páez* v. *Peru* (Reparations), Inter-Am. Ct HR, 27 November 1998, Ser. C, No. 43, para. 50; *Paniagua Morales et al.* v. *Guatemala* (Reparations, 2001), para. 78.

[2] *Factory at Chorzów* (Merits), 1928 PCIJ (Ser. A) No. 17, at 29 (13 September), cited in *Velásquez Rodríguez* v. *Honduras* (Compensatory Damages), Inter-Am. Ct HR, 21 July 1989, Ser. C, No. 7, para. 25; *Paniagua Morales et al.* v. *Guatemala* (Reparations), Inter-Am. Ct HR, 25 May 2001, Ser. C, No. 76, para. 75; *Baena Ricardo et al. (270 Workers* v. *Panama)* (Merits), Inter-Am. Ct HR, 2 February 2001, Ser. C, No. 72, para. 201; *Loayza Tamayo* (Reparations), Inter-Am. Ct HR, 27 November 1998, Ser. C, No. 42, para. 84.

[3] *Blake* v. *Guatemala* (Reparations), Inter-Am. Ct HR, 22 January 1999, Ser. C, No. 48, para. 31.

[4] *Castillo Páez* v. *Peru* (Reparations), Inter-Am. Ct HR, 27 November 1998, Ser. C, No. 43, para. 49; *Garrido and Baigorria* v. *Argentina* (Reparations), Inter-Am. Ct HR, 27 August 1998, Ser. C, No. 39, para. 42; *Paniagua Morales et al.* v. *Guatemala* (Reparations, 2001), para. 77.

[5] *Castillo Páez* v. *Peru* (Reparations, 1998), para. 49; *Garrido and Baigorria* v. *Argentina* (Reparations, 1998), para. 42; *Paniagua Morales et al.* v. *Guatemala* (Reparations, 2001), para. 77.

possible, any injuries caused as a result of a State's failure to meet those standards.[6]

A State may incur international obligations under customary international law or through the ratification of a treaty. Historically, under the international law of injury to aliens, a State violated an international obligation to another State when it injured a citizen of another State.[7] Only a State could sue another State and demand reparation for the injuries inflicted on its citizens. The injured individual did not have a directly enforceable claim against the State that violated his or her rights. This principle was expressed in the *Factory at Chorzów Case*, in which the Permanent Court of International Justice stated that '[t]he rules of law governing the reparation are the rules of international law in force between the two States concerned, and not the law governing relations between the State which has committed a wrongful act and the individual who has suffered damage'.[8]

Historically, an individual had no international recourse in the case of a violation by his or her own government. This aspect of international law has changed in the last half century. States have ratified human rights treaties that create international obligations owed by the Contracting States to individuals. If the State violates these obligations, the treaties may require the State to remedy the violation by making reparations to the injured party.[9] Most States have ratified treaties under which they have voluntarily assumed an international obligation to protect human rights and have granted jurisdiction to international authorities to oversee their compliance.[10]

[6] Marjorie Whiteman, *Damages in International Law*, at 23–4 (Government Printing Office, Washington DC, 1937).

[7] See *Mavrommatis Palestine Concessions* (Jurisdiction), 1924 PCIJ (Ser. A) No. 2, at 13 (30 August).

[8] *Factory at Chorzów* (Merits), 1928 PCIJ (Ser. A) at 28. See Richard B. Lillich and Burns H. Weston, *International Claims: Contemporary European Practice* (University Press of Virginia, 1982).

[9] See International Covenant on Civil and Political Rights, opened for signature 16 December 1966, Arts. 2, 2(3)(a) and 9(5), 999 UNTS 171 (entered into force 23 March 1976); Universal Declaration of Human Rights, Art. 8, GA Res. 217A (III), UN GAOR, 3rd Sess., Pt 1, at 71 (1948), UN Doc. A/810 (1948); European Convention for the Protection of Human Rights and Fundamental Freedoms, as amended by Protocol No. 11, Rome, 4 November 1950, Art. 41; African Charter of Human and Peoples' Rights (Banjul Charter), 27 June 1981, Art. 21(2), 21 ILM 59 (1982) (limited right to a remedy). See also *Restatement (Third) of the Foreign Relations Law of the United States*, § 906 (1990).

[10] See Statute of the International Court of Justice, 59 Stat. 1055 (entered into force 24 October 1945), Art. 36.

In the Americas, the States Parties to the American Convention on Human Rights have undertaken an international obligation to protect and ensure the rights delineated in the treaty and to provide reparations to the injured parties if the State violates those rights. If the State charged with violation of the American Convention accepts responsibility or the Inter-American Court of Human Rights attributes responsibility for the violation to the State, the Court may then order the State to make reparations to the individual in accordance with the American Convention.[11] The Court has stated in this regard that '[w]hen a wrongful act occurs that is imputable to a State, the State incurs international responsibility for the violation of international law, with the resulting duty to make reparation, and the duty to put an end to the consequences of the violation'.[12]

The duty to make reparations when an individual's rights are violated should be ordered first and foremost by domestic courts. The Inter-American Court has held that the absence of an effective domestic remedy is itself a violation of the American Convention.[13] The resort to the international human rights system can be made only after the domestic system has failed to provide the victim with an effective remedy. Even when domestic justice is not available, however, only a minority of these cases are actually considered by an international court. Thus, the majority of victims who suffer similar abuses are never compensated. In Honduras, for example, from 1981 to 1984, one hundred to one hundred and fifty persons disappeared.[14] The Honduran Human Rights Commissioner and former President of the Inter-American Commission opined that it was unfair that only those whose cases were before the Inter-American Court received reparations.[15] He recommended that all proven cases of disappearances should receive economic reparations.[16]

[11] American Convention on Human Rights, Art. 63(1), 22 November 1969, 9 ILM 673, OEA/Ser.K/XVI/I.1, doc. 65 rev. 1 corr. 1 (1970), reprinted in 2001 Basic Documents.

[12] *Blake* v. *Guatemala* (Reparations, 1999), para. 33.

[13] *Constitutional Court Case (Aguirre Roca, Rey Terry and Revoredo Marsano* v. *Peru)* (Merits), Inter-Am. Ct HR, 31 January 2001, Ser. C, No. 71, para. 89, citing *Judicial Guarantees in States of Emergency (Articles 27(2), 25 and 8 American Convention on Human Rights)*, Advisory Opinion OC-9/87 of 6 October 1987, Ser. A, No. 9, para. 24.

[14] *Velásquez Rodríguez* v. *Honduras* (Merits), Inter-Am. Ct HR, 29 July 1988, Ser. C, No. 4, para. 147(a).

[15] Comisionado Nacional de Protección de los Derechos Humanos, *Los Hechos Hablan por sí Mismos, Informe Preliminar Sobre los Desaparecidos en Honduras 1980–1993*, 409 (Editorial Guaymuras, Honduras, 1994).

[16] *Ibid.*

The Inter-American Court's authority to award victim reparations

When the Court has determined that the State is liable for a violation of the American Convention or the State voluntarily accepts responsibility for the violation, Article 63(1) of the Convention authorizes victim reparations. Article 63(1) provides that:

> [i]f the Court finds that there has been a violation of a right or freedom protected by this Convention, the Court shall rule that the injured party be ensured the enjoyment of his right or freedom that was violated. It shall also rule, if appropriate, that the consequences of the measure or situation that constituted the breach of such right or freedom be remedied and that fair compensation be paid to the injured party.[17]

Article 63(1) codifies a canon of customary law and a fundamental principle of international law, that 'every violation of an international obligation which results in harm creates a duty to make adequate reparation'.[18] This provision grants the Court the most expansive formal powers to order reparations of any human rights organ.

The legislative history of Article 63(1) reveals that the drafters intended by its language to give the Court broad powers to order reparations for the injured party. The original draft of the reparations provision of the Convention provided for only compensatory damages.[19] That provision read: '[a]fter it has found that there was a violation of a right or freedom protected by this Convention, the Court shall be competent to determine the amount of compensation to be paid to the injured party'.[20] The Guatemalan representative then successfully proposed strengthening and expanding the provision. Under the Guatemalan proposal, which was essentially the provision as it stands today, if the Court recognized a violation of the Convention, it could provide '[t]hat the consequences of the decision or measure that has impaired those rights be stopped; [t]hat the injured party be guaranteed the enjoyment of his violated right or

[17] American Convention, Art. 63(1).

[18] *Velásquez Rodríguez* v. *Honduras* (Compensatory Damages, 1989), para. 25 (citing *Factory at Chorzów* (Jurisdiction), 1927 PCIJ at 21, and *Factory at Chorzów* (Merits), 1928 PCIJ at 26); *Reparation for Injuries Suffered in the Service of the United Nations*, Advisory Opinion, 1949 ICJ Reports 184; see also *Paniagua Morales et al.* v. *Guatemala* (Reparations, 2001), para. 78; *Blake* v. *Guatemala* (Reparations, 1999), para. 33.

[19] Draft American Convention on Protection of Human Rights, Art. 52(1), OEA/Ser.L/II.19 doc. 48 (English) rev. 1 (2 October 1968), reprinted in Buergenthal and Norris (eds.), *Human Rights: The Inter-American System*, booklet 13, vol. 2, at 1, 20.

[20] *Ibid.*

freedom, and [t]he payment of just compensation to the injured party'.[21] After the Drafting Committee's affirmative vote on the Guatemalan proposal, Committee minutes reveal that it had 'approved a text which is broader and more categorically in defense of the injured party than was the Draft'.[22] The subsequent report of the United States Delegation was in agreement, explaining that the final wording of the provision strengthened and expanded the draft provision which had only authorized the Court to determine compensation.[23] The legislative history offered no further explanation of the reasoning underlying the decision to strengthen the reparations provision. There are statements elsewhere in the legislative history, however, which indicate that the drafters of the American Convention intended to enhance the protection of human rights within the unique circumstances of the Western hemisphere.[24]

The Court's authority to order reparations under Article 63(1) is much broader than that of its European counterpart. The corresponding provision of the European Convention, Article 41 (formerly Article 50), authorizes the European Court of Human Rights to 'afford just satisfaction to the injured party' if necessary when the domestic law of the State concerned allows for only partial reparation.[25] The European Court of Human Rights has determined that that provision limits it to ordering financial compensation.[26] The European Court has regularly declared that,

[21] Observations by the Governments of the Member States on the Draft Inter-American Convention on Protection of Human Rights: Guatemala, OEA/Ser.K/XVI/1.1 doc. 24 (English) (8 November 1969), reprinted in Buergenthal and Norris (eds.), *Human Rights: The Inter-American System*, Booklet 13, vol. 2, at 119, 132.

[22] Report of Committee II: Organs of Protection and General Provisions, OEA/Ser.K/ XVI/1.1 doc. 71 (English) rev. 1 (30 January 1970), reprinted in Buergenthal and Norris (eds.), *Human Rights: The Inter-American System*, Booklet 12, vol. 2, at 225, 232. The wording of the provision was later modified slightly.

[23] Report of the US Delegation, at 54 reprinted in Buergenthal and Norris (eds.), *Human Rights: The Inter-American System*, Booklet 15, vol. 3, at i, 54.

[24] See, e.g., Sydney Liskofksy, 'Report on the Convention on Human Rights Adopted by Inter-American Specialized Conference on Human Rights', reprinted in Buergenthal and Norris (eds.), *Human Rights: The Inter-American System*, Booklet 15, vol. 3, at 87, 88.

[25] European Convention, Art. 41.

[26] See P. van Dijk and G. J. H. van Hoof, *Theory and Practice of the European Convention on Human Rights*, at 258 (3rd edn, Kluwer, The Hague, 1998). See also A. H. Robertson and J. G. Merrills, *Human Rights in Europe: A Study of the European Convention on Human Rights*, 311 (3rd edn, Manchester University Press, 1993); Montserrat Enrich Mas, 'Right to Compensation under Article 50', in *The European System for the Protection of Human Rights*, 775, 778 (R. St J. Macdonald *et al.* eds., 1993), stating that '[a] number of applicants have requested the Court to annul an internal decision or measure, to issue an injunction and to give some directions to the respondent State. The Court has answered that it had no jurisdiction to do so.'

in the European system, 'it is for the State to choose the means to be used in its domestic legal system to redress the situation that has given rise to the violation of the Convention'.[27] The representative of the Council of Europe observing the American drafting conference reported on the reparations provision thus: '[t]he Inter-American Court of Human Rights will have considerably wider powers than the European Court'.[28] The extent of the future African Court's authority to order reparations is unclear. The relevant provision provides that the Court 'shall make appropriate orders to remedy the violation, including the payment of fair compensation or reparation'.[29] Although the wording leaves room for interpretation, the provision does not appear on its face to have the breadth of the reparations provision of the American Convention.

Persons who may be awarded reparations

The American Convention specifies that it is the 'injured party' who shall receive reparations.[30] The term 'injured party' is synonymous with the term 'victim', meaning the person or persons affected by the violation. For certain types of human rights violations, especially extra-judicial executions and forced disappearances, the Court may consider the injured party to be not only the person who was killed or disappeared but also that person's next of kin who suffered as a result of losing a loved one and who was denied recourse by State authorities.[31] The Court's Rules define 'next of kin' as the 'direct ascendants and descendants, siblings, spouses or permanent companions, or those determined by the Court, if applicable'.[32] The UN General Assembly, in its Declaration of Basic Principles of Justice for Victims of Crime and Abuse of Power, declared that '[t]he term "victim" also includes, where appropriate, the immediate

[27] *Zanghì* v. *Italy*, 194-C ECHR (Ser. A), para. 26 (1991). See also *Belilos* v. *Switzerland*, 131 ECHR (Ser. A), para. 78 (1988).

[28] Council of Europe Report, reprinted in Buergenthal and Norris (eds.), *Human Rights: The Inter-American System*, Booklet 15, vol 3, at 81; see also Robertson and Merrills, *Human Rights in Europe*, at 311.

[29] Protocol to the African Charter of Human and Peoples' Rights on the Establishment of an African Court of Human and Peoples' Rights, adopted 9 June 1998, Art. 27(1).

[30] American Convention, Art. 63(1).

[31] *Trujillo Oroza* v. *Bolivia* (Reparations), Inter-Am. Ct HR, 27 February 2002, Ser. C, No. 92, para. 54; *Bámaca Velásquez* (Merits), Inter-Am. Ct HR, 25 November 2000, Ser. C, No. 70, para. 160; *Garrido and Baigorria* (Reparations, 1998), para. 50.

[32] 2001 Rules of Procedure of the Inter-Am. Ct HR, entered into force on 1 June 2001, approved by the Court at its forty-ninth regular session held 25 November 2000, Art. 2(15).

family or dependants of the direct victim'.[33] The European Commission also defined the term 'victim' as 'not only the direct victim or victims of the alleged violation, but also any person who would indirectly suffer prejudice as a result of such violation or who would have a valid personal interest in securing the cessation of such violation'.[34]

The Court especially considers that forced disappearances cause the family of the disappeared person suffering and anguish, a sense of insecurity, and frustration and impotence due to the authorities' failure to investigate.[35] In this regard, the Court has stated that, when a person is forcibly disappeared, 'the violation of the mental and moral integrity of the next of kin is precisely a direct consequence of the forced disappearance'.[36] For example, in the *Blake Case*, in which the State was held responsible for a denial of justice in covering up the disappearance and death of the victim, but not for the victim's death due to lack of jurisdiction *ratione temporis*, the Court held that the deceased's family members were the direct victims of the denial of justice, and thus the injured parties.[37] In the *Street Children Case*, the Court also considered the mothers of the murdered youths to be direct victims of the State's violation of their rights to a fair trial and judicial protection.[38] In that case, the Court held that the deceased and their representatives were prevented from exercising their right to 'effective recourse' before a competent domestic tribunal and were, therefore, direct victims of that violation.[39]

The damages caused to the family or other dependants by the death or permanent disappearance of a victim can be claimed by them in their own right.[40] Although the burden of proof is on the person claiming damages, there is a presumption that immediate family, including spouse, children, parents and siblings, suffer moral damages for egregious human

[33] GA Res. 40/34, UN GAOR 3rd Comm., 40th Sess., Annex, para. 2, UN Doc. A/C.3/40/L.21 (1985).

[34] *X* v. *Federal Republic of Germany*, App. No. 4185/69, 35 Eur. Comm. HR, DR 140, 142 (1970); see also *Koolen* v. *Belgium*, App. No. 1478/62, 13 Eur. Comm. HR, DR 71, 89 (1963). See A. A. Cançado Trindade, 'Co-existence and Co-ordination of Mechanisms of International Protection of Human Rights (at Global and Regional Levels)', 202 *Recueil des Cours* 9, 265–6 (1987); van Dijk and van Hoof, *Theory and Practice*, at 56.

[35] *Blake* v. *Guatemala* (Merits, 1998), para. 114, cited in *Bámaca Velásquez* (Merits, 2000), para. 160.

[36] *Ibid.* [37] *Blake* v. *Guatemala* (Reparations, 1999), para. 38.

[38] *Villagrán Morales et al.* v. *Guatemala (The Street Children Case)* (Merits), Inter-Am. Ct HR, 19 November 1999, Ser. C, No. 63, para 238.

[39] *Ibid.*, para. 236. [40] *Trujillo Oroza* v. *Bolivia* (Reparations, 2002), para. 56.

rights violations committed against the direct victim.[41] The presumption shifts the burden to the State. The Inter-American Court has cited with approval the factors considered by the European Court of Human Rights in determining whether the next of kin of a direct victim are also victims of a human rights violation. These factors include 'the closeness of the family relationship, the particular circumstances of the relationship with the victim, the degree to which the family member was a witness of the events related to the disappearance, the way in which the family member was involved in attempts to obtain information about the disappearance of the victim and the State's response to the steps undertaken'.[42]

In accordance with traditional principles on causation, the Inter-American Court holds that the State must make reparations solely to those persons who suffer the immediate effects of its unlawful acts. The Court stated that '[t]o compel the perpetrator of an illicit act to erase all the consequences produced by his action is completely impossible, since that action caused effects that multiplied to a degree that cannot be measured'.[43] Consequently, the Court has not awarded reparations to all those who have claimed to be injured by the State's breach of its human rights violations. The Court has ruled, however, that the State's obligation to make reparation is sometimes extended to persons who are not immediate family of the victims, but who suffered some consequence of the unlawful act.[44] This category of claimant the Court referred to as 'dependants'.[45] Examples might include other relatives or companions who were supported by the victim.

The Court has established a three-pronged test to determine whether the claim of a non-successor dependant will be honoured. First, the victim must have previously made payments to the claimant, even if the victim did not have a legal obligation to pay such support.[46] These payments must have been 'regular, periodic payments either in cash, in kind, or in services'.[47] A 'series of sporadic contributions' would not be sufficient to meet this criterion.[48] Secondly, 'the nature of the relationship between the victim and the claimant should be such that it provides some basis for

[41] *Ibid.*

[42] *Bámaca Velásquez* (Merits, 2000), para. 163, citing *Timurtas* v. *Turkey*, ECHR, Judgment of 13 June 2000, para. 95; and *Çakici* v. *Turkey*, ECHR Judgment of 8 July 1999, para. 98.

[43] *Aloeboetoe et al.* v. *Suriname* (Reparations), Inter-Am. Ct HR, 10 September 1993, Ser. C, No. 15, para. 48. But see Dinah Shelton, 'The Jurisprudence of the Inter-American Court of Human Rights', 10 *American University Journal of International Law and Policy*, 333, 363–4 (1994).

[44] *Aloeboetoe et al.* v. *Suriname* (Reparations, 1993), para. 67.

[45] *Ibid.*, para. 71. [46] *Ibid.*, para. 68. [47] *Ibid.* [48] *Ibid.*

the assumption that the payments would have continued had the victim not been killed'.[49] Thirdly, the claimant must have had a financial need that was met by the contributions of the victim.[50] The Court clarified that '[t]his does not necessarily mean that the person should be indigent, but only that it be somebody for whom the payment represented a benefit that, had it not been for the victim's attitude, it would not have been able to obtain on his or her own'.[51] The Court's test for non-successor dependants is equitable in that it compensates those who can prove that they suffered a serious loss as a result of the victim's death.

The Inter-American Court has refused to expand the principle of injured party beyond that of the victim's next of kin and dependants. In the *Aloeboetoe Case*, for instance, the Court did not act on the request of the Commission to award moral damages to the Saramaca tribe as a whole.[52] The Commission argued that the members of the tribe 'constitute a family in the broad sense of that term',[53] and thus should have been awarded moral damages. The Commission reasoned that tribal society is unique in that a person is a member of the family group, the village community and the tribe.[54] The Court, however, did not attribute special significance to the tribal culture: rather, it found that all persons are members of families and citizens of a State, and also belong to intermediate communities[55] and that moral compensation does not extend to such communities.[56] Thus, the Court is unlikely to expand the concept of injured party to include the community itself, even when a State has undertaken a systematic practice of gross violations of human rights designed to intimidate the community into submissiveness.[57] In such instances, there is an argument that the community is a victim to which it may be appropriate to award damages.

The Inter-American Commission attempts to ensure that more victims are treated equitably in that it refers cases to the Court involving multiple victims. For instance, in the *Baena Ricardo et al. Case*, the victims were 270 workers who had been discharged from their jobs.[58] In the *Hilaire,*

[49] *Ibid.* [50] *Ibid.*

[51] *Ibid.* See also *Paniagua Morales et al.* v. *Guatemala* (Reparations, 2001), para. 85.

[52] *Aloeboetoe et al.* v. *Suriname* (Reparations, 1993), para. 83.

[53] *Ibid.*, para. 19. [54] *Ibid.* [55] *Ibid.*, para. 83. [56] *Ibid.*

[57] See Cecilia Medina Quiroga, *The Battle of Human Rights: Gross Systematic Violations and the Inter-American System*, at 16 (Kluwer, 1988); Report of the Commission on Truth for El Salvador, 'From Madness to Hope: The 12-Year War in El Salvador', 10 (United Nations, 1993); National Commission for the Protection of Human Rights, 'The Facts Speak for Themselves: Preliminary Report on the Disappeared in Honduras 1980–1993', at 217–18 (1994).

[58] *Baena Ricardo et al. (270 Workers* v. *Panama)* (Merits, 2001).

Constantine and Benjamin et al. Cases, the victims were thirty-two prisoners on death row in Trinidad and Tobago.[59] The Commission's Rules of Procedure provide that most cases in which the State has not complied with Commission recommendations will be sent to the Court,[60] and the Court's Rules allow for joinder of similar cases.[61] Despite these attempts at providing justice for more victims, the reality of the situation remains that only a few victims receive State reparations ordered by the Inter-American Court. This can be viewed as a failure of the system. Van Boven, however, argues positively that international tribunals 'can play a vital role for the benefit of those persons whose rights are immediately affected but also, in a wider sense, as catalysts to influence the international and domestic legal orders in favour of larger sectors of victimized people'.[62]

The goal of full restitution (*restitutio in integrum*)

The Inter-American Court holds that:

> reparation for damage caused by a breach of an international obligation requires, whenever possible, full restitution (*restitutio in integrum*), which consists of reestablishing the previous situation. If that [is] not possible, the international court must order that steps be taken to guarantee the rights infringed, redress the consequences of the infringements, and determine payment of indemnification as compensation for damage caused.[63]

The Court has also specified that *restitutio in integrum* may include compensation, satisfaction and assurances that the violations will not be repeated.[64] The reparations awarded under this principle must be proportionate to the injury caused by the violations.[65]

59 *Hilaire, Constantine and Benjamin et al.* v. *Trinidad and Tobago* (Merits), Inter-Am. Ct HR, 21 June 2002, Ser. C, No. 94, para. 58.

60 See 2001 Rules of Procedure of the Inter-American Commission on Human Rights, approved by the Commission at its 109th special session held on 4–8 December 2000, entered into force 1 May 2001, Art. 44(1).

61 2001 Rules of Procedure of the Inter-Am. Ct HR, Art. 28.

62 Van Boven, 'Reparations: A Requirement of Justice', in *El Sistema Interamericano de Protección de los Derechos Humanos en el Umbral del Siglo XXI: Memoria del Seminario Noviembre de 1999*, vol. I, 653, at 656 (2001).

63 *Barrios Altos (Chumbipuma Aguirre et al.* v. *Peru)* (Reparations), Inter-Am. Ct HR, 30 November 2001, Ser. C, No. 87, para. 25; see also *Cesti Hurtado* v. *Peru* (Reparations), Inter-Am. Ct HR, 31 May 2001, Ser. C, No. 78, para. 33; *Paniagua Morales et al.* v. *Guatemala* (Reparations, 2001), para. 76; *Velásquez Rodríguez* v. *Honduras* (Compensatory Damages, 1989), para. 26.

64 *Castillo Páez* v. *Peru* (Reparations, 1998), para. 48.

65 *Ibid.*, para. 51.

In certain cases, however, the Court has stated that *restitutio in integrum* 'may not be possible, sufficient or appropriate'.[66] Full restitution is not 'possible', for example, in the case of an extrajudicial execution or a disappearance in which the victim is most likely deceased, because the Court cannot restore to the victim the enjoyment of the right to life that has been violated. When restitution is not possible, the Court will require that the State take a series of measures that, to the extent possible, repair the consequences of the violations and pay compensation for the injuries.

The Court has not explained when full restitution would not be 'appropriate'. Garcia-Amador stated in his study *The Changing Law of International Claims* that certain forms of reparations may not be appropriate if they prove 'incompatible with the municipal law of the respondent state, offend national honor and dignity, or [are] seriously out of proportion to the injury sustained or the character of the act or omission imputed to the State'.[67] Under these criteria, however, States could find that any form of satisfaction, such as the duty to investigate the violation and punish the violators, is inappropriate. State discretion of this magnitude would unduly limit the type of reparations that could be awarded for human rights violations. The law of international claims has evolved since Garcia-Amador's study. Although it remains true that the reparations ordered cannot be disproportionate to the injury, the domestic law of the offending State must now be amended to comply with the international commitments the State has violated. Moreover, the offence to the nation's honour and dignity should not be viewed as resulting from the reparations ordered, but rather from the violation that took place.

The State must ensure the injured party the enjoyment of the right or freedom violated

Article 63(1) of the American Convention authorizes the Inter-American Court to order the State to ensure that the victim be permitted to enjoy the right or freedom that the State violated.[68] In some instances, this could be viewed as a type of injunctive relief.[69] It is a form of reparation that is

[66] *Aloeboetoe et al.* v. *Suriname* (Reparations, 1993), para. 49 (emphasis in the original).

[67] F. V. Garcia-Amador, *The Changing Law of International Claims*, 596 (Oceana, New York, 1984).

[68] American Convention, Art. 63(1).

[69] See W. Michael Reisman, 'Compensation for Human Rights Violations: The Practice of the Past Decade in the Americas', in *State Responsibility and the Individual: Reparation in*

only available if the victim is living. Thus, if the victim is in prison, and the Court holds that the detention is illegal, the Court has the statutory authority to order the State to free the victim. For example, in the *Loayza Tamayo Case*, the victim, a female college professor, had been imprisoned since 1993.[70] She had been first tried in military courts before 'faceless judges' and then in civilian courts, in violation of the American Convention's prohibition of double jeopardy and other due process rights.[71] During her time in captivity, she was subject to cruel, inhuman and degrading treatment.[72] In its judgment of 17 September 1997 on the merits of the case, the Court ordered Peru 'in accordance with its domestic legislation, [to] order the release of Ms. María Elena Loayza-Tamayo within a reasonable time'.[73] On 20 October 1997, Peru informed the Court that she had been released from prison.[74]

When the victim's rights to due process have been violated, the Court can order that the State guarantee the victim a new trial, as it did in the *Castillo Petruzzi et al. Case*.[75] The Court also can order and has ordered that the victim be reinstated to former employment. In the *Baena Ricardo et al. Case*, in which the Court held that 270 Panamanian workers were wrongfully discharged from their jobs, the Court ordered that they be reinstated to their former employment or to commensurate positions with all benefits.[76] Similarly, in the *Loayza Tamayo Case*, the Court ordered the State to reinstate the victim to her former teaching positions.[77] The Court specified that she be reinstated with salary and benefits equal to those she received when she was arrested plus appreciation to the date of judgment and be guaranteed full retirement benefits, including those owed for the time of her detention.[78] These are efforts to ensure that the victim enjoy some of the rights violated.

Instances of Grave Violations of Human Rights, 65, at 73 (A. Randelzhofer and C. Tomuschat eds., 1999).

70 *Loayza Tamayo* v. *Peru* (Merits), Inter-Am. Ct HR, 17 September 1997, Ser. C, No. 33, para. 3.

71 *Ibid.*, para. 46 and Resolutions 1 and 3–4.

72 *Ibid.*, para. 56 and Resolution 2.

73 *Ibid.*, para. 84 and Resolution 5.

74 *Loayza Tamayo Case*, Letter from the State of Peru of 20 October 1997 concerning compliance with the Judgment of the Court, reprinted in 1997 Annual Report of the Inter-Am. Court, at 245.

75 *Castillo Petruzzi et al.* v. *Peru* (Merits), Inter-Am. Ct HR, 30 May 1999, Ser. C, No. 52, Resolution 13.

76 *Baena Ricardo et al. (270 Workers* v. *Panama)* (Merits, 2001), para. 203.

77 *Loayza Tamayo* v. *Peru* (Reparations, 1998), para. 113 and Resolution 1.

78 *Ibid.*, para. 113.

The State must take measures to remedy the consequences of the violation

Under the American Convention, the Court, if it is appropriate in a specific case, can order a State to take measures to remedy the consequences of the human rights violation.[79] Traditionally, those consequences were considered to be the injuries that had already been caused to the individual victim by the violation. Thus, the Court has required that the State provide medical care to a torture victim who continues to suffer health problems as a result of inhumane treatment, or the Court can order the State to exhume the victim's body and bring it to the location chosen by his family.[80] The law has evolved, however, to include in the remedy of the consequences of the violation a duty to deter future violations. If the State does not take action against the perpetrators of human rights violations, a direct consequence is that there is neither specific nor general deterrence and impunity prevails.

Duty to investigate, identify, publicize and punish

The Court holds that State action to investigate the facts of the violation and to punish those responsible 'constitute[s] a part of the reparation of the consequences of the violation of rights or freedoms'.[81] The Court consistently orders the State to thoroughly investigate the violation and to identify, prosecute and punish the violators.[82] The State's obligation in this respect persists until it has fully complied with this duty.[83] Moreover, the State's duty to investigate the violation must be undertaken:

> in a serious manner and not as a mere formality preordained to be ineffective. An investigation must have an objective and be assumed by the State as its own legal duty, not as a step taken by private interests that depends upon the initiative of the victim or his family or upon their offer of proof, without an effective search for the truth by the Government.[84]

[79] American Convention, Art. 63(1).

[80] *Paniagua Morales et al.* v. *Guatemala* (Reparations, 2001), para. 204.

[81] *Velásquez Rodríguez* v. *Honduras* (Compensatory Damages, 1989), para. 33.

[82] *Cantoral Benavides* v. *Peru* (Merits, 2000), operative para. 12; *Villagrán Morales et al.* v. *Guatemala (The Street Children Case)* (Merits, 1999), operative para. 8; *Paniagua Morales et al.* v. *Guatemala* (Reparations, 2001), operative para. 2; *Barrios Altos (Chumbipuma Aguirre et al.* v. *Peru)* (Merits), Inter-Am. Ct HR, Judgment of 14 March 2001, Ser. C, No. 75, operative para. 5.

[83] *Trujillo Oroza* v. *Bolivia* (Reparations, 2002), para. 111.

[84] *Bámaca Velásquez* v. *Guatemala* (Merits), Inter-Am. Ct HR, 25 November 2000, Ser. C, No. 70, para. 212, quoting *Villagrán Morales et al.* v. *Guatemala (The Street Children Case)* (Merits), Inter-Am. Ct HR, 19 November 1999, Ser. C, No. 63, para. 226.

The Court holds that the relatives of the victims have the right to know all the facts.[85] However, it has not adopted the principle that society has a right to the truth. In the *Bámaca Velásquez Case*, the Court held that the 'right to the truth is subsumed in the right of the victim or his next of kin to obtain clarification of the facts relating to the violations'.[86] As the Court limited its holding to the circumstances of the particular case, it is not clear whether, in the future, the Court will expand its jurisprudence to include a societal right to the truth.

The State's duty to investigate and identify those responsible includes a duty to publish the results of the investigation.[87] Publication of the results of the investigation will rehabilitate the reputations of the victims by revealing the truth of the violations. In some instances, States that abused human rights pursued policies that maligned victims by accusing them of being subversives, terrorists, enemies of the State or common criminals.[88] This practice was recognized in the decree that established the Chilean Truth Commission.[89] The decree explained the rationale underlying the rehabilitation of the victim's reputation in stating: 'only the knowledge of truth will restore the dignity of the victims in the public mind, allow their relatives and mourners to honor them fittingly, and in some measure make it possible to make amends for the damage done'.[90]

States are now voluntarily accepting the duty to clear the victim's reputation. In the *Benavides Cevallos Case*, Ecuador's agent before the Court said at the public hearing:

> I wish to state for the record that my country accepts and acknowledges its responsibility in the disappearance and death of Professor Consuelo Benavides Cevallos . . . [and that] the name of Professor Benavides has also been cleared in all the spoken and written media in [Ecuador], as the struggle that her family has waged for so many years to bring the truth to light has been publicized at all levels.[91]

This is a positive step in the evolution of respect for human rights.

[85] *Las Palmeras* v. *Colombia* (Merits), Inter-Am. Ct HR, 6 December 2001, Ser. C, No. 90, para. 69.

[86] *Bámaca Velásquez* v. *Guatemala* (Merits, 2000), para. 201.

[87] *Barrios Altos Case (Chumbipuma Aguirre et al.* v. *Peru)* (Merits, 2001), operative para. 5; *Bámaca Velásquez* v. *Guatemala* (Merits, 2000), operative para. 8.

[88] See *ibid.*, para. 93(a), expert testimony of Helen Mack.

[89] Decree Establishing the National Commission on Truth and Reconciliation, Supreme Decree No. 365 (25 April 1990), reprinted in *Report of the Chilean National Commission on Truth and Reconciliation* (Philip E. Barryman trans., 1993).

[90] *Ibid.*

[91] *Benavides Cevallos* v. *Ecuador* (Merits), Inter-Am. Ct HR, 19 June 1998, Ser. C, No. 38, para. 35.

The second prong of Article 63(1), that the consequences of the violation be remedied, encompasses the duty to punish human rights violators. The State must punish the 'intellectual authors' or 'masterminds' of the violation as well as the individuals who carried it out.[92] Punishment will also serve as a force against impunity by acting as both a specific and a general deterrent. The State has a duty to combat impunity by attempting to ensure that the type of violation attributed to it is not repeated in the future. The Court defines impunity as 'the total lack of investigation, prosecution, capture, trial and conviction of those responsible for violations of the rights protected by the American Convention'.[93] The Court reasons that the State is obliged to use all legal means to combat impunity, which if unchecked 'fosters chronic recidivism of human rights violations and total defenselessness of victims and their relatives'.[94] When State authorities have acted with impunity, a thorough investigation and publication of the facts of the violation will have a deterrent effect on both the individual perpetrators and others who would be dissuaded from committing similar violations. Van Boven explained that:

> [i]n many situations where impunity has been sanctioned by the law or where *de facto* impunity prevails with regard to persons responsible for gross violations of human rights, the victims are effectively barred from seeking and receiving redress and reparation. In fact, once the State authorities fail to investigate the facts and to establish criminal responsibility, it becomes very difficult for victims or their relatives to carry on effective legal proceedings aimed at obtaining just and adequate reparation.[95]

Where impunity persists, a victim's right to reparation for gross violations of human rights and fundamental freedoms 'is likely to become illusory'.[96]

[92] *Blake* v. *Guatemala* (Reparations, 1999), para. 55; *Constitutional Court* v. *Peru* (Merits, 2001), para. 123.

[93] *Constitutional Court* v. *Peru* (Merits, 2001), para. 123, quoting *Bámaca Velásquez* (Merits, 2000), para. 211.

[94] *Bámaca Velásquez* (Merits, 2000), para. 211, quoting *Paniagua Morales et al.* v. *Guatemala (The White Van Case)* (Merits, 1998), para. 173.

[95] Theo Van Boven, 'Study Concerning the Right to Restitution, Compensation and Rehabilitation for Victims of Gross Violations of Human Rights and Fundamental Freedoms', UN Human Rights Commission E/CN.4/Sub.2/1993/8 (2 July 1993), 16, para. 51.

[96] *Ibid.*, para. 130.

Court order that the State amend, adopt or repeal domestic laws or judgments

The scope of the Inter-American Court's authority under the American Convention to order the State to take measures to remedy the consequences of the violation is sufficiently broad to allow the Court to order the adoption, amendment or repeal of national laws or judgments. The American Convention provides that '[t]he States Parties to this Convention undertake to respect the rights and freedoms recognized herein and to ensure to all persons subject to their jurisdiction the free and full exercise of those rights and freedoms'.[97] The Court clarified that 'the general obligations of the State, established in Article 2 of the Convention, include the adoption of measures to suppress laws and practices of any kind that imply a violation of the guarantees established in the Convention, and also the adoption of laws and the implementation of practices leading to the effective observance of the said guarantees'.[98] Consequently, if the State has adopted a law or other measure that is incompatible with its international obligations under the American Convention, the Court will order the State to take the appropriate action to remedy the conflict. Even if the law in question has not been enforced against the victims in the case, the Court may find it to be *per se* in violation of the Convention.[99]

Measures to remedy the consequences of a human rights violation originally did not include those consequences that could possibly be caused in the future if the law that resulted in the measure continued in force.[100] This interpretation had the unfortunate result of requiring every subsequent victim of offending domestic laws to pursue fruitless and costly cases before national tribunals in order to exhaust domestic remedies,[101] and then to turn to the international human rights system to remedy the violation. It not only prolonged human misery but also caused a flood of similar cases before international human rights bodies. For instance, under this interpretation, if the Inter-American Court were to rule that a

[97] American Convention, Art. 1(1).

[98] *'The Last Temptation of Christ' (Olmedo Bustos et al.* v. *Chile)* (Merits), Inter-Am. Ct HR, 5 February 2001, Ser. C, No. 73, para. 85, quoted in *Trujillo Oroza* v. *Bolivia* (Reparations, 2002), para. 96.

[99] *Hilaire, Constantine and Benjamin et al.* v. *Trinidad and Tobago* (Merits, 2002), paras. 114–16.

[100] Garcia-Amador, *The Changing Law of International Claims*, at 583.

[101] A victim must first exhaust domestic remedies before he or she may file a complaint for international relief. See American Convention, Art. 46(1)(a).

domestic law violated the Convention by authorizing detention without adequate guarantees of due process, reparations would be limited to an order that the victim's prison term be annulled. The Court would not be authorized to order that the State amend the law. The domestic effect of the Court's ruling would then depend upon whether the State concerned adhered to a monistic or dualistic view of international law, and thus whether the Inter-American Court judgments were self-executing.[102] It is illogical and archaic that a domestic law, which has been declared in violation of a State's international legal obligations, should be allowed to remain in force. This limitation on the power of international human rights courts was a remnant of exaggerated State sovereignty.

Order to adopt laws or procedures

The American Convention mandates that 'the States Parties [must] undertake to adopt, in accordance with their constitutional processes and the provisions of this Convention, such legislative or other measures as may be necessary to give effect to those rights or freedoms'.[103] The Court explained that:

> [t]his general obligation of the State party implies that the measures of domestic law must be effective (the principle of *effet utile*). This means that the State must adopt all measures so that the provisions of the Convention are effectively fulfilled in its domestic legal system, as Article 2 of the Convention requires. Such measures are only effective when the State adjusts its actions to the Convention's rules of protection.[104]

Pursuant to this provision, in the *Trujillo Oroza Case* the Court ordered Bolivia to pass legislation, that was pending in the Bolivian Congress, to make forced disappearance a crime.[105] Likewise, in the *Paniagua Morales Case*, in which people had been taken into custody and then murdered by members of the national police, the Court ordered Guatemala to set up

[102] See generally Thomas Buergenthal, 'Self-Executing and Non-Self-Executing Treaties in National and International Law', 235 *Recueil des Cours*, 303 (1992). See also Thomas Buergenthal, 'International Tribunals and National Courts: The Internationalization of Domestic Adjudication', in *Recht Zwischen Umbruch und Bewahrung*, 687, 695–9 (Max-Planck, 1995), for a discussion of the Argentine Supreme Court's holding that a particular provision of the American Convention is directly self-executing in Argentina. *Ekmekdjian* v. *Sofovich*, Corte Suprema de Justicia de la Nación 315 Fallos 1492 (1992).

[103] American Convention, Art. 2.

[104] *'The Last Temptation of Christ' (Olmedo Bustos et al.* v. *Chile)* (Merits), Inter-Am. Ct HR, 5 February 2001, Ser. C, No. 73, para. 87, quoted in *Trujillo Oroza* v. *Bolivia* (Reparations, 2002), para. 96.

[105] *Trujillo Oroza* v. *Bolivia* (Reparations, 2002), para. 98, operative para. 2.

a registry of those who have been detained by the authorities.[106] In the *Mayagna (SUMO) Awas Tingni Community Case*, in which the Government of Nicaragua granted a forestry concession on lands claimed by an indigenous community, the Court ordered the State to adopt 'legislative, administrative, and any other measures necessary to create an effective mechanism for delimitation, demarcation, and titling of the property of indigenous communities, in accordance with their customary law, values, customs and mores'.[107]

Order to amend laws

The Court has taken the well-reasoned and statutorily justifiable position that, if the State has not voluntarily conformed its laws to the American Convention, it is within the scope of the Court's remedial authority to order the State to amend any law that violates the Convention. In this regard, the Court has stated that:

> [i]n international law, customary law establishes that a State which has ratified a human rights treaty must introduce the necessary modifications to its domestic law to ensure the proper compliance with the obligations it has assumed. This law is universally accepted, and is supported by jurisprudence. The American Convention establishes the general obligation of each State Party to adapt its domestic law to the provisions of this Convention, in order to guarantee the rights that it embodies.[108]

The Court reasoned that, if States have a positive obligation to adopt measures to guarantee human rights, 'it follows, then, that they also must refrain both from promulgating laws that disregard or impede the free exercise of these rights, and from suppressing or modifying the existing laws protecting them'.[109] Accordingly, in *'The Last Temptation of Christ' Case*,[110] the Court ordered Chile to take the appropriate measures to amend its domestic laws respecting prior censorship so as to protect the freedom of thought and expression protected by the American Convention.

[106] *Paniagua Morales et al.* v. *Guatemala* (Reparations, 2001), para. 203.

[107] *Mayagna (SUMO) Awas Tingni Community* v. *Nicaragua* (Merits), Inter-Am. Ct HR, 31 August 2001, Ser. C, No. 79, para. 164 and operative para. 3. See generally S. James Anaya and Robert A. Williams Jr, 'The Protection of Indigenous Peoples' Rights Over Lands and Natural Resources Under the Inter-American Human Rights System', 14 *Harvard Human Rights Journal*, 33, n. 20 (2001).

[108] *'The Last Temptation of Christ' (Olmedo Bustos et al.* v. *Chile)* (Merits, 2001), para. 87, quoted in *Trujillo Oroza* v. *Bolivia* (Reparations, 2002), para. 96.

[109] *Hilaire, Constantine and Benjamin et al.* v. *Trinidad and Tobago* (Merits, 2002), para. 113.

[110] *Ibid.*, paras. 97–8, operative para. 4.

Likewise, in the *Hilaire, Constantine and Benjamin et al. Case*, the Court ordered Trinidad and Tobago to modify the domestic law that mandatorily imposed the death penalty on any person convicted of murder, so as to bring it into compliance with the American Convention and other international norms.[111] In the *Loayza Tamayo* and *Castillo Petruzzi Cases*, the Court ordered Peru to adapt certain anti-terrorism and treason laws to conform to the American Convention.[112] Peru did comply with the Court's decision and amended the laws.[113]

The Court's orders to a State that it must conform its domestic laws to the American Convention are general in nature. Typically, they do not specify the exact means required of the State to meet its international obligations. The State, in its sovereignty, is allowed a margin of appreciation as to what measures it will take. For example, in the *Street Children Case*, the Court held that Guatemala had a duty to implement legislative, administrative or whatever other measures were necessary to conform its domestic law to protect the rights of the child as set forth in Article 19 of the American Convention.[114] The Court generally will not substitute its judgment for that of the State to determine which measures would be most appropriate. In the *Street Children Case*, the Court stated that it could not establish what measures the State must take to fulfil the requirements of the Convention.[115]

Declaration that domestic law lacks legal effect

The Court is also empowered to declare that a domestic law in violation of the American Convention lacks legal effect.[116] In this regard, the Court holds that laws granting amnesty for grave violations of human rights are in violation of the Convention.[117] In the *Barrios Altos Case*, the Court held that Peru's amnesty laws, which grant immunity to the perpetrators of human rights violations, are incompatible with the American Convention and, therefore, are without legal effect.[118] The Court took a broad stance against amnesty laws, stating:

[111] *Hilaire, Constantine and Benjamin et al.* v. *Trinidad and Tobago* (Merits, 2002), paras. 86 and 212 and operative para. 8.

[112] *Loayza Tamayo* v. *Peru* (Reparations, 1998), operative para. 5; *Castillo Petruzzi et al.* v. *Peru* (Merits, 1999), operative para. 14.

[113] *Cantoral Benavides* v. *Peru* (Reparations, 2001), para. 76.

[114] *Villagrán Morales et al.* v. *Guatemala (The Street Children Case)* (Reparations), Inter-Am. Ct HR, 26 May 2001, Ser. C, No. 77, para. 98.

[115] *Ibid.*

[116] *Barrios Altos (Chumbipuma Aguirre et al.* v. *Peru)* (Merits), Inter-Am. Ct HR, 14 March 2001, Ser. C, No. 75, operative para. 4.

[117] *Ibid.*, para. 41.

[118] *Ibid.*, operative para. para. 4.

> [t]his Court considers that all amnesty provisions, provisions on prescription [statutes of limitation] and the establishment of measures designed to eliminate responsibility are inadmissible, because they are intended to prevent the investigation and punishment of those responsible for serious human rights violations such as torture, extrajudicial, summary, or arbitrary execution and forced disappearance, all of them prohibited because they violate non-derogable rights recognized by human rights law.[119]

The Court subsequently quoted this language in the *Trujillo Oroza Case*, in which Bolivia had released from custody the defendants, who were charged with torturing and forcibly disappearing the victim, because the statute of limitations had run.[120]

The Court's ruling on amnesty laws provides international judicial precedent which supports individuals, organizations and authorities that are battling impunity domestically. The Bolivian State welcomed an internationally mandated solution to its domestic problem of impunity. In its reparations brief to the Court in the *Trujillo Oroza Case*, Bolivia declared that it did not object to the trial of those charged with the forced disappearance of the victim, although they had been released pursuant to domestic law, or to a Court-ordered solution whereby the judgment of the Inter-American Court would amend or modify the decisions of the domestic courts.[121]

Authority to rule on existing domestic law if the State accepts responsibility

The Court has resolved that, even when the State accepts responsibility for a human rights violation, the Court will rule on an existing domestic law that allegedly violates the American Convention. In the *Barrios Altos Case*, although Peru accepted international responsibility, the Court held that Peru's amnesty laws contravened the American Convention and were thus without legal effect.[122] In earlier cases, the Court had not assessed the compatibility of the laws in question, such as the Venezuelan Code of Military Justice in the *El Amparo Case*, after the State acknowledged responsibility.[123]

Once a claim that a domestic law violates an individual's human rights is before the Court, the Court has a duty to those who may become future

[119] *Ibid.*, para. 41.

[120] *Trujillo Oroza* v. *Bolivia* (Reparations, 2002), para. 106; see also *Del Caracazo* v. *Venezuela* (Reparations), Inter-Am. Ct HR, 29 August 2002, Ser. C, No. 95, para. 119.

[121] *Ibid.*, para. 93(a).

[122] *Barrios Altos* v. *Peru* (Merits, 2001), para. 41.

[123] *El Amparo* v. *Venezuela* (Merits), Inter-Am. Ct HR, 18 January 1995, Ser. C, No. 19, para. 4.

victims of the law and to the development of human rights law to rule on its compatibility with the State's international obligations. This is necessary although a State may be more likely to accept international responsibility if it can thereby avoid such a decision of the Court.

No action if the domestic law or judgment is no longer in effect

When a domestic law that contravenes the American Convention has already been repealed or is no longer in effect at the time of the Court's ruling, the Court holds that the issue is moot and there is no need for the Court to take further action. For example, in the *Ivcher Bronstein Case*, Peru had already acted upon a Commission recommendation and had nullified the resolution that had abrogated the victim's Peruvian citizenship.[124] Therefore, the Court considered the Commission's request for a Court ruling on the law to be immaterial. Similarly, in the *Suárez Rosero Case*, in which the Court had held in its judgment on the merits that a provision of the Ecuadorian Criminal Code was in violation of the American Convention, the Court did not take measures in the reparations stage because the Ecuadoran Constitutional Court had already declared the provision to be unconstitutional.[125] Likewise, in the *Baena Ricardo Case*, the law providing for retroactive application against the workers was no longer in force.[126] In such instances, the Court will merely pronounce that a former domestic law was in violation of the American Convention but take no further action.[127] Such a ruling may be effective in inhibiting the promulgation of future similar laws in the offending State or in other States. No other measures are useful or necessary. When appropriate, the State should be commended for bringing its domestic law into compliance with its international obligations.

Court order to annul or execute a domestic judgment or ruling

The State's duty extends not only to laws but also to 'other measures'.[128] As such, the Court can order the State to annul a domestic judgment or ruling that was issued in violation of the State's obligations under the American Convention. In the *Cesti Hurtado Case*, the Court held that the

[124] *Ivcher Bronstein* v. *Peru* (Merits), Inter-Am. Ct HR, 6 February 2001, Ser. C, No. 74, para. 179.

[125] *Suárez Rosero* v. *Ecuador* (Reparations) (Art. 63(1) American Convention on Human Rights), Inter-Am. Ct HR, 20 January 1999, Ser. C, No. 44, paras. 81–3.

[126] *Baena Ricardo et al. (270 Workers* v. *Panama)* (Merits, 2001), para. 211.

[127] *Ibid.*, para. 211; *Ivcher Bronstein* v. *Peru* (Merits, 2001), para. 179.

[128] American Convention, Art. 2.

proceeding against the victim in the military justice system was incompatible with the American Convention.[129] The Court, therefore, ordered Peru to annul the action and any and all effects deriving from it to the detriment of the victim.[130] During a subsequent stage of the proceedings, the State notified the Court that 'the orders against [Mr. Cesti] that restricted his freedom and embargoed his property are suspended'.[131] Also, in the *Cantoral Benavides Case*, the Court held that the victim had been subjected to proceedings based on a law that was incompatible with the American Convention.[132] Consequently, it ordered the State to nullify his conviction and 'all judicial or administrative, criminal, or police proceedings against [him] in connection with the events of the present case and [to] expunge the corresponding records'.[133] In the *Loayza Tamayo Case*, the Court ordered the State to take all necessary internal legal measures to ensure that no decision against the victim had any adverse legal effect.[134]

The Court may also order the State to execute a domestic decision. In the *Cesti Hurtado Case*, the Court found that a petition for *habeas corpus* met the requirements established by the American Convention.[135] The decision granting *habeas corpus* had been issued by the Public Law Chamber of Lima, the competent tribunal in the domestic case, but the State had refused to execute it for over two years.[136] In its decision on the merits, the Court ordered the State to execute the domestic *habeas corpus* decision.[137] The *habeas corpus* decision was executed, and Cesti Hurtado was released from prison before the reparations stage of the case.[138]

Order to the State to take action or refrain from taking action

The Inter-American Court can order a State to take specific action or to refrain from taking action. For example, in the *Hilaire, Constantine and Benjamin et al. Case*, the Court ordered Trinidad and Tobago to retry the

[129] *Cesti Hurtado* v. *Peru* (Merits), Inter-Am. Ct HR, 29 September 1999, Ser. C, No. 56, operative para. 8.

[130] *Ibid.* [131] *Ibid.*

[132] *Cantoral Benavides* v. *Peru* (Reparations), Inter-Am. Ct HR, 3 December 2001, Ser. C, No. 88, para. 77.

[133] *Ibid.*, paras. 77 and 78.

[134] *Loayza Tamayo* v. *Peru* (Reparations, 1998), operative para. 3.

[135] *Cesti Hurtado* v. *Peru* (Merits, 1999), para. 193. [136] *Ibid.* [137] *Ibid.*

[138] *Cesti Hurtado* v. *Peru* (Request for Interpretation of the Judgment of 29 September 1999), Inter-Am. Ct HR, Order of 19 November 1999, Ser. C, No. 62, para. 6, OEA/Ser.L/V/III.47, doc. 6, 24 January 2000.

thirty-one petitioners who were on death row, to refrain from executing them regardless of the results of the new trials, and to improve its prison conditions to comply with international human rights standards.[139] In *Cantos*, the Court ordered Argentina to refrain from charging the victim domestic court costs and a fine for their late payment.[140] In the *Mayagna (SUMO) Awas Tingni Community* v. *Nicaragua Case*, the Court ordered Nicaragua to demarcate and title the lands of the indigenous community[141] and to refrain from any actions that would affect the use, value or enjoyment of the land in the geographical area claimed by the community until after the boundary of its property was established.[142] The Court has also ordered States to take some well-publicized action which would serve to verify that those who were killed or who remain disappeared were innocent victims. In the *Street Children Case*, the Court ordered Guatemala to name an education centre after the victims and to place a plaque in the centre with their names.[143] The Court reasoned that the centre would memorialize the victims. It would also serve to awaken the conscience of the nation and thus avoid the repetition of crimes against street children in the future. In the *Trujillo Oroza Case*, the Court ordered Bolivia to fulfil its offer to name a school for the victim.[144] Victims' families have long requested this type of satisfaction from the Court. This is another step in the direction of humanizing reparations in international human rights law, going beyond the order to pay monetary compensation.

When confronted with victims who have been forcibly disappeared, the Court has ordered the State to remedy the consequences of the violation to the extent possible, by using all means available to inform the families of the victim's fate and to locate the remains.[145] If the victim was extrajudicially executed and buried in an unmarked grave, the Court has ordered the State to exhume the body of the victim, to return it to the family at

[139] *Hilaire, Constantine and Benjamin et al.* v. *Trinidad and Tobago* (Merits, 2002), para. 217 and operative paras. 9, 11 and 14.

[140] *Cantos* v. *Argentina* (Merits), Inter-Am. Ct HR, 28 November 2002, Ser. C, No. 96, para. 70(a) and Resolution 1.

[141] *Mayagna (SUMO) Awas Tingni Community* v. *Nicaragua* (Merits, 2001), para. 164.

[142] *Ibid.*

[143] *Villagrán Morales et al.* v. *Guatemala (The Street Children Case)* (Reparations, 2001), paras. 103 and 115(7).

[144] *Trujillo Oroza* v. *Bolivia* (Reparations, 2002), operative paras. 6 and 4.

[145] *Aloeboetoe et al.* v. *Suriname* (Reparations, 1993), para. 109 (quoting *Godínez Cruz* v. *Honduras* (Merits), Inter-Am. Ct HR, 29 January 1989, Ser. C, No. 5, para. 191 and *Velásquez Rodríguez* v. *Honduras* (Merits, 1988), para. 181).

the State's expense and to pay burial expenses.[146] In the *Street Children Case*, in which the tortured bodies of the victims had been dumped in an uninhabited area and exposed to inclement weather and animals, the Court ordered that the bodies be returned to the families at no cost to them.[147] The Court reasoned that the families have a right to bury the victims in accordance with their customs and religious beliefs.[148]

Other acts would be beneficial and would serve as a general deterrent. The Court could order the State to provide training in human rights to its police and military personnel. There is some precedent for this in that the Inter-American Convention to Prevent and Punish Torture requires that States Parties take measures in police training to emphasize the prohibition of torture.[149] Also, although the Court has not ordered a State to ratify relevant international conventions, States have voluntarily offered to do so as one means of reparation. In the *Benavides Cevallos Case*, Ecuador stated that it welcomed the Commission's recommendation that it ratify the Inter-American Convention on Forced Disappearance of Persons in the interest of deterrence.[150] Likewise, in the voluntary agreement reached between the victims' representatives and the State in the *Barrios Altos Case*, Peru agreed to promote ratification of the International Convention on the Non-Applicability of Statutory Limitations to War Crimes and Crimes Against Humanity.[151]

Apology as satisfaction

A State can remedy, to some small extent, the consequences of the violation by apologizing to the victim or the family of a deceased victim. An official apology provides acknowledgment of State responsibility for the human rights violation. Under the international law of State responsibility for injury to aliens, an official State apology is a form of satisfaction. The

146 *Las Palmeras* v. *Colombia* (Reparations), Inter-Am. Ct HR, Judgment of 26 November 2002, paras. 76–7 and Resolution 4. See also *Villagrán Morales et al.* v. *Guatemala (The Street Children Case)* (Reparations, 2001), para. 102; *Paniagua Morales et al.* v. *Guatemala* (Reparations, 2001), operative para. 3.

147 *Villagrán Morales et al.* v. *Guatemala (The Street Children Case)* (Reparations, 2001), para. 102.

148 *Ibid.*

149 Inter-American Convention to Prevent and Punish Torture, signed at Cartagena de Indias, Colombia, on 9 December 1985 at the fifteenth regular session of the General Assembly of the OAS, entered into force on 28 February 1987, Art. 7.

150 *Benavides Cevallos* v. *Ecuador* (Merits, 1998), para. 52.

151 *Barrios Altos (Chumbipuma Aguirre et al.* v. *Peru)* (Reparations, 2001), para. 44(c).

apology is extended from one State to another, and not from a State to an injured individual.[152] International law has evolved over time, and States now have direct obligations to individuals as well as to other sovereign States. The time has come in the history of human rights litigation for a Court to require that the State publicly apologize to the victim or the family of a deceased victim for the violation of the victim's human rights. The Inter-American Court has taken this next step. In the *Cantoral Benavides Case*, in which a young man was illegally imprisoned and tortured by State agents, the Court ordered the State to 'make a public apology acknowledging its responsibility'.[153]

It is a sign of the true advancement of human rights when a State accepts international responsibility, and, as an act of grace, voluntarily and publicly apologizes to the victim or the family. Bolivia voluntarily accepted international responsibility for the disappearance of the victim in the *Trujillo Oroza Case* and informed the Court in the public hearing that it had sent a written apology to the victim's family.[154] Likewise, Peru volunteered to publicly apologize to the victims in the *Durand and Ugarte*[155] and the *Barrios Altos Cases*.[156] Bolivia and Peru should be commended for taking this step in promoting civility in the resolution of human rights violations. A Court order to apologize to a victim may be more acceptable to States in the future as other States have voluntarily apologized to the families of victims. An apology should not be considered a blemish on the honour of the State; it should instead be a mark of integrity for the State to disavow abusive acts and express its regret that those acts were perpetrated in its jurisdiction.

State must pay fair compensation

The Inter-American Court has the authority to order the State to pay the victim 'fair compensation'.[157] The amount of compensation that the

[152] Garcia-Amador, *The Changing Law of International Claims*, at 569.

[153] *Cantoral Benavides* v. *Peru* (Reparations, 2001), para. 81.

[154] *Trujillo Oroza* v. *Bolivia* (Merits), Inter-Am. Ct HR, 26 January 2000, Ser. C, No. 64, para. 37.

[155] *Durand and Ugarte* v. *Peru* (Reparations), Inter-Am. Ct HR, 3 December 2001, Ser. C, No. 92, para. 39(b).

[156] *Barrios Altos (Chumbipuma Aguirre et al.* v. *Peru)* (Reparations, 2001), para. 44(e).

[157] American Convention, Art. 63(1). A discrepancy exists between the meaning of the term 'justa indemnización' in Spanish and its translation to 'fair compensation' in English. Reisman opined that the term should be interpreted to mean a 'lawful measure' of compensation. Reisman, 'Compensation for Human Rights Violations', at 73.

Court may order a State to pay to the victims of human rights abuse is determined by the 'American Convention and the applicable principles of international law'.[158] It is not 'limited by the defects, imperfections or deficiencies of national law'.[159] In the *Velásquez Rodríguez Case*, the Court rejected Honduras' argument that the amount of compensation paid to the victim's next of kin should be based on the most favourable benefits provided by Honduran legislation in the case of accidental death.[160] Although the Court does consider information on national wage rates, actuarial tables, etc., in determining the compensation to award, it does not limit itself to the remedy available under domestic law.[161] The Court does not have complete discretion in determining the amount of compensation for actual damages; rather, it must adhere to the ordinary methods established in case law to determine the award.[162]

The Inter-American Commission, when attributing a human rights violation to a State, often makes a general recommendation in its final report that the State pay compensation. The Commission does not, however, determine the amount of compensation owing. The Commission relies on the State's domestic law to determine the amount that should be paid. Although there is no official information available, Reisman stated that, to his knowledge, no State has ever paid victim compensation in compliance with a Commission recommendation.[163] If the Commission were to award a specific amount of compensation, which was in line with an amount likely to be ordered by the Court, it might stimulate settlement efforts.

Material damages (pecuniary damages)

The Court generally awards compensation for material damages. As generally understood, the term 'material damages', or 'pecuniary damages', may include loss of earnings, medical expenses, the costs incurred in searching for the victim when State authorities engage in a cover-up and fail to investigate, and other expenses of a pecuniary character that are caused by the violation.[164] Shelton defines pecuniary losses to include 'the value of the very thing to which the plaintiff was entitled and any

158 *Velásquez Rodríguez* v. *Honduras* (Compensatory Damages, 1989), para. 31.
159 *Ibid.*, para. 30. 160 *Ibid.*, para. 43. 161 *Ibid.*, para. 46.
162 *Aloeboetoe et al.* v. *Suriname* (Reparations, 1993), para. 87.
163 Reisman, 'Compensation for Human Rights Violations', at 71.
164 See *Trujillo Oroza* v. *Bolivia* (Reparations, 2002), para. 74(a).

special/consequential harms or losses, such as lost profits, resulting from harm to the thing to which the plaintiff was entitled'.[165]

Loss of earnings and benefits

Compensation for the victim's loss of earnings, *lucro cessans*, is one form of actual damages. The Inter-American Court maintains that compensation should be granted for the injury suffered by the victim of human rights violations during the period when he or she was unable to work due to the actions or omissions of the State.[166] Calculations of lost wages can be particularly complex, especially if the victim is partially disabled and can work only at a job paying less than he or she previously earned. Moreover, if the victim worked at another job while awaiting judgment, those earnings should be subtracted from the amount of lost wages owing. There could also be questions concerning mitigation of damages. The Inter-American Court has also awarded lost earnings to family members who left their jobs to search for their missing relatives.[167] For example, the Court awarded Jennifer Harbury, the wife of Bámaca Velásquez, compensation for her lost earnings for the period during which she gave up her job to search for her missing husband.[168]

Calculation of loss of earnings When a surviving victim has been unable to work due to the human rights violation, compensation for lost wages is based on the time the victim was unemployed and the actual wages and other benefits they failed to receive during that time.[169] This situation could occur when a victim has been disabled either temporarily or permanently due to actions attributable to the State, when the victim was wrongfully imprisoned,[170] or when the victim was illegally dismissed from his or her job.

When the victim has died as a result of the human rights violation, the Court will base its calculations on evidence of the victim's age and life expectancy at the time of death and the victim's actual salary.[171] The

[165] Dinah Shelton, *Remedies in International Human Rights Law* (Oxford, 1999).

[166] *Bámaca Velásquez* v. *Guatemala* (Reparations), Inter-Am. Ct HR 22 February 2002, Ser. C, No. 91, para. 54(a).

[167] *Ibid.* [168] *Ibid.*

[169] *Constitutional Court Case* (Merits, 2001), para. 120; *Suárez Rosero* v. *Ecuador* (Reparations, 1999), para. 59; *El Amparo* v. *Venezuela* (Reparations, 1996), para. 28; *Baena Ricardo et al. (270 Workers* v. *Panama)* (Merits, 2001), para. 205.

[170] *Loayza Tamayo* v. *Peru* (Reparations, 1998), paras. 3 and 113.

[171] *El Amparo* v. *Venezuela* (Reparations, 1996), para. 28; *Neira Alegría et al.* v. *Peru* (Reparations), Inter-Am. Ct HR, 19 September 1996, Ser. C, No. 29, para. 49.

victim's life expectancy is based on official tables that estimate the number of additional years the victim would have lived had he or she died a natural death, taking into account the data on the victim's age, sex and geographic zone of residence.[172] Tables estimating life expectancy at the victim's birth are not adequate due to the high rate of infant mortality in some underdeveloped countries in the system.[173] If reliable information about the victim's actual salary is not available, and there is no evidence that the victim had any skill or training, the Court employs the presumption that the victim would have earned the equivalent of the minimum wage in the State.[174] The Court calculated lost earnings of the street children killed in the *Villagrán Morales Case* based on Guatemala's minimum wage, even though the victims had not been regularly employed at the time of their deaths.[175] In the *Neira Alegría Case*, the Court was not provided with official figures on the minimum wage in Peru; citing equity and the actual economic and social situation, the Court estimated the probable income of the victims.[176]

The Court has also based its determination of lost wages on equitable factors when it has not been able to determine the nature of the victim's employment had he lived.[177] If the parties do not produce adequate evidence, and the level at which the victim would have been employed cannot be established, the Court will determine lost wages based on the principles of equity and the actual economic and social situation in Latin America.[178] In the *Bámaca Velásquez Case*, the victim was a thirty-five-year old guerilla leader who had played a part in negotiating the Guatemalan peace accords.[179] He had left his native Mam Indian village to join the guerrillas at the age of eighteen. His only work until that time had been as an uneducated labourer in the fields.[180] The State argued that his lost wages should be based on the wages of an agricultural worker.[181] However, a Mayan indigenous leader and former Guatemalan congressional representative testified that, had Bámaca Velásquez lived, he could have been involved in politics after the peace accords.[182] As there was no

[172] *Paniagua Morales et al.* v. *Guatemala* (Reparations, 2001), para. 68. [173] *Ibid.*

[174] *Del Caracazo* v. *Venezuela* (Reparations, 2002), para. 50(d); see also *El Amparo* v. *Venezuela* (Reparations, 1996), para. 28; *Neira Alegría et al.* v. *Peru* (Reparations, 1996), para. 49.

[175] *Villagrán Morales et al.* v. *Guatemala (The Street Children Case)* (Reparations, 2001), para. 79.

[176] *Neira Alegría et al.* v. *Peru* (Reparations, 1996), para. 50.

[177] *Bámaca Velásquez* v. *Guatemala* (Reparations, 2002), para. 51(b).

[178] *Neira Alegría et al.* v. *Peru* (Reparations, 1996), paras. 49–50.

[179] *Bámaca Velásquez* v. *Guatemala* (Reparations, 2002), para. 29.

[180] *Ibid.* [181] *Ibid.*, para. 48(a). [182] *Ibid.*, para. 54(d).

certain evidence to assist the Court in a determination of the victim's prospective occupation and earnings, the Court set the amount based on equitable principles.[183]

Alternatively, the Court has based its calculations on the *canasta alimentaria basica* (basic food basket), a measure based on the consumer price index for subsistence goods, if that measure is higher than the minimum wage in the area.[184] Whichever measure the Court applies in determining the amount of lost wages, the Court then deducts an estimate of the personal expenses which the victim would have incurred had he or she lived (approximately 25 per cent of the total).[185] The Court's award of lost earnings also includes interest from the date of the violation to the time of judgment.[186] It does not, however, include adjustments for future inflation or salary increases. The amount is then adjusted to reflect the present value of the future earnings.[187]

The Court's efforts to determine lost earnings have often been thwarted by the seasonal employment of the victims, the lack of employment and tax records, and geographical and cultural impediments. In the *Aloeboetoe Case*, for example, the victims, members of the Saramaca tribe, lived in the jungles of south-central Suriname far from the Caribbean coast.[188] The tribe does not use written documents and most of its members are functionally illiterate.[189] Moreover, the victims did not have stable employment: they had periodically travelled to the coasts of Suriname and French Guiana to work at construction jobs.[190] Even with the assistance of expert witnesses, it was difficult to establish evidence of lifetime loss of earnings 'in a culture and economy in which pay stubs, tax returns, and other ordinary means of verification are not customarily employed'.[191]

The parties may present expert testimony to establish proof of lost earnings when appropriate. Thus, in the *Aloeboetoe Case*, the Commission introduced an anthropological expert, who testified about relevant factors in Saramacan culture, and an affidavit from the accounting firm of Coopers and Lybrand, which calculated the projected earnings of the victims using the 'present value added' method of accounting.[192] The

[183] *Ibid.*, para. 51(b). [184] *El Amparo* v. *Venezuela* (Reparations, 1996), para. 28.

[185] *Ibid.*; *Neira Alegría et al.* v. *Peru* (Reparations, 1996), para. 50; *Paniagua Morales et al.* v. *Guatemala* (Reparations, 2001), para. 117.

[186] *Neira Alegría et al.* v. *Peru* (Reparations, 1996), para. 50.

[187] *Paniagua Morales et al.* v. *Guatemala* (Reparations, 2001), para. 117.

[188] Padilla, 'Reparations in Aloeboetoe v. Suriname', at 545.

[189] *Aloeboetoe et al.* v. *Suriname* (Reparations, 1993), para. 72.

[190] Padilla, 'Reparations in Aloeboetoe v. Suriname', at 546.

[191] *Ibid.*, at 552. [192] *Ibid.*, at 546.

Court may also employ experts or make use of its own staff in determining appropriate reparations *proprio motu*.[193] In the *El Amparo Case*, the Court employed an actuarial counsellor to calculate the amount of damages.[194] In the *Aloeboetoe Case*, the Deputy Secretary of the Court went to Suriname to make an *in situ* verification of the loss of earnings figures.[195] At that time, the Court had not yet established the presumption that the victim would have earned at least the minimum wage in the State.

In recent complex cases in which the Court has determined merits and reparations in the same judgment, and the Court has lacked the information to determine the amount of lost wages and job-related benefits, the Court has referred the victims to the national courts for a determination of lost wages and other job or business-related losses.[196] In the *Baena Ricardo et al. Case*, in which the Court held that 270 workers had their jobs terminated illegally and were, consequently, owed back pay and other economic benefits, the Court mandated that the State pay material damages in accordance with its national labour laws.[197] In the *Cesti Hurtado Case*, the Court determined that 'in view of the particularities of this case and the nature of the reparations requested, this Court considers that they should be determined by the mechanisms established in the domestic laws'.[198] In the *Ivcher Bronstein Case*, the Court did not resolve the question of the compensation that the victim should be awarded for the loss of dividends and other payments which he would have received had he continued as majority shareholder in the company as he was legally entitled to do.[199] The Court specified that he should submit the claim to the competent national authorities.[200] When doing so, the Court has established certain parameters that must be considered by the national courts.[201]

On the one hand, this seems to be another costly burden to place on the victim who has already spent years exhausting domestic remedies and then litigating the case before the Inter-American Commission and Court. Conversely, the Court sits part-time and does not have sufficient time or resources to determine complex cases involving domestic employment

193 2001 Rules of Procedure of the Inter-Am. Ct HR, Art. 44(3) and (4).
194 *El Amparo* v. *Venezuela* (Reparations, 1996), para. 12.
195 *Aloeboetoe et al.* v. *Suriname* (Reparations, 1993), para. 87.
196 *Constitutional Court Case* (Merits, 2001), para. 121; *Baena Ricardo et al. (270 Workers* v. *Panama)* (Merits, 2001), para. 205.
197 *Ibid.* 198 *Cesti Hurtado* v. *Peru* (Reparations, 2001), para. 46.
199 *Ivcher Bronstein* v. *Peru* (Merits, 2001), para. 181. 200 *Ibid.*, operative para. 8.
201 *Baena Ricardo et al. (270 Workers* v. *Panama)* (Merits, 2001), para. 205; *Durand and Ugarte* v. *Peru* (Merits), Inter-Am. Ct HR, 16 August 2000, Ser. C, No. 68.

laws or commercial and business law. Especially when the State has shown a willingness to comply with the measures ordered by the Court, and the victim is capable of litigating the case before the national courts, this avenue can be attempted. The Court maintains the authority to oversee State compliance with the judgment.[202]

Distribution of lost earnings of deceased victims The lost earnings of a deceased victim are paid to the successors (beneficiaries) of the victim. The Inter-American Court makes the determination of the beneficiaries of the damages awarded to the victim. Those beneficiaries need not first meet the requirements of the inheritance law of the State to be considered the victim's heirs in the Court.[203] In the absence of international customary or conventional rules that would determine a person's successors,[204] the Court applies general principles of law recognized by civilized nations to determine the issue.[205] The Court has repeatedly held that:

> [i]t is a norm common to most legal systems that a person's successors are his or her children. It is also generally accepted that the spouse has a share in the assets acquired during a marriage; some legal systems also grant the spouse inheritance rights along with the children. If there is no spouse or children, private common law recognizes the ascendants as heirs. It is the Court's opinion that these rules, generally accepted by the community of nations, should be applied in the instant case, in order to determine the victims' successors for purposes of compensation.[206]

The Court generally divides the lost wages of the deceased victim between the spouse or companion[207] and the children, if there are any.[208] The wife or companion of the victim receives half of the compensation for lost wages and the other half is divided equally among the victim's children.[209] This resolution of the division of lost wages is preferable to some of the Court's earlier rulings, and also the ruling in the later *Del Caracazo Case*

[202] *Baena Ricardo et al.* (*270 Workers* v. *Panama*) (Merits, 2001), operative para. 10.

[203] *Velásquez Rodríguez* v. *Honduras* (Compensatory Damages, 1989), para. 54.

[204] *Aloeboetoe et al.* v. *Suriname* (Reparations, 1993), para. 61.

[205] *Ibid.*; see also Statute of the ICJ, Art. 38(1).

[206] *Bámaca Velásquez* v. *Guatemala* (Reparations, 2002), para. 32; *Aloeboetoe et al.* v. *Suriname* (Reparations, 1993), para. 62; *Paniagua Morales et al.* v. *Guatemala* (Reparations, 2001), para. 84.

[207] In many States in Latin America some of the poor do not officially marry but rather live together as *compañeros* and raise their children. The Court has awarded damages to the victim's *compañera* or *compañero*. See *Paniagua Morales et al.* v. *Guatemala* (Reparations, 2001), para. 118.

[208] *Ibid.*, para. 229. [209] *Ibid.*

in which the Court awarded the wife of the victim only a one-quarter to one-third share of each category of damages. The larger portion was paid to the victim's children, and, in some cases, the compensation was also divided with the parents of the victim.[210]

Parents receive the victim's lost wages when the victim is not succeeded by either a wife, permanent companion or children.[211] In the *Bámaca Velásquez Case*, however, the Court deviated from its normal allocation rules. It took into account the request of the representatives of the victim and the Commission that the Court observe the customs of the Mam people of Guatemala.[212] According to custom, the eldest son in a family contributes to the support of his parents and siblings.[213] Therefore, as the victim in the case was the eldest son, the Court awarded the victim's lost wages in equal shares between his wife, father, and two sisters.[214]

Medical expenses of victims and family members

When the surviving direct victim or an indirect victim of a human rights violation suffers physically or emotionally, the Court may order that the State compensate that person for the medical expenses incurred during the time of the violation as well as for continuing treatment. Surviving direct victims, such as the two women who each had a leg amputated and the man who remained a paraplegic due to human rights violations in the *Del Caracazo Case*, may have health problems which have been treated or which must be treated in the future.[215] In the *Loayza Tamayo Case*, in which a female university professor was illegally imprisoned and subjected to cruel, inhuman and degrading punishment for more than four years, the victim suffered serious health problems during her incarceration.[216] The Court found that some of the severe physical and psychological health disorders brought on by her imprisonment could be irreversible.[217] Likewise, in the *Cantoral Benavides Case*, the Court ordered that the victim, who had been incarcerated at the age of twenty and who had been tortured, be reimbursed for the medical expenses incurred

[210] *Velásquez Rodríguez* v. *Honduras* (Compensatory Damages, 1989), para. 58; *Godínez Cruz* (Compensatory Damages, 1990), para. 53; *Del Caracazo* (Reparations, 2002), para. 91.

[211] *Trujillo Oroza* v. *Bolivia* (Reparations, 2002), para. 73; *Villagrán Morales et al.* v. *Guatemala (The Street Children Case)* (Reparations, 2001), operative para. 1.

[212] *Bámaca Velásquez* v. *Guatemala* (Reparations, 2002), para. 52.

[213] *Ibid.* [214] *Ibid.* [215] *Del Caracazo* (Reparations, 2002), para. 87.

[216] *Loayza Tamayo* v. *Peru* (Reparations, 1998), para. 106(i) and (j).

[217] *Ibid.*, para. 106(j).

while he was incarcerated as well as for future psychotherapy and medical expenses.[218]

The family of those who were disappeared, extra-judicially executed or illegally imprisoned may also suffer health consequences that require medical or psychological treatment. In the *Trujillo Oroza Case*, in which the mother of the victim claimed medical expenses for treatment for the stress and uncertainty resulting from her son's disappearance, the Court awarded her damages to recompense her medical costs.[219] Also, in the *Bámaca Velásquez Case*, in which the victim's wife, Jennifer Harbury, suffered related health problems and incurred medical costs, the Court ordered damages to cover those expenses.[220] In the *Durand and Ugarte Case*, Peru agreed to provide psychological support and to cover the costs of the health services and medications for the life of the beneficiaries.[221] Although it is not possible to project the exact amount of the future health-related expenses that the victim will bear, the Court attempts to order their reimbursement.

Expenses of searching for the victim

The Court holds that material damages include the expenses incurred by those who search for a family member who has been forcibly disappeared. These costs may include visits to jails, morgues, hospitals and public authorities, travel expenses such as plane tickets, lodging and food, telephone calls, and other miscellaneous expenses.[222] Should the body be located, material damages may include funeral expenses. The Court holds that there is a presumption that funeral expenses are borne by the family of the victim and should be indemnified.[223]

It is not clear what proof the Court will require to establish expenses. In the *Velásquez Rodríguez* and *Godínez Cruz Cases*, the Court stated that the expenses incurred by the family in investigating the whereabouts of the victim are theoretically a part of the damages which may be awarded, but it did not award expenses in these cases because they had been neither pleaded nor proved.[224] In the *Bámaca Velásquez Case*, however, the Court

218 *Cantoral Benavides* v. *Peru* (Reparations, 2001), para. 51.

219 *Trujillo Oroza* v. *Bolivia* (Reparations, 2002), paras. 53(g) and 75.

220 *Bámaca Velásquez* v. *Guatemala* (Reparations, 2002), para. 54(b).

221 *Durand and Ugarte* v. *Peru* (Reparations, 2001), paras. 36–8.

222 *Trujillo Oroza* v. *Bolivia* (Reparations, 2002), para. 74(a); *Bámaca Velásquez* v. *Guatemala* (Reparations, 2002), para. 54(c).

223 *Del Caracazo* (Reparations, 2002), para. 50(c).

224 *Godínez Cruz* (Compensatory Damages, 1989), para. 40; *Velásquez Rodríguez* v. *Honduras* (Compensatory Damages, 1989), para. 42.

awarded damages to cover these expenses, even though the victim's wife did not have receipts for all expenses incurred.[225] The Court commented in this regard that the facts of the case revealed, and the government had recognized, the series of attempts she had made to find her husband.[226]

Compensation for other material injuries

In addition to compensating for loss of earnings, pecuniary damages may also include the restitution of money or material possessions taken from the victims. The American Convention provides that '[n]o one shall be deprived of his property' except for public purposes and in return for just compensation.[227] If property has been stolen from the victim or has been subject to eminent domain, the victim must be compensated. The Court held that Nicaragua violated the right to property in the *Mayagna (SUMO) Awas Tingni Community Case*, in which Nicaragua had granted a logging concession on indigenous lands.[228] The Court did not award monetary compensation, because material damages were not proved.[229]

The reallocation of economic resources to housing, education, health care or employment may qualify as material damages. As an example of the reallocation of economic resources, in the *Aloeboetoe Case*, the Court ordered the State to open and staff the school and medical dispensary in the area of the victims' beneficiaries.[230] The Court reasoned that part of the compensation awarded to the victims' children was meant to enable them to complete their education, a remedy which could not be realized if the State did not provide a school in the area of the tribe.[231] The Court's order to open basic educational and health facilities would seem to be well in keeping with the letter and spirit of the American Convention, which provides for the progressive development of economic, social and cultural rights.[232]

[225] *Bámaca Velásquez* v. *Guatemala* (Reparations, 2002), para. 54(c).
[226] *Ibid.* [227] American Convention, Art. 21(2).
[228] *Mayagna (SUMO) Awas Tingni Community* v. *Nicaragua* (Merits, 2001), operative para. 2.
[229] *Ibid.*, para. 165.
[230] *Aloeboetoe et al.* v. *Suriname* (Reparations, 1993), para. 96. [231] *Ibid.*
[232] American Convention, Art. 26. The Additional Protocol to the American Convention on Human Rights in the Area of Economic, Social and Cultural Rights, Arts. 10(2)(a) and 13(1), provides a right to primary health care and education. See 'Protocol of San Salvador', signed at San Salvador, El Salvador, on 17 November 1988 at the eighteenth regular session of the General Assembly, and entered into force on 16 November 1999.

Minimal compensation when violation inferred

The Inter-American Court awarded only minimal compensation in the instance in which it was forced to infer that the State was responsible for a violation of the Convention due to the State's failure to produce information requested by the Court.[233] Parties to a case before the Court are obligated to provide information in their possession when the Court requests it.[234] Should the State neglect to respond to the Court's request for information, and other factors concur, the Court may infer State responsibility. In the *Gangaram Panday Case*, the Court inferred State responsibility for an illegal detention when Suriname failed to provide the Court with pertinent information that would have determined State responsibility.[235] The Court then awarded only minimal compensation to the family of the victim because the violation was inferred rather than proved.[236] Court awards of only minimal compensation in such cases could lead to the unfortunate result that, where evidence is incriminating, the State may choose to withhold it so as to limit its exposure. It may be that the Court's ruling in *Gangaram Panday* was an anomaly, and that the Court will apply the same reparations criteria in all cases in which it has determined that the Convention has been violated.

Moral damages

The term 'moral damages' or 'non-pecuniary damages' in international law includes damages for the suffering and afflictions caused to the direct victim, the emotional distress of the family members, and non-material changes in the living conditions of the victim, if alive, and the family.[237] Moral damages are not economic in nature. In the *Aloeboetoe Case*, for example, the Court held that the victims suffered moral injuries when they were illegally taken into custody by the military, beaten and then killed.[238] The Court stated that '[t]he beatings received, the pain of knowing they were condemned to die for no reason whatsoever, [and] the torture of having to dig their own graves' was part of the moral damage suffered by the victims who died.[239] The one victim who did not die immediately also suffered the moral injury of bearing 'the pain of his wounds being

233 *Gangaram Panday* v. *Suriname* (Merits, 1994), para. 70.

234 2001 Rules of Procedure of the Inter-Am. Ct HR, Art. 44(2).

235 *Gangaram Panday* v. *Suriname* (Merits, 1994), paras. 50 and 51.

236 *Ibid.*, para. 70.

237 *Trujillo Oroza* v. *Bolivia* (Reparations, 2002), para. 77. *Velásquez Rodríguez* v. *Honduras* (Compensatory Damages, 1989), para. 27.

238 *Aloeboetoe et al.* v. *Suriname* (Reparations, 1993), para. 51.

239 *Ibid.*

infested by maggots and of seeing the bodies of his companions being devoured by vultures'.[240]

Those who have a close emotional relationship with the victim, such as the victim's spouse, children, parents and siblings, may also suffer emotional distress, and thus may be awarded moral damages in their own right.[241] The Court explained that, when the violation is sufficiently serious, the moral suffering of the victims and their families must be compensated.[242] The European Court has also awarded moral or non-pecuniary damages to the family of direct victims.[243] In the *Colozza Case*, the victim, Mr. Colozza, suffered a violation of his right to a fair trial. He died before the case was decided by the Court. The widow claimed, in addition to pecuniary damages, that the violation had occasioned 'both for him and her, physical and mental suffering'.[244] The Court stated that non-pecuniary damages 'undoubtedly suffered by him and *by his widow*' had to be added to the pecuniary damages.[245]

Determination of amount of moral damages

The amount of moral damages awarded by the Inter-American Court is grounded in 'the principles of equity' as it is in the European system.[246] Moral damages cannot be calculated mathematically by the use of a precise formula.[247] Nonetheless, the victim or family member should receive an amount approximating the loss, if possible.[248] Although the Court's jurisprudence is a factor in establishing moral damages, the Court will also consider the particular circumstances of each victim.[249] For example, in the *Aloeboetoe Case*, six of the seven victims who were murdered were awarded the same amount of moral damages, because no evidence indicated that there had been differences in the ill-treatment or injuries they received. The other victim, who watched his companions die and then lived for a month after the assault, was awarded a greater amount in

240 *Ibid.* 241 *Velásquez Rodríguez* v. *Honduras* (Compensatory Damages, 1989), para. 50.

242 *El Amparo* v. *Venezuela* (Reparations, 1996), para. 35; *Neira Alegría et al.* v. *Peru* (Reparations, 1996), para. 56.

243 *Colozza* v. *Italy*, 89 ECHR (Ser. A) (1985), para. 38.

244 *Ibid.*, para. 36. 245 *Ibid.*, para. 38 (emphasis added).

246 *Velásquez Rodríguez* v. *Honduras* (Compensatory Damages, 1989), para. 27; *Godínez Cruz* (Compensatory Damages, 1990), para. 25, cited in *Aloeboetoe et al.* v. *Suriname* (Reparations, 1993), para. 86; see also *H.* v. *Belgium*, No. 127-B ECHR (Ser. A), para. 60 (1987).

247 Garcia-Amador, *The Changing Law of International Claims*, at 579. 248 *Ibid.*, at 580.

249 *Paniagua Morales et al.* v. *Guatemala* (Reparations, 2001), para. 104; *El Amparo* v. *Venezuela* (Reparations, 1996), para. 34; *Neira Alegría et al.* v. *Peru* (Reparations, 1996), para. 58.

moral damages.[250] Moreover, the Court presumes that victims who are minors at the time of death are especially vulnerable and therefore awards them additional moral damages.[251]

At one stage in its jurisprudence, it appeared that the Court had determined to award a set amount of moral damages in each case where moral damages were at issue, regardless of the amount of suffering borne by the victim. Thus, in the *El Amparo Case*, in which fourteen fishermen were murdered and two escaped, the Court without explanation set US$20,000 as the moral damages awarded to the living victims and to the beneficiaries of the deceased victims.[252] In the *Neira Alegría Case*, in which three victims perished, the Court also established US$20,000 as moral damages for each victim.[253] While it may be advantageous for settlement purposes to establish one amount for moral damages because the parties can then better anticipate the Court's judgment, the practice nevertheless undermines the Court's assertion that it will consider the facts of each case and be guided by equitable factors. Equitable principles properly applied would require that the Court take into account the right violated and the individual suffering of each victim when determining moral damages.

In determining what equitable factors affect the amount of moral damages to be awarded, the Court has reasoned that it may reduce the amount of moral damages if the State accepts international responsibility for the human rights violations because the acceptance itself constitutes moral satisfaction for the victims.[254] Yet moral damages for the suffering of deceased victims should not be reduced if the State accepts international responsibility for the violation, because the amount of their suffering does not change with the acceptance of responsibility. The moral suffering of families and surviving victims may be ameliorated, however, with State acceptance of responsibility for the violation. In such a case, it may be equitable for the Court to reduce the award of damages for moral suffering of the families and surviving victims. The Court distinguished the large awards of moral damages in the *Velásquez Rodríguez* and *Godínez Cruz Cases* against Honduras from the lesser awards in the *Aloeboetoe* and *El Amparo Cases* on the basis that Suriname accepted responsibility for the violations in *Aloeboetoe* and Venezuela accepted responsibility in

250 *Aloeboetoe et al.* v. *Suriname* (Reparations, 1993), para. 91.
251 *Del Caracazo* (Reparations, 2002), para. 102.
252 *El Amparo* v. *Venezuela* (Reparations, 1996), para. 37.
253 *Neira Alegría et al.* v. *Peru* (Reparations, 1996), para. 58.
254 *El Amparo* v. *Venezuela* (Reparations, 1996), para. 34.

El Amparo.[255] If the Court does decrease moral damages when the State voluntarily accepts responsibility, it may influence States to accept responsibility in future cases. This possible influence was undermined, however, when the Court awarded the same amount of moral damages in *Neira Alegría*, in which Peru did not accept responsibility for the violations, as it did in *El Amparo* in which Venezuela accepted responsibility. Identical awards of moral damages per victim in both cases negates the Court's assertion that acceptance of international responsibility may reduce moral damages, and, therefore, it may undermine the State's incentive to accept responsibility. If the Court is going to reduce awards for moral damages when the State accepts responsibility for a violation, it must do so consistently to encourage State acknowledgment of human rights violations.

Proof of moral injury

Moral injury to the direct victim can be evident from the type of abuse. The Court noted that 'it is characteristic of human nature' that any person subjected to aggression and abuse will experience moral suffering.[256] When the State accepts responsibility for the violation or the Court attributes responsibility to the State, no evidence is required to prove moral damages to the direct victims in cases of extrajudicial execution, torture or disappearance.[257]

When the Court orders reparations for the related suffering of others, the Court considers the relationship of the claimants to the direct victim in determining whether the moral injury must be proved. There is a rebuttable presumption that the parents, children, spouse or companion, and siblings of a direct victim suffer moral injuries when the direct victim was subject to grave human rights violations and also when there is impunity for the violations.[258] In the *Aloeboetoe Case*, for instance, the Court held that the moral suffering of the parents could be presumed as a result of the cruel death of their sons.[259] The Court reasoned that 'it is essentially human for all persons to feel pain at the torment of their

[255] *Ibid.*

[256] *Aloeboetoe et al.* v. *Suriname* (Reparations, 1993), para. 52; *Neira Alegría et al.* v. *Peru* (Reparations, 1996), para. 57; *Garrido and Baigorria* (Reparations, 1998), para. 49.

[257] *Garrido and Baigorria* v. *Argentina* (Reparations, 1998), para. 49.

[258] *Cesti Hurtado* v. *Peru* (Reparations, 2001), para. 54; *Del Caracazo* (Reparations, 2002), para. 64; *Paniagua Morales et al.* v. *Guatemala* (Reparations, 2001), paras. 108 and 125; *Villagrán Morales et al.* v. *Guatemala (The Street Children Case)* (Reparations, 2001), para. 68.

[259] *Aloeboetoe et al.* v. *Suriname* (Reparations, 1993), para. 76.

child'.[260] The family need not produce evidence unless the State rebuts the presumption.[261] In the early *Velásquez Rodríguez* and *Godínez Cruz Cases*, the Commission produced expert psychiatric testimony as to the psychological problems suffered by the wives and children of the men who had disappeared.[262] Such testimony may still be useful to prove the extent of the moral injuries, but it is not necessary.

The presumption that siblings suffer moral injury as a result of an egregious human rights violation to a brother or sister has developed gradually in the jurisprudence of the Court.[263] In *Villagrán Morales et al.* v. *Guatemala*, the Court stated that 'according to the most recent jurisprudence of the Court, it may be presumed that the death of a person results in non pecuniary damage to his siblings'.[264] This holding eliminates the need for the Court to evaluate evidence relating to the relationship between siblings and the victim, unless the State produces evidence to refute a close relationship.

The Court's award of moral damages has not consistently specified what portion of the amount awarded is for the suffering of the deceased or disappeared victim and what portion is for the suffering of the victim's family. In two judgments issued against Guatemala on consecutive days, the Court revealed this inconsistency. In the *Street Children Case*, the Court specified the amount of moral damages awarded for the suffering of the deceased victims, which was to be paid to the mothers as their next-of-kin, and the amount of moral damages it awarded for the emotional distress and other violations suffered by the mothers directly.[265] In the *White Van Case*, however, the Court awarded a lump sum in moral damages for the suffering of the deceased victim and the next-of-kin without designating the amounts attributable to the different violations.[266] This lack of precision does not enhance settlement possibilities between victims and States. When the parties can more easily determine the amount

[260] *Ibid.*

[261] *Paniagua Morales et al.* v. *Guatemala* (Reparations, 2001), para. 143; see *Cesti Hurtado* v. *Peru* (Reparations, 2001), para. 54.

[262] *Godínez Cruz* v. *Honduras* (Compensatory Damages, 1989), para. 49; *Velásquez Rodríguez* v. *Honduras* (Compensatory Damages, 1989), para. 51.

[263] See *Paniagua Morales et al.* v. *Guatemala* (Reparations, 2001), Separate Opinion of Judge de Roux Rengifo (outlining the changes in the Court's jurisprudence).

[264] *Villagrán Morales et al.* v. *Guatemala (The Street Children Case)* (Reparations, 2001), para. 68

[265] *Ibid.*, para. 93.

[266] *Paniagua Morales et al.* v. *Guatemala* (Reparations, 2001), para. 145.

of reparations the Court is likely to order in specific circumstances, the parties are more likely to reach a settlement and obviate the need to rely on the Court.

Beneficiaries of victim's moral damages

When the victim is deceased or remains disappeared, the Inter-American Court holds that the victim's entitlement to moral damages for injuries suffered until the time of death automatically passes to his or her heirs by succession.[267] As stated, the victim's heirs by succession generally are the spouse and children, if there are any, and, if not, the victim's parents.[268] In the *Velásquez Rodríguez* and *Godínez Cruz Cases*, both victims were married and had children. The Court directed that the reparations be made to each victim's wife and children.[269] In cases in which the victim was not legally married but had a permanent companion, the Court awards the spouse's share to the companion.

The issue of beneficiaries was complicated in the *Aloeboetoe Case*, in which, in accordance with tribal custom, some of the deceased victims had practised polygamy, an illegal practice in Suriname. Additionally, the marriages and births of the tribe were not legally recognized, because they had not been officially registered with the State as required under Surinamese law.[270] The Court ruled that the determination of the children, spouse and ascendants of the deceased was to be made in accordance with local family law.[271] Although local law would normally be the law of the State, in the *Aloeboetoe Case* the Court found that Surinamese family law did not apply to the tribe.[272] The Court had two bases for this holding. First, the tribe was unaware of State law and lived by its own rules; secondly, the State did not provide the facilities necessary to legalize the marriages and register the births of the tribe.[273]

[267] *Garrido and Baigorria* v. *Argentina* (Reparations, 1998), para. 50, citing *Aloeboetoe et al.* v. *Suriname* (Reparations, 1993), para. 54; *El Amparo* v. *Venezuela* (Reparations, 1996), paras. 43 and 46; *Neira Alegría et al.* v. *Peru* (Reparations, 1996), paras. 63 and 65; and *Caballero Delgado and Santana* v. *Colombia* (Reparations), Inter-Am. Ct HR, 29 January 1997, Ser. C, No. 31, paras. 60 and 61.

[268] *Bámaca Velásquez* v. *Guatemala* (Reparations, 2002), para. 32; *Aloeboetoe et al.* v. *Suriname* (Reparations, 1993), para. 62; *Paniagua Morales et al.* v. *Guatemala* (Reparations, 2001), para. 84.

[269] *Godínez Cruz* (Compensatory Damages, 1989), paras. 51–3; *Velásquez Rodríguez* v. *Honduras* (Compensatory Damages, 1989), paras. 56–8.

[270] *Aloeboetoe et al.* v. *Suriname* (Reparations, 1993), para. 63.

[271] *Ibid.*, para. 62. [272] *Ibid.*, para. 58. [273] *Ibid.*

Judgment may suffice as moral damages

The judgment of an international tribunal which attributes responsibility to the State for a human rights violation is *per se* a form of moral damages.[274] In *'The Last Temptation of Christ' Case*, in which the Court held that Chile had violated the right to freedom of thought and expression by its prior censorship of a movie, the Court held that the judgment itself was a sufficient form of reparations and moral satisfaction in the case.[275] Also, in the *Cesti Hurtado Case*, the Court held that its judgment in his favour constituted adequate reparation for damage to the victim's reputation and honour occasioned by his illegal imprisonment for fraud.[276] However, the Court did grant the victim moral damages in the form of pecuniary compensation for other violations.

The judgment alone does not constitute sufficient moral compensation and must be supplemented by pecuniary damages when the injured party has suffered extensively.[277] For violations that involve the illegal detention, torture, disappearance or death of the victim, the Court generally mandates that, in addition to the judgment, the State provide pecuniary moral compensation or its equivalent to the victims and their families.[278]

Damages to the victim's life plan

The Inter-American Court is laying the jurisprudential framework for the institution of an innovative type of damages in human rights cases, tentatively called damages to the victim's 'life plan'. A person's life plan is individual and is a composite of that person's ambitions, particular circumstances, and potential.[279] It is composed of the reasonable goals a person sets and that person's potential for attainment of those goals.[280] The Court stated in this regard that:

> [t]he concept of a 'life plan' is akin to the concept of personal fulfillment, which in turn is based on the options that an individual may have for leading his life and achieving the goal that he sets for himself. Strictly speaking, those options are the manifestation and guarantee of freedom. An individual can

[274] *Cantos* v. *Argentina* (Merits, 2002), para. 71; *El Amparo* v. *Venezuela* (Reparations, 1996), para. 56; *Paniagua Morales et al.* v. *Guatemala* (Reparations, 2001), para. 105.

[275] *'The Last Temptation of Christ' (Olmedo Bustos et al.* v. *Chile)* (Merits, 2001), para. 99.

[276] *Cesti Hurtado* v. *Peru* (Reparations, 2001), para. 59.

[277] *Paniagua Morales et al.* v. *Guatemala* (Reparations, 2001), para. 105; *Castillo Páez* v. *Peru* (Reparations, 1998), para. 84.

[278] *Paniagua Morales et al.* v. *Guatemala* (Reparations, 2001), para. 105; *Castillo Páez* v. *Peru* (Reparations, 1998), para. 84.

[279] *Loayza Tamayo* v. *Peru* (Reparations, 1998), para. 147.

[280] *Ibid.*

> hardly be described as truly free if he does not have options to pursue in life and to carry that life to its natural conclusion. Those options, in themselves, have an important existential value. Hence, their elimination or curtailment objectively abridges freedom and constitutes the loss of a valuable asset, a loss that this Court cannot disregard.[281]

In its decision on reparations in the *Loayza Tamayo Case*, the Court sympathetically discussed at length the victim's claim for damages to her 'life plan' (*proyecto de vida*).[282] The Court had determined that university professor María Elena Loayza Tamayo had been subjected to cruel, inhuman and degrading punishment during her illegal incarceration that resulted in severe psychological and physical disorders.[283] According to expert testimony accepted by the Court, following her release she was living in a foreign country, not employed, and receiving ongoing medical treatment.[284] The Court explained that interference with the 'life plan' of the victim may curtail the person's opportunity to attain the full realization of one's potential.[285]

Human rights violations of the type suffered by Loayza Tamayo, which subject the victim to prolonged loss of freedom and continuing physical and psychological damage, are particularly disruptive of a victim's life plan. Even when the person physically recovers, he or she may remain fearful, less trusting and less able to experience healthy future relationships and joy in living. This is no small loss. Reparations, as generally awarded under international law, do not take account of these elusive but very real limitations superimposed on the victim's remaining life. The Court pointed out that, although the material and moral damages awarded served as compensation, 'it would be difficult to restore or offer back to her the options for personal fulfillment of which she has been unjustly deprived'.[286] Similarly, in the *Cantoral Benavides Case*, in which the victim had been a twenty-year-old college student when he was illegally imprisoned, the Court held that '[t]he best way to restore Luis Alberto Cantoral Benavides' life plan' was for the State to assist the victim to attain a professional degree.[287]

The Court also indirectly referred to the disruption in the life plan of the mother of a disappeared victim when it set compensation for the moral damages suffered by her. In the *Trujillo Oroza Case*, the victim's mother

[281] *Ibid.*, para. 148. [282] *Ibid.*, para. 147. [283] *Ibid.*, para. 106(i) and (j).
[284] *Ibid.*, para. 106(m). [285] *Ibid.*, para. 147.
[286] *Loayza Tamayo* v. *Peru* (Reparations, 1998), para. 154.
[287] *Cantoral Benavides* v. *Peru* (Reparations, 2001), para. 80.

had spent twenty-eight years trying to find her son and seeking justice for his disappearance on the domestic and international planes.[288] The Court cited its earlier statements on life plan in the *Loayza Tamayo* and *Cantoral Benavides Cases*, in stating that the violations had occasioned a grave alteration in the course that the victim's mother's life normally would have followed.[289]

Non-monetary compensation for moral damages

The Court may order the State to compensate for moral damages through a monetary substitute. For example, in the *Mayagna (SUMO) Awas Tingni Community* v. *Nicaragua Case*, the Court ordered Nicaragua to invest, in consultation with the Community, a sum of money 'in works or services of collective interest for the benefit of the Awas Tingni Community'.[290] Also, in the *Cantoral Benavides Case*, in which the victim was imprisoned at the age of twenty, the Court ordered the State to grant the victim a scholarship to allow him to pursue his university studies and to defray his living expenses for the duration of his studies.[291] Although these projects are worthwhile, they could embroil the Court, as monitor of judgment compliance, in future disputes between the parties.

No punitive damages

The Inter-American Court has not awarded punitive damages for even the most egregious human rights violations. The Court has stated that the reparations ordered must be proportionate to the violation.[292] Thus, the nature and amount of the reparations depend on the injuries caused by the violations. The Court interprets the American Convention requirement that 'fair compensation be paid to the injured party' to include only compensatory and not punitive damages.[293] It has stated often that reparations are not intended to enrich or impoverish the victim or heirs.[294] This interpretation is not surprising in that punitive damages are not

288 *Trujillo Oroza* v. *Bolivia* (Reparations, 2002), para. 66(a).

289 *Ibid.*, para. 88(c), citing *Loayza Tamayo* v. *Peru* (Reparations, 1998), paras. 147–54; *Cantoral Benavides* v. *Peru* (Reparations, 2001), para. 60.

290 *Mayagna (SUMO) Awas Tingni Community* v. *Nicaragua* (Merits, 2001).

291 *Cantoral Benavides* v. *Peru* (Reparations, 2001), operative para. 6.

292 *Castillo Páez* v. *Peru* (Reparations, 1998), para. 51.

293 *Velásquez Rodríguez* v. *Honduras* (Compensatory Damages, 1989), para. 38.

294 *Castillo Páez* v. *Peru* (Reparations, 1998), para. 53; *Garrido and Baigorria* (Reparations, 1998), para. 43; *Paniagua Morales et al.* v. *Guatemala* (Reparations, 2001), para. 79.

authorized in civil law systems, and, even in the United States, they are often under attack.[295] In the Anglo-American system, domestic courts may award punitive damages when a wrongful act was aggravated by violence, oppression, malice or wanton and wicked conduct by the defendant.[296] The award of punitive damages is then meant to punish the defendant for the evil behaviour or outrageous conduct and to set a deterring example for similar wrongdoers.[297] Such an award is above and beyond the amount necessary to compensate the plaintiff for loss[298] and is often considered to be an unjustified windfall to the plaintiff.

The Inter-American Court has stated that it is not a penal court and, therefore, does not have the power to award exemplary or punitive damages.[299] Although the Court did not award punitive damages in its initial cases, it had not precluded the possibility of a future punitive award. In its early cases, the Court acknowledged that punitive damages are awarded in some domestic courts, but held that the principle of awarding punitive damages 'is not applicable in international law at this time'.[300] The qualification 'at this time' appeared to allow for the possibility that at some future time punitive damages might be awarded in the Inter-American system. If punitive damages were not awarded in the *Velásquez Case*, however, where the violation was so egregious and the State did not accept international responsibility, it was difficult to imagine a case in which punitive damages would be awarded by the Court.

Some commentators have argued that punitive damages are justifiable in cases of gross and systematic violations of human rights.[301] Although they may be justifiable, widespread poverty in many countries in the Inter-American system and the large number of victims who go uncompensated militate against the award of large sums to relatively few victims. Punitive damages would be paid out of public coffers, rather than out of the pockets of individual violators. Large payments to a few victims could possibly result in a domestic backlash against the Court.

295 'High Court Examines, Gingerly, Issue of Punitive Damages' Limit', *New York Times*, 12 October 1995, at A18.

296 Prosser and Keeton, *Prosser and Keeton on the Law of Torts*, at 9–10.

297 *Ibid.* 298 *Ibid.*, at 9.

299 *Garrido and Baigorria* (Reparations, 1998), para. 43.

300 *Velásquez Rodríguez* v. *Honduras* (Compensatory Damages, 1989), para. 38; *Godínez Cruz* (Compensatory Damages, 1989), para. 36. See Whiteman, *Damages in International Law*, at 36; Christine Gray, *Judicial Remedies in International Law*, at 26–8 (Oxford, 1991).

301 Shelton, *Remedies in International Human Rights Law*, at 290.

Ex gratia compensation

Under the international law of injury to aliens, States at times refuse to accept legal responsibility for a violation, but nonetheless, 'as an act of grace', pay *ex gratia* compensation to the State of the injured party.[302] An '*ex gratia* payment' is defined by *Black's Law Dictionary* as a '[p]ayment made by one who recognizes no legal obligation to pay but who makes payment to avoid greater expense'. In the European human rights system, the United Kingdom's offer of *ex gratia* compensation was accepted by the applicant in *G* v. *United Kingdom*, and the European Commission therefore struck the case from its list.[303] This type of situation has not yet arisen in the Inter-American system, but can be envisioned. For instance, a government elected in a State involved in a case in which the previous government is accused of human rights violations could offer to make reparations to the injured party *ex gratia*, but refuse to admit liability for the alleged violation. An advantage to the new government in this scenario is that it would not then be ordered to investigate the violation and to punish the violators, acts which might jeopardize the stability of the new government.

An offer of *ex gratia* compensation would normally be made during negotiations for a friendly settlement. If the victim or family of the victim refused to accept the State's offer of *ex gratia* compensation, the case would then presumably go forward in the Commission. If the case were already before the Court when the victim rejected the State's offer, presumably the Court would make a determination on State responsibility and, if appropriate, issue a judgment on reparations.

Costs and expenses

The Court may order the State to pay costs and expenses to the successful victim who requests them.[304] These may include the costs and expenses involved in taking the necessary actions to exhaust domestic remedies and in bringing a case before the Inter-American Commission and Court,

[302] Garcia-Amador, *The Changing Law of International Claims*, at 575 (quoting Jackson H. Ralston, *The Law and Procedure of International Tribunals*, at 57–8 (1926)).

[303] European Commission on Human Rights, Application No. 10172/82 (1988).

[304] 2001 Rules of Procedure of the Inter-Am. Ct HR, Art. 55(1)(h). See Sergio García Robles, 'Las Reparaciones en el Sistema Interamericano de Protección de los Derechos Humanos', in *El Sistema Interamericano de Protección de los Derechos Humanos en el Umbral del Siglo XXI: Memoria del Seminario Noviembre de 1999*, vol. I, 149, at 150 (2001).

including the fees paid for legal assistance in doing so.[305] In addition, although the Commission and Court do not levy filing fees, there are other expenses, such as those involved in producing the necessary documents, and bringing witnesses and representatives to hearings. The Court reasons that costs are a natural consequence of the efforts made on behalf of the victim to obtain a court judgment that holds the State liable for human rights violations and for the duty to make reparations.[306]

The reimbursement of costs, expenses and attorney fees is directly related to the individual victim's access to justice. A sophisticated regional human rights system providing remedies is of little value to petitioners who do not have the financial resources necessary to pursue those remedies before the enforcement organs. If the petitioner is not reimbursed for the financial outlays and commitments incurred as a result of human rights violations, the Convention's mandate that reparations be awarded to remedy the consequences of the violation will not be fulfilled.[307]

Determination of costs based in equity

The costs awarded must be 'necessary and reasonable according to the specifics of each case'.[308] The Court's determination of what costs are reasonable is based in equity and on considerations of fairness.[309] In making the determination, the Court considers the connection between the costs and the results achieved in the case.[310] This requires that the Court make a 'prudent estimate' of the costs by considering any circumstances particular to the case that are different from those of other cases and by reviewing receipts and vouchers.[311]

The Court may award costs and expenses even when there is a lack of evidence of the exact amount incurred.[312] Originally, the Court required that expenses be pleaded and proved by the Commission. It was often difficult, however, for the Commission to provide adequate proof of

305 See *Caballero Delgado and Santana* v. *Colombia* (Merits, 1995), paras. 71 and 72(6); *Aloeboetoe et al.* v. *Suriname* (Reparations, 1993), paras. 94, 95 and 111; *'The Last Temptation of Christ' (Olmedo Bustos et al.* v. *Chile)* (Merits, 2001), para. 100.

306 *Loayza Tamayo* v. *Peru* (Reparations, 1998), para. 176; *Garrido and Baigorria* (Reparations, 1998), para. 79.

307 See *Garrido and Baigorria* v. *Argentina* (Reparations, 1998), para. 79; American Convention, Art. 63(1).

308 *Garrido and Baigorria* v. *Argentina* (Reparations, 1998), para. 80.

309 *Constitutional Court* v. *Peru* (Merits, 2001), para. 125.

310 *Garrido and Baigorria* v. *Argentina* (Reparations, 1998), para. 80.

311 *Ibid.*, para. 82. See also *Loayza Tamayo* v. *Peru* (Reparations, 1998), para. 179; *Paniagua Morales et al.* v. *Guatemala* (Reparations, 2001), para. 212.

312 *Paniagua Morales et al.* v. *Guatemala* (Reparations, 2001), para. 213.

expenses incurred where the living conditions of the families hampered conservation of receipts.[313] In the *El Amparo* and *Neira Alegría Cases*, the Court ruled that, even when no evidence as to the amount of expenses had been presented, in equity it would award US$2,000 to each victim's family as compensation for expenses incurred in the domestic arena.[314] The decision of the Court to award a set amount avoided the socio-economic difficulties of providing proof of expenses and provided a basis for settlement of the case. Conversely, it left the Court vulnerable to charges that the awards were arbitrary. For instance, in the *El Amparo Case*, the Court ordered Venezuela to pay fourteen families of victims and two surviving victims US$2,000 each, a total of US$32,000 in expenses.[315] One would assume that the families acted in concert in bringing actions before the domestic authorities and that the award, therefore, probably multiplies the expenses actually incurred. The Court's present practice of awarding damages based in equity, considering all factors available, is preferable to not awarding damages that cannot be proved or ordering a set amount of damages regardless of proof.

Representation-related expenses

The Court has recognized the legitimacy of representation-related expenses before the organs of the Inter-American system,[316] since it first amended its Rules of Procedure to grant the victim the right independently to produce evidence at the reparations stage of the Court proceedings.[317] The costs referred to in the Court's Rules of Procedure include the victim's necessary and reasonable expenses, including attorney fees, in bringing the case before domestic courts and the organs of the Inter-American system.[318] The reimbursement of these costs will be even more necessary as victims can now autonomously call witnesses and provide evidence in all stages of the proceedings before the Court.[319] The Court's Rules of Procedure provide that the party offering the evidence must cover the costs of its production.[320] Victims need legal representation to present a

[313] *El Amparo* v. *Venezuela* (Reparations, 1996), para. 18.

[314] *Ibid.*, para. 21; *Neira Alegría et al.* v. *Peru* (Reparations, 1996), para. 42.

[315] *El Amparo* v. *Venezuela* (Reparations, 1996), para. 21.

[316] *Garrido and Baigorria* v. *Argentina* (Reparations, 1998), para. 81.

[317] 1996 Rules of Procedure of the Inter-American Court of Human Rights, approved by the Court at its twenty-fourth regular session, held 9–20 September 1996, Art. 44(2).

[318] *Cesti Hurtado* v. *Peru* (Reparations, 2001), para. 71; 2001 Rules of Procedure of the Inter-Am. Ct HR, Art. 55(1)(h).

[319] 2001 Rules of Procedure of the Inter-Am. Ct HR, Art. 23(1).

[320] *Ibid.*, Art. 45.

persuasive case and financial support to offset the burden of defraying the cost of producing the evidence.

The determination of the attorney fees to be awarded to a successful victim is based on the Court's assessment of the attorney's performance, evidence introduced, and factors that demonstrated the relevance and quality of the work performed.[321] As is logical, attorneys who represent their clients throughout the entire process in domestic and Inter-American proceedings will receive higher compensation than those who represent them only before the Inter-American Court.[322] The Court will not necessarily order payment of the full amount of fees requested, even when the victim presents documentation. The Court decides claims for costs and expenses, including attorney fees, 'with restraint'.[323] In the *Cesti Hurtado Case*, the victim requested almost a half-million dollars for the reimbursement of costs and expenses.[324] The Court awarded him only US$20,000. The Court has explicitly rejected State suggestions that it set attorney fees as a percentage of the compensation awarded when evidence is available to make a determination of the attorney's work.[325] The Court in some later cases has ordered that attorney fees be paid through the Inter-American Commission.[326]

The Court will only order the payment of attorney fees that the victim has actually paid or promised to pay.[327] The Court is now willing to order attorney fees for attorneys who work for non-governmental organizations. In the *Suárez Rosero Case*, it awarded attorney fees to an attorney who was employed by the American University's Human Rights Clinic.[328] The Court also awarded attorney fees to the Center for Justice and International Law in various cases, including for its representation of the families of the murdered street children in the *Villagrán Morales Case* and in the *Las Palmeras Case*, although the Court award may be minimal.[329] This evolution is important because non-governmental organizations do

321 *Garrido and Baigorria* (Reparations, 1998), para. 83.

322 *Paniagua Morales et al.* v. *Guatemala* (Reparations, 2001), para. 216.

323 *Cesti Hurtado* v. *Peru* (Reparations, 2001), para. 72.

324 *Ibid.*, para. 68.

325 *Paniagua Morales et al.* v. *Guatemala* (Reparations, 1998), para. 214; *Garrido and Baigorria* v. *Argentina* (Reparations, 1998), para. 83.

326 *'The Last Temptation of Christ' Case* (Merits, 2001), para. 101; *Baena Ricardo et al.* v. *Panama* (Merits, 2001), operative para. 6.

327 *Garrido and Baigorria* v. *Argentina* (Reparations, 1998), para. 80.

328 *Suárez Rosero* v. *Ecuador* (Interpretation of the Judgment on Reparations), Inter-Am. Ct HR, 29 May 1999, Ser. C, No. 51, para. 38.

329 *Villagrán Morales et al.* v. *Guatemala (The Street Children Case)* (Reparations, 2001), para. 109; *Las Palmeras* v. *Colombia* (Reparations, 2002), Resolution 9.

not have unlimited funds. They should not be compelled to refuse services to legitimate petitioners whose cases will prove unduly expensive. The arrangements with these petitioners, however, must specify that, in the event of success, the attorneys must be paid.

The award of attorney fees is also important because the caseload of the enforcement organs has grown exponentially, making it impossible for the few public interest attorneys to represent all those who need assistance. Many victims now have local representation at the domestic level. These victims should have the option of continuing the case with the same attorneys. However, their attorneys normally cannot carry the case forward on the international plane unless they are reimbursed for their time and expenses. Thus, an additional benefit brought about by Court-ordered attorney fees is that attorney compensation should result in a body of national attorneys who are experienced in bringing cases before the Inter-American system, making it likely that justice will be provided to additional victims. Moreover, if the State is confronted by well-documented cases, and is aware that it must pay the costs for both parties if it loses the cases, this may encourage the State to investigate thoroughly and acknowledge international responsibility when appropriate. When more cases are brought before the regional organs, it may serve to reduce the incidence of national human rights abuses.

In the European system, the Court generally requires that the applicant be represented by an advocate who is authorized to practise law.[330] The European system provides free legal aid to needy applicants.[331] Should the victim be vindicated and the Court award attorney fees, the amount of legal aid received by the victim may be deducted from the award.[332] The compensation awarded by the Court to a successful applicant includes attorney fees and other expenses paid by the victim to bring a case at the domestic level and before the European human rights system.[333] In determining the amount of an award of costs and expenses, the European Court ascertains 'whether the costs and expenses claimed were actually

[330] European Court of Human Rights, Rules of Court, Art. 36, entered into force on 1 November 1998. The European Court's Rules further provide that '[t]he President of the Chamber may, where representation would otherwise be obligatory, grant leave to the applicant to present his or her own case, subject, if necessary, to being assisted by an advocate or other approved representative'. *Ibid.*, Art. 36(4)(b).

[331] *Ibid.*, Arts. 91–6.

[332] *McCann and Others* v. *United Kingdom*, 324 ECHR (Ser. A), para. 222 (1995).

[333] European Court of Human Rights, Rules of Court, Art. 74(j); *Belilos* v. *Switzerland*, 132 ECHR (Ser. A), para. 79 (1988). See van Dijk and van Hoof, *Theory and Practice*, at 234.

incurred, necessarily incurred and reasonable as to quantum'.[334] Thus, if the applicants are not under an obligation to pay the attorney, the European Court holds that the costs have not been 'necessarily incurred' and does not compensate for them.[335]

The Inter-American system does not have the funding to provide legal aid at this time. Should adequate funding be available in the future, it would be beneficial if the OAS allocated funds for legal aid in that it would encourage local attorneys to pursue cases within the Inter-American system.

No award for costs incurred by the Commission and Court

The State is not charged for the costs incurred by the Inter-American Commission or Court. In the *Caballero Delgado and Santana Case*, the Commission requested that the State be ordered to pay the costs incurred by the counsel of the Commission in bringing witnesses to testify.[336] The Court denied this request, stating that 'the Commission cannot demand that expenses incurred as a result of its own internal work structure be reimbursed through the assessment of costs. The operation of the human rights organs of the American system is funded by the Member States by means of their annual contributions.'[337] It is generally recognized, however, that the funding of the Inter-American human rights organs is inadequate.[338] The Court's failure to award costs may result in a serious limitation on the number and types of cases that the Commission can afford to refer to the Court. It is not in keeping with the spirit of the enforcement of human rights if the Commission must first consider whether the financial burden of bringing a particular case before the Court is acceptable. The Commission's decision should be based solely on the merits of the individual case and its precedential value for international human

334 *Inze* v. *Austria*, 126 ECHR (Ser. A), para. 53 (1987). See van Dijk and van Hoof, *Theory and Practice*, at 250. The European Court awarded the costs incurred by the victim for an expert witness who testified in proceedings before the domestic court. *Inze* v. *Austria*, 126 ECHR (Ser. A), para. 54 (1987).

335 *McCann and Others* v. *United Kingdom*, 324 ECHR (Ser. A), paras. 220–1 (1995).

336 *Caballero Delgado and Santana* v. *Colombia* (Merits, 1995), para. 23(6); see also *Aloeboetoe et al.* v. *Suriname* (Reparations, 1993), para. 114.

337 *Caballero Delgado and Santana* v. *Colombia* (Merits, 1995), para. 70 (quoting *Aloeboetoe et al.* v. *Suriname* (Reparations, 1993), para. 114).

338 See *El Financiamiento del Sistema Interamericano de Derechos Humanos*, Report produced by the Office of the Secretary General of the Organization of American States by the *Ad Hoc* Working Group on Human Rights created by the Ministers of Foreign Relations, meeting on 22 November 1999 in San José, Costa Rica (28 April 2000); Pasqualucci, 'The Inter-American Human Rights System', at 355–9.

rights law. If the States that are liable for human rights violations are not required to pay the costs of the case, the OAS must adequately fund the Commission and the Court. The decision of the Court to allow the victim to present his or her own case and to award costs to the successful victim partially remedies this situation. It does, however, put a major burden on the victim who is unsuccessful before the Court. Although that victim may have an arrangement with the attorney which provides that the attorney shall only be paid in the event of success, the victim will still be responsible for expenses incurred in transporting witnesses to the Court in San José, Costa Rica, and paying their expenses while they are there.

State/victim agreements

The State and victim may negotiate a reparations agreement without a Court order. Alternatively, when the State has accepted international responsibility, the Court may rule that reparations be determined by agreement between the State, the representative of the victim, and the Commission.[339] The Court's jurisprudence on reparations is now sufficiently consistent that States and victims have been able in some instances to reach agreement.[340] In the *Benavides Cevallos Case*, the State of Ecuador and the family of the deceased victim reached a friendly settlement in which the State publicly cleared the victim's name, paid compensation to the family, and agreed to name a public place in her honour and to punish those responsible.[341] In the *Durand and Ugarte Case*, the parties' negotiated agreement included most areas covered in the Inter-American Court's latest decisions on reparations.[342] Peru agreed, *inter alia*, to make pecuniary reparations, to pay for part of the construction of the beneficiaries' houses, to pay the beneficiaries' health care costs, to publish and circulate the Court's judgment on the merits, to publicly apologize to the victims' families, to investigate the crime and punish the perpetrators, and to attempt to locate and deliver the victims' mortal remains to their families.[343] In the *Barrios Altos Case*, the State and representatives of the victims agreed, *inter alia*, that the State would erect a monument in memory of the victims.[344]

339 *Barrios Altos (Chumbipuma Aguirre et. al* v. *Peru)* (Merits), Inter-Am. Ct HR, 14 March 2001, Ser. C, No. 75, operative para. 6.

340 See *Benavides Cevallos* v. *Ecuador* (Merits, 1998), para. 55 and operative para. 3; *Durand and Ugarte* v. *Peru* (Reparations, 2001), para. 17.

341 *Benavides Cevallos* v. *Ecuador* (Merits, 1998), paras. 35 and 50.

342 *Durand and Ugarte* v. *Peru* (Reparations, 2001), para. 17.

343 *Ibid.*, paras. 36–9.

344 *Barrios Altos (Chumbipuma Aguirre et al.* v. *Peru)* (Reparations, 2001), para. 44(f), operative para. 5(f).

The Court, on receiving the agreement, will request the Commission's view on its feasibility.[345] The Commission has been involved in the case and is, therefore, more likely to know whether the victims have been pressured to settle, whether all the beneficiaries have been included, and whether the proposed settlement is fair. The Court reserves the right to approve agreements, to monitor State compliance, and to settle all problems of interpretation.[346] It is the Court's role to:

> assess whether the agreement on reparations is fully compatible with the relevant provisions of the American Convention, and verify whether it guarantees payment of just compensation to the victims and, where appropriate, to their next of kin, and if it repairs the consequences of the situation resulting from the violation of their human rights.[347]

The Court then enters a judgment ordering the measures to which the parties agreed. The Court has specified that 'any controversy or difference which may arise will be decided by the Court', and it will only close the case when the State has complied fully with the judgment.[348]

When the agreement envisions a long-term, multi-faceted State commitment to the beneficiaries of the reparations, the Court might do better to assign the resolution of future problems to a third party for mediation or arbitration. In the *Barrios Altos Case*, the State agreed to provide life-time health care and educational benefits to the beneficiaries.[349] The educational benefits include the ongoing provision of uniforms, workbooks and class materials for several beneficiaries.[350] One can foresee multiple problems in regard to this type of reparation which would not be of sufficient international importance to require the attention of the Inter-American Court.

Manner of compliance

States Parties must comply promptly and completely with all judgments of the Court to which they are a party.[351] States have an obligation under customary international law, as expressed in the principle of *pacta sunt servanda*, to comply in good faith with their international legal obligations.[352] All authorities of the State – the executive, legislative and judicial – are

[345] *Durand and Ugarte* v. *Peru* (Reparations, 2001), para. 18; *Barrios Altos (Chumbipuma Aguirre et al.* v. *Peru)* (Reparations, 2001), para. 17.

[346] *Durand and Ugarte* v. *Peru* (Reparations, 2001), paras. 41, 43 and 44.

[347] *Barrios Altos (Chumbipuma Aguirre et al.* v. *Peru)* (Reparations, 2001), para. 23.

[348] *Ibid.*, para. 48, operative para. 6. [349] *Ibid.*, paras. 42 and 43.

[350] *Ibid.*, para. 43. [351] American Convention, Art. 68.

[352] Vienna Convention on the Law of Treaties, Art. 26.

bound by the Court's judgments. Inter-American Court judgments are 'final and not subject to appeal',[353] and a State cannot rely on its domestic law to justify a failure to comply with a judgment.[354]

The Inter-American Court has developed consistent jurisprudence on the manner in which the State must comply with Court orders to make pecuniary reparations. The Court generally orders the State to pay compensation and costs in US dollars or in the equivalent amount in local currency when the payment is made.[355] The Court specifies that the exchange rate is the 'selling rate for the United States Dollar and the [local currency] quoted on the New York market on the day before the date of payment'.[356] By requiring that the amount of compensation be calculated in hard currency rather than the sometimes unstable and fluctuating currencies of some American states, the Court avoids the problem that arose in the *Honduran Disappearance Cases*, in which the Court-ordered payment in Honduran currency lost a significant portion of its purchasing power through a currency devaluation before the State complied with the judgment.[357] The Court subsequently ordered the State to adjust the amount paid by the government to compensate for the decline in the purchasing power of the currency during the delay in payment.[358]

The Court-ordered compensation is to be free from 'any national, provincial or municipal tax or duty that exists now or that may be legislated in the future'.[359] Thus, for example, if the State normally charges a tax on banking transactions for the deposit of cash or a cheque, the State must arrange domestically to forego that tax on the reparations ordered by the Court.[360] In most instances, any interest subsequently earned or any use made of that compensation is subject to domestic tax laws.[361]

353 American Convention, Art. 67.

354 Vienna Convention on the Law of Treaties, Art. 27.

355 *Garrido and Baigorria* v. *Argentina* (Reparations, 1998), para. 87; *Aloeboetoe et al.* v. *Suriname* (Reparations, 1993), para. 99; *Constitutional Court* v. *Peru* (Merits, 2001), para. 126.

356 *Aloeboetoe et al.* v. *Suriname* (Reparations, 1993), para. 99. The European Court of Human Rights now specifies damages awards in euros.

357 *Godínez Cruz* (Interpretation of the Compensatory Damages, 1990), paras. 40–3.

358 *Ibid.*

359 *Garrido and Baigorria* v. *Argentina* (Reparations, 1998), para. 89; see also *Velásquez Rodríguez* v. *Honduras* (Compensatory Damages, 1989), para. 57; *Neira Alegría et al.* v. *Peru* (Reparations, 1996), operative para. 3; *Blake* v. *Guatemala* (Reparations, 1999), operative para. 4; *Caballero Delgado and Santana* v. *Colombia* (Reparations, 1997), para. 64.

360 *Suárez Rosero* v. *Ecuador* (Interpretation of the Judgment on Reparations, 1999), para. 28.

361 *Ibid.*, para. 29.

There is, however, an exemption from taxation of interest earned by trust accounts established for the benefit of minors. The interest earned on trust accounts may be added to the principal, and the total is distributed to the beneficiary when he or she reaches the age of majority.[362] Thereafter, it is subject to taxation. All costs, including attorney fees, ordered by the Court as part of the reparations are also free of taxation.[363] Ecuador unsuccessfully attempted to challenge this decision in the *Suárez Rosero Case*, arguing that the attorney should be subject to the same taxes paid by other attorneys.[364]

The Court generally allows a State six months from the time it is notified of the Court's judgment to comply with the reparations judgment.[365] In the past, the Court has on occasion specified an exact date by which the State must pay,[366] but it seems to have abandoned this practice in favour of the six-month deadline. If the State does not make payment during the time period established by the Court, it must pay interest on the amount owing.[367] The interest rate that the State must pay for the period that it is in arrears is the current bank rate in the offending State.[368]

Compensatory damages and costs are generally paid directly to the adult victims or other beneficiaries of the award.[369] When that person has died, the payment is to be paid to his or her heirs.[370] If the named beneficiary does not claim the compensation during a prescribed time, the State must deposit the compensation in US dollars or in its equivalent in national currency in a trust fund established in that person's name at a bank of recognized solvency 'under the most favorable banking terms'.[371] The compensation will escheat to the State after ten years if it has not been claimed by the named beneficiary.[372] Even if the proceeds eventually escheat to the State, the reparations judgment shall be considered to have been honoured.[373]

362 *Ibid.*, para. 32. 363 *Ibid.*, para. 41. 364 *Ibid.*, paras. 18 and 34.

365 *Paniagua Morales et al.* v. *Guatemala* (Reparations, 2001), para. 220; *Loayza Tamayo* v. *Peru* (Reparations, 1998), para. 183; *Garrido and Baigorria* v. *Argentina* (Reparations, 1998), para. 86; *Gangaram Panday* v. *Suriname* (Merits, 1994), operative para. 4.

366 *Aloeboetoe et al.* v. *Suriname* (Reparations, 1993), para. 116.

367 *Garrido and Baigorria* v. *Argentina* (Reparations, 1998), para. 90.

368 See *Garrido and Baigorria* v. *Argentina* (Reparations, 1998), para. 90; *Paniagua Morales et al.* v. *Guatemala* (Reparations, 2001), para. 227; *Villagrán Morales et al.* v. *Guatemala (The Street Children Case)* (Reparations, 2001), para. 121.

369 *Paniagua Morales et al.* v. *Guatemala* (Reparations, 2001), para. 221; *Gangaram Panday* v. *Suriname* (Merits, 1994), para. 70.

370 *Loayza Tamayo* v. *Peru* (Reparations, 1998), para. 186.

371 *Paniagua Morales et al.* v. *Guatemala* (Reparations, 2001), para. 224; *Loayza Tamayo* v. *Peru* (Reparations, 1998), para. 187.

372 *Ibid.* 373 *Ibid.*

Generally, when the beneficiaries of the Court-ordered compensation are minors (or in one instance uneducated adults),[374] the Court attempts to preserve the purchasing power of the compensation by requiring that it be deposited in a trust fund. The State must set up the trust and bear the costs associated with it.[375] Interest earned by the trust is accumulated. The entire amount of principal and accumulated interest is payable to the beneficiary when he or she reaches the age of majority.[376] In case of death of the minor, the trust passes to his or her heirs.[377] The Court prefers a trust, rather than a bank account, because trusts are institutions designed to increase the real value of the assets.[378]

The Court has not only ordered the establishment of the trust funds, it has even specified many of their operational details.[379] The trust fund must be established in a sound and solvent domestic financial institution.[380] It must also be set up 'under the most favorable conditions consistent with banking practice'.[381] The Court interpreted the term 'most favorable conditions' as follows:

> any act or measure by the trustee must ensure that the amount assigned maintains its purchasing power and generates sufficient earnings or dividends to increase it; the phrase *permitted by... banking practice* indicates that the trustee must faithfully perform his task as would a good head of family and that he has the power and obligation to select diverse types of investment, whether through deposits in strong currencies, such as the United States dollars or others, the purchase of mortgage bonds, real estate, guaranteed securities or any other investment recommended by... banking practice, precisely as ordered by the Court.[382]

Moreover, the Court has established a State duty 'to take the necessary measures to protect the minor's interests against inflation, insolvency,

[374] *Aloeboetoe et al.* v. *Suriname* (Reparations, 1993), paras. 101–2.

[375] *Suárez Rosero* v. *Ecuador* (Fulfillment of Judgment), Inter-Am. Ct HR, 4 December 2001, operative para. 1.

[376] *Paniagua Morales et al.* v. *Guatemala* (Reparations, 2001), para. 223; *Suárez Rosero* v. *Ecuador* (Reparations, 1999), para. 107.

[377] *Suárez Rosero* v. *Ecuador* (Reparations, 1999), para. 107.

[378] *Godínez Cruz* (Interpretation of the Compensatory Damages, 1990), para. 32; *Velásquez Rodríguez* v. *Honduras* (Interpretation of Compensatory Damages, 1990), para. 32.

[379] *Aloeboetoe et al.* v. *Suriname* (Reparations, 1993), paras. 100–2.

[380] *Suárez Rosero* v. *Ecuador* (Reparations, 1999).

[381] *Aloeboetoe et al.* v. *Suriname* (Reparations, 1993), para. 100; *Velásquez Rodríguez* v. *Honduras* (Compensatory Damages, 1989), para. 58.

[382] *Velásquez Rodríguez* v. *Honduras* (Interpretation of the Compensatory Damages, 1990), para. 31; *Godínez Cruz* (Interpretation of the Compensatory Damages, 1990), para. 31.

negligence or the incompetence of the trustee'.[383] This State duty not only protects the beneficiaries but also protects the Court. In one early case, the Court put itself at future risk by involving itself in crafting the administrative structure of the trust funds. In the *Aloeboetoe Case*, the Court set up a foundation to administer the trusts and went so far as to name the foundation members.[384] This paternalistic stance could result in complaints from beneficiaries who were not given control of their money should the foundation trustees named by the Court abuse their fiduciary duties. The Court should avoid this well-meaning practice in the future.

In limited instances the Court has not ordered that compensation be placed in trust for minor beneficiaries. In the case of one minor beneficiary who was close to the age of majority, the Court determined that the time-consuming formalities involved in establishing a trust fund were unwarranted. Instead the Court ordered that the compensation be deposited 'in an interest-bearing, fixed-term certificate of deposit, at the most favorable terms under banking practice in Peru'.[385] Another possible exception arose in the *Gangaram Panday Case*, in which the Court ordered that half of the nominal compensation awarded be paid to the children 'if any'. The Court did not set up a trust fund. This may be due to the fairly small amount of the children's share, which was US$5,000, or the fact that the Court did not know if the decedent had children.[386]

Court procedures in determining reparations

In the interest of procedural efficiency and economy, the Court has expedited the deadlines to submit claims for reparations and costs and, whenever possible, reduced the number of phases in the proceedings. The applicant must now include a prayer for reparations in the application to the Court.[387] If necessary, the application can be amended subsequently to include additional information or claims. The Court cited the Permanent Court of International Justice in holding that 'in proceedings before an international court a party may modify its application, provided that

383 *Suárez Rosero* v. *Ecuador* (Interpretation of the Judgment on Reparations, 1999), para. 32.
384 *Aloeboetoe et al.* v. *Suriname* (Reparations, 1993), para. 103.
385 *Loayza Tamayo* v. *Peru* (Reparations, 1998), para. 184.
386 *Gangaram Panday* v. *Suriname* (Merits, 1994), para. 70.
387 2001 Rules of Procedure of the Inter-Am. Ct HR, Art. 33.

the other party has the procedural opportunity to state its views on the subject'.[388]

The Court may set reparations in the judgment on the merits, in a separate reparations judgment, partially in both the merits and reparations judgments, or by accepting an independent agreement arrived at between the parties. The procedure used by the Court is dependent on the facts of the case. If the Court has sufficient information, it sets reparations in the judgment on the merits.[389] When more information is required, it opens the reparations and costs phase of the proceedings.[390] Likewise, in the European Court, the decision on just satisfaction may be made simultaneously with the judgment on the merits of the case if the Court finds that the issue is ready for decision. If it is not yet ready, the Court may reserve the decision for a further procedure.[391]

The reparations stage of the proceedings is usually initiated when the President of the Court requests the victim's representative, the Commission and the State to submit briefs on reparations. The consistent practice of the Court allows the parties to indicate in these briefs the evidence they intend to produce at the reparations stage.[392] The Court has interpreted the rule requiring the submission of all evidence in the application and answer to allow the parties to tender evidence 'in the original brief each party submits for each stage of the proceeding'.[393] The Court may also initiate any studies that it deems necessary and call for a public hearing.[394] At the public hearing, the Court hears the arguments of the parties, which includes the representatives of the victims or of their families.[395] Although the victims or their next-of-kin have the opportunity of presenting evidence, they may not be available or aware of the proceedings. In the *Street Children* and *White Van Cases* against Guatemala, all the beneficiaries of the victims could not be located. The Court ordered the State to publicize the case in the national newspapers and on radio and television, so that the victims' relatives could participate.[396]

388 *Aloeboetoe et al.* v. *Suriname* (Reparations, 1993), para. 81 (citing *Factory at Chorzów* (Merits), 1928 PCIJ (Ser. A) No. 17, at 7 (13 September)).

389 See *Baena Ricardo et al. (270 Workers* v. *Panama)* (Merits, 2001), operative paras. 6–9.

390 2001 Rules of Procedure of the Inter-Am. Ct HR, Art. 56(1); see *Villagrán Morales et al.* v. *Guatemala (The Street Children Case)* (Merits, 1999), operative para. 9.

391 See van Dijk and van Hoof, *Theory and Practice*, at 173.

392 *Cesti Hurtado* v. *Peru* (Reparations, 2001), para. 20; *Castillo Páez* v. *Peru* (Reparations, 1998), para. 37.

393 *Loayza Tamayo* v. *Peru* (Reparations, 1998), para. 15(b).

394 *Velásquez Rodríguez* v. *Honduras* (Compensatory Damages, 1989), para. 4.

395 2001 Rules of Procedure of the Inter-Am. Ct HR, Art. 23(1).

396 *Paniagua Morales et al.* v. *Guatemala* (Reparations, 2001), para. 13; *Villagrán Morales et al.* v. *Guatemala (The Street Children Case)* (Reparations, 2001), para. 17.

Testimony or other evidence introduced at any prior stage of the proceedings before the Court may be considered by the Court in its determination of damages.[397] In the *Blake Case*, in which the family of the victim wished to introduce into evidence statements made at the oral hearing on the merits, the Court agreed, reasoning that '[t]he body of evidence of a case is unique and indivisible and is made up of the evidence submitted during all the stages of the proceeding'.[398] When determining reparations, the Court will use as a base of reference the findings of fact from its decision on the merits.[399] There are no rebuttals or rejoinders permitted at the reparations stage.[400] Formerly, the Court allowed the Commission and the State a period of six months following the judgment on the merits to agree on reparations. The Court retained jurisdiction over the case to verify that any agreement reached was fair or to institute the subsequent stage should the parties fail to reach an agreement. Usually, the Commission and the State could not reach an agreement during the prescribed period. The only result was that an additional six months had passed before the Court entered into the reparations stage. For a time, the Court eliminated the practice of allowing a period for negotiations. More recently, when the State has recognized and accepted international responsibility for its actions, the Court has reinstituted the negotiations. In the *Barrios Altos Case*, in which the Court granted the State, the Commission and the victims or their representatives three months to notify the Court on their agreement as to reparations,[401] the parties were able to reach an agreement. In all cases, there is no bar to the parties reaching a friendly settlement while the Court considers the issue of reparations.

When deciding on reparations or when reviewing a reparations agreement reached by the parties, the Court deliberates in private and subsequently issues its judgment.[402] Whenever possible, the same judges who decided the merits of the case make the decision as to reparations, and supervise compliance with the Court's judgment.[403] The Rules of the Court no longer provide that the judgment be issued in public, which

397 *Paniagua Morales et al.* v. *Guatemala* (Reparations, 2001), para. 67.

398 *Blake* v. *Guatemala* (Reparations, 1999), para. 28.

399 *Ibid.*, para. 87; *Villagrán Morales et al.* v. *Guatemala (The Street Children Case)* (Reparations, 2001), para. 69.

400 *Loayza Tamayo* v. *Peru* (Reparations, 1998), para. 15(b).

401 *Barrios Altos* v. *Peru* (Merits, 2001), operative para. 6.

402 2001 Rules of Procedure of the Inter-Am. Ct HR, Art. 57(1).

403 Order of the Inter-American Court of Human Rights of 19 September 1995, reprinted in 1995 Annual Report of the Inter-Am. Ct HR, at 129, OAS/Ser.L/V/III.33 doc. 4, 22 January 1996.

allows for judgments to be issued in a more timely manner. The Convention mandates that the State Party to a case comply with the Court's judgment.[404] All judgments of the Court are final and not subject to appeal.[405] If there is disagreement about its scope or meaning, the parties may ask the Court to interpret the judgment.[406] Any judgment ordering compensatory damages may be directly executed in the State in accordance with the domestic procedures that govern the execution of judgments against the State.[407] The Court supervises compliance with the reparations judgment and maintains the case on its docket until full reparations are made.[408] At the conclusion of 2002, the Court was monitoring compliance with its judgments in twenty-seven contentious cases.[409]

Resort to political organs

If the State does not comply with a judgment of the Court, the Court shall note the specific instances of non-compliance and formulate pertinent recommendations in its annual report to the General Assembly of the OAS.[410] The Court's attempted use of this procedure to force Honduras to comply with its judgment as interpreted in the *Velásquez Rodríguez* and *Godínez Cruz Cases* was unsuccessful. Although Honduras had paid the compensation originally ordered by the Court in these cases, albeit late, it refused to pay the Court-ordered interest and additional amount resulting from its failure to make the payment on time, before the devaluation of its currency. Consequently, the Court included a resolution detailing Honduras' non-compliance in its yearly report, which it expected to

[404] American Convention, Art. 68(1). [405] *Ibid.*, Art. 67. [406] *Ibid.*

[407] *Ibid.*, Art. 68(2). The observer from the European human rights system, in commenting that the Inter-American Court has 'considerably wider powers than the European Court', added: 'Thirdly, not only do Contracting Parties undertake (as in the European Convention) to abide by the judgment of the Court (Article 68), but an order for damages will be directly enforceable in the State concerned . . . a provision recalling Articles 187 and 192 of the Rome Treaty.' Council of Europe, 'Report on the Inter-American Specialized Conference on Human Rights' (Strasbourg, 22 December 1969), reprinted in *Human Rights: The Inter-American System*, Booklet 15, vol. 3, at 81 (Thomas B. Buergenthal and Robert E. Norris eds., 1982).

[408] *Paniagua Morales et al.* v. *Guatemala* (Reparations, 2001), para. 228; *Aloeboetoe et al.* v. *Suriname* (Reparations, 1993), para. 116(6); *Gangaram Panday* v. *Suriname* (Merits, 1994), operative para. 5. See *Gangaram Panday*, 27 November 1998 Order of the Inter-Am. Ct HR, operative paras. 1 and 2 (resolving that the State of Suriname had complied with the Court's judgment by depositing the required amount in a special account in the name of the beneficiaries and therefore closing the case).

[409] See 2002 Annual Report of the Inter-Am. Ct HR.

[410] American Convention, Art. 65.

present to the General Assembly of the OAS. Due to the extensive lobbying campaign of Honduras, however, this statement was never officially presented to the General Assembly. Honduras reportedly threatened to withdraw its acceptance of the contentious jurisdiction of the Court if the General Assembly were to read the Court's condemnation. The General Assembly's refusal to even mildly denounce Honduras for its initial failure to fulfil the judgment of the Court limits the Court's ability to command enforcement of its judgments. Although the Honduran Government, after an extended delay, fully paid the compensation ordered by the Court,[411] its successful campaign to block OAS efforts to oversee compliance with Court judgments may make that avenue untenable. The General Assembly must censure States that do not comply in full with Court judgments.

Conclusion

The Inter-American Court's progress in the area of reparations is perhaps its most important contribution to the evolution of international human rights law. As a result of its judgments, reparations are no longer limited to the payment of compensation. The Inter-American Court has successfully ordered States to adopt laws to bring the State into compliance with its international obligations. It has also ordered States to amend or repeal domestic laws that are not in compliance with the American Convention. The Court has held that domestic laws, such as the amnesty laws of Peru, are without legal effect, because they violate protected international rights, and domestic courts have given judgments in accordance with this holding. Domestic court rulings may also be the subject of Court-ordered reparations. The Court may order a State to annul or execute a domestic court decision. In this way, the Court has, for example, ordered that the victim be released from prison.

The Court has also ordered other more innovative types of reparations, particularly suited to human rights cases. The Court has ordered the State to exhume bodies and thus allow the family to give the victim a proper burial at State expense, to pay for the victim's schooling, or to build and staff a school and health clinic in the area of the beneficiaries. In the interest of deterrence and of awakening the conscience of the nation, the

[411] *Velásquez Rodríguez* (Interpretation of the Compensatory Damages, 1990), Inter-Am. Ct HR, 17 August 1990, Ser. C, No. 9; *Godínez Cruz* (Interpretation of the Compensatory Damages, 1990); *La Tribuna* (Tegucigalpa, Honduras), 8 February 1996, Nacionales Section, at 13.

Court has ordered that victims be memorialized in monuments, street names or names of educational centres. These forms of satisfaction have long been requested by victims' families. Most recently, the Court has ordered the State to publicly apologize to the victim or the family of the victim. The States have complied with these orders.

The Court is attempting, albeit not yet very successfully, to counter impunity through its orders of reparation. The Court consistently orders the State to investigate, prosecute and punish the 'intellectual authors' (masterminds) and perpetrators of human rights violations. The Court will not close the case until this aspect of reparations is satisfied.

Except for the duty to punish violators, States are, for the most part, complying with Court-ordered reparations. Moreover, States are entering into reparations agreements with the victims without the need for a Court order.

PART III

Provisional measures

6

Provisional measures

> [I]n international human rights law, the nature of provisional measures is not only preventative in the sense that they preserve a juridical situation, but fundamentally protective, because they protect human rights. Provided the basic requirements of extreme gravity and urgency and the prevention of irreparable damage to persons are met, provisional measures become a genuine jurisdictional guarantee of a preventive nature.[1]

Introduction

The usual time-consuming approach of international proceedings is inadequate in urgent situations that may result in the death or torture of the victim. Under traditional human rights law, little could be done formally to provide immediate assistance to those who were in imminent danger. The Inter-American human rights system can, however, provide timely assistance to victims in special circumstances. The American Convention authorizes the Inter-American Commission in 'cases of extreme gravity and urgency' to circumvent its time-consuming intermediary procedures and to request immediately that the Inter-American Court adopt provisional measures.[2] Also, when the case is before the Court, the Court at the request of a party or on its own motion may order the government involved to take or refrain from taking certain measures.[3]

[1] *The La Nación Newspaper Case* (Costa Rica), Provisional Measures, Inter-Am. Ct HR, Order of 6 December 2001, Ser. E. 'Considering' section, para. 4; *Gallardo Rodriguez Case* (Mexico), Provisional Measures, Inter-Am. Ct HR, Order of 14 February 2002, Ser. E, 'Considering' section, para. 5; *Peace Community of San José de Apartadó* (Colombia), Provisional Measures, Inter-Am. Ct HR, Order of 18 June 2002, Ser. E, 'Considering' section, para. 4.

[2] American Convention on Human Rights, Art. 63(2), 22 November 1969, 9 ILM 673, OEA/Ser.K/XVI/I.1, doc. 65 rev. 1 corr. 1 (1970), reprinted in 2001 Basic Documents; see also 2001 Rules of Procedure of the Inter-American Commission on Human Rights, entered into force on 1 May 2001, approved by the Commission at its 109th special session held 4–8 December 2000, Art. 74.

[3] American Convention, Art. 63(2); 2001 Rules of Procedure of the Inter-American Court of Human Rights, Art. 25(1), entered into force on 1 June 2001, approved by the Court

Although a State Party to the American Convention has an obligation, *erga omnes*, to protect all persons subject to its jurisdiction,[4] the Court may use its authority to call upon the State to take special measures to protect persons who are in immediate danger. An order of provisional measures may require that the government take positive action such as providing police protection to witnesses in a case being considered by the Commission or Court. Conversely, provisional measures may require that the State not take action, such as in the *James et al. Case*, in which the Court ordered Trinidad and Tobago not to execute named prisoners until their cases were resolved by the Commission.[5] Various terms are used to denote the same meaning in international documents: 'provisional measures', 'interim measures', 'interim measures of protection', 'precautionary measures', 'emergency measures', 'urgent measures' and 'conservatory measures'. The term 'provisional measures' will be used in this book except when the applicable source uses an alternative term.

Interim measures have developed into a dynamic tool to combat human rights violations in the Inter-American system owing to the urgent character of many of the human rights claims.[6] The potential for irreparable damage to persons in these cases often requires an immediacy of response that can only be provided by the implementation of provisional measures. This preventive function, when there is a possibility of imminent and irreparable damage to persons, is in many ways more valuable than the compensatory function of a final judgment.

Interim measures in general

The role of provisional measures under domestic legal systems and under international human rights systems differs. The Inter-American Court explained that 'the purpose of provisional measures, under the national legal systems (domestic procedural law) in general, is to preserve the rights of the contending parties, ensuring that the future judgment on the merits is

at its forty-ninth regular session held 25 November 2000. See Jerome B. Elkind, *Interim Protection: A Functional Approach*, 3 (Nijhoff, The Hague, 1981); Jerzy Sztucki, *Interim Measures in the Hague Court: An Attempt at a Scrutiny*, 72 (Kluwer, Netherlands, 1983).

4 *Peace Community of San José de Apartadó* (Colombia), Provisional Measures, Inter-Am. Ct HR, Order of 18 June 2002, Ser. E, para. 7.

5 *James et al.* (Trinidad and Tobago), Provisional Measures, Inter-Am. Ct HR, Order of 25 May 1999, Ser. E, operative para. 2(b).

6 See Verónica Gómez, 'Inter-American Commission on Human Rights and the Inter-American Court of Human Rights: New Rules and Recent Cases', 1 *Human Rights Law Review*, 111 (2001).

not harmed by their actions *pendente lite*'.[7] Under the international law of human rights, however, 'the purpose of provisional measures goes further, as, besides their essentially preventive character, they effectively protect fundamental rights, inasmuch as they seek to avoid irreparable damage to persons'.[8] In international human rights law, provisional measures are often adopted to protect a potential victim from extradition, torture or death.

The authority to adopt provisional measures has an historical basis in both domestic and international legal systems. In US domestic courts, the equivalent of an order of provisional measures is an interlocutory injunction, also referred to as a preliminary injunction. Orders of provisional measures also exist under civil law.[9] On the international plane, the doctrine and practice of the International Court of Justice (ICJ) served as a model for provisional measures in the European and Inter-American human rights systems.[10] Consequently, there are parallels between the procedures in the three systems. The United Nations Human Rights Committee has a more limited authority, in that it can inform a State of the Committee's 'views as to whether interim measures may be desirable to avoid irreparable damage to the victim of the alleged violation'.[11] The Inter-American human rights system has expanded the application of provisional measures and adapted the doctrine and practice of their use to the unique conditions of the Americas.

Precautionary measures ordered by the Commission

Petitioners before the Commission may request that the Commission order a State to take interim measures. Although neither the American Convention nor the Statute of the Inter-American Commission licenses

[7] *Constitutional Court* (Peru), Provisional Measures, Inter-Am. Ct HR, Order of the President, 7 April 2000, 'Considering' section, para. 10.

[8] *Ibid.*, para. 11. *Loayza Tamayo* (Peru), Provisional Measures, Inter-Am. Ct HR, Order of 3 February 2001, 'Considering' section, para. 8.

[9] See *Codigo de Procedimientos Civiles de Costa Rica*, Arts. 449–64 (1987); *Codigo de Procedimientos Civiles de Chile*, Art. 280 (1983); *Codigo Procesal Civil y Comercial de la Nación*, Arts. 195–210 (Argentina) (1987); see Elkind, *Interim Protection*, at 26–8.

[10] See Hector Gros Espiell, 'El Procedimiento Contencioso Ante la Corte Interamericana de Derechos Humanos' [Contentious Procedure Before the Inter-American Court of Human Rights], in *La Corte Interamericana de Derechos Humanos* [The Inter-American Court of Human Rights], 67, 73 and 83 (Inter-American Institute of Human Rights, Costa Rica, undated).

[11] Rules of Procedure of the United Nations Human Rights Committee, Rule 86, UN Doc. CCPR/C/3/Rev.6 (24 April 2001).

the Commission to order a State to adopt interim measures, the Commission's Rules of Procedure authorize the Commission to request that 'the State concerned adopt precautionary measures to prevent irreparable harm to persons'.[12] The Commission's Rules give the Commission the discretion to request such measures 'in serious and urgent cases' and 'whenever necessary according to the information available'.[13] Although it can be assumed that interim measures would most often be required in serious and urgent cases, this broad-based authority is preferable to the Court's more limiting rules. The Commission's initial standard, which authorized the Commission to request interim measures 'in cases where the denounced facts are true',[14] was unworkable in that it appeared to require a prejudging of the merits of the case.[15] Provisional measures do not prejudge a decision on the merits of the case.[16]

The Commission need not wait for a party to request precautionary measures; it can take such measures on its own initiative.[17] When the Commission is not in session, the President of the Commission or, if he or she is not available, one of the Vice-Presidents, shall consult with the other members of the Commission to make the decision.[18] The circumstances may be such that it is not reasonable to take the time to consult with the other members, in which case the President or Vice-President can make the decision on behalf of the Commission.[19] The Commission may then request relevant information on the matter from the interested parties.[20]

A *prima facie* determination that a petition meets the requirements of admissibility, made by the Secretariat of the Commission, should be all that is required before the Commission may request that the State adopt precautionary measures. The Commission maintains that the urgent risk of irreparable damage to persons absolves the Commission from the prior necessity of making a formal decision on the admissibility of a complaint before requesting that the State take precautionary measures.[21] In this regard, the Commission stated that 'such precautionary measures may be requested even when the admissibility of a case has not yet been defined by the Commission pursuant to Article 46 of the Convention, since, by their

[12] 2001 Rules of Procedure of the Inter-Am. Comm. HR, Art. 25(1).

[13] *Ibid.* [14] Regulations of the Inter-Am. Comm. HR, approved 29 June 1987, Art. 29(2).

[15] See Jo M. Pasqualucci, 'Provisional Measures in the Inter-American Human Rights System: An Innovative Development in International Law', 26 *Vanderbilt Journal of Transnational Law*, 803 (1993).

[16] 2001 Rules of Procedure of the Inter-Am. Comm. HR, Art. 25(4). [17] *Ibid.*

[18] *Ibid.*, Art. 25(2). [19] *Ibid.* [20] *Ibid.*, Art. 25(3).

[21] Request for Provisional Measures in Case 10.548, Inter-Am. Ct HR 25, 27, OEA/Ser.G/CP, doc. 2146 (1991).

very nature, provisional measures arise from a reasonable presumption of extreme and urgent risk of irreparable damage to persons'.[22] This decision is supported by the Commission's Rules which provide that in 'exceptional circumstances' the Commission may defer its decision on admissibility.[23] Under this provision, the Commission is authorized to make a *prima facie* determination that the petition meets the requirements of admissibility and thereby accept the petition 'in principle'.[24] This should be sufficient to allow the Commission to order the State to take precautionary measures.

The Court holds that there is a presumption that Court-ordered provisional measures are necessary when the Commission has previously ordered precautionary measures on its own authority that were not effective, and another threatening event has subsequently occurred.[25] Such was the situation in the *Urso Branco Prison Case*, in which several prisoners had been killed by other inmates.[26] The Commission had requested that the Government of Brazil take precautionary measures to protect those imprisoned and disarm the inmates that had weapons.[27] The Commission's request was ineffective, in that subsequently five more inmates were killed.[28] The Court stated that, as the Commission's request had not produced the necessary protection and the subsequent events resulted in a presumption that the lives and personal integrity of the other prisoners were in danger, it would order provisional measures.[29] The presumption is a practical means for the Court to encourage States to comply with Commission orders of precautionary measures. State compliance with the measures ordered by the Commission will save lives, reduce the ever-mounting case load of the Court and allow the State to take positive action to ameliorate a situation before it is exposed to additional international scrutiny.

In early cases, the Court required that the Commission first request on its own authority that the State Party take precautionary measures. Only when that avenue did not prove effective would the Court entertain a Commission request that the Court adopt provisional measures. This step was unnecessary in the Inter-American system, because the Commission's adoption of precautionary measures is neither statutorily required nor

[22] *Ibid.* [23] 2001 Rules of the Inter-Am. Comm. on Human Rights, Art. 37(3).

[24] *Velásquez Rodríguez* v. *Honduras* (Preliminary Objections), Inter-Am. Ct HR, 26 June 1987, Ser. C, No. 3, para. 39.

[25] *Digna Ochoa y Plácido et al.* (Mexico) Provisional Measures, Inter-Am. Ct HR, Order of 17 November 1999, Ser. E, 'Considering' section, para. 6.

[26] *Urso Branco Prison Case* (Brazil), Provisional Measures, Inter-Am. Ct HR, Order of 18 June 2002, Ser. E, para. 1.

[27] *Ibid.* [28] *Ibid.* [29] *Ibid.*, para. 5

authorized. Furthermore, it entailed a passage of time that cannot be afforded in urgent cases. In the *Vogt Case*, for instance, the Commission unsuccessfully requested that Guatemala take precautionary measures to protect a priest who received death threats on three occasions over a period of two years before the Commission turned to the Court.[30] Governments are less likely to comply with measures requested by the Commission.

Under the Court's current practice, irrespective of whether the Commission has independently asked the State to take precautionary measures, the Commission may request that the Court order the State to take provisional measures. The Court gives substantial weight to a request for provisional measures submitted by the Commission.

Inherent authority of the Court to order provisional measures

The Inter-American Court has decreed its inherent authority to order provisional measures.[31] The Court, in ordering provisional measures in the *Honduran Disappearance Cases*,[32] based its authority on its 'character as a judicial body and the powers that derive therefrom',[33] as well as on the American Convention. The inherent nature of the Court's authority is especially important, because the Court's statutory authority is limited. Buergenthal explained that it may have been reliance on its inherited powers that permitted the Court to order Honduras to adopt measures to clarify that every person enjoys the right to appear before the Commission and Court.[34]

Whether a court has inherent authority to order provisional measures has been a subject of dispute. Experts have long argued in relation to the power of the ICJ that '[t]he judicial process which is entrusted to the Court includes as one of its features, indeed as one of its essential features, this power to indicate provisional measures which ought to be taken'.[35] Elkind

[30] *Vogt* (Guatemala), Provisional Measures, Inter-Am. Ct HR, Order of the President, 12 April 1996, Ser. E, para. 3(i).

[31] *Velásquez Rodríguez* v. *Honduras* (Merits), Inter-Am. Ct HR, 29 July 1988, Ser. C, No. 4, para. 45. See Thomas Buergenthal, 'Interim Measures in the Inter-American Court of Human Rights', in *Interim Measures Indicated by International Courts*, 69, 83–4 (R. Bernhardt ed., 1994).

[32] *Velásquez Rodríguez* (Merits, 1988), para. 45; *Godínez Cruz* (Merits), Inter-Am. Ct HR, 20 January 1989, Ser. C, No. 5, para. 43; *Fairén Garbi and Solís Corrales* (Merits), Inter-Am. Ct HR, 15 March 1989, Ser. C, No. 6, para. 64.

[33] *Velásquez Rodríguez* v. *Honduras* (Merits, 1989), para. 45.

[34] Buergenthal, 'Interim Measures in the Inter-American Court of Human Rights', at 84, quoting *Velásquez Rodríguez* v. *Honduras* (Merits, 1988), para. 45(2).

[35] Elkind, *Interim Protection*, at 162, quoting from Manley Hudson, *The Permanent Court of International Justice, 1920–1942: A Treatise*, 425–6 (Arno Press, New York, 1943).

contends that the Court's power to order provisional measures is a general principle of international law, and that this general principle supports the contention that such measures are an inherent part of the judicial function.[36] The European Court, however, does not claim inherent powers in lieu of the statutory authority to order provisional measures.[37] The lack of a provision in the European Convention on provisional measures is in contrast to Article 41 of the Statute of the ICJ and Article 63(2) of the American Convention, both of which provide those courts with statutory authority. The sole authority for the adoption of provisional measures in the European human rights system is contained in that Court's self-authorized Rules of Procedure.[38]

Although the Inter-American Court has emphasized its inherent authority to order provisional measures, the legislative history of the American Convention does not clarify the drafters' intent. The initial draft of the Convention, which was the principal working paper at the conference for the adoption of the Convention,[39] did not include any reference to provisional measures. Costa Rica then proposed that the Court be given the power, common to all world tribunals, to act in serious and urgent situations.[40] The Costa Rican delegate introduced a broad-ranging provision which provided that '[t]he Court shall be able to take provisional measures that it considers pertinent, in urgent situations and when there is sufficient cause to justify it, for the protection of the right allegedly violated'.[41] This provision, which was not passed in committee, could have been interpreted to permit the Court to order provisional measures to protect any right protected by the Convention. Although no State voted against the initial version, all but one State abstained from voting.[42] Subsequently, Costa Rica proposed the current provision which was unanimously adopted without discussion or objections.[43]

[36] *Ibid.*, citing Cheng, *General Principles of Law as Applied by International Courts and Tribunals*, 267–76 (Stevens, London, 1953).

[37] *Cruz Varas* v. *Sweden*, 201 ECHR (Ser. A), paras. 95–9 (1991); but see *Mamatkulov and Abdurasulovic* v. *Turkey*, ECHR (Ser. A), 6 February 2003, paras. 109–11, holding that provisional measures are binding.

[38] European Court of Human Rights, Rules of Court, Rule 39, entered into force on 1 November 1998.

[39] San José Conference. See the text of the Draft Inter-American Convention on Protection of Human Rights, *1968 Inter-American Yearbook of Human Rights*, 389 (1973).

[40] Minutes of the Sixth Session of Committee II, Summary Version, 20 November 1969, in Thomas Buergenthal and Robert Norris (eds.), *Human Rights: The Inter-American System*, vol. 2, at 214.

[41] *Ibid.*, at 215. [42] *Ibid.*, at 214.

[43] Minutes of the Third Plenary Session, Summary Version, 21 November 1969, in Buergenthal and Norris (eds.), *Human Rights: The Inter-American System*, vol. 2, at 262.

The question of whether a Court has inherent powers to order provisional measures is no longer controversial, since this power is essential to protect human rights. The object and purpose of the American Convention is the protection of the rights of individuals,[44] and 'the final result of the international procedure must have some practical relevance for the person concerned'.[45] The Court must have the legal authority to order provisional measures in any case in which there will be immediate and irreparable damage, even after the Court determines the rights of the parties in the case. This power is necessary for the effective functioning of the Inter-American human rights system.

Statutory basis of the Court's authority to order provisional measures

Article 63(2) of the American Convention expressly provides statutory authority for the Inter-American Court to adopt provisional measures. This provision reads:

> In cases of extreme gravity and urgency, and when necessary to avoid irreparable damage to persons, the Court shall adopt such provisional measures as it deems pertinent in matters it has under consideration. With respect to a case not yet submitted to the Court, it may act at the request of the Commission.[46]

The adoption of provisional measures is discretionary, as it is before the ICJ[47] and the European Court.[48] The Inter-American Court makes an *ad hoc* determination considering all the facts and circumstances of each case. The Court's Rules of Procedure further support this discretionary nature by providing that the Court may order any provisional measures which it 'deems pertinent'.[49] Thus, the Court has discretion to determine whether

[44] *Effect of Reservations on the Entry into Force of the American Convention on Human Rights (Arts. 74 and 75)*, Inter-Am. Ct HR, Advisory Opinion OC-2/82 of 24 September 1982, para. 29.

[45] Rudolf Bernhardt, 'Interim Measures of Protection under the European Convention on Human Rights', in *Interim Measures Indicated by International Courts*, 95 at 102 (Bernhardt ed., 1994).

[46] American Convention, Art. 63(2).

[47] See Statute of the International Court of Justice, 59 Stat. 1055, entered into force 24 October 1945, Art. 41(1); Leo Gross, 'The Case Concerning United States Diplomatic Consular Staff in Tehran: Phase of Provisional Measures', 74 *American Journal of International Law*, 395, 406 (1980); see also Sztucki, *Interim Measures in the Hague Court*, at 61.

[48] Rules of Court of the European Court of Human Rights, Rule 39(1).

[49] 2001 Rules of Procedure of the Inter-Am. Ct HR, Art. 25(1).

it will order provisional measures, and, if so, what type of measures are justified in a particular situation. The Court has stated, however, that this power of the Court is not to be exercised lightly. The Court's adoption of provisional measures is 'an extraordinary instrument, one which becomes necessary in exceptional circumstances'.[50] The exceptional circumstances are present when there is a *prima facie* situation of grave and imminent danger.[51]

A presumption that a *prima facie* situation of grave and imminent danger exists when the Commission makes the request for provisional measures.[52] The Court has stated in this regard that:

> in view of the fact that the request comes from the Commission, the Court accords credibility to these statements and finds that they endow the situation *prima facie* with the characteristics of extreme gravity and urgency that justify adoption by the Court of whatever provisional measures it deems necessary to avoid irreparable damage to the persons on whose behalf they have been requested.[53]

The Court relies on a Commission request, inasmuch as the Commission is the organ most closely involved in monitoring the matters before it. When time is of the essence, as it is in the consideration of a request for provisional measures, the Court does not have the time nor the resources to independently reappraise the situation underlying the request.

The Court has changed its practice in this area. In early provisional measures requests, the Court required that the Commission provide evidence to the Court to support a presumption of the truth of the allegations.[54] The Court requested corroborating evidence even when the petitioners were independent human rights monitoring organizations, such as Americas Watch and the Center for Justice and International Law, that had investigated and verified the abuses and filed a detailed petition with the

[50] *Chunimá*, Request for Provisional Measures, Inter-Am. Ct HR, 42, 45, OAS/Ser.L/V/III.25, doc. 7 (1991).

[51] *Digna Ochoa Plácido et al.* (Mexico), Provisional Measures, Inter-Am. Ct HR, Order of 17 November 1999, Ser. E. 'Considering' section, para. 5.

[52] *Caballero Delgado and Santana* (Colombia), Provisional Measures, Inter-Am. Ct HR, Order of 7 December 1994, Ser. E, 'Considering' section, para. 3.

[53] *Ibid.*

[54] *Peruvian Prisons* (Peru), Provisional Measures, Inter-Am. Ct HR, Order of 14 December 1992, Ser. E, 'Considering' section, para. 6; *Chipoco* (Peru), Provisional Measures, Inter-Am. Ct HR, Order of the President, 14 December 1992, Ser. E, 'Considering' section, para. 2; *Chunimá* (Guatemala), Provisional Measures, Inter-Am. Ct HR, Order of 1 August 1991, Ser. E, 'Considering' section, para. 7.

Commission providing the dates, places and facts.[55] This practice resulted in an unnecessary passage of time before provisional measures could be ordered.

The Court's authority to adopt provisional measures may extend, in exceptional instances, to advisory opinion proceedings. The Convention's authorization specifies that the Court may adopt provisional measures in 'matters it has under consideration'.[56] Dunshee de Abranches posited that the choice of the word 'matters' in place of 'cases'[57] raises the possibility that the Court may also adopt provisional measures in the context of a request for an advisory opinion if there is an imminent danger of irreparable damage to a person.[58] Traditional international law has not made provisional measures available in advisory matters except perhaps when two States agree to request an advisory opinion in a veiled contentious situation.[59] Provisional measures could be instrumental in advisory proceedings when, for instance, the issue is whether a State can apply the death penalty to prisoners whose rights arguably had not been observed. Nothing in the American Convention bars this use should provisional measures prove pertinent in an advisory proceeding.

Current situation of extreme gravity and urgency

The Court may order whatever provisional measures it deems appropriate, but only in cases of 'extreme gravity and urgency'.[60] Thus, the situation must be sufficiently serious; otherwise provisional measures are not called for. The situation must also be urgent in that the possibility of injury is imminent and calls for immediate action by the Court. The *Chunimá Case* presented such an urgent situation, as five people had already been killed and others, including the judges who issued the arrest warrants for the suspects, had received death threats and were in hiding.[61]

In the *Chipoco Case*, by contrast, the Court did not find that the situation involved imminent danger. In *Chipoco*, the Commission requested provisional measures to protect Peruvian human rights activist Carlos Chipoco, who had previously cooperated with the Commission when Peru was accused of violating human rights. Chipoco subsequently had

[55] *Chunimá*, para. 1 and 'Considering' section, para. 7.
[56] American Convention, Art. 63(2).
[57] Carlos Alberto Dunshee de Abranches, 'The Inter-American Court of Human Rights', 30 *American University Law Review*, 80, 109 (1980).
[58] *Ibid.*, at 125. [59] See Sztucki, *Interim Measures in the Hague Court*, at 139.
[60] American Convention, Art. 63(2).
[61] *Chunimá* (Guatemala), Request for Provisional Measures, Inter-Am. Ct HR, 42.

been criminally charged in Peru with the crime of 'activities in support of subversion' for working with human rights organizations and criticizing the State,[62] a conviction which could have resulted in his loss of Peruvian nationality and twenty years in prison.[63] Although Chipoco was in the United States at the time of the indictment, the legal possibility existed that he could be tried *in absentia* in Peru. At that stage of the proceedings, while Chipoco was in the United States and before an arrest warrant had been issued, the Commission requested that the Court adopt provisional measures in the case. The Court was not sitting at the time of the request, and the President refused to adopt the urgent measures requested. The President found that, since an arrest warrant for the alleged victim had not been issued, the conditions did not exist to justify the adoption of urgent measures.[64] At the plenary Court's next session, the Court also refused to adopt provisional measures, finding that the Commission had not submitted sufficient information to the Court to support the request.[65] Likewise, in *'The Last Temptation of Christ' Case*, when Chile had not eliminated prior censorship of movies within the period ordered in the Court's judgment, the Court did not find a situation of extreme gravity and urgency sufficient to order provisional measures.[66]

Irreparable damage

The threat must be of irreparable damage. Irreparable damage is serious and irreversible. When there are threats to the lives of witnesses before the Court or Commission, for example, the Court will order a State to take provisional measures to protect them. Also, when it is alleged that a person is being subjected to torture or cruel and inhumane punishment or is scheduled for execution, there is the imminent possibility of irreparable damage and the Court will order provisional measures. The Court's initial orders of provisional measures were limited to cases in which a person was in imminent danger of irreparable damage through death or physical abuse. The *Reggiardo Tolosa Case* extended the standard to protect the psychological integrity of the alleged victims from irreparable damage.

62 *Chipoco* (Peru), Provisional Measures, Inter-Am. Ct HR, Order of the President, 14 December 1992, para. 3.

63 *Ibid.*, para. 5. 64 *Ibid.*, 'Whereas' section, para. 6.

65 *Chipoco* (Peru), Provisional Measures, Inter-Am. Ct HR, Order of 27 January 1993, Ser. E, 'Considering' section, para. 2.

66 *'The Last Temptation of Christ' (Olmedo Bustos et al.* v. *Chile)* (Compliance with Judgment), Inter-Am. Ct HR, Resolution of 28 November 2002, para. 5.

It is questionable whether the requisites of the possibility of irreparable injury to persons were present in the *Reggiardo Tolosa Case*. In that case, which was not before the Court, the Commission requested that the Court order the Government of Argentina to adopt provisional measures to protect the psychological well-being of sixteen-year-old twin boys, who were the natural children of a young couple who had been forcibly disappeared in 1976 during the 'dirty war' in Argentina. According to the request, the twins had been born during the clandestine captivity of their mother, who was pregnant at the time of the arrest. Immediately after their birth, the twins were taken by a sub-commissioner of the Federal Police, Samuel Miara. He and his wife then registered the birth of the children and raised them as if they were their natural children.[67] Despite blood tests proving that the children belonged to relatives that were searching for them, the Argentine courts left them with the Miaras. In 1991, the Grandmothers of the Plaza de Mayo presented petitions to the Inter-American Commission, and in 1993, the Commission asked the Court to order provisional measures.[68] The Court was not in session at the time of the request, but the President ordered the State to take urgent measures.[69] Argentina then took action, and subsequently reported to the Court that the boys had been sent to live with the family of an uncle.[70] Reports showed that the boys did not choose to leave the home in which they had been raised. The frustration of the petitioners at not being able to force the Argentine courts to enforce the law was understandable, but a situation that threatened irreparable damage to the children, sufficient to warrant provisional measures, arguably did not exist.

In more recent cases, the Court appears to have broadened its interpretation of irreparable damage to include any type of irreparable damage to persons. For example, a person or community of persons can suffer irreparable damage if their ancestral grounds are logged and denuded of trees. Persons may also suffer irreparable damage in certain cases if their personal possessions or livelihood are taken from them. The Court should

[67] 'Los Crímenes Impunes del Comisario Miara', *Madres de Plaza de Mayo* newspaper, 20 May 1989.

[68] *Reggiardo Tolosa* (Argentina), Commission Request for Provisional Measures in Case 10.959, Inter-Am. Comm. HR, Request of October 1993, reprinted in 1993 Annual Report of the Inter-Am. Ct HR, OAS/Ser.L/V/III.29 doc. 4, 10 January 1994.

[69] *Reggiardo Tolosa* (Argentina), Provisional Measures, Inter-Am. Ct HR, Order of the President, 19 November 1993, Ser. E, Resolution 1.

[70] *Reggiardo Tolosa* (Argentina), Provisional Measures, Inter-Am. Ct HR, Order of 19 January 1994, Ser. E, para. 4.

be concerned as to whether the threatened action will damage a person in such a way that a monetary judgment in the case will not compensate him or her for the loss. If that be the case, and the injury is serious, the Court should order provisional measures.

Beneficiaries of provisional measures

The Convention authorizes provisional measures 'to avoid irreparable damage to persons'.[71] After its initial order of provisional measures, the Court may order the expansion of the measures to include additional persons who are considered at risk. In the *Colotenango Case*, for example, provisional measures were expanded to include the daughter of a beneficiary of provisional measures.[72] The daughter had been abducted, anaesthetized by her abductors, and held for ransom.[73] It is not uncommon that threats are made or action is taken against family members of the beneficiaries of provisional measures or against the judges or prosecutors who are attempting to investigate the allegations. These additional people are then also in need of protection.

An issue that has come to the forefront is whether the persons for whom the Court orders provisional measures must be individually named or whether it is sufficient that they belong to an identifiable group. The Court has been confronted with requests to order provisional measures of a collective nature to protect groups or communities of people.[74] For instance, in *Haitians and Dominicans of Haitian Descent in the Dominican Republic Case*, the Commission asked the Court to order provisional measures to prevent the Dominican Republic from engaging in the massive expulsion of thousands of Haitians and Dominicans of Haitian descent, that was taking place without the necessary due process.[75] The Court issued provisional measures to protect the few persons who had been identified by the Commission as representatives of the types of violations

[71] American Convention, Art. 63(2).

[72] *Colotenango* (Guatemala), Provisional Measures, Inter-Am. Ct HR, Order of 2 February 2000, Ser. E, operative para. 2.

[73] *Ibid.*, para. 12.

[74] See *Peace Community of San José de Apartadó* (Colombia), Provisional Measures, Inter-Am. Ct HR, Order of 24 November 2000, Ser. E; *Haitians and Dominicans of Haitian Descent in the Dominican Republic* (Dominican Republic), Provisional Measures, Inter-Am. Ct HR, Order of 18 August 2000, Ser. E.

[75] *Haitians and Dominicans of Haitian Descent in the Dominican Republic* (Dominican Republic), Provisional Measures, Inter-Am. Ct HR, Order of 18 August 2000, Ser. E, para. 2.

occurring.[76] The Court refused, however, to issue provisional measures for the protection of the thousands of unnamed persons who were in danger of illegal deportation and possible separation from their families. In doing so, the Court stated:

> [t]his Court deems it indispensable to identify individually the persons in danger of suffering irreparable damage, for which reason it is not feasible to order provisional measures without specific names, for protecting generically those in a given situation or those who are affected by certain measures: however, it is possible to protect the individualized members of a community.[77]

The Court's position in that case was more restrictive than its prior practice would support. In earlier cases, the Court had required the State to protect unnamed persons who could be identified by their activities and affiliation. In the *Digna Ochoa and Plácido et al. Case*, the Court not only specified the names of the members of the human rights NGO that the Government of Mexico was ordered to protect, but also extended the measures to cover other unnamed persons who worked at or visited the offices of the organization.[78] Also, in the *Alvarez et al. Case*, the Government of Colombia was ordered not only to protect specific human rights workers but also to take any necessary measures to ensure that all persons related to the NGO could function without danger to their lives or personal integrity.[79]

Subsequent to the *Haitians and Dominicans of Haitian Descent in the Dominican Republic Case*, the Court ordered provisional measures to include persons who were identifiable but who were not named individually. In the *Peace Community of San José de Apartadó Case*, the Commission requested provisional measures to protect the inhabitants of a community in Colombia that was attempting to maintain its neutrality in the midst of civil conflict.[80] Forty-seven of the approximately twelve hundred to thirteen hundred community members had been murdered in a nine-month period.[81] The Commission, while requesting provisional measures to protect the entire community, listed 189 names in light of the Court's

[76] *Ibid.*, operative para. 1. [77] *Ibid.*, 'Considering' section, para. 8.

[78] *Digna Ochoa Plácido et al.* (Mexico), Provisional Measures, Inter-Am. Ct HR, Order of 17 November 1999, Ser. E, operative paras. 1 and 2.

[79] *Álvarez et al.* (Colombia), Provisional Measures, Inter-Am. Ct HR, Order of 12 November 2000, Ser. E, operative para. 4.

[80] *Peace Community of San José de Apartadó* (Colombia), Provisional Measures, Inter-Am. Ct HR, Order of 24 November 2000, Ser. E, para. 9(c).

[81] *Ibid.*, para. 2.

earlier decision requiring the individualization of those to be protected.[82] Gómez explained that individually identifying the residents of the Peace Community in Colombia was 'problematic, not because of their large number but because of the stigmatization implied by bringing a complaint alleging human rights violations before an international body'.[83] The naming of specific individuals may place those persons in danger of reprisals. In the *Peace Community of San José de Apartadó Case*, the Court acknowledged its earlier requirement that people be individualized, but heeded the Commission's arguments in favour of provisional measures to protect an identifiable group.[84] The Court ordered provisional measures to protect all members of the community without requiring that the population be named individually, because the group had 'special characteristics' that differentiated it from earlier situations considered by the Court.[85] According to the Court, these characteristics included the limited size of the community, its organization, its location in a determined geographic place, the ability to identify and individualize its members, and the similar risks to the members' lives and personal integrity resulting solely by virtue of belonging to the community.[86] Later, when paramilitaries had killed three truck and bus drivers who were delivering goods or persons to or from the community, the Court expanded the measures to include any persons who provided services to the community.[87] These persons were not named. The expansion of the Court's orders to cover groups of persons who are identifiable but who for relevant reasons are not listed individually by name represents an advance in human rights law. It does not put an unacceptable burden on the State, provided that there is a means to establish protection.

It is not certain, however, whether the Court will limit its orders to protect identifiable groups, without naming specific individuals, to situations in which naming the individuals would put them in danger. In the *Urso Branco Prison Case*, after thirty-seven inmates were killed by other inmates, the Court ordered provisional measures to protect all those who were imprisoned there.[88] This broadly stated order should have been

82 *Ibid.*, para. 5; and Gómez, 'New Rules and Recent Cases', at 125.

83 Gómez, 'New Rules and Recent Cases' at 125.

84 *Peace Community of San José de Apartadó* (Colombia), Provisional Measures, Inter-Am. Ct HR, Order of 24 November 2000, Ser. E, 'Considering' section, para. 7.

85 *Ibid.* 86 *Ibid.*

87 *Peace Community of San José de Apartadó* (Colombia), Provisional Measures, Inter-Am. Ct HR, Order of 18 June 2002, Ser. E, para. 6 and operative para. 2.

88 *Urso Branco Prison Case* (Brazil), Provisional Measures, Inter-Am. Ct HR, Order of 18 June 2002, Ser. E, operative para. 1.

sufficient under the *Peace Community* test, as the inmates were an identifiable group – all those incarcerated in the Urso Branco Prison. The Court, however, also required that the State supply a list of names of the prisoners and update that list every two months.[89] It is unclear if individual names are needed for the protection of the prisoners. If not, the requirement that the State supply the names of the inmates seems to be a needless formality.

Procedures applicable to a request for provisional measures

Due to the urgent nature of a provisional measures request and the part-time status of the Court, it is essential that the Court have expedited procedures for dealing with the ever-increasing number of requests for provisional measures. The Court's procedures depend to some extent on whether the case in which the orders are requested is before the Court or is still being considered by the Commission. They also depend on whether the Court is in session when the measures are requested.

The Court may order a State to take provisional measures only if the Court has jurisdiction over the State. Therefore, a State must have ratified the American Convention and accepted the jurisdiction of the Inter-American Court. The only objection to the Court's jurisdiction has thus far been made by Trinidad and Tobago, which had denounced the jurisdiction of the Court prior to the Court-ordered measures.[90] In the *James et al. Case*, in which the Court ordered the delay of the executions of certain prisoners in Trinidad and Tobago, the State objected that the Court no longer had jurisdiction *ratione temporis*.[91] The initial orders of provisional measures had been made before Trinidad and Tobago denounced the American Convention on 26 May 1998. The denunciation was effective one year later on 26 May 1999. The Court issued provisional measures on two occasions after that date. In doing so, the Court reasoned that, in accordance with international law, the denunciation did not release the State from its liability for acts in violation of the Convention which occurred prior to the effective date of the denunciation.[92]

The Inter-American Court should resolve any objections to its jurisdiction to order provisional measures by making a *prima facie* determination of jurisdiction. Due to the urgency and gravity of the matters considered,

[89] *Ibid.*, operative paras. 3 and 4.

[90] *James et al.* (Trinidad and Tobago), Provisional Measures, Inter-Am. Ct HR, Order of 16 August 2000, Ser. E, 'Considering' section, para. 6.

[91] *Ibid.* [92] *Ibid.*

the Court should not hold a separate preliminary stage of the proceedings to entertain the objection. The necessity for immediate action should encourage the Court to follow the relevant precedent of the ICJ. The ICJ holds that, when considering a request for provisional measures and a corresponding objection to jurisdiction, the ICJ need only satisfy itself that there appears to be a *prima facie* basis for the ICJ's jurisdiction. The ICJ need not satisfy itself that it has jurisdiction on the merits of the case.[93] A *prima facie* basis of jurisdiction should also be adequate for the Inter-American Court when it considers requests for provisional measures.

The President's adoption of urgent measures pending convocation of the Court

When there is a request for provisional measures and the Court is not in session, the Rules of the Court authorize its President to 'call upon' a government to adopt urgent measures.[94] In making the decision to call for urgent measures, the President should consult with the Permanent Commission of the Court and, whenever possible, with the other judges.[95] Urgent measures may be 'necessary to ensure the effectiveness of any provisional measures subsequently ordered by the Court'.[96] The Court considers that the State has an obligation to adopt the President's order in such instances.[97]

When the President has ordered a State to take urgent measures, the Court will consider the request at its next session.[98] Previously, the Rules required that the President, after adopting urgent measures, call the Court into session immediately. With the proliferation in the number of requests for provisional measures, the number of additional special sessions which would be necessary would be beyond the budget of the Court. The Court, therefore, adopted a procedural modification to counterbalance the need for provisional measures with the financial limitations of the Court. Rather than meeting in special session, the President can adopt urgent measures, and the Court will consider the request and the President's response to it at its next regular session.[99] This procedural change enhances judicial efficiency.

93 *Military and Paramilitary Activities In and Against Nicaragua (Nicaragua* v. *US)*, 23 ILM, 468, 473 (ICJ, 1984).

94 2001 Rules of Procedure of the Inter-Am. Ct HR, Art. 25(4).

95 *Ibid.*

96 *Constitutional Court* (Peru), Provisional Measures, Inter-Am. Ct HR, Order of the President, 7 April 2000, Ser. E, para. 13.

97 *Ibid.*, 'Considering' section, para. 8

98 2001 Rules of Procedure of the Inter-Am. Ct HR, Art. 25(4).

99 *Ibid.*

Plenary Court's consideration of provisional measures requests

When the President's order of urgent measures is adopted in accordance with the law and is consistent with the facts and circumstances of the situation, the plenary Court will ratify the President's order.[100] The Court did not initially provide as much support for the President's orders, holding that the emergency measures requested by the President do not result in a *fait accompli,* and thus were not subsequently binding on the plenary Court.[101] The Court asserted that those measures ordered by the President serve to avoid irreparable actions until the Court can meet to study the matter.[102] The Court's ambivalent support of the President's orders did not encourage State compliance, and thus jeopardized the well-being of the potential victims. To date, the Court has ratified all provisional measures adopted by the President and ordered the State to maintain those measures.[103]

In response to a request for provisional measures, the Court or the President may summon the parties to a public hearing before the plenary Court to consider their arguments.[104] Although public hearings on provisional measures requests are not required, the Court usually holds public hearings. The hearing publicizes the urgent situation, making the State more likely to take action to remedy it. It also allows the parties to meet face-to-face, which could serve to promote understanding of the problem and provide the Court with much-needed information. The victim may participate in the proceedings when the case has already been submitted to the Court, but the Commission also must supply the Court with all relevant information. If the case has not been submitted to the Court, it is the responsibility of the Commission to present the position of the potential beneficiaries at a public hearing.

Entities authorized to request provisional measures

When a case is not yet before the Court, only the Commission is authorized to request the Court to order provisional measures.[105] If the Commission

[100] *Constitutional Court* (Peru), Provisional Measures, Inter-Am. Ct HR, Order of 14 August 2000, Ser. E, para. 13.

[101] *Chunimá* (Guatemala), Order of the Inter-Am. Ct HR, 52, 55.

[102] *Ibid.*

[103] See *Bámaca Velásquez* (Guatemala), Provisional Measures, Inter-Am. Ct HR, Order of 29 August 1998, Ser. E, operative para. 1; *Serech and Saquic* (Guatemala), Provisional Measures, Inter-Am. Ct HR, Order of 28 June 1996, Ser. E, operative para. 1.

[104] 2001 Rules of Procedure of the Inter-Am. Ct HR, Art. 25(5).

[105] American Convention, Art. 63(2); *Colotenango* (Guatemala), Provisional Measures, Inter-Am. Ct HR, Order of 5 September 2001, Ser. E, para. 18, citing its Decision of 29 August 2001.

is not in session when it is notified of the need for provisional measures, the Commission's President may make the request.[106] When the case has already been submitted to the Court, any party to the case can request provisional measures, including the victim.[107] It is reasonable for the Court to respond to a direct request by the victim. Undue time would be lost if the victim had first to resort to the Commission, and then the Commission were to make the request of the Court. The right to request provisional measures directly of the Court should not, however, be provided to a petitioner in a matter before the Commission. In that situation, the Commission is more familiar with the facts of the case and is in a better position to determine the truth of the allegations and whether provisional measures are warranted. The Court's credibility would be in jeopardy were it to order measures in reliance solely on the allegations of unknown petitioners. Moreover, the floodgates of the Court would be opened if it were to accept provisional measures requests from the petitioners in the hundreds of cases before the Commission.

The Court, or its President when the Court is not in session, may order provisional measures *ex officio*, when appropriate.[108] In the *Constitutional Court Case*, the alleged victim requested that the Court adopt provisional measures to protect her and her husband.[109] The Court's Rules of Procedure provide that a 'party' can present a request for provisional measures.[110] The Court's 2001 Rules of Procedure, which make the victim a party before the Court, were not yet in effect and thus there was no provision for the victim to request provisional measures at that time. Therefore, the Court's President ordered urgent measures on his own motion,[111] reasoning that the purpose of such measures is 'to avoid irreparable damage to persons' in grave and urgent circumstances, and that therefore, when necessary, the Court or the President must be able to order measures on its or his own motion.[112] This authority, however, should seldom be required under the Court's latest Rules of Procedure

[106] 2001 Rules of Procedure of the Inter-Am. Comm. HR, Art. 74(2).

[107] American Convention, Art. 63(2).

[108] *Constitutional Court* (Peru), Provisional Measures, Inter-Am. Ct HR, Order of the President, 7 April 2000, Ser. E, para. 4.

[109] *Ibid.*, para. 2.

[110] 2001 Rules of Procedure of the Inter-Am. Ct HR, Art. 25(1); 1996 Rules of Procedure of the Inter-American Court of Human Rights, approved by the Court at its twenty-fourth regular session held 9–20 September 1996, Art. 25(1).

[111] *Constitutional Court* (Peru), Provisional Measures, Inter-Am. Ct HR, Order of the President, 7 April 2000, Ser. E, para. 4.

[112] *Ibid.*

except perhaps to order the protection of other witnesses in the case who alert the Court that they are in danger.

Monitoring provisional measures

The Court monitors State compliance with provisional measures orders by relying on State and Commission reports. Periodically, the State must submit reports which provide a detailed update on the provisional measures that it is taking to protect the beneficiaries of the Court's order.[113] To do so, it may be necessary for a representative of the State to meet with the beneficiaries of the measures. The State must also report on the investigation and punishment of the perpetrators of the acts that led to the Court-ordered provisional measures.[114] The Commission is charged with oversight of a government's compliance with the measures ordered and with a concurrent duty to report to the Court. The Commission is in the optimum position to report to the Court on the effectiveness of the measures, because it is generally in contact with the beneficiaries. Therefore, the Court relays the State reports on the measures taken to the Commission and requires the Commission's observations on those reports.[115]

Margin of appreciation in Court-ordered provisional measures

The Court's provisional measures orders are general in nature, often mandating that 'the State adopt, without delay, whatever measures are necessary to protect' certain persons.[116] The State is allowed a margin of appreciation in how it will implement such measures. The Court does not initially specify particular actions that the government must take to

[113] See *Colotenango* (Guatemala), Provisional Measures, Inter-Am. Ct HR, Order of 22 June 1994, Ser. E, operative paras. 1 and 2; *Digna Ochoa Plácido et al.* (Mexico), Provisional Measures, Inter-Am. Ct HR, Order of 17 November 1999, Ser. E, operative para. 5.

[114] *Digna Ochoa Plácido et al.* (Mexico), Provisional Measures, Inter-Am. Ct HR, Order of 17 November 1999, Ser. E, operative para. 3; *Colotenango* (Guatemala), Provisional Measures, Inter-Am. Ct HR, Order of 2 February 2000, Ser. E, operative para. 5; *Aléman Lacayo* (Nicaragua), Provisional Measures, Inter-Am. Ct HR, Order of 2 February 1996, Ser. E, operative para. 2.

[115] See *Digna Ochoa Plácido et al.* (Mexico), Provisional Measures, Inter-Am. Ct HR, Order of 17 November 1999, Ser. E, operative para. 5; *Aléman Lacayo* (Nicaragua), Provisional Measures, Inter-Am. Ct HR, Order of 2 February 1996, Ser. E, operative para. 3.

[116] *Digna Ochoa Plácido et al.* (Mexico), Provisional Measures, Inter-Am. Ct HR, Order of 17 November 1999, Ser. E, operative para. 1; *Chunimá* (Guatemala), Order of the Inter-Am. Ct HR, 52, 53; *Peruvian Prisons*, Order of the President of the Inter-Am. Ct HR, 101, 102, OAS/Ser.L/V/III.27, doc. 10 (1992).

fulfil its obligations of protection, despite the sometimes particularized requests made by the Commission. Thus, the Court, in the absence of the opportunity to educate itself about the appropriate possibilities of protection in each State, appears to refrain from ordering specific measures; instead, it will allow the government in its sovereignty a margin of appreciation to determine what measures will fulfil the Court's general demands of protection. One means that the Court uses to encourage the State to adopt meaningful measures of protection is to require that the State consult with the beneficiaries of the measures to determine the most effective and least intrusive means of protecting them.[117]

Should the measures adopted prove inadequate, it is the province of the Commission to notify the Court and suggest more adequate alternatives.[118] This option minimizes the burden on the Court by putting the Commission in the position of overseer. Only when the initial measures adopted by a government prove to be inadequate will the Court specify measures which the State must take to fulfil its obligation to the Court.

The duration of provisional measures

The duration of provisional measures is specific to the facts and circumstances of each request. Once ordered, provisional measures must be maintained while the basic circumstances that led to their adoption continue to exist.[119] The Court is likely to extend its orders of provisional measures when the Commission verifies that the extreme gravity and urgency of the threat continues.[120] In many cases, the grave and urgent situation may extend for a period of years, thereby forcing the Court repeatedly to extend the orders. In the *Colotenango Case*, for example, the Court first ordered provisional measures in 1994 to protect the lives and physical integrity of persons who had witnessed an attack by Guatemalan civil patrols against an unarmed human rights demonstration as well as to protect the relatives and attorneys of those witnesses.[121]

117 See *Colotenango* (Guatemala), Provisional Measures, Inter-Am. Ct HR, Order of 2 February 2000, Ser. E, operative para. 4.

118 *Ibid.*

119 *Constitutional Court* (Peru), Provisional Measures, Inter-Am. Ct HR, Order of 14 March 2001, Ser. E, 'Considering' section, para. 3.

120 See *Constitutional Court* (Peru), Provisional Measures, Inter-Am. Ct HR, Order of 14 August 2000, Ser. E, 'Considering' section, para. 6.

121 *Colotenango* (Guatemala), Provisional Measures, Inter-Am. Ct HR, Order of 22 June 1994, Ser. E, para. 3 and operative para. 1.

The measures were periodically expanded to cover additional persons who were at risk.[122] In February 2000, the Court extended the orders for the eighth time, because the civil patrol members who had been convicted in the case had escaped from prison and a family member of one of the beneficiaries had been abducted.[123] The provisional measures were still active as of 1 January 2003.[124]

It is likely that the number of provisional measures requests will continue to increase, and that the duration of provisional measures orders will continue for extended periods. At the conclusion of 2001, the Court was overseeing active provisional measures in thirteen cases. This burden on the part-time Court and Commission with their limited staff threatens to overwhelm the functioning of the Inter-American human rights system.

The Court will terminate provisional measures when the circumstances of gravity and urgency that resulted in the Court's adoption of provisional measures no longer exist. In the *Aléman Lacayo Case*, for example, in which the Court originally ordered provisional measures to protect a presidential candidate, the measures were terminated at the request of the Commission because the beneficiary of the measures was elected President of Nicaragua.[125] In the *Suárez Rosero Case*, the urgent measures ordered by the President of the Court were lifted by the plenary Court at the request of the Commission when the beneficiary of the measures was released from prison.[126] In the *Constitutional Court Case*, the Court lifted provisional measures when the beneficiary of the measures was reinstated on the Peruvian Constitutional Court.[127] Provisional measures were lifted in the *Ivcher Bronstein Case* subsequent to Peru's cancellation of arrest warrants, annulment of court proceedings against the victim, and restoration of the alleged victim's Peruvian nationality and shareholder status in the television station.[128] In the *Vogt Case*, at the request of the

[122] *Colotenango* (Guatemala), Provisional Measures, Inter-Am. Ct HR, Orders of 1 December 1994, 19 September 1997 and 2 February 2000, Ser. E.

[123] *Colotenango* (Guatemala), Provisional Measures, Inter-Am. Ct HR, Order of 2 February 2000, Ser. E, para. 12, 'Considering' section, para. 6 and operative para. 1.

[124] To be printed in 2002 Annual Report of the Inter-American Court of Human Rights.

[125] *Aléman Lacayo* (Nicaragua), Provisional Measures, Inter-Am. Ct HR, Order of 6 February 1997, Ser. E, 'Considering' section, paras. 2 and 3.

[126] *Suárez Rosero* (Ecuador), Provisional Measures, Inter-Am. Ct HR, Order of 28 June 1996, Ser. E, 'Considering' section, para. 2 and Resolution.

[127] *Constitutional Court* (Peru), Provisional Measures, Inter-Am. Ct HR, Order of 14 March 2001, 'Considering' section, para. 3.

[128] *Ivcher Bronstein* (Peru), Provisional Measures, Inter-Am. Ct HR, Order of 14 March 2001.

Commission, the Court terminated the provisional measures protecting a priest in Guatemala because 'the petitioners ha[d] informed the Commission that owing to the effective and timely intervention of the Honorable Court those threats and direct and specific acts of harassment had abated considerably and [that] Father Vogt [was] conducting his pastoral activity in a normal manner'.[129]

In some instances, the Court will lift provisional measures for one or more beneficiaries who are no longer in need of protection, while maintaining the protective measures for the other persons covered by the measures. For instance, in the *James et al. Case*, in which the Court ordered provisional measures to protect several prisoners who were on death row in Trinidad and Tobago, the Court lifted the measures for two prisoners who had been re-sentenced for manslaughter and were, therefore, no longer in need of protection.[130] When the Commission petitions the Court to lift provisional measures, it generally declares that it will monitor the situation for any future problems.[131] States are more likely to comply with Court-ordered provisional measures if the Court lifts those measures when they are no longer warranted for particular persons.

The conclusion of a case before the Court does not necessarily allow the Court to lift provisional measures. The Court was unduly hasty in terminating the provisional measures ordered to protect the witnesses in the *Caballero Delgado and Santana Case* two days after it issued its judgment on reparations.[132] Only days later, the former beneficiaries of the measures petitioned the Court to reinstate the measures at least until the domestic proceedings and investigations had ended.[133] All parties

[129] *Vogt* (Guatemala), Provisional Measures, Inter-Am. Ct HR, Order of 11 November 1997, Ser. E, para. 4, quoting the Commission's brief of 27 October 1997. See also *Serech and Saquic* (Guatemala), Provisional Measures, Inter-Am. Ct HR, Order of 19 September 1997, Ser. E, para. 4 and Resolution 1; *Cesti Hurtado* (Peru) Provisional Measures, Inter-Am. Ct HR, Order of 14 August 2000, Ser. E, 'Considering' section, paras. 8 and 9 and Resolution 1; and *Paniagua Morales et al. and Vásquez et al.* (Guatemala), Provisional Measures, Inter-Am. Ct HR Order of 27 November 1998, Ser. E.

[130] *James et al.* (Trinidad and Tobago), Provisional Measures, Inter-Am. Ct HR, Order of 2 September 2002, Ser. E, para. 6 and Resolution 1; see also *Giraldo Cardona et al.* (Colombia), Provisional Measures, Inter-Am. Ct HR, Order of 19 June 1998, Ser. E, 'Considering' section, para. 2 and Resolution 1; *Caballero Delgado and Santana* (Colombia), Provisional Measures, Inter-Am. Ct HR, Order of 3 June 1999, Ser. E, para. 4 and Resolution 1.

[131] *Serech and Saquic* (Guatemala), Provisional Measures, Inter-Am. Ct HR, Order of 19 September 1997, Ser. E, para. 6.

[132] *Caballero Delgado and Santana* (Colombia), Provisional Measures, Inter-Am. Ct HR, Order of 31 January 1997, Ser. E, 'Considering' section, paras. 1 and 2 and Resolution 1.

[133] *Caballero Delgado and Santana* (Colombia), Provisional Measures, Inter-Am. Ct HR, Order of 16 April 1997, Ser. E, paras. 4–6.

involved, including the Commission and the State, concurred that the measures should be reinstated and the Court did so.[134] Witnesses in cases before the Inter-American human rights organs may continue to be targeted long after the case has been closed.

The Court may refuse to lift provisional measures when it cannot be verified that the situation that precipitated the request has improved.[135] In the *Clemente Teherán et al. Case*, the Commission could no longer establish contact with the members of the indigenous community who had initially reported the human rights violations. The Commission reported that 'it was clear that persons who supplied information to the authorities [of the Zenú indigenous community] would be in serious danger and may therefore be reluctant to participate fully in the investigations'.[136] Subsequently, after a period of prolonged lack of communication with the petitioners, the Commission and the State requested that the Court terminate the provisional measures.[137] The Court refused the request stating that neither the Commission nor the State had provided the Court with 'sufficient reasons to indicate that the "*situation of extreme gravity and urgency*" has ceased, whereby this Tribunal feels that the lifting of the provisional measures is not justified'.[138] The Court's decision may be frustrating to the Commission, which has limited resources for verifying the situations of petitioners. It is positive, however, in that it may serve to minimize State attempts at intimidating petitioners to the Inter-American system into abandoning their petitions.

The binding nature of provisional measures

The Inter-American Court has proclaimed that its orders of provisional measures are binding and mandatory.[139] In the *Constitutional Court Case*, the Court held that:

> the provision established in Article 63(2) of the Convention makes it mandatory for the state to adopt the provisional measures ordered by this Tribunal, since there stands 'a basic principle of the law of international

[134] *Ibid.*, Resolution 1.

[135] *Clemente Teherán et al.* (Colombia), Provisional Measures, Inter-Am. Ct HR, Order of 19 June 1998, Ser. E, para. 3.

[136] *Ibid.*, para. 6.

[137] *Clemente Teherán et al.* (Colombia), Provisional Measures, Inter-Am. Ct HR, Order of 12 August 2000, Ser. E, paras. 3 and 11.

[138] *Ibid.* 'Considering' section, para. 7.

[139] See *Constitutional Court* (Peru), Provisional Measures, Inter-Am. Ct HR, Order of 14 August 2000, Ser. E, para. 14.

> state responsibility, supported by international jurisprudence, according to which states must fulfil their conventional international obligations in good faith (*pacta sunt servanda*)'.[140]

In earlier orders in the *James et al. Case*, the Court had implied the mandatory nature of its orders of provisional measures in stating that 'States parties must not take any action that may frustrate the *restitutio in integrum* of the rights of the alleged victims.'[141] That wording, however, although mandatory in nature, did not provide a definitive statement on the as-then-unresolved binding nature of the measures in the Inter-American system. The Court's statement in the *Constitutional Court Case* is definite and leaves no measure of doubt as to the Court's resolution of this question.[142]

The Court's decision that provisional measures are binding is supported by the wording and location in the American Convention of the provision authorizing provisional measures. Article 63(2) of the American Convention is located in the chapter entitled 'Jurisdiction and Functions', thus eliminating what was once a potent argument in the ICJ for the non-binding nature of the measures. That argument was based on the location of the provision on interim measures in the Statute of the ICJ, in the chapter on procedure rather than in the chapter on the competence of the Court, which relates to jurisdictional matters.[143] Consequently, it was sometimes argued that provisional measures were not binding in the ICJ, because they are merely procedural rather than jurisdictional.[144] The ICJ has since held in the *LaGrand Case (Germany* v. *United States of America)* that provisional measures are binding on the parties.[145] The ICJ stated that its order that the US take provisional measures 'was not a mere exhortation', and that its order 'was consequently binding in character and created a legal obligation for the United States'.[146]

140 *Ibid.*

141 *James et al.* (Trinidad and Tobago), Provisional Measures, Inter-Am. Ct HR, Order of 29 August 1998, Ser. E, 'Considering' section, para. 7 and Order of 27 May 1999, 'Considering' section, para. 9.

142 *Constitutional Court* (Peru), Provisional Measures, Inter-Am. Ct HR, Order of 14 August 2000, Ser. E, para. 14.

143 Elkind, *Interim Protection*, at 155 and 156 (citing Hammarskjold).

144 *Ibid.* See also J. Peter Bernhardt, 'The Provisional Measures Procedure of the International Court of Justice through US Staff in Tehran: Fiat Iustitia, Pereat Curia?', 20 *Virginia Journal of International Law*, 557, 561 (1980).

145 *LaGrand* (*FRG* v. *US*), 2001 ICJ Reports No. 104 (Merits) (Judgment 27 June).

146 *Ibid.*, para. 110.

The strength of the wording of the Article on provisional measures may affect the extent to which the provision is considered to be binding. The wording of the Statute of the ICJ, that the Court has the power to 'indicate' provisional measures that 'ought to be taken', was at one time argued to imply that the Court's adoption of interim measures is a mere suggestion to be complied with out of the good will of the State.[147] This argument against the binding character of the measures is no longer successful in the European system, which also adopted the word 'indicate' in its rules on provisional measures.[148] In contrast, the phrasing of the Article on provisional measures in the American Convention avoids the traditional but controversial term 'indicate', instead providing that the Court 'shall adopt' the measures that it deems pertinent,[149] a more forceful term that goes beyond mere suggestion. This more forceful language, combined with the placement of the provisional measures Article in the jurisdictional chapter, suggests that the drafters of the American Convention, by eliminating the basis for the traditional arguments against the binding nature of the measures, intended provisional measures to be binding in the Inter-American system.

Should a State Party fail to comply with an order of provisional measures, the only recourse of the Court is to specify the failure in its annual report to the OAS General Assembly.[150] A problem in the case of provisional measures, however, is that the General Assembly meets only once a year for a fairly short period.[151] Considering the urgent character of provisional measures, this recourse to the OAS General Assembly will not be particularly useful unless, by chance, the meeting occurs at the point of a State's failure to comply with provisional measures. Even then, no action will be taken unless the General Assembly has the political will to act.

Circumstances repeatedly giving rise to orders of provisional measures

The Court's decision as to whether it will adopt provisional measures is fact-specific. The factual situation must demonstrate the requisites of gravity and urgency to justify the adoption of the extraordinary remedy of provisional measures. The Court has ordered provisional measures in

[147] Elkind, *Interim Protection*, at 153–66.

[148] Rules of the European Court of Human Rights, Rule 39(1); *Mamatkulov and Abdurasulovic v. Turkey*, ECHR (Ser. A), 6 February 2003, paras. 109–11, holding that provisional measures are binding.

[149] American Convention, Art. 63(2).

[150] *Ibid.*, Art. 65.

[151] See Davidson, *The Inter-American Court of Human Rights*, at 9.

varied situations: to protect a presidential candidate in Nicaragua whose motorcade had been attacked by heavily armed men;[152] to protect members of a Colombian indigenous reservation who were allegedly being victimized to force them from their land;[153] to protect a priest in the highlands of Guatemala;[154] and to protect television social commentators in Venezuela.[155] Certain factual situations, however, have repeatedly resulted in Court-ordered provisional measures.

Protection of witnesses before the Court and Commission

On several occasions, the Court has ordered provisional measures to protect witnesses who have testified or who have been called to testify before the Inter-American Commission and Court.[156] Often State nationals who testify before the organs of the Inter-American system about governmental abuses of human rights are considered to be enemies of the State, who have publicly sullied the State's reputation. These witnesses may face retaliation and require measures for their protection. Thus, the Court may order the State to take provisional measures to protect witnesses. In this regard, the Court has stated that 'it is the responsibility of the State to adopt security measures to protect all those who are subject to its jurisdiction; this obligation is even more evident as regards those who are involved in proceedings before the supervisory organs of the American Convention'.[157]

The Court initially ordered provisional measures to protect witnesses in the *Honduran Disappearance Cases*.[158] In those cases, the Court ordered

[152] *Aléman Lacayo* (Nicaragua), Provisional Measures, Inter-Am. Ct HR, Order of 2 February 1996, Ser. E, para. 3.

[153] *Clemente Teherán et al.* (Colombia), Provisional Measures, Inter-Am. Ct HR, Order of 19 June 1998, Ser. E, para. 2(b).

[154] *Vogt* (Guatemala), Provisional Measures, Inter-Am. Ct HR, Order of the President, 12 April 1996, Ser. E.

[155] *Luisiana Ríos et al.* (Venezuela), Provisional Measures, Inter-Am. Ct HR, Order of 27 November 2002, Ser. E, para. 1 and Resolution 1.

[156] See *Bámaca Velásquez* (Guatemala), Provisional Measures, Inter-Am. Ct HR, Order of 29 August 1998, Ser. E, para. 2; *Caballero Delgado and Santana* (Colombia), Provisional Measures, Inter-Am. Ct HR, Order of 31 January 1997, Ser. E, para. 1; *Serech and Saquic* (Guatemala), Provisional Measures, Inter-Am. Ct HR, Order of the President, 14 April 1996, Ser. E, para. 7; *Paniagua Morales* v. *Guatemala* (Reparations), Inter-Am. Ct HR, Judgment of 25 May 2001, Ser. C, No. 76, para. 44.

[157] *Digna Ochoa and Plácido et al.* (Mexico), Provisional Measures, Inter-Am. Ct HR, Order of 17 November 1999, Ser. E, 'Considering' section, para. 7; *Liliana Ortega et al.* (Venezuela), Provisional Measures, Inter-Am. Ct HR, Order of 27 November 2002, Ser. E, 'Considering' section, para. 7.

[158] *Velásquez Rodríguez* v. *Honduras* (Merits, 1988), para. 45; *Godínez Cruz* (Merits, 1989), para. 45.

the State to adopt measures to protect specific persons and to make clear that an individual's participation as a witness before the organs of the Inter-American system 'is a right enjoyed by every individual and is recognized as such by Honduras as a party to the Convention'.[159] At a public hearing on the merits of the cases, Honduran nationals had testified for the Commission. On their return to Honduras following the hearings, two witnesses received death threats. The Commission then requested that the Court adopt measures for the protection of those witnesses.[160] The President of the Court requested that the Government of Honduras take all measures necessary to guarantee the safety of the lives and property of the two witnesses threatened.[161] In response, Honduras informed the Court that it would protect the two named witnesses.[162] Although those two witnesses were not subsequently harmed, shortly thereafter three other past and prospective witnesses were assassinated in Honduras.[163] The Court, sitting on the date of the final assassination, required Honduras immediately to adopt provisional measures necessary 'to prevent further infringements on the basic rights of those who have appeared or have been summoned' to appear before the Court.[164] Thereafter, no additional witnesses were harmed.

The Court also may order the protection of witnesses appearing before the Commission. In the *Bustios Rojas Case*, for example, a Peruvian journalist had been killed and another wounded *en route* to investigate a murder.[165] An eyewitness to the attack, who had accused members of the Peruvian military of responsibility, was subsequently murdered.[166] The military also allegedly threatened and detained two other eyewitnesses, and both the wife of the assassinated journalist and the journalist who survived the attack received death threats. The petitioner, the Committee for the Protection of Journalists, claimed that, under the circumstances, the very filing of a petition before the Commission placed the lives of the surviving victim and the witnesses further at risk.[167] Therefore, the petitioners submitted that 'there was an urgent need for precautionary measures to compel the government to cease and desist from intimidating the victims and witnesses and to guarantee their lives and personal safety until a final decision on the

159 *Velásquez Rodríguez* v. *Honduras* (Merits, 1988), para. 45. 160 *Ibid.*, para. 39.
161 *Ibid.* 162 *Ibid.* 163 *Ibid.*, paras. 40–1. 164 *Ibid.*, para. 41.
165 *Bustios-Rojas* (Peru), Request for Provisional Measures, Inter-Am. Ct HR 25, 28, OEA/Ser.G/CP, doc. 2146 (1991).
166 *Ibid.* 167 *Ibid.*, at 25.

merits of the petition was rendered'.[168] The Commission directly requested that the Government of Peru take precautionary measures to protect the lives and personal integrity of the seven named persons[169] and, in the same resolution, requested that the Court also order that the State adopt provisional measures in the case.[170] The Court granted the request and ordered Peru to adopt provisional measures to protect the witnesses.[171]

The provisional measures ordered to protect witnesses must often be expanded to protect the families of the witnesses.[172] Acts of retaliation are not limited to the witnesses but rather often extend to the witnesses' family members and loved ones. Consequently, those related to witnesses may also find themselves at risk. In the *Bámaca Velásquez Case*, a witness testified against specific Guatemalan State agents at a public hearing of the Court.[173] Those agents were never taken into custody.[174] Upon the witness' return to Guatemala, the Court granted the Commission's request for protective measures for all family members living with him.[175]

Even after the case is resolved and the State has made the prescribed reparations, the witnesses may continue to be in need of provisional measures of protection. In the *Blake Case*, in which Nicholas Blake, an American, disappeared in the highlands of Guatemala, provisional measures were necessary to protect the key witness and his family.[176] The witness had been the object of death threats because he had testified before the Court and Commission and had earlier informed the US Embassy officials about Blake's assassination and those involved in it.[177] Subsequent to the closure of the case, Guatemala requested that the provisional measures be terminated.[178] The Commission countered that several persons who had allegedly participated in the criminal acts against Nicholas Blake had not

[168] See Petition to the Inter-American Commission on Human Rights, Violations of the Human Rights of Peruvian Journalists Hugo Bustios Saavedra and Eduardo Rojas Arce (3 May 1990) (submitted by the Committee to Protect Journalists, 16 East 42nd Street, Third Floor, New York, NY 10017, USA) (on file with author).

[169] *Bustios-Rojas* (Peru), Request for Provisional Measures, Inter-Am. Ct HR 25, 28.

[170] *Ibid.* [171] *Ibid.*, 33 and 37.

[172] *Bámaca Velásquez* (Guatemala), Provisional Measures, Inter-Am. Ct HR, Order of 29 August 1998, Ser. E, para. 5 and Resolution 2.

[173] *Ibid.*, para. 2. [174] *Ibid.* [175] *Ibid.*, para. 5 and Resolution 2.

[176] *Blake* (Guatemala), Provisional Measures, Inter-Am. Ct HR, Order of 22 September 1995, para. 3.

[177] *Ibid.*, para. 4.

[178] *Blake* (Guatemala), Provisional Measures, Inter-Am. Ct HR, Order of 18 August 2000, Ser. E, para. 4.

been investigated or arrested, and thus were a threat to the beneficiaries of the measures.[179] The Court decided to continue the provisional measures but to require the government to report on the measures every six months rather than every two months, as it had been required to do previously.[180]

Protection of human rights activists and organizations

The Commission often requests provisional measures to protect human rights activists who are threatened or persecuted because of their human rights advocacy and activities.[181] In the *Digna Ochoa Plácido Case*, the Court ordered provisional measures after an attorney for a Mexican non-governmental organization was kidnapped, two members were threatened, and the office of the organization was ransacked.[182] Digna Ochoa, the primary beneficiary of the provisional measures, was a Mexican human rights activist. The Court ordered Mexico to adopt measures to protect her life and physical integrity as well as those of the named members of the organization, and to ensure that those working at and visiting the human rights centre could do so without danger.[183] On 28 August 2001, almost two years later, the Court lifted and terminated the provisional measures at the request of the State and with the concurrence of the Commission.[184] The acts of harassment and threats had ceased, and attorney Digna Ochoa was reportedly confident that human rights violations against her and the workers at the human rights centre 'could not happen in present day Mexico'.[185] Nonetheless, in October 2001, Digna Ochoa was found shot to death at close range in her colleague's office.[186] Her

179 *Ibid.*, para. 7. 180 *Ibid.*, Resolutions 1 and 3.

181 *Álvarez et al.* (Colombia), Provisional Measures, Inter-Am. Court HR, Order of 22 July 1997, Ser. E; *Giraldo Cardona et al.* (Colombia), Inter-Am. Ct HR, Order of 28 October 1996, Ser. E; *Digna Ochoa Plácido et al.* (Mexico), Inter-Am. Ct HR, Order of 17 November 1999, Ser. E.

182 *Digna Ochoa Plácido et al.* (Mexico), Provisional Measures, Inter-Am. Ct HR, Order of 17 November 1999, Ser. E, para. 2.

183 *Ibid.*, Resolutions 1 and 2.

184 *Digna Ochoa Plácido et al.* (Mexico), Provisional Measures, Inter-Am. Ct HR, Order of 28 August 2001, Ser. E, paras. 2–4 and Resolutions 1–2.

185 *Ibid.*, paras. 2–4; *Miguel Agustín Pro Juárez Human Rights Center et al.* (Mexico), Provisional Measures, Inter-Am. Ct HR, Order of 30 November 2001, Ser. E, paras. 8 and 10.

186 *New York Times*. 22 October 2001, International Section, A6, Ginger Thompson byline.

assassination occurred less than two months after she was no longer protected under the provisional measures. The President of the Court immediately ordered urgent measures to protect the other members of the human rights centre and the victim's family, and these measures were ratified by the Court.[187]

Similarly, in the *Girardo Cardona Case*, the president of and attorney for a Colombian human rights organization was assassinated while he was under the precautionary measures ordered by the Commission.[188] The Court subsequently ordered Colombia to take provisional measures to protect the other human rights workers in the organization and the family of the deceased attorney.[189] In the *Chunimá Case* the Commission requested provisional measures after several members of a Guatemalan Indian human rights monitoring group had been murdered and others threatened with death.[190] Americas Watch and the Center for Justice and International Law had filed the petition with the Commission.[191] As the Court was not sitting at the time of the request, the President ordered Guatemala to adopt urgent measures of protection for those named.[192] The President also convened a special session of the Court and ordered the Government of Guatemala and the Commission to appear at a public hearing.[193] Guatemala, although it twice requested postponement of the hearing, did appear and presented its position.[194] Furthermore, at the hearing, Guatemala announced the arrest and incarceration of the principal suspects, in accordance with the arrest warrants issued and in accordance with the request of the Commission.[195] Although provisional measures have not been consistently successful in protecting human rights advocates, they have been instrumental in eliminating future harm in many cases.

[187] *Miguel Agustín Pro Juárez Human Rights Center et al.* (Mexico), Provisional Measures, Inter-Am. Ct HR, Order of 30 November 2001, Ser. E, Resolutions 1–3.

[188] *Giraldo Cardona et al.* (Colombia), Provisional Measures, Inter-Am. Ct HR, Order of 27 November 1999, Ser. E, Resolutions 1 and 2.

[189] *Giraldo Cardona et al.* (Colombia), Inter-Am. Ct HR, Order of 28 October 1996, Ser. E.

[190] *Chunimá* (Guatemala), Request for Provisional Measures, Inter-Am. Ct HR, 43.

[191] *Ibid.*, at 42.

[192] *Chunimá* (Guatemala), Provisional Measures, Inter-Am. Ct HR, Order of the President of 15 July 1991, Ser. E., Resolution 1.

[193] *Ibid.*, Resolution 2. At the time of the President's Order, the Rules of Procedure of the Court required that the President convoke the Court immediately upon receiving a request for provisional measures.

[194] *Ibid.*, at 54. [195] *Ibid.*

Death penalty cases

The Inter-American Court has issued provisional measures in several joined death penalty cases.[196] In the *James et al. Case*, the Commission requested that the Court order Trinidad and Tobago to stay the imminent executions of several prisoners on death row until the Commission made determinations in their cases.[197] The State executed two of the prisoners, but subsequently stayed the executions of the others.[198] The Commission also has ordered the United States to take precautionary measures to stay the execution of prisoners on death row. The United States did not comply with these orders. The Commission could not request provisional measures from the Court in these cases, because the United States has not ratified the American Convention or accepted the jurisdiction of the Court.

Protection to allow persons to return to their homes

The Court has repeatedly issued provisional measures ordering a State to provide security so persons could return to their country or, if internally displaced, to their homes within a State. Some victims of human rights violations, family members of victims, or those who have received threats against their lives or safety have left their homes and even their countries out of fear. For example, in the *Loayza Tamayo Case*, in which Peru released the victim from prison in response to a Court order, she immediately left Peru and resided in Chile. The Court responded to a request on her behalf for provisional measures by ordering Peru *inter alia* to 'guarantee to Ms. Loayza Tamayo the necessary conditions of security for her to be able to return to the country without fear of suffering negative consequences to her physical safety, mental health and moral integrity'.[199] In its order of provisional measures in *Haitians and Dominicans of Haitian Descent in the Dominican Republic*,[200] which responded to the mass expulsions

[196] *James et al.* (Trinidad and Tobago), Provisional Measures, Inter-Am. Ct HR, Order of 16 August 2000, Ser. E.

[197] *James et al.* (Trinidad and Tobago), Provisional Measures, Inter-Am. Ct HR, Order of 29 August 1998, Ser. E, para. 1.

[198] *James et al.* (Trinidad and Tobago), Provisional Measures, Inter-Am. Ct HR, Order of 16 August 2000, Ser. E, para. 12.

[199] *Loayza Tamayo* (Peru), Provisional Measures, Order of 3 February 2001, 'Considering' section, para. 10.

[200] *Haitians and Dominicans of Haitian Descent in the Dominican Republic* (Dominican Republic), Provisional Measures, Inter-Am. Ct HR, Order of 7 August 2000.

of persons from the Dominican Republic to Haiti on the basis of skin colour[201] without the requisite due process, the Court ordered the State to permit those who had been deported to return to its territory.[202] In *Peace Community of San José de Apartadó*, in which the members of the community had left due to threats and acts of aggression, the Court ordered Colombia to provide the necessary conditions for those who had been forced to leave, to return to their homes.[203] These orders appear to have been most successful when the beneficiary is a single person or family rather than a group.

Conclusion

Provisional measures will never be a panacea for all human rights problems in the western hemisphere. These measures realistically can protect only a few people in limited situations. The threat of their adoption by the Court, however, and the attention drawn to a situation when such measures are adopted, can have a chilling effect on human rights abuses in the area and are another step towards ending these abuses in the region.

Requests for Court-ordered provisional measures have mushroomed. Moreover, in most instances, the measures, once instated, cannot be lifted, because the beneficiaries continue to be in danger for several years. The monitoring of each situation by the Commission and by the Court is putting pressure on the already limited resources of these organs. Although the institution of provisional measures and their oversight are arguably one of the most important functions of the system, because they save lives rather than merely providing reparations after the event, should such requests continue to proliferate the system may sink beneath their weight.

201 *Ibid.*, para. 2(d). 202 *Ibid.*, Resolution 4.

203 *Peace Community of San José de Apartadó* (Colombia), Provisional Measures, Inter-Am. Ct HR, Order of 24 November 2000, Ser. E, 'Considering' section, para. 8; see also *Giraldo Cardona et al.* (Colombia), Provisional Measures, Inter-Am. Ct HR, Order of 5 February 1997, Ser. E, 'Considering' section, para. 5.

7

Conclusion: the effectiveness of the Inter-American Court

> Compliance and non-compliance by states with their international obligations depends less on the formal status of a judgment and its abstract enforceability. Much more important is its impact as a force capable of legitimating governmental conduct and the perception of governments about the political cost of non-compliance.[1]

The effect of the Inter-American Court on the emergence of international human rights law

The judgments and opinions rendered by the Inter-American Court have significantly contributed to the development of international human rights law and to its doctrinal divergence from traditional international law. International human rights law principally developed following the atrocities of the Second World War. Even then, acceptance of the discipline was gradual. As late as the 1960s, influential members of the American Society of International Law argued that human rights was not a part of international law.[2] Sohn describes the advent of human rights law as a 'revolution'.[3] He writes that:

> [j]ust as the French Revolution ended the divine rights of kings, the human rights revolution that began at the 1945 San Francisco Conference of the United Nations has deprived the sovereign states of the lordly privilege of being the sole possessors of rights under international law. States have had to concede to ordinary human beings the status of subjects of international

1 Thomas Buergenthal, 'The Inter-American System for the Protection of Human Rights', in *Human Rights in International Law: Legal and Policy Issues*, 439, 470 (Theodore Meron ed., 1984).

2 Sonia Picado Sotela, 'Thomas Buergenthal', in *The Modern World of Human Rights/El Mundo Moderno de los Derechos Humanos: Essays in Honour of Thomas Buergenthal*, 19, 27 (1996).

3 See Louis Sohn, 'The New International Law: Protection of the Rights of Individuals Rather Than States', 32 *American University Law Review*, 1 (1982).

> law, to concede that individuals are no longer mere objects, mere pawns in the hands of states.[4]

The emergence of international human rights law as a separate and formal branch of public international law necessitates a re-evaluation of the foundational concepts of public international law. The Inter-American Court has reassessed many of the canons of international law to determine if they are applicable to a law that benefits individuals rather than States. The foundational principle of traditional international law is State sovereignty, which allows a State almost complete freedom in the conduct of its internal affairs, unless the State voluntarily relinquishes certain aspects of its sovereignty. Without that voluntary relinquishment, external forces, such as other States or international organizations, ordinarily cannot interfere. Even a State's treatment of its nationals was traditionally considered to be a matter of State sovereignty and not subject to outside intervention. A State's voluntary act, however, has long been held to cede to international law subject matter that was originally under the State's sovereignty. The State may do so by ratifying a treaty or by failing to persistently object to an emerging principle of customary international law. This positivist or classic view provides that international law derives from the voluntary will of the State. It was expressed in the celebrated statement of the Permanent Court of International Justice in the *Lotus Case* which provided that:

> [i]nternational law governs relations between independent States. The rules of law binding upon States therefore emanate from their own free will as expressed in conventions or by usages generally accepted as expressing principles of law and established in order to regulate the relations between these co-existing independent communities or with a view to the achievement of common aims. Restrictions upon the independence of States cannot therefore be presumed.[5]

The voluntary aspect of international law was defensible when international law pertained exclusively to obligations between States. It is untenable today when international law is envisioned as also regulating State obligations to individuals, organizations and the global environment. Gradually, human rights law has begun to chip away at the foundation of consent and State sovereignty in international law. As the rights of the individual are recognized, this liberalization results in non-governmental organizations and scholars demanding even greater rights for individuals,

[4] *Ibid.* [5] *SS 'Lotus' (France* v. *Turkey)*, 1927 PCIJ Ser. A, No. 10, at 18 (7 September).

groups and organizations. More recently, international courts and commentators have gone to the extent of suggesting that the voluntary nature of State obligations, at least in the area of human rights, is inappropriate.

The Inter-American Court has also proclaimed that the concept of 'reciprocity' that has characterized treaty obligations between States is not applicable to human rights treaties.[6] The Inter-American Court differentiates human rights treaties from other treaties, reasoning that they:

> are not multilateral treaties of the traditional type concluded to accomplish the reciprocal exchange of rights for the mutual benefit of the contracting States. Their object and purpose is the protection of the basic rights of individual human beings, irrespective of their nationality, both against the State of their nationality and all other contracting States.[7]

Cançado Trindade cites several factors supporting the *sui generis* character of human rights treaties, including the objective nature of human rights obligations, the independence of treaty terms from the domestic law of the State, the collective guarantee underlying human rights treaties, the broad scope of the protection, and the narrow interpretation of the express restrictions permitted.[8] He reasons that together these factors fulfil the object and purpose of human rights treaties, maintain the integrity of the treaties and establish limits on the voluntary nature of State responsibilities. Cançado Trindade asserts that there is 'a new vision of relations between the public power and the human being, that comes down, in the final analysis, to the recognition that the State exists for the human being and not *vice versa*'.[9]

The Inter-American Court does not impose a static interpretation of human rights on the American Convention. The concept of the basic rights owing to individuals has expanded over time. These rights have been elaborated in the light of the changing societal conditions that have enriched human rights law in the previous fifty years. The Court interprets the Convention 'within the framework of the entire legal system prevailing at the time of the interpretation',[10] thus permitting the evolution of the rights.

[6] *Effect of Reservations on the Entry into Force of the American Convention on Human Rights (Arts. 74 and 75)*, Inter-Am. Ct HR, Advisory Opinion OC-2/82 of 24 September 1982, Ser. A, No. 2, para. 29.

[7] *Ibid.*

[8] *Blake* v. *Guatemala* (Reparations), Inter-Am. Ct HR, 22 January 1999, Ser. C, No. 48, Separate Opinion of Judge Cançado Trindade, para. 33.

[9] *Ibid.*

[10] *Right to Information on Consular Assistance Within the Framework of the Guarantees of Legal Due Process*, Inter-Am. Ct HR, Advisory Opinion OC-16/99 of 1 October 1999, Ser. A, No. 16, para. 113.

The Court has also given its judicial imprimatur to principles of law that have been controversial or unsettled. Notably, the Court has underscored the fundamental principle that an effective and functioning democracy is the essential form of government for the protection and enforcement of human rights, contradicting the opposing view that the form of government is immaterial.[11] The Court has also emphasized that human rights are universal rather than culturally relative in character.[12] The Court reasoned that, if it were to recognize distinctions based on a regional character of human rights obligations, it would 'deny the existence of the common core of basic human rights standards'.[13] The principle that rights are culturally relative would allow for distinctions and exceptions on the basis of religious or cultural differences, distinctions which sometimes support human rights violations.

The Court has clarified that the concept of the non-derogability of select fundamental human rights includes specific judicial guarantees such as *habeas corpus* which are essential to the protection of those rights.[14] The Court held that, even in times of emergency, the State may not derogate from certain judicial guarantees as they are essential to the protection of other non-derogable rights such as the right to life and the right to humane treatment. The Court stated that '[h]abeas corpus performs a vital role in ensuring that a person's life and physical integrity are respected, in preventing his disappearance or the keeping of his whereabouts secret and in protecting him against torture or cruel, inhumane, or degrading punishment or treatment'.[15]

Significantly, the Court holds that States cannot make reservations to rights which are defined as being non-derogable by the American Convention. In this regard, the Court made the important pronouncement

[11] *Word 'Laws' in Article 30 of the American Convention on Human Rights*, Inter-Am. Ct HR, Advisory Opinion OC-6/86 of 9 May 1986, Ser. A, No. 6, para. 32; *Compulsory Membership in an Association Prescribed by Law for the Practice of Journalism (Arts. 13 and 29 of the American Convention on Human Rights)*, Inter-Am. Ct HR, Advisory Opinion OC-5/85 of 13 November 1985, Ser. A, No. 5, para. 42.

[12] *'Other Treaties' Subject to the Consultative Jurisdiction of the Court (Art. 64 of the American Convention on Human Rights)*, Inter-Am. Ct HR, Advisory Opinion OC-1/82, of 24 September 1982, Ser. A, No. 1, para. 40.

[13] *Ibid.*

[14] *Habeas Corpus in Emergency Situations (Arts. 27(2) and 7(6) of the American Convention on Human Rights)*, Inter-Am. Ct HR, Advisory Opinion OC-8/87 of 30 January 1987, Ser. A, No. 8, para. 11.

[15] *Judicial Guarantees in States of Emergency (Arts. 27(2), 25 and 8 of the American Convention on Human Rights)*, Inter-Am. Ct HR, Advisory Opinion OC-9/87 of 6 October 1987, Ser. A, No. 9, para. 35.

that 'a reservation which was designed to enable a State to suspend any of the non-derogable fundamental rights must be deemed to be incompatible with the object and purpose of the Convention, and, consequently, not permitted by it'.[16]

The Court reinforced the well-accepted principle of non-discrimination in human rights law, but went on to clarify that all differences are not discriminatory, effectively condoning affirmative action. The Court found that discrepancies in legal treatment are *per se* discriminatory only when they have 'no objective and reasonable justification'.[17] According to the Court, certain inequalities may be instrumental in attaining justice for those who are in a 'weak legal position'.[18]

The Court is also making inroads into the traditional concept that a State may commit itself to protect human rights on an international plane by ratifying a human rights treaty, but that those rights may not be self-executing on the domestic plane. The Court has stated that '[i]n concluding these human rights treaties, the States can be deemed to submit themselves to a legal order within which they, for the common good, assume various obligations, not in relation to other States, but towards all individuals within their jurisdiction'.[19] Given this reality, provisions in human rights treaties which are sufficiently definite should be considered to be inherently self-executing and, therefore, automatically incorporated into the law of domestic States that ratify the human rights convention. It should be understood that, if a domestic law conflicts with the State's international treaty obligations, the State is in violation of its international obligations, and the Court may order the State to amend or repeal the law so as to comply with the treaty provisions. This authority has been asserted by the Court. It now orders States to adopt laws or amend and repeal laws that are in conflict with the American Convention. Domestic courts and legislatures are complying with these judgments and advisory opinions. The European Court of Justice has long assumed this authority based on the States' renunciation of certain sovereign rights in accepting the legal system of the European Union and on the principle of effectiveness. The principle of effectiveness provides that, unless international law is given

[16] *Restrictions to the Death Penalty (Arts. 4(2) and 4(4) of the American Convention on Human Rights)*, Inter-Am. Ct HR, Advisory Opinion OC-3/83, of 8 September 1983, Ser. A, No. 3, para. 61.

[17] *Proposed Amendments to the Naturalization Provisions of the Constitution of Costa Rica*, Inter-Am. Ct HR, Advisory Opinion OC-4/84 of 19 January 1984, Ser. A, No. 4, para. 56.

[18] *Ibid.* [19] *Ibid.*

priority over State law, international law cannot be applied in a reasonable and useful way.[20] This reasoning is even more applicable when the subject matter of the laws in question is the protection of individual human rights.

Domestic and institutional change resulting from the application of the American Convention and the rulings of the Inter-American Court

The mere existence of the American Convention and the Inter-American Court has a chilling effect on human rights abuses within States. Domestic courts in some States Parties have incorporated the American Convention into domestic law, and have relied on it in domestic rulings. For example, Chilean superior courts have ruled that, pursuant to the American Convention which has been ratified by Chile and is therefore incorporated into national law, no one can be imprisoned for debt, and torture may not be used during interrogations.[21] In Peru, even before the Inter-American Court held that the amnesty laws contravened the American Convention, a judge refused to dismiss criminal cases pending in her court against State officials, because she held that the amnesty laws violated the Peruvian Constitution and the international obligations undertaken by Peru pursuant to its ratification of the American Convention.[22] The Judicial Committee of the Privy Council, Trinidad and Tobago's highest appeals court, ordered the State to stay all executions until the prisoners' cases were resolved by the Inter-American Court and Commission.[23] It held that the failure to do so 'would constitute a breach of the constitutional rights of the alleged victims'.[24]

It may be sufficient for a case to be referred to the Court to bring about change within a State. Several States Parties, including Argentina,[25]

[20] *Ibid.*

[21] See *'The Last Temptation of Christ' (Olmedo Bustos et al.* v. *Chile)*, Inter-Am. Ct HR, 5 February 2001, Ser. C, No. 73, para. 45(d).

[22] *Barrios Altos (Chumbipuma Aguirre et al.* v. *Peru)* (Merits), Inter-Am. Ct HR, 14 March 2001, Ser. C, No. 75, para. 2(k).

[23] *Hilaire, Constantine and Benjamin et al.* v. *Trinidad and Tobago* (Merits), Inter-Am. Ct HR, 21 June 2002, Ser. C, No. 94, para. 84(q), citing *Thomas and Hilaire* v. *Batiste et al*, Privy Council Appeal No. 60 of 1998.

[24] *Ibid.*

[25] *Garrido and Baigorria* v. *Argentina* (Merits), Inter-Am. Ct HR, 2 February 1996, Ser. C, No. 26, para. 25.

Bolivia,[26] Ecuador,[27] Peru,[28] Venezuela[29] and Suriname,[30] have accepted international responsibility for human rights violations when confronted with litigation before the Court. In the *Trujillo Oroza Case*, for example, when the case was submitted to the Court, Bolivia accepted responsibility for the detention, torture and murder of a university student, who had disappeared after he was taken into custody by government agents.[31] Also, in the *Del Caracazo Case* against Venezuela, it was only when the case was before the Court in 1999 that the government accepted responsibility for several deaths resulting from the military crackdown on civil disturbances which took place in 1989.[32] Peru, after first renouncing its acceptance of the jurisdiction of the Court, later reversed its position and also accepted international responsibility in the cases pending before it, including the *Barrios Altos Case*,[33] the *Constitutional Court Case*[34] and the *Ivcher Bronstein Case*.[35] The contentious judgments, advisory opinions and provisional measures of the Court have also resulted in changes both nationally and internationally.

Domestic and institutional implementation of the Court's advisory opinions

Inter-American Court advisory opinions are influencing the implementation of human rights law on a national basis. National courts are relying

[26] *Trujillo Oroza* v. *Bolivia* (Merits), Inter-Am. Ct HR, 26 January 2000, Ser. C, No. 64, paras. 36–7.

[27] *Benavides Cevallos* v. *Ecuador* (Merits), Inter-Am. Ct HR, 19 June 1998, Ser. C, No. 38, para. 35.

[28] *Barrios Altos (Chumbipuma Aguirre et al.* v. *Peru)* (Merits), Inter-Am. Ct HR, 14 March 2001, Ser. C, No. 75, para. 31(1); *Castillo Páez, Loayza Tamayo, Castillo Petruzzi et al., Ivcher Bronstein and Constitutional Court* v. *Peru Cases* (Compliance with Judgment), Inter-Am. Ct HR, Order of 1 June 2001, para. 11, citing Peru's acceptance of responsibility in the *Ivcher Bronstein* and *Constitutional Court Cases.*

[29] *El Amparo* v. *Venezuela* (Merits), Inter-Am. Ct HR, 18 January 1995, Ser. C, No. 19, para. 19; *Del Caracazo* v. *Venezuela* (Merits), Inter-Am. Ct HR, 11 November 1999, Ser. C, No. 58, para. 37.

[30] *Aloeboetoe et al.* v. *Suriname* (Merits), Inter-Am. Ct HR, 4 December 1991, Ser. C, No. 11, para. 22.

[31] *Trujillo Oroza* v. *Bolivia* (Merits, 2000), paras. 36–7.

[32] *Del Caracazo* v. *Venezuela* (Merits), Inter-Am. Ct HR, 11 November 1999, Ser. C, No. 58, para. 37.

[33] *Barrios Altos (Chumbipuma Aguirre et al.* v. *Peru)* (Merits, 2001), paras. 31 and 34–5.

[34] The *Castillo Páez, Loayza Tamayo, Castillo Petruzzi et al., Ivcher Bronstein and Constitutional Court* v. *Peru Cases* (Compliance with Judgment), Inter-Am. Ct HR, Order of 1 June 2001, para. 11.

[35] *Ibid.*

on and citing the Inter-American Court's advisory opinions in the interpretation of their domestic laws. For example, the Costa Rican Supreme Court's Constitutional Chamber has nullified or reinterpreted domestic laws found by the Inter-American Court to be incompatible with the American Convention.[36] In response to the Inter-American Court's advisory opinion *Compulsory Membership in an Association Prescribed by Law for the Practice of Journalism*, the Costa Rican Supreme Court's Constitutional Chamber nullified a domestic law mandating the compulsory membership of journalists and reporters in an association which limited membership to university graduates who had specialized only in certain fields.[37] In the advisory opinion, the Inter-American Court advised Costa Rica that the law was incompatible with freedom of expression under the Convention, because it denied 'any person access to the full use of the news media as a means of expressing opinions or imparting information'.[38] The Constitutional Chamber reiterated the reasoning of the Inter-American Court in its decision.[39] The Constitutional Chamber also stated that, when a State requests an advisory opinion on the compatibility of its domestic laws with the American Convention or other treaties, the opinion is binding and obligatory on the government that requested it.[40] In another Costa Rican opinion, the Constitutional Chamber declared, in accordance with the Inter-American Court's advisory opinion *Proposed Amendments to the Naturalization Provisions of the Constitution of Costa Rica*, that a State law on nationalization of spouses could not discriminate on the basis of gender.[41]

The Argentine Supreme Court, relying on the advisory opinion *Enforceability of the Right to Reply or Correction*, held that the American

[36] Acción de Incost, No. 421-S-80, *Roger Ajun Blanco, Art. 22 Ley Org. Col. de Periodistas*, Sala Constitucional de la Corte Suprema de Justicia (9 May 1995) (Costa Rica).

[37] See Pedro Nikken, 'La Función Consultiva de la Corte Interamericana de Derechos Humanos', in *El Sistema Interamericano de Protección de los Derechos Humanos en el Umbral del Siglo XXI: Memoria del Seminario Noviembre de 1999*, vol. I, 161, at 178 (2001), citing the Constitutional Chamber of the Supreme Court of Justice of Costa Rica Exp. 0421-S-90.-No. 2313-95 (9 May 1995).

[38] *Compulsory Membership in an Association Prescribed by Law for the Practice of Journalism*, Advisory Opinion OC-5/85, para. 85 (citing Costa Rican Law No. 4420).

[39] Acción de Incost, No. 421-S-80, *Roger Ajun Blanco, Art. 22 Ley Org. Col. de Periodistas*, Sala Constitucional de la Corte Suprema de Justicia (9 May 1995) (Costa Rica).

[40] See Nikken, 'La Función Consultiva', at 179, citing the Constitutional Chamber of the Supreme Court of Justice of Costa Rica Exp. 0421-S-90.-No. 2313-95 (9 May 1995).

[41] Expediente 2965-S-91, Voto: 3435-92, *Ricardo Fliman Wargraft* v. *Director y Jefe de la Sección de Opciones y Naturalizaciones*, Sala Constitucional de la Corte Suprema de Justicia (11 November 1992) (Costa Rica).

Convention creates a directly enforceable right of reply in Argentina without the need for separate domestic legislation.[42] The applicable provision of the American Convention provides that a person 'injured by inaccurate or offensive statements or ideas disseminated to the public in general by a legally regulated medium of communication has the right to reply or to make a correction using the same communications outlet, under such conditions as the law may establish'.[43] The Inter-American Court stated in its advisory opinion that 'any State Party that does not already ensure the free and full exercise of the right to reply or correction is under an obligation to bring about that result, be it by legislation or whatever other measures may be necessary under its domestic legal system'.[44]

Every advisory opinion has not necessarily met a positive response in domestic courts but may nonetheless influence human rights. Following the Inter-American Court's advisory opinion in *The Right to Consular Assistance*, which determined that the Vienna Convention on Consular Relations requires that law enforcement authorities who arrest a foreigner inform the detainee of the right to notify his or her consulate,[45] foreign nationals have unsuccessfully attempted to rely on the advisory opinion in US courts.[46] Although most US courts have not granted relief to these defendants, the negative publicity raised by the Inter-American Court's advisory opinion and the ICJ's decision in the *LaGrand Case*[47] have resulted in positive changes for foreigners arrested in the US in the wake of those decisions. Shortly after submission of *The Right to Consular Assistance* advisory request to the Inter-American Court, the US Department of State issued and distributed to all US law enforcement agencies a handbook entitled *Consular Notification and Access: Instructions for Federal, State and Local Law Enforcement and Other Officials Regarding Foreign Nationals in the United States and the Rights of Consular*

[42] Thomas Buergenthal, 'International Tribunals and National Courts: The Internationalization of Domestic Adjudication', in *Recht zwischen Umbruch und Bewahrung*, 687, 695 (Max-Planck, 1995) (citing *Ekmekdjian* v. *Sofovich*, No. E. 64. XXIII, 315 Fallos 1492, 1511–15 (Argentina, Corte Suprema de Justicia de la Nación, 1992)).

[43] American Convention, Art. 14(1).

[44] *Enforceability of the Right to Reply or Correction (Arts. 14(1), 1(1) and 2 of the American Convention on Human Rights)*, Inter-Am. Ct HR, Advisory Opinion OC-7/86 of 29 August 1986, Ser. A, No. 7, para. 33.

[45] *Right to Information on Consular Assistance in the Framework of the Guarantees of Legal Due Process*, Advisory Opinion OC-16/99, operative para. 1.

[46] *United States* v. *Li*, 206 F 3d 56 (1st Cir. 2000) (*en banc*); *United States* v. *José Lombera-Camorlinga*, 206 F 3d 882, 882–3 (2000) (*en banc*).

[47] See *LaGrand (Germany* v. *United States)*, 2001 ICJ Reports 104 (27 June).

Officials to Assist Them.[48] The handbook informs arresting authorities of the rights provided to foreign nationals by the Vienna Convention on Consular Relations. It provides detailed instructions to detaining officials that the foreign individual who is detained has a mandatory right to consular notification.[49] Moreover, it encourages enforcement officers to employ the golden rule. It explains that '[t]hese are mutual obligations that also pertain to American citizens abroad. In general, you should treat a foreign national as you would want an American citizen to be treated in a similar situation in a foreign country.'[50] The State Department's instructions to US law enforcement authorities are at least partially in response to the Inter-American Court's advisory opinion and the negative worldwide publicity it generated regarding the US failure to comply with the Convention.

Not all States have revised their domestic laws to correspond with the Court's advisory opinions. Some States, for instance, continue to have laws that authorize the derogation of the right of *habeas corpus* during a state of emergency. This practice ignores two advisory opinions interpreting the American Convention as prohibiting the suspension of *habeas corpus.*[51]

The mere institution of advisory opinion proceedings may encourage a State to examine its laws and actions and bring them into compliance with its human rights obligations. One example of such governmental action was made evident at a public hearing on an advisory opinion request concerning the legality of Guatemala's extension of the death penalty.[52] In 1982, following a military coup by General Efriam Rios Montt, Guatemala established special courts to combat subversion.[53] These Courts of Special Jurisdiction typically met in secret and arguably did not provide even minimum due process guarantees to defendants.[54] The government had also extended the death penalty to crimes which were not punishable by death at the time Guatemala ratified the American Convention.[55] Guatemala executed those defendants found guilty under the new laws.[56] Despite pleas from the Inter-American Commission and from

[48] See State Department, Pub. No. 10518, *Consular Notification and Access: Instructions for Federal, State and Local Law Enforcement and Other Officials Regarding Foreign Nationals in the United States and the Rights of Consular Officials to Assist Them* (January 1998).

[49] *Ibid.*, at 251. [50] *Ibid.*

[51] See *Judicial Guarantees in States of Emergency*, Advisory Opinion OC-9/87, *Habeas Corpus in Emergency Situations*, Advisory Opinion OC-8/87, para. 36.

[52] *Restrictions to the Death Penalty*, Advisory Opinion OC-3/83.

[53] Charles Moyer and David Padilla, 'Executions in Guatemala as Decreed by the Courts of Special Jurisdiction in 1982–83: A Case Study', 6 *Human Rights Quarterly*, 507 (1984).

[54] *Ibid.*, at 508. [55] *Ibid.*, at 509. [56] *Ibid.*, at 511.

Pope John Paul II, who was about to visit Guatemala, the State proceeded with the executions.[57] Although Guatemala had not accepted the Court's jurisdiction, and thus could not be brought before it in a contentious case, the Commission sought an advisory opinion from the Court.[58] Guatemala objected to the admissibility of the advisory opinion petition,[59] but attended the public hearing on the matter. At the public hearing Guatemala unexpectedly announced the suspension of the executions,[60] which were never resumed. The public exposure caused by the Court's consideration of the issue resulted in this change of policy. Moreover, Guatemala subsequently withdrew the reservation to the Convention that had resulted in the advisory opinion.[61] Thus, advisory opinions interpreting the substantive provisions of the American Convention and determining the compatibility of a State's domestic laws with its international legal obligations have encouraged States to revise their domestic laws and actions.

Advisory opinions on the procedural provisions of the American Convention have also contributed to the refinement of the application of those procedures by the Inter-American Commission. States have twice requested that the Court interpret the provisions of the American Convention specifying procedures that the Commission must follow.[62] In part, responding to the Court's advisory opinions as well as to preliminary objections in contentious cases, the Commission has revised its procedures in handling individual complaints. The Commission now registers petitions, makes an express declaration of admissibility, requires a friendly settlement phase, and follows guidelines to determine which cases shall be referred to the Court.

Finally, the Court's advisory opinion *The Effect of Reservations* resulted in a change of policy in the OAS. Prior to the advisory opinion, States that ratified the American Convention with reservations were not immediately considered to be parties to the treaty. Subsequent to the Court's advisory opinion, which held the opposite, the new OAS Legal Advisor advised the Secretary General that Argentina had become a State Party on the date

57 *Ibid.*, at 508. 58 Advisory Opinion OC-3/83. 59 *Ibid.*, para. 11.

60 Moyer and Padilla, 'Executions in Guatemala', at 516 and 520.

61 See Nikken, 'La Función Consultiva', at 177, citing the Guatemalan Acuerdo Gubernativo No. 281-86 of 20 May 1986.

62 *Certain Attributes of the Inter-American Commission on Human Rights*, Inter-Am. Ct HR, Advisory Opinion OC-13/93 of 16 July 1993, Ser. A, No. 13; and *Reports of the Inter-American Commission on Human Rights*, Inter-Am. Ct HR, Advisory Opinion OC-15/97 of 14 November 1997, Ser. A, No. 15.

of its ratification despite doing so with reservations.[63] Thus, the Court's advisory opinions are contributing to the development of human rights law on several levels: institutional, national and international.[64]

Domestic implementation of provisional measures

In general, governments have made an effort to comply with both the initial orders of urgent measures made by the President of the Court and the orders for provisional measures taken by the full Court. For instance, in the *Gallardo Rodríguez Case*, a Mexican general had been imprisoned since 1995, allegedly for criticizing abuses of power within the Mexican army.[65] The Inter-American Commission and the United Nations Working Group on Arbitrary Detention had studied the case and had declared his detention to be illegal.[66] The President of the Inter-American Court, in conjunction with all the judges of the Court, ordered urgent measures to protect General Gallardo Rodríguez and called for a public hearing to be held before the plenary Court on 18 February 2001. Mexico released the long-time prisoner before the hearing took place.[67] Another impressive demonstration of government compliance occurred at the public hearing on provisional measures in the *Chunimá Case*.[68] There, the Guatemalan Government made the surprise announcement that, in accordance with a Commission request, it had arrested the civil patrol leaders who were allegedly responsible for the assassinations.[69]

Although it is difficult to prove that the reason that persons were not harmed was because a government adopted provisional measures for their protection, it is interesting to note the occurrences in the *Honduran Disappearance Cases*. When two witnesses who had appeared before the Court received death threats,[70] the President of the Court requested that the

[63] See Thomas Buergenthal, 'The Advisory Practice of the Inter-American Human Rights Court', 79 *American Journal of International Law*, 1, at 4 (1985).

[64] *Ibid.*, at 2.

[65] *Gallardo Rodriguez Case* (Mexico), Provisional Measures, Inter-Am. Ct HR, Order of the President, 20 December 2001.

[66] *Ibid.*

[67] See Statement of the Secretary of Foreign Affairs, Jorge G. Castañeda, During the Joint Conference with the Secretary of the Interior, Santiago Creel, Mexico City, 7 February 2002.

[68] *Chunimá* (Guatemala), Provisional Measures of the Inter-Am. Ct HR, Order of 1 August 1991, para. 4.

[69] *Ibid.*

[70] *Velásquez Rodríguez Case* (Merits), Inter-Am. Ct HR, Judgment of 29 July 1988, Ser. C, No. 4, para. 39.

Government of Honduras protect those particular witnesses. The government duly informed the Court that it would guarantee their safety as requested.[71] Although those named witnesses were not harmed, three other witnesses who had appeared before the Court or who were scheduled to give evidence were subsequently murdered.[72]

Not all governments, however, have complied with provisional measures orders. Trinidad and Tobago executed two prisoners who were covered by Court-ordered provisional measures.[73] The measures required that the State 'take all measures to preserve [their] lives' so as not to hinder the processing of their cases before the Inter-American system.[74] The State did not, however, execute the other beneficiaries of the measures.

Domestic implementation of Court orders in contentious cases

The Inter-American Court has been particularly effective in advancing the development of reparations in international human rights law. The Court has gone further than the European system by ordering States to amend domestic laws that are in violation of the American Convention,[75] to annul domestic court judgments that were reached in violation of the Convention, and to execute domestic court judgments that States have refused to execute in favour of individuals.[76] The Court has also ordered that victims who did not receive due process guarantees be released from prison, and the States concerned have complied with the Court's orders.

Inter-American Court rulings that State laws violate the American Convention have resulted in the repeal or amendment of those laws. For example, in the *Suárez Rosero Case*, Ecuador's Constitutional Court declared a provision in its criminal code to be unconstitutional after the Inter-American Court found it to be in violation of the American Convention.[77] In Peru, the Supreme Court of Military Justice complied with the Inter-American Court's ruling that it annul its domestic judgment against Mr Cesti Hurtado.[78] The State thereafter notified the Court that 'the

[71] *Ibid.* [72] *Ibid.*, paras. 40–1.

[73] *James et al.* (Trinidad and Tobago), Provisional Measures, Inter-Am. Ct HR, Order of 16 August 2000, Ser. E, paras. 4 and 12.

[74] *Ibid.*, quoting Orders of 29 August 1998, 25 May 1999 and 27 May 1999.

[75] See Chapter 5, pp. 247–8 above.

[76] *Ibid.*; *Cesti Hurtado* v. *Peru* (Merits), paras. 193 and 194.

[77] *Suárez Rosero* v. *Ecuador* (Reparations) (Art. 63(1) American Convention of Human Rights), Inter-Am. Ct HR, 20 January 1999, Ser. C, No. 44, paras. 81–3.

[78] *Cesti Hurtado* v. *Peru* (Reparations), Inter-Am Ct HR, 31 May 2001, Ser. C, No. 78, para. 15.

orders against the victim that restricted his freedom and embargoed his property are suspended',[79] and that the victim was released from prison before the reparations stage of the case.[80]

In general, States are making Court-ordered monetary reparations, although compliance is not universal. Some of those that have paid the beneficiaries include Suriname in the *Gangaram Panday Case*,[81] Guatemala in the *Blake Case*,[82] Ecuador in the *Benavides Cevallos Case*,[83] Honduras in the *Velásquez Rodríguez* and *Godínez Cruz Cases*,[84] Argentina in the *Garrido and Baigorria Case*[85] and Venezuela in the *El Amparo Case*, although it still owes interest for delay in payment.[86] Peru made full payment in *Castillo Páez*,[87] *Neira Alegría*,[88] *Loayza Tamayo*[89] and the *Constitutional Court Cases*,[90] and partial payment in the *Durand and Ugarte*[91] and the *Ivcher Bronstein Cases*.[92] It is not sufficient, however, that States pay compensation and neglect to comply with other Court-ordered reparations which are meant to deter future violations. States should not be perceived to pay for their actions that violate human rights.

States have been less responsive to Court orders to end impunity and identify, prosecute and punish those responsible for human rights

79 *Ibid.*

80 *Cesti Hurtado* v. *Peru* (Request for Interpretation of the Judgment of 29 September 1999), Inter-Am. Ct HR, Order of 19 November 1999, Ser. C, No. 62, para. 6.

81 *Gangaram Panday*, Order of the Inter-Am. Ct HR, 27 November 1998, Ser. C, para. 1.

82 2000 Annual Report of the Inter-American Court of Human Rights, OEA/Ser.L/V/III.50, doc. 4, 29 January 2000, at 39.

83 *Benavides Cevallos* v. *Ecuador* (Merits), Inter-Am. Ct HR, 19 June 1998, Ser. C, No. 38, para. 56.

84 *Velásquez Rodríguez* (Interpretation of the Compensatory Damages), Inter-Am. Ct HR, 17 August 1990, Ser. C, No. 9; *Godínez Cruz* (Interpretation of the Compensatory Damages); *La Tribuna* (Tegucigalpa, Honduras), 8 February 1996, Nacionales Section, at 13.

85 *Garrido and Baigorria* v. *Peru* (Compliance with Judgment), Inter-Am. Ct HR, Resolution of 27 November 2002, 'Considering' section, para. 6.

86 *El Amparo* v. *Venezuela* (Compliance with Judgment), Inter-Am. Ct HR, Resolution of 28 November 2002, Resolution 2.

87 *Castillo Páez* v. *Peru* (Compliance with Judgment), Inter-Am. Ct HR, Resolution of 28 November 2002, paras. 7 and 10.

88 *Neira Alegría et al.* v. *Peru* (Compliance with Judgment), Inter-Am. Ct HR, Resolution of 28 November 2002, 'Considering' section, para. 6.

89 *Loayza Tamayo* v. *Peru* (Compliance with Judgment), Inter-Am. Ct HR, Resolution of 27 November 2002, 'Considering' section, para. 6.

90 *Constitutional Court* v. *Peru*, status of compliance with judgment, in 2001 Annual Report of the Inter-Am. Ct HR, OEA/Ser.L/V/III.54, doc. 4, at 50.

91 *Durand and Ugarte* v. *Peru* (Compliance with Judgment), Inter-Am. Ct HR, Resolution of 27 November 2002, para. 3.

92 *Ivcher Bronstein* v. *Peru*, status of compliance with judgment, in 2001 Annual Report of the Inter-Am. Ct HR, OEA/Ser.L/V/III.54, doc. 4, at 50.

violations. One of those responsible for the murder of Nicholas Blake in Guatemala has been tried, convicted and condemned to twenty-eight years in prison.[93] However, in most other cases, States do not appear to have made good-faith efforts to comply with this aspect of the Court's reparations decision.

Limitations on the Inter-American system

Limitations on the Inter-American human rights system have an adverse effect on its ability to protect and promote human rights. The ultimate success or failure of the Inter-American human rights system rests upon the financial, political and moral support of the OAS member States. State action or inaction influences the effectiveness of the Inter-American system, and, in particular, the Inter-American Court. The Court today confronts limitations that include the lack of universality, the necessity for domestic implementation, the failure of the political organs of the OAS to carry out the role assigned to them by the American Convention, inadequate funding, and the absence of a control mechanism to review the qualifications of nominees to the Court.

Lack of universality

The proper functioning of the Inter-American human rights system requires universality of State ratification or accession to the American Convention and acceptance of the jurisdiction of the Court. Twenty-four of the thirty-five Member States of the OAS are currently parties to the American Convention.[94] The States that have failed to ratify the Convention are the United States and Canada, as well as Belize, Guyana and several Caribbean nations. Twenty-one of the States Parties have accepted the compulsory jurisdiction of the Inter-American Court.[95]

The lack of universality complicates the functioning of the Inter-American Commission, which must apply different criteria depending on whether a State is or is not a party to the American Convention. The OAS Charter authorizes the Commission 'to promote the observance and protection of human rights' in all Member States.[96] Under its Statute, the Commission must apply the human rights provisions of the American

[93] 2001 Annual Report of the Inter-Am. Ct HR, OEA/Ser.L/V/III.54, doc. 4, at 43–4.
[94] See text at Chapter 1, note 19. [95] See text at Chapter 1, note 64.
[96] OAS Charter, Art. 106.

Declaration of the Rights and Duties of Man – and not the Convention – to those OAS Member States that are not parties to the Convention.[97] To further complicate matters, not all States Parties to the Convention have accepted the compulsory jurisdiction of the Court. The Commission may automatically refer cases to the Court only where the State concerned has accepted jurisdiction.[98] Finally, States may make reservations to rights protected by the Convention, thereby altering the system of protection in that State.

Every year the OAS General Assembly calls upon the American States to ratify or accede to the American Convention.[99] When Canada joined the OAS in 1990, it was committed to ratifying the American Convention. Canada's Counselor and Alternate Permanent Representative to the OAS explained that the delay in ratification was due to Canadian jurisdictional issues, in that human rights fall primarily under the jurisdiction of the provinces rather than under federal jurisdiction. While the Canadian federal government has the treaty-making authority, it must engage in consultations with the provincial governments prior to ratification.[100] The consultations have not yet been fruitful, reportedly due in part to the text of the right to life provision as well as other problems.[101] Likewise, the United States has a federal system in which criminal law falls to the individual states. If the US were to ratify the American Convention, it would most likely do so with reservations and understandings to certain provisions. For example, the US would presumably make reservations to the provision that the death penalty not be reinstituted in States that have abolished it, and that it shall not be inflicted on anyone who has committed a crime before reaching the age of majority.[102] Also, the right to life provision that specifies that life begins, in general, at conception[103] would require a reservation, because of the US Supreme Court's ruling on abortion. When the United States ratified the Genocide Convention and the Torture Convention after several years, it did so with reservations

[97] Statute of the Inter-American Commission on Human Rights, Art. 1(1), approved by General Assembly Resolution 447 at its ninth regular session, held in La Paz, Bolivia, Arts. 19 and 20(a), October 1979, reprinted in 2001 Basic Documents, at 119.

[98] American Convention, Art. 62.

[99] OAS General Assembly Resolution Evaluating the Workings of the Inter-American System, para. 3(a).

[100] See Brian Tittemore, 'Canada and the OAS – The First Five Years', *Human Rights Brief*, 2 (1995), available at http://www.wcl.american.edu/hrbrief/v2i3/canada23.htm.

[101] William A. Schabas, 'Canadian Ratification of the American Convention on Human Rights', 16 *Netherlands Quarterly of Human Rights*, 315 (1998).

[102] American Convention, Art. 4(3) and (5).

[103] *Ibid.*, Art. 4(1).

and understandings. It is questionable, however, whether such reservations would be compatible with the object and purpose of the American Convention.

It can be argued that, by ratifying the American Convention, even with multiple reservations, the United States and Canada would strengthen human rights protections in the Americas. According to this reasoning, until ratification of the American Convention is universal and all States Parties have accepted the jurisdiction of the Court, the system will continue to operate in a complicated piecemeal fashion. Conversely, it has been asserted that multiple reservations to the American Convention violate the integrity of the treaty and weaken the Inter-American human rights system.[104] Under this view, the lack of integrity of the American Convention caused by multiple reservations may be considered a greater problem than the lack of universality.[105]

Necessity for domestic implementation

The universality of the system is irrelevant if States do not domestically implement the rights protected by the Convention, the judgments of the Court, and the recommendations of the Commission. The American Convention mandates that States give domestic legal effect to the rights it delineates.[106] All States Parties 'undertake to adopt, in accordance with their constitutional processes and the provisions of this Convention, such legislative or other measures as may be necessary to give effect to those rights or freedoms'.[107] Thus, States Parties must take steps to internalize the international human rights norms which they committed themselves to ensure and protect when they ratified the Convention. When States fulfil their duties to ensure and protect rights on the domestic plane, the burden on the international enforcement organs will be lightened.

States Parties must take legal measures to make the judgments of the Court self-executing in their domestic courts. States Parties also have a duty to comply promptly with all judgments of the Court.[108] Moreover, they should also take steps to ensure compliance with the

[104] See Hernán Salgado Pesantes, 'Las Reservas en los Tratados de Derechos Humanos', in *Liber Amicorum Héctor Fix-Zamudio*, vol. I, 1, at 12–13 (1998).

[105] See Andrés E. Montalvo, 'Reservations to the American Convention on Human Rights: A New Approach', 16 *American University International Law Review*, 269, 271 (2001); Hernán Salgado Pesantes, 'Las Reservas en los Tratados de Derechos Humanos', at 12–13.

[106] American Convention, Art. 2.

[107] *Ibid.*

[108] See *Loayza Tamayo* v. *Peru* (Compliance with Judgment), Inter-Am. Ct HR, Resolution of 17 November 1999, decision 1; *Durand and Ugarte* v. *Peru* (Compliance with Judgment), Inter-Am. Ct HR, Resolution of 27 November 2002, Resolution 1.

recommendations of the Commission. The Court has ruled that the principle of good faith obligates a State to endeavour to comply with the Commission's recommendations.[109] The Court added that by ratifying the American Convention States Parties commit themselves to fulfil the Commission's recommendations.[110] Conversely, the Court has also stated that State compliance with Commission recommendations is not obligatory[111] and the Court will not hold the State liable for failure to fulfil Commission recommendations.[112] The Court is giving contrary indications to States which could retard their acceptance of Commission recommendations and, thus, increase the cases referred to the Court. The State should be required to comply with Commission recommendations. If the State is not in agreement with the Commission's attribution of State responsibility or its recommendations, the State should submit the case to the Court for its judgment.[113] If it does not do so, and does not comply, the State should be held to be in violation of its international obligations. The observance of the human rights obligations enshrined in the American Convention and their national enforcement requires changes to those domestic laws that contravene Convention provisions. States Parties to the American Convention must pass legislation to that effect.

Failure of the political organs to adequately support the human rights system

The political organs of the OAS have not fulfilled their intended role of providing formal support to the Commission and the Court. The failure of the political organs to exert political pressure on States Parties as foreseen by the drafters of the American Convention has been a notably unsuccessful aspect of the functioning of the Inter-American system. The Convention does not provide for formal enforcement of judgments. It provides only that the Court shall present its annual report to the OAS

109 *Loayza Tamayo* v. *Peru* (Merits), Inter-Am. Ct HR, 15 September 1997, Ser. C, No. 33, para. 80.

110 *Ibid.*, para. 81.

111 *Caballero Delgado and Santana* v. *Colombia* (Merits), Inter-Am. Ct HR, 8 December 1995, Ser. C, No. 22, para. 67, quoted in *Genie Lacayo* (Merits), Inter-Am. Ct HR, 29 January 1997, Ser. C, No. 30, para. 93.

112 *Baena Ricardo et al. (270 Workers* v. *Panama)* (Merits), Inter-Am. Ct HR, 2 February 2001, Ser. C, No. 72, 193.

113 American Convention, Art. 51. See Manuel Ventura Robles, 'El Futuro de la Corte Interamericana de Derechos Humanos', *Revista Instituto Interamericano de Derechos Humanos*, 129, 137 (2001) (special edition), reporting on the suggestions resulting from the meetings of experts held by the Inter-American Court at the end of 1999 and the beginning of 2000.

General Assembly.[114] The Court's report individually denotes cases in which States have not complied with Court judgments.[115] The General Assembly may then discuss the State's non-compliance and, if appropriate, adopt political measures against the delinquent state. This provision was introduced to correlate in some degree to the role of the Committee of Ministers in the European human rights system, which can supervise the execution of a judgment. Commenting on this procedure, the European system's observer to the American drafting conference expressed the expectation that 'the reporting of a state for non-compliance to the General Assembly, which will be attended by several hundred delegates and widely publicized, is undoubtedly a procedure which most governments would prefer to avoid'.[116]

Political pressure to comply with the Inter-American Court's judgments has not materialized. The Court's annual reports are not directly reviewed by the OAS General Assembly and receive only perfunctory recognition each year.[117] The General Assembly has never issued a comment on State non-compliance with Court judgments. Moreover, the General Assembly has failed to recognize, much less act, in more egregious situations. For example, when Trinidad and Tobago denounced the Convention, the General Assembly remained silent on the withdrawal. Subsequently, when Trinidad and Tobago rejected the provisional measures ordered by the Court in death penalty cases, the OAS ignored requests to include the matter on the agenda of the General Assembly.[118] Theoretically, the General Assembly's censure of States in this context could have a positive influence on State compliance. In other contexts, political pressure by the OAS General Assembly has proved effective. For example, after the OAS Meeting of Consultation of Ministers of Foreign Affairs passed a resolution condemning the Somoza government's

[114] American Convention, Art. 65. [115] *Ibid.*; Statute of the Inter-Am. Ct HR, Art. 30.

[116] Council of Europe, *Report on the Inter-American Specialized Conference on Human Rights* (Strasbourg, 22 December 1969), reprinted in Buergenthal and Norris (eds.), *Human Rights: The Inter-American System*, booklet 15, vol. 3, at 67.

[117] See generally Approval of the 1998 Annual Report of the Inter-American Court, in the 1999 Annual Report of the Inter-American Court of Human Rights, 47, OEA/Ser.L/V/III.47, doc. 6, 24 January 2000; see Verónica Gómez, 'The Interaction Between the Political Actors of the OAS, the Commission and the Court', in *The Inter-American System of Human Rights*, 173, 192–201 (Harris and Livingstone eds., 1998).

[118] See Douglass Cassel, 'Peru Withdraws from the Court: Will the Inter-American Human Rights System Meet the Challenge?', 20 *Human Rights Law Journal*, 167, 173 (1999), citing letters signed by the Inter-American Court judges to the President of the OAS Permanent Council, dated 14 and 25 May 1999, and to the OAS Secretary-General, dated 27 May 1999.

treatment of the Nicaraguan people, Somoza finally resigned. In doing so, he stated: 'What role do I play when I have the OAS down my neck?'[119] One would expect that a State's concern that it could be censured by the OAS would improve implementation of judgments of the Inter-American Court.

Fear of adverse international publicity has often been a powerful tool in discouraging human rights violations. It has proven most effective when regional or international organs, such as the OAS General Assembly or the UN General Assembly, condemn the violator. Optimally, widespread publicity would accompany the Court's annual report; and the General Assembly would debate the contents of the report, single out States that had not complied with judgments, and then call upon those States to fulfil their duties under the Convention. The General Assembly should then include on its agenda for subsequent meetings all failures of State compliance. Not surprisingly, most States are sensitive about their international reputations and world image. According to a former member of the UN Commission on Human Rights, '[d]espite the harsh realities of power politics, world opinion is a force to be reckoned with. Governments do devote much time and energy, both in and out of the UN, to defending and embellishing their own human-rights image and demeaning that of others.'[120] When Argentine government agents reportedly caused thousands of people to disappear during the 'Dirty War',[121] Argentina hired a high-powered public relations firm in New York to improve its international image.[122] The threat of embarrassment or shame is a principal tool currently in use to prevent human rights abuses.[123] The likelihood of negative publicity often persuades governments to comply with their international human rights obligations. It

[119] See Christina Cerna, 'Human Rights in Conflict with the Principle of Non-Intervention: The Case of Nicaragua Before the Seventeenth Meeting of Consultation of Ministers of Foreign Affairs', in *Derechos Humanos, Direitos Humanos, Human Rights en Las Americas, Homage to the Memory of Carlos A. Dunshee de Abranches* (1984).

[120] Morris B. Abram, 'The UN and Human Rights', 47 *Foreign Affairs*, 363, 371 (1969).

[121] Comisión Nacional Sobre la Desaparición de Personas, *Nunca Mas* [National Commission on the Disappearance of Persons, *Never Again*], 479 (Editorial Universitaria de Buenos Aires 14a. ed., 1986).

[122] David Weissbrodt and Maria L. Bartolomei, 'The Effectiveness of International Human Rights Pressures: The Case of Argentina, 1976–1983', 75 *Minnesota Law Review*, 1009, 1030 (1991).

[123] David Weissbrodt and Teresa O'Toole, 'The Development of International Human Rights Law', in *The Universal Declaration of Human Rights 1948–1988: Human Rights, the United Nations and Amnesty International*, 17, 25 (AIUSA Legal Support Network, New York, 1988).

would, therefore, be beneficial for the OAS political organs to play their intended role in the Inter-American human rights system. However, it appears that until participation in the Inter-American system is universal – or at least includes the United States and Canada – the OAS General Assembly may not be willing to chastise those States that have ratified the Convention and accepted the jurisdiction of the Court.

Inadequate funding of the Court and the Commission

Although the promotion and protection of human rights in the Americas is a priority, the OAS does not adequately fund the Court and the Commission. Lack of funding means a shortage of staff attorneys. The size of the legal staffs of the secretariats of the Commission and Court has not kept pace with their expanding case loads. In recent years, the vast majority of the complaints filed with the Commission have not been referred to the Court in part due to the limited staff and resources of both institutions.[124]

Limited funding also translates into fewer Court sessions. Hearings at the seat of the Court require the presence of the judges and corresponding expenditures. Sessions of the Court have been postponed because of budgetary problems.[125] Since its inception in 1979, the Court has functioned on a part-time basis. Judges are at the disposal of the Court and, thus, are expected to travel to the seat of the Court as needed.[126] Most judges have full-time positions in their countries of residence. The requirement that judges be readily available reflects the urgent nature of many cases within the Court's competency. In the years immediately following the Court's inception, the infrequent meetings may have been adequate, but they are not sufficient to deal efficiently with the ever-increasing caseload of the Court. Only twelve advisory opinions were issued and three joined contentious cases were decided in the Court's first ten years of existence.[127] The number of cases and provisional measures requests has been increasing

[124] See Thomas Buergenthal and Douglass Cassel, 'The Future of the Inter-American Human Rights System', in *El Futuro del Sistema Interamericano de los Derechos Humanos*, 539, 546 (Méndez and Cox, eds., Inter-American Institute of Human Rights, 1998).

[125] *Mayagna (SUMO) Awas Tingni Community* v. *Nicaragua* (Merits), Inter-Am. Ct HR, 31 August 2001, Ser. C, No. 79, para. 46.

[126] Statute of the Inter-Am. Ct HR, Art. 16.

[127] Note that the Court did not accept the contentious case of the Government of Costa Rica. *In The Matter of Viviana Gallardo et al.*, Inter-Am. Ct HR, Decision of 13 November 1981, Ser. A, No. G101/81.

steadily since that time. The caseload of the Court should increase more dramatically under the Commission's 2001 Rules of Procedure which provide that every case against a State that has accepted the Court's jurisdiction will be referred to the Court 'unless there is a reasoned decision by an absolute majority of the members of the Commission to the contrary'.[128] This change will necessitate more frequent Court sessions. The Court's draft Statute originally envisioned a permanent court with full-time judges. The OAS General Assembly found this proposal unjustified until such time as the Court had a substantial caseload.[129] In 2001, the OAS General Assembly ordered the Permanent Council to study the possibility of a permanent Commission and Court.[130]

An increase in sessions of the Court will require a corresponding increase in financing. Unfortunately, the OAS, which finances the Court, experiences almost continual shortfalls that show no signs of abating.[131] In 2000, the OAS General Assembly resolved to recommend a substantial increase in funding for the Court and Commission.[132] The OAS General Assembly subsequently instructed the Permanent Council to 'take concrete steps' to substantially increase the operating budgets of both the Commission and the Court within a reasonable time through the establishment of a fund to encourage voluntary contributions.[133] Nikken argues convincingly that organizations that make voluntary contributions regulate their use, requiring that the money finance predetermined special projects and not salaries and ordinary expenses.[134] If the OAS cannot obtain additional voluntary funding for the Court and Commission, then the OAS will need to re-evaluate its priorities and eliminate all but

128 2001 Rules of Procedure of the Inter-American Commission on Human Rights, entered into force on 1 May 2001, approved by the Commission at its 109th special session held 4–8 December 2000, Art. 44(1).

129 Thomas Buergenthal, 'The Inter-American Court of Human Rights', 76 *American Journal of International Law*, 231, 232–3, nn. 11 and 17 (1982) (citing the draft Statute, OEA/Ser.P/AG/doc.1112/79 (10 October 1979), Arts. 20 and 22).

130 General Assembly Resolution Evaluating the Workings of the Inter-American System, para. 1(e).

131 See Thomas Buergenthal, 'The Inter-American Court and the OAS', 7 *Human Rights Law Journal*, 157 (1986).

132 OAS AG/RES. 1701 (XXX-O/00), Resolution 4.

133 General Assembly Resolution Evaluating the Workings of the Inter-American System, para. 1(d).

134 Pedro Nikken, 'Observaciones Sobre el Fortalecimiento del Sistema Interamericano de Derechos Humanos en Visperas de la Asamblea General de la OEA', 13 *Revista Inter-Americano Instituto de Derechos Humanos*, 38 (2001) (special edition).

the most essential spending. A top priority in the Inter-American system must be the promotion and protection of human rights, as the violation of human rights is one of the gravest problems facing the Americas. This priority is not reflected in the budget of the OAS. The OAS allocates funding to various social and cultural programmes and studies,[135] and, while these programmes are no doubt valuable, their impact pales when compared to that of monitoring and enforcing human rights in the Americas.[136]

Quality control of judges elected to the Court

The bench of the Inter-American Court has been graced with several excellent human rights jurists and scholars. Their judicial opinions and decisions reflect a depth of understanding of public international law in general and international human rights law in particular. The first judges to be elected were among the most impressive names in human rights law in the western hemisphere. Moreover, the members of the original Court themselves had first-hand experience in human rights – four of the Court's first judges had been jailed for political reasons at different times of their lives.[137] Subsequent nominations to the Court have not been of such uniformly commanding quality. Despite the Convention's requirements, governments may intentionally or unintentionally undermine the Court by nominating judges who lack high-level expertise.[138] Some nominations have reflected cronyism rather than qualifications.[139] Politics have sometimes influenced the elections; certain nations have

[135] Organization of American States, Proceedings, vol. I, Twenty-Second Regular Session, Nassau, The Bahamas, 18–23 May 1992, OEA/Ser.P/XXII.0.2, 21 June 1992, Court Budget, 77–88.

[136] Canada, which joined the OAS on 8 January 1990, has urged that the OAS increase financial support for the Inter-American human rights system. See Address by the Honorable Barbara McDougall, Canadian Secretary of State for Foreign Affairs to the XXIII OAS General Assembly (7 June 1993). Furthermore, Canada has advocated that funding be curtailed to certain OAS committees including the Inter-American Defense Board. Conversation with Harold Hickman, Counsellor and Alternative Representative of the Canadian Mission to the OAS (October 1993).

[137] Carlos Roberto Reina, Rodolfo Piza Escalante, Maximo Cisneros and Thomas Buergenthal. Thomas Buergenthal, Talk to Human Rights Class of 22 September 1995 at George Washington University Law School. Notes on file with the author.

[138] See Douglass Cassel Jr, 'Somoza's Revenge: A New Judge for the Inter-American Court of Human Rights', 13 *Human Rights Law Journal*, 137, 139 (1992).

[139] Martin Anderson, 'Human Rights Nominee Has Clouded Past', *Miami Herald*, 7 April 1994, A11.

reportedly voted in block to elect a candidate despite weak qualifications.[140] With only seven judges[141] as compared to more than forty on the European Court of Human Rights, the Inter-American Court must be ever-vigilant as to the qualifications of its judges.[142]

The OAS should provide for more transparent and less politicized election procedures to ensure the quality of judges. One means of ensuring greater transparency would be to publish the names of proposed candidates and to invite comments from domestic bar associations and institutions.[143] In the European system, a committee of the Parliamentary Assembly of the Council of Europe reviews the *curriculum vitae* and interviews all judicial candidates.[144] In addition, the European Committee of Ministers has an informal procedure to 'weed out (off-the-record) any unacceptable or totally unmeritorious candidatures'.[145] This examination of candidates takes place before the list is formally submitted to the Parliamentary Assembly.[146] A similar practice in the OAS could derail nominations of unqualified or undedicated judges or commissioners.

Conclusion

The Inter-American Court of Human Rights and the Inter-American Commission on Human Rights have made significant advances in the protection of human rights in the region. Many of these advances are directly attributable to the evolution of the practice and procedures of the Court and the Commission. The new autonomy granted to the victim before the Court and the expedited procedures of both organs bring justice within the reach of individuals. Through its liberalized procedures the Court has also paved the way for non-governmental organizations, that often espouse the position of the human rights community, to express their views before the Court. Much still needs to be done. As

[140] See Buergenthal and Cassel, 'The Future of the Inter-American Human Rights System', at 544–5; Cassel, 'A New Judge for the Inter-American Court', at 139.

[141] American Convention, Art. 52(1).

[142] The European Court has one judge for each High Contracting Party. European Convention for the Protection of Human Rights and Fundamental Freedoms, as amended by Protocol No. 11, Art. 20.

[143] Buergenthal and Cassel, 'The Future of the Inter-American Human Rights System', at 545.

[144] See Andrew Drzemczewski, 'The European Human Rights Convention: Protocol No. 11 Entry into Force and First Year of Application', in *El Sistema Interamericano de Protección de los Derechos Humanos en el Umbral del Siglo XXI*, 357, 367 (2001).

[145] *Ibid.*, at 367. [146] *Ibid.*

explained by Buergenthal, however, '[e]ven some success in the international human rights field, however small, will make this world a little better place to live in. And that, after all, is what law is all about.'[147] The Inter-American Court is having greater success than many would have expected.

[147] Remarks by Thomas Buergenthal, American Society of International Law, Annual Meeting, 24 April 1981, Proceedings.

Appendix 1

American Convention on Human Rights

Signed at the Inter-American Specialized Conference on Human Rights, San José, Costa Rica, 22 November 1969

Preamble

The American states signatory to the present Convention,

Reaffirming their intention to consolidate in this hemisphere, within the framework of democratic institutions, a system of personal liberty and social justice based on respect for the essential rights of man;

Recognizing that the essential rights of man are not derived from one's being a national of a certain state, but are based upon attributes of the human personality, and that they therefore justify international protection in the form of a convention reinforcing or complementing the protection provided by the domestic law of the American states;

Considering that these principles have been set forth in the Charter of the Organization of American States, in the American Declaration of the Rights and Duties of Man, and in the Universal Declaration of Human Rights, and that they have been reaffirmed and refined in other international instruments, worldwide as well as regional in scope;

Reiterating that, in accordance with the Universal Declaration of Human Rights, the ideal of free men enjoying freedom from fear and want can be achieved only if conditions are created whereby everyone may enjoy his economic, social, and cultural rights, as well as his civil and political rights; and

Considering that the Third Special Inter-American Conference (Buenos Aires, 1967) approved the incorporation into the Charter of the Organization itself of broader standards with respect to economic, social, and educational rights and resolved that an inter-American convention on human rights should determine the structure, competence, and procedure of the organs responsible for these matters,

Have agreed upon the following:

Part I
State Obligations and Rights Protected

Chapter I
General Obligations

Article 1
Obligation to Respect Rights

1. The States Parties to this Convention undertake to respect the rights and freedoms recognized herein and to ensure to all persons subject to their jurisdiction the free and full exercise of those rights and freedoms, without any discrimination for reasons of race, color, sex, language, religion, political or other opinion, national or social origin, economic status, birth, or any other social condition.

2. For the purposes of this Convention, 'person' means every human being.

Article 2
Domestic Legal Effects

Where the exercise of any of the rights or freedoms referred to in Article 1 is not already ensured by legislative or other provisions, the States Parties undertake to adopt, in accordance with their constitutional processes and the provisions of this Convention, such legislative or other measures as may be necessary to give effect to those rights or freedoms.

Chapter II
Civil and Political Rights

Article 3
Right to Juridical Personality

Every person has the right to recognition as a person before the law.

Article 4
Right to Life

1. Every person has the right to have his life respected. This right shall be protected by law and, in general, from the moment of conception. No one shall be arbitrarily deprived of his life.

2. In countries that have not abolished the death penalty, it may be imposed only for the most serious crimes and pursuant to a final judgment rendered by a competent court and in accordance with a law establishing such punishment, enacted prior to the commission of the crime. The application of such punishment shall not be extended to crimes to which it does not presently apply.

3. The death penalty shall not be reestablished in states that have abolished it.

4. In no case shall capital punishment be inflicted for political offenses or related common crimes.

5. Capital punishment shall not be imposed upon persons who, at the time the crime was committed, were under 18 years of age or over 70 years of age; nor shall it be applied to pregnant women.

6. Every person condemned to death shall have the right to apply for amnesty, pardon, or commutation of sentence, which may be granted in all cases. Capital punishment shall not be imposed while such a petition is pending decision by the competent authority.

Article 5
Right to Humane Treatment

1. Every person has the right to have his physical, mental, and moral integrity respected.

2. No one shall be subjected to torture or to cruel, inhuman, or degrading punishment or treatment. All persons deprived of their liberty shall be treated with respect for the inherent dignity of the human person.

3. Punishment shall not be extended to any person other than the criminal.

4. Accused persons shall, save in exceptional circumstances, be segregated from convicted persons, and shall be subject to separate treatment appropriate to their status as unconvicted persons.

5. Minors while subject to criminal proceedings shall be separated from adults and brought before specialized tribunals, as speedily as possible, so that they may be treated in accordance with their status as minors.

6. Punishments consisting of deprivation of liberty shall have as an essential aim the reform and social readaptation of the prisoners.

Article 6
Freedom from Slavery

1. No one shall be subject to slavery or to involuntary servitude, which are prohibited in all their forms, as are the slave trade and traffic in women.

2. No one shall be required to perform forced or compulsory labor. This provision shall not be interpreted to mean that, in those countries in which the penalty established for certain crimes is deprivation of liberty at forced labor, the carrying out of such a sentence imposed by a competent court is prohibited. Forced labor shall not adversely affect the dignity or the physical or intellectual capacity of the prisoner.

3. For the purposes of this article, the following do not constitute forced or compulsory labor:

a. work or service normally required of a person imprisoned in execution of a sentence or formal decision passed by the competent judicial authority. Such work or service shall be carried out under the supervision and control of public authorities, and any persons performing such work or service shall not be placed at the disposal of any private party, company, or juridical person;
b. military service and, in countries in which conscientious objectors are recognized, national service that the law may provide for in lieu of military service;
c. service exacted in time of danger or calamity that threatens the existence or the well-being of the community; or
d. work or service that forms part of normal civic obligations.

Article 7
Right to Personal Liberty

1. Every person has the right to personal liberty and security.

2. No one shall be deprived of his physical liberty except for the reasons and under the conditions established beforehand by the constitution of the State Party concerned or by a law established pursuant thereto.

3. No one shall be subject to arbitrary arrest or imprisonment.

4. Anyone who is detained shall be informed of the reasons for his detention and shall be promptly notified of the charge or charges against him.

5. Any person detained shall be brought promptly before a judge or other officer authorized by law to exercise judicial power and shall be entitled to trial within a reasonable time or to be released without prejudice to the continuation of the proceedings. His release may be subject to guarantees to assure his appearance for trial.

6. Anyone who is deprived of his liberty shall be entitled to recourse to a competent court, in order that the court may decide without delay on the lawfulness of his arrest or detention and order his release if the arrest or detention is unlawful. In States Parties whose laws provide that anyone who believes himself to be threatened with deprivation of his liberty is entitled to recourse to a competent court in order that it may decide on the lawfulness of such threat, this remedy may not be restricted or abolished. The interested party or another person in his behalf is entitled to seek these remedies.

7. No one shall be detained for debt. This principle shall not limit the orders of a competent judicial authority issued for nonfulfillment of duties of support.

Article 8
Right to a Fair Trial

1. Every person has the right to a hearing, with due guarantees and within a reasonable time, by a competent, independent, and impartial tribunal, previously established by law, in the substantiation of any accusation of a criminal nature made against him or for the determination of his rights and obligations of a civil, labor, fiscal, or any other nature.

2. Every person accused of a criminal offense has the right to be presumed innocent so long as his guilt has not been proven according to law. During the proceedings, every person is entitled, with full equality, to the following minimum guarantees:

a. the right of the accused to be assisted without charge by a translator or interpreter, if he does not understand or does not speak the language of the tribunal or court;
b. prior notification in detail to the accused of the charges against him;

c. adequate time and means for the preparation of his defense;
d. the right of the accused to defend himself personally or to be assisted by legal counsel of his own choosing, and to communicate freely and privately with his counsel;
e. the inalienable right to be assisted by counsel provided by the state, paid or not as the domestic law provides, if the accused does not defend himself personally or engage his own counsel within the time period established by law;
f. the right of the defense to examine witnesses present in the court and to obtain the appearance, as witnesses, of experts or other persons who may throw light on the facts;
g. the right not to be compelled to be a witness against himself or to plead guilty; and
h. the right to appeal the judgment to a higher court.

3. A confession of guilt by the accused shall be valid only if it is made without coercion of any kind.

4. An accused person acquitted by a nonappealable judgment shall not be subjected to a new trial for the same cause.

5. Criminal proceedings shall be public, except insofar as may be necessary to protect the interests of justice.

Article 9
Freedom from Ex Post Facto Laws

No one shall be convicted of any act or omission that did not constitute a criminal offense, under the applicable law, at the time it was committed. A heavier penalty shall not be imposed than the one that was applicable at the time the criminal offense was committed. If subsequent to the commission of the offense the law provides for the imposition of a lighter punishment, the guilty person shall benefit therefrom.

Article 10
Right to Compensation

Every person has the right to be compensated in accordance with the law in the event he has been sentenced by a final judgment through a miscarriage of justice.

Article 11
Right to Privacy

1. Everyone has the right to have his honor respected and his dignity recognized.

2. No one may be the object of arbitrary or abusive interference with his private life, his family, his home, or his correspondence, or of unlawful attacks on his honor or reputation.

3. Everyone has the right to the protection of the law against such interference or attacks.

Article 12
Freedom of Conscience and Religion

1. Everyone has the right to freedom of conscience and of religion. This right includes freedom to maintain or to change one's religion or beliefs, and freedom to profess or disseminate one's religion or beliefs, either individually or together with others, in public or in private.

2. No one shall be subject to restrictions that might impair his freedom to maintain or to change his religion or beliefs.

3. Freedom to manifest one's religion and beliefs may be subject only to the limitations prescribed by law that are necessary to protect public safety, order, health, or morals, or the rights or freedoms of others.

4. Parents or guardians, as the case may be, have the right to provide for the religious and moral education of their children or wards that is in accord with their own convictions.

Article 13
Freedom of Thought and Expression

1. Everyone has the right to freedom of thought and expression. This right includes freedom to seek, receive, and impart information and ideas of all kinds, regardless of frontiers, either orally, in writing, in print, in the form of art, or through any other medium of one's choice.

2. The exercise of the right provided for in the foregoing paragraph shall not be subject to prior censorship but shall be subject to subsequent imposition of liability, which shall be expressly established by law to the extent necessary to ensure:

a. respect for the rights or reputations of others; or
b. the protection of national security, public order, or public health or morals.

3. The right of expression may not be restricted by indirect methods or means, such as the abuse of government or private controls over newsprint, radio broadcasting frequencies, or equipment used in the dissemination of information, or by any other means tending to impede the communication and circulation of ideas and opinions.

4. Notwithstanding the provisions of paragraph 2 above, public entertainments may be subject by law to prior censorship for the sole purpose of regulating access to them for the moral protection of childhood and adolescence.

5. Any propaganda for war and any advocacy of national, racial, or religious hatred that constitute incitements to lawless violence or to any other similar action against any person or group of persons on any grounds including those of race, color, religion, language, or national origin shall be considered as offenses punishable by law.

Article 14
Right of Reply

1. Anyone injured by inaccurate or offensive statements or ideas disseminated to the public in general by a legally regulated medium of communication has the right to reply or to make a correction using the same communications outlet, under such conditions as the law may establish.

2. The correction or reply shall not in any case remit other legal liabilities that may have been incurred.

3. For the effective protection of honor and reputation, every publisher, and every newspaper, motion picture, radio, and television company, shall have a person responsible who is not protected by immunities or special privileges.

Article 15
Right of Assembly

The right of peaceful assembly, without arms, is recognized. No restrictions may be placed on the exercise of this right other than those imposed in conformity with the law and necessary in a democratic society in the interest of national security, public safety or public order, or to protect public health or morals or the rights or freedom of others.

Article 16
Freedom of Association

1. Everyone has the right to associate freely for ideological, religious, political, economic, labor, social, cultural, sports, or other purposes.

2. The exercise of this right shall be subject only to such restrictions established by law as may be necessary in a democratic society, in the interest of national security, public safety or public order, or to protect public health or morals or the rights and freedoms of others.

3. The provisions of this article do not bar the imposition of legal restrictions, including even deprivation of the exercise of the right of association, on members of the armed forces and the police.

Article 17
Rights of the Family

1. The family is the natural and fundamental group unit of society and is entitled to protection by society and the state.

2. The right of men and women of marriageable age to marry and to raise a family shall be recognized, if they meet the conditions required by domestic laws, insofar as such conditions do not affect the principle of nondiscrimination established in this Convention.

3. No marriage shall be entered into without the free and full consent of the intending spouses.

4. The States Parties shall take appropriate steps to ensure the equality of rights and the adequate balancing of responsibilities of the spouses as to marriage, during marriage, and in the event of its dissolution. In case of dissolution, provision shall be made for the necessary protection of any children solely on the basis of their own best interests.

5. The law shall recognize equal rights for children born out of wedlock and those born in wedlock.

Article 18
Right to a Name

Every person has the right to a given name and to the surnames of his parents or that of one of them. The law shall regulate the manner in which this right shall be ensured for all, by the use of assumed names if necessary.

Article 19
Rights of the Child

Every minor child has the right to the measures of protection required by his condition as a minor on the part of his family, society, and the state.

Article 20
Right to Nationality

1. Every person has the right to a nationality.
2. Every person has the right to the nationality of the state in whose territory he was born if he does not have the right to any other nationality.
3. No one shall be arbitrarily deprived of his nationality or of the right to change it.

Article 21
Right to Property

1. Everyone has the right to the use and enjoyment of his property. The law may subordinate such use and enjoyment to the interest of society.
2. No one shall be deprived of his property except upon payment of just compensation, for reasons of public utility or social interest, and in the cases and according to the forms established by law.
3. Usury and any other form of exploitation of man by man shall be prohibited by law.

Article 22
Freedom of Movement and Residence

1. Every person lawfully in the territory of a State Party has the right to move about in it, and to reside in it subject to the provisions of the law.
2. Every person has the right lo leave any country freely, including his own.
3. The exercise of the foregoing rights may be restricted only pursuant to a law to the extent necessary in a democratic society to prevent crime or to protect national security, public safety, public order, public morals, public health, or the rights or freedoms of others.

4. The exercise of the rights recognized in paragraph 1 may also be restricted by law in designated zones for reasons of public interest.

5. No one can be expelled from the territory of the state of which he is a national or be deprived of the right to enter it.

6. An alien lawfully in the territory of a State Party to this Convention may be expelled from it only pursuant to a decision reached in accordance with law.

7. Every person has the right to seek and be granted asylum in a foreign territory, in accordance with the legislation of the state and international conventions, in the event he is being pursued for political offenses or related common crimes.

8. In no case may an alien be deported or returned to a country, regardless of whether or not it is his country of origin, if in that country his right to life or personal freedom is in danger of being violated because of his race, nationality, religion, social status, or political opinions.

9. The collective expulsion of aliens is prohibited.

Article 23
Right to Participate in Government

1. Every citizen shall enjoy the following rights and opportunities:

a. to take part in the conduct of public affairs, directly or through freely chosen representatives;
b. to vote and to be elected in genuine periodic elections, which shall be by universal and equal suffrage and by secret ballot that guarantees the free expression of the will of the voters; and
c. to have access, under general conditions of equality, to the public service of his country.

2. The law may regulate the exercise of the rights and opportunities referred to in the preceding paragraph only on the basis of age, nationality, residence, language, education, civil and mental capacity, or sentencing by a competent court in criminal proceedings.

Article 24
Right to Equal Protection

All persons are equal before the law. Consequently, they are entitled, without discrimination, to equal protection of the law.

Article 25
Right to Judicial Protection

1. Everyone has the right to simple and prompt recourse, or any other effective recourse, to a competent court or tribunal for protection against acts that violate his fundamental rights recognized by the constitution or laws of the state concerned or by this Convention, even though such violation may have been committed by persons acting in the course of their official duties.

2. The States Parties undertake:

a. to ensure that any person claiming such remedy shall have his rights determined by the competent authority provided for by the legal system of the state;
b. to develop the possibilities of judicial remedy; and
c. to ensure that the competent authorities shall enforce such remedies when granted.

Chapter III
Economic, Social, and Cultural Rights

Article 26
Progressive Development

The States Parties undertake to adopt measures, both internally and through international cooperation, especially those of an economic and technical nature, with a view to achieving progressively, by legislation or other appropriate means, the full realization of the rights implicit in the economic, social, educational, scientific, and cultural standards set forth in the Charter of the Organization of American States as amended by the Protocol of Buenos Aires.

Chapter IV
Suspension of Guarantees, Interpretation, and Application

Article 27
Suspension of Guarantees

1. In time of war, public danger, or other emergency that threatens the independence or security of a State Party, it may take measures

derogating from its obligations under the present Convention to the extent and for the period of time strictly required by the exigencies of the situation, provided that such measures are not inconsistent with its other obligations under international law and do not involve discrimination on the ground of race, color, sex, language, religion, or social origin.

2. The foregoing provision does not authorize any suspension of the following articles: Article 3 (Right to Juridical Personality), Article 4 (Right to Life), Article 5 (Right to Humane Treatment), Article 6 (Freedom from Slavery), Article 9 (Freedom from *Ex Post Facto* Laws), Article 12 (Freedom of Conscience and Religion), Article 17 (Rights of the Family), Article 18 (Right to a Name), Article 19 (Rights of the Child), Article 20 (Right to Nationality), and Article 23 (Right to Participate in Government), or of the judicial guarantees essential for the protection of such rights.

3. Any State Party availing itself of the right of suspension shall immediately inform the other States Parties, through the Secretary General of the Organization of American States, of the provisions the application of which it has suspended, the reasons that gave rise to the suspension, and the date set for the termination of such suspension.

Article 28
Federal Clause

1. Where a State Party is constituted as a federal state, the national government of such State Party shall implement all the provisions of the Convention over whose subject matter it exercises legislative and judicial jurisdiction.

2. With respect to the provisions over whose subject matter the constituent units of the federal state have jurisdiction, the national government shall immediately take suitable measures, in accordance with its constitution and its laws, to the end that the competent authorities of the constituent units may adopt appropriate provisions for the fulfillment of this Convention.

3. Whenever two or more States Parties agree to form a federation or other type of association, they shall take care that the resulting federal or other compact contains the provisions necessary for continuing and rendering effective the standards of this Convention in the new state that is organized.

Article 29
Restrictions Regarding Interpretation

No provision of this Convention shall be interpreted as:

a. permitting any State Party, group, or person to suppress the enjoyment or exercise of the rights and freedoms recognized in this Convention or to restrict them to a greater extent than is provided for herein;
b. restricting the enjoyment or exercise of any right or freedom recognized by virtue of the laws of any State Party or by virtue of another convention to which one of the said states is a party;
c. precluding other rights or guarantees that are inherent in the human personality or derived from representative democracy as a form of government; or
d. excluding or limiting the effect that the American Declaration of the Rights and Duties of Man and other international acts of the same nature may have.

Article 30
Scope of Restrictions

The restrictions that, pursuant to this Convention, may be placed on the enjoyment or exercise of the rights or freedoms recognized herein may not be applied except in accordance with laws enacted for reasons of general interest and in accordance with the purpose for which such restrictions have been established.

Article 31
Recognition of Other Rights

Other rights and freedoms recognized in accordance with the procedures established in Articles 76 and 77 may be included in the system of protection of this Convention.

Chapter V
Personal Responsibilities

Article 32
Relationship Between Duties and Rights

1. Every person has responsibilities to his family, his community, and mankind.

2. The rights of each person are limited by the rights of others, by the security of all, and by the just demands of the general welfare, in a democratic society.

PART II
MEANS OF PROTECTION

CHAPTER VI
COMPETENT ORGANS

Article 33

The following organs shall have competence with respect to matters relating to the fulfillment of the commitments made by the States Parties to this Convention:

a. the Inter-American Commission on Human Rights, referred to as 'The Commission'; and
b. the Inter-American Court of Human Rights, referred to as 'The Court.'

CHAPTER VII
INTER-AMERICAN COMMISSION ON HUMAN RIGHTS

SECTION 1
ORGANIZATION

Article 34

The Inter-American Commission on Human Rights shall be composed of seven members, who shall be persons of high moral character and recognized competence in the field of human rights.

Article 35

The Commission shall represent all the member countries of the Organization of American States.

Article 36

1. The members of the Commission shall be elected in a personal capacity by the General Assembly of the Organization from a list of candidates proposed by the governments of the member states.

2. Each of those governments may propose up to three candidates, who may be nationals of the states proposing them or of any other member state of the Organization of American States. When a slate of three is proposed, at least one of the candidates shall be a national of a state other than the one proposing the slate.

Article 37

1. The members of the Commission shall be elected for a term of four years and may be reelected only once, but the terms of three of the members chosen in the first election shall expire at the end of two years. Immediately following that election the General Assembly shall determine the names of those three members by lot.

2. No two nationals of the same state may be members of the Commission.

Article 38

Vacancies that may occur on the Commission for reasons other than the normal expiration of a term shall be filled by the Permanent Council of the Organization in accordance with the provisions of the Statute of the Commission.

Article 39

The Commission shall prepare its Statute, which it shall submit to the General Assembly for approval. It shall establish its own Regulations.

Article 40

Secretariat services for the Commission shall be furnished by the appropriate specialized unit of the General Secretariat of the Organization. This unit shall be provided with the resources required to accomplish the tasks assigned to it by the Commission.

Section 2
Functions

Article 41

The main function of the Commission shall be to promote respect for and defense of human rights. In the exercise of its mandate, it shall have the following functions and powers:

a. to develop an awareness of human rights among the peoples of America;
b. to make recommendations to the governments of the member states, when it considers such action advisable, for the adoption of progressive measures in favor of human rights within the framework of their domestic law and constitutional provisions as well as appropriate measures to further the observance of those rights;
c. to prepare such studies or reports as it considers advisable in the performance of its duties;
d. to request the governments of the member states to supply it with information on the measures adopted by them in matters of human rights;
e. to respond, through the General Secretariat of the Organization of American States, to inquiries made by the member states on matters related to human rights and, within the limits of its possibilities, to provide those states with the advisory services they request;
f. to take action on petitions and other communications pursuant to its authority under the provisions of Articles 44 through 51 of this Convention; and
g. to submit an annual report to the General Assembly of the Organization of American States.

Article 42

The States Parties shall transmit to the Commission a copy of each of the reports and studies that they submit annually to the Executive Committees of the Inter-American Economic and Social Council and the Inter-American Council for Education, Science, and Culture, in their respective fields, so that the Commission may watch over the promotion of the rights implicit in the economic, social, educational, scientific, and cultural standards set forth in the Charter of the

Organization of American States as amended by the Protocol of Buenos Aires.

Article 43

The States Parties undertake to provide the Commission with such information as it may request of them as to the manner in which their domestic law ensures the effective application of any provisions of this Convention.

Section 3
Competence

Article 44

Any person or group of persons, or any nongovernmental entity legally recognized in one or more member states of the Organization, may lodge petitions with the Commission containing denunciations or complaints of violation of this Convention by a State Party.

Article 45

1. Any State Party may, when it deposits its instrument of ratification of or adherence to this Convention, or at any later time, declare that it recognizes the competence of the Commission to receive and examine communications in which a State Party alleges that another State Party has committed a violation of a human right set forth in this Convention.
2. Communications presented by virtue of this article may be admitted and examined only if they are presented by a State Party that has made a declaration recognizing the aforementioned competence of the Commission. The Commission shall not admit any communication against a State Party that has not made such a declaration.
3. A declaration concerning recognition of competence may be made to be valid for an indefinite time, for a specified period, or for a specific case.
4. Declarations shall be deposited with the General Secretariat of the Organization of American States, which shall transmit copies thereof to the member states of that Organization.

Article 46

1. Admission by the Commission of a petition or communication lodged in accordance with Articles 44 or 45 shall be subject to the following requirements:

a. that the remedies under domestic law have been pursued and exhausted in accordance with generally recognized principles of international law;
b. that the petition or communication is lodged within a period of six months from the date on which the party alleging violation of his rights was notified of the final judgment;
c. that the subject of the petition or communication is not pending in another international proceeding for settlement; and
d. that, in the case of Article 44, the petition contains the name, nationality, profession, domicile, and signature of the person or persons or of the legal representative of the entity lodging the petition.

2. The provisions of paragraphs 1.a and 1.b of this article shall not be applicable when:

a. the domestic legislation of the state concerned does not afford due process of law for the protection of the right or rights that have allegedly been violated;
b. the party alleging violation of his rights has been denied access to the remedies under domestic law or has been prevented from exhausting them; or
c. there has been unwarranted delay in rendering a final judgment under the aforementioned remedies.

Article 47

The Commission shall consider inadmissible any petition or communication submitted under Articles 44 or 45 if:

a. any of the requirements indicated in Article 46 has not been met;
b. the petition or communication does not state facts that tend to establish a violation of the rights guaranteed by this Convention;
c. the statements of the petitioner or of the state indicate that the petition or communication is manifestly groundless or obviously out of order; or

d. the petition or communication is substantially the same as one previously studied by the Commission or by another international organization.

SECTION 4
PROCEDURE

Article 48

1. When the Commission receives a petition or communication alleging violation of any of the rights protected by this Convention, it shall proceed as follows:

a. If it considers the petition or communication admissible, it shall request information from the government of the state indicated as being responsible for the alleged violations and shall furnish that government a transcript of the pertinent portions of the petition or communication. This information shall be submitted within a reasonable period to be determined by the Commission in accordance with the circumstances of each case.
b. After the information has been received, or after the period established has elapsed and the information has not been received, the Commission shall ascertain whether the grounds for the petition or communication still exist. If they do not, the Commission shall order the record to be closed.
c. The Commission may also declare the petition or communication inadmissible or out of order on the basis of information or evidence subsequently received.
d. If the record has not been closed, the Commission shall, with the knowledge of the parties, examine the matter set forth in the petition or communication in order to verify the facts. If necessary and advisable, the Commission shall carry out an investigation, for the effective conduct of which it shall request, and the states concerned shall furnish to it, all necessary facilities.
e. The Commission may request the states concerned to furnish any pertinent information and, if so requested, shall hear oral statements or receive written statements from the parties concerned.
f. The Commission shall place itself at the disposal of the parties concerned with a view to reaching a friendly settlement of the matter on the basis of respect for the human rights recognized in this Convention.

2. However, in serious and urgent cases, only the presentation of a petition or communication that fulfills all the formal requirements of admissibility shall be necessary in order for the Commission to conduct an investigation with the prior consent of the state in whose territory a violation has allegedly been committed.

Article 49

If a friendly settlement has been reached in accordance with paragraph 1.f of Article 48, the Commission shall draw up a report, which shall be transmitted to the petitioner and to the States Parties to this Convention, and shall then be communicated to the Secretary General of the Organization of American States for publication. This report shall contain a brief statement of the facts and of the solution reached. If any party in the case so requests, the fullest possible information shall be provided to it.

Article 50

1. If a settlement is not reached, the Commission shall, within the time limit established by its Statute, draw up a report setting forth the facts and stating its conclusions. If the report, in whole or in part, does not represent the unanimous agreement of the members of the Commission, any member may attach to it a separate opinion. The written and oral statements made by the parties in accordance with paragraph 1.e of Article 48 shall also be attached to the report.

2. The report shall be transmitted to the states concerned, which shall not be at liberty to publish it.

3. In transmitting the report, the Commission may make such proposals and recommendations as it sees fit.

Article 51

1. If, within a period of three months from the date of the transmittal of the report of the Commission to the states concerned, the matter has not either been settled or submitted by the Commission or by the state concerned to the Court and its jurisdiction accepted, the Commission may, by the vote of an absolute majority of its members, set forth its opinion and conclusions concerning the question submitted for its consideration.

2. Where appropriate, the Commission shall make pertinent recommendations and shall prescribe a period within which the state is to

take the measures that are incumbent upon it to remedy the situation examined.

3. When the prescribed period has expired, the Commission shall decide by the vote of an absolute majority of its members whether the state has taken adequate measures and whether to publish its report.

Chapter VIII
Inter-American Court of Human Rights

Section 1
Organization

Article 52

1. The Court shall consist of seven judges, nationals of the member states of the Organization, elected in an individual capacity from among jurists of the highest moral authority and of recognized competence in the field of human rights, who possess the qualifications required for the exercise of the highest judicial functions in conformity with the law of the state of which they are nationals or of the state that proposes them as candidates.

2. No two judges may be nationals of the same state.

Article 53

1. The judges of the Court shall be elected by secret ballot by an absolute majority vote of the States Parties to the Convention, in the General Assembly of the Organization, from a panel of candidates proposed by those states.

2. Each of the States Parties may propose up to three candidates, nationals of the state that proposes them or of any other member state of the Organization of American States. When a slate of three is proposed, at least one of the candidates shall be a national of a state other than the one proposing the slate.

Article 54

1. The judges of the Court shall be elected for a term of six years and may be reelected only once. The term of three of the judges chosen in the first election shall expire at the end of three years. Immediately after the

election, the names of the three judges shall be determined by lot in the General Assembly.

2. A judge elected to replace a judge whose term has not expired shall complete the term of the latter.

3. The judges shall continue in office until the expiration of their term. However, they shall continue to serve with regard to cases that they have begun to hear and that are still pending, for which purposes they shall not be replaced by the newly elected judges.

Article 55

1. If a judge is a national of any of the States Parties to a case submitted to the Court, he shall retain his right to hear that case.

2. If one of the judges called upon to hear a case should be a national of one of the States Parties to the case, any other State Party in the case may appoint a person of its choice to serve on the Court as an *ad hoc* judge.

3. If among the judges called upon to hear a case none is a national of any of the States Parties to the case, each of the latter may appoint an *ad hoc* judge.

4. An *ad hoc* judge shall possess the qualifications indicated in Article 52.

5. If several States Parties to the Convention should have the same interest in a case, they shall be considered as a single party for purposes of the above provisions. In case of doubt, the Court shall decide.

Article 56

Five judges shall constitute a quorum for the transaction of business by the Court.

Article 57

The Commission shall appear in all cases before the Court.

Article 58

1. The Court shall have its seat at the place determined by the States Parties to the Convention in the General Assembly of the Organization; however, it may convene in the territory of any member state of the Organization of American States when a majority of the Court considers

it desirable, and with the prior consent of the state concerned. The seat of the Court may be changed by the States Parties to the Convention in the General Assembly by a two-thirds vote.

2. The Court shall appoint its own Secretary.

3. The Secretary shall have his office at the place where the Court has its seat and shall attend the meetings that the Court may hold away from its seat.

Article 59

The Court shall establish its Secretariat, which shall function under the direction of the Secretary of the Court, in accordance with the administrative standards of the General Secretariat of the Organization in all respects not incompatible with the independence of the Court. The staff of the Court's Secretariat shall be appointed by the Secretary General of the Organization, in consultation with the Secretary of the Court.

Article 60

The Court shall draw up its Statute which it shall submit to the General Assembly for approval. It shall adopt its own Rules of Procedure.

Section 2
Jurisdiction and Functions

Article 61

1. Only the States Parties and the Commission shall have the right to submit a case to the Court.

2. In order for the Court to hear a case, it is necessary that the procedures set forth in Articles 48 and 50 shall have been completed.

Article 62

1. A State Party may, upon depositing its instrument of ratification or adherence to this Convention, or at any subsequent time, declare that it recognizes as binding, *ipso facto*, and not requiring special agreement, the jurisdiction of the Court on all matters relating to the interpretation or application of this Convention.

2. Such declaration may be made unconditionally, on the condition of reciprocity, for a specified period, or for specific cases. It shall be presented to the Secretary General of the Organization, who shall transmit copies thereof to the other member states of the Organization and to the Secretary of the Court.

3. The jurisdiction of the Court shall comprise all cases concerning the interpretation and application of the provisions of this Convention that are submitted to it, provided that the States Parties to the case recognize or have recognized such jurisdiction, whether by special declaration pursuant to the preceding paragraphs, or by a special agreement.

Article 63

1. If the Court finds that there has been a violation of a right or freedom protected by this Convention, the Court shall rule that the injured party be ensured the enjoyment of his right or freedom that was violated. It shall also rule, if appropriate, that the consequences of the measure or situation that constituted the breach of such right or freedom be remedied and that fair compensation be paid to the injured party.

2. In cases of extreme gravity and urgency, and when necessary to avoid irreparable damage to persons, the Court shall adopt such provisional measures as it deems pertinent in matters it has under consideration. With respect to a case not yet submitted to the Court, it may act at the request of the Commission.

Article 64

1. The member states of the Organization may consult the Court regarding the interpretation of this Convention or of other treaties concerning the protection of human rights in the American states. Within their spheres of competence, the organs listed in Chapter X of the Charter of the Organization of American States, as amended by the Protocol of Buenos Aires,* may in like manner consult the Court.

2. The Court, at the request of a member state of the Organization, may provide that state with opinions regarding the compatibility of any of its domestic laws with the aforesaid international instruments.

* Current Chapter VIII of the OAS Charter.

Article 65

To each regular session of the General Assembly of the Organization of American States the Court shall submit, for the Assembly's consideration, a report on its work during the previous year. It shall specify, in particular, the cases in which a state has not complied with its judgments, making any pertinent recommendations.

Section 3
Procedure

Article 66

1. Reasons shall be given for the judgment of the Court.
2. If the judgment does not represent in whole or in part the unanimous opinion of the judges, any judge shall be entitled to have his dissenting or separate opinion attached to the judgment.

Article 67

The judgment of the Court shall be final and not subject to appeal. In case of disagreement as to the meaning or scope of the judgment, the Court shall interpret it at the request of any of the parties, provided the request is made within ninety days from the date of notification of the judgment.

Article 68

1. The States Parties to the Convention undertake to comply with the judgment of the Court in any case to which they are parties.
2. That part of a judgment that stipulates compensatory damages may be executed in the country concerned in accordance with domestic procedure governing the execution of judgments against the state.

Article 69

The parties to the case shall be notified of the judgment of the Court and it shall be transmitted to the States Parties to the Convention.

Chapter IX
Common Provisions

Article 70

1. The judges of the Court and the members of the Commission shall enjoy, from the moment of their election and throughout their term of office, the immunities extended to diplomatic agents in accordance with international law. During the exercise of their official function they shall, in addition, enjoy the diplomatic privileges necessary for the performance of their duties.

2. At no time shall the judges of the Court or the members of the Commission be held liable for any decisions or opinions issued in the exercise of their functions.

Article 71

The position of judge of the Court or member of the Commission is incompatible with any other activity that might affect the independence or impartiality of such judge or member, as determined in the respective statutes.

Article 72

The judges of the Court and the members of the Commission shall receive emoluments and travel allowances in the form and under the conditions set forth in their statutes, with due regard for the importance and independence of their office. Such emoluments and travel allowances shall be determined in the budget of the Organization of American States, which shall also include the expenses of the Court and its Secretariat. To this end, the Court shall draw up its own budget and submit it for approval to the General Assembly through the General Secretariat. The latter may not introduce any changes in it.

Article 73

The General Assembly may, only at the request of the Commission or the Court, as the case may be, determine sanctions to be applied against members of the Commission or judges of the Court when there are justifiable grounds for such action as set forth in the respective statutes.

A vote of a two-thirds majority of the member states of the Organization shall be required for a decision in the case of members of the Commission and, in the case of judges of the Court, a two-thirds majority vote of the States Parties to the Convention shall also be required.

PART III
GENERAL AND TRANSITORY PROVISIONS

CHAPTER X
SIGNATURE, RATIFICATION, RESERVATIONS, AMENDMENTS, PROTOCOLS, AND DENUNCIATION

Article 74

1. This Convention shall be open for signature and ratification by or adherence of any member state of the Organization of American States.
2. Ratification of or adherence to this Convention shall be made by the deposit of an instrument of ratification or adherence with the General Secretariat of the Organization of American States. As soon as eleven states have deposited their instruments of ratification or adherence, the Convention shall enter into force. With respect to any state that ratifies or adheres thereafter, the Convention shall enter into force on the date of the deposit of its instrument of ratification or adherence.
3. The Secretary General shall inform all member states of the Organization of the entry into force of the Convention.

Article 75

This Convention shall be subject to reservations only in conformity with the provisions of the Vienna Convention on the Law of Treaties signed on May 23, 1969.

Article 76

1. Proposals to amend this Convention may be submitted to the General Assembly for the action it deems appropriate by any State Party directly, and by the Commission or the Court through the Secretary General.
2. Amendments shall enter into force for the States ratifying them on the date when two-thirds of the States Parties to this Convention have

deposited their respective instruments of ratification. With respect to the other States Parties, the amendments shall enter into force on the dates on which they deposit their respective instruments of ratification.

Article 77

1. In accordance with Article 31, any State Party and the Commission may submit proposed protocols to this Convention for consideration by the States Parties at the General Assembly with a view to gradually including other rights and freedoms within its system of protection.

2. Each protocol shall determine the manner of its entry into force and shall be applied only among the States Parties to it.

Article 78

1. The States Parties may denounce this Convention at the expiration of a five-year period from the date of its entry into force and by means of notice given one year in advance. Notice of the denunciation shall be addressed to the Secretary General of the Organization, who shall inform the other States Parties.

2. Such a denunciation shall not have the effect of releasing the State Party concerned from the obligations contained in this Convention with respect to any act that may constitute a violation of those obligations and that has been taken by that state prior to the effective date of denunciation.

Chapter XI
Transitory Provisions

Section 1
Inter-American Commission on Human Rights

Article 79

Upon the entry into force of this Convention, the Secretary General shall, in writing, request each member state of the Organization to present, within ninety days, its candidates for membership on the Inter-American Commission on Human Rights. The Secretary General shall prepare a list in alphabetical order of the candidates presented, and transmit it to the member states of the Organization at least thirty days prior to the next session of the General Assembly.

Article 80

The members of the Commission shall be elected by secret ballot of the General Assembly from the list of candidates referred to in Article 79. The candidates who obtain the largest number of votes and an absolute majority of the votes of the representatives of the member states shall be declared elected. Should it become necessary to have several ballots in order to elect all the members of the Commission, the candidates who receive the smallest number of votes shall be eliminated successively, in the manner determined by the General Assembly.

Section 2
Inter-American Court of Human Rights

Article 81

Upon the entry into force of this Convention, the Secretary General shall, in writing, request each State Party to present, within ninety days, its candidates for membership on the Inter-American Court of Human Rights. The Secretary General shall prepare a list in alphabetical order of the candidates presented and transmit it to the States Parties at least thirty days prior to the next session of the General Assembly.

Article 82

The judges of the Court shall be elected from the list of candidates referred to in Article 81, by secret ballot of the States Parties to the Convention in the General Assembly. The candidates who obtain the largest number of votes and an absolute majority of the votes of the representatives of the States Parties shall be declared elected. Should it become necessary to have several ballots in order to elect all the judges of the Court, the candidates who receive the smallest number of votes shall be eliminated successively, in the manner determined by the States Parties.

[*The following text is not part of the Convention.*]

The Convention was signed at San José, Costa Rica, on 22 November 1969. It entered into force on 18 July 1978 in accordance with Article 74(2) of the Convention. The following table shows the status of ratifications of and accessions to the Convention and acceptances of the jurisdiction of the Inter-American Court.

Signatory States	Date of deposit of ratification or accession	Date of acceptance of the jurisdiction of the Court
Argentina*	5 September 1984	5 September 1984
Barbados	27 November 1982	4 June 2000
Bolivia	19 July 1979	27 July 1993
Brazil	25 September 1992	10 December 1998
Chile*	21 August 1990	21 August 1990
Colombia*	31 July 1973	21 June 1985
Costa Rica*	8 April 1970	2 July 1980
Dominica	3 June 1993	
Dominican Republic	19 April 1978	25 March 1999
Ecuador*	28 December 1977	13 August 1984
El Salvador	23 June 1978	6 June 1995
Grenada	18 July 1978	
Guatemala	25 May 1978	9 March 1987
Haiti	27 September 1977	20 March 1998
Honduras	8 September 1977	9 September 1981
Jamaica*	7 August 1978	
Mexico	2 March 1981	16 December 1998
Nicaragua	25 September 1979	12 February 1991
Panama	22 June 1978	9 May 1990
Paraguay	24 August 1989	26 March 1993
Peru*	28 July 1978	21 January 1981
Suriname	12 November 1987	12 November 1987
Trinidad and Tobago	28 May 1991	28 May 1991
United States		
Uruguay*	19 April 1985	19 April 1995
Venezuela*	9 August 1977	24 June 1981

* States that have accepted the competence of the Inter-American Commission on Human Rights to receive and examine communications in which a State Party alleges that another State Party has violated the human rights set forth in the American Convention: Argentina (5 September 1984); Chile (21 August 1990); Colombia (21 June 1985); Costa Rica (2 July 1980); Ecuador (13 August 1984); Jamaica (7 August 1978); Peru (21 January 1981); Uruguay (19 April 1985); and Venezuela (9 August 1977).

Appendix 2

Rules of Procedure of the Inter-American Court of Human Rights

Approved by the Court at its forty-ninth regular session, 16–25 November 2000

Preliminary Provisions

Article 1
Purpose

1. These Rules regulate the organization and establish the procedure of the Inter-American Court of Human Rights.
2. The Court may adopt such other Rules as may be necessary to carry out its functions.
3. In the absence of a provision in these Rules or in case of doubt as to their interpretation, the Court shall decide.

Article 2
Definitions

For the purposes of these Rules:

1. the term '**Agent**' refers to the person designated by a State to represent it before the Inter-American Court of Human Rights;
2. the term '**Deputy Agent**' refers to the person designated by a State to assist the Agent in the discharge of his duties and to replace him during his temporary absences;
3. the expression '**General Assembly**' refers to the General Assembly of the Organization of American States;
4. the term '**Commission**' refers to the Inter-American Commission on Human Rights;
5. the expression '**Permanent Commission**' refers to the Permanent Commission of the Inter-American Court of Human Rights;

6. the expression '**Permanent Council**' refers to the Permanent Council of the Organization of American States;

7. the term '**Convention**' refers to the American Convention on Human Rights ('Pact of San José', Costa Rica);

8. the term '**Court**' refers to the Inter-American Court of Human Rights;

9. the term '**Delegates**' refers to the persons designated by the Commission to represent it before the Court;

10. the expression '**original claimant**' refers to the person, group of persons, or nongovernmental entity that instituted the original petition before the Commission, pursuant to Article 44 of the Convention;

11. the term '**day**' shall be understood to be a natural day;

12. the expression '**States Parties**' refers to the States that have ratified or adhered to the Convention;

13. the expression '**Member States**' refers to the States that are members of the Organization of American States;

14. the term '**Statute**' refers to the Statute of the Court adopted by the General Assembly of the Organization of American States on 31 October 1979 (AG/RES. 448 [IX-0/79]), as amended;

15. the expression '**next of kin**' refers to the immediate family, that is, the direct ascendants and descendants, siblings, spouses or permanent companions, or those determined by the Court, if applicable;

16. the expression '**report of the Commission**' refers to the report provided for in Article 50 of the Convention;

17. the term '**Judge**' refers to the judges who compose the Court for each case;

18. the expression '**Titular Judge**' refers to any judge elected pursuant to Articles 53 and 54 of the Convention;

19. the expression '**Interim Judge**' refers to any judge appointed pursuant to Articles 6(3) and 19(4) of the Statute;

20. the expression '**Judge ad hoc**' refers to any judge appointed pursuant to Article 55 of the Convention;

21. the term '**month**' shall be understood to be a calendar month;

22. the acronym '**OAS**' refers to the Organization of American States;

23. the expression '**parties to the case**' refers to the victim or the alleged victim, the State and, only procedurally, the Commission;

24. the term '**President**' refers to the President of the Court;

25. the term '**Secretariat**' refers to the Secretariat of the Court;

26. the term '**Secretary**' refers to the Secretary of the Court;

27. the expression ‘**Deputy Secretary**’ refers to the Deputy Secretary of the Court;

28. the expression ‘**Secretary General**’ refers to the Secretary General of the Organization of American States;

29. the expression ‘**Vice-President**’ refers to the Vice-President of the Court;

30. the expression ‘**alleged victim**’ refers to the person whose rights under the Convention are alleged to have been violated;

31. the term ‘**victim**’ refers to the person whose rights have been violated, according to a judgment pronounced by the Court.

TITLE I
ORGANIZATION AND FUNCTIONING OF THE COURT

CHAPTER I
THE PRESIDENCY AND VICE-PRESIDENCY

Article 3
Election of the President and the Vice-President

1. The President and the Vice-President shall be elected by the Court for a period of two years and may be reelected. Their term shall begin on the first day of the first session of the corresponding year. The election shall take place at the last regular session held by the Court during the preceding year.

2. The elections referred to in this Article shall be by secret ballot of the Titular Judges present. The judge who wins four or more votes shall be deemed to have been elected. If no candidate receives the required number of votes, a ballot shall take place between the two judges who have received the most votes. In the event of a tie, the judge having precedence in accordance with Article 13 of the Statute shall be deemed to have been elected.

Article 4
Functions of the President

1. The functions of the President are to:

a. represent the Court;

b. preside over the meetings of the Court and to submit for its consideration the topics appearing on the agenda;
c. direct and promote the work of the Court;
d. rule on points of order that may arise during the meetings of the Court. If any judge so requests, the point of order shall be decided by a majority vote;
e. present a biannual report to the Court on the activities he has carried out as President during that period;
f. exercise such other functions as are conferred upon him by the Statute or these Rules, or entrusted to him by the Court.

2. In specific cases, the President may delegate the representation referred to in paragraph 1(a) of this Article to the Vice-President, to any of the judges or, if necessary, to the Secretary or to the Deputy Secretary.

3. If the President is a national of one of the parties to a case before the Court, or in special situations in which he considers it appropriate, he shall relinquish the Presidency for that particular case. The same rule shall apply to the Vice-President or to any judge called upon to exercise the functions of the President.

Article 5
Functions of the Vice-President

1. The Vice-President shall replace the President in the latter's temporary absence, and shall assume the Presidency when the absence is permanent. In the latter case, the Court shall elect a Vice-President to serve out the rest of the term. The same procedure shall be followed if the absence of the Vice-President is permanent.

2. In the absence of the President and the Vice-President, their functions shall be assumed by the other judges in the order of precedence established in Article 13 of the Statute.

Article 6
Commissions

1. The Permanent Commission shall be composed by the President, the Vice-President and any other judges the President deems it appropriate to appoint, according to the needs of the Court. The Permanent Commission shall assist the President in the exercise of his functions.

2. The Court may appoint other commissions for specific matters. In urgent cases, they may be appointed by the President if the Court is not in session.

3. The commissions shall be governed by the provisions of these Rules, as applicable.

Chapter II
The Secretariat

Article 7
Election of the Secretary

1. The Court shall elect its Secretary, who must possess the legal qualifications required for the position, a good command of the working languages of the Court, and the experience necessary for discharging his functions.

2. The Secretary shall be elected for a term of five years and may be re-elected. He may be removed at any time if the Court so decides. A majority of no fewer than four judges, voting by secret ballot in the presence of a quorum, is required for the appointing or removal of the Secretary.

Article 8
Deputy Secretary

1. The Deputy Secretary shall be appointed on the proposal of the Secretary, in the manner prescribed in the Statute. He shall assist the Secretary in the performance of his functions and replace him during his temporary absences.

2. If the Secretary and the Deputy Secretary are both unable to perform their functions, the President may appoint an Interim Secretary.

Article 9
Oath

1. The Secretary and the Deputy Secretary shall take an oath or make a solemn declaration before the President undertaking to discharge their duties faithfully, and to respect the confidential nature of the facts that come to their attention while exercising their functions.

2. The staff of the Secretariat, including any persons called upon to perform interim or temporary duties, shall, upon assuming their functions, take an oath or make a solemn declaration before the President undertaking to discharge their duties faithfully and to respect the confidential nature of the facts that come to their attention while exercising their functions. If the President is not present at the seat of the Court, the Secretary shall administer the oath.

3. All oaths shall be recorded in a document to be signed by the person being sworn in and by the person administering the oath.

Article 10
Functions of the Secretary

The functions of the Secretary shall be to:

a. communicate the judgments, advisory opinions, orders and other rulings of the Court;
b. keep the minutes of the meetings of the Court;
c. attend the meetings of the Court held at its seat or elsewhere;
d. deal with the correspondence of the Court;
e. direct the administration of the Court, pursuant to the instructions of the President;
f. prepare the drafts of the working schedules, rules and regulations, and budgets of the Court;
g. plan, direct and coordinate the work of the staff of the Court;
h. carry out the tasks assigned to him by the Court or by the President;
i. perform any other duties provided for in the Statute or in these Rules.

Chapter III
Functioning of the Court

Article 11
Regular Sessions

During the year, the Court shall hold the sessions needed for the exercise of its functions on the dates decided upon by the Court at the previous session. In exceptional circumstances, the President may change the dates of these sessions after prior consultation with the Court.

Article 12
Special Sessions

Special sessions may be convoked by the President on his own initiative or at the request of a majority of the judges.

Article 13
Quorum

The quorum for the deliberations of the Court shall consist of five judges.

Article 14
Hearings, Deliberations and Decisions

1. Hearings shall be public and shall be held at the seat of the Court. When exceptional circumstances so warrant, the Court may decide to hold a hearing in private or at a different location. The Court shall decide who may attend such hearings. Even in these cases, however, minutes shall be kept in the manner prescribed in Article 42 of these Rules.

2. The Court shall deliberate in private, and its deliberations shall remain secret. Only the judges shall take part in the deliberations, although the Secretary and the Deputy Secretary or their substitutes may attend, as well as such other Secretariat staff as may be required. No other persons may be admitted, except by special decision of the Court and after taking an oath or making a solemn declaration.

3. Any question that calls for a vote shall be formulated in precise terms in one of the working languages. At the request of any of the judges, the Secretariat shall translate the text thereof into the other working languages and distribute it prior to the vote.

4. The minutes of the deliberations of the Court shall be limited to a statement of the subject of the discussion and the decisions taken. Separate opinions, dissenting and concurring, and declarations made for the record shall also be noted.

Article 15
Decisions and Voting

1. The President shall present, point by point, the matters to be voted upon. Each judge shall vote either in the affirmative or the negative; there shall be no abstentions.

2. The votes shall be cast in inverse order to the order of precedence established in Article 13 of the Statute.

3. The decisions of the Court shall be adopted by a majority of the judges present at the time of the voting.
4. In the event of a tie, the President shall have a casting vote.

Article 16
Continuation in Office by the Judges

1. Judges whose terms have expired shall continue to exercise their functions in cases that they have begun to hear and that are still pending. However, in the event of death, resignation or disqualification, the judge in question shall be replaced by the judge who was elected to take his place, if applicable, or by the judge who has precedence among the new judges elected upon expiration of the term of the judge to be replaced.
2. All matters relating to reparations and indemnities, as well as supervision of the implementation of the judgments of the Court, shall be heard by the judges comprising it at that stage of the proceedings, unless a public hearing has already been held. In that event, they shall be heard by the judges who had attended that hearing.
3. All matters relating to provisional measures shall be heard by the Court composed of Titular Judges.

Article 17
Interim Judges

Interim Judges shall have the same rights and functions as Titular Judges, except for such limitations that have been expressly established.

Article 18
Judges *Ad Hoc*

1. In a case arising under Article 55(2) and 55(3) of the Convention and Article 10(2) and 10(3) of the Statute, the President, acting through the Secretariat, shall inform the States referred to in those provisions of their right to appoint a Judge *ad hoc* within 30 days of notification of the application.
2. When it appears that two or more States have a common interest, the President shall inform them that they may jointly appoint one Judge ad hoc, pursuant to Article 10 of the Statute. If those States have not communicated their agreement to the Court within 30 days of the last notification of the application, each State may propose its candidate within 15 days. Thereafter, and if more than one candidate has been

nominated, the President shall choose a common Judge *ad hoc* by lot, and shall communicate the result to the interested parties.

3. Should the interested States fail to exercise their right within the time limits established in the preceding paragraphs, they shall be deemed to have waived that right.

4. The Secretary shall communicate the appointment of Judges *ad hoc* to the other parties to the case.

5. The Judge *ad hoc* shall take an oath at the first meeting devoted to the consideration of the case for which he has been appointed.

6. Judges *ad hoc* shall receive honoraria on the same terms as Titular Judges.

Article 19
Impediments, Excuses and Disqualification

1. Impediments, excuses and disqualification of Judges shall be governed by the provisions of Article 19 of the Statute.

2. Motions for impediments and excuses must be filed prior to the first hearing of the case. However, if the grounds therefor were not known at the time, such motions may be submitted to the Court at the first possible opportunity, so that it can rule on the matter immediately.

3. When, for any reason whatsoever, a judge is not present at one of the hearings or at other stages of the proceedings, the Court may decide to disqualify him from continuing to hear the case, taking all the circumstances it deems relevant into account.

Title II
Procedure

Chapter I
General Rules

Article 20
Official Languages

1. The official languages of the Court shall be those of the OAS, which are Spanish, English, Portuguese and French.

2. The working languages shall be those agreed upon by the Court each year. However, in a specific case, the language of one of the parties may be adopted as a working language, provided it is one of the official languages.

3. The working languages for each case shall be determined at the beginning of the proceedings, unless they are the same as those already being employed by the Court.

4. The Court may authorize any person appearing before it to use his own language if he does not have sufficient knowledge of the working languages. In such circumstances, however, the Court shall make the necessary arrangements to ensure that an interpreter is present to translate that testimony into the working languages. The interpreter must take an oath or make a solemn declaration, undertaking to discharge his duties faithfully and to respect the confidential nature of the facts that come to his attention in the exercise of his functions.

5. The Court shall, in all cases, determine which text is authentic.

Article 21
Representation of the States

1. The States Parties to a case shall be represented by an Agent, who may, in turn, be assisted by any persons of his choice.

2. If a State replaces its Agent, it shall so notify the Court, and the replacement shall only take effect once the notification has been received at the seat of the Court.

3. A Deputy Agent may be designated who will assist the Agent in the exercise of his functions and replace him during his temporary absences.

4. When appointing its Agent, the State in question shall indicate the address at which all relevant communications shall be deemed to have been officially received.

Article 22
Representation of the Commission

The Commission shall be represented by the Delegates it has designated for the purpose. The Delegates may be assisted by any persons of their choice.

Article 23
Participation of the Alleged Victims

1. When the application has been admitted, the alleged victims, their next of kin or their duly accredited representatives may submit their requests, arguments and evidence, autonomously, throughout the proceeding.

2. When there are several alleged victims, next of kin or duly accredited representatives, they shall designate a common intervenor who shall be the only person authorized to present requests, arguments and evidence during the proceedings, including the public hearings.

3. In case of disagreement, the Court shall make the appropriate ruling.

Article 24
Cooperation of the States

1. The States Parties to a case have the obligation to cooperate so as to ensure that all notices, communications or summonses addressed to persons subject to their jurisdiction are duly executed. They shall also facilitate compliance with summonses by persons who either reside or are present within their territory.

2. The same rule shall apply to any proceeding that the Court decides to conduct or order in the territory of a State Party to a case.

3. When the performance of any of the measures referred to in the preceding paragraphs requires the cooperation of any other State, the President shall request the corresponding government to provide the requisite assistance.

Article 25
Provisional Measures

1. At any stage of the proceedings involving cases of extreme gravity and urgency, and when necessary to avoid irreparable damage to persons, the Court may, at the request of a party or on its own motion, order such provisional measures as it deems pertinent, pursuant to Article 63(2) of the Convention.

2. With respect to matters not yet submitted to it, the Court may act at the request of the Commission.

3. The request may be made to the President, to any judge of the Court, or to the Secretariat, by any means of communication. In every case, the recipient of the request shall immediately bring it to the President's attention.

4. If the Court is not sitting, the President, in consultation with the Permanent Commission and, if possible, with the other judges, shall call upon the government concerned to adopt such urgent measures as may be necessary to ensure the effectiveness of any provisional measures that may be ordered by the Court at its next session.

5. The Court, or its President if the Court is not sitting, may convoke the parties to a public hearing on provisional measures.

6. In its Annual Report to the General Assembly, the Court shall include a statement concerning the provisional measures ordered during the period covered by the report. If those measures have not been duly implemented, the Court shall make such recommendations as it deems appropriate.

Article 26
Filing of Briefs

1. The application, the reply thereto, and any other briefs addressed to the Court, may be presented in person, by courier, facsimile, telex, mail or any other method generally used. If they are dispatched by electronic means, the original documents must be submitted within 15 days.

2. The President may, in consultation with the Permanent Commission, reject any communication from the parties which he considers patently inadmissible, and shall order that it be returned to the interested party, without further action.

Article 27
Default Procedure

1. When a party fails to appear in or continue with a case, the Court shall, on its own motion, take such measures as may be necessary to complete the consideration of the case.

2. When a party enters a case at a later stage of the proceedings, it shall take up the proceedings at that stage.

Article 28
Joinder of Cases and Proceedings

1. The Court may, at any stage of the proceedings, order the joinder of interrelated cases, when there is identity of parties, subject-matter and ruling law.

2. The Court may also order that the written or oral proceedings of several cases, including the introduction of witnesses, be carried out jointly.

3. After consulting the Agents and the Delegates, the President may direct that two or more cases be conducted simultaneously.

Article 29
Decisions

1. The judgments and orders for discontinuance of a case shall be rendered exclusively by the Court.

2. All other orders shall be rendered by the Court if it is sitting, and by the President if it is not, unless otherwise provided. Decisions of the President that are not purely procedural may be appealed before the Court.

3. Judgments and orders of the Court may not be contested in any way.

Article 30
Publication of Judgments and Other Decisions

1. The Court shall order the publication of:

a. its judgments and other decisions, including separate opinions, dissenting or concurring, whenever they fulfill the requirements set forth in Article 55(2) of these Rules;
b. documents from the dossier, except those considered irrelevant or unsuitable for publication;
c. records of the hearings;
d. any other document that the Court considers suitable for publication.

2. The judgments shall be published in the working languages used in each case. All other documents shall be published in their original language.

3. Documents relating to cases already adjudicated, and deposited with the Secretariat of the Court, shall be made accessible to the public, unless the Court decides otherwise.

Article 31
Application of Article 63(1) of the Convention

Application of this provision may be invoked at any stage of the proceedings.

Chapter II
Written Proceedings

Article 32
Institution of the Proceedings

For a case to be referred to the Court under Article 61(1) of the Convention, the application shall be filed in the Secretariat of the Court in the working languages. Whereas the filing of an application in only one working language shall not suspend the proceeding, the translations into the other language or languages must be submitted within 30 days.

Article 33
Filing of the Application

The brief containing the application shall indicate:

1. the claims (including those relating to reparations and costs); the parties to the case; a statement of the facts; the orders on the opening of the proceeding and the admissibility of the petition by the Commission; the supporting evidence, indicating the facts on which it will bear; the particulars of the witnesses and expert witnesses and the subject of their statements; the legal arguments, and the pertinent conclusions. In addition, the Commission shall include the name and address of the original petitioner, and also the name and address of the alleged victims, their next of kin or their duly accredited representatives, when this is possible.
2. The names of the Agents or the Delegates.

If the application is filed by the Commission, it shall be accompanied by the report referred to in Article 50 of the Convention.

Article 34
Preliminary Review of the Application

When, during a preliminary review of the application, the President finds that the basic requirements have not been met, he shall request the applicant to correct any deficiencies within 20 days.

Article 35
Notification of the Application

1. The Secretary of the Court shall notify of the application to:

a. the President and the judges of the Court;
b. the respondent State;
c. the Commission, when it is not the applicant;
d. the original claimant, if known;
e. the alleged victim, his next of kin, or his duly accredited representatives, if applicable.

2. The Secretary shall inform the other States Parties, the Permanent Council of the OAS through its President, and the Secretary General of the OAS, of the filing of the application.

3. When notifying, the Secretary shall request the respondent States to designate their Agent, and the Commission to appoint its Delegates, within one month. Until the Delegates are duly appointed, the Commission shall be deemed to be properly represented by its President for all purposes of the case.

4. When the application has been notified to the alleged victim, his next of kin or his duly accredited representatives, they shall have a period of 30 days to present autonomously to the Court their requests, arguments and evidence.

Article 36
Preliminary Objections

1. Preliminary objections may only be filed in the brief answering the application.

2. The document setting out the preliminary objections shall set out the facts on which the objection is based, the legal arguments, and the conclusions and supporting documents, as well as any evidence which the party filing the objection may wish to produce.

3. The presentation of preliminary objections shall not cause the suspension of the proceedings on the merits, nor the respective time periods or terms.

4. Any parties to the case wishing to submit written briefs on the preliminary objections may do so within 30 days of receipt of the communication.

5. When the Court considers it indispensable, it may convene a special hearing on the preliminary objections, after which it shall rule on the objections.

6. The Court may decide on the preliminary objections and the merits of the case in a single judgment, under the principle of procedural economy.

Article 37
Answer to the Application

1. The respondent shall answer the application in writing within two months of the notification. The requirements indicated in Article 33 of these Rules shall apply. The Secretary shall communicate the said answer to the persons referred to in Article 35(1) above.

2. In its answer, the respondent must state whether it accepts the facts and claims or whether it contradicts them, and the Court may consider accepted those facts that have not been expressly denied and the claims that have not been expressly contested.

Article 38
Other Steps in the Written Proceedings

Once the application has been answered, and before the opening of the oral proceedings, the parties may seek the permission of the President to enter additional written pleadings. In such a case, the President, if he sees fit, shall establish the time limits for presentation of the relevant documents.

Chapter III
Oral Proceedings

Article 39
Opening

The President shall announce the date for the opening of the oral proceedings and shall call such hearings as may be necessary.

Article 40
Conduct of the Hearings

1. The President shall direct the hearings. He shall prescribe the order in which the persons eligible to take part shall be heard, and determine the measures required for the smooth conduct of the hearings.

2. The provisions of Article 23 of these Rules of Procedure shall be observed, with regard to who may speak for the victims or the alleged victims, their next of kin or their duly accredited representatives.

Article 41
Questions Put During the Hearings

1. The judges may ask all persons appearing before the Court any questions they deem proper.

2. The witnesses, expert witnesses and any other persons the Court decides to hear may, subject to the control of the President, be examined by the persons referred to in Articles 21, 22 and 23 of these Rules.

3. The President is empowered to rule on the relevance of the questions posed and to excuse the person to whom the questions are addressed from replying, unless the Court decides otherwise. Leading questions shall not be permitted.

Article 42
Minutes of the Hearings

1. Minutes shall be taken at each hearing and shall contain the following:

a. the names of the judges present;
b. the names of those persons referred to in Articles 21, 22 and 23 of these Rules, who are present at the hearing;
c. the names and personal information of the witnesses, expert witnesses and other persons appearing at the hearing;
d. statements made expressly for the record by the States Parties, by the Commission, by the victims or alleged victims, by their next of kin or their duly accredited representatives;
e. the statements of the witnesses, expert witnesses and other persons appearing at the hearing, as well as the questions posed to them and the replies thereto;
f. the text of the questions posed by the judges and the replies thereto;
g. the text of any decisions rendered by the Court during the hearing.

2. The Agents, Delegates, victims or alleged victims, their next of kin or their duly accredited representatives, and also the witnesses, expert witnesses and other persons appearing at the hearing, shall receive a copy of the relevant parts of the transcript of the hearing to enable them, subject to the control of the Secretary, to correct any errors in transcription. The Secretary shall set the time limits for this purpose, in accordance with the instructions of the President.

3. The minutes shall be signed by the President and the Secretary, and the latter shall attest to their accuracy.

4. Copies of the minutes shall be transmitted to the Agents, the Delegates, the victims and the alleged victims, their next of kin or their duly accredited representatives.

Chapter IV
Evidence

Article 43
Admission

1. Items of evidence tendered by the parties shall be admissible only if previous notification thereof is contained in the application and in the reply thereto and, when appropriate, in the document setting out the preliminary objections and in the answer thereto.

2. Evidence tendered to the Commission shall form part of the file, provided that it has been received in a procedure with the presence of both parties, unless the Court considers it essential that such evidence should be repeated.

3. Should any of the parties allege *force majeure*, serious impediment or the emergence of supervening events as grounds for producing an item of evidence, the Court may, in that particular instance, admit such evidence at a time other than those indicated above, provided that the opposing parties are guaranteed the right of defense.

4. In the case of the alleged victim, his next of kin or his duly accredited representatives, the admission of evidence shall also be governed by the provisions of Articles 23, 35(4) and 36(5) of the Rules of Procedure.

Article 44
Procedure for Taking Evidence

The Court may, at any stage of the proceedings:

1. Obtain, on its own motion, any evidence it considers helpful. In particular, it may hear as a witness, expert witness, or in any other capacity, any person whose evidence, statement or opinion it deems to be relevant.

2. Request the parties to provide any evidence within their reach or any explanation or statement that, in its opinion, may be useful.

3. Request any entity, office, organ or authority of its choice to obtain information, express an opinion, or deliver a report or pronouncement on any given point. The documents may not be published without the authorization of the Court.

4. Commission one or more of its members to conduct measures in order to gather evidence.

Article 45
Cost of Evidence

The party requesting the production of an item of evidence shall cover its cost.

Article 46
Convocation of Witnesses and Expert Witnesses

1. The Court shall determine when the parties are to call their witnesses and expert witnesses whom the Court considers it necessary to hear. They shall be summoned in the manner deemed most suitable by the Court.

2. The summons shall indicate:

a. the name of the witness or expert witness;
b. the facts on which the examination will bear or the object of the expert opinion.

Article 47
Oath or Solemn Declaration by Witnesses and Expert Witnesses

1. After his identity has been established and before giving evidence, every witness shall take an oath or make a solemn declaration in which he shall state that he will speak the truth, the whole truth and nothing but the truth.

2. After his identity has been established and before performing his task, every expert witness shall take an oath or make a solemn declaration in which he shall state that he will discharge his duties honorably and conscientiously.

3. The oath shall be taken, or the declaration made, before the Court or the President or any of the judges so delegated by the Court.

Article 48
Objections to Witnesses

1. Any party may object to a witness before he testifies.

2. If the Court considers it necessary, it may nevertheless hear, for purposes of information, a person who is not qualified to be heard as a witness.

3. The Court shall assess the value of the testimony and of the objections made by the parties.

Article 49
Objections to Expert Witnesses

1. The grounds for disqualification applicable to judges under Article 19(1) of the Statute shall also apply to expert witnesses.

2. Objections shall be presented within 15 days of notification of the appointment of the expert witness.

3. If the expert witness who has been challenged contests the ground invoked against him, the Court shall rule on the matter. However, when the Court is not in session, the President may, after consultation with the Permanent Commission, order the evidence to be presented. The Court shall be informed thereof and shall rule on the value of the evidence.

4. Should it become necessary to appoint a new expert witness, the Court shall rule on the matter. Nevertheless, if the evidence needs to be heard as a matter of urgency, the President, after consultation with the Permanent Commission, shall make the appointment and inform the Court accordingly. The Court shall rule on the value of the evidence.

Article 50
Protection of Witnesses and Expert Witnesses

States may neither institute proceedings against witnesses or expert witnesses nor bring illicit pressure to bear on them or on their families on account of declarations or opinions they have delivered before the Court.

Article 51
Failure to Appear or False Evidence

The Court shall inform the States when those persons summoned to appear or declare, fail to appear or refuse to give evidence without good reason, or when, in the opinion of the Court, they have violated their oath or solemn declaration, so that the appropriate action may be taken under the relevant domestic legislation.

Chapter V
Early Termination of the Proceedings

Article 52
Discontinuance of a Case

1. When the party that has brought the case notifies the Court of its intention not to proceed with it, the Court shall, after hearing the opinions of the other parties thereto, decide whether to discontinue the hearing and, consequently, to strike the case from its list.

2. If the respondent informs the Court of its acquiescence to the claims of the party that has brought the case, the Court, after hearing the opinions of the other parties to the case [shall determine][1] whether such acquiescence and its juridical effects are acceptable. In that event, the Court shall determine the appropriate reparations and indemnities.

Article 53
Friendly Settlement

When the parties to a case before the Court inform it of the existence of a friendly settlement, compromise, or any other occurrence likely to lead to a settlement of the dispute, the Court may strike the case from its list.

Article 54
Continuation of a Case

The Court may, notwithstanding the existence of the conditions indicated in the preceding paragraphs, and bearing in mind its responsibility

[1] The words in square brackets have been added by the present author, to correspond to the Spanish text.

to protect human rights, decide to continue the consideration of a case.

Chapter VI
Judgments

Article 55
Contents of the Judgment

1. The judgment shall contain:

a. the names of the President, the judges who rendered it, the Secretary and Deputy Secretary;
b. the identity of the parties and their representatives;
c. a description of the proceedings;
d. the facts of the case;
e. the conclusions of the parties;
f. the legal arguments;
g. the ruling on the case;
h. the decision, if any, on reparations and costs;
i. the result of the voting;
j. a statement indicating which text is authentic.

2. Any judge who has taken part in the consideration of a case is entitled to append a separate opinion, concurring or dissenting, to the judgment. These opinions shall be submitted within a time limit to be fixed by the President, so that the other judges may take cognizance thereof prior to notification of the judgment. The said opinions shall only refer to the issues covered in the judgment.

Article 56
Judgment on Reparations

1. When no specific ruling on reparations has been made in the judgment on the merits, the Court shall set the time and determine the procedure for the deferred decision thereon.

2. If the Court is informed that the parties to the case have reached an agreement in regard to the execution of the judgment on the merits, it shall verify the fairness of the agreement and rule accordingly.

Article 57
Delivery and Communication of the Judgment

1. When a case is ready for judgment, the Court shall deliberate in private and adopt the judgment, which shall be notified to the parties by the Secretariat.

2. The texts, legal arguments and votes shall all remain secret until the parties have been notified of the judgment.

3. Judgments shall be signed by all the judges who participated in the voting and by the Secretary. However, a judgment signed by the majority of the judges and the Secretary shall also be valid.

4. Separate opinions, dissenting or concurring, shall be signed by the judges submitting them and by the Secretary.

5. The judgments shall conclude with an order, signed by the President and the Secretary and sealed by the latter, providing for the communication and execution of the judgment.

6. The originals of the judgments shall be deposited in the archives of the Court. The Secretary shall dispatch certified copies to the States Parties, the parties to the case, the Permanent Council through its President, the Secretary General of the OAS, and any other interested person who requests them.

Article 58
Request for Interpretation

1. The request for interpretation, referred to in Article 67 of the Convention, may be made in connection with judgments on the merits or on reparations and shall be filed with the Secretariat. It shall state with precision the issues relating to the meaning or scope of the judgment of which the interpretation is requested.

2. The Secretary shall transmit the request for interpretation to the parties to the case and shall invite them to submit any written comments they deem relevant, within the time limit established by the President.

3. When considering a request for interpretation, the Court shall be composed, whenever possible, of the same judges who delivered the judgment of which the interpretation is being sought. However, in the event of death, resignation, impediment, excuse or disqualification,

the judge in question shall be replaced pursuant to Article 16 of these Rules.

4. A request for interpretation shall not suspend the effect of the judgment.

5. The Court shall determine the procedure to be followed and shall render its decision in the form of a judgment.

Title III
Advisory Opinions

Article 59
Interpretation of the Convention

1. Requests for an advisory opinion under Article 64(1) of the Convention shall state with precision the specific questions on which the opinion of the Court is being sought.

2. Requests for an advisory opinion submitted by a Member State or by the Commission shall, in addition, identify the provisions to be interpreted, the considerations giving rise to the request, and the names and addresses of the Agent or the Delegates.

3. If the advisory opinion is sought by an OAS organ other than the Commission, the request shall also specify, further to the information listed in the preceding paragraph, how it relates to the sphere of competence of the organ in question.

Article 60
Interpretation of Other Treaties

1. If the interpretation requested refers to other treaties concerning the protection of human rights in the American states, as provided for in Article 64(1) of the Convention, the request shall indicate the name of, and parties to, the treaty, the specific questions on which the opinion of the Court is being sought, and the considerations giving rise to the request.

2. If the request is submitted by an OAS organ, it shall indicate how the subject of the request falls within the sphere of competence of the organ in question.

Article 61
Interpretation of Domestic Laws

1. A request for an advisory opinion presented pursuant to Article 64(2) of the Convention shall indicate the following:

a. the provisions of domestic law and of the Convention or of other treaties concerning the protection of human rights to which the request relates;
b. the specific questions on which the opinion of the Court is being sought;
c. the name and address of the applicant's Agent.

2. Copies of the domestic laws referred to in the request shall accompany the application.

Article 62
Procedure

1. On receipt of a request for an advisory opinion, the Secretary shall transmit copies thereof to all the Member States, the Commission, the Permanent Council of the OAS through its President, the Secretary General of the OAS and the OAS organs within whose spheres of competence the subject of the [...][2] request falls, as appropriate.

2. The President shall establish the time limits for the filing of written comments by the interested parties.

3. The President may invite or authorize any interested party to submit a written opinion on the issues covered by the request. If the request is governed by Article 64(2) of the Convention, he may do so after prior consultation with the Agent.

4. At the conclusion of the written proceedings, the Court shall decide whether there should be oral proceedings and shall fix the date for such a hearing, unless it delegates the latter task to the President. Prior consultation with the Agent is required in cases governed by Article 64(2) of the Convention.

[2] The words omitted read 'revision of', and were omitted by the present author in order to correspond to the Spanish text.

Article 63
Application by Analogy

The Court shall apply the provisions of Title II of these Rules to advisory proceedings, to the extent that it deems them to be compatible.

Article 64
Delivery and Content of Advisory Opinions

1. The delivery of advisory opinions shall be governed by Article 57 of these Rules.

2. Advisory opinions shall contain:

a. the name of the President, the judges who rendered the opinion, the Secretary and Deputy Secretary;
b. the issues presented to the Court;
c. a description of the proceedings;
d. the legal arguments;
e. the opinion of the Court;
f. a statement indicating which text is authentic.

3. Any judge who has taken part in the delivery of an advisory opinion is entitled to append a separate opinion, dissenting or concurring, to the opinion of the Court. These opinions shall be submitted within a time limit to be fixed by the President, so that the other judges can take cognizance thereof before the advisory opinion is rendered. They shall be published in accordance with Article 30(1)(a) of these Rules.

4. Advisory opinions may be delivered in public.

Title IV
Final and Transitory Provisions

Article 65
Amendments to the Rules of Procedure

These Rules of Procedure may be amended by the decision of an absolute majority of the Titular Judges of the Court. Upon their entry into force, they shall abrogate the previous Rules of Procedure.

Article 66
Entry into Force

These Rules of Procedure, the Spanish and English versions of which are equally authentic, shall enter into force on 1 June 2001.

Done at the seat of the Inter-American Court of Human Rights in San José, Costa Rica on this twenty-fourth day of November, 2000.

Appendix 3

Statute of the Inter-American Court of Human Rights

Adopted by the General Assembly of the OAS at its ninth regular session, held in La Paz, Bolivia, October 1979 (Resolution No. 448)

Chapter I
General Provisions

Article 1
Nature and Legal Organization

The Inter-American Court of Human Rights is an autonomous judicial institution whose purpose is the application and interpretation of the American Convention on Human Rights. The Court exercises its functions in accordance with the provisions of the aforementioned Convention and the present Statute.

Article 2
Jurisdiction

The Court shall exercise adjudicatory and advisory jurisdiction:

1. Its adjudicatory jurisdiction shall be governed by the provisions of Articles 61, 62 and 63 of the Convention, and
2. Its advisory jurisdiction shall be governed by the provisions of Article 64 of the Convention.

Article 3
Seat

1. The seat of the Court shall be San José, Costa Rica; however, the Court may convene in any member state of the Organization of American States (OAS) when a majority of the Court considers it desirable, and with the prior consent of the State concerned.

2. The seat of the Court may be changed by a vote of two-thirds of the States Parties to the Convention, in the OAS General Assembly.

Chapter II
Composition of the Court

Article 4
Composition

1. The Court shall consist of seven judges, nationals of the member states of the OAS, elected in an individual capacity from among jurists of the highest moral authority and of recognized competence in the field of human rights, who possess the qualifications required for the exercise of the highest judicial functions under the law of the State of which they are nationals or of the State that proposes them as candidates.

2. No two judges may be nationals of the same State.

Article 5
Judicial Terms[1]

1. The judges of the Court shall be elected for a term of six years and may be reelected only once. A judge elected to replace a judge whose term has not expired shall complete that term.

2. The terms of office of the judges shall run from January 1 of the year following that of their election to December 31 of the year in which their terms expire.

3. The judges shall serve until the end of their terms. Nevertheless, they shall continue to hear the cases they have begun to hear and that are still pending, and shall not be replaced by the newly elected judges in the handling of those cases.

Article 6
Election of the Judges – Date

1. Election of judges shall take place, insofar as possible, during the session of the OAS General Assembly immediately prior to the expiration of the term of the outgoing judges.

[1] Amended by Resolution 625 (XII-0/82) of the twelfth regular session of the OAS General Assembly.

2. Vacancies on the Court caused by death, permanent disability, resignation or dismissal of judges shall, insofar as possible, be filled at the next session of the OAS General Assembly. However, an election shall not be necessary when a vacancy occurs within six months of the expiration of a term.

3. If necessary in order to preserve a quorum of the Court, the States Parties to the Convention, at a meeting of the OAS Permanent Council, and at the request of the President of the Court, shall appoint one or more interim judges who shall serve until such time as they are replaced by elected judges.

Article 7
Candidates

1. Judges shall be elected by the States Parties to the Convention, at the OAS General Assembly, from a list of candidates nominated by those States.

2. Each State Party may nominate up to three candidates, nationals of the state that proposes them or of any other member state of the OAS.

3. When a slate of three is proposed, at least one of the candidates must be a national of a state other than the nominating state.

Article 8
Election – Preliminary Procedures[2]

1. Six months prior to expiration of the terms to which the judges of the Court were elected, the Secretary General of the OAS shall address a written request to each State Party to the Convention that it nominate its candidates within the next ninety days.

2. The Secretary General of the OAS shall draw up an alphabetical list of the candidates nominated, and shall forward it to the States Parties, if possible, at least thirty days before the next session of the OAS General Assembly.

3. In the case of vacancies on the Court, as well as in cases of the death or permanent disability of a candidate, the aforementioned time periods shall be shortened to a period that the Secretary General of the OAS deems reasonable.

[2] Modified by AG/RES. 1098 (XXI-91).

Article 9
Voting

1. The judges shall be elected by secret ballot and by an absolute majority of the States Parties to the Convention, from among the candidates referred to in Article 7 of the present Statute.

2. The candidates who obtain the largest number of votes and an absolute majority shall be declared elected. Should several ballots be necessary, those candidates who receive the smallest number of votes shall be eliminated successively, in the manner determined by the States Parties.

Article 10
Ad Hoc Judges

1. If a judge is a national of any of the States Parties to a case submitted to the Court, he shall retain his right to hear that case.

2. If one of the judges called upon to hear a case is a national of one of the States Parties to the case, any other State Party to the case may appoint a person to serve on the Court as an *ad hoc* judge.

3. If among the judges called upon to hear a case, none is a national of the States Parties to the case, each of the latter may appoint an *ad hoc* judge. Should several States have the same interest in the case, they shall be regarded as a single party for purposes of the above provisions. In case of doubt, the Court shall decide.

4. The right of any State to appoint an *ad hoc* judge shall be considered relinquished if the State should fail to do so within thirty days following the written request from the President of the Court.

5. The provisions of Articles 4, 11, 15, 16, 18, 19 and 20 of the present Statute shall apply to ad hoc judges.

Article 11
Oath

1. Upon assuming office, each judge shall take the following oath or make the following solemn declaration: 'I swear' – or 'I solemnly declare' – 'that I shall exercise my functions as a judge honorably, independently and impartially and that I shall keep secret all deliberations.'

2. The oath shall be administered by the President of the Court and, if possible, in the presence of the other judges.

Chapter III
Structure of the Court

Article 12
Presidency

1. The Court shall elect from among its members a President and Vice-President who shall serve for a period of two years; they may be reelected.

2. The President shall direct the work of the Court, represent it, regulate the disposition of matters brought before the Court, and preside over its sessions.

3. The Vice-President shall take the place of the President in the latter's temporary absence, or if the office of the President becomes vacant. In the latter case, the Court shall elect a new Vice-President to serve out the term of the previous Vice-President.

4. In the absence of the President and the Vice-President, their duties shall be assumed by other judges, following the order of precedence established in Article 13 of the present Statute.

Article 13
Precedence

1. Elected judges shall take precedence after the President and Vice-President according to their seniority in office.

2. Judges having the same seniority in office shall take precedence according to age.

3. Ad hoc and interim judges shall take precedence after the elected judges, according to age. However, if an ad hoc or interim judge has previously served as an elected judge, he shall have precedence over any other ad hoc or interim judge.

Article 14
Secretariat

1. The Secretariat of the Court shall function under the immediate authority of the Secretary, in accordance with the administrative standards of the OAS General Secretariat, in all matters that are not incompatible with the independence of the Court.

2. The Secretary shall be appointed by the Court. He shall be a full-time employee serving in a position of trust to the Court, shall have his office

at the seat of the Court and shall attend any meetings that the Court holds away from its seat.

3. There shall be an Assistant Secretary who shall assist the Secretary in his duties and shall replace him in his temporary absence.

4. The Staff of the Secretariat shall be appointed by the Secretary General of the OAS, in consultation with the Secretary of the Court.

Chapter IV
Rights, Duties and Responsibilities

Article 15
Privileges and Immunities

1. The judges of the Court shall enjoy, from the moment of their election and throughout their term of office, the immunities extended to diplomatic agents under international law. During the exercise of their functions, they shall, in addition, enjoy the diplomatic privileges necessary for the performance of their duties.

2. At no time shall the judges of the Court be held liable for any decisions or opinions issued in the exercise of their functions.

3. The Court itself and its staff shall enjoy the privileges and immunities provided for in the Agreement on Privileges and Immunities of the Organization of American States, of May 15, 1949, *mutatis mutandis*, taking into account the importance and independence of the Court.

4. The provisions of paragraphs 1, 2 and 3 of this article shall apply to the States Parties to the Convention. They shall also apply to such other member states of the OAS as expressly accept them, either in general or for specific cases.

5. The system of privileges and immunities of the judges of the Court and of its staff may be regulated or supplemented by multilateral or bilateral agreements between the Court, the OAS and its member states.

Article 16
Service

1. The judges shall remain at the disposal of the Court, and shall travel to the seat of the Court or to the place where the Court is holding its sessions as often and for as long a time as may be necessary, as established in the Regulations.

2. The President shall render his service on a permanent basis.

Article 17
Emoluments

1. The emoluments of the President and the judges of the Court shall be set in accordance with the obligations and incompatibilities imposed on them by Articles 16 and 18, and bearing in mind the importance and independence of their functions.

2. The *ad hoc* judges shall receive the emoluments established by Regulations, within the limits of the Court's budget.

3. The judges shall also receive per diem and travel allowances, when appropriate.

Article 18
Incompatibilities

1. The position of judge of the Inter-American Court of Human Rights is incompatible with the following positions and activities:

a. Members or high-ranking officials of the executive branch of government, except for those who hold positions that do not place them under the direct control of the executive branch and those of diplomatic agents who are not Chiefs of Missions to the OAS or to any of its member states;
b. Officials of international organizations;
c. Any others that might prevent the judges from discharging their duties, or that might affect their independence or impartiality, or the dignity and prestige of the office.

2. In case of doubt as to incompatibility, the Court shall decide. If the incompatibility is not resolved, the provisions of Article 73 of the Convention and Article 20(2) of the present Statute shall apply.

3. Incompatibilities may lead only to dismissal of the judge and the imposition of applicable liabilities, but shall not invalidate the acts and decisions in which the judge in question participated.

Article 19
Disqualification

1. Judges may not take part in matters in which, in the opinion of the Court, they or members of their family have a direct interest or in which they have previously taken part as agents, counsel or advocates,

or as members of a national or international court or an investigatory committee, or in any other capacity.

2. If a judge is disqualified from hearing a case or for some other appropriate reason considers that he should not take part in a specific matter, he shall advise the President of his disqualification. Should the latter disagree, the Court shall decide.

3. If the President considers that a judge has cause for disqualification or for some other pertinent reason should not take part in a given matter, he shall advise him to that effect. Should the judge in question disagree, the Court shall decide.

4. When one or more judges are disqualified pursuant to this article, the President may request the States Parties to the Convention, in a meeting of the OAS Permanent Council, to appoint interim judges to replace them.

Article 20
Disciplinary Regime

1. In the performance of their duties and at all other times, the judges and staff of the Court shall conduct themselves in a manner that is in keeping with the office of those who perform an international judicial function. They shall be answerable to the Court for their conduct, as well as for any violation, act of negligence or omission committed in the exercise of their functions.

2. The OAS General Assembly shall have disciplinary authority over the judges, but may exercise that authority only at the request of the Court itself, composed for this purpose of the remaining judges. The Court shall inform the General Assembly of the reasons for its request.

3. Disciplinary authority over the Secretary shall lie with the Court, and over the rest of the staff, with the Secretary, who shall exercise that authority with the approval of the President.

4. The Court shall issue disciplinary rules, subject to the administrative regulations of the OAS General Secretariat insofar as they may be applicable in accordance with Article 59 of the Convention.

Article 21
Resignation – Incapacity

1. Any resignation from the Court shall be submitted in writing to the President of the Court. The resignation shall not become effective until the Court has accepted it.

2. The Court shall decide whether a judge is incapable of performing his functions.

3. The President of the Court shall notify the Secretary General of the OAS of the acceptance of a resignation or a determination of incapacity, for appropriate action.

Chapter V
The Workings of the Court

Article 22
Sessions

1. The Court shall hold regular and special sessions.

2. Regular sessions shall be held as determined by the Regulations of the Court.

3. Special sessions shall be convoked by the President or at the request of a majority of the judges.

Article 23
Quorum

1. The quorum for deliberations by the Court shall be five judges.

2. Decisions of the Court shall be taken by a majority vote of the judges present.

3. In the event of a tie, the President shall cast the deciding vote.

Article 24
Hearings, Deliberations, Decisions

1. The hearings shall be public, unless the Court, in exceptional circumstances, decides otherwise.

2. The Court shall deliberate in private. Its deliberations shall remain secret, unless the Court decides otherwise.

3. The decisions, judgments and opinions of the Court shall be delivered in public session, and the parties shall be given written notification thereof. In addition, the decisions, judgments and opinions shall be published, along with judges' individual votes and opinions and with such other data or background information that the Court may deem appropriate.

Article 25
Rules and Regulations

1. The Court shall draw up its Rules of Procedure.

2. The Rules of Procedure may delegate to the President or to Committees of the Court authority to carry out certain parts of the legal proceedings, with the exception of issuing final rulings or advisory opinions. Rulings or decisions issued by the President or the Committees of the Court that are not purely procedural in nature may be appealed before the full Court.

3. The Court shall also draw up its own Regulations.

Article 26
Budget, Financial System

1. The Court shall draw up its own budget and shall submit it for approval to the General Assembly of the OAS, through the General Secretariat. The latter may not introduce any changes in it.

2. The Court shall administer its own budget.

Chapter VI
Relations with Governments and Organizations

Article 27
Relations with the Host Country, Governments and Organizations

1. The relations of the Court with the host country shall be governed through a headquarters agreement. The seat of the Court shall be international in nature.

2. The relations of the Court with governments, with the OAS and its organs, agencies and entities and with other international governmental organizations involved in promoting and defending human rights shall be governed through special agreements.

Article 28
Relations with the Inter-American Commission on Human Rights

The Inter-American Commission on Human Rights shall appear as a party before the Court in all cases within the adjudicatory jurisdiction of the Court, pursuant to Article 2(1) of the present Statute.

Article 29
Agreements of Cooperation

1. The Court may enter into agreements of cooperation with such nonprofit institutions as law schools, bar associations, courts, academies and educational or research institutions dealing with related disciplines in order to obtain their cooperation and to strengthen and promote the juridical and institutional principles of the Convention in general and of the Court in particular.

2. The Court shall include an account of such agreements and their results in its Annual Report to the OAS General Assembly.

Article 30
Report to the OAS General Assembly

The Court shall submit a report on its work of the previous year to each regular session of the OAS General Assembly. It shall indicate those cases in which a State has failed to comply with the Court's ruling. It may also submit to the OAS General Assembly proposals or recommendations on ways to improve the inter-American system of human rights, insofar as they concern the work of the Court.

Chapter VII
Final Provisions

Article 31
Amendments to the Statute

The present Statute may be amended by the OAS General Assembly, at the initiative of any member state or of the Court itself.

Article 32
Entry into Force

The present Statute shall enter into force on January 1, 1980.

Appendix 4

Rules of Procedure of the Inter-American Commission on Human Rights

Approved by the Commission at its 109th special session held 4–8 December 2000.

Title I
Organization of the Commission

Chapter I
Nature and Composition

Article 1
Nature and Composition

1. The Inter-American Commission on Human Rights is an autonomous organ of the Organization of American States whose principal functions are to promote the observance and defense of human rights and to serve as an advisory body to the Organization in this area.

2. The Commission represents all the Member States of the Organization.

3. The Commission is composed of seven members elected in their individual capacity by the General Assembly of the Organization. They shall be persons of high moral character and recognized competence in the field of human rights.

Chapter II
Membership

Article 2
Duration of the Term of Office

1. The members of the Commission shall be elected for four years and may be re-elected only once.

2. In the event that new members of the Commission have not been elected to replace those completing their term of office, the latter shall continue to serve until the new members are elected.

Article 3
Precedence

The members of the Commission shall follow the President and Vice-Presidents in order of precedence according to their seniority in office. When there are two or more members with equal seniority, precedence shall be determined according to age.

Article 4
Incompatibility

1. The position of member of the Inter-American Commission on Human Rights is incompatible with the exercise of activities which could affect the independence or impartiality of the member, or the dignity or prestige of the office.

2. The Commission, with the affirmative vote of at least five of its members, shall decide whether a situation of incompatibility exists.

3. The Commission, prior to taking a decision, shall hear the member whose activities are claimed to be incompatible.

4. The decision with respect to the incompatibility, together with all the background information, shall be sent to the General Assembly, through the Secretary General of the Organization, for the purposes set forth in Article 8(3) of the Commission's Statute.

Article 5
Resignation

The resignation of a member of the Commission shall be submitted to the President of the Commission in writing. The President shall immediately notify the Secretary General of the OAS for the appropriate purposes.

Chapter III
Board of Officers of the Commission

Article 6
Composition and Functions

The Commission shall have as its board of officers a President, a First Vice-President and a Second Vice-President, who shall perform the functions set forth in these Rules of Procedure.

Article 7
Elections

1. Only members present shall participate in the election of each of the officers referred to in the preceding article.

2. Elections shall be by secret ballot. However, with the unanimous consent of the members present, the Commission may decide on another procedure.

3. The affirmative vote of an absolute majority of the members of the Commission shall be required for election to any of the positions referred to in Article 6.

4. Should it be necessary to hold more than one ballot for election to any of these positions, the names receiving the lowest number of votes shall be eliminated successively.

5. Elections shall be held on the first day of the Commission's first session of the calendar year.

Article 8
Duration of Term of Officers

1. The term of office of the officers is one year. The term runs from the date of their election until the elections held the following year for the new board, pursuant to Article 7, paragraph 5. The members of the board of officers may be re-elected to their respective positions only once during each four-year period.

2. In the event that the term of office of a Commission member expires, and he or she is President or Vice-President, the provisions of Article 9, paragraphs 2 and 3 of these Rules of Procedure shall apply.

Article 9
Resignation, Vacancy and Replacements

1. If a member of the board of officers resigns from that position or ceases to be a member of the Commission, the Commission shall fill the position at the next period of sessions for the remainder of the term of office.

2. The First Vice-President shall serve as President until the Commission elects a new President under the provisions of paragraph 1 of this article.

3. In addition, the First Vice-President shall replace the President if the latter is temporarily unable to perform his or her duties. In the event of the absence or disability of the First Vice-President, or if that position is vacant, the Second Vice-President shall serve as President. In the event of the absence or disability of the Second Vice-President, the member with the greatest seniority according to Article 3 shall serve as President.

Article 10
Powers of the President

1. The powers of the President shall be:

a. to represent the Commission before the other organs of the Organization and other institutions;
b. to convoke sessions of the Commission in accordance with the Statute and these Rules of Procedure;
c. to preside over sessions of the Commission and submit to it for consideration all matters appearing on the agenda of the work program approved for the corresponding session; to decide the points of order raised during the deliberations; and to submit matters to a vote in accordance with the applicable provisions of these Rules of Procedure;
d. to give the floor to the members in the order in which they have requested it;
e. to promote the work of the Commission and oversee compliance with its program-budget;
f. to present a written report to the Commission at the beginning of its period of sessions on what he or she has done during its recesses to carry out the functions assigned to him or her by the Statute and these Rules of Procedure;
g. to seek compliance with the decisions of the Commission;

h. to attend the meetings of the General Assembly of the OAS and other activities related to the promotion and protection of human rights;
i. to travel to the headquarters of the Commission and remain there for as long as he or she considers necessary to carry out his or her functions;
j. to designate special committees, ad hoc committees and subcommittees composed of several members to carry out any mandate within his or her area of competence; and
k. to perform any other functions that may be conferred upon him or her in these Rules of Procedure or other tasks entrusted to him or her by the Commission.

2. The President may delegate to one of the Vice-Presidents or to another member of the Commission the powers specified in paragraphs (a), (h) and (k).

Chapter IV
Executive Secretariat

Article 11
Composition

The Executive Secretariat of the Commission shall be composed of an Executive Secretary and at least one Assistant Executive Secretary, with the professional, technical and administrative staff needed to carry out its activities.

Article 12
Powers of the Executive Secretary

1. The powers of the Executive Secretary shall be:

a. to direct, plan, and coordinate the work of the Executive Secretariat;
b. to prepare, in consultation with the President, the draft program-budget of the Commission, which shall be governed by the budgetary provisions in force for the OAS, and with respect to which he or she shall report to the Commission;
c. to prepare the draft work program for each session in consultation with the President;
d. [to] advise the President and members of the Commission in the performance of their duties;
e. to present a written report to the Commission at the beginning of each period of sessions on the activities of the Secretariat since the preceding

period of sessions, and on any general matters that may be of interest to the Commission; and

f. to implement the decisions entrusted to him or her by the Commission or its President.

2. The Assistant Executive Secretary shall replace the Executive Secretary in the event of his or her absence or disability. In the absence or disability of both, the Executive Secretary or the Assistant Executive Secretary, as the case may be, shall designate one of the specialists of the Executive Secretariat as a temporary replacement.

3. The Executive Secretary, Assistant Executive Secretary and staff of the Secretariat must observe the strictest discretion in all matters the Commission considers confidential.

Article 13
Functions of the Executive Secretariat

The Executive Secretariat shall prepare the draft reports, resolutions, studies and any other work entrusted to it by the Commission or by the President. In addition, it shall receive and process the correspondence, petitions and communications addressed to the Commission. The Executive Secretariat may also request that interested parties provide any information it deems relevant, in accordance with the provisions of these Rules of Procedure.

Chapter V
Functioning of the Commission

Article 14
Periods of Sessions

1. The Commission shall hold at least two regular periods of sessions per year for the duration previously determined by it and as many special sessions as it deems necessary. Prior to the conclusion of each period of sessions, the date and place of the next period shall be determined.

2. The sessions of the Commission shall be held at its headquarters. However, the Commission may decide to meet elsewhere, pursuant to the vote of an absolute majority of its members and with the consent or at the invitation of the State concerned.

3. Each period of sessions shall consist of the number of sessions necessary to carry out its activities. The sessions shall be confidential, unless the Commission determines otherwise.

4. Any member who because of illness or for any other serious reason is unable to attend all or part of any session of the Commission, or to fulfill any other function, shall notify the Executive Secretary to this effect as soon as possible. The Executive Secretary shall so inform the President and ensure that those reasons appear in the record.

Article 15
Rapporteurships and Working Groups

1. The Commission may create rapporteurships to better fulfill its functions. The rapporteurs shall be designated by the vote of an absolute majority of the members of the Commission and may be Commission members or other persons. The Commission shall determine the characteristics of the mandate entrusted to each rapporteurship. The rapporteurs shall periodically present their work plans to the plenary of the Commission.

2. The Commission may also create working groups or committees to prepare its periods of sessions or to carry out special programs or projects. The Commission shall constitute working groups as it sees fit.

Article 16
Quorum for Sessions

The presence of an absolute majority of the members of the Commission shall be necessary to constitute a quorum.

Article 17
Discussion and Voting

1. The sessions shall conform primarily to the Rules of Procedure and secondarily to the pertinent provisions of the Rules of Procedure of the Permanent Council of the OAS.

2. Members of the Commission may not participate in the discussion, investigation, deliberation or decision of a matter submitted to the Commission in the following cases:

a. if they are nationals of the State which is the subject of the Commission's general or specific consideration, or if they were accredited or carrying out a special mission as diplomatic agents before that State; or

b. if they have previously participated in any capacity in a decision concerning the same facts on which the matter is based or have acted as an adviser to, or representative of, any of the parties interested in the decision.

3. If a member considers that he or she should abstain from participating in the study or decision of a matter, that member shall so inform the Commission, which shall decide if the disqualification is warranted.

4. Any member may raise the issue of the disqualification of another member on the basis of the grounds set forth in paragraph 2 of this article.

5. When the Commission is not meeting in regular or special session, the members may deliberate and decide on matters within their competence by the means they consider appropriate.

Article 18
Special Quorum to Take Decisions

1. The Commission shall decide the following matters by an absolute majority vote of its members:

a. election of the board of officers of the Commission;
b. interpretation of the application of these Rules of Procedure;
c. adoption of a report on the situation of human rights in a specific State; and
d. for matters where such a majority is required under the provisions of the American Convention, the Statute or these Rules of Procedure.

2. In respect of other matters, the vote of the majority of the members present shall be sufficient.

Article 19
Explanation of Vote

1. Whether or not members agree with the decision of the majority, they shall be entitled to present a written explanation of their vote, which shall be included following the text of that decision.

2. If the decision concerns the approval of a report or preliminary report, the explanation of the vote shall be included following the text of that report or preliminary report.

3. When the decision does not appear in a separate document, the explanation of the vote shall be included in the minutes of the meeting, following the decision in question.

Article 20
Minutes of the Sessions

1. Summary minutes shall be taken of each session. They shall state the day and time at which it was held, the names of the members present, the matters dealt with, the decisions taken, and any statement made by a member especially for inclusion in the minutes. These minutes are confidential internal working documents.

2. The Executive Secretariat shall distribute copies of the summary minutes of each session to the members of the Commission, who may present their observations to the Secretariat prior to the period of sessions at which those minutes are to be approved. If there has been no objection as of the beginning of that period of sessions, the minutes shall be considered approved.

Article 21
Compensation for Special Services

Pursuant to the approval of an absolute majority of its members, the Commission may entrust any member with the preparation of a special study or other specific work to be carried out individually outside the sessions. Such work shall be compensated in accordance with the funds available in the budget. The amount of the fees shall be set on the basis of the number of days required for the preparation and drafting of the work.

Title II
Procedure

Chapter I
General Provisions

Article 22
Official Languages

1. The official languages of the Commission shall be Spanish, French, English and Portuguese. The working languages shall be those decided on by the Commission every two years, in accordance with the languages spoken by its members.

2. Any member of the Commission may dispense with the interpretation of debates and preparation of documents in his or her language.

Article 23
Presentation of Petitions

Any person or group of persons or nongovernmental entity legally recognized in one or more of the Member States of the OAS may submit petitions to the Commission, on their own behalf or on behalf of third persons, concerning alleged violations of a human right recognized in, as the case may be, the American Declaration of the Rights and Duties of Man, the American Convention on Human Rights, the Additional Protocol in the Area of Economic, Social and Cultural Rights, the Protocol to Abolish the Death Penalty, the Inter-American Convention to Prevent and Punish Torture, the Inter-American Convention on Forced Disappearance of Persons, and/or the Inter-American Convention on the Prevention, Punishment and Eradication of Violence Against Women, in accordance with their respective provisions, the Statute of the Commission, and these Rules of Procedure. The petitioner may designate an attorney or other person to represent him or her before the Commission, either in the petition itself or in another writing.

Article 24
Consideration Motu Proprio

The Commission may also, *motu proprio,* initiate the processing of a petition which, in its view, meets the necessary requirements.

Article 25
Precautionary Measures

1. In serious and urgent cases, and whenever necessary according to the information available, the Commission may, on its own initiative or at the request of a party, request that the State concerned adopt precautionary measures to prevent irreparable harm to persons.

2. If the Commission is not in session, the President, or, in his or her absence, one of the Vice-Presidents, shall consult with the other members, through the Executive Secretariat, on the application of the provision in the previous paragraph. If it is not possible to consult within a reasonable period of time under the circumstances, the President or, where

appropriate, one of the Vice-Presidents shall take the decision on behalf of the Commission and shall so inform its members.

3. The Commission may request information from the interested parties on any matter related to the adoption and observance of the precautionary measures.

4. The granting of such measures and their adoption by the State shall not constitute a prejudgment on the merits of a case.

Chapter II
Petitions Referring to the American Convention on Human Rights and Other Applicable Instruments

Article 26
Initial Review

1. The Executive Secretariat of the Commission shall be responsible for the study and initial processing of petitions lodged before the Commission that fulfill all the requirements set forth in the Statute and in Article 28 of these Rules of Procedure.

2. If a petition or communication does not meet the requirements called for in these Rules of Procedure, the Executive Secretariat may request that the petitioner or his or her representative satisfy those that have not been fulfilled.

3. If the Executive Secretariat has any doubt as to whether the requirements referred to have been met, it shall consult the Commission.

Article 27
Condition for Considering the Petition

The Commission shall consider petitions regarding alleged violations of the human rights enshrined in the American Convention on Human Rights and other applicable instruments, with respect to the Member States of the OAS, only when the petitions fulfill the requirements set forth in those instruments, in the Statute, and in these Rules of Procedure.

Article 28
Requirements for the Consideration of Petitions

Petitions addressed to the Commission shall contain the following information:

a. the name, nationality and signature of the person or persons making the denunciation; or in cases where the petitioner is a nongovernmental entity, the name and signature of its legal representative(s);
b. whether the petitioner wishes that his or her identity be withheld from the State;
c. the address for receiving correspondence from the Commission and, if available, a telephone number, facsimile number, and email address;
d. an account of the act or situation that is denounced, specifying the place and date of the alleged violations;
e. if possible, the name of the victim and of any public authority who has taken cognizance of the fact or situation alleged;
f. the State the petitioner considers responsible, by act or omission, for the violation of any of the human rights recognized in the American Convention on Human Rights and other applicable instruments, even if no specific reference is made to the article(s) alleged to have been violated;
g. compliance with the time period provided for in Article 32 of these Rules of Procedure;
h. any steps taken to exhaust domestic remedies, or the impossibility of doing so as provided in Article 31 of these Rules of Procedure; and
i. an indication of whether the complaint has been submitted to another international settlement proceeding as provided in Article 33 of these Rules of Procedure.

Article 29
Initial Processing

1. The Commission, acting initially through the Executive Secretariat, shall receive and carry out the initial processing of the petitions presented as follows:

a. it shall receive the petition, register it, record the date of receipt on the petition itself and acknowledge receipt to the petitioner;
b. if the petition does not meet the requirements of these Rules of Procedure, it may request that the petitioner or his or her representative complete them in accordance with Article 26(2) of these Rules;
c. if the petition sets forth distinct facts, or if it refers to more than one person or to alleged violations not interconnected in time and place, the claims may be divided and processed separately, so long as all the requirements of Article 28 of these Rules of Procedure are met;

d. if two or more petitions address similar facts, involve the same persons, or reveal the same pattern of conduct, they may be joined and processed together;
e. in the situations provided for in subparagraphs c and d, it shall give written notification to petitioners.

2. In serious or urgent cases, the Executive Secretariat shall immediately notify the Commission.

Article 30
Admissibility Procedure

1. The Commission, through its Executive Secretariat, shall process the petitions that meet the requirements set forth in Article 28 of these Rules of Procedure.

2. For this purpose, it shall forward the relevant parts of the petition to the State in question. The identity of the petitioner shall not be revealed without his or her express authorization. The request to the State for information shall not constitute a prejudgment with regard to any decision the Commission may adopt on the admissibility of the petition.

3. The State shall submit its response within two months counted from the date the request is transmitted. The Executive Secretariat shall evaluate requests for extensions of this period that are duly founded. However, it shall not grant extensions that exceed three months from the date of the first request for information sent to the State.

4. In serious or urgent cases, or when it is believed that the life or personal integrity of a person is in real or imminent danger, the Commission shall request the promptest reply from the State, using for this purpose the means it considers most expeditious.

5. Prior to deciding upon the admissibility of the petition, the Commission may invite the parties to submit additional observations, either in writing or in a hearing, as provided for in Chapter VI of these Rules of Procedure.

6. Once the observations have been received or the period set has elapsed with no observations received, the Commission shall verify whether the grounds for the petition exist or subsist. If it considers that they do not exist or subsist, it shall order the case archived.

Article 31
Exhaustion of Domestic Remedies

1. In order to decide on the admissibility of a matter, the Commission shall verify whether the remedies of the domestic legal system have been pursued and exhausted in accordance with the generally recognized principles of international law.

2. The provisions of the preceding paragraph shall not apply when:

a. the domestic legislation of the State concerned does not afford due process of law for protection of the right or rights that have allegedly been violated;
b. the party alleging violation of his or her rights has been denied access to the remedies under domestic law or has been prevented from exhausting them; or
c. there has been unwarranted delay in rendering a final judgment under the aforementioned remedies.

3. When the petitioner contends that he or she is unable to prove compliance with the requirement indicated in this article, it shall be up to the State concerned to demonstrate to the Commission that the remedies under domestic law have not been previously exhausted, unless that is clearly evident from the record.

Article 32
Deadline for the Presentation of Petitions

1. The Commission shall consider those petitions that are lodged within a period of six months following the date on which the alleged victim has been notified of the decision that exhausted the domestic remedies.

2. In those cases in which the exceptions to the requirement of prior exhaustion of domestic remedies are applicable, the petition shall be presented within a reasonable period of time, as determined by the Commission. For this purpose, the Commission shall consider the date on which the alleged violation of rights occurred and the circumstances of each case.

Article 33
Duplication of Procedures

1. The Commission shall not consider a petition if its subject matter:

a. is pending settlement pursuant to another procedure before an international governmental organization of which the State concerned is a member; or
b. essentially duplicates a petition pending or already examined and settled by the Commission or by another international governmental organization of which the State concerned is a member.

2. However, the Commission shall not refrain from considering petitions referred to in paragraph 1 when:

a. the procedure followed before the other organization is limited to a general examination of the human rights situation in the State in question and there has been no decision on the specific facts that are the subject of the petition before the Commission, or it will not lead to an effective settlement; or
b. the petitioner before the Commission or a family member is the alleged victim of the violation denounced and the petitioner before the other organization is a third party or a nongovernmental entity having no mandate from the former.

Article 34
Other Grounds for Inadmissibility

The Commission shall declare any petition or case inadmissible when:

a. it does not state facts that tend to establish a violation of the rights referred to in Article 27 of these Rules of Procedure;
b. the statements of the petitioner or of the State indicate that it is manifestly groundless or out of order; or
c. supervening information or evidence presented to the Commission reveals that a matter is inadmissible or out of order.

Article 35
Desistance

The petitioner may at any time desist from his or her petition or case, to which effect he or she must so state in writing to the Commission. The statement by the petitioner shall be analyzed by the Commission, which may archive the petition or case if it deems this appropriate, or continue to process it in the interest of protecting a particular right.

Article 36
Working Group on Admissibility

A working group shall meet prior to each regular session in order to study the admissibility of petitions and make recommendations to the plenary of the Commission.

Article 37
Decision on Admissibility

1. Once it has considered the positions of the parties, the Commission shall make a decision on the admissibility of the matter. The reports on admissibility and inadmissibility shall be public and the Commission shall include them in its Annual Report to the General Assembly of the OAS.

2. When an admissibility report is adopted, the petition shall be registered as a case and the proceedings on the merits shall be initiated. The adoption of an admissibility report does not constitute a prejudgment as to the merits of the matter.

3. In exceptional circumstances, and after having requested information from the parties in keeping with the provisions of Article 30 of these Rules of Procedure, the Commission may open a case but defer its treatment of admissibility until the debate and decision on the merits. The case shall be opened by means of a written communication to both parties.

Article 38
Procedure on the Merits

1. Upon opening the case, the Commission shall set a period of two months for the petitioners to submit additional observations on the merits. The pertinent parts of those observations shall be transmitted to the State in question so that it may submit its observations within two months.

2. Prior to making its decision on the merits of the case, the Commission shall set a time period for the parties to express whether they have an interest in initiating the friendly settlement procedure provided for in Article 41 of these Rules of Procedure. The Commission may also invite the parties to submit additional observations in writing.

3. If it deems it necessary in order to advance in its consideration of the case, the Commission may convene the parties for a hearing, as provided for in Chapter VI of these Rules of Procedure.

Article 39
Presumption

The facts alleged in the petition, the pertinent parts of which have been transmitted to the State in question, shall be presumed to be true if the State has not provided responsive information during the maximum period set by the Commission under the provisions of Article 38 of these Rules of Procedure, as long as other evidence does not lead to a different conclusion.

Article 40
On-Site Investigation

1. If it deems it necessary and advisable, the Commission may carry out an on-site investigation, for the effective conduct of which it shall request and the State concerned shall furnish all pertinent facilities.

2. However, in serious and urgent cases, only the presentation of a petition or communication that fulfills all the formal requirements of admissibility shall be necessary in order for the Commission to conduct an on-site investigation with the prior consent of the State in whose territory a violation has allegedly been committed.

Article 41
Friendly Settlement

1. On its own initiative or at the request of any of the parties, the Commission shall place itself at the disposal of the parties concerned, at any stage of the examination of a petition or case, with a view to reaching a friendly settlement of the matter on the basis of respect for the human rights recognized in the American Convention on Human Rights, the American Declaration and other applicable instruments.

2. The friendly settlement procedure shall be initiated and continue on the basis of the consent of the parties.

3. When it deems it necessary, the Commission may entrust to one or more of its members the task of facilitating negotiations between the parties.

4. The Commission may terminate its intervention in the friendly settlement procedure if it finds that the matter is not susceptible to such a resolution or any of the parties does not consent to its application, decides

not to continue it, or does not display the willingness to reach a friendly settlement based on respect for human rights.

5. If a friendly settlement is reached, the Commission shall adopt a report with a brief statement of the facts and of the solution reached, shall transmit it to the parties concerned and shall publish it. Prior to adopting that report, the Commission shall verify whether the victim of the alleged violation or, as the case may be, his or her successors, have consented to the friendly settlement agreement. In all cases, the friendly settlement must be based on respect for the human rights recognized in the American Convention on Human Rights, the American Declaration and other applicable instruments.

6. If no friendly settlement is reached, the Commission shall continue to process the petition or case.

Article 42
Decision on the Merits

1. The Commission shall deliberate on the merits of the case, to which end it shall prepare a report in which it will examine the arguments, the evidence presented by the parties, and the information obtained during hearings and on-site observations. In addition, the Commission may take into account other information that is a matter of public knowledge.

2. The Commission shall deliberate in private, and all aspects of the discussions shall be confidential.

3. Any question put to a vote shall be formulated in precise terms in one of the official languages of the OAS. At the request of any member, the text shall be translated by the Secretariat into one of the other official languages and distributed prior to the vote.

4. The minutes referring to the Commission's deliberations shall restrict themselves to the subject of the debate and the decision approved, as well as any separate opinions and any statements made for inclusion in the minutes.

Article 43
Report on the Merits

After the deliberation and vote on the merits of the case, the Commission shall proceed as follows:

1. If it establishes that there was no violation in a given case, it shall so state in its report on the merits. The report shall be transmitted to the

parties, and shall be published and included in the Commission's Annual Report to the OAS General Assembly.

2. If it establishes one or more violations, it shall prepare a preliminary report with the proposals and recommendations it deems pertinent and shall transmit it to the State in question. In so doing, it shall set a deadline by which the State in question must report on the measures adopted to comply with the recommendations. The State shall not be authorized to publish the report until the Commission adopts a decision in this respect.

3. It shall notify the petitioner of the adoption of the report and its transmittal to the State. In the case of States Parties to the American Convention that have accepted the contentious jurisdiction of the Inter-American Court, upon notifying the petitioner, the Commission shall give him or her one month to present his or her position as to whether the case should be submitted to the Court. When the petitioner is interested in the submission of the case, he or she should present the following:

a. the position of the victim or the victim's family members, if different from that of the petitioner;
b. the personal data relative to the victim and the victim's family members;
c. the reasons he or she considers that the case should be referred to the Court;
d. the documentary, testimonial, and expert evidence available; and
e. the claims concerning reparations and costs.

Article 44
Referral of the Case to the Court

1. If the State in question has accepted the jurisdiction of the Inter-American Court in accordance with Article 62 of the American Convention, and the Commission considers that the State has not complied with the recommendations of the report approved in accordance with Article 50 of the American Convention, it shall refer the case to the Court, unless there is a reasoned decision by an absolute majority of the members of the Commission to the contrary.

2. The Commission shall give fundamental consideration to obtaining justice in the particular case, based, among others, on the following factors:

a. the position of the petitioner;
b. the nature and seriousness of the violation;

c. the need to develop or clarify the case-law of the system;
d. the future effect of the decision within the legal systems of the Member States; and,
e. the quality of the evidence available.

Article 45
Publication of the Report

1. If within three months from the transmittal of the preliminary report to the State in question the matter has not been solved or, for those States that have accepted the jurisdiction of the Inter-American Court, has not been referred by the Commission or by the State to the Court for a decision, the Commission, by an absolute majority of votes, may issue a final report that contains its opinion and final conclusions and recommendations.

2. The final report shall be transmitted to the parties, who, within the time period set by the Commission, shall present information on compliance with the recommendations.

3. The Commission shall evaluate compliance with its recommendations based on the information available, and shall decide on the publication of the final report by the vote of an absolute majority of its members. The Commission shall also make a determination as to whether to include it in the Annual Report to the OAS General Assembly, and/or to publish it in any other manner deemed appropriate.

Article 46
Follow-Up

1. Once the Commission has published a report on a friendly settlement or on the merits in which it has made recommendations, it may adopt the follow-up measures it deems appropriate, such as requesting information from the parties and holding hearings in order to verify compliance with friendly settlement agreements and its recommendations.

2. The Commission shall report on progress in complying with those agreements and recommendations as it deems appropriate.

Article 47
Certification of Reports

The originals of the reports signed by the Commissioners who participated in their adoption shall be deposited in the files of the Commission.

The reports transmitted to the parties shall be certified by the Executive Secretariat.

Article 48
Interstate Communications

1. A communication presented by a State Party to the American Convention on Human Rights that has accepted the competence of the Commission to receive and examine such communications against other States Parties shall be transmitted to the State Party in question, whether or not it has accepted the Commission's competence in this respect. If that competence has not been accepted, the communication shall be transmitted in order that the State concerned may exercise its option under Article 45, paragraph 3 of the Convention, to recognize that competence in the specific case that is the subject of the communication.

2. If the State in question has accepted the Commission's competence to consider a communication from another State Party, the respective procedure shall be governed by the provisions of the present Chapter II, insofar as they apply.

Chapter III
Petitions Concerning States That Are Not Parties to the American Convention on Human Rights

Article 49
Receipt of the Petition

The Commission shall receive and examine any petition that contains a denunciation of alleged violations of the human rights set forth in the American Declaration of the Rights and Duties of Man in relation to the Member States of the Organization that are not parties to the American Convention on Human Rights.

Article 50
Applicable Procedure

The procedure applicable to petitions concerning Member States of the OAS that are not parties to the American Convention shall be that provided for in the general provisions included in Chapter I of Title II; in Articles 28 to 43 and 45 to 47 of these Rules of Procedure.

Chapter IV
On-Site Observations

Article 51
Designation of the Special Commission

On-site observations shall in each case be conducted by a Special Commission named for that purpose. The number of members of the Special Commission and the designation of its President shall be determined by the Commission. In cases of great urgency, such decisions may be made by the President subject to the approval of the Commission.

Article 52
Disqualification

A member of the Commission who is a national of or who resides in the territory of the State in which the on-site observation is to be conducted shall be disqualified from participating in it.

Article 53
Schedule of Activities

The Special Commission shall organize its own activities. To that end, it may assign any activity related to its mission to its own members and, in consultation with the Executive Secretary, to any staff members or necessary personnel of the Executive Secretariat.

Article 54
Necessary Facilities and Guarantees

In extending an invitation for an on-site observation or in giving its consent thereto, the State shall furnish to the Special Commission all necessary facilities for carrying out its mission. In particular, it shall commit itself not to take any reprisals of any kind against any persons or entities cooperating with or providing information or testimony to the Special Commission.

Article 55
Other Applicable Standards

Without prejudice to the provisions in the preceding article, any on-site observation agreed upon by the Commission shall be carried out in accordance with the following standards:

a. the Special Commission or any of its members shall be able to interview any persons, groups, entities or institutions freely and in private;
b. the State shall grant the necessary guarantees to those who provide the Special Commission with information, testimony or evidence of any kind;
c. the members of the Special Commission shall be able to travel freely throughout the territory of the country, for which purpose the State shall extend all the corresponding facilities, including the necessary documentation;
d. the State shall ensure the availability of local means of transportation;
e. the members of the Special Commission shall have access to the jails and all other detention and interrogation sites and shall be able to interview in private those persons imprisoned or detained;
f. the State shall provide the Special Commission with any document related to the observance of human rights that the latter may consider necessary for the presentation of its reports;
g. the Special Commission shall be able to use any method appropriate for filming, photographing, collecting, documenting, recording, or reproducing the information it considers useful;
h. the State shall adopt the security measures necessary to protect the Special Commission;
i. the State shall ensure the availability of appropriate lodging for the members of the Special Commission;
j. the same guarantees and facilities that are set forth in this article for the members of the Special Commission shall also be extended to the staff of the Executive Secretariat;
k. the expenses incurred by the Special Commission, each of its members and the staff of the Executive Secretariat shall be borne by the OAS, subject to the pertinent provisions.

Chapter V
Annual Report and Other Reports of the Commission

Article 56
Preparation of Reports

The Commission shall submit an annual report to the General Assembly of the OAS. In addition, the Commission shall prepare the studies and reports it deems advisable for the performance of its functions and shall publish them as it sees fit. Once their publication is approved, the Commission shall transmit them, through the General Secretariat, to the Member States of the OAS and its pertinent organs.

Article 57
Annual Report

1. The Annual Report presented by the Commission to the General Assembly of the OAS shall include the following:

a. An analysis of the human rights situation in the hemisphere, along with recommendations to the States and organs of the OAS as to the measures necessary to strengthen respect for human rights;
b. a brief account of the origin, legal bases, structure and purposes of the Commission, as well as the status of ratifications of the American Convention and all other applicable instruments;
c. a summary of the mandates and recommendations conferred upon the Commission by the General Assembly and the other competent organs, and of the status of implementation of such mandates and recommendations;
d. a list of the periods of sessions held during the time period covered by the report and of other activities carried out by the Commission to achieve its purposes, objectives and mandates;
e. a summary of the activities of the Commission carried out in cooperation with other organs of the OAS and with regional or universal organs of the same type, and the results achieved;
f. the reports on individual petitions and cases whose publication has been approved by the Commission, as well as a list of the precautionary measures granted and extended, and of its activities before the Inter-American Court;

g. a statement on the progress made in attaining the objectives set forth in the American Declaration of the Rights and Duties of Man, the American Convention on Human Rights and all other applicable instruments;
h. any general or special report the Commission considers necessary with regard to the situation of human rights in the Member States, and, as the case may be, follow-up reports noting the progress achieved and the difficulties that have existed with respect to the effective observance of human rights; and
i. any other information, observation or recommendation that the Commission considers advisable to submit to the General Assembly, as well as any new activity or project that implies additional expenditures.

2. For the preparation and adoption of the reports provided for in paragraph 1(h) of this article, the Commission shall gather information from all the sources it deems necessary for the protection of human rights. Prior to its publication in the Annual Report, the Commission shall provide a copy of said report to the respective State. That State may send the Commission the views it deems pertinent within a maximum time period of one month from the date of transmission. The contents of the report and the decision to publish it shall be within the exclusive discretion of the Commission.

Article 58
Report on Human Rights in a State

The preparation of a general or special report on the status of human rights in a specific State shall meet the following standards:

a. after the draft report has been approved by the Commission, it shall be transmitted to the government of the Member State in question so that it may make any observations it deems pertinent;
b. the Commission shall indicate to that State the deadline within which it must present its observations;
c. once the Commission has received the observations from the State, it shall study them and, in light thereof, may maintain or modify its report and decide how it is to be published;
d. if no observation has been submitted by the State as of the expiration of the deadline, the Commission shall publish the report in the manner it deems appropriate;

e. after its publication, the Commission shall transmit it through the General Secretariat to the Member States and General Assembly of the OAS.

Chapter VI
Hearings Before the Commission

Article 59
Initiative

The Commission may decide to hold hearings on its own initiative or at the request of an interested party. The decision to convoke the hearings shall be made by the President of the Commission, at the proposal of the Executive Secretary.

Article 60
Purpose

The hearings may have the purpose of receiving information from the parties with respect to a petition or case being processed before the Commission, follow-up to recommendations, precautionary measures, or general or particular information related to human rights in one or more Members States of the OAS.

Article 61
Guarantees

The State in question shall grant the necessary guarantees to all the persons who attend a hearing or who in the course of a hearing provide information, testimony or evidence of any type to the Commission. That State may not prosecute the witnesses or experts, or carry out reprisals against them or their family members because of their statements or expert opinions given before the Commission.

Article 62
Hearings on Petitions or Cases

1. Hearings on petitions or cases shall have as their purpose the receipt of oral or written presentations by the parties relative to new facts and information additional to that which has been produced during the

proceeding. The information may refer to any of the following issues: admissibility; the initiation or development of the friendly settlement procedure; the verification of the facts; the merits of the matter; follow-up on recommendations; or any other matter pertinent to the processing of the petition or case.

2. Requests for hearings must be submitted in writing at least 40 days prior to the beginning of the respective session of the Commission. Requests for hearings shall indicate their purpose and the identity of the participants.

3. If the Commission accedes to the request or decides to hold a hearing on its own initiative, it shall convoke both parties. If one party, having been duly notified, does not appear, the Commission shall proceed with the hearing. The Commission shall adopt the necessary measures to maintain in confidence the identity of the experts and witnesses if it believes that they require such protection.

4. The Executive Secretariat shall inform the parties as to the date, place and time of the hearing at least one month in advance. However, that time period may be reduced if the participants grant the Executive Secretariat prior and express consent to that effect.

Article 63
Presentation and Production of Evidence

1. During the hearing, the parties may present any document, testimony, expert report or item of evidence. At the request of a party or on its own initiative, the Commission may receive the testimony of witnesses or experts.

2. With respect to the documentary evidence submitted during the hearing, the Commission shall grant the parties a prudential time period for submitting their observations.

3. A party that proposes witnesses or experts for a hearing shall so state in its request. For this purpose, it shall identify the witness or expert and the purpose of his or her witness or expert testimony.

4. Upon deciding on the request for a hearing, the Commission shall also determine whether to receive the witness or expert testimony proposed.

5. When one party offers witness and expert testimony, the Commission shall notify the other party to that effect.

6. In extraordinary circumstances and for the purpose of safeguarding the evidence, the Commission may, at its discretion, receive testimony

in hearings without satisfying the terms of the previous paragraph. In such circumstances, it shall take the measures necessary to guarantee the procedural balance between the parties in the matter submitted for its consideration.

7. The Commission shall hear one witness at a time; the other witnesses shall remain outside the hearing room. Witnesses may not read their presentations to the Commission.

8. Prior to giving their testimony, witnesses and experts shall identify themselves and take an oath or make a solemn promise to tell the truth. At the express request of the interested person, the Commission may maintain the identity of a witness or expert in confidence when necessary to protect him or her or other persons.

Article 64
Hearings of a General Nature

1. Persons who are interested in presenting testimony or information to the Commission on the human rights situation in one or more States, or on matters of general interest, shall direct a request for a hearing to the Executive Secretariat with proper notice prior to the respective session.

2. Persons making such a request shall indicate the purpose of their appearance, a summary of the information they will furnish, the approximate time required for that purpose, and the identity of the participants.

Article 65
Participation of the Commission Members

The President of the Commission may form working groups to participate in the program of hearings.

Article 66
Attendance

Attendance at the hearings shall be limited to the representatives of the parties, the Commission, the staff of the Executive Secretariat, and the Recording Secretaries. The decision to allow the presence of other persons shall vest exclusively in the Commission, which shall so inform the parties prior to beginning the hearing, orally or in writing.

Article 67
Expenses

The party that proposes the production of evidence at a hearing shall cover all of the attendant expenses.

Article 68
Documents and Minutes of the Hearings

1. A summary of the minutes of the hearing shall be prepared and shall record the day and time it was held, the names of the participants, the decisions adopted, and the commitments assumed by the parties. The documents submitted by the parties in the hearing shall be attached as annexes to the minutes.

2. The minutes of the hearings are internal working documents of the Commission. If a party so requests, the Commission shall provide a copy, unless, in the view of the Commission, its contents could entail some risk to persons.

3. The Commission shall make a tape of the testimony and shall make it available to the parties that so request.

Title III
Relations with the Inter-American Court of Human Rights

Chapter I
Delegates, Advisers, Witnesses and Experts

Article 69
Delegates and Assistants

1. The Commission shall entrust one or more persons to represent it and participate as delegates in the consideration of any matter before the Inter-American Court of Human Rights. If the petitioner so requests, the Commission shall include him or her as a delegate.

2. In appointing such delegates, the Commission shall issue any instructions it considers necessary to guide their actions before the Court.

3. When it designates more than one delegate, the Commission shall assign to one of them the responsibility of resolving situations that are

not foreseen in the instructions, or of clarifying any doubts raised by a delegate.

4. The delegates may be assisted by any person designated by the Commission. In the discharge of their functions, the advisers shall act in accordance with the instructions of the delegates.

Article 70
Witnesses and Experts

1. The Commission may also request the Court to summon other persons as witnesses or experts.

2. The summoning of such witnesses or experts shall be in accordance with the Rules of Procedure of the Court.

Chapter II
Procedure Before the Court

Article 71
Notification of the Petitioner

If the Commission decides to refer a case to the Court, the Executive Secretary shall immediately give notice of that decision to the petitioner and to the victim. With that communication, the Commission shall transmit all the elements necessary for the preparation and presentation of the application.

Article 72
Presentation of the Application

1. When, in accordance with Article 61 of the American Convention on Human Rights, the Commission decides to bring a case before the Court, it shall submit an application specifying the:

a. claims on the merits, and reparations and costs sought;
b. parties in the case;
c. presentation of the facts;
d. information on the opening of the procedure and admissibility of the petition;
e. individualization of the witnesses and experts and the purpose of their statements;

f. legal grounds and the pertinent conclusions;
g. available information on the original complainant, the alleged victims, their family members or duly accredited representatives;
h. names of its delegates; and
i. the report provided for in Article 50 of the American Convention.

2. The Commission's application shall be accompanied by certified copies of the items in the file that the Commission or its delegate considers pertinent.

Article 73
Transmittal of other Elements

The Commission shall transmit to the Court, at its request, any other evidence, document or information concerning the case, with the exception of documents concerning futile attempts to reach a friendly settlement. The transmittal of documents shall in each case be subject to the decision of the Commission, which shall withhold the name and identity of the petitioner, if the latter has not authorized that this be revealed.

Article 74
Provisional Measures

1. The Commission may request that the Court adopt provisional measures in cases of extreme gravity and urgency, and when it becomes necessary to avoid irreparable damage to persons in a matter that has not yet been submitted to the Court for consideration.

2. When the Commission is not in session, that request may be made by the President, or in his or her absence, by one of the Vice-Presidents in order of precedence.

Title IV
Final Provisions

Article 75
Calendar Computation

All time periods set forth in the present Rules of Procedure – in numbers of days – will be understood to be counted as calendar days.

Article 76
Interpretation

Any doubt that might arise with respect to the interpretation of these Rules of Procedure shall be resolved by an absolute majority of the members of the Commission.

Article 77
Amendment of the Rules of Procedure

The Rules of Procedure may be amended by an absolute majority of the members of the Commission.

Article 78
Transitory Provision

These Rules of Procedure, whose texts in Spanish and English are equally authentic, shall enter into force on May 1, 2001.

Appendix 5

Form for presenting petitions on human rights violations

The following form, prepared by the Executive Secretariat of the Inter-American Commission on Human Rights, is intended to assist the presentation of petitions regarding violations of human rights alleged to have been committed by member states of the Organization of American States, by the victims of such violations, their families, civil society organizations and other persons.

The form is based upon the information required under the Commission's Rules of Procedure for processing petitions filed with the Commission and for determining whether there have been violations of human rights protected by international instruments binding upon the State accused of the violations. The necessary information is set out in Article 28 of the Commission's Rules of Procedure, which reads as follows:

> **Article 28. Requirements for the Consideration of Petitions.**
> Petitions addressed to the Commission shall contain the following information:
>
> a. the name, nationality and signature of the person or persons making the denunciation; or in cases where the petitioner is a nongovernmental entity, the name and signature of its legal representative(s);
> b. whether the petitioner wishes that his or her identity be withheld from the State;
> c. the address for receiving correspondence from the Commission and, if available, a telephone number, facsimile number, and email address;
> d. an account of the act or situation that is denounced, specifying the place and date of the alleged violations;
> e. if possible, the name of the victim and of any public authority who has taken cognizance of the fact or situation alleged;
> f. the State the petitioner considers responsible, by act or omission, for the violation of any of the human rights recognized in the American Convention on Human Rights and other applicable instruments, even if no specific reference is made to the article(s) alleged to have been violated;

g. compliance with the time period provided for in Article 32 of these Rules of Procedure;
h. any steps taken to exhaust domestic remedies, or the impossibility of doing so as provided in Article 31 of these Rules of Procedure; and
i. an indication of whether the complaint has been submitted to another international settlement proceeding as provided in Article 33 of these Rules of Procedure.

Before completing the attached form, please read the following instructions carefully.

Instructions

The form should be filled in as completely as possible and include all of the information available regarding the particular situation that is alleged to constitute one or more violations of human rights by an OAS member state.[1] The wording of the responses should be simple and direct, without political rhetoric. Where the information requested is not available or does not apply you should indicate 'information not available' or 'not applicable' as appropriate.

In cases where the life or physical integrity of a person or group of persons is in imminent danger despite having approached appropriate domestic authorities, you may submit the pertinent information to the Commission even if information concerning the exhaustion of domestic remedies is not currently available.

Once completed, the form can be presented to the Executive Secretariat of the Commission by mail to:

Inter-American Commission on Human Rights
1889 F Street NW
Washington DC 20006
USA

by fax at the number (202) 458 3992, or by e-mail at cidhoea@oas.org.

[1] The Member States of the OAS are Antigua and Barbuda, Argentina, Bahamas, Barbados, Belize, Bolivia, Brazil, Canada, Chile, Colombia, Costa Rica, Cuba, Dominica, Dominican Republic, Ecuador, El Salvador, Grenada, Guatemala, Guyana, Haiti, Honduras, Jamaica, Mexico, Nicaragua, Panama, Paraguay, Peru, Saint Lucia, Saint Vincent and the Grenadines, Saint Kitts and Nevis, Suriname, Trinidad and Tobago, the United States, Uruguay and Venezuela.

Form

I. PERSON OR GROUP OF PERSONS PRESENTING THE PETITION ON VIOLATIONS ALLEGEDLY COMMITTED AGAINST THEM ('VICTIM(S)') OR COMMITTED AGAINST ANOTHER PERSON OR GROUP OF PERSONS ('PETITIONER(S)')

Name:____
(in the case of a nongovernmental entity also include the name of its legal or non-legal representative(s))

Contact information

Address: ____

____

Telephone number:__________________________________

Fax number:_______________________________________

Do you want the Commission to keep the identity of the petitioner(s) confidential during the procedure?________________

II. MEMBER STATE OF THE OAS RESPONSIBLE FOR THE HUMAN RIGHTS VIOLATIONS ALLEGED BY THE PETITIONER(S): ____

____

III. INCIDENT OR SITUATION DENOUNCED

Explain the incident or situation complained of in as much detail as possible, specifying the place and date of the alleged human rights violations: ____

____

____

____

____

____

____

Available evidence

Describe the documents that might assist in proving the violations described above and that can be provided to the Commission, for example portions of judicial procedures, forensic reports, photographs, films, etc. (Do not submit the original documents but rather copies. In principle it is not necessary for copies of documents to be certified by a public official or notary public.):____

____

____

____

____

Identify witnesses to the violations described above. In the event that witnesses have given statements or depositions before judicial authorities, you should also file copies of this testimony or indicate whether it will be possible to do so in the future:______________

____

____

____

Identify the persons and/or authorities responsible for the alleged violations described above:____________________________

____

____

____

IV. HUMAN RIGHTS VIOLATED **(Where possible, specify the provisions of the American Convention and other applicable instruments that you consider to have been violated as a result of the situation described above):**________________________

____

____

____

V. NAME AND DETAILS OF THE PERSON OR PERSONS AFFECTED BY THE HUMAN RIGHTS VIOLATIONS ALLEGED ABOVE, IN THE EVENT THAT THEY ARE DISTINCT FROM THE PERSON OR PERSONS PRESENTING THE PETITION (see point I):__________

Name: ____

____

____

Contact information

Address:______________________________________

____

Telephone: ____________________________________

Fax number: ___________________________________

Where the victim is no longer alive, please identify their next-of-kin:

____

VI. JUDICIAL REMEDIES AVAILABLE TO REMEDY THE SITUATION DENOUNCED

Detail the steps taken by the victim(s) or the petitioner(s) before the courts, tribunals or administrative authorities of the country responsible for the alleged violations. Also indicate whether you have not been able to initiate or complete such steps because (1) the domestic legislation of the State does not provide due process of law for the protection of the right or rights that have allegedly been violated; (2) the victim(s) or petitioner(s) have been denied access to the remedies under domestic law or have been prevented from exhausting them; or (3) there has been unreasonable delay in rendering a final judgment on the remedies described above:______

____

____

____

In cases where the situation denounced involves crimes or other violations of public law (e.g. murder, torture), indicate whether there has been a corresponding judicial investigation and the result, or whether there has been an unreasonable delay in rendering a result in such an investigation:

____

____

____

In cases where domestic remedies have been exhausted, indicate the date on which the victim was notified of the final decision: ____

____

____

VII. INDICATE WHETHER THE COMPLAINT HAS BEEN SUBMITTED TO THE UNITED NATIONS HUMAN RIGHTS COMMITTEE OR ANOTHER INTERNATIONAL ORGANIZATION WITH SIMILAR CHARACTERISTICS: ______________________________

____

____

____

SIGNATURE: ______________________________________

DATE: ____

BIBLIOGRAPHY

Books

Bayefsky, Anne (ed.), *The UN Human Rights System in the 21st Century* (Kluwer, The Hague, 2000)

Bissonnette, Pierre André, *La Satisfaction Comme Mode de Réparation en Droit International* (Annemasse, 1952)

Broun, Kenneth S., George E. Dix, Michael H. Graham, D. H. Kaye, Robert P. Mosteller and E. F. Roberts, *McCormick on Evidence* (John William Strong ed., 4th edn, West, St Paul, MN, 1992)

Brownlie, Ian, *Principles of Public International Law* (5th edn, Oxford, 1998)

Buergenthal, Thomas B. and Robert E. Norris (eds.), *Human Rights: The Inter-American System* (Oceana, New York, 1982)

Buergenthal, Thomas, and Dinah Shelton, *Protecting Human Rights in the Americas: Cases and Materials* (4th edn, Engel, 1995)

Cançado Trindade, A. A. *The Application of the Rule of Exhaustion of Local Remedies in International Law* (Cambridge, 1983)

Co-existence and Co-ordination of Mechanisms of International Protection of Human Rights (at Global and Regional Levels) (Nijhoff, The Hague, 1990)

Comisionado Nacional de Protección de los Derechos Humanos, *Los Hechos Hablan por sí Mismos, Informe Preliminar Sobre los Desaparecidos en Honduras 1980–1993* (Editorial Guaymuras, Honduras, 1994)

La Corte Interamericana de Derechos Humanos: Estudios y Documentos (Instituto Interamericano de Derechos Humanos, San José, Costa Rica, 1986)

Crawford, James, *International Law Commission's Articles on State Responsibility: Introduction, Text and Commentaries* (Cambridge University Press, Cambridge, 2002)

Davidson, Scott, *The Inter-American Court of Human Rights* (Dartmouth, 1992)

Elkind, Jerome B., *Interim Protection, A Functional Approach* (Nijhoff, The Hague, 1981)

Friedenthal, Jack H., *et al.*, *Civil Procedure* (2nd edn, West, St Paul, MN, 1993)

Garcia-Amador, F. V., *The Changing Law of International Claims* (Oceana, New York, 1984)

García Ramírez, Sergio, *Los Derechos Humanos y la Jurisdicción Interamericana* (Universidad Nacional Autónoma de México, 2002)

Ghandhi, P. R., *The Human Rights Committee and the Right of Individual Communication: Law and Practice* (Ashgate, Dartmouth, 1998)

Gomien, Donna, D. J. Harris and Leo Zwaak, *Law and Practice of the European Convention on Human Rights and the European Social Charter* (Council of Europe Publishing, Strasbourg, 1996)

Gray, Christine, *Judicial Remedies in International Law* (Oxford, 1991)

Gros Espiell, Hector, *La Convención Americana y la Convención Europea de Derechos Humanos: analisis comparativo* (Editorial Juridica de Chile, Santiago, Chile, 1991)

Harris, David J. and Stephen Livingstone, eds., *The Inter-American System of Human Rights* (Oxford University Press, Oxford, and Clarendon Press, New York, 1998)

Hitters, Juan Carlos, *Derecho Internacional de los Derechos Humanos*, vol. II (Ediar Sociedad Anonima Editora, Buenos Aires, 1993)

Hudson, Manley O., *The Permanent Court of International Justice, 1920–1942* (Macmillan, New York, 1943)

Kazazi, Mojtaba, *Burden of Proof and Related Issues: A Study of Evidence Before International Tribunals* (Kluwer, The Hague, 1996)

Keeton, W. Page and William Prosser, *Prosser and Keeton on the Law of Torts* (5th edn, West, St Paul, MN, 1984)

Keith, Kenneth, *The Extent of the Advisory Jurisdiction of the ICJ* (A. W. Sijthoff, Leyden, 1971)

Lillich, Richard, ed., *Fact Finding Before International Tribunals: Eleventh Sokol Colloquium* (Transnational Publishers, Ardsley-on-Hudson, NY, 1992)

Lillich, Richard B. and Burns H. Weston, *International Claims: Contemporary European Practice* (University Press of Virginia, 1982)

Lilly, Graham C., *An Introduction to the Law of Evidence* (3rd edn, West, St Paul, MN, 1996)

Mani, V. S., *International Adjudication: Procedural Aspects* (Nijhoff, The Hague, 1980)

McGoldrick, Dominic, *The Human Rights Committee: Its Role in the Development of the International Covenant on Civil and Political Rights* (Oxford, 1991)

McWhinney, Edward, *Judicial Settlement of International Disputes: Jurisdiction, Justiciability and Judicial Law-Making on the Contemporary International Court* (Nijhoff, 1991)

Medina Quiroga, Cecilia, *The Battle of Human Rights: Gross Systematic Violations and the Inter-American System* (Kluwer, 1988)

Méndez, Juan and Francisco Cox (eds.), *El Futuro del Sistema Interamericano de los Derechos Humanos* (Instituto Interamericano de Derechos Humanos, Costa Rica, 1998)

Newman, Frank and David Weissbrodt, *International Human Rights: Law, Policy and Process* (Anderson, Cincinnati, 1990)

Nieto Navia, Rafael, *La Corte y el Sistema Interamericano de Derechos Humanos* (Corte Interamericana de Derechos Humanos, San José, Costa Rica, 1994)

Nikken, Pedro, *La Protección Internacional de los Derechos Humanos: su Desarrollo Progresivo* (Instituto Interamericano de Derechos Humanos, San José, Costa Rica, 1987)

Orlu Nmehielle, Vincent O., *The African Human Rights System: Its Laws, Practice, and Institutions* (Martinus Nijhoff, The Hague, 2001)

Pinto, Monica, *La Denuncia ante la Comisión Interamericana de Derechos Humanos* (Editores del Puerto, Buenos Aires, 1993)

Pomerance, Michla, *The Advisory Function of the International Court in the League and UN Eras* (Johns Hopkins, Baltimore, 1973)

Pratap, Dharma, *The Advisory Jurisdiction of the International Court* (Clarendon Press, Oxford, 1972)

Ralston, Jackson H., *The Law and Procedure of International Tribunals* (Stanford University Press, 1926)

Robertson, A. H. and J. G. Merrills, *Human Rights in Europe: A Study of the European Convention on Human Rights* (3rd edn, Manchester University Press, 1993)

Rosenne, Shabtai, *The Law and Practice of the International Court, 1920–1996* (3rd edn, Nijhoff, The Hague and Boston, 1997)

Procedure in the International Court: A Commentary on the 1978 Rules of the International Court of Justice (Nijhoff Kluwer, The Hague and Boston, 1983)

The Time Factor in the Jurisdiction of the International Court of Justice (A. W. Sijthoff, Leyden, 1960)

Sandifer, Durward, *Evidence Before International Tribunals* (2nd edn, University Press of Virginia, Charlottesville, 1975)

Santoscoy, Bertha, *La Commission interaméricaine des droits de l'homme et le développement de sa compétence par le système des petitions individuelles* (Presses Universitaires de France, Paris, 1995)

Schachter, Oscar, *International Law in Theory and Practice* (Martinus Nijhoff, The Hague, 1991)

Shelton, Dinah, *Remedies in International Human Rights Law* (Oxford, 1999)

Sieghart, Paul, *The International Law of Human Rights* (Oxford, 1983)

Sztucki, Jerzy, *Interim Measures in the Hague Court: An Attempt at a Scrutiny* (Kluwer, The Hague, 1983)

Van Dijk, P. and G. J. H. van Hoof, *Theory and Practice of the European Convention on Human Rights* (3rd edn, Kluwer, The Hague, 1998)

Ventura, Manuel E. and Daniel Zovatto, *La Función Consultiva de le Corte Interamericana de Derechos Humanos: Naturaleza y Principios 1982–1987* (Instituto Interamericano de Derechos Humanos, San José, Costa Rica, 1989)

Whiteman, Marjorie, *Damages in International Law* (Government Printing Office, Washington DC, 1937)

Wright, Charles Alan, *Law of Federal Courts* (5th edn, West, St Paul, MN, 1994)

Zovatto, Daniel, *Los Estados de Excepción y los Derechos Humanos en America Latina* (Editorial Juridica Venezolana, 1990)

Zwart, Tom, *The Admissibility of Human Rights Petitions: The Case Law of the European Commission of Human Rights and the Human Rights Committee* (Kluwer, Boston, 1994)

Articles and chapters in edited volumes

Abram, Morris B., 'The UN and Human Rights', 47 *Foreign Affairs*, 363 (1969)

'The Inter-American Court of Human Rights', 30 *American University Law Review*, 80 (1980–1)

Anaya, S. James and Robert A. Williams Jr, 'The Protection of Indigenous Peoples' Rights over Lands and Natural Resources under the Inter-American Human Rights System', 14 *Harvard Human Rights Journal*, 33 (2001)

Bernhardt, Peter, 'The Provisional Measures Procedure of the International Court of Justice through US Staff in Tehran: Fiat Iustitia, Pereat Curia?', 20 *Virginia Journal of International Law*, 557 (1980)

Bernhardt, Rudolf, 'Interim Measures of Protection under the European Convention on Human Rights', in *Interim Measures Indicated by International Courts*, 95 (Bernhardt ed., Springer-Verlag, Berlin and New York, 1994)

Buergenthal, Thomas, 'The Advisory Practice of the Inter-American Human Rights Court', 79 *American Journal of International Law*, 1 (1985)

'The American and European Conventions on Human Rights: Similarities and Differences', 30 *American University Law Review*, 155 (1980–1)

'The American Convention on Human Rights: Illusions and Hopes', 21 *Buffalo Law Review*, 121 (1971)

'The Inter-American Court and the OAS', 7 *Human Rights Law Journal*, 157 (1986)

'The Inter-American Court of Human Rights', 76 *American Journal of International Law*, 231 (1982)

'The Inter-American System for the Protection of Human Rights', in *Human Rights in International Law: Legal and Policy Issues* (Theodore Meron ed., 1984)

'Interim Measures in the Inter-American Court of Human Rights', in *Interim Measures Indicated by International Courts*, 69 (R. Bernhardt ed., Springer-Verlag, Berlin and New York, 1994)

'International Tribunals and National Courts: The Internationalization of Domestic Adjudication', in *Recht zwischen Umbruch und Bewahrung: Völkerrecht, Europarecht, Staatsrecht: Festschrift für Rudolf Bernhardt*, 687 (Springer-Verlag, Berlin and New York, 1995)

'Judicial Fact-Finding: The Inter-American Human Rights Court', in *Fact-Finding Before International Tribunals: Eleventh Sokol Colloquium*, 263 (Richard Lillich ed., Transnational Publishing, New York, 1992)

'The Normative and Institutional Evolution of International Human Rights', 19 *Human Rights Quarterly*, 703 (1997)

'Proliferation of International Courts and Tribunals: Is it Good or Bad?', 14 *Leiden Journal of International Law*, 267 (2001)

'Self-Executing and Non-Self-Executing Treaties in National and International Law', 235 *Recueil des Cours*, 303 (1992)

Buergenthal, Thomas and Douglass Cassel, 'The Future of the Inter-American Human Rights System', in *El Futuro del Sistema Interamericano de los Derechos Humanos*, 539 (Juan Méndez and Francisco Cox eds., Instituto Interamericano de Derechos Humanos, Costa Rica, 1998)

Cançado Trindade, Antonio Augusto, 'Co-existence and Co-ordination of Mechanisms of International Protection of Human Rights (at Global and Regional Levels)', 202 *Recueil des Cours*, 9 (1987)

'The Inter-American Human Rights System at the Dawn of the New Century: Recommendations for Improvement of its Mechanism of Protection', in *The Inter-American System of Human Rights*, 417 (Harris and Livingstone eds., Oxford, 1998)

Cassel, Douglass Jr, 'Fact-Finding in the Inter-American System', in *The UN Human Rights Treaty System in the 21st Century*, 105 (Bayefsky ed., Kluwer, The Hague, 2000)

'Peru Withdraws from the Court: Will the Inter-American Human Rights System Meet the Challenge?', 20 *Human Rights Law Journal*, 167 (1999)

'Somoza's Revenge: A New Judge for the Inter-American Court of Human Rights', 13 *Human Rights Law Journal*, 137 (1992)

Cerna, Christina, 'Commission Organization and Petitions', in *The Inter-American System of Human Rights*, 65 (Harris and Livingstone eds., Oxford, 1998)

'Human Rights in Conflict with the Principle of Non-Intervention: The Case of Nicaragua Before the Seventeenth Meeting of Consultation of Ministers of Foreign Affairs', in *Derechos Humanos, Direitos Humanos, Human Rights en Las Americas, Homage to the Memory of Carlos A. Dunshee de Abranches* (OAS, Washington DC, 1984)

'The Structure and Functioning of the Inter-American Court of Human Rights (1979–1992)', 63 *British Yearbook of International Law*, 135 (1992)

Cornell, Angela and Kenneth Roberts, 'Democracy, Counterinsurgency, and Human Rights: The Case of Peru', 12 *Human Rights Quarterly*, 529 (1990)

Cox, Francisco, 'Analyzing the Inter-American Commission on Human Rights under Three Theories of Compliance', 28 *Revista Inter-American Institute of Human Rights*, 11 (Instituto Interamericano de Derechos Humanos, San José, Costa Rica, 1998)

Crawford, James, Pierre Bodeau and Jacqueline Peel, 'The ILC's Draft Articles on State Responsibility: Toward Completion of a Second Reading', 94 *American Journal of International Law*, 660 (2000)

Dankwa, E. V. O., 'Conference on Regional Systems of Human Rights Protection in Africa, the Americas and Europe', 13 *Human Rights Law Journal*, 314 (1992)

Drzemczewski, Andrew, 'The European Human Rights Convention: Protocol No. 11 Entry into Force and First Year of Application', in *El Sistema Interamericano de Protección de los Derechos Humanos en el Umbral del Siglo XXI*, 357 (Corte Interamericana de Derechos Humanos, San José, Costa Rica, 2001)

Dumas, Nanette, 'Enforcement of Human Rights Standards: An International Human Rights Court and Other Proposals', 13 *Hastings International and Comparative Law Review*, 585 (1990)

Dunshee de Abranches, Carlos A., 'La Corte Interamericana de Derechos Humanos', in *La Convención Americana de Derechos Humanos*, 117 (OAS, 1980)

Enrich Mas, Montserrat, 'Right to Compensation under Article 50', in *The European System for the Protection of Human Rights*, 775 (R. St J. Macdonald *et al.* eds., Nijhoff, Dordrecht and Boston, 1993)

Farer, Tom J., 'The OAS at the Crossroads: Human Rights', 72 *Iowa Law Review*, 401 (1987)

'The Rise of the Inter-American Human Rights Regime: No Longer a Unicorn, Not Yet an Ox', in *The Inter-American System of Human Rights*, 36 (Harris and Livingstone eds., Oxford, 1998)

Farrior, Stephanie, 'State Responsibility for Human Rights Abuses by Non-State Actors', 92 *American Society of International Law Proceedings*, 299 (1998)

Faulkner, Elizabeth, 'The Right to Habeas Corpus: Only in the Americas', 9 *American University Journal of International Law and Policy*, 653 (1994)

Fix-Zamudio, Hectór, 'Lineamientos Procesales de Los Procedimientos Ante la Corte Interamericana de Derechos Humanos', in *La Corte y el Sistema Interamericano de Derechos Humanos*, 147 (Corte Interamericana de Derechos Humanos, San José, Costa Rica, 1994)

García Robles, Sergio, 'Las Reparaciones en el Sistema Interamericano de Protección de los Derechos Humanos', in *El Sistema Interamericano de Protección de los Derechos Humanos en el Umbral del Siglo XXI: Memoria del Seminario Noviembre de 1999*, vol. I, 149 (Corte Interamericana de Derechos Humanos, San José, Costa Rica, 2001)

Gaviria, Cesar, 'Toward a New Vision of the Inter-American Human Rights System', 4 *Journal of Latin American Affairs*, 4 (1996)

Goldsworthy, Peter J., 'Interim Measures of Protection in the International Court of Justice', 68 *American Journal of International Law*, 258 (1974)

Gómez, Verónica, 'Inter-American Commission on Human Rights and the Inter-American Court of Human Rights: New Rules and Recent Cases', 1 *Human Rights Law Review*, 111 (2001)

'The Interaction Between the Political Actors of the OAS, the Commission and the Court', in *El Futuro del Sistema Interamericano de los Derechos Humanos*, 192 (Harris and Livingstone eds., Oxford, 1998)

Gross, Leo, 'The Case Concerning United States Diplomatic Consular Staff in Tehran: Phase of Provisional Measures', 74 *American Journal of International Law*, 395 (1980)

Grossman, Claudio, 'Disappearances in Honduras: The Need for Direct Victim Representation in Human Rights Litigation', 15 *Hastings International and Comparative Law Review*, 363 (1992)

'Strengthening the Inter-American Human Rights System: The Current Debate', 92 *American Society of International Law Proceedings*, 186 (1998)

Harris, David, 'Regional Protection of Human Rights: The Inter-American Achievement', in *The Inter-American System of Human Rights*, 1 (Harris and Livingstone eds., Oxford, 1998)

Heffernan, Liz, 'The Nuclear Weapons Opinions: Reflections on the Advisory Procedure of the International Court of Justice', 28 *Stetson Law Review*, 133 (1998)

Kristjansdottir, Edda, 'The Legality of the Threat or Use of Nuclear Weapons under Current International Law: The Arguments Behind the World Court's Advisory Opinion', 30 *New York University Journal of International Law and Policy*, 291 (1997–8)

Luna, Erik G. and Douglas J. Sylvester, 'Beyond Breard', 17 *Berkeley Journal of International Law*, 147 (1999)

Medina Quiroga, Cecilia, 'The Inter-American Commission on Human Rights and the Inter-American Court of Human Rights: Reflections on a Joint Venture', 12 *Human Rights Quarterly*, 439 (1990)

'The Role of Country Reports in the Inter-American System of Human Rights', in *El Futuro del Sistema Interamericano de los Derechos Humanos*, 115 (Harris and Livingstone eds., Oxford, 1998)

Méndez, Juan E., 'La Participación de la Victima Ante la Corte Interamericana de Derechos Humanos', in *La Corte y el Sistema Interamericano de Derechos Humanos*, 321 (Corte Interamericana de Derechos Humanos, San José, Costa Rica, 1994)

Méndez, Juan and Jose Vivanco, 'Disappearances and the Inter-American Court: Reflections on a Litigation Experience', 13 *Hamline Law Review*, 507 (1990)

Montalvo, Andrés E., 'Reservations to the American Convention on Human Rights: A New Approach', 16 *American University International Law Review*, 269 (2001)

Morawa, Alexander H. E., 'The Individual as a Party to International Human Rights Litigation, with Particular Reference to the Issue of "Abuse of the Right to Petition"', 4 *Journal of International Relations*, 11 (1997)

Moyer, Charles, 'Friendly Settlement in the Inter-American System: The Verbitsky Case – When Push Needn't Come to Shove', in *La Corte y el Sistema Interamericano de Derechos Humanos*, 347 (Corte Interamericana de Derechos Humanos, San José, Costa Rica, 1994)

'The Role of Amicus Curiae in the Inter-American Court of Human Rights', in *La Corte Interamericana de Derechos Humanos: Estudios y Documentos*, 103 (Corte Interamericana de Derechos Humanos, San José, Costa Rica, 1986)

Moyer, Charles and David Padilla, 'Executions in Guatemala as Decreed by the Courts of Special Jurisdiction in 1982–83: A Case Study', 6 *Human Rights Quarterly*, 507 (1984)

Nikken, Pedro, 'Observaciones Sobre el Fortalecimiento del Sistema Interamericano de Derechos Humanos en Vísperas de la Asamblea General de la OEA', 13 *Revista Inter-Americano Instituto de Derechos Humanos* (2001). (special edition)

Norgaard, Carl A. and Hans C. Kruger, 'Interim and Conservatory Measures under the European System of Protection of Human Rights', in *Progress in the Spirit of Human Rights*, 109 (1988)

Norris, Robert, 'Leyes de Impunidad y los Derechos Humanos en Las Americas: Una Respuesta Legal', 15 *Instituto Interamericano de Derechos Humanos Revista*, 47 (1992)

Orlu Nmehielle, Vincent O., 'Towards an African Court of Human Rights: Structuring and the Court', 6 *Annual Survey of International and Comparative Law*, 27 (2000)

Padilla, David, 'The Inter-American Commission on Human Rights of the Organization of American States: A Case Study', 9 *American University Journal of International Law and Policy*, 95 (1993)

'Reparations in Aloeboetoe v. Suriname', 17 *Human Rights Quarterly*, 541 (1995)

Parassram Concepción, Natasha, 'The Legal Implications of Trinidad and Tobago's Withdrawal from the American Convention on Human Rights', 16 *American University International Law Review*, 847 (2001)

Pasqualucci, Jo M., 'The Advisory Practice of the Inter-American Court of Human Rights: Contributing to the Evolution of International Human Rights Law', 38 *Stanford Journal of International Law* 241 (2002)

'The Inter-American Human Rights System: Establishing Precedents and Procedure in Human Rights Law', 26 *University of Miami Inter-American Law Review*, 297 (1994–5)

'Preliminary Objections Before the Inter-American Court of Human Rights', 40 *Virginia Journal of International Law*, 1 (1999)

'Provisional Measures in the Inter-American Human Rights System: An Innovative Development in International Law', 26 *Vanderbilt Journal of Transnational Law*, 803 (1993)

'Thomas Buergenthal: Holocaust Survivor to Human Rights Advocate', 18 *Human Rights Quarterly*, 877 (1996)

'Victim Reparations in the Inter-American Human Rights System: A Critical Assessment of Current Practice and Procedure', 18 *Michigan Journal of International Law*, 1 (1996)

'The Whole Truth and Nothing but the Truth: Truth Commissions, Impunity and the Inter-American Human Rights System', 12 *Boston University International Law Journal*, 321 (1994)

Paust, Jordan J., 'Breard and Treaty-Based Rights under the Consular Convention', 92 *American Journal of International Law*, 691 (1998)

Reina, Ana María, 'Las Excepciones Preliminares en el Sistema Interamericano de Derechos Humanos', in *La Corte y el Sistema Interamericano de Derechos Humanos*, 421 (Corte Interamericana de Derechos Humanos, San José, Costa Rica, 1994)

Reisman, W. Michael, 'Compensation for Human Rights Violations: The Practice of the Past Decade in the Americas', in *State Responsibility and the Individual: Reparation in Instances of Grave Violations of Human Rights*, 63 (A. Randelzhofer and C. Tomuschat eds., 1999)

Reisman, Michael and Janet Koven Levit, 'Fact-Finding Initiatives for the Inter-American Court of Human Rights', in *La Corte y el Sistema Interamericano de Derechos Humanos*, 443 (Rafael Nieto Navia ed., Corte Interamericana de Derechos Humanos, San José, Costa Rica, 1994)

Robinson, Patrick L., 'The Inter-American Human Rights System', 17 *West Indian Law Journal*, 8 (1992)

Rodriguez Pinzon, Diego, 'The Victim Requirement, the Fourth Instance Formula and the Notion of "Person" in the Individual Complaint Procedure of the Inter-American Human Rights System', 7 *International Law Students Association Journal of International and Comparative Law*, 369 (2001)

Rodríguez Rescia, Victor Manuel, 'Eficacia Jurídica de la Jurisprudencia de la Corte Inter-Americanos de Derechos Humanos', in *La Corte y el Sistema Interamericano de Derechos Humanos*, 459 (Rafael Nieto Navia ed., Corte Interamericana de Derechos Humanos, San José, Costa Rica, 1994)

Roht-Arriaza, Naomi, 'State Responsibility to Investigate and Prosecute Grave Human Rights Violations in International Law', 78 *California Law Review*, 449 (1990)

Ruda, J. M., 'Reservations to Treaties', 146 *Recueil des Cours*, 95 (1973)

Rudolf, Beate, 'International Decision: Loizidou v. Turkey', 91 *American Journal of International Law*, 532 (1997)

Ryssdal, Rolv, 'The Future of the European Court of Human Rights', ECOUR90296.AB, 4 (1990)

Salgado Pesantes, Hernán, 'Las Reservas en los Tratados de Derechos Humanos', in *Liber Amicorum Héctor Fix-Zamudio*, vol. I, 1 (Corte Interamericana de Derechos Humanos, San José, Costa Rica, 1998)

Schwebel, Stephen M., 'Authorizing the Secretary-General of the United Nations to Request Advisory Opinions of the International Court of Justice', 78 *American Journal of International Law*, 869 (1984)

'Widening the Advisory Jurisdiction of the International Court of Justice Without Amending its Statute', 33 *Catholic University Law Review*, 355 (1984)

Shelton, Dinah, 'The Jurisprudence of the Inter-American Court of Human Rights', 10 *American University Journal of International Law and Policy*, 333 (1994)

'The Participation of Nongovernmental Organizations in International Judicial Proceedings', 88 *American Journal of International Law*, 611 (1994)

Sohn, Louis B., 'Broadening the Advisory Jurisdiction of the International Court of Justice', 77 *American Journal of International Law*, 124 (1983)

'The New International Law: Protection of the Rights of Individuals Rather than States', 32 *American University Law Review*, 1 (1982)

Sohn, Louis and R. Baxter, 'Responsibility of States for Injuries to the Economic Interests of Aliens', 55 *American Journal of International Law*, 545 (1961)

Solano Monge, Auxiliadora, 'La Prueba Pericial Ante la Corte Interamericana de Derechos Humanos', in *Liber Amicorum Héctor Fix-Zamudio*, vol. II, 1451 (Corte Interamericana de Derechos Humanos, San José, Costa Rica, 1998)

Urbina Briceño, Adalberto José, 'La Competencia Consultiva de la Corte Interamericana de Derechos Humanos', 90 *Revista de la Facultad de Ciencias Jurídicas y Políticas, Universidad Central de Venezuela*, 355 (Caracas, 1993)

Van Boven, Theo, 'Reparations: A Requirement of Justice', in *El Sistema Interamericano de Protección de los Derechos Humanos en el Umbral del Siglo XXI: Memoria del Seminario Noviembre de 1999*, vol. I, 653 (Corte Interamericana de Derechos Humanos, San José, Costa Rica, 2001)

Ventura Robles, Manuel, 'The Discontinuance and Acceptance of Claims in the Jurisprudence of the Inter-American Court of Human Rights', 5 *International Law Students Association Journal of International and Comparative Law*, 603 (1999)

'El Futuro de la Corte Interamericana de Derechos Humanos', *Revista Instituto Interamericano de Derechos Humanos*, 129 (2001)

'Los Articulos 50 y 51 de la Convención Americana sobre Derechos Humanos', in *La Corte y el Sistema Interamericano de Derechos Humanos*, 553 (Corte Interamericana de Derechos Humanos, San José, Costa Rica, 1994)

Vivanco, José Miguel and Lisa L. Bhansali, 'Procedural Shortcomings in the Defense of Human Rights: An Inequality of Arms', in *The Inter-American System of Human Rights*, 421 (Harris and Livingstone eds., Oxford, 1998)

Volio, Fernando, 'The Inter-American Commission on Human Rights', 30 *American University Law Review*, 65 (1980)

Weissbrodt, David and Maria L. Bartolomei, 'The Effectiveness of International Human Rights Pressures: The Case of Argentina, 1976–1983', 75 *Minnesota Law Review*, 1009 (1991)

Weissbrodt, David and Teresa O'Toole, 'The Development of International Human Rights Law', in *The Universal Declaration of Human Rights 1948–1988: Human Rights, the United Nations and Amnesty International* (AIUSA Legal Support Network, New York, 1988)

Weston, Burns H., 'Regional Human Rights Regimes: A Comparison and Appraisal', 20 *Vanderbilt Journal of Transnational Law*, 585 (1987)

Websites

Organization of American States
http://www.oas.org

Inter-American Court of Human Rights
http://www.corteidh.or.cr

Inter-American Commission on Human Rights
http://www.cidh.oas.org

Council of Europe
http://www.coe.int

European Court of Human Rights
http://www.echr.coe.int

Covenant of the League of Nations (including amendments adopted to December 1924)
http://www.tufts.edu/departments/fletcher/multi/www/league-covenant.html

International Court of Justice
http://www.icj-cij.org

Treaty Establishing the European Community, as amended by subsequent treaties, Rome, 25 March 1957
http://www.hri.org/docs/Rome57/

Other international reports and documents

2001 Basic Documents Pertaining to Human Rights in the Inter-American System, OEA/Ser.L/V/I.4 rev. 8 (22 May 2001)

Cerna, Christina M., 'Questions of International Law Raised by Peru's "Withdrawal" from the Inter-American Court of Human Rights' (unpublished manuscript on file with the author, 2001)

Comisión Nacional Sobre la Desaparición de Personas, *Nunca Mas* [National Commission on the Disappearance of Persons, *Never Again*], (Editorial Universitaria de Buenos Aires 14a. ed., 1986)

Council of Europe, 'Report on the Inter-American Specialized Conference on Human Rights' (Strasbourg, 22 December 1969), reprinted in *Human Rights: The Inter-American System*, Booklet 15, vol. 3, 67 (Thomas B. Buergenthal and Robert E. Norris eds., 1982)

'Los Crímenes Impunes del Comisario Miara', *Madres de Plaza de Mayo* newspaper, 20 May 1989

Gibbings, Wesley, 'Controversy Reigns as Gallows are Readied', Inter Press Service, 25 June 1998, available in 1998 WL 5987954

'High Court Examines, Gingerly, Issue of Punitive Damages' Limit', *New York Times*, 12 October 1995, A18

Informe de la Comisión Nacional de Verdad y Reconciliación, Chile [National Commission on Truth and Reconciliation Report, Chile] (March 1991)

International Commission for Central America Recovery and Development, 'Poverty, Conflict and Hope: A Turning Point in Latin America' (1989)

Lopez Miranda, Lillian J., 'Analysis of the Use of Preliminary Objections in the Inter-American Court of Human Rights: 1979–1996' (1999)

National Commission for the Protection of Human Rights, 'The Facts Speak for Themselves: Preliminary Report on the Disappeared in Honduras 1980–1993' (1994)

Office of the Secretary General of the Organization of American States, Report prepared for the Ad Hoc Working Group on Human Rights, created by the Foreign Ministers' meeting of 22 November 1999, 'Financing the Inter-American Human Rights System' (28 April 2000)

Organization of American States General Secretariat, 'The Inter-American System: Treaties, Conventions and Other Documents' (F. V. Garcia-Amador ed., 1983)

Restatement (Third) of Foreign Relations Law of the United States (1986)

Statement by US Department of State on US Withdrawal from Nicaragua Proceedings, 18 January 1985, 79 *American Journal of International Law*, 431, 438–9 (1985), 24 ILM 1743 (1985)

Statement of Mr Pierre-Henri Imbert, Director General of Human Rights at the Council of Europe, delivered at the 57th session of the United Nations Commission on Human Rights, Geneva, 29 March 2001

UN Secretary-General, Report of the World Conference on Human Rights, 1993 Vienna Declaration on Human Rights, UN Doc. A/Conf.157/24 (1993)

UN Secretary-General, 'Report of the Secretary-General Summarizing the Views of Various Governments Concerning the Role of the International Court of Justice', UN Doc. A/8382 (1971)

UN Truth Commission Report for El Salvador, 'From Madness to Hope: The Twelve-Year War in El Salvador' (United Nations, New York and San Salvador, 1993)

United States, Department of State, Letter and Statement Concerning Termination of Acceptance of ICJ Compulsory Jurisdiction, 7 October 1985, reprinted in 24 ILM 1742 (1985)

Van Boven, Theo, 'Study Concerning the Right to Restitution, Compensation and Rehabilitation for Victims of Gross Violations of Human Rights and Fundamental Freedoms', 16, UN Human Rights Commission, E/CN.4/Sub.2/1993/8 (2 July 1993)

INDEX